HOME EDUCATION:
RIGHTS AND REASONS

HOME EDUCATION: RIGHTS AND REASONS

John W. Whitehead
Alexis Irene Crow

CROSSWAY BOOKS • WHEATON, ILLINOIS
A DIVISION OF GOOD NEWS PUBLISHERS

Home Education: Rights and Reasons.

Copyright © 1993 by The Rutherford Institute.

Published by Crossway Books
a division of
Good News Publishers
1300 Crescent Street
Wheaton, Illinois 60187

Photography: Jim Whitmer

Art Direction/Design: Mark Schramm

First printing, 1993

Printed in the United States of America

Note: This book is not intended to be, and does not constitute, the giving of legal advice. Particular court decisions may not apply to particular factual situations, or may not be legally binding in particular jurisdictions. The existence of unfavorable decisions indicates that reliance should not be placed on favorable decisions as necessarily dispositive or assuring a successful outcome in litigation. Moreover, this book is not intended to substitute for individual reliance on privately retained legal counsel.

Library of Congress Cataloging-in-Publication Data
Home education : rights and reasons / John W. Whitehead . . . [et al.].
    p.   cm.
    Includes bibliographical references (p.) and index.
    1. Home schooling—Law and legislation—United States. 2.
Civil rights—United States. I. Whitehead, John W., 1946- .
KF4221.H65 1993   344.73'071—dc20 [347.30471]   92-38994
ISBN 0-89107-655-7

01		00		99		98		97		96		95		94		93
15	14	13	12	11	10	9	8	7	6	5	4	3	2	1

CONTENTS

ACKNOWLEDGMENTS

The authors appreciate and wish to thank The Rutherford Institute law clerks, interns, and secretaries for their enthusiasm for this project, their overall assistance, and their very long hours.

In particular, the authors wish to acknowledge the research and technical assistance of the following individuals: Mike Brickhill, Laurence Beckemeyer, Julie Carlson, Melanie Davis, Susan Graham, Renee Ladd, Eric Larson, Scott McGraw, Annie Mecias, Marsha Peavy, Colleen Koontz Pinyan, Clint Pinyan, Debbie Summers, and Keith Williams, and the secretarial assistance of Tracy Cosner Gardner, Peggy Kelly, Sally Mason, and Fran Wilhelmson.

Finally, the authors wish to thank their families for their support and encouragement. Without them, this book would not have been written.

The Authors

FOREWORD

Late one night in the Fall of 1978, I was awakened from my sleep by a telephone call. The man on the line, Peter Nobel, told me that he and his wife, Ruth, had recently been charged with a crime and that they needed a lawyer. In response to my question concerning their "crime," Peter replied that they had been charged with the misdemeanor of not having their children in a school approved under Michigan law.

The Nobels, I found out, were home schooling five of their seven children.

I asked why they did not have their children in a public or private school. The Nobels were quite adamant that because of their religious beliefs they had no alternative but to home school their children.

Intrigued, I took their case. I assembled a number of experts and prepared my case for court.

I argued that the Nobels' right to the free exercise of their religion, guaranteed by the United States Constitution, protected their right to educate their children in their home. The attorneys for the State of Michigan countered that even though the academic achievements of the Nobel children were high, the children were not properly socialized. Therefore, Michigan argued, the state had a compelling interest in overriding the religious beliefs of the Nobel family.

My experts, however, showed in their testimony that peer pressure in the public schools is often damaging and that, because of the positive family setting, the Nobel children were, on the whole, better socialized than the majority of public school children.

We won our case!

However, not everyone agrees on home education or its results. In legislatures and courts throughout the United States (and even in other countries), the right to educate one's children at home continues to be challenged. This occurs despite undisputed favorable historical precedent, favorable Supreme Court and other court decisions, and favorable expert opinion on academics and socialization.

This valuable right, as well as the importance of protecting the integrity of the family as a whole, is imperative. At The Rutherford Institute, we count these important issues high on our scale of priorities.

Thus, it is the object of this book not only to set forth the case for home education, but also to document the numerous ways in which home education has benefited and continues to benefit society. The constitutional arguments that establish the right to educate one's children at home are also presented. Finally, current legislative status of laws affecting home schools are referenced, along with some practical suggestions as to how you, the reader, can protect your right, and perhaps the rights of others, to have a home school.

John W. Whitehead
President
The Rutherford Institute

PART ONE

The Public Education Milieu

If an unfriendly foreign power had attempted to impose on America the mediocre education performance that exists today, we might well have viewed it as an act of war.

National Commission on Excellence in Education
A Nation at Risk

1

The Crisis in Contemporary Public Education

FACE OF THE CRISIS

We live in a time of great social crisis. Our children rank at the bottom of nineteen industrial nations in reading, writing, and arithmetic. The world's narcotic economy is based upon our own consumption of this commodity. If we didn't buy so many powdered dreams the business would collapse—and schools are an important sales outlet. Our teenage suicide rate is the highest in the world—and suicidal kids are rich kids for the most part, not the poor.

Our school crisis is a reflection of this greater social crisis. We seem to have lost our identity. Children and old people are penned up and locked away from the business of the world to a degree without precedent; nobody talks to them anymore. Without children and old people mixing in daily life, a community has no future and no past, only a continuous present. In fact, the name "community" hardly applies to the way we interact with each other. We live in networks, not communities, and everyone I know is lonely because of that. In some strange way school is a major actor in this tragedy, just as it is a major actor in the widening gulf among social classes. Using school as a sorting mechanism, we appear to be on the way to creating a caste system, complete with untouchables who wander through subway trains begging and [sleeping] on the streets.

I've noticed a fascinating phenomenon in my twenty-five years of teaching—that schools and schooling are increasingly irrelevant to the great enterprises of the planet.[1]

New York City's Teacher of the Year for 1990 spoke these words upon his acceptance of his award.

A noted critic in the field of education writes, "When *Newsweek* begins to sound like the *Blumenfeld Education Letter* when describing the failures of public education, then we can assume that the most ardent defenders of the public schools among our businessmen and politicians and journalists are well aware of the seemingly insoluble problems the system faces."[2]

As James Kilpatrick writes, "The good old days, some wit has remarked, never were. But in the field of education the aphorism may not hold true."[3]

Consider the following two students:

The first, an eleven-year-old Kansas student, proudly recalls the questions that qualified her for her eighth grade diploma:

> The "orthography" quiz . . . asked us to spell twenty words, including "abbreviated," "obscene," "elucidation," "assassination" and "animosity." . . . In Reading we were required to tell what we knew of the writings of Thomas Jefferson, and for another of the ten questions to "indicate the pronunciation and give the meanings of the following words: Zenith, deviated, coliseum, misconception, panegyric, Spartan, talisman, eyrie, triton, crypt." . . . In grammar's ten were two directing us to analyze and diagram: "There is a tide in the affairs of men, which taken at the flood, leads on to fortune." . . .
>
> In history we were to "give a brief account of the colleges, printing, and religion in the colonies prior to the American Revolution," to "name the principal campaigns and military leaders of the Civil War," and to "name the principal political questions which have been advocated since the Civil War and the party which advocated each."[4]

That student was graduating from the eighth grade in a one-room school in Kansas in 1907.[5] The contrast between the foregoing recollection and the following situation is a striking example of the crisis in contemporary public education.

One morning in April 1986, several Virginia high school students entered the Advanced Placement (AP) biology examination with knowledge of the test's contents. Sophia, who at the beginning of the school year moved to Virginia from Taiwan, was responsible for the illegal knowledge. Her boyfriend, Max, took the AP test at an American school in Taiwan, then called Sophia in Virginia. Since Taiwan lies just over the International Date Line, Sophia had over nine hours to prepare her essay responses. She also called her friends to alert them to the essay and multiple choice questions. By morning on the East Coast, Sophia and her friends were prepared for an examination the contents of which they already knew.

Sophia's efforts were remarkable. The AP testing service, which had not previously encountered such a situation, sent a special investigative team to the Virginia high school. Much was at stake. AP examinations, given in subjects ranging from calculus to foreign languages, allow students to receive college credit for high school studies. Some students earn a semester or even a year of credit at participating colleges and universities. To ensure an even standard, the testing service utilizes an extensive security program. But Sophia evaded those security measures on that April morning. She was turned in by a classmate who learned of her cheating, but Sophia was nonetheless admitted to a southwestern university, and her test records simply state, "Test not graded by request."

The problems with contemporary public education in the United States are not, strictly speaking, recent phenomena. Problems such as low motivation, the lack of resources, and overcrowded classrooms are old obstacles. On the other hand, reform of American education is not a new concept. During the Progressive Era of the late 1800s and early 1900s, schools were a favorite target of reformers.[6] Later, in the 1950s and 1960s, massive efforts were made to reform the schools by desegregating them.[7] Reforms of the 1980s came from the same mold.[8]

The Difference in Modern Reform

Despite some similarities, there is a major difference between early reform movements and the one that began in the 1980s: the reform movement that began in the 1980s had no single purpose to accomplish. Whereas the progressives wanted a *universal* opportunity for education, and the desegregationists wanted an end to racial segregation, the 1980s reformers sought "excellence."[9] The "Excellence Movement" began in 1981 with the creation of the National Commission on Excellence in Education (NCEE).[10] It continued into 1989, when President George Bush convened the Education Summit with the nation's governors.[11] It has lived on into the 1990s. Indeed, in 1991 President Bush, the so-called "Education President," unveiled his nine-year "America 2000" plan.[12]

Obviously, the generalized goal of "excellence" is nebulous. It is so nebulous that educators and others involved with or affected by the American public education system honestly can disagree about how to achieve "excellence" and whether "excellence," in fact, has been achieved.[13]

Meanwhile, the problems of American education have not abated.[14] The same concerns of illiteracy, declining test scores, curriculum weaknesses, and an expanding moral crisis continue to exist in this last decade of the Twentieth Century. As *Newsweek* magazine notes:

> How bad are eighth graders' math skills? So bad that half are scoring just above the proficiency level expected of fifth-grade students. Even the best students did miserably; at the top-scoring schools, the average was well below grade level. Hardly any students have the background to go beyond simple computation; most of these kids can add, but they have serious trouble thinking through simple problems. These grim statistics [in June 1991], released in the first large-scale state-by-state study of math

achievement, prompted Education Secretary Lamar Alexander to declare a math emergency in the nation's schools. "None of the states are cutting it," he said. "This is an alarm bell that should ring all night throughout this country."

What's really frightening about these results is that the alarm has been ringing since the 1983 publication of "A Nation at Risk," the federally sponsored study that highlighted vast problems in the public schools. Yet despite years of talk about reform—and genuine efforts at change in a few places—American students are still not making the grade and remain behind their counterparts in other industrialized nations.[15]

In this chapter we will examine, first, how American education is evaluated: how are measurements of achievement made, and what do such measurements mean? Second, our focus will be on the major impetus of the Excellence Movement and the reforms suggested by that movement. Finally, we will examine several goals of the Excellence reformers and will conclude that the reforms implemented have not yet achieved such goals.

HOW IS AMERICAN EDUCATION EVALUATED?

Evaluation of Schools

The process of evaluating schools takes many forms. Some are extremely subjective—for example, using parent or student surveys. Other evaluations are more objective, taking into account test scores or graduation rates. Still other studies incorporate both subjective and objective methods in order to obtain a comprehensive result.[16] Conclusions will vary, of course, according to the method of evaluation used. Moreover, any study is necessarily dependent on the schools chosen. For example, a sample consisting entirely of parochial schools will present a different result than that based on a sample of inner-city public schools.

Evaluation of Student Achievement

The process of evaluating student achievement also takes many forms. One form of evaluation focuses on the student as an individual. These evaluations will ask, first, what the student learned, and, second, how well the student is doing in comparison with peers.[17] This kind of evaluation is generally accomplished in contemporary American schools through one of three methods.

Perhaps the method most familiar to American parents and students is the classroom test which determines whether a child can recall specific information in response to teacher-given questions.[18] Such classroom tests include "essay, short-answer, oral-recitation, true/false, multiple choice," and matching.[19] As one professor explains: "The mainstay of classroom evaluations [i.e., tests], are essentially one-shot, single-direction evaluations.

That is, the teacher asks a question and the child has one opportunity to demonstrate his knowledge."[20]

The second method of student achievement evaluation is based upon student-teacher interaction.[21] Either inside or outside the classroom, the teacher will evaluate a student's knowledge through a discussion or conference. The results of these forms of evaluation will be communicated to the parents through report card comments or scheduled conferences.[22]

The third method of evaluating student achievement is the Advanced Placement (AP) examination. High school students who demonstrate sufficient mastery of a given subject can receive college credit for related high school work.

The second type of student achievement evaluation compares the individual student to other students, or the individual student to an established standard, or the individual student's knowledge to his own prior knowledge. The last comparison—a "before and after" evaluation of the student—is rarely used for determining grades.[23] However, such examinations are used to encourage disadvantaged students and to motivate gifted students.

> For example, if a pretest indicates that a child already knows 50 percent of the vocabulary words, the teacher might require a score of 95 percent for that child to get an A. Another child with a pretest score of 20 percent might only need to get an 80 for an A. After all, to achieve 80 percent the second child would have learned more new words than the first child.[24]

The other two comparisons (one student with other students or one student against a given standard) are used more often in contemporary American public schools. The American College Testing Assessment (ACT) and the Scholastic Aptitude Test (SAT) are both commonly used to compare students with other students.[25] When students are compared with one another, the usual approach is to develop a middle point or norm. On the SAT, for example, each test-taker receives a "raw score", or the number of questions correctly answered.[26] The raw score is then converted to a standardized score so that there are as many students scoring above the middle as there are below the middle.[27] This process is known as a "normal" distribution and is often called the "bell-shaped curve."[28] Typically scores are assigned in the same manner as teachers who "grade on the curve."[29] This means that a teacher will assign mostly C's, with a few A's and B's and a few D's and F's. Under this method, receiving an A no longer represents mastery of the material, but rather doing better than the other classroom students.

On some occasions, students are evaluated against some established criterion. Several examinations—for example, the Comprehensive Test of Basic Skills (CTBS)—test whether a student can meet a social standard of basic living skills.[30]

However, these types of evaluations are subject to considerable criticism. For example, one professor has observed: "Increasingly some teachers feel coerced into teaching to the test because their own evaluations rest on how well their students perform."[31] Also, tests of basic skills confuse the measurement of "what the child learned [with] the overall worth of the learner, the teacher, or the school."[32]

Evaluation Through Public Opinion

Education evaluation, however, often focuses on more than just the students. Opinion polls and surveys examine how communities feel about their schools. If community support is low, a school might find funding decreased after the next school board election. Property values are often affected by school performance. While these methods of evaluation are highly subjective, they profoundly affect the way schools operate. Together, objective and subjective criteria indicate where an educational system has been—and they shape the future of the system.

WHAT HAS THE EVALUATION OF AMERICAN PUBLIC EDUCATION SHOWN?

On August 26, 1981, the U. S. Secretary of Education created the National Commission on Excellence in Education (NCEE).[33] Its eighteen-member panel[34] was directed "to examine the quality of education in the United States and to make a report to the Nation."[35] From October 1981 until April 1983, the NCEE performed its duties. Commission members read papers from education experts; heard testimony of administrators, teachers, students, and parents; analyzed existing studies of education; received letters from concerned citizens; and discussed alternative education programs.[36] In April 1983, the NCEE finished its task.

The Committee's report, entitled *A Nation at Risk*, indicated that the American educational system was in disarray. *A Nation at Risk* warned the nation that educational reform was imperative. One observer remarked that "the report made a forceful entry onto the educational scene, using provocative language to present a caustic analysis of the pervading weaknesses of American public education."[37] Prior to the NCEE's report, some educators feared that the Committee would dwell in vagueness, never addressing specific problems. A New York high school teacher cautioned: "I think it is the responsibility of a committee to list specific problems to be addressed so that it will know what to look for in the investigation."[38] The NCEE addressed these concerns and identified the specific ailments of an American education system at risk before it suggested changes.[39]

The Risk: Mediocrity Is the Norm

At the heart of the Commission's concern was its discovery of widespread mediocrity in America's schools. Two NCEE staff members noted that an "essential message from the Commission is that mediocrity, not excellence, is the norm in American education. *A Nation at Risk* paid tribute to 'heroic' examples of educational excellence, but it made clear the fact that, on balance, 'a rising tide of mediocrity' threatens to overwhelm the educational foundations of American society."[40] According to the Commission, this mediocrity endangered the nation's health; compared to the rest of the world, America was losing its competitive advantage at a time when "an abundance of natural resources and inexhaustible human enthusiasm" was no longer enough.[41] The risk, however, encompassed more than just America's world standing: it also threatened "the intellectual, moral, and spiritual strengths of [the] people which knit together the very fabric of [American] society."[42] In fact, the NCEE wrote, "If an unfriendly foreign power had attempted to impose on America the mediocre education performance that exists today, we might well have viewed it as an act of war."[43]

The Commission's discovery of such widespread mediocrity in the nation's public schools was a serious one because of the obvious importance of education to society.[44] The NCEE explained:

> Citizens know intuitively what some of the best economists have shown in their research, that education is one of the chief engines of a society's material well-being. They know, too, that education is the common bond of a pluralistic society and helps tie us to other cultures around the globe.[45]

Symptoms of the Risk

Nearly three hundred people testified before the Commission through oral testimony and written papers, and from these testimonies the Commission selected startling examples to identify the risk:

—On 19 international assessments of student achievement academic tests, American students never finished first or second when compared to students from other industrialized nations; actually, American students finished in last place seven times.

—Forty percent of high school upperclassmen cannot draw inferences from written materials, and eighty percent are incapable of writing a persuasive essay.

—Only one out of three American 17-year-olds can solve a mathematics problem requiring several steps.[46]

These examples are merely illustrative of the discoveries made by the NCEE. The Commission concluded in general that "declines in educational performance are in large part the result of disturbing inadequacies in the way the educational process itself is often conducted."[47] In 1983, the nation's schools were "homogenized, diluted, and diffused";[48] almost half of U.S. high school students migrated from vocational and college preparatory courses to "general track" courses.[49] Furthermore, while students left the challenging classes, the schools lowered their expectations of high school graduates. In 1980, no state required foreign language instruction for graduation, and thirty-five states required no more than one year of science and mathematics.[50] Under such conditions, the Commission must not have been surprised that colleges and universities also had to lower their admission standards[51] and increase the offering of remedial mathematics courses.[52]

PROPOSED REMEDIES

After its indictment of the public schools, the Commission outlined its proposals for reform. The primary goal of the NCEE, as its name suggests, was to suggest ways of returning excellence to the nation's schools, rather than allowing them to continue in mediocrity. *A Nation at Risk* states:

> Our recommendations are based on the beliefs that everyone can learn, that everyone is born with an *urge* to learn which can be nurtured, that a solid high school education is within the reach of virtually all, and that life-long learning will equip people with the skills required for new careers and for citizenship.[53]

The Committee made five recommendations to help alleviate the risk faced by the nation's schools—public, private, and parochial alike.

Strengthened Graduation Requirements

First, the NCEE believed that high schools must strengthen their graduation requirements to include: "(a) 4 years of English, (b) 3 years of mathematics, (c) 3 years of science, (d) 3 years of social studies, and (e) one-half year of computer science."[54] Furthermore, the Commission advised the nation that the eight grades prior to high school should provide a strong foundation for the more demanding high school curriculum. Those years in particular should develop each individual's gifts and talents.[55]

More Rigorous College Admissions Standards

Second, while the high schools were urged to strengthen their curricula, colleges and universities were advised to adopt rigorous admissions standards. Overall, the educational system should challenge students toward excellence, rather than fostering average achievement. The Commission relied on the term "rigorous" when describing its proposals for the curriculum and for expectations of the students.[56]

Increased Time in Classrooms

Third, *A Nation at Risk* asserted that a rigorous program of study and higher standards would require more time in the classroom. It therefore recommended that schools more effectively use the school day, adopt a longer school day, or lengthen the school year: "School districts and State legislatures should strongly consider 7-hour school days, as well as a 200- to 220-day school year."[57]

Improved Teacher Preparation

Fourth, the Commission suggested improvement in the preparation of teachers and changes to make teaching "a more rewarding and respected profession."[58] Implementing these recommendations might attract the best teachers and retain them in the profession. A merit-based evaluation system was recommended along with salary increases to make teaching competitive with other careers.

Increased Fiscal Support for Schools

Naturally, such programs led to the fifth recommendation, which was to encourage fiscal support of the school system.[59] The Commission strongly claimed that our nation's citizens must "hold educators and elected officials" accountable for the status of the country's schools.[60] Without grassroots level action and support, the Committee's proposals would remain mere theories rather than actual reform. And without such reform, the NCEE seemed convinced that American schools were in grave danger. The concluding paragraph to *A Nation at Risk* states:

> It is [our children's] America, and the America of all of us, that is at risk; it is to each one of us that this imperative is addressed. It is by our willingness to take up the challenge, and our resolve to see it through, that America's place in the world will be either secured or forfeited. Americans have succeeded before and so we shall again.[61]

THE NATIONAL RESPONSE

Although some observers criticized the NCEE's report,[62] Americans appeared generally to concur with its findings. In the 1983 Gallup Poll of the public's attitudes toward the public schools, people were asked if they had heard of the Commission's report or had read it. About 30 percent were familiar with *A Nation at Risk*, and 87 percent of that informed group agreed with the report's findings. Yet, even among those who were unfamiliar with the report, 75 percent agreed with the statement that "the quality of education in the [United States'] public schools is only fair and not improving."[63] Whether the Commission's report was exactly correct seemed irrelevant—the American populace agreed that the nation's schools were at risk.

More recently, it has been reported in the popular press that:

> The nation's faith in its public schools is fading fast. A steady stream of reports from the nation's classrooms about drugs, violence, bureaucratic bloat and ill-educated students is eroding public confidence in the American tradition of "common" schooling that reaches back to the early

19th century. In one unnerving harbinger, fully 85 percent of the parents polled by the *Houston Post* in September [1991] believed their kids were unsafe in that city's public schools. And despite a decade of effort to turn things around, there is a deepening perception that the entire enterprise of public education is foundering without any real hope of rescue, especially in the nation's cities.[64]

MEETING THE CHALLENGE

Less than eight months after the publication of *A Nation at Risk*, the NCEE prepared another report for the U. S. Secretary of Education: *Meeting the Challenge*.[65] This report documented the nation's positive response to exposure of the risks facing education. All across the country, schools reevaluated their curricula and teaching methods. Some areas formed citizen groups to make particular recommendations for local needs. The NCEE reported that forty-four states were changing graduation requirements and forty-two were reforming their curricula following the release of *A Nation at Risk*.[66] If nothing else, the NCEE brought education directly to the public's attention, and people eagerly discussed educational issues with a sense of urgency "not felt since the Soviet Satellite [Sputnik] shook American confidence in its public schools in 1957."[67]

Yet, the response has not been wholly positive: "the number of private schools increased by nearly 30 percent during the 1980s . . . while the number of public schools declined 3 percent. . . . The shift to private schools is being led in many cases by baby-boomer parents who are turning their backs on the public-education system in which they were raised. . . . And more and more parents say they would opt for a private school if they could afford one."[68]

WOULD EDUCATIONAL BUREAUCRACIES RESPOND TO *A NATION AT RISK*?

The question that remained was whether the public's response to *A Nation at Risk* since 1983 would result in actual improvement in the public school system and the education of America's children. Three major concerns of the NCEE remain essentially unimproved: first, continuing illiteracy; second, weakness of the average contemporary school curriculum; third, a continuing deficit in standardized test scores. As a fourth concern, this chapter examines the continuing moral crisis in contemporary American public schools.

ILLITERACY

Literacy should be the fundamental goal of America's educational system. Freedom depends on the ability of citizens to participate and make informed decisions. As Shirley Chisholm, the first African American woman to be elected to the Congress of the United States, remarked: "How can you use the ballot box if you cannot read the newspapers, the referendums, and the political literature in order to be cognizant of the issues? Reading is almost synonymous with knowledge, and knowledge is power."[69]

Many Americans have attained basic literacy.[70] Basic literacy, although the criteria are not well-defined, means an ability to write a shopping list or to read at a certain grade level (for example, at a fourth grade level).[71] The problem arises, however, in that fewer and fewer Americans are able to perform complex and challenging literary tasks beyond a basic level.[72] According to one education expert, in 1984 there were twenty-five million American adults who could read either not at all or at less than a fifth grade level; another thirty-five million adults read at less than a ninth grade level.[73] In practical terms, ninth grade proficiency is required to read antidote instructions on bottles of household cleaners, and twelfth grade competence is required for reading a life insurance form.[74] From a larger perspective, sixty million adults reading at less than a ninth grade level represent one-third of American adults.[75]

The 1984 figure of sixty million illiterates and semi-literates demonstrates a three-fold increase over the numbers in 1975.[76] Approximately four million adults joined the ranks of illiterates each year during the period 1975-84. These increases are offset somewhat by the recent efforts to increase adult literacy.[77] However, such efforts to ameliorate adult illiteracy do not address the four million persons annually who slip through the schools without an ability to read. Further additions to the ranks of illiterates threaten in the future. As one expert concludes: "Every bit of evidence we have at hand suggests that we will see an increase in the numbers of illiterate adults within another fifteen years."[78] While adult literacy programs are moderately successful in minimizing the damage, the schools are not plugging the leak of four million new illiterate adults each year.

Evidence supports the concept of a "cycle of illiteracy."[79] This means that children of illiterates also tend to be illiterate. Studies show that children seem to learn better in school when they already have learned at home during their preschool years.[80] The cycle of illiteracy is not irreparable, but it is nevertheless a real problem and one that may be further complicated by the fact that the symptoms may not be readily apparent until late in the child's school career. In a 1976 Cleveland study, 75 percent of kindergarten students were at or above the national norm for reading development, and there "was no significant divergence between races."[81] However, by eleventh grade, 72 percent of white students were at or above the norm, yet only 41 percent of black students met or exceeded the norm.[82] Factoring in the adult illiteracy rate of 44 percent for black adults—compared to only 16 percent for white adults—the cycle of illiteracy becomes apparent between generations of black Americans.[83]

This cycle of illiteracy may not manifest itself, however, until at least the fourth grade:[84]

Up to the end of third grade, and for much of the fourth, the content of the books that children read is insubstantial. Starting in fourth grade, but more clearly in the fifth, content in itself grows more important. Up to that point, a child learns to read. After that point, the child reads to learn.[85]

A unique irony is created. Learning to read is facilitated by preschool stimulation, but those students who most need help in learning to read—the children of illiterates—cannot obtain preschool preparation from their illiterate parents. Unfortunately, the schools are failing to accomplish that task for the four million students each year who enter adulthood without the ability to read.[86] Although the public schools are in a unique position to help, the task appears too difficult for the current system.

Cultural Literacy

Another aspect of illiteracy raised concern in the late 1980s—i.e., "cultural illiteracy," which was publicized by Professor E. D. Hirsch, Jr.[87] According to Hirsch, cultural literacy is not the mental process of decoding written words, but rather:

> It is the background information stored in [readers'] minds, that enables them to take up a newspaper and read it with an adequate level of comprehension, getting the point, grasping the implications, *relating what they read to the unstated context* which alone gives meaning to what they read.[88]

Cultural literacy is as important to reading comprehension as the ability to decode the alphabet into intelligible words. An illustration might be useful. Take the letters *f*, *e*, *d*, *e*, *r*, *a*, and *l*. By themselves (for a literate person), this word is *fed-er-al* and it is an adjective describing the central government of the United States. The term *literacy* thus describes this process of decoding sequential letters so as to match some concept in the reader's memory.

But cultural literacy takes the process one step further. For example, the word *federal* certainly describes the central government of the United States. However, much more context is involved. For example, when the United States was formed, its first charter of government—the Articles of Confederation—left the central government so weak that it could not even provide for a national army. Concerned with this and other deficiencies, the founders created the Constitution. This document in turn created a "federal" government that divided powers between the states and the central government. In America, the word *federal* might also evoke the cultural concept of the Civil War—the result of which determined that states cannot secede from the Federal Union. Cultural literacy thus describes this process of placing a word or phrase into an unstated cultural context:

The reader's mind is constantly inferring meanings that are not directly stated by the words of a text but are nonetheless part of its essential content. The explicit meanings of a piece of writing are the tip of an iceberg of meaning; the larger part lies below the surface of the text and is composed of the reader's own relevant knowledge.[89]

Cultural literacy is the process that allows a reader *to see* as well as to look, *to hear* as well as to listen, and *to understand* as well as to comprehend.

Empirical evidence supports the conclusion that cultural literacy is still at risk in the United States today. On October 8, 1985, the chairperson of the National Endowment for the Humanities reported, "[T]wo-thirds of the seventeen-year-old students tested could not place the Civil War in the correct half century; a third did not know the Declaration of Independence was signed between 1750 and 1800 . . . [and] a third did not know that Columbus sailed for the New World before '1750.'"[90] This study indicates that many of the nation's schoolchildren lack cultural literacy.

A large part of the responsibility for cultural literacy has been assigned to the nation's public schools: "In the modern age, the role assigned to our schools is to prepare our children for the broader activities of society and to train them in the literate public culture."[91] Yet, contemporary American public schools no longer stress the content of traditional American public culture.[92] This trend away from content is a "fundamental educational mistake" that has caused "a gradual decline in our ability to communicate . . . [and] has therefore been a chief cause of illiteracy, which is a subcategory of the inability to communicate."[93] An inability to communicate creates a clear hazard in cultural literacy that has not improved—and perhaps has worsened—in recent years.

One of Hirsch's colleagues demonstrates the importance of cultural literacy in a scientific context. Professor James Trefil raises two issues that probably concern most Americans: first, the Strategic Defense Initiative (SDI), and second, the safety of nuclear reactors.[94] Both issues are affected whenever Americans vote for the Senators and members of Congress who appropriate billions of dollars for the highly technical programs. For persons living in close proximity to nuclear power plants, the viability of safety devices is crucial to peace of mind. Both issues involve complex technical aspects of electronics, physics, and engineering. Without a cultural understanding of science, American voters cannot vote knowledgeably on either SDI or nuclear regulation. And if the scientists who actually understand the technology cannot communicate in common terms with the general public, then potential social benefits might be lost in the confusion. Trefil concludes: "It is part of the basic responsibility of scientists to translate the essential elements of science into general, non-technical terms."[95]

Other areas also present the risk of miscommunication, including genetic engineering, the greenhouse effect, and chemical warfare. If Americans continue to lack cultural literacy in these areas, the result may be that Americans will lose their democratic powers over strategic scientific matters.

In fact, the American form of democracy might very well depend on cultural literacy. Without a common reservoir of culture that brings Americans together, divisions will undoubtedly occur since "literate culture has become the common currency for social and economic exchange in our democracy, and the only available ticket to full citizenship."[96] As American schoolchildren learn less content, the ability to rely on unstated background assumptions while communicating is sacrificed. Communication necessarily becomes inefficient. And as inefficiencies rise, efforts to communicate will decline in number. The current trend of process without content might lead to schoolchildren with lots to say and write—but fewer to understand what is being said and written.

CURRICULUM

The term *curriculum* involves several objectives. First, a curriculum is a long-term lesson plan or extended course of study. In many schools, certain objectives must be met each year for students to complete the curriculum. A kindergarten curriculum, for example, might include learning the alphabet, counting to ten, and recognizing colors.

Second, any curriculum is an attempt to standardize the educational process. Different teachers will utilize different instructional methods, but a curriculum will ensure that everyone has a similar starting and ending point.

Finally, curricula are programs for achieving social goals. One objective of society is a high level of literacy. This is accomplished by learning the alphabet in kindergarten, learning to spell in second grade, and writing term papers in seventh grade. Schools are also "intended to produce, through the application of formulae, formulaic human beings whose behavior can be predicted and controlled."[97]

Although the term *curriculum* can be used to describe various objectives, the achievement of each objective is sought in the same setting: the nation's schools. When changes are necessary in education, the curriculum is thus generally the target of reform. This truism has been proved in recent efforts to improve American schools.

National Curriculum Objectives: America 2000

In 1991, President George Bush unveiled his new plan for improving America's public schools.[98] The plan—called a "crusade" by Education Secretary Lamar Alexander—aimed to restore American dominance in mathematics and science.[99] President Bush also sought a high school graduation rate of 90 percent.[100] Since some schools suffer nearly a 40 percent dropout rate,[101] the Bush approach would require three-quarters of dropouts not only to stay in school but also to graduate. At the same time President Bush sought to increase the graduation rate, he also sought to make the high school and primary school curriculum more difficult. The President's plan, called America 2000, included proposals for establishing high national curriculum standards in English, math, science, history, and geography.[102]

America 2000 demonstrates the truism that education changes include alterations in school curricula.[103] Yet a high graduation rate and raised national standards may be mutually exclusive goals.[104]

The school curriculum changes rapidly from "readin', 'ritin', and 'rithmetic" as a student progresses through the grades. One education commentator believes that a diverse curriculum is the inevitable result of society's goal of graduating a large percentage of the population.[105] When attendance is compulsory and graduation rates make the headlines, schools face enormous pressure to provide something for everyone.[106] Thus, computer science becomes as important as English, and mechanics takes on equal importance with biology. Such equivalence between traditional and vocational education may make sense in light of today's rising technology. Since 75 percent of technical jobs do not require a college degree, "a good vocational education can be a surer route to a career than the traditional academic skills."[107]

To entice a maximum number of student-customers, the schools expand their curriculum choices and place no value emphasis on any particular choice.[108] The necessity for an expanded curriculum also follows from the fact that teenage students have radically diverse lifestyles from one another. Some know before entering high school that colleges and graduate schools are in their futures. Others have children or parents to support. And still others see extracurricular high school activities as a ticket to professional athletics or other careers. With so much diversity, a pure curriculum of English, math, science, computers, history, and foreign languages would include some students and exclude others. Thus, to attract such a diverse student population, schools often resort to diverse curriculum content.

Format Changes

In light of high dropout rates, other schools have adopted innovative approaches to their extracurricular content and to the format of their curricula. Administrators of these schools apparently believe that creativity is required to capture the attention of students.

For instance, the principal at Sousa Junior High School in Southeast Washington, D.C., adopted two changes to help curb the dropout rate. First, the school gymnasium opens around sunrise each morning, and students are allowed to play basketball—but in return they must stay for classes during the day.[109] Second, each class period was reduced by eight minutes, creating an extra time period with the minutes saved.[110] The idea behind both changes was apparently to accommodate the attention span of the students. Early-morning basketball might bring the students to school, and shorter periods might keep the pupils there. Since half of the District of

Columbia's dropouts claim to feel alienated from education,[111] approaches like this are implemented to keep those students in school by appealing to their interests. The theory apparently is that these children will somehow benefit just by attending school. These activities change the format, but not the content, of the curriculum.

Curriculum Changes

America 2000, however, focuses on the precise knowledge students should have before entering society. Its theory apparently is that society benefits more from a 90 percent rate of superior graduates than a 100 percent rate of mediocre graduates.

Despite these differences, both approaches share a common focus: enticing dropouts to return to education.[112] For those dropouts who perceive school as boring, either a more challenging curriculum or more interesting extracurricular activities are seen as avoiding boredom. Nonetheless, one proponent of public schools argues that the "first lesson private schools teach is that schools need a clear mission and they need to be simple. . . . It's a false assumption that because public schools are publicly funded they have to be all things to all people. Public-school authorities should create portfolios of schools, each with a different focus, in math and science, say, or vocational education."[113]

Changes in Classroom Dynamics: Negotiations and Treaties

There is an additional aspect to the curriculum that transcends the formal boundaries of class subjects and class times: the classroom itself. Teachers and students will act in a manner that sometimes deviates from the formal curriculum. In the past, teachers usually served to bridge the gap between students and the subject matter. Today, many public school teachers act more like a third team on a baseball diamond and have no more influence than students on the subject taught.[114] In response to the "third-team scenario," students and teachers negotiate "treaties" to either engage in learning or avoid learning.[115]

An example of the negotiation process is the recent phenomenon of "Walkman tolerance." Increasingly teachers are allowing students to bring their portable radios to class if the students will use earphones and refrain from talking during instruction.[116] Three terms are important to these classroom treaties: time, relationship, and intensity.[117] The first term, *time*, basically contains two components. Class attendance is the first component, and it is negotiated by the number of times a student can be late for class or "cut" the class entirely.[118] Sometimes class attendance is modified when the teacher discusses non-curriculum subjects during the first few minutes of class or when the teacher dismisses the class a few minutes early.[119]

Homework is the second time component and is most likely to be subject to bargaining.[120] Some teachers continue to collect and grade homework, but others simply assume homework will get done. Interestingly, teachers do not seem willing to abandon homework entirely. The ultimate bargain is to "relocat[e] homework to the classroom. Class time is used for [homework activity] that would otherwise be done out of class."[121] Time negotiation is a crucial process when a main goal of education is universal graduation. When some children have no desire to attend school, teachers have incentive to bargain for strong learning some of the time rather than weak learning all of the time.

The second and third terms of negotiation are related to one another. *Intensity* within the classroom clearly depends on the *relationship* between the teacher and the students. As one education author explains: "Behind all the treaties lies a deeply felt preference by most students and most teachers for relations they usually call open, friendly, and caring. No student definition of a good teacher was more common than someone who could 'relate' to them."[122]

However, "relating" to students is more of a continuum than an isolated quality. One version of "relating" is when a teacher is nurturing toward students and cares deeply about their personal lives.

An opposite extreme occurs when a teacher relates to students by an entirely professional, pragmatic approach (although, to some students, this may represent a more acceptable relationship).[123] These versions of the teacher-student relationship translate into certain levels of intensity within the classroom. For college-bound students, a professional relationship culminates in an intense study of the subject matter. Humorist Dave Barry describes the classroom intensity of a prior generation:

> [Back in the 1950s], math was taught by what professional educators refer to as: the Noogie Method. At least this was the method used by Mr. O'Regan, a large man who taught me the times tables. Mr. O'Regan would stand directly behind you and yell: "9 TIMES 7!" And if you didn't state the answer immediately, Mr. O'Regan would give you a noogie.[124]

Intensity is thus expressed in various ways. Treaties may well be formed "that regard subjects not as vehicles for the development of thinking but as materials to be endured with as little passion and commitment as possible."[125] Within these two extremes is a spectrum open for intraclassroom negotiation. A treaty might cycle between a nurturing and a professional relationship, or some subjects might be taught with intensity while others will be avoided.

With the existence of classroom treaties, a curriculum contains both formal and informal components. For education reform to be successful, both aspects must be altered. Perhaps needless to say, the formal curriculum is dependent on the resources available.

Financial Resources

The U.S. Department of Education reported in September 1991 that it would spend "a record $413.8 billion on education this year. About $248.6

billion of that total will be going to public primary and secondary education, making an average per-pupil investment of just under $6,000. The Education Department's annual 'Back to School' forecast shows that per-pupil spending in the public schools has increased nearly $3,000 in the last ten years."[126] It seems apparent that limits on financial resources, in general, are not the source of the problems in America's schools.[127] As one authority on education matters notes:

> The public schools' problems are rooted in the way public schools are governed—from the top down. They are designed to be responsive to political entities—school boards, state legislatures and the interest groups that influence them. By their nature, they steal vital authority away from schools. People work harder and smarter when they have autonomy, but teachers and principals in public education simply don't have very much autonomy. The alternative to the current political and bureaucratic system of public education is a market-driven system, one where individual schools are given lots of autonomy but are kept in check by permitting parents and students to choose freely among schools. Such a system would have a great deal of accountability in it, but an accountability that would motivate educators to work harder and smarter rather than to follow rules and regulations.[128]

Some state governments appear to be addressing needs for financial support, and some state courts appear to be ordering a rough equivalence of expenditures between school authorities.[129] While these changes may help alleviate the current disparity between rich and poor school districts, increased funding will more than likely not resolve the problems of contemporary public education.[130] As one senior researcher has said:

> There are school systems—Los Angeles, Miami, parts of New York—that are grossly overcrowded due to immigration. There are cities like Memphis where per-pupil spending is under $3,000 a year. These are places where more money is absolutely required. But there's no reason why school systems can't create the kind of simple, focused schools I'm talking about with the same amount of money we typically spend on the chaotic schools we've got now.[131]

DEFICIT IN STANDARDIZED TEST SCORES

As noted earlier, one measure of classroom performance is a student's score on standardized tests. Different schools and different classrooms may use differing methods of instruction, although most will offer a balance of lectures and interactive activities in their curricula. Thus, one of the strongest justifications for standardized tests is that they "provide some basis for comparing students applying [to college] from schools of very different quality and grading standards."[132]

These tests can also be used to compare school systems. When standardized test scores are publicized, parents and other community leaders look to see if their schools are "better" or "worse" than schools elsewhere. Above-average scores can contribute to community pride, while low scores may raise concern. According to the theory of standardized tests, as many students should score above the average—or "norm"—as those who score below. This means that for every community taking pride in its schools, there is another neighborhood with raised concerns. Over the past three decades, however, a different concern has been raised: the average score has fallen.[133] The average composite score on the Scholastic Aptitude Test (SAT), which is administered by the Educational Testing Service,[134] fell from 970 in 1963 to 890 in 1980.[135] On the math portion, the average dropped from 500 to 470;[136] the verbal average fell from 480 to 420.[137] By 1989, the average score had not improved very much, despite many improvement efforts:[138] the average for the math portion was 476 and for the verbal portion 427.[139] Furthermore, a huge disparity in scores exists between students of different minority groups: white students average 200 points higher than black students on the combined SAT score.[140] More recently, a new low of 422 has been reached in the national SAT verbal score; the previous low of 424 was reached in 1980.[141] According to the College Board: "The mean verbal score has declined for the fifth consecutive year to a new all-time low, two points below its previous low in 1980, 1981, and 1990."[142]

As average scores have fallen, colleges and universities ironically have come to rely increasingly on standardized tests as a primary admission factor. As of 1989, 84 percent of American four-year colleges required taking the SAT for entrance.[143] For scholarships, the use of SAT scores only (without any other criteria) has been declared unconstitutional in New York.[144] But overall in the United States, the importance of SAT scores has risen. With the rise in importance, however, also has come an incentive to cheat. One guidance counselor remarked that one "can certainly steal these [SAT] exams. . . . There are lots of kids today who will do anything they can to get a higher score."[145]

In one well-publicized instance, New York school officials refused to cancel a statewide chemistry exam despite knowledge of widespread distribution of the answers.[146] The *New York Post* decided, therefore, to publish the answers as a way of exposing the massive cheating involved; only after the *Post's* actions did education officials cancel the exam. Apparently it took a *Post* reporter only "about 15 minutes to locate a high school student on the telephone who was able to send by fax a copy of the test's answer key."[147] While the company responsible for administering the SAT contends that its security measures are sufficient, examples of cheating on other standardized tests appear to be growing.

THE MORAL CRISIS
Cheating
If the increasing number of incidents of standardized test cheating is any indication, American schools are in a moral crisis as well as an educational

crisis.[148] Within the schools, children are no longer able to focus entirely on the learning process.

Clothing Becomes a Catalyst for Death and Violence

As gangs have proliferated in urban areas, even the clothing students wear has become a matter of life and death. Students have been shot for wearing certain clothes. At least one student athlete was killed for his "high-tech" basketball shoes. In response to the violence attached to clothing, some schools have reintroduced dress codes in order to stifle gang identification and peer pressure.[149]

In other cases, a hard look or a flared temper can result in school violence. Between 1987 and 1989, New York City schools recorded nearly 6,500 serious incidents—including robbery, weapons possession, assault, sex offenses, and drug use or possession.[150] These incidents finally culminated in the installation of metal detectors in five New York City high schools; in the first year of operation, 820 weapons were confiscated.[151] By December 1989, the president of the United Federation of Teachers was calling for the installation of metal detectors in any New York City high school that requested them.[152]

Many guidance counselors and school administrators agree that drastic measures such as dress codes and metal detectors might be necessary to alleviate the rise in both the incidence and the intensity of school violence.[153]

In any event:

> More than 400,000, or about 2% of the US's 12-19 year olds were victims of violent crimes at their own schools, the Federal Government just reported in its National Crime Victimization Survey. About 430,000 students (over 2% of the 21.6 million students in the 12-19 year old range) carry weapons to school to protect themselves (i.e., guns, knives, brass knuckles, razor blades, and spiked jewelry). The report said one out of five high school students and one out of three high school boys carries a weapon to school, while 43% said they had been armed four or more times in the previous month. Rape, aggravated assault, and robbery are common crimes at U.S. schools. The same government survey said that one in two teenagers drinks and one in three smokes.[154]

Violence Near School Grounds

Yet, the moral crisis is not limited to the school grounds. Many students are most afraid of the violence that occurs "just outside the schools, often when classes are through for the day."[155] Often this violence is drug-related.[156]

Drugs

In fact, the emerging drug culture may be a dominant force in the American moral crisis. Schools are beginning to address the drug problem through radical new programs, which seem to be necessary "as the crack epidemic touches the lives of younger children across the country."[157]

"Personal Trait" Programs

These programs attempt to develop personal traits in children that help them to resist drugs.[158] However, it is not certain whether these new efforts will have a positive effect on the nation's schoolchildren. Since most of these recent "personal trait" programs take place at the elementary school level, any success will not appear for several years, since the decision to use drugs generally is made during high school.[159]

Indeed, according to recent statistics, the rates of drug and alcohol use among high school students have risen dramatically. In 1962, only 4 percent of high school seniors had tried marijuana; by 1982, 59 percent had used the drug.[160] In addition, 90 percent of the high school class of 1985 had used alcohol[161]—which is especially alarming since in most states the legal drinking age is twenty-one years old. More recently:

> A new study released by the Department of Health and Human Services reports that 8 million, or about 40%, of junior and senior-high school students drink weekly, and together consume approximately 35% of all wine coolers sold in America. More than 3 million students say they drink alone, more than 4 million drink when they are upset, and nearly 3 million drink because they are bored, the study reported. U.S. Surgeon General Antonia Novella commented while releasing the report that, "many of these kids are already alcoholics ... [and] the rest may well be on their way." The report was based upon a survey of 956 students grades 7 through 12 in eight states and is consistent with other federal studies showing alcohol as the drug choice for American adolescents.[162]

AIDS Education

Another area for moral concern is the subject of human sexuality. As the AIDS virus has spread, schools have assumed responsibility for teaching students about AIDS and methods of preventing the spread of the virus. Since 1988, at least twenty-eight states have required AIDS education for every public school child.[163] Nonetheless:

> From January 1987 through December 1991, the cumulative number of acquired immunodeficiency syndrome (AIDS) cases among adolescents aged 13-19 years in the United States increased from 127 to 789, and in 1989, AIDS became the sixth leading cause of death for persons aged 15-24 years. Because the median incubation period between infection with human immunodeficiency virus (HIV) and onset of AIDS is nearly 10 years, many 20-29-year-olds with AIDS may have been infected during adolescence.[164]

"Tragically, the condom emphasis is breeding a false sense of security among people in high-risk categories: anyone sexually active outside of a mutually monogamous marriage. The research clearly shows that reliance on condoms for safety from HIV is trifling with death."[165] And yet, many state statutes mandating AIDS education do not require parental *consent*, in contrast to parental *notification*. This deprives parents of the right to direct the education of their children in an area where the wrong information can cost their children their lives.

At least two states make a distinction between sex education and AIDS education and thereby circumvent their state's statutory parental notification requirements for sex education. In Louisiana, the state attorney general issued an opinion holding that Louisiana school districts either can teach AIDS education as part of their sex education programs or can teach AIDS education as part of their communicable disease curriculum—without adopting a sex education program.[166] Although the state permits parents to remove their children from sex education classes,[167] because AIDS education is distinguished from sex education, it appears that a local Louisiana school board would not have to follow the notification requirements under the sex education statutes. Although such schools must limit AIDS education so that it will not constitute sex education, if Louisiana school districts have not elected to place it within a sex education program,[168] children, nonetheless, may be exposed to a secular discussion of issues without the benefit of an express excusal provision for AIDS education.

The Michigan Attorney General has also distinguished AIDS education from sex education.[169] In Michigan, parents may exclude their children from the traditional sex education courses.[170] Although the communicable diseases/AIDS education statute in Michigan does not include an excusal provision,[171] the Attorney General has stated that "students must be excused from instruction concerning characteristics or symptoms of [AIDS] if requested by a parent or guardian for religious reasons."[172]

Since AIDS education often includes perspectives and information that are antithetical to the religious and moral teaching of some parents or, at a minimum, includes information with which parents disagree on factual or other grounds, legislation of this sort is troubling for numerous reasons, including the fact that parents must often pass high hurdles before they can remove their children from such classes, and state statutes may even attempt to preclude excusal entirely. For example, the Tennessee legislature only allows excusal after a parent submits a written statement requesting excusal and after the parents personally examine the materials or confer with teachers or school officials.[173] In Washington, the ability of parents to remove their children from sex education courses is conditioned upon their attendance at a presentation of the materials and curricula.[174] Such burdensome requirements make it unduly difficult to obtain excusal.

Condom Distribution

Many schools now encourage children to make their own decisions about when to engage in sex and with whom, and the use of contraceptives is explained.[175] Sexual intercourse within the bounds of marriage is presented as simply one of several options. The schools' failure to teach abstinence until marriage is indicated through the statistics on teenage pregnancy: although the *number* of adolescent mothers has remained constant, at about 470,000 per year since the 1970s, the *proportion* of unmarried teenage mothers has risen from three-tenths to seven-tenths.[176]

The New York City public high school system instituted a condom availability program in 1991 that was challenged by numerous parents and students in the City's public high schools.[177] Although parents had a right to request that their children not participate in that part of the required classroom instruction concerning the methods of prevention of AIDS,[178] there is no provision for excusal with respect to the City's voluntary condom availability program. In denying the request of the parents and students for declaratory and injunctive relief, the Supreme Court of New York said: "The school is not compelling the students to participate and sanctions are not imposed if they choose not to participate. As a result of these characteristics, a State benefit is not being conditioned upon conduct prohibited by one's faith, nor is a benefit denied due to conduct mandated by one's faith. Petitioners are not being asked to modify their behavior or violate their beliefs . . . all the program does is expose the children to other ideas on the subject, distasteful as they may be to petitioners."[179] The New York Supreme Court notes: "The program may arguably make it more difficult to practice one's religion, but such burdens are merely incidental and do not rise to the level of free exercise violations."[180] The Court continues: "Although the Petitioners argue that indirect coercion, mainly peer pressure and the school's promulgation of the condom program, are subject to scrutiny under the First Amendment, the effects of the voluntary program are at best incidental."[181]

California legislation provides that minors may receive contraceptives without parental consent.[182]

Condoms are currently available, sometimes without parental notification or consent, in many public schools across the country, either from condom-dispensing machines installed in the public school rest rooms or school-based "health clinics" that are sometimes staffed by non-school personnel.

CONCLUSION

American education is still in a crisis. Illiteracy is growing, and standardized test scores continue to decline. The average school curriculum remains weak. Furthermore, most American students are engulfed in a moral crisis framed by a drug culture and widespread sexual misconduct. The crisis persists despite a massive effort to reform American education throughout the

1980s. Educators are questioning whether the crisis has peaked or whether reform efforts simply can do no more to improve the system. The conclusion to this debate will emerge over the next decade as the Excellence Movement continues with President Bush's America 2000 plan and the education agenda of President Bill Clinton.

However, it seems likely that the ultimate vision of reformers cannot be met in the current public school system. The American student body is as varied as the country's populace. Yet, Excellence reform seeks not only universal graduation but also universal literacy. Furthermore, while reformers assert the need for increased resources, the additional resources are slow in coming. True reform requires national leadership, local action, and fiscal support. Unfortunately these components have not yet been present simultaneously.

The conclusion is that successful Excellence reform in American public schools is possible but improbable. There are too many competing demands for all the reform goals to be met together. The nation's schools are still at risk, and before much longer, the risk may become reality.

Nonetheless, many Americans do not accept hopelessness. As New York's 1990 Teacher of the Year said: "Genuine reform is possible, but it shouldn't cost anything. We need to rethink the fundamental premises of schooling and decide what it is we want all children to learn, and why."[183]

Meanwhile, some will continue to seek "excellence" in America's public schools. Entrepreneurs and businessmen will undoubtedly attempt to implement new and innovative technical approaches to education.[184]

Parochial schools will fight the battle in their own ways.[185] Some preparatory schools are becoming partners with the public schools.[186]

Home schools will continue to flourish and increase in number. As one source notes: "The number of students educated at home has swelled from 10,000 in 1970 to over 300,000 today, an increase that shows no sign of slackening. About 75 percent of home schoolers are conservative Christians who stress the Bible in their teachings and who lament what they see as a decline in traditional values in public schools. Still others believe that public schools don't set high enough academic standards."[187]

All of this raises the ultimate question: "[Will] such a public-education system lead to the fragmentation of society and the further segregation of the nation's students by race and class? Ultimately, the question is whether common schooling is necessary for the common good."[188]

2

The History and Philosophy of Public Education

Although *A Nation At Risk*[1] documents many of the problems of contemporary American public education and contains many recommendations to cure its ills, the report's analytical framework rarely extends beyond the schools. Families and churches are essentially absent from the report, as either a part of the problem or its solution.[2]

Historically, however, both the family and the church have played a critical role in American public education.[3] Over time, schools in America have increased in importance as a source of education, but the home and family remain steadfast as the primary source of all instruction and training.

EDUCATION IN COLONIAL AMERICA, 1600–1765

The people who originally came to America, especially the English, brought with them educational philosophies, institutions, and instructional methods which they tried to reestablish in the colonies.[4] The colonists wanted to preserve the European civilizations they had left behind by copying the educational institutions of their homelands.[5] They also brought with them an interrelationship between home, church and school that taught the values of piety, civility and learning, with the school as the least important institution for such teaching.[6]

There were major differences between American colonial regions in the area of education, but some things were universal among the colonists. For example, all the colonists were instilled with a strong sense of religious commitment.[7] In general, local or church authorities built and financed what schools there were, with little outside supervision from the civil government.[8] Although there was more social mobility in the colonies than in Europe, schools remained class-centered.[9] While the upper classes sent their sons to formal schools, middle and working class parents apprenticed their sons to tradesmen to learn skills, as was the practice in Europe.[10]

THE NEW ENGLAND COLONIES

The New England colonies included Massachusetts, Connecticut, New Hampshire, Vermont and Rhode Island.[11] The primary influence on education in the New England colonies was religion, in particular that of the Puritans.[12] The center of Puritanism is the belief in the Bible as the inspired Word of God, giving people the rules for conduct and worship.[13] In their view, everyone was a sinner and the world was full of evil and temptation.[14] Predestination was a fundamental concept in Puritan theology. A chosen few among the descendants of Adam would be saved through the sacrifice of Jesus Christ on earth. Others were condemned to an afterlife of eternal suffering.[15]

To the Puritans, education played a very important role in teaching the principles of religion, morals and earning a living.[16] Since Calvinism centered on the Bible, good Calvinists had to be literate.[17] In the hope of being accepted by God, work and education became primary concerns: "[T]o achieve nobility and attain salvation, man must transcend his physical surroundings by education, work, and great personal struggle."[18]

Geographical conditions in New England also promoted education. The farm land was not fertile, so settlers turned from agriculture to building, manufacturing and trade.[19] Businesses thus needed employees who could work with numbers and documents. It was an economic necessity to have people who could read, write and do mathematics.[20] Nonetheless, the primary philosophy of the schools remained the furtherance of religion.[21]

In order to fulfill these goals, Massachusetts enacted legislation in 1642 requiring all children to be educated to certain minimal standards.[22] This law was enacted in response to the court's conclusion that many parents were neglecting the education of their children.[23]

This law was followed in 1647 by the "Old Deluder Satan Act." "Based upon the premise that ignorant people were prone to evil, the Law of 1647 sought to train up a literate population sufficiently schooled to resist the temptations of the devil."[24] The first tax on property for local schools was in Dedham, Massachusetts, in 1648.[25]

There were many different methods of instruction in the New England colonies. In remote areas, a teacher would travel from one settlement to another to provide instruction, then move on to other settlements.[26] Wealthy families sometimes employed tutors who lived in the home and instructed the children.[27] There were also schools with one master for a roomful of children of varying ages.[28]

Puritan children were expected to be seen and not heard, with schooling as a method of taming the propensity of children toward evil and idleness.[29] This was implemented by hard work, discipline and corporal punishment.[30] "Severe floggings were administered for misbehavior or breaking the rules, since Puritan philosophy called for literally beating the Devil out of the child."[31] Children were constantly reminded of "the shortness of life, the torments of hell and the fear that one's behavior might not be acceptable for salvation."[32] Children also did chores such as carrying in firewood, milking cows, and working in the fields as a form of informal education.[33]

The first reading source many children used was the "hornbook." This was a piece of paper with the alphabet, some syllables, a benediction, and the Lord's Prayer on it; the paper was attached to a board and was covered with transparent horn.[34] One of the most widely used books was the *New England Primer*, which first appeared in 1690.[35] This book combined the substance of the hornbook (the alphabet and syllables) with religious lessons such as the Lord's Prayer and the Ten Commandments.[36] Writing with ink and quill pens and arithmetic, or ciphering as it was called, were also taught.[37]

THE MIDDLE ATLANTIC COLONIES

The Middle Atlantic colonies were New York, Pennsylvania, Delaware and New Jersey.[38] The Middle Atlantic colonies were marked by diversity in both language and religion.[39] Among the religious denominations found in these colonies were the Dutch Reformed Church, Anglicans, Quakers, Lutherans, Moravians, Dunkers, Anabaptists, Presbyterians, French Huguenots, Roman Catholics from Ireland and Germany, and Jews.[40] With all this diversity, the state gave up control of the schools, in favor of private control by each sect.[41] The only laws in place were those giving the royal governor the right to license teachers.[42]

In New Amsterdam, later to become New York, control of the schools was shared by the Dutch West India Company which supported the schools financially, the Dutch Reformed Church which exercised control of the curriculum, and the colonial governor who licensed teachers.[43] Formal education was limited since the Anglicans believed that education was a private matter for the family and church to oversee.[44] There were schools operated by the Society for the Propagation of the Gospel in Foreign Parts (SPG) for poor children, as well as private schools that were run for profit.[45]

Pennsylvania was established as a refuge for Quakers by William Penn, its first governor.[46] Quakers rejected the idea of a specially trained ministry but advocated literacy. Instruction in the Quaker schools was therefore not oriented to the memorization of doctrines.[47] Quaker schools were of excellent quality[48] and were open to everyone, including girls, African Americans, and Indians.[49]

A night school was opened in Philadelphia in 1731 which taught writing and arithmetic.[50] Although the New England colonies were the leaders in universal education during this period, there was a high level of educational activity at the elementary level in the Middle Colonies.[51]

THE SOUTHERN COLONIES

The Southern colonies were Maryland, Virginia, Georgia, North Carolina, and South Carolina.[52] The Southern colonies were relatively small, with a population that was spread out over a large area of land.[53] In addition, most of the settlers in this area were Anglican.[54] As mentioned earlier, the Anglicans believed education was a private matter to be left to families and the church.[55] These factors combined to make formal schooling most rare in the Southern colonies.[56]

The strict class structure in Europe was transported to the colonial South.[57] For the landed gentry, tutorial education was a common practice.[58] Sons of the planter class were taught the Greek and Roman classics along with English literature, the Bible, and painting and architecture.[59] Efforts were made to provide schools for poor children and Indians, but these efforts failed.[60]

Old Field Schools, schools built by members of the community on fallow fields, and Dame Schools, instruction by women in their own homes, were also tried in the South.[61] For the most part, however, schooling remained informal due to the scattered population and general belief that each family was responsible for the education of its own children, not those of others.[62]

EDUCATION AND THE AMERICAN REVOLUTION, 1776–1812

The American Revolution changed the way Americans thought about themselves. This necessitated a change in educational theory and practice. Democracy threatened the dual system of education in which only the privileged enjoyed the benefits of the educational system.[63] "In the republican society that flows from Locke's and Jefferson's contract theory, political roles are based on election by the governed rather than on birth. In fact, no one knows whose children are going to become political leaders."[64] Universal education becomes much more important in a democratic society where no one knows who is destined to govern. All citizens need to be prepared to govern; and since all citizens choose their governors, everyone needs to be competent to exercise this duty.[65]

In contrast to the Puritan belief that everyone is evil, the Enlightenment theorists, especially Jean Jacques Rousseau, believed in the inherent goodness of human beings.[66] Other challenges to old ideas also developed. The Enlightenment thinkers appealed "to *human* reason rather than divine law, to *natural* rights rather than supernatural rights, to *scientific* method rather than to established truths, to *social* agreements and *individual* freedom rather than authoritarian control, and to *humanitarian* and *democratic* faith rather than aristocratic privilege."[67]

The Revolutionary War itself had a damaging impact on education. The energies and resources of the people were drawn away from education and into the war.[68] Rural schools had to shut down, and larger town schools were severely hampered, so illiteracy increased.[69] Teachers left to fight the war, and schools were turned into barracks.[70] English support, especially the Anglican SPG, was terminated and never resumed.[71]

Prior to the adoption and ratification of the Constitution, the national government enacted two ordinances regarding education. The Land Ordinance of 1785 set aside the sixteenth section of government land in each township for schools.[72] Article Three of the Northwest Ordinance of 1787 expressed a commitment to education in stating: "Religion, morality, and knowledge being necessary to good government and the happiness of mankind, schools and the means of education shall forever be encouraged."[73]

When the founding fathers drafted the Constitution and the Bill of Rights, they did not include any provision for education.[74] The Reserved Powers Clause of the Tenth Amendment left control over education with each state.[75] There were many proposals for a national school system, but they all failed.[76] Most states made a commitment to education in their state constitutions, however.[77]

EDUCATIONAL LEADERS

Colonial educational reform was led by a few key men. Benjamin Franklin was a self-made and largely self-educated man who favored schools with English as the instructional language, a curriculum that embodied scientific and practical skills, and knowledge with the aim of preparing people to make useful contributions to society, politics, government and business.[78] He also wanted good manners, etiquette, ethics and morals to be taught in the schools.[79] These were a sharp break with the traditional mode of studying the classics and religion.[80]

Thomas Jefferson had an enormous impact on public education. Unlike Franklin, Jefferson was educated at formal educational institutions.[81] Jefferson was particularly concerned about educating people for their roles in the emerging democratic society.[82] Jefferson said that the best defense against tyranny is to "illuminate as far as practicable, the minds of the people at large."[83] Jefferson recognized that everyone had equal rights but unequal abilities. He hoped to remedy this situation through civic education.[84] Replacing an aristocracy in the European mold would be a "natural aristocracy" based on "talent and ability" rather than birth and wealth.[85]

In 1779, Jefferson introduced a "Bill for the More General Diffusion of Knowledge" to the Virginia legislature.[86] Although Jefferson's bill was defeated for economic reasons, it was significant because it sought to establish state-sponsored elementary education.[87]

Another important educational leader during the end of the Eighteenth Century was Noah Webster. Webster supported free schools so American children could learn "the virtues of liberty, just laws, morality, hard work, and patriotism."[88] To inculcate these values, he called for teaching training, class sizes of no more than twenty-five students, interesting presentation of subjects, and promotion of student motivation to achieve academically.[89] Webster believed that "a national language" would be the "bond of national union," so he wanted to develop a distinctively American language and literature.[90]

Webster wrote several textbooks that were very popular in America, especially his spelling book.[91] Noah Webster's most famous work is his *American Dictionary of the English Language*, which was completed in 1825.[92]

THE COMMON SCHOOL MOVEMENT, 1812–1865

The beginning of the Nineteenth Century saw many changes in American society. Along with those changes, education began to take on the form that would continue through the Twentieth Century. "The 1830's saw the growth of the conception that any citizen could effectively manage positions of public trust and responsibility."[93] With this further democratization came new calls for universal public education.

The American common school movement was aimed at establishing tax-supported, locally controlled elementary schools that would be available to all children.[94] As a result, thousands of local school districts were formed, with schools that followed a generalized version of Protestant Christianity.[95] The common school movement took hold at different rates in different areas of the country. As expected, the New England states moved rapidly, while the southern states did not establish common schools until after the Civil War.[96]

THE INDUSTRIAL REVOLUTION AND IMMIGRATION

The first half of the Nineteenth Century saw the beginning of the Industrial Revolution.[97] At the same time that America was industrializing, there was massive immigration.[98] Industrialization increased the gross national product and spurred economic growth, but it also created complex social problems.[99] In the East, large factory towns were built up on water power sources.[100] New transportation modes facilitated the industrial growth.[101]

The shift from an agrarian rural economy to an industrial urban economy brought many problems. Large numbers of children were gathered in central locations, and factories and mills needed educated managers and trained workers.[102] Immigration produced a heterogeneous population with non-English speakers and non-Protestant people.[103] Common schooling was a way to solve these problems. It worked both as a way to increase social and economic mobility and as a way of controlling immigrants by imposing the language, beliefs and values of the dominant group on outsiders.[104]

Westward expansion also helped the common school movement. As people moved west, the belief that people should have equal opportunity without "the stigma of charity" spurred universal education with universal suffrage in the large frontier communities.[105] Obtaining tax money to support the theories of minimum public education for every child was not as easy, however.[106]

HORACE MANN AND THE COMMON SCHOOL

Horace Mann was one of the leading proponents of common schooling. He learned to read in school, then primarily self-educated himself until he entered Brown University.[107] He combined the Puritanism of his childhood with his study of Transcendentalism to create his theories on education.[108] He believed that the future of the nation depended on universal public education.[109]

Mann was able to convince a coalition of businessmen, workers, farmers and members of different religious denominations that public education would benefit them all.[110] His model of the common school was to be attended by all children, regardless of class background or religion.[111] It was also a public institution to be funded by the public, administered by public officials, and accountable to the community.[112]

The curriculum of Mann's common school was to enable students to perform their societal duties. The curriculum should therefore include the skills needed for life, for ethical behavior, and for responsible citizenship.[113] The moral values stressed were those of "hard work, effort, honesty, diligence, thrift, literacy, respect for property, and respect for reason."[114] Mann rejected sectarianism in favor of a general Christian Protestant ethic that was rejected by Roman Catholics.[115]

Catholics were not the only ones who opposed the common schools. Some private schools feared that common schools would make their schools obsolete. They also feared that common schools would lower admissions requirements, lower academic standards, and weaken the curriculum.[116] Some people opposed the common schools because they did not believe the public had a responsibility to finance education.[117] Others were apprehensive that the common schools would give the government too much control in indoctrinating children.[118] In addition, people who wanted to preserve their ethnicity opposed the threat of the creation of a common language, morality, and religion.[119]

As mentioned earlier, the common schools were based on a general Christian Protestant ethic. The McGuffey readers were widely read in the common schools.[120] These readers contributed to the grading movement, i.e., the organization of schools in eight-year elementary schools.[121]

EDUCATIONAL ALTERNATIVES

The "monitorial" method of education was used in several nations at the beginning of the Nineteenth Century.[122] Under monitorial education, a master teacher trains a number of teaching assistants called monitors who then teach students.[123] Joseph Lancaster was the major developer of this system, and he came to America in 1818 to promote it.[124] The primary benefit of the system was that it was cheap, and this accounted for the system being so popular in the densely populated urban areas.[125]

The New Harmony, Indiana, attempt at "communitarian" schools was engineered by Robert Owen and William Maclure.[126] The New Harmony schools attempted to use the philosophies of Swiss educator Heinrich Pestalozzi.[127] Pestalozzi emphasized sense realism in the development of children's perceptive powers.[128] He believed that an atmosphere of love and security was essential to the child's learning.[129] Although the New Harmony experiment eventually failed, it was important because the schools offered educational opportunities to both boys and girls.[130]

THE FORMATION OF HIGH SCHOOLS

The first American high school was opened in 1821 in Boston to meet the needs of boys who did not plan to attend college.[131] Up until this time, upper schools, called Latin Grammar Schools, were reserved for the children of wealthy families to prepare them for college.[132] The Latin Grammar Schools accepted boys who could already read and write English and taught them for four or five years. The curriculum was focused on Latin and Greek, with additional studies in history, geography, and mathematics.[133]

The academy eventually replaced the Latin grammar school for secondary education.[134] The academy made secondary education more attainable for larger numbers of people during the democratization of the United States.[135] The academies were privately run, so they were focused on business-related subjects such as bookkeeping and accounting to attract a large number of students.[136] Religious denominations that had withdrawn from elementary schooling also opened academies for secondary schooling.[137]

THE CIVIL WAR TO THE TURN OF THE CENTURY, 1865–1900

The Civil War severely restricted the educational development of southern American schools.[138] "The war left southern states in physical and economic ruin with crops destroyed, buildings burned, livestock slaughtered, and the labor force demoralized."[139]

By the end of the Nineteenth Century, the United States had established the educational system in place today: a ladder from first grade through college in a series of yearly steps.[140] After the Civil War, the industrialization of the North proceeded rapidly and stimulated the growth of large cities such as New York, Chicago and Philadelphia.[141] Economic growth produced an expanded tax base and a sophisticated industrial system that required skilled workers.[142]

The common school movement earlier in the century established the precedent for tax-supported education on the elementary level.[143] Controversy surrounded the move to finance public high schools. The best known case in this area is *Stuart v. School District No. 1 of Kalamazoo.*[144] Three taxpayers brought suit to restrain the school board from collecting and using taxes to support the high school.[145] Writing for the Michigan Supreme Court, Justice Cooley held that high schools constitute a vital link between elementary schools and state universities, and so taxes could be spent on them.[146] This decision became the precedent which established the right of states to raise taxes for public high schools.[147]

THE MOVE TOWARD STANDARDIZATION

The lack of uniform standards in secondary schools prompted the National Education Association to form "The Committee of Ten" in 1892 to make recommendations about methods, standards and programs.[148] The Committee was chaired by Charles W. Eliot, then president of Harvard, and was made up of five college presidents and one professor; two headmasters of private secondary schools; one principal of a public high school; and the United States Commissioner of Education.[149] With such a makeup, the committee was controversial,[150] and, to no one's surprise, it recommended reinforcing the high school as a college prepatory institution.[151]

PROGRESSIVISM: 1900 TO THE EARLY 1950s

The progressive period in America occurred "within the first two decades of the twentieth century."[152] While the progressive period in education paralleled "the larger national movement chronologically," it "extended into the early 1950s and still exercises an impact today."[153] An analysis of the impact of the progressive education period is complex because the educational period sometimes parallels the national progressive movement and at other times is distinct from it.[154]

The national progressive movement had several basic themes which were also reflected in education. These were:

(1) Government should regulate economic power in the public interest.

(2) Expert knowledge and the scientific method should be applied to solving social, political, economic, and educational problems.

(3) The national environment should be conserved and its quality enhanced.

(4) Political institutions and processes should be reformed to make government more efficient.

(5) The spirit of community should be revitalized in the burgeoning urban areas.

(6) Educational institutions and processes should facilitate democratic participation and scientific efficiency.[155]

The progressive movement in education occurred in four stages. These were:

(1) the genesis period of progressive education, from 1900 to 1919, when it was part of a general climate of opinion that sought to reform American political, economic, and educational institutions and processes;

(2) the period from 1919 to 1930, when progressive education was dominated by child-centered educators associated with private schools who pioneered educational innovation and experimentation;

(3) the tumultuous era of the Great Depression and World War II, from 1930 to 1945, during which an internal ideological conflict arose between child-centered educators and social reconstructionists; and

(4) the 1950s, which saw major critics charging that progressive education, by then identified with life adjustment education, had contributed to the decline of educational standards in the United States.[156]

The progressive education movement was an umbrella movement in which those individuals opposed to traditionalism became united, although the progressives never developed a specific educational philosophy.[157] Traditional education adapted the corporate structure to the organization of schools; it emphasized efficiency and uniformity, order and discipline.[158] "The major function of organized education was conservative in that it was to preserve the cultural heritage by transmitting it to the young."[159] The major criticisms of traditional education included:

In their movement toward organizational maturity, urban public schools had grown excessively formal, routine, and bureaucratic. They generally preserved the status quo and resisted change. Throughout the United States, especially in the rural areas, teachers in thousands of small one-room schoolhouses were still emphasizing memorization, drill, rote learning, recitation, and moral values drawn from the McGuffey readers.[160]

Progressivism as an educational philosophy and movement evolved from the philosophy of pragmatism:

An American philosopher, Charles S. Peirce (1839-1914), founded the philosophical system called pragmatism. This philosophy held that meaning and value of ideas could be found only in their practical results. Later, William James (1842-1910) extended Peirce's theory of meaning into a theory of truth. James went further and asserted that the satisfactory working of an idea constitutes its whole truth. Pragmatism was carried much further by John Dewey (1859-1952), who was a widely known and influential philosopher and educator. Dewey's philosophy was called experimentalism by some because he insisted that ideas must always be tested by experiment. His experimental beliefs carried over into his educational philosophy, which became the basis for what was usually described as progressive education.[161]

LEADERS OF THE PROGRESSIVE MOVEMENT

One of the leaders of reform in this initial phase of the progressive movement was Jane Addams. Jane Addams, a social worker, opened Hull House, a settlement house on the west side of Chicago.[162] Hull House was a social and educational center designed to serve the immigrant population with the goals of easing immigrants' transition into American society while encouraging social and economic integration.[163] Through her work at Hull House, Jane Addams developed a philosophy of *socialized education*, a philosophy which viewed learning occurring in school (formal) and out of school in the environment (informal) as "reciprocal rather than exclusionary," which meant that education should be involved with "the city's social, economic, and political life."[164] Addams believed education should include:

(1) practical experiences and activities related to industrial training and home economics;

(2) an historical examination of the development of industry and the role that labor played in that development; and

(3) the development and exercise of aesthetic values in the creating of industrial products.[165]

Other educational trends occurring during this time were the conservation movement, agricultural education, and nature study.

Liberty Hyde Bailey, "a professor of horticulture and dean of the College of Agriculture at Cornell University, was a pioneer in the emerging field of scientific agriculture."[166] He advocated the Nature Study Movement and encouraged "an educated awareness among the general population about the relationships between nature, science, and agriculture."[167] Bailey's Nature Study Movement had both a direct and indirect influence on education.

For example: agriculture entered the secondary curriculum of rural schools; teachers in rural areas received pre- and in-service preparation in agriculture; nature study entered the general curriculum in many schools, and textbooks incorporated materials on nature study.[168]

John Dewey is perhaps the one individual most associated with the progressive educational movement. In 1896, Dewey founded the Laboratory School of the University of Chicago in order to put his educational ideas into practice.[169] This school "was to be (as its name indicates) a laboratory—a place to implement, test, verify, or reject innovative practices."[170] Some of the elements of Dewey's educational theory and practice were that instruction was related "to stages of child growth and development,"[171] instruction occurred in small groups due to "the social nature of learning,"[172] activity was considered important, and "curriculum emphasized concomitant learning."[173] One of the most important and central themes of Dewey's educational philosophy is "the complete act of thought."[174]

> Dewey held that learning grows out of ongoing activity which must be meaningful to the learner. Activity involves the individual in the relationship between an act and its consequences. This implies schools must foster purposeful activity by building on the common interests of children, such as communication, inquiry, construction, and artistic expression. Although activity is required for learning, no progress will be made so long as the activity is routine and the student operates on the basis of habit.[175]

Dewey saw learning as occurring in several definite stages: a difficulty or problem is created which prevents the continuation of an activity; the problem creates motivation for learning; information and data are gathered concerning a possible solution; an educated hypothesis or guess is generated by weighing the probable consequences of certain actions; and finally, the best hypothesis is chosen and tested.[176]

THE SECOND PHASE

The second phase of progressivism was from 1919 to 1930. During this time period "the United States moved from World War I, through the prosperity of the 1920s, to the Great Depression of the 1930s."[177] In 1919, the Progressive Education Association was organized, and in the 1920s those educators involved in private experimental schools were the most outspoken members.[178] The Progressive Education Association never developed a specific philosophy, but it did create a purpose: "The aim of Progressive Education is the freest and fullest development of the individual, based upon the scientific study of his mental, physical, and social characteristics and needs."[179] The organization adopted the following seven principles on March 15, 1919:

> Freedom to develop naturally, Interest as the motive for all work, The teacher as a guide, not a taskmaster, Scientific study of pupil development, Greater attention to all that affects the child's physical development, Co-operation . . . to meet the needs of child life, and The progressive school a leader in educational movements.[180]

During the 1920s, the child-centered philosophy was in favor in the progressivism movement. This philosophy of education held that children should be free to learn.[181] The focus of the school was centered around the child and the child's needs and interests and included such innovations as open classroom design, instruction based on the child's and group's immediate interests, and active learning via group or individual projects.[182] It was thought that children would learn the basic skills such as reading, writing, mathematics, science, history, etc., as a result of these projects.[183]

There were also innovations in teaching methods during this phase. William Heard Kilpatrick was an educator responsible for the development of the "project method."[184]

> The project method united Dewey's "complete act of thought," or problem solving according to the scientific method, with the learners' purposeful efforts in planning, directing, and executing their work by solving problems arising in their own individual and group experience. In uniting thought and action, the project method would provide teachers with a usable way to instill the scientific method and cultivate a sense of community in their students.[185]

THE THIRD PHASE

The third phase of the progressivism movement occurred from 1930 to 1945. It was during the Great Depression that a major controversy arose in the progressivism movement which created a schism within the Progressive Education Association.[186] This controversy transpired between the child-centered school and the philosophy of social reconstructionism. The individual who gave momentum to this educational philosophy is George S. Counts.[187] Counts delivered a speech at the Progressive Education Association Convention of 1932 entitled, "Dare Progressive Education Be Progressive?" and later wrote a book, *Dare the School Build a New Social Order?*[188] "Counts' address charged that progressives had romanticized the child's nature and had ignored the social reality in which children lived."[189] Counts believed schools needed to become involved with the current political, economic and social issues and problems.[190] He believed "that schools should be active in altering society"[191] and urged progressives to "point the way to the creation of a new society—a cooperative democracy":[192]

> Social Reconstructionists argue that civilization is in a profound state of cultural crisis. If schools continue to mirror the social status quo, then Reconstructionists claim that schooling will merely transmit societal ills and injustices. Schools will really be training children to play roles required in an archaic and self-destructive society. . . . Reconstructionist educators use the findings and methods of such social sciences as economics, anthropology, sociology, and psychology to provide the basis for their plans of social reform.
>
> Social Reconstructionists want to use education as a means of designing policies that will bring about a new society. Such education . . . cannot be neutral but must be committed to bringing about deliberate social

change. It must prepare future generations to be social engineers who can use science and technology to create a new and better world society.[193]

The social reconstructionist educational movement is one which is focused on helping children both cope with tumultuous change and improve their world.

THE FINAL PHASE

In the fourth and final phase of the progressivism movement, which occurred in the 1950s, life adjustment education became popular. "Life adjustment emphasized the need to provide youth with functional experiences in practical arts, home and family life, health, physical fitness, recreation, and civic competency."[194] (More will be said about life adjustment education in a later section.) The life adjustment movement became associated with the progressive movement.[195] It was severely criticized as being anti-intellectual and was blamed for lowering academic standards in America.[196] With the launching of Sputnik in 1957, there was a "reemphasis on academic subjects and disciplines," and progressivism, having become associated with life adjustment education, lost favor and support.[197]

NORMALCY AND PROSPERITY: THE 1920s

In the 1920s, there were two elements that influenced education: internationalism versus isolationism, and the Red Scare of 1919-1920. In education, the struggle between internationalists and isolationists made itself manifest in debates regarding curricula. "Isolationists believed that citizenship education should concentrate on the study of American history and government and cultivate a 'pro-American' rather than internationalist attitude."[198]

Related to the issue of internationalism versus isolationism was the Red Scare of 1919-1920. The Tsarist regime collapsed, the provisional government of Prince Lvov and Alexander Kerensky fell, and Lenin was brought to power by the Bolshevik Revolution.[199] The Red Scare directly and indirectly impacted education:

> Committees of citizens were formed to examine school textbooks and libraries to eliminate anti-Americanism, as they defined the term. Textbooks in history and the social studies were scrutinized for "unpatriotic" and "un-American" passages. Patriotic organizations wanted more military history. . . .
> Teachers, too, were scrutinized to make sure that they did not deviate from "true patriotism." . . .
> During the 1920s, when nativist sentiments and antiforeign prejudices were strong in many sections of the country, American public schools were often dominated by a climate of opinion that considered the true

national character to be white, Protestant, and Anglo-Saxon. The tone of the country's schools, although there were rare exceptions, was assimilationist and sought to educate American youngsters to fit into a homogenized society.[200]

Throughout the 1920s there appeared to be a split in America between small-town/rural society and the big cities.[201] This split resulted in a clash of values.[202] In education, this clash of values could be seen in the Scopes "monkey" trial of 1924 in which Williams Jennings Bryan and Clarence Darrow debated creationism versus evolution.[203]

Industrialization and the assembly line had a great impact on education. The focus of education was on efficiency. Utilizing the innovative method of the school survey, educators attempted to apply new industrial technology to schools, particularly to the management of schools, in the hopes of "improving their educational efficiency and instructional delivery."[204]

Two other significant trends in education at this time were the "development of a more permissive attitude toward children, and the social prolonging of adolescence."[205] "Many educators during the 1920s urged greater freedom for children. . . . Through activities and projects, children were encouraged to express themselves freely and creatively without fear of adult prescription or censorship."[206]

Due to the compulsory attendance laws and child labor restrictions, greater numbers of adolescents were attending and finishing high school.[207] This led to a "youth or teen-age culture." Some educators advocated changing the conception of high school from preparation for college to a multipurpose institution.[208]

THE GREAT DEPRESSION OF THE 1930s

The prosperity of the 1920s ended abruptly with the stock market crash of 1929. The crash had a profound impact on education:

(1) Fiscal retrenchment due to a shrinking tax base caused a reduction in the teaching force and educational programs. (2) Many began to seriously question traditional American values, particularly those associated with business ethics and the free enterprise system. (3) The alliance between businessmen and school administrators weakened. Of the three areas of impact, the fiscal pressures upon the schools were the most direct.[209]

In practical terms, the impact of the Depression meant the length of the school year was reduced, many schools were closed, the number of teachers was reduced, teachers were unable to be paid, class sizes were increased, and the number of courses was reduced.[210] The Depression also affected children and families by increasing malnutrition among children, adding to the psychological stress suffered by families with no means of financial support, and increasing the number of adolescents who became "tramps."[211]

In 1933, President Franklin D. Roosevelt developed his New Deal policies, and several of these had an indirect effect on education. Roosevelt created the Civilian Conservation Corps (CCC) in 1933, which was "designed to alleviate unemployment through 'the performance of useful public works.'"[212] "Those eligible to admission to the CCC were unemployed, unmarried males between the ages of seventeen and twenty-three."[213] The CCC also offered education, with each camp having an educational advisor.[214] The following is a list of educational objectives for CCC educational programs:

(1) development of powers of self-expression, self-entertainment and self-culture;
(2) development of pride and satisfaction in cooperative work;
(3) development of an understanding of social and economic conditions;
(4) preservation and strengthening of good habits of health and mind;
(5) improvement of employment opportunities by vocational training and counseling; and
(6) development of an appreciation of nature and rural life.[215]

There was no uniform curriculum in the CCC; however, "courses were offered in such subjects as citizenship, botany, English, forestry, first aid, hygiene, surveying, zoology, algebra, astronomy, bookkeeping, entomology, geology, history, music, and painting."[216] Literacy courses were also offered.[217]

The Works Progress Administration (WPA) "also undertook projects of a broadly educational and artistic nature."[218]

During the 1930s, two educational philosophies gained prominence. These were the social reconstructionist and essentialist educational movements. George S. Counts was representative of the social reformist progressive philosophy discussed above. Counts urged educators to create a new social order, and "instead of accepting the status quo, Counts challenged teachers to 'deliberately reach for power' and 'to fashion the curriculum and the procedures of the school' so that they could shape the 'social attitudes, ideals, and behavior of the coming generation.'"[219]

Essentialism, a reaction to the progressive movement in American education and to social reconstructionalists, urged "a return to basic skills and subjects . . . the essentialists recommended that educators concentrate their efforts on schooling rather than on reforming society."[220] The primary function of the school, according to essentialism, is "preserving the basic elements of the cultural heritage by deliberately transmitting it to the young."[221] The essentialist movement began in 1938 and was led by William C. Bagley.[222] "They said the essential skills of reading, writing, and arithmetic should be found in every elementary curriculum together with history, literature, and geography. For the secondary school, curriculum was the western cultural heritage, including academic subjects in the arts and sciences."[223]

POSTWAR AMERICA: 1945 TO 1960

Several trends after World War II greatly influenced education. These were: the expansion of the middle class, the relocation by many Americans from cities to the suburbs, and the increase in population (also known as the baby boom).[224] The increase in the suburban population led to a need for new schools and teachers in these areas.[225] Since the suburban population primarily consisted of the affluent upper-middle class, the suburbs had abundant financial resources with which to build schools and fund educational programming, and the schools themselves had strong support and commitment from the upper-middle class, who viewed education as the way for their children to succeed.[226] For cities, however, this relocation had negative consequences. Cities experienced shrinking financial support for schools.[227] When schools in the city physically deteriorated, fewer new schools could be built due to a lack of financial resources; this in turn led to overcrowding in existing schools.[228] The relocation also led to racial and economic segregation.[229]

Civil rights were a major issue at this time and profoundly affected education. "In 1946, President Truman appointed the Presidential Committee on Civil Rights."[230] Specifically relating to education, the Committee found "racially segregated schooling as unfair to black children."[231] In 1954, racial segregation was directly addressed in the public schools in the court case of *Brown v. Board of Education of Topeka*. Thurgood Marshall, a NAACP attorney later to become a United States Supreme Court Justice, successfully "argued that racially segregated schools violated the due process clause of the Fourteenth Amendment, denied black children equality of educational opportunity, and caused them psychological damage."[232] The separate-but-equal doctrine which had been in effect since the *Plessy v. Ferguson* case in 1896 was overturned.[233] One year after the *Brown v. Board of Education* case, the Supreme Court ordered racial integration to proceed "with all deliberate speed."[234]

THE COLD WAR

The Cold War, beginning in the years of the Truman administration, also had its effects on education. Intellectuals', educators', and writers' loyalty was suspected.[235] "The 1950s saw state legislatures and occasional school districts requiring professors, teachers, and educational personnel to sign oaths attesting to their loyalty to federal and state governments," and "they encouraged a mood of censorship, in which textbooks and other educational materials were examined for allegedly un-American or subversive views."[236] During the Joseph McCarthy era, "mere accusation of 'Red Influence' was sufficient to frighten many school officials into firing teachers or removing books from the school libraries."[237]

Finally, it was believed that "American students, especially at the junior high, high school, and college levels, needed to be educated about the dangers of communism."[238]

On June 1, 1945, life adjustment education originated from Charles A. Prosser at an invitational meeting of vocational educators sponsored by the Division of Vocational Education of the Office of Education in Washington, D.C.[239] Prosser was concerned about the "estimated 60 percent of American youth who were being trained for neither skilled occupations nor college."[240] Life adjustment education was a significant movement from 1945 to 1954 when it came under attack.[241] Life adjustment education was viewed as a response to "the social and psychological uneasiness produced by the cultural changes that followed immediately after World War II," such as rising divorce rates, increases in juvenile delinquency, and living in communities which were evolving.[242] "For children and adolescents, the new patterns of postwar life were unstable and unsettling. Life-adjustment education promised a degree of social stability by providing youth with coping and adjusting skills that would serve them in changing situations."[243] This educational movement was also in response to the prolonging of adolescence.[244]

Educators were "to devise a widely varied functional curriculum that would be of interest and be immediately useful to these noncollege preparatory students."[245] Life adjustment education "was a broad and ill-defined movement" which varied between schools.[246] "It might be an introduction to careers, on-the-job training, a course in correct social manners, or learning how to baby-sit, decorate a room, or develop a pleasing and popular personality."[247] "Twenty-nine states developed some kind of curriculum revision associated with Life Adjustment by 1954. Many school systems became interested in how to meet the needs of those who seemed not to benefit from standard courses."[248] One benefit of life adjustment education was that it "gave attention to the concern for equal educational opportunity and the problems of cultural deprivation which later brought about such programs as Head Start and the Job Corps."[249]

EDUCATION CRITICS

During the 1950s, a number of education critics appeared, the most notable of which were Arthur E. Bestor, Jr., Admiral Hyman Rickover, Max Rafferty, and Robert Hutchins.[250] These critics attacked life adjustment education and progressive education (which they did not distinguish from life adjustment education).[251] "Generally, the critics of the 1950's sought to redirect public education by charging that: 1. American public schooling had grown pedagogically weak due to life-adjustment education; 2. American public schools were academically inferior to European schools; amd 3. An overly permissive attitude in American schools had lowered civic and moral standards."[252] These critics "claimed that equality of opportunity did not mean the same education for everyone, and that the national welfare demanded special provisions for the gifted."[253]

"In October 1957, the Soviet Union launched a space satellite, *Sputnik*, into orbit around the earth."[254] This event "stimulated widespread demands for more rigorous academic standards and programs, especially in mathematics and science."[255] Basic sciences, mathematics, and foreign languages were emphasized.[256] Congress enacted the National Defense Education Act (NDEA) in 1958, which provided "assistance to programs designed to improve instruction in mathematics, science, and foreign languages" and also provided matching grants to the states to improve secondary school guidance and counseling programs.[257]

At the end of the 1950s, James B. Conant issued several reports on American education. Generally these reports found American education wanting:

> Conant's recommendations sought to revitalize the high school curriculum. He sought to instill academic rigor and standards by recommending that half of every student's program be based on academic disciplines such as mathematics, English, science, and social science. However, he did not neglect the high school's role regarding students' general development. For example, Conant's recommendations included more counseling services, individualized instruction, and elective courses to meet differing interests and career goals.[258]

THE NEW FRONTIER AND THE GREAT SOCIETY: 1960 TO 1970

During this era, President Lyndon Johnson was able to influence Congress to enact the Elementary and Secondary Education Act of 1965 (ESEA).[259] "As part of Johnson's War on Poverty, the major thrust of the ESEA sought to equalize educational opportunities, especially in inner-city and rural poverty areas."[260]

> This measure provided funds for textbooks and other instructional materials and services in public and private elementary and secondary schools. The primary purpose was to ensure that children from low-income families had access to adequate materials. Control of the funds was in state and local hands rather than those of federal agencies. The act also included one hundred million dollars for research in the field of education to be administered by the United States Office of Education.[261]

The Johnson administration also passed the Economic Opportunity Act of 1965, "which created a number of early childhood education programs, known collectively as Operation Head Start. These programs were designed to give economically and culturally disadvantaged children a concerted early educational opportunity before they entered school."[262] The Johnson administration also created the Job Corps, "designed for high school dropouts who needed special vocational training to learn saleable skills that would prepare them for employment."[263] During this era, African

Americans, Hispanic Americans, and women raised America's consciousness about their heritage and culture.[264] This consciousness raising resulted in ethnic and multicultural studies programs which examined their contributions to America.[265] As a result of Hispanic consciousness raising, the Bilingual Education Act of 1968 was passed, which "provided federal funds to local school districts to help them meet the needs of students of limited English-speaking ability." And "in 1970 the Office of Civil Rights of the Department of Health, Education, and Welfare issued guidelines requiring districts enrolling more than 5 percent non-English-speakers to take 'affirmative steps to rectify the language deficiency' so that such students could participate effectively in the educational program."[266] The women's liberation movement also had an impact on education in that it discredited the sex stereotyping of education programs and occupations.[267]

In the early 1960s, attempts were made at revising curriculums in the schools.[268] The strategy for these reforms was to have teams of academic experts in mathematics and the sciences, primarily dominated by university professors, examine and revise existing curriculums.[269] The revised curricula, frequently called New Math, New Chemistry, etc., was to be taught to small groups of teachers who would teach these revisions in their own schools.[270] "Underlying the various curricular reforms was the learning theory of Jerome Bruner, which emphasized the structure of disciplines and the use of inquiry, or discovery, method."[271]

> By the mid-1960s, a new breed of educational critics appeared. The new critics argued that schools were overly centralized, bureaucratic, formalized, routine, mindless, and stifling of children's freedom and teachers' creativity. They urged a flexibility that would permit learners and teachers to shape their own educational environments along more humanistic contours.[272]

These critics were sometimes referred to as the "Romantic critics" after the romanticism movement characterized by Rousseau.[273] "These romantic critics were anti-institutional and urged that children should be free to follow their own curiosity, interests, and inclinations. Teachers, in turn, were to be enthusiastic, exciting, and creative."[274]

SOCIETY AND EDUCATION IN THE 1970s

In the 1970s, the bleak economy greatly affected education. Students were interested in career paths which would provide them with "economic security and status."[275] Another trend which was having an effect on education at this time "was that the United States was approaching zero population growth. This meant the number of school-age children, especially those of elementary age, was declining."[276] This meant decreasing financial resources for the schools. Inflation was also negatively affecting schools, with the result being "that while school revenues decreased or remained fixed, expenditures increased."[277] This economic situation brought about school closings and reduction in the force of teachers.[278] The Watergate scandal had an effect on education by promoting "a revival of civic education."[279]

Another phenomenon of the 1970s was the energy crisis precipitated by the OPEC oil embargo.

> The energy crisis had several educational consequences: (1) Federal policies were developed to both educate Americans about the crisis and to reduce America's reliance on imported oil. (2) Educators began to talk about "energy education" and "energy conservation programs" designed to inform young people of the realities of the energy scarcity. (3) In a very practical way, educational administrators sought to make teachers and students "energy conscious" and to effect energy savings in heating and insulating school buildings.[280]

Yet another trend affecting education was the relocation of business and industries to the Sunbelt.[281] Northern schools in particular suffered declining enrollments and revenues, while southern and western states "experienced a need to expand their school facilities and to hire additional teachers."[282]

In the administration of President Jimmy Carter an important benefit for education was the creation of the U. S. Department of Education.[283] Shirley Hufstedler was appointed the first Secretary of Education.[284]

> Among Secretary Hufstedler's priorities for the new department were: (1) ensuring equal educational opportunities for all, (2) supporting state and local efforts for educational improvement, (3) promoting educational research and evaluation, (4) disseminating information about education, and (5) coordinating, managing, and accounting for federally supported education programs.[285]

In the 1970s, several pieces of legislation were enacted which benefitted special learners. The first was the Vocational Rehabilitation Act of 1973 which:

> [P]rovided for vocational training in mainstream settings, the promotion and expansion of employment opportunities, and the removal of architectural and transportation barriers. The act sought to encourage more handicapped individuals to enter the nation's workforce and to remove unnecessary obstacles to their hiring and in their working conditions.[286]

The second was the All Handicapped Children Act of 1975, which "established a national policy that the nation's handicapped children between the ages of three and twenty-one would be assured an 'appropriate public education,' designed to meet their unique needs."[287]

SOCIETY AND EDUCATION IN THE 1980s

The 1980s was a period in which education was critically examined and "saw the issuing of many reports that examined 'the crisis in education.'" By far the most publicized of these reports was *A Nation at Risk: The Imperative for Educational Reform*, the report of the National Commission on Excellence. America's educational achievement was compared with other nations and found to be inferior, particularly to that of Japan and West Germany.[288] "The commission issued a series of recommendations on curriculum reform, the use of institutional time, and teacher effectiveness."[289] The Commission's recommendations called for "a return to the basic subjects," and in particular for students to have a foundation in the Five New Basics which include English, mathematics, social studies, computer science, and foreign language.[290] President Ronald Reagan believed the following academic reforms were needed:

(1) restoration of "good old-fashioned discipline";
(2) ending drug and alcohol abuse by children and youth;
(3) raising academic standards and expectations;
(4) encouraging good teaching by paying and promoting teachers on "the basis of their competence and merit";
(5) revitalizing the educational role of parents and local and state governments; and
(6) emphasizing basic academic skills and subjects.[291]

The educational policies of President Reagan and Terrell Bell, then U.S. Secretary of Education, were designed to:

(1) focus national attention on the need for educational reform, (2) reduce federal spending for education, (3) encourage state and local educational reforms and initiatives, and (4) use the presidency and the Department of Education as a bully pulpit to emphasize basic education, merit pay for teachers, and the restoration of traditional values in the schools.[292]

Finally, the educational program of President George Bush,[293] President Bill Clinton, and each succeeding President means that the history and philosophy of public education will continue to be important to American citizens, including those who educate their children at home.

3

Freedom and
Educational Diversity

BRAVE NEW WORLD

In 1932, Aldous Huxley predicted the future of the world and described in
detail the education and preparation of the young for this "brave new
world." He described a society which preserved social class or "caste"
through genetic programming and educational programs in which the
state's prescribed values would be inculcated through intense conditioning:

INFANT NURSERIES. NEO-PAVLOVIAN CONDITIONING ROOMS, announced
the notice board.

The Director opened a door.... Half a dozen nurses ... were engaged
in setting out bowls of roses in a long row across the floor....

"Set out the books," he said curtly....

"Now bring in the children."

They hurried out of the room and returned in a minute or two, each
pushing a kind of tall dumbwaiter laden, on all its four wire-netted
shelves, with eight-month-old babies, all exactly alike (a Bokanovsky
Group, it was evident) and all (since their caste was Delta) dressed in
khaki.

"Put them down on the floor."

The infants were unloaded.

"Now turn them so that they can see the flowers and books." ...

The swiftest crawlers were already at their goal. Small hands reached
out uncertainly, touched, grasped, unpetaling the transfigured roses,
crumpling the illuminated pages of the books. The Director waited until

all were happily busy. Then, "Watch carefully," he said. And, lifting his hand, he gave the signal.

The Head Nurse, who was standing by a switchboard at the other end of the room, pressed down a little lever.

There was a violent explosion. Shriller and ever shriller, a siren shrieked. Alarm bells maddeningly sounded.

The children started, screamed; their faces were distorted with terror.

"And now," the Director shouted (for the noise was deafening), "now we proceed to rub in the lesson with a mild electric shock."

He waved his hand again, and the Head Nurse pressed a second lever. The screaming of the babies suddenly changed its tone. There was something desperate, almost insane, about the sharp spasmodic yelps to which they now gave utterances. Their little bodies twitched and stiffened; their limbs moved jerkily as if to the tug of unseen wires. . . .

"Offer them the flowers and books again."

The nurses obeyed; but at the approach of the roses, at the mere sight of those gaily-coloured images of pussy and cock-a-doodle-doo and baa-baa black sheep, the infants shrunk away in horror; the volume of their howling suddenly increased.

"Observe," said the Director triumphantly, "observe."

Books and loud noises, flowers and electric shocks—already in the infant mind these couples were compromisingly linked; after two hundred repetitions of the same or a similar lesson they would be wedded indissolubly. What man has joined, nature is powerless to put asunder. . . .

Roses and electric shocks, the khaki of Deltas and a whiff of asafoetida—wedded indissolubly before the child can speak. But wordless conditioning is crude and wholesale; cannot bring home the finer distinctions, cannot inculcate the more complex courses of behaviour. For that there must be words, but words without reason. In brief, hypnopaedia.

"The greatest moralizing and socializing force of all time. . ."

Not so much like drops of water, though water, it is true, can wear holes in the hardest granite; rather, drops of liquid sealing-wax, drops that adhere, incrust, incorporate themselves with what they fall on, till finally the rock is all one scarlet blob.

"Till at last the child's mind *is* these suggestions, and the sum of the suggestions *is* the child's mind. And not the child's mind only. The adult's mind too—all his life long. The mind that judges and desires and decides—made up of these suggestions. But all these suggestions are *our* suggestions!" The Director almost shouted in his triumph. "Suggestions from the State. . . ."[1]

This passage depicting the classroom and educational methods of the future acknowledges that education is a powerful tool for shaping and molding society. Many would say there is no comparison between America's current system of education and that which Huxley prophesied.

Yet, it is also likely that critics of this country's public education system would see similarities between the two: the mass age-segregated education of children, education's maintenance of the society's socioeconomic levels, the inculcation of values in the schools, and the virtual monopoly of public education, to name but a few. As was depicted in *Brave New World*, the purpose of state education is far more than imparting knowledge: state education is a socializing institution. Education is a means of transmitting values, beliefs, opinions, ideas, culture and worldviews to the members of our society to whom the future is entrusted. It profoundly influences the very consciences of children. Thus, whoever controls education has the power to influence society. Historically, the family has had this power, but increasingly it resides with the government-run public schools.

Many Americans assume there is considerable freedom in education and that families have many choices available to them in educating their children. However, the reality is that educational choice is limited and in some cases nonexistent for American families. All too frequently the educational options available to a family are dependent upon the ability to afford them. Thus, for many families, public education might be seen as the only option. For these families, home schooling could be an affordable option that would allow them to assume control of their children's education and socialization. Those families who choose to take back the power of education through home schooling often encounter great difficulty with public school authorities in doing so. Frequently, the struggle between parents wishing to home school their children and public school authorities escalates into battles so intense that a resolution in accord with constitutional freedoms may only be achieved by the courts. These cases tangibly demonstrate the limits of freedom in education in the United States.

This chapter will examine the benefits society receives when freedom in educational choice is allowed to flourish and the dangers of limiting educational choice. Particular attention will be focused on the option of home schooling. Two categories of issues will be discussed. These areas correspond to the two broad categories of parents who home school: those who home school for ideological reasons and those who home school for pedagogical reasons.[2]

IDEOLOGICAL ISSUES

Conflicts between families and school officials regarding home schooling reveal a widespread concern about the influence of the public schools on children and within the family. This concern often centers on the values being taught or, as some believe, inculcated by the schools. In order to fully understand this concern, a brief review of the history of schooling in America is necessary.[3]

Changes in American Schooling That Have Increased the Influence of Schools

Several changes in American education have occurred which have served to increase the influence of the public schools. The most important is the advent of compulsory public schooling. Prior to the nineteenth century, schooling was primarily home-based.[4] Parents were solely responsible for selecting and providing the types and amounts of education they believed their children needed.[5] "Thus, from the founding of the original colonies of Puritan New England until the early years following the adoption of the Constitution, home education was one of the major forms, if not the predominant form, of education."[6]

In the mid- to late Nineteenth Century, taxpayer-supported public schools became available.[7] Nonetheless, the assumption of parental control of their children's education persisted. Stephen Arons, Director of Legal Studies at the University of Massachusetts, has extensively studied family/school value conflicts, including conflicts involving home schooling. He views the "right of excusal" as evidence of this assumption:

> Even after public schools provided at taxpayer expense became available in the late 19th century the presumption of family responsibility and control remained. The strength of this parental prerogative in education can be gauged by the "right of excusal." At common law prior to the early 20th century, state courts generally upheld the right of parents to have their children excused from any course or program of study to which the parents objected. No questions were asked concerning the parents' motivation for such excusals; and although the effect on the efficiency and good order of the schools was considered, this was not interpreted to block parental wishes. School was regarded as an opportunity to which children were entitled, not as a requirement to be imposed, complete with specified content, upon dissenting parents.[8]

During this period parents ". . . remained in legally recognized control of the content of individual education."[9] In addition to the assumption of parental control of education, an assumption of parental competency regarding the education of their children existed: "It was assumed that parents were as competent as school personnel to determine what their children were to learn and how they ought to be taught."[10]

In the early Twentieth Century, public education became compulsory.[11] Besides being compulsory, a public school education became more popular and provided greater status.[12] "Americanization was a central objective of early compulsory education. Formal public schooling sought to remove the stamp of individual and ethnic orientations that immigrant, family-related learning environments promoted."[13] During this period, there was a strong belief in the "Melting Pot" concept of America: "America is God's Crucible, the great Melting-Pot where all the races of Europe are melting and reforming. . . . God is making the American."[14] "Another objective of educational reformers, as exemplified in the early common schools and later in the schools of the 20th century, was to counteract undesirable characteristics perceived in the lower classes."[15] Education at this time was believed by many Americans to be the "great equalizer" among the social classes and capable of counteracting the negative influences of poverty.

The institution of compulsory public education in the United States created changes in the assumptions of Nineteenth-Century Americans. The compulsion to attend school shifted the focus of education from the individual to the group. With this shift in the focus of education, there was a corresponding shift in the assumption of parental competence in the area of education: "Parents began to be viewed as presumptively incompetent in the area of education as schooling became less an issue of individual development and family aspiration and more an issue of social needs and group values."[16]

The assumption of parental incompetence in education shifted the locus of responsibility for the education of children from parents to the public schools:

> The effect of the compulsion to attend was to reverse the presumption of parental control in education and to shift the locus of responsibility from the family to an institutionalized school operated by the government and responsive to the group rather than individual demands.[17]

The acceptance of these assumptions, that public schools are more competent in the area of education and are therefore responsible for the education of children, has increased the public schools' control over the upbringing and education of American children while diminishing that of the family. Many families have lost several important functions that were once traditionally theirs, and consequently a very large and important part of child-rearing has been taken from the family and assumed by the schools. The public schools have become the educator, socializer, and transmitter of culture and values for many American children. The net effect of these changes in education and shifts in assumptions is that public schools now occupy a central and prominent position within many families.

Changes in the Family That Have Increased the Influence of Schools

Several changes *within the family* have also combined to increase the influence of and reliance on the public schools. These changes have led to a decrease in the time families spend together and have served to decrease the influence of families on children. One change has been the increase in two-career families or families in which both parents work. "The 'Norman Rockwell' family—a working father, a housewife mother, and two children of school age—constitutes only 6% of U.S. households today."[18] This statistic indicates that many American children no longer have the amount of access they once did to one parent whose primary occupation is the care of the home and children. In addition, census statistics reveal that during the 1980s children were less likely to live within a traditional family structure (two parents and siblings): "Every kind of 'atypical' family increased in number during the decade, while the 'typical' family—married couple with children—actually declined in number."[19]

This statistic is related to the increase in single-parent families. "Today, almost 50% of America's young people will spend some years before they reach age 18 being raised by a single parent."[20] It is reported that fifteen million children are being reared by single mothers, and "in 1988, 4.3 million children were living with a mother who had never been married (up 678% since 1970)."[21] It is also reported that there are two and a half million single fathers rearing children, and "371,000 children are being reared by a never-married father."[22]

These statistics indicate that children are spending far less time with both parents, and perhaps less quality time, as parents are fatigued from working. Consider, for example, the depressing statistics which reveal that "at least two million school-age children have no adult supervision at all after school. Two million more are being reared by *neither* parent."[23] According to a recent study from the American Academy of Pediatrics, "12- and 13-year-old 'latch-key kids,' who take care of themselves for 11 or more hours a week, are almost twice as likely to drink alcohol and much more likely to use marijuana than supervised kids."[24]

Families today tend to spend a great deal of time away from one another, with members involved in their own individual activities. This is particularly so when work involves a great deal of travel and parents maintain a high level of involvement in social and community service commitments.[25] Children spend long hours in school (which are longer if they are involved in afterschool activities) and frequently are involved in sports and clubs outside of school.[26]

Today families are smaller with fewer children and often have little or no contact with extended families (grandparents, uncles, aunts, cousins, etc.).[27] Traditionally, extended families provided vital assistance to parents in child-rearing and were an important source in the transmission of values and the socialization of children. This lack of contact with families, because of the relational vacuum it creates, has greatly increased the influence of schools in the lives of children. Due to a lack of time, energy and resources, many parents have increasingly relied on the schools to teach values, socialize, and educate their children.

Societal Changes That Have Increased the Influence of Schools

Several societal changes have led to a decrease in the contact of children with caring and concerned adults in their community. There has been a decrease in small towns and an increase in urban and suburban towns and cities.[28] While there are more people in larger towns and cities, these are often impersonal environments where people tend to have fewer close and personal relationships with others, in contrast with small towns where everyone often knows everyone else.[29] Children may thus have fewer opportunities for truly meaningful relationships with adults.[30] In smaller towns, neighbors frequently act as guardians when children are away from their parents, and children know that, if they misbehave, neighbors will step in and their parents will surely find out.[31] This aspect of small towns enables children to go out into the neighborhood without the necessity of excessive parental concern.[32]

Another change in United States society is that it has become age-segregated, and the contacts children have with adults and even with children of different ages has been decreased.[33] "Much of this age-segregation mentality has been provided us by the public education system."[34] The result of this age-segregation has been that children frequently have more contact with peers than with adults: "Mass state education has forced children into horizontal peer relationships, thereby abrogating the traditional vertical relationships with adults."[35] There are several negative effects from such strong peer relationships facilitated by the schools. Conformity and peer pressure are very strong: "Conformity to behavior and beliefs of fellow-students is at very best strong. Sometimes conformity becomes an obsessive drive of students. It almost always has a harmful effect on parent-child relations."[36] Another problem with conformity in the schools is the effect on a nonconforming student who may be perceived as deviant by his or her peer group and rejected or stigmatized.[37]

In a study regarding the effects of peer pressure, Professor Urie Bronfenbrenner questioned 766 sixth grade students who reported they spent an average of only two to three hours a day with their parents during the weekend.[38] During this time, these students spent about twice as much time with their friends.[39] The children indicated this was their preference when asked "with whom they would rather spend a free weekend afternoon."[40] However, these children seemed to be influenced more "by a *lack* of attention and concern at home than by the attractiveness of the peer group."[41] The findings of this study indicated, "in general, the peer-oriented children held rather negative views of themselves and the peer group. They also expressed a dim view of their own future."[42] These children also indicated that they participated in more antisocial behavior such as illegal activities, skipping school, "lying," "teasing other children," and so forth.[43] Professor Bronfenbrenner sums up the study's findings:

> [I]t would seem that the peer-oriented child is more a product of parental disregard than of the attractiveness of the peer group—that he turns to his age-mates less by choice than by default. The vacuum left by the withdrawal of parents and adults from the lives of children is filled with an undesired— and possibly *undesirable*—substitute of any age-segregated peer group.[44]

A problem with children having less contact with parents and adults is that they may fail to learn appropriate and beneficial behavior through the observation and imitation of parents and adults. Albert Bandura has demonstrated the connection between observation and learning in children through a classic experiment on aggression.[45] In the experiment, four- to five-year-old boys and girls observed an adult playing aggressively with a blow-up clown, commonly called a Bobo doll. The adult "model" sat on the Bobo doll, kicked it, hit it on the nose and on the head with a mallet, and threw it around the room while making aggressive verbal statements. Other children observed the same situation by watching a videotape or watching a videotape created in a cartoon format with the room designed to look like a cartoon and the model dressed as a cat. A fourth group of children did not observe the model but went directly on to the next part of the experiment. In this part of the experiment, all children were given an opportunity to play with the doll on their own. The results indicated that the children who observed the model acting aggressively with the doll, whether through direct observation or by viewing the videotape (including the cartoon video), acted aggressively with the doll in the same manner. Those children who did not observe the model did not act aggressively with the doll.[46]

This experiment suggests that children require frequent contact with their parents and other caring adults in order to learn socially appropriate behavior. It appears from Bronfenbrenner's study[47] that children who lack this contact must rely on their peers, and this seems to have negative consequences.

The changes in public schooling, the family, and society have created a void in the lives of many children. This void has increasingly been filled by schools that have assumed many of the traditional responsibilities and functions of the family. The schools have become more powerful and influential, and the changes discussed above have weakened the power and influence of the family in the lives of their children. Thus, the school now has a more central position within many families.

Loss of Mediating Structures

These changes have also weakened the mediating structure of the family in society and have strengthened the state itself. "Mediating structures are such institutions as neighborhoods, families, churches, schools, and voluntary associations."[48] When these mediating structures are properly intact, they serve to limit the growth of the state.[49] With the breakdown of traditional family structure, society is losing its most basic mediating structure.[50] Mediating structures, particularly the family, are the agencies that generate and maintain values in our society.[51] "Therefore, when these structures break down, society—that is, people—must look to the megastructures, such as the state, as a source of values. In America, we see the state-financed public schools assuming the role of providing 'values.'"[52]

Public School Monopoly

Another factor which has increased the power of public schools in America is their status as a virtual monopoly. There is a clear lack of viable alternatives to public education for most families. "In spite of the escape-valve theory of alternatives to government education, the right of educational choice remains a prerogative of the wealthy."[53]

Value Inculcation in the Schools

The increased power and influence of the public schools has led to a concern over the values being taught in the schools. This concern has sparked a great deal of debate and an increase in conflict between families and schools regarding value inculcation in the public schools. There are several options for parents who object to the values being transmitted in the public schools, but the option which is perceived as the most radical and has received the most publicity is home schooling.[54]

As mentioned previously, research on parents who have chosen to home educate their children indicates that they fall into two broad categories: those who object to the ideology taught or transmitted in the schools (including values) and/or want to strengthen their relationships with their children, and those who object to the quality of education; the first group is slightly larger than the second.[55] For many of the families who home school, the values taught in the public schools run counter to their own values (and specifically religious values); what is at stake is the development of their children's consciences. Parents choosing to home school their children often encounter great resistance from the public school personnel, and frequently these conflicts must be resolved by the courts. These court cases have prompted a close examination of value inculcation in the public schools and its constitutionality.

Values and the First Amendment

There apparently is an implicit belief held by members of the United States Supreme Court that as long as the values being taught in the public schools are held by the majority, there is no unconstitutional interference with individual freedom: "[T]he Court has implied a shift from equating secularism with neutrality to viewing the inculcation of secular values in school as consistent with individual freedom so long as they are majority values that are forced upon students."[56] In the 1922 case *Pierce v. Society of Sisters*, the Supreme Court considered the state's power to standardize its children by forcing students to attend only public schools after the State of Oregon passed legislation banning private schools.[57] Oregon's law was declared unconstitutional, and the Court said that "the child is not the mere creature of the state."[58] In quoting the Court, one author interprets the ruling:

> "[The] fundamental theory of liberty excludes any general power of the state to standardize its children by forcing them to accept instruction from public teachers only." The right of families to attend nongovernment

schools in satisfaction of the compulsory education laws was thus affirmed, but the Court also implied that states could make reasonable regulations of private schools.[59]

However, what has remained unclear is the extent to which private schools, including home schools, may be regulated by the state and at what point this regulation becomes unconstitutional. Later, the Court held "that the right to attend an alternative to government-controlled schools could not be obliterated by a scheme of regulation of private schools so detailed that the difference between government and private schools became insignificant."[60] This statement, however, continues to leave the boundary between reasonable and unreasonable governmental regulation unclear: "As the struggles of some dissenting families have shown, the point at which state regulation of private schooling crosses the line of constitutional permissibility has remained ill marked."[61] The Court's failure to delineate clearly the constitutional limits of such state regulation may be "due in part to the Court's failure to address the First Amendment consequences of government control of the value content of schooling."[62]

There are several difficulties with the Supreme Court's position on teaching values in the public schools. It is likely that, outside of the school setting, imposing a set of values and beliefs accepted by the majority on a captive audience would be seen as unconstitutional. There is a lack of acknowledgment and understanding of the extent of secular ideology inculcated in the schools or its effects on the formation of beliefs in children: "If such statist thinking were to leave the realm of *obiter dictum* and find its way into the Court's doctrine, it would fly in the face of every known conception of individual liberty and First Amendment freedom."[63] As such, one author contends that "the present political and financial structure of American schooling is unconstitutional."[64]

Families choosing to home school who have been involved in conflict with public school authorities have raised the issue of "whether majority control of schooling is compatible with fundamental liberties in general and the First Amendment to the Constitution in particular."[65] Those families who have no other options but the public schools find their children forced to learn the values, beliefs and opinions of the majority even if these values, beliefs and opinions are abhorrent or run counter to the families'. The financial structure of public schooling limits free choice in education. Indeed:

> We have created a system of school finance that provides free choice for the rich and compulsory socialization for everyone else. The present method of financing American education discriminates against the poor and the working class and even a large part of the middle class by conditioning the exercise of First Amendment rights of school choice upon an ability to pay while simultaneously eroding the ability to pay through the regressive collection of taxes used exclusively for government schools.[66]

Reasons Violation of First Amendment Rights Is Tolerated

One commentator has theorized that this unconstitutionality is legally tolerated for three reasons that together constitute an imperfect understanding of family-school value conflict.[67] First, there is a lack of understanding of the centrality of the public schools within the family and in the upbringing and socialization of children. Second, there is a lack of acknowledgment of the relationship between the *formation* and the *expression* of belief and opinions. Finally, there is a lack of attention to the imposition of secular ideology in the public schools. As this commentator writes:

> To date, this pattern and practice of violating basic constitutional rights has been tolerated by the law in all but a few instances because of a flawed understanding of the problem of family/school value conflict. Most judges and legislators have not perceived the centrality of school socialization to the lives of families and the raising of children; neither have they acknowledged the relationship between the formation of world views in children and the expression of opinion protected by the First Amendment. And finally, the courts have been so preoccupied with preventing religious impositions in publicly supported schools that they have virtually ignored the more significant impositions of ideology.[68]

The centrality of the public schools within the family and the imposition of ideology (value inculcation) has been previously discussed. There is an undeniable connection between formation and expression of values, beliefs and opinions, and protection of the First Amendment in education, as will be discussed below.

The Formation/Expression Connection of Beliefs and the First Amendment

One reason conflicts regarding value inculcation in the public schools and conflicts involving parents seeking alternatives to public school, such as home schooling, continue to occur is that the courts have failed to address in a straightforward and consistent manner the relationship between the influence of the public schools on the development of values in children and the First Amendment.[69] Children in their developing years, especially young children, are incapable of exploring and comparing values and choosing those values which are most beneficial for them. Children are dependent on adults to help them accomplish this task. Traditionally, this has been the responsibility of the family, primarily the parents. Yet, as discussed above, the public education system has been increasingly assuming this function.

The development of values in children (which later translate into beliefs and opinions) is particularly important to the sovereignty and dignity of the individual because it precedes the expression of these values. Government-run public schools are inculcating the values, beliefs and opinions of the political majority during the most sensitive years of a child's development. This inculcation of majority-held values may interfere with a family's right to teach its own values, and it also impedes the free expression of belief by influencing the development of values. The strong connection between formation and expression of belief and the unavailability of alternatives to public education for all families would make it seem that the inculcation of majority values in the public schools is a violation of the First Amendment right to freedom of expression. This means:

> The connection between expression and formation of beliefs is so close they are nearly inseparable. Freedom of expression makes possible the unfettered formulation of belief and opinion in an atmosphere of open exchange unconstricted by government. In turn, the governmentally uncoerced formulation of beliefs and opinions is essential to freedom of expression.[70]

Applying the First Amendment to Public Schooling

This conclusion suggests the First Amendment should be applied differently to public schooling. Specifically, the First Amendment should be expanded to include the formation of beliefs. There is a forceful argument for the necessity of this expansion:

> If the most sensitive point in the transmission of beliefs and the definition of knowledge were not protected by the First Amendment, an originating point of the consent of the governed would be controlled by the government, and all communication, learning, speech, voting, and assembling would be colored and distorted by this coercive tampering with individual consciousness.[71]

> If the government were able to use schooling to regulate the development of ideas and opinions by controlling the transmission of culture and the socialization of children, freedom of expression would become a meaningless right; just as government control of expression would make the formation of belief and opinion a state-dominated rather than an individually based process. If the First Amendment protected only the communication and not the formation of ideas, totalitarianism and freedom of expression could be characteristics of the same society. In modern times the opportunity to coerce consciousness precedes, and may do away with, the need to manipulate expression.[72]

> The expression/formation connection between the First Amendment's emphasis on the dignity of the individual and education's inevitable influence on personal development and transmission of culture suggests a formulation of First Amendment principles as follows: the development as well as the expression of those beliefs, opinions, world views, and aspects of conscience that constitute individual consciousness should be free of government coercion through schooling.[73]

The existence of home schooling and other alternatives to public education serves to protect First Amendment rights by protecting the formation of beliefs from government manipulation. By expanding the First Amendment to include the formation of beliefs, it would be necessary to make alternatives to public education, such as home schooling, available to all families and to prevent unreasonable government regulation of these alternatives as a means of protecting the First Amendment right to freedom of expression. As Stephen Arons writes:

> The consequences of applying this First Amendment principle to the present structure of schooling are clear. Eliminating family educational choice or permitting government regulation of content of schooling renders individual expression, self-fulfillment, and personal development meaningless. So long as individual dignity matters, the individual ought to control his own education; where the individual is too young to make an informed and voluntary choice, his parents ought to control it.[74]

Applying this First Amendment principle to the present structure of schooling would also require that freedom of school choice must be made available to all families, not just the wealthy. The current system of school finance would have to be redesigned to prevent discrimination against educational choices of the nonwealthy.[75]

Larger Issues in Family-School Value Conflicts

Value conflicts between families and public school officials have at their core a larger concern than the expression of minority values, beliefs and opinions. The outcome of these conflicts will greatly affect political participation in the future: "Public-school officials and the political majorities they claim to represent are engaged in attempts to control the opinions upon which their present and future power depends."[76] Perhaps this explains the reason home schooling, which research shows is frequently motivated by value conflict with the public schools, has triggered an uproar out of proportion to a relatively small movement.

For families, education and socialization of children is a method of preserving the family, its values, and its understandings of life. If the family is part of a minority group or community, the ability to educate and socialize their children is a way of ensuring political representation and power in the future.[77] Thus, schooling conflicts are vital to the health and well-being of our democratic society and serve an important function for the society:

> Dissent developed and expressed in the process of schooling is therefore an important resource for the future growth of culture and the establishment of political consensus. The dead hand of orthodoxy not only deprives substantial numbers of families of the ability to participate in culture and public life, it threatens to end the process of growth altogether and replace it with what Jung called "the spiritual and moral darkness of

State Absolutism." This darkness is one which we are accustomed to thinking about as the condition of totalitarian societies.[78]

However:

Up to this point no major court has struck a clear and comprehensible balance between the power of the family and the power of the school to control the education of the child. When such an occasion does finally arrive, the court will not succeed in resolving the conflict over home education unless it abandons attention to superficial issues and takes up the question of whether the right to preserve family values and privacy is so fundamental, and the right to an alternative to public school so basic to freedom of belief, that the state must have a compelling justification for any regulation it makes of home education.[79]

There have been three compelling justifications which have demonstrated longevity. These are: 1. that a child must receive an education, but not a specific type; 2. that the education must eliminate racism as outlined in the Thirteenth, Fourteenth and Fifteenth Amendments; and 3. that children must be protected from abuse.[80]

Dangers in Limiting Freedom of School Choice

Limiting viable alternatives to public education and allowing strict government regulation of these alternatives creates an environment conducive to certain dangers. One of the gravest potential dangers occurs when individuals with great power and influence occupy key positions within the government in this environment, thus creating the possibility for government to manipulate the formation of values, beliefs and opinions through public schooling to ensure the preservation of the government. Should this occur, individualism and diversity, the cornerstones of American democracy, would be severely restricted, and public orthodoxy would result. First Amendment rights would become meaningless. If such a situation should occur, American society could potentially slip toward totalitarianism. Historical examples abound.

For instance, the consequences of such an occurrence in Nazi Germany provide a historical lesson. Adolf Hitler understood the importance of utilizing education to inculcate values, beliefs and opinions in children to ensure the preservation of the Third Reich. Hitler began by abolishing private education, making public school attendance compulsory, and reorganizing and centralizing public education.[81]

In a speech on November 6, 1933, Hitler spoke of his strategy to utilize children in the development and preservation of his Third Reich:

When an opponent declares, "I will not come over to your side," . . . I calmly say, "Your child belongs to us already. . . . What are you? You will pass on. Your descendants, however, now stand in the new camp. In a short time they will know nothing else but this new community."[82]

And later, in a speech on May 1, 1937, Hitler declared: "This new Reich will give its youth to no one, but will itself take youth and give to youth its own education and its own upbringing."[83] According to William L. Shirer, author of *The Rise and Fall of the Third Reich*: "It was not an idle boast; that was precisely what was happening."[84]

Other changes in education under Hitler included a shift in the focus of education from the individual to the community. "Hitler and other Nazis . . . emphasized the need to subordinate the individual to the community. Education, then, had to be geared not to the development of the individual but to the needs of the community."[85] The Nazi Minister of the Interior, Dr. Wilhelm Frick, pronounced: "The period in which the task of the school was considered to be to develop the individual is past. The new school proceeds on principle from the idea of the community, which is the age-old legacy of our Germanic ancestors."[86]

The Nazi regime created the Hitler Youth, an organization for children and adolescents in which membership became compulsory, initially to supplement, and later to assume responsibility for, education. "To Adolf Hitler it was not so much the public schools, from which he himself had dropped out so early in life, but the organizations of the Hitler Youth on which he counted to educate the youth of Germany for the ends he had in mind."[87] Hitler hoped that as individuals who became leaders in the Hitler Youth graduated from the organization they would replace the teachers in the schools to ensure a supply of teachers supportive and loyal to the Third Reich. "The final aim was that out of the Hitler Youth would eventually come 'the youth leader and educator of the future.' . . ."[88] By merging formal public schooling and Hitler Youth Service, education would become an invaluable tool for the indoctrination of the young citizenry and would ensure the growth and preservation of the Third Reich.[89] Parents who attempted to prohibit their children from joining the Hitler Youth were subject to long prison sentences or the danger that their children would be taken away from them.[90]

Several rough parallels can be drawn between the system of education in Nazi Germany and our present-day system of public education. First, both systems made public education compulsory. While a difference exists between the two systems in that Nazi Germany abolished private education and the American system permits it, this difference may not be as large as it first appears because, as discussed previously, for many American families there are limited alternatives to public education. Second, in both systems the focus of education shifted from the individual to the community, with responsibility for socialization and education of children being increasingly assumed by government-run schools. Third, in the American system of public education, as in Nazi Germany, there appears to be an acceptance of the appropriateness of inculcating the values of political majority. Finally, as occurred in Nazi Germany, there have been some parents who, by keeping their children out of public school because of objections to ideology, have received prison sentences or had their children taken from them. For example:

> In Iowa parents who educate their nine-year-old son at home are convicted of criminal violations. They appeal, are acquitted, and are threatened with renewed prosecution the next year. In Michigan a family is forced to send three of their children to a boarding school 150 miles from home to avoid the threat of having their children made wards of the court and sent to foster homes. In Massachusetts a family is accused of parental neglect for educating two teenagers at home, and the children are removed to the custody of the welfare department. After a long struggle, the family is split up and scattered over three states. Another family is told by a judge to comply with school requirements or move out of the state. In Rhode Island a couple is arrested for educating their daughters, aged eight and nine, at home. In Missouri a woman spends time behind bars because she does not believe her seven-year-old is ready for school.[91]

Protecting First Amendment Rights

The presence of these rather rough parallels or similarities does not imply that the United States is metamorphosing into a totalitarian society, but, rather, it underscores the need to protect education from becoming a force and tool of orthodoxy and manipulation by ensuring freedom in educational choice for all families. By doing so, First Amendment rights will be protected, particularly the right to freedom of expression, without which the American democracy could not survive: "[I]f belief formation is not protected, all freedom is jeopardized."[92] Furthermore, "[i]f families are allowed to operate unfettered, they produce the form of diversity and pluralism that is essential to free societies. This avoids the uniformity that is associated with authoritarian states."[93]

Benefits to Society from Freedom in Educational Choice

Freedom in educational choice, specifically the option of home schooling, offers important benefits to American society. Home schooling and other alternatives to public education protect the formation or development of belief, which subsequently protects the First Amendment right to freedom of expression. Specifically, educational alternatives serve to limit the power of the state to inculcate, through public schools, the values of the political majority and to manipulate the consciousness of children:

> The society that can utilize institutional power to reduce the individual's control over the development of personal consciousness has made that individual politically impotent. Under these conditions the government becomes a kind of political perpetual motion machine, legitimizing its policies through the public opinion it helps create.[94]

Home schooling and other alternatives contribute to the growth of culture and the establishment of political consensus.[95] These alternatives to public education help to promote social cohesion by preventing the enforcement of political majority values. Allowing home schooling and other alternatives strengthens the family. They restore the presumption of competence in education to families and return to the family the responsibility for the education, socialization and transmission of culture and values to their children. They allow individual families ". . . to explore, create, and pass on beliefs that might become more useful to social survival than public orthodoxy."[96] They ensure political representation and power for minority families.[97] Finally, home schooling and other alternatives promote the diversity and pluralism necessary to free societies.[98]

PEDAGOGICAL ISSUES

This section will discuss ways in which the home schooling alternative benefits American society by promoting excellence in education. While home schooling may not be desirable for all parents and children, this form of education, which can be exciting and innovative, offers numerous advantages that public schools do not. David and Micki Colfax, for example, have home schooled their four children and received widespread attention when three of their sons were accepted to and attended Harvard. They have referred to home schooling as "perhaps the most dynamic and creative educational movement in decades."[99]

There are many problems with formal schooling which can prevent children from achieving their maximum potential. Home schooling eliminates some of these problems. The following is a discussion of the problems found in formal schooling which interfere with children receiving optimum benefit from education. The discussion will conclude with the advantages of home schooling and school choice.

Perpetuation of Stereotypes and Social Inequalities

Schools are often unable to serve children from broad and diverse backgrounds equally well and thus they often perpetuate stereotypes and social inequalities:

> *The long-held assumption* that schools serve children from broad and diverse backgrounds equally well has been all but discredited. Evidence mounts from critics of both public and private schools that formal and hidden curriculums of schools contribute to the reproduction of social inequalities rather than equalizing opportunity.[100]

There are many dynamics at work in the classroom that mitigate against equal and fair treatment and opportunity for all students. For purposes of this discussion, the term *dynamics* refers to interpersonal interactions between two or more people. These dynamics may operate with or without the knowledge or awareness of those involved.

Schemas

One dynamic in the classroom is the use of schemas, particularly by teachers. Schemas are abstract cognitive representations or categories that individuals utilize to classify and understand stimuli in their environment.[101] Schemas aid people in understanding their environment by inferring information, specifically information regarding characteristics or behaviors, about stimuli of which they have no direct knowledge or experience.[102] An example of how people use schemas is described as follows:

> [I]f you see a person who is shy, quiet, and timid, you might search through your categories [schemas] until you encounter a match with these characteristics: This person is *introverted* . . . recognizing a person as introverted allows you to infer that the person probably is also reserved, hesitant, bashful, and oversensitive.[103]

Schemas may be extremely useful and beneficial because they allow people to quickly understand stimuli in the environment and predict information without having to observe all characteristics and behaviors of the stimuli: "Using a schema allows us to store information with a great deal of economy. In other words, using abstract concepts reduces the need to remember many redundant pieces of information."[104]

While schemas may be beneficial, they also have a negative aspect: they color people's perception and can thus result in the inference of inaccurate or faulty information. This negative aspect of schemas can especially cause problems when people are classified or categorized. Once an individual classifies a person as fitting into a particular schema, the individual may recall information regarding the person's characteristics or behaviors *which he or she did not actually observe* but are consistent with that schema. Unfortunately, the information recalled may not be true. Conversely, an individual may fail to recall information which they observed but which is inconsistent with the schema.

In the school setting, these errors caused by schemas can have devastating consequences for students. A possible example follows: A teacher holds a schema for problem children. At the beginning of the school year, the teacher has a child in class who has trouble adjusting to the classroom structure after a relatively unstructured summer. The child is disruptive in class, refusing to remain quiet or sit relatively still. The teacher may categorize this child as a "problem child." By doing so, the teacher may recall seeing negative behaviors from the child which are consistent with the schema but which he or she did not actually observe. The teacher also may fail to recall observations of positive behavior from the child which are inconsistent with the schema. Later, the child adjusts to the structure and routine of the classroom and settles down. If the teacher is feeling stressed and overwhelmed, he or she may be unlikely to be attentive to the behavior changes of this particular child and may continue to observe only behavior consistent with the schema. How is this teacher likely to describe this child during a parent-teacher conference? Probably in a very negative way, since the teacher categorized the child as a problem child and is unlikely to observe the changes in the child's behavior. A problem is created when it need not have been. Perhaps this dynamic may partially account for "personality conflicts" between teachers and students.

These types of problems have led researchers to conclude of schemas:

> While this may be an efficient way to make an overwhelming amount of information more manageable, it can sometimes lead us to error. Some have suggested that using schemas to simplify a complex task can result in the perceiver becoming inflexible and sloppy because the task is not being attended to closely.[105]

What task can be considered more complex than teaching twenty or thirty children? The act of teaching requires flexibility and attentiveness. In summary, the schemas teachers hold have the ability to profoundly affect their relationships with students and, even more importantly, students' progress.

Stereotypes

A related dynamic at work in the classroom is the holding of stereotypes by teachers. Stereotypes are types of schemas. Stereotypes are defined as "a set of characteristics believed by the perceiver to be held in common by all members placed into a category. A stereotype can be seen as a schema used to represent a group of people who have a particular feature or attribute in common."[106]

As with schemas, stereotypes are often difficult to dispel because information which would dispel the stereotype may not be recalled.[107] "Stereotypes, like other schemas, can be reflected in the information that is remembered. And the remembered information is likely to be consistent with the stereotyped expectations. We tend to remember what we expect to find."[108] Stereotypes can act as self-fulfilling prophecies (self-fulfilling prophecies will be discussed in greater detail below) in which an individual's or society's belief that something will happen leads it to happen.[109]

Socioeconomic Stereotypes

While most people are aware of stereotypes regarding race, ethnicity, sex, and gender, research shows an even wider variety of stereotypes which may affect how children and students are viewed in the classroom. A study by John Darley and Paget Gross examined the effect of socioeconomic stereotypes on teachers' predictions of academic performance.[110]

> They gave schoolteachers a case history in which a young girl was fully described, including personal details. The teachers also saw photographs

of the child in her home environment. Although all teachers saw photographs of the same child and received the same basic history, Darley
and Gross varied whether the child was photographed in front of a house
in an obviously lower-class neighborhood or in an obviously middle-class
neighborhood. After a teacher had read the case history and had seen the
photograph of the child, a videotape was played showing the child taking an achievement test—working on the test and answering the tester's
questions. In some portions of the videotape the child looked interested
and attentive, while in others she appeared distracted and bored. Thus,
in some parts of the tape the child looked like a good student, and in others she looked like a poor student. All of the teachers saw the same videotape and read the same basic history with the alterations about the
background related to socioeconomic status.

After watching the videotape, each teacher was asked to predict the
child's academic performance in classes and to support the predictions
with evidence they had detected in the videotape of the test performance.
The teachers thought the lower-class child would be a poor performer
and the middle-class child would be a good performer. . . . When asked
to support their predictions, teachers who had watched the "middle-
class" child recalled the instances in the videotape when the child acted
like a good student. Those who watched the "lower-class" child recalled
the instances when the child acted like a poor student.[111]

This research suggests that a teacher's perceptions of a student's academic performance may be colored by the child's perceived socioeconomic
status. This stereotype most affects the children of minorities and single
mothers, who make up a disproportionately large part of the lower socioeconomic levels.

Physical Attractiveness Stereotypes

Another stereotype affecting students in the classroom which has been studied is physical attractiveness. Research on attraction has demonstrated that
people frequently develop judgments regarding a person's character and
behavior based on the person's physical attractiveness, and these judgments
carry a great deal of weight.[112] Attraction research has revealed a commonly
held physical attractiveness stereotype: "[A]ttractive people are viewed as
more interesting, kind, exciting, sensitive . . . and as having better futures
in store."[113] Even attractive children are favorably stereotyped.[114]

A study which examined the effect of physical attractiveness in children
on the evaluations of teachers "found that when compared with unattractive children, physically attractive children are thought by teachers to be
more intelligent, to have greater educational prospects, and even to have
parents with better attitudes towards school."[115] Another study "found that
the quality of an essay and the essay writer's ability were both rated more
favorably when the writer was thought to be attractive."[116] In other
research, it was "found that physically attractive people were guided toward

better job opportunities than were unattractive ones—even though the job recommendations were made by experienced personnel consultants."[117] In yet another study it was demonstrated that physical attractiveness influenced judgments of character.

> Adults read teachers' reports of severe classroom disturbances committed by children. If the subjects thought the child was good looking, they judged the transgression less negatively than if they thought an unattractive child was the offender. In addition, attractive children were seen as less likely to commit future transgressions. But when the child was unattractive, the offense was more likely to be seen as reflecting a lasting quality.[118] Other research offers the sobering suggestion that this can result in a self-fulfilling prophecy: juvenile delinquents have been found to be low in attractiveness.[119]

In a related study, researchers found "subjects are more lenient when assigning punishment to attractive students who cheat than they are to unattractive students who cheat."[120] The research described above predicts dismal and frightening consequences for the child who is unattractive.

Self-fulfilling Prophecy

A final dynamic at work in the classroom is self-fulfilling prophecy. Self-fulfilling prophecy is a phenomenon by which "people's expectations about the future events lead them to behave in particular ways that, on occasion, can cause the expected event to occur."[121] "In psychology, as in other fields, people tend to find what they are looking for. More than that, they may even tend unwittingly to *create* what they seek."[122]

Research has demonstrated the phenomenon of self-fulfilling prophecy. Robert Rosenthal has extensively studied self-fulfilling prophecies. These studies have implications for labeling and its subsequent effect on achievement.

> In one experiment . . . research participants were led to believe they would be serving as experimenters. Their task was to show photographs of faces to students. The task of the students was to rate the degree of success they felt was reflected in each of the photographed faces. Prior to this, however, some of the research participants had been led to expect the students would give high ratings of success; others were led to believe the students would give low ratings. Even though the photographs shown to the two groups of students were identical, research participants who expected high ratings got significantly higher ratings than did those who expected low ratings. In fact, the ratings of the two groups did not even overlap. Somehow, through posture or gestures or subtle voice cues, the research participants (acting as experimenters) communicated their expectations to the students.[123]

Thus, it was the experimenter's expectations that determined the results of the study and not the photographs.

In another study, experimenters were to train albino rats. The experimenters were given rats which were no different from one another.

Some were told that their rats had been specially bred for intelligence; others were told their rats were particularly dull. Those experimenters who had the "bright" rats found faster learning than the others. The mechanism of the bias in this case was that the experimenters who had the "bright" rats handled them more than did those who had the "dull" rats.[124]

In this study, the labels of "bright" and "dull" and the experimenters' expectations were responsible for the amount of learning which took place in the rats. Robert Rosenthal took his research a step further and conducted an experiment involving labeling children in the classroom.

Robert Rosenthal . . . told a group of elementary-school teachers that certain pupils had obtained high scores on some special tests and so were sure to show unusual intellectual development during the school year. [Teachers were informed that these students would demonstrate large academic gains during the school year.] Actually these pupils were no different from others who had not been labeled potential "late bloomers." Later in the year, the teachers rated the late bloomers as more interested, more curious, and happier than other students. And when all the children were given IQ tests at the end of the year, those who had been labeled late bloomers showed a significantly greater gain in IQ than did their classmates.[125]

These self-fulfilling prophecy studies point out the potential and inherent problems in labeling, ability grouping, and tracking students in the schools. This research suggests that labeling could be extremely detrimental, especially for those children labeled below average, mentally retarded, learning disordered, and/or emotionally disordered. Once a child is given such a label, it can lower teachers' expectations of the child and cause them to interact with the child in such a manner that the label becomes accurate: a self-fulfilling prophecy. The child may also accept this label and never discover his or her true capabilities. "Critics of these practices argue that labeling students by single dimensions of ability and homogenous grouping relegates children placed in lower groups to an inferior education and prepares them for a limited future."[126] Moreover, the effects of educational tracking have been likened to the detrimental effects of racial segregation that the Supreme Court recognized in Brown v. Board of Education.[127]

The dynamics in the classroom described above, the holding of schemas and stereotypes, and self-fulfilling prophecies, are just a few of the possible dynamics occurring in the classroom which mitigate against children doing their best and achieving their maximum potential. These dynamics make up a part of what has been called the hidden curriculum in schools and is one of the reasons schools do not serve all children equally well.

Difficulty of Serving Children with Unique Learning Styles or Needs

Another reason schools do not serve children equally well is that schools have great difficulty properly serving children with unique learning styles or needs. Children with unique learning styles and needs include gifted children, children with mental retardation, and children with learning or emotional difficulties. Research on parents' motivations for home schooling reveal that a large number of parents decided to home school their children because formal school structures are often not suited for dealing appropriately with such children:

> [T]he schools are often unwilling or unable to serve children with unique learning styles or scholarly needs, and they [parents] believed that their children would suffer from the schools' shortcomings. In these families, the parents believed their children would only learn if they were freed from comparison with group norms of achievements.[128]

Jane A. Van Galen, who studies home schooling families, reports, "[F]requently in these families, children found themselves to be in trouble in school, and the parents felt that they had exhausted the schools' resources for solving the problem."[129] Van Galen shares the accounts of two mothers of their children's difficulties in school that resulted in their decision to home school:

> Jim's situation was absolutely intolerable. He came up against a teacher who absolutely had a very straight and narrow attitude about the way everything had to be done. . . . She started labeling him emotionally disturbed. She said that he was going to be a drug addict when he grew up.

> It was a difficult situation [for him] to be in a classroom at that young an age, and to feel the stress accumulating with the academics and to feel behind, you know, "I can't, I can't." Emotionally, I felt that we were all beat, and he was just a 7-year-old.[130]

Schools, by their very structure, lack the ability to individually tailor education to each child's special abilities and needs. In public schools, children are expected to learn material in the time allotted and to move on. Children's differences in learning are not addressed. Frequently, there are not enough personnel or specially trained personnel to help children pursue special interests, develop their abilities to the fullest, and master subjects and skills with which they are having difficulty. Home schooling, on the other hand, frees children from being compared with their peers and from the limited definition of success in schools as "getting all A's." Home schooling parents are able to focus all of their attention on their child, rather than twenty or thirty children, and to individually tailor schooling to their child's needs.

Self-directed Learning

Another area in which schools are lacking is in teaching the skills for self-directed learning that are increasingly required in today's world.

> [Self-directed learning is a] process in which individuals take the initiative, with or without the help of others, in diagnosing their learning needs, formulating learning goals, identifying human and material resources for learning, choosing and implementing appropriate learning strategies, and evaluating learning outcomes.[131]

In short, self-directed learning is the process of learning how to learn.[132] By contrast, formal schooling primarily utilizes teacher-directed learning, which teaches the student the skills and process of learning how to be taught.

Malcolm Knowles, in his book *Self-Directed Learning*, discusses the differences in the body of theory and practice and assumptions between self-directed and teacher-directed learning.[133] "Andragogy" is the term used to refer to the body of theory and practice of self-directed learning; it is derived from the Greek *aner*, which means "man," and *agogus*, which means "leader."[134] The body of theory and practice of teacher-directed learning is referred to as "pedagogy"; it is derived from the Greek word *paid*, which means "child," and *agogus*, or "leader."[135] According to Knowles, "andragogy is defined . . . as the art and science of helping adults (or, even better, maturing human beings) learn."[136] "Pedagogy has come to be defined as the art and science of teaching, but its tradition is in the teaching of children."[137]

Knowles discusses five assumptions along which self-directed and teacher-directed learning differ. These assumptions are: concept of the learner, the role of the learner's experience, readiness to learn, orientation to learning, and motivation.[138]

Concept of the Learner

In the first assumption, self-directed learning holds a concept of the learner as an "increasingly self-directed organism" and "assumes that the human being grows in capacity (and need) to be self-directing as an essential component of maturing, and that this capacity should be nurtured to develop as rapidly as possible."[139] In contrast, teacher-directed learning conceptualizes the learner as "a dependent personality . . . the teacher has the responsibility of deciding what and how the learner should be taught."[140]

Role of the Learner's Experience

In the second assumption, self-directed learning perceives the learner's growing experiences as "an increasingly rich resource for learning which should be exploited along with the resources of experts."[141] Teacher-directed learning, on the other hand, views the learner's experiences as something "to be built on more than used" and "assumes that the learner's experience is of less value than that of the teacher, the textbook writers and materials producers as a resource for learning, and that therefore the teacher has the responsibility to see to it that the resources of these experts are transmitted to the learner."[142]

Readiness to Learn

Self-directed learning, in the third assumption, "assumes that individuals become ready to learn what is required to perform their evolving life tasks or to cope more adequately with their life problems, and that each individual therefore has a somewhat different pattern of readiness from other individuals."[143] "Teacher-directed learning assumes that students become ready to learn different things at different levels of maturation, and that a given set of learners will therefore be ready to learn the same things at a given level of maturation."[144]

Orientation to Learning

In the fourth assumption, self-directed learning assumes that the natural orientation of human beings to learning "is task- or problem-centered, and that therefore learning experiences should be organized as task-accomplishing or problem-solving learning projects," whereas "teacher-directed learning assumes that students enter into education with a subject-centered orientation to learning (they see learning as accumulating subject matter) and that therefore learning experiences should be organized according to units of content."[145]

Motivation

In the fifth assumption, "self-directed learning assumes that learners are motivated by internal incentives, such as the need for esteem (especially self-esteem), the desire to achieve, the urge to grow, the satisfaction of accomplishment, the need to know something specific, and curiosity."[146] "Teacher-directed learning assumes that students are motivated to learn in response to external rewards and punishments, such as grades, diplomas, awards, degrees, and fear of failure."[147]

The comparison of assumptions between self- and teacher-directed learning does not indicate that teacher-directed learning is without value. Both types of learning are useful and valuable, and there are certain times when teacher-directed learning is required, such as when the learner is beginning a study of an unfamiliar area. In this case, it is probable the learner will have little or no experience to bring as a resource to the area of study and will likely be dependent on others who are more knowledgeable to accumulate information on the subject under study. There are times when learning readiness really does depend on maturation level and cases when the learner will be motivated by external rewards or punishments.[148] However, Malcolm Knowles states:

> Perhaps what makes the difference between pedagogical and andragogical education is not so much the difference in the assumptions underlying their theory and practice as it is the attitude of learners. If self-directed learners recognize that there are occasions on which they will need to be taught, they will enter into those taught-learning situations in a searching, probing frame of mind and will exploit them as resources for learning without losing their self-directedness.[149]

The importance of the skill of self-directed learning to survival in the present and future cannot be underestimated. Alvin Toffler, author of *Future Shock*, discusses the reasons this skill will be so important in the future:

> Given further acceleration, we can conclude that knowledge will grow increasingly perishable. Today's "fact" becomes tomorrow's "misinformation" . . . a society in which the individual constantly changes his job, his place of residence, his social ties and so forth, places an enormous premium on learning efficiency. Tomorrow's schools must therefore teach not merely data, but ways to manipulate it. Students must learn how to discard old ideas, how and when to replace them. They must, in short, learn how to learn.[150]

Toffler quotes psychologist Herbert Gerjuoy of the Human Resources Research Organization:

> The new education must teach the individual how to classify and reclassify information, how to evaluate its veracity, how to change categories when necessary, how to move from the concrete to the abstract and back, how to look at problems from a new direction—how to teach himself. Tomorrow's illiterate will not be the man who can't read; he will be the man who has not learned how to learn.[151]

Although Toffler writes about the future, the need to learn how to learn is upon us today. For example, Richard Nelson Bolles, author of *What Color Is Your Parachute?*, states that the average person goes job hunting eight times during his or her life,[152] and Carole Hyatt, author of *Shifting Gears*, reports "12 million people are currently engaged in switching to a new career, and 12 million more are actively planning the change. Indeed, trends indicate that the average person will have three distinct careers in her working life."[153]

These statistics underscore the need for people to understand how to prepare themselves for new and different jobs and careers. It is not always practical or efficient for people to return to school every time they require preparation, and exploring different job and career areas often requires an individual to research options by gathering information from both human and material sources to make the best career decision for himself or herself. Even when an individual chooses to return to school, he or she may need to gather information on prospective schools and programs, financial aid, and admission procedures. In order to handle job or career transitions smoothly and efficiently and to make the best choices for themselves, these people must possess the skills of self-directed learning. If people do not take the initiative and responsibility for learning what is available and best suits them, allowing decisions affecting their life to be left to others or chance, they are likely to be dissatisfied. For individuals to explore their options they must know how to learn.

John W. Gardner outlines the changes in our perception of education which must occur to encourage lifelong learning:

> The ultimate goal of the educational system is to shift to the individual the burden of pursuing his own education. This will not be a widely shared pursuit until we get over our odd conviction that education is what goes on in school buildings and nowhere else. Not only does education continue when schooling ends, but it is not confined to what may be studied in adult education courses. The world is an incomparable classroom, and life is a memorable teacher for those who aren't afraid of her.[154]

Advantages of Home Schooling

Home schooling is well suited to the development of self-directed learning skills in children and eliminates or decreases the dynamics of schemas, stereotypes and labeling which occur in the classroom. David and Micki Colfax, mentioned previously, declare that home schooling is superior to other approaches in at least four areas: 1. the ability to exercise control over content, methods, timing and personnel; 2. greater efficiency in learning; 3. increased autonomy; and 4. creativity.[155] In discussing the superiority of home schooling with regard to control over content, the Colfaxes assert that the curriculum in schools does not address individual differences in children's maturation, aptitudes, and ability to assimilate and accommodate new information.[156] The Colfaxes declare that public school curriculum is, in fact, senseless:

> The public school curriculum—which embodies, at least theoretically, *what* is to be learned and *when*—is in fact nothing more than a hodge-podge of materials and assumptions resulting from the historical interplay of educational theories, political expedience, educational fads and fashions, pretensions to culture, demagoguery, and demography.[157]

> But because the curriculum is devised by "specialists" who are presumed, at least within the ranks of the educational bureaucracy, to know just

what should be taught and when, the notion that learning is a top-down, externally imposed process, a "laying-on of culture," is perpetuated and reinforced, unchallenged, daily.[158]

For the most part any standardized, official curriculum is largely meaningless, incoherent, and irrelevant to the lives of most children. It is rather a control mechanism, one which interferes with and undermines education.[159]

The Colfaxes point out that home schooling provides the milieu to individually tailor programs of study to children's needs, interests, skills and abilities once the basics of reading, writing and mathematics have been mastered. It supplies the freedom for parents and children to work together to create and design programs of study which are meaningful and interesting to the child, take into account the child's capabilities, and meet both short- and long-term goals.[160]

Home schooling parents have the freedom to experiment with and test teaching methods and curriculum, to retain those which they find most effective, and to discard those they find ineffective. They also have the ability to be truly eclectic and to use what works best in furthering the education of their children. Not being tied to any particular method or material, they can quickly change course when something isn't working and respond rapidly to the child's individual needs.[161] According to the Colfaxes:

Unlike teachers and administrators, who sometimes seem to have a trained susceptibility to commercially promoted gimmickry, parents can be skeptically eclectic in their choice of and commitment to methods and materials . . . of all kinds without having to worry about professional orthodoxies, fads or fashions.[162]

Home schooling, moreover, offers parents and children control over timing. Teaching can be geared to the individual child's readiness to learn specific material. Because home schooling is individually based and parents are in the unique position of intimately knowing their child, they can vary and match the pace and flow of the information and material taught to the needs and readiness of their child; they can press forward to assure their child is adequately challenged in certain subjects, while simultaneously slowing down to ensure difficult subjects are mastered.[163] In addition, experience suggests children learn best when they are ready to learn:

It seems obvious, yet its implications are almost universally ignored: children learn best when they are intellectually, emotionally, and socially *ready* to learn. And because children are not universally *ready* when age-graded oriented teachers are, learning often does not take place when and as it should.[164]

Home schooling offers control over personnel as well. Who hasn't endured a school year or seen a child endure a school year with a teacher he or she did not like? A poor, difficult or abusive teacher wastes valuable time in a child's life at best and at worst can turn a child off to learning or leave emotional or intellectual scars.[165] Loving parents who have their child's best interests at heart and facilitate their child's learning at the child's own pace can help to create a love of learning which lasts a lifetime.

A second area in which home schooling is superior to other approaches is in its efficiency. Simple mathematics documents home schooling as far more efficient than the public school environment:

The numbers are straightforward and irrefutable. The child who attends public school typically spends approximately 1,100 hours a year there, but only twenty percent of these—220—are spent, as the educators say, "on task." Nearly 900 hours, or eighty percent, are squandered on what are essentially organizational matters.

In contrast, the homeschooled child who spends only two hours a day, seven days a week, year-round, on basics alone, logs over *three times* as many hours "on-task" in a given year than does his counterpart. Moreover, unlike the public school child, whose day is largely taken up by non-task activities, the homeschooled child has ample time left each day to take part in other activities—athletics, art, history, etc.—without having to sacrifice other interests, as is commonly the case in school where, for example, one may have to choose between playing sports or playing in the orchestra simply because of time constraints.[166]

A third area in which home schooling is superior to other options is autonomy. Home schooled children have the autonomy to pursue different and varied interests and decide the amount of time and effort they will devote to learning projects. This characteristic of home schooling encourages children to take responsibility for their learning—in short, to become self-directed learners.[167]

Unconstrained by an overly long school day, the homeschooled child can become educationally autonomous, as it were, and capable of dealing with learning not as something "out there" and "run by them," as commonly understood, but as an integral part of everyday life, something for which one has to take responsibility.[168]

The fourth and final area that David and Micki Colfax identify as superior to other options is creativity. By virtue of its freedom in control over content, methods, timing and personnel, its efficiency, and the autonomy it provides, home schooling encourages children to become self-directed learners and for parents and children to be creative in discovering what works best for them and what interests them.[169]

This is, of course, not an exhaustive list of the benefits of home schooling, but only a general one, and it is certain the list is longer.

Advantages of School Choice Within Public Schools

While home schooling is perhaps the educational option which offers parents and their children the most freedom and choice, school choice in public schools has also shown beneficial effects in children, teachers and the schools. One benefit of choice in public schools is that it creates competition among schools and forces schools to offer superior programming to attract students and remain viable and open. Thomas Toch, Educational Correspondent for *U.S. News and World Report*, has reviewed the results of competition between public schools and discusses one successful program in New York City's District 4.[170] Toch believes the marketplace in public education can be successful when it is well established.[171] Toch quotes a deputy school superintendent who has held his position for many years on the effects of competition between public schools: "No school is going to stand still in the face of competition."[172] The results of this competition speak for themselves:

> In 1980, District 4 had hundreds of empty classrooms; now it attracts more than a thousand students from other parts of the city. It's unlikely these students would venture into East Harlem's often-dangerous neighborhoods if they and their parents didn't think it was educationally worth their while.[173]

> The school system's academic performance has improved dramatically since the introduction of choice. One measure is the number of District 4 students admitted annually to New York City's four specialized high schools, which require rigorous tests for admission. That number has increased from 10 before open enrollment to 250 today.[174]

In addition to improving the academic curriculum, competition also has the effect of making the public schools more accountable. Toch believes "introduction of a marketplace into public education helps create the accountability that school reformers have sought, even as it diminishes the necessity of prescriptive mandates."[175] One of the most exciting benefits of school choice is what occurs in students and teachers: feelings of apathy and alienation decrease, and the sense of ownership and community in the school increases.[176]

> If permitting students to select the schools they attend represents a powerful source of reform in public education, the reason has as much to do with the capacity of choice to create a strong sense of community in schools as it does with market forces. One of the greatest barriers to increased academic achievement in schools is an extraordinary level of alienation among junior and senior high school students; large

numbers of them, in rich and poor schools alike, simply don't care about learning.[177]

This increased feeling of ownership and community increases motivation and dedication to learning in students, thereby creating a positive attitude toward learning, and this positive attitude promotes greater academic achievement.[178] According to Toch:

> But when students have a say in selecting their schools, they frequently develop strong ties to them. Having chosen or "invested" in their schools, they typically identify with them. That sense of ownership, in turn, seems to be a powerful source of motivation, strengthening students' dedication to their studies. . . .
>
> When they're permitted to select from schools that are educationally special, students' identification with their schools is heightened even further. . . .
>
> The positive attitude toward learning among students permitted to select their schools typically translates into greater academic achievement.[179]

Consequences of Failure in Education to Society

Freedom in education, specifically school choice, whether it is the freedom to choose alternatives to public education or to choose schools within the public education system, has the beneficial effect of greater academic achievement. While it seems obvious that excellence in education is vital to our democratic society and the healthy growth and well-being of our country, this point is made startlingly clear when the consequences of failure in education to our society are examined. The failure of a child to receive a good education costs our society a great deal. There is a strong relationship between education and poverty and between education and crime: "A good generalization is that increased levels of education will reduce the chances of living in poverty better than anything else. This is widely accepted."[180] From a taxpayer's point of view, it is much less expensive to prevent people from going into poverty than to pay for the consequences of poverty— namely, supporting these individuals and their children on welfare.[181] Since education has been shown to reduce poverty, it appears to be a worthwhile and wise investment.

Perhaps the most startling consequence for our society of the failure of children to receive a good education is revealed in the strong relationship between education and crime:

> Today, more than 80% of America's one million prisoners are high school dropouts. Each prisoner costs taxpayers upwards of $20,000 a year. Moreover, the investment in prisoners is a bad one, in that 63% of released inmates are back in jail for serious crimes within three years. Taxpayers spend more by far on a prisoner than on *any other kind* of tax-

supported individual. . . . Indeed, in Pennsylvania it is seven times more expensive for taxpayers to maintain someone in the *state pen* than it is to maintain someone at Penn State![182]

Statistics on dropout, graduation, and prisoner rates demonstrate this relationship:

> It is interesting to note that, with one exception, the states with the lowest dropout rates also have the lowest rates of prisoners per 100,000 people. With two exceptions, the states with the lowest graduation rates have the highest rates of prisoners per 100,000 people.[183]

According to one expert on the subject, "America's prison population *doubled* in less than a decade, reaching 1.1 million prisoners in 1990. (The U.S. incarceration rate in 1991 was the highest in the world, ahead of the Soviet Union and South Africa. In fact, in 1988 a black male in the U.S. was about five times as likely to be in prison as a black male in South Africa.)"[184] Moreover, "the cost of our prisons is increasing faster than that of *any other* social service, including education and health."[185] It is truly ironic that we invest more on our prisoners than on education when increased levels of education has been shown to reduce crime rates.[186]

Hodgkinson also points out the relationship between poverty, crime and education. He states:

> For young high school dropouts working minimum-wage jobs, there is little chance that the American Dream will become reality—unless, of course, they turn to crime. In 1989, four million Americans worked full-time but were still eligible for poverty benefits! Since Ben Franklin, America's deal with its citizens has been: if you work hard, you shouldn't be poor. Where is the reward for the work ethic for these four million people?
>
> However, we know that as educational levels increase, so do earnings. And as earnings increase, the propensity for crime decreases. If you can make your way in the mainstream, a risky criminal "career" becomes less and less inviting.[187]

The consequences of a lack of education make it essential that the United States take the actions necessary to ensure that its future citizens will be well-educated. Freedom in education is an essential part of the solution. School choice, whether it involves alternatives outside the public education system such as home schooling, or within the public education system, seems to facilitate parents' and their children's investment in their education and their dedication and commitment to academic achievement. While alternatives to public education, such as home schooling, may not be desirable for all parents and children, if these alternatives help even a few children to obtain a good education, experience academic success, and develop a lifelong love of learning, it is well worth supporting these alternatives and keeping them viable. Consider the consequences to society of not doing so:

> It behooves us all to make sure that *every* child in America has a good education and access to a good job. We cannot, as a nation, afford to throw *any* child away; we need them all to become successful adults if the economy, the community, the work force, the military—indeed, the nation—are to thrive.[188]

SUMMARY

We have examined the benefits American society receives from diversity in educational opportunities. Its focus has been on alternatives to public education, primarily the alternative of home schooling, but the benefits of school choice within the public education system were also briefly examined. Two categories of issues which were discussed, ideological and pedagogical, correspond to the reasons families choose to home school.

With regard to ideological issues, when alternatives to public education are given the freedom to flourish without unreasonable government regulation, First Amendment rights are protected. When these alternatives are made available to all families (with availability not being based on wealth), families are able to choose education for their children which teaches or transmits the values, beliefs and opinions they endorse. This freedom prevents the forced inculcation of majority values which presently occurs for those families unable to afford alternatives. It allows families to protect the development or formation of beliefs in their children, which in turn protects individuals' First Amendment right of freedom of expression.

Giving families choices in education limits the power of the state to inculcate political majority values and manipulate the consciousness of children through schooling. By returning control over education and restoring the presumption of competence in education to families, the mediating structure of the family in society is strengthened, and this also serves to limit the power of the state.[189] Families belonging to a minority group or community are ensured of future political representation and power.[190] Home schooling and other alternatives to public education limit public orthodoxy in the society, contribute to the growth of culture and political consensus, and promote social cohesion.[191] Finally, freedom in education helps to promote the diversity and pluralism necessary to free societies by allowing families to operate unfettered.[192]

Freedom in education also helps to promote excellence in education. Home schooling helps eliminate dynamics occurring in classrooms which mitigate against children achieving their maximum potential. These dynamics include schemas and stereotypes held by school personnel, labeling, and self-fulfilling prophecies. Home education frees children from comparison with others and allows them to experience varied forms of success rather than just getting good grades. Children have the freedom to develop their special skills, interests and abilities (their talents) to the fullest. This enhances children's self-esteem. This type of education is conducive to the development of individualized programs to meet the particular learning styles and needs of each child and particularly benefits children with unique styles and needs such as the gifted, the mentally retarded, and emotional and/or learning disordered children. The child's best interest is the priority rather than the best interest of the class or group.

Home schooling also provides an important milieu for self-directed learning, which is increasingly required for survival in today's world. David and Micki Colfax assert home schooling is superior in the areas of exercising control (over content, methods, timing and personnel), efficiency in learning, autonomy, and creativity.[193]

School choice within the public education system has also been shown to have beneficial effects. Creating a marketplace and competition within the public education system has prompted schools to improve academic programming and remain accountable.[194] It decreases feelings of apathy and alienation, while increasing a sense of ownership and community among students and school personnel.[195] Consequently, the motivation and dedication to learning of students, parents and school personnel increases the promotion of greater academic achievement.[196] Perhaps the most compelling argument for choice in education has to do with the consequences when students fail in the traditional education system. A lack of education correlates very strongly with poverty and crime.[197] As a society, Americans cannot afford to allow children to fail in education. Freedom in education, specifically school choice, is an essential part of the solution.

4

Free Market Choice in Education

School choice is an issue that has been debated for years. However, with its politicization during the past few years, school choice is now a seemingly important issue of national public policy. Thus, while it has only recently become a topic of debate and discussion among national leaders and candidates, limited school choice plans have long been under consideration at the state and national level. This convergence of newfound national attention with long-standing interest and experimentation has made school choice one of the most discussed topics of the 1990s.

A precise definition of school choice is difficult. It is, generally, an option for parents and their children to select an educational experience other than their local public school.[1] This, in and of itself, is not a particularly controversial proposition. Specialized public schools, such as those which emphasize science, mathematics, or the arts,[2] or schools which help disabled or troubled students, have existed for years. Almost everyone would agree that these schools often benefit their students and should continue to exist.

However, this is merely the beginning of the issue of school choice. Proposals for school choice run the gamut from ideas such as specialized schools to options allowing students to attend any public school they wish within their own district to recommendations that the government remove itself entirely from the business of running public schools. This tremendous range of options illustrates the difficulty of defining the school choice movement.

While this huge disparity in notions about school choice exists, many Americans are certain of their dissatisfaction with what they have and would like to be able to do something more about it. For example, Gallup and *Phi Delta Kappan* magazine conducted a poll regarding the feelings of

Americans about their educational system which showed that the majority of Americans are in favor of some sort of options in choosing schools.[3] Substantial numbers of minority respondents to this poll favored choice, probably because their children are often in the worst public schools.[4] It is clear that people no longer want just one option.

Thus, several states now provide students at least limited choice among public schools.[5] Indeed, at least two other states and one city have gone further to allow students to lessen the economic blow of choosing private schools where the public ones are inadequate.[6] Furthermore, both of the major party candidates in the 1992 presidential election favored extension of school choice, though to fundamentally different degrees.[7]

Why did this all come to a head at this point in American history? Some say that it comes as a part of the general bipartisan move toward privatization, deregulation, and the ending of government monopolies that has been occurring in the United States throughout the Carter, Reagan and Bush presidencies.[8] For example, close to the time that President Bush announced a proposed budget which included an educational voucher plan of payments to low- and middle-income parents who want to send their children to private schools,[9] he was signing an executive order to allow municipalities to sell off public facilities to private contractors,[10] his Secretary of Housing and Urban Development was formulating plans to speed the sale of public housing projects to their tenants,[11] and the Postmaster General, who had done more than any other to privatize the Postal Service, was retiring.[12]

This growing privatization is not, however, solely an American phenomenon. Eastern and Central European countries are rapidly privatizing services,[13] some African countries are denationalizing airlines and postal services,[14] and America's closest neighbors and trading partners, Mexico and Canada, are ending government monopolies at breakneck speed.[15] It is perhaps natural that educational systems would follow suit.

However, the daily news about the dismal academic performance of American students is speeding along the trend toward privatization and competition.[16] People are becoming disgruntled with the ever-present evidence that something is terribly wrong with the educational system. Because almost 90 percent of children in the United States attend public schools,[17] with almost all of those attending their local community public schools, the general public in various respects is concluding that the problem is not with a distant educational system but with their own local public schools.

WHAT IS SCHOOL CHOICE?
Public School Choice Options
Many of the more moderate proponents of school choice favor various types of choice among public schools. There are many kinds of public school choice options. Some, such as the creation of magnet or alternative schools, involve setting up specialized schools that students from anywhere within a state or district can attend. Another public school choice option

involves allowing students at the high school level to take college courses. The final, and most complete, method of public school choice involves allowing families to send their students to any public school they choose either within their district or within their state.

Magnet Schools

Through magnet schools, parents can select a public school that caters to a child's special interests and talents.[18] For example, children with strong science skills can attend special state-run science schools, while children with musical talents can attend a public school for the performing arts.[19] Therefore, students with special talents and abilities can develop these skills in ways not possible in the typical public school.[20]

Magnet schools have sometimes been used by school districts to desegregate urban schools following "white flight," the movement of whites to suburbs to leave predominantly black inner-city schools.[21] To try to achieve racial integration, school officials have created magnet schools in many urban areas in the hope that white students would enroll because of the schools' unique features or strong academic reputations.[22] These magnet schools are generally open to district-wide enrollment.[23]

Today magnet schools have, to some extent, outgrown their link to desegregation.[24] These unique programs serve the additional purposes of attracting government funding for innovative education and of building a strong foundation for and encouraging school reform.[25] The growth of magnet schools—by the late 1980s, the number of magnet schools reached 2,500[26]—demonstrates that if the chance is offered and it is made economically feasible, families will often choose to send their children to creative, specialized schools that suit the needs and ambitions of those children.

Second-chance Programs

Second-chance programs, which are also relatively familiar, seek to assist at-risk students and dropouts, encouraging them to finish high school and providing them with the resources to do so. Minnesota is one state which implements such a program.[27] Eligible participants in the state's Area Learning Centers and Alternative Programs include those with "low test scores or grades, chemical dependencies, excessive truancy or expulsion."[28]

Postsecondary Options

Postsecondary options provide another form of choice within the public school system. This option usually allows high school juniors and seniors to enroll in certain courses at local vocational-technical institutions, community colleges, or four-year colleges or universities for high school or college credit.[29] Typically, the state pays for tuition, books and fees.[30] Upon acceptance into many programs, students may either enroll on a full-time basis at the college or may split their time between the high school and the college.[31] Participation in a program offering postsecondary options, however, does not interfere with the privilege of participation in high school extracurricular activities.[32]

Public School Choice

When many people think of public school choice, they are not thinking of magnet or alternative schools or of taking courses at the local college. The basic concept of public school choice essentially means that within a certain group of public schools, students can pick the school they would like to attend. As two commentators say, in these plans "every school is a school of choice."[33]

Intradistrict choice permits parents and students to select any public school within the school district in which they reside.[34] There are two variations of intradistrict public school choice. Some districts utilize an "open enrollment" plan, which is a more pure form of choice because students can truly attend the public schools of their choice in that district.[35] On the other hand, some districts, in efforts to maintain racial balances, elect "controlled" intradistrict choice.[36]

The second form of public school choice is interdistrict choice, meaning district boundaries do not limit choice.[37] Parents can send their children to public schools in other districts within the state.

Public school choice, while not as expansive as letting parents direct their tax dollars to either public or private schools, nevertheless serves as a "powerful means" of reform.[38] Precisely because the plans do not include assistance to private and parochial schools, they have attracted overwhelming support.[39] This allows experimentation with school choice at the state and local level, providing parents and students the opportunity to have more control over their educational experiences, without causing the outcry that would undoubtedly ensue from initially supporting students' attendance at private or parochial schools.

Thus, it appears that "[t]he most promising choice systems now in operation are those that have moved aggressively toward the elimination of fixed jurisdictions and assignments."[40] Two experiments exemplify the potential promise of this reform effort. On the intradistrict level, Cambridge, Massachusetts, has developed one of the most aggressive public school choice programs in the United States.[41] In the early 1980s, after integration efforts failed, Cambridge switched to a "controlled choice" system.[42] Parents and students had the freedom to select the school best suited to their needs.[43] The school system provided parents with special liaisons to assist parents in making their school choice and in completing the application process.[44] Parents and students ranked their top four choices,[45] and a school administrator made the assignments by giving weight to such factors as racial diversity and proximity.[46] The vast majority of families received their first choice,[47] and those who did not could appeal the decisions.[48] The results show that more students are returning to public schools in Cambridge.[49]

Among the states on the edge of interdistrict choice is Minnesota.[50] In

Minnesota, children can attend schools outside their jurisdiction provided the district has opened itself to enrollment from outsiders—which most districts are encouraged to do.[51] While the program is new, and a final evaluation is not yet available, early response is positive,[52] and those involved are reportedly pleased with the results.[53]

Nonetheless, such plans are not sufficient.[54] For true and meaningful reform to occur, many proponents of school choice believe that governments—federal, state, and local—must take the next step.

TUITION TAX CREDITS AND VOUCHER PLANS

The most radical types of school choice proposals revolve not around choice among publicly-run schools but are rather proposals to "privatize" educational services and bring market forces into play. Although there are many proposals that would assist in privatization,[55] the most commonly proposed methods of privatizing education involve providing either tuition tax credits or vouchers that would allow parents to reclaim tax money to pay for tuition at any school of their choice, public or private. Through economic incentives, these plans promote a wider range of choice because parents are not required to pay taxes to support a local public school system they do not choose to use and then to carry alone the burden of tuition at the school of their choosing.

In addition to the economic benefits for individual families, proponents of school choice indicate that the entire educational system will benefit because parents will be more flexible in choosing schools. Every school, both public and private, will be forced to cater to students' needs and desires or risk losing students to other public and private schools. Those recommending reform through "privatization" of educational services suggest that introducing more market forces into education would have enormous positive effects,[56] which would "actively promote and nurture . . . the kinds of schools people want."[57]

These two methods would operate in slightly different manners.

Tuition tax credit plans indirectly transfer funds to parents who choose to send their children to private schools by giving them income tax credits or deductions for expenses related to their children's education.[58] Although they are called tuition tax credit plans, that is a misnomer in two respects. First, the plans are not necessarily limited only to tuition, since some plans include other educational expenses, such as fees for transportation and textbooks.[59] Second, plans which include deductions, as well as credits, are both usually grouped under the name "tuition tax credit."[60]

Vouchers are a more direct form of transfer. The government, when giving vouchers, generally returns a grant to the parents that they can apply to the tuition of their children at the public or private school of their choice.[61] Voucher plans directly return money to parents, including parents whose taxable income is so low that they would not benefit from tax credits.[62] These plans allow more parents to have a wider range of educational choices.[63]

The 1973 United States Supreme Court decision in *Committee for Public Education v. Nyquist*[64] dimmed the possibility of granting either tuition tax credits or vouchers.[65] The year before the decision, New York had passed an education statute which, in part, provided for tuition reimbursement, or what would more commonly be called vouchers, for tuition paid to private schools by low-income parents.[66] It also offered tax deductions for private school tuition paid for by higher-income parents.[67]

The Supreme Court, in an opinion authored by Justice Powell, overturned both of these provisions as violating the Establishment Clause. First, the Court said that the vouchers constituted thinly veiled direct support of religion in violation of the Establishment Clause:

> By reimbursing parents for a potion of their tuition bill, the State seeks to relieve their financial burdens sufficiently to assure that they continue to have the option to send their children to religion-oriented schools. And while the other purposes for that aid . . . are certainly unexceptionable, the effect of the aid is unmistakably to provide desired financial support for nonpublic, sectarian institutions.[68]

The Court also found that in the tax deduction provision, "[t]he qualifying parent . . . receives the same form or encouragement and reward for sending his children to nonpublic schools" as he did in the voucher plan.[69]

In 1983, however, the Court upheld a Minnesota statute that provided a tuition tax credit that was essentially the same as the New York plan except in one respect: it provided tax credits for expenses for both private *and* public education, instead of only private education, as had been the case in the New York statute. The Court, in a 5-4 decision led by Justice Rehnquist, held, in *Mueller v. Allen*,[70] that this was the primary distinction which made the Minnesota statute valid. The petitioners argued that because 96 percent of children in private schools at the time attended religiously affiliated institutions, most of the deductions would be claimed by families for expenses in religious schools.[71]

The Supreme Court rejected any introduction of statistics on who would benefit, saying: "We would be loath to adopt a rule grounding the constitutionality of a facially neutral law on annual reports reciting the extent to which various classes of private citizens claimed benefits under the law."[72] And this, the Court ruled, was a facially valid law, potentially benefiting all parents equally:

> Unlike the assistance at issue in *Nyquist*, [the Minnesota statute] permits *all* parents—whether their children attend public school or private—to deduct their children's educational expenses. . . . [A] program . . . that

neutrally provides state assistance to a broad spectrum of citizens is not readily subject to challenge under the Establishment Clause.[73]

The Court indicated that a less important factor that contributed to the constitutionality of the Minnesota plan was the fact that it was a tax deduction instead of a tax credit or an outright grant or voucher, as were the provisions in the New York statute.[74] The Court indicated that the specific structure of the New York plan had been of questionable constitutionality.[75] However, even in *Nyquist* the Court had reserved the question of whether "a program having the elements of a 'genuine tax deduction' would be constitutionally acceptable."[76]

So, as this specific form of tuition tax credit became acceptable, the constitutionality of other types of tax credits and vouchers remained in doubt.

Current Tuition Tax Credit Systems

The Minnesota statute approved in *Mueller* is not simply a tax credit program covering tuition because it allows a tax deduction for a portion of the amount paid to others for "tuition, textbooks, and transportation."[77] It allows these educational expenses to be deducted for students:

> [A]ttending an elementary or secondary school situated in Minnesota, North Dakota, South Dakota, Iowa, or Wisconsin, wherein a resident of this state may legally fulfill the state's compulsory attendance laws, which is not operated for profit, and which adheres to the provisions of the Civil Rights Act of 1964 and chapter 363.[78]

These expenses, thus, may be paid to sectarian religious schools; however, they cannot include costs of textbooks used for subjects not "legally and commonly taught in public elementary and secondary schools in th[e] state."[79] Thus, textbooks entitled to reimbursement do not "include instructional books and materials used in the teaching of religious tenets, doctrines, or worship, the purpose of which is to instill such tenets, doctrines, or worship."[80]

Iowa's plan, which is the only other state tuition tax credit program,[81] is modeled on the Minnesota plan and differs from it only in minor details. First, the Iowa program offers both a deduction[82] and a tax credit.[83] Second, while the Minnesota statute covers the expenses inside the state and in the neighboring states,[84] the Iowa statute is valid only for expenses incurred in Iowa.[85] In addition, the Iowa statute covers only "tuition and textbooks" and excludes transportation.[86] Finally, and most importantly, the Iowa statute prohibits those families with combined net income of $45,000 or more from taking the deduction.[87]

Vouchers

Even though educational vouchers were disapproved in *Nyquist*, and the *Mueller* Court indicated that it might not view vouchers as part of a "genuine system of tax laws,"[88] vouchers remain a matter of debate in the United States.

One commentator believes that the distinctions drawn between tax deductions, tax credits, and outright grants or vouchers in *Mueller* constituted, as Justice Marshall's dissent said, merely a "formalistic distinction."[89] One professor of constitutional law believes that this distinction was effectively withdrawn in *Witters v. Washington Department of Services for the Blind*.[90] The case involved a Washington program in which the blind could receive education in any vocational school for the blind of his or her choice, either public or private, through the use of a voucher.[91] The recipient was studying to follow a career as "a pastor, missionary or youth director" at a Christian college.[92] The Supreme Court opinion, written by Justice Marshall, indicated that because the program was available equally to all schools, public and private, secular and religious, and because it had not been overused to support religion in the past, its primary effect was not to advance religion, and therefore it did not violate the Establishment Clause.

An understanding of the Court's position on vouchers in secondary and elementary education may be found in the concurring opinions for the case.[93] Justice Powell, joined by then Chief Justice Burger and Justice Rehnquist, concurred, indicating that the Court should have relied more heavily on *Mueller*.[94] Justice Powell likened this particular voucher program to the secondary and elementary tax deduction which had been upheld in *Mueller*, and said that it should be validated for the same reason the Minnesota plan was upheld: because the program was available to an entire class of people without reference to religion.[95] Justices White and O'Connor also agreed that *Mueller* was applicable in this case.[96] Thus, the five Justices who were in the majority in *Mueller* agreed in their concurrences that their decision there was applicable to the situation in *Witters*.[97] According to Professor Choper: "[V]ouchers are now valid but, on the other hand, if aid is provided directly to the schools, it will usually be held invalid. That is where the law stands."[98]

Current Voucher Systems

Only one voucher system is currently underway,[99] and it apparently is the best (publicized) case of educational choice in the United States.[100] In 1989, Democratic state legislator Annette "Polly" Williams pushed a parental choice program through the Wisconsin legislature. Williams, who represents inner-city Milwaukee residents, sponsored a bill, the Milwaukee Parental Choice Program,[101] which proposed a limited and specific voucher program as an experiment for low-income families.[102] Among the restrictions of the program: it is only open to those with income under a certain low level; it is only open to transfers who are currently in the public school systems; and, last, students are not eligible to transfer into religious schools. This last restriction raised the question of the program's constitutionality, but the Wisconsin Supreme Court has ruled that the Milwaukee Parental Choice Program is an acceptable form of voucher program.[103] This decision was no doubt welcome, as the voucher program had been well-received by the families and the students.[104]

Spurred by the popularity of the Milwaukee program,[105] President George Bush, in his January 1992 State of the Union address, proposed a $500 million nationwide program that would provide vouchers to low- and middle-income parents that would enable them to send their children to any private, public, or parochial school of their choice.[106] He then included this item in his Department of Education budget for 1993.[107] As of this writing, this budget had yet to be passed, but the future for the program was not bright. Just before the budget was submitted, by a 57-36 vote, the Senate rejected a low-income tuition tax credit plan that would have appropriated $30 million to create six small school choice demonstration projects.[108]

To understand school choice issues, it may be helpful to to review some history on the issue. The public schools have not always held this near-monopoly in the field of education. As one author points out,[109] in the early history of the United States, most schools, with some exceptions, were privately owned and run, and it was not until the 1820s and 1830s that public schools began to become more commonplace.[110]

It was at this time that Horace Mann, known as the father of the common school movement, became active in shaping educational theory.[111] Mann, the secretary of the Massachusetts Board of Education in the 1830s and 1840s, believed that public schools were necessary to create a political community in which all social groups could be mixed and thus learn to live together in accordance with the political and moral principles necessary for good citizenship.[112] Mann's ideas coincided with a working-class demand for government-sponsored schools.[113]

However, these schools were usually run by local groups of parents and citizens until the early decades of this century.[114] Because local citizens had the final say in most matters of spending, curriculum, and finance, these early public schools remained highly responsive to parental and local concerns.

The public school system, as we know it, began to develop around the turn of the century when education professionals began to demand that school boards be less politically controlled.[115] As school boards became smaller and non-partisan, the position of school board members became more elite and professional.[116] School board members in the reconstituted boards began delegating power to school administrators, ostensibly in the interest of lessening political control in school management.[117]

Thus, by the 1930s, in most places control over the business of education had evolved into the province of the professionals, who could perform in the best interests of the children without having to be responsive to widespread parental control.

Finally, in the 1950s and 1960s, the federal government assumed a role with respect to state school systems, prescribing certain cures for educational shortfalls,[118] and the role of parents in the public education system was further reduced.

OVERALL EFFECT OF SCHOOL CHOICE

In 1962, Nobel laureate economist Milton Friedman proposed the application of greater free market forces to education in his book *Capitalism and Freedom*.[119] In a short chapter on education, Professor Friedman set forth the guiding rationale for school choice plans and claimed that the "indiscriminate extension of governmental responsibility" into education was not necessary.[120] Friedman asserted that governmental regulation was acceptable,[121] and governmental financing was even tolerable,[122] but he thought that governmental administration of schools should not be accepted.[123] He wrote: "[T]he actual administration of educational institutions by the government, the 'nationalization,' as it were, of the bulk of the 'education industry' is much more difficult to justify on . . . any . . . grounds."[124]

Friedman's specific solution for this problem was the distribution of vouchers to students.[125] However, more important than his specific proposals were his thoughts on what had gone wrong with the education system and how choice would correct it. Friedman believed that compulsory public school attendance statutes might lead to a lack of freedom of thought and belief.[126] Furthermore, he thought that since parental school dollars are already being spent in public schools through taxation, very few would be willing to withdraw their children.[127] This, in and of itself, Friedman believed, led to stagnation and a lack of parental input, because schools need not listen to parents in order to survive, and parental views may only be shared through "cumbrous political channels."[128]

School choice could correct these problems in many ways: a wide variety of schools would develop to respond to the increased demand;[129] competition would increase flexibility and responsiveness to parental and student desires;[130] and conformity of education would be reduced.[131]

HOME EDUCATION AND SCHOOL CHOICE PROPONENTS

Fears about the lack of parental input and options are where proponents of home education and school choice meet. Home schoolers are concerned enough about their input into the education of their children to take complete control of that education. They believe that it is important to emphasize the subjects and methods most suitable to their children, thereby individualizing the education of their children. These concerns mirror those of the school choice proponents as expressed by Professor Friedman.

PUBLIC SCHOOL CONCERNS REGARDING SCHOOL CHOICE

School officials sometimes assert that all that is necessary to correct the problems in American public education is more money. It is common for them to tie the ability to reform to the need for more money, and consequently more administrative control.

In a recent controversy regarding the education budget in Massachusetts, in which Governor William Weld proposed additional reforms without any additional funds, administration officials repeatedly stressed the link between quality and money.[132] One official said: "It is fraudulent to look at school reform without looking at finances and the need for more money."[133]

The response of another official demonstrated that both money and reform were inextricably linked to the thing about which administrators are most concerned: control. When the budgetary planning was carried out by the elected officials of Massachusetts without consultation with the education professionals and administrators, the spokesman said: "People in education in this state don't know what is going on. We have not been filled in. No education people have been involved in the planning."[134]

THE FUTURE OF HOME SCHOOLING IN THE AGE OF SCHOOL CHOICE

One authority has commented that educational reforms, as with all governmental changes, move in stages.[135]

This authority theorizes that it is not completely incomprehensible to think in the long-term about the "unthinkable"—namely, the dismantling of public schools.[136]

The changes in tax reduction and rebate that are instituted through school choice programs may eventually be available to home schoolers. Though the effect may be small now, as legislatures warm to the idea of school choice and as the current experiments show positive results, policymakers may become more inclined toward including home schools in their plans.

There are some benefits to home educators from current school legislation in Minnesota and Iowa.[137] Neither of these states specify that a student must be attending a school full-time in order for the family's educational expenses to be deductible.[138] This means that if, as a home schooler, a parent decides to send a child part-time to an accredited public or private school for certain classes, some expenses may be deductible under the statutes of both states.[139]

It is impossible to foresee to what extent home schools may be included in future legislation. Parents and concerned citizens, however, have the advantage of being able to influence legislation at the beginning of the school choice movement.

The timing is right, before school choice laws become too standardized from state to state. Home schoolers should lobby their legislatures to prevent the inequities of laws and proposed laws that favor choice among public and private schools, and even religious schools, but ignore home schools.

One concern about the school choice movement might be how it will affect the home school movement. The ranks of those who educate their children themselves are growing steadily.[140] If American cities and states continue to adopt forms of choice, will the two movements collide and lead to the extinction of home schooling as families abandon home schools for innovative public schools or newly affordable private schools?

The application of economic theory to this question would, perhaps surprisingly, lead to the answer that there would be limited effect in the number of those home schooling their children.

Obviously, the immediate effect of an increase in choice among public schools might be a slight decrease in those home schooling. The flight back to public schools might occur within those families where a parent has withdrawn a student from public schools to teach them at home for one specific reason—for example, because of a lack of discipline, a violent environment in a local school, or a weakness in a program desired by the student or his family. If the option opens for such a family to send its child to a school which does not possess that specific deficiency, that parent may be likely to send his child to that more appropriate school.

However, a return to public schools by some families will not likely drain the home schooling movement of its strength. There are some parental preferences that public schools cannot provide, given the current judicial and legislative interpretations of the United States Constitution and of the various state constitutions. Studies have shown that the majority of families have chosen home schooling because they hold certain religious beliefs that influence their conceptions of education and the morals and character-building that it should entail.[141] For many of these, no amount of choice among public schools will matter. For those who favor prayer as an educational tool, or the teaching of creationism, or just the teaching of certain values and ethics, there will never be an acceptable public school under present law.

The exodus from home schools might be theoretically even greater if people are given the option to use vouchers to choose between public schools and private schools but cannot apply the vouchers to home schools. Those moving to the private schools who otherwise might not have left their home schools might include students from families who want certain religious precepts taught.[142] Those who want unconventional specialized schools, perhaps equestrian or astronomy schools, which might crop up with the creation of smaller, more innovative private schools, might also leave.

However, a very interesting point can be made which will further mitigate against the tendency of home school children to leave when school choice is offered. One survey of home school families concluded that proportionally more students leave private schools than public schools to be educated in the home.[143] Furthermore, according to this survey, these families are not leaving for economic reasons: they are not leaving because they can no longer afford private school tuition.[144] This surely must explode the myths that home school families make their choices *merely* because they want school prayer or some other straightforward religious objective. In almost any town or county anywhere, parochial schools exist which provide prayer or the teaching of creationism. It would be simple enough for parents to utilize these schools if those pieces of the curriculum were all they desired. However, there exists this large number of families who apparently have the resources to send their children to private schools but choose not to do so.

These families want not just school prayer, but a certain type of school prayer. They want the very specific type of education they feel is best for their children. Private schools may come closer to providing the education they desire, but they cannot provide the total package—the education to the family's exact specifications. And private schools cannot provide what studies say is one of the most important elements of home education: focused time in which parents can personally, painstakingly pass on the important lessons of life to their children.[145]

This last element is the one that will keep home schooling parents from sending their children to private schools, even if they could receive vouchers for private schools but not for their educational expenses in home schooling. There is an economic concept known as "opportunity cost." The opportunity cost of doing something is the value of the thing that you could otherwise be doing. If John takes an afternoon off from work to play golf with his friends, he will not only lose the money we normally think of as "costs," for example, greens and cart fees for playing the course, but he will be paying the opportunity cost of the wages he would have received by working that afternoon.

In a larger sense, occupational choices have tremendous opportunity costs. If professional basketball player Michael Jordan had decided that he enjoyed being a postman instead of being an entertainment conglomerate, the opportunity costs to him might have been well over $100 million in the course of his lifetime.

The opportunity costs of home schooling illustrate why the home schooling movement will probably not see many students leaving to attend private schools. Parents who choose to leave public or private schools make much more difficult sacrifices than being forced to purchase books, supplies, and equipment and foregoing their tax payments. The process of educating a child takes a good deal of time. How much time do parents spend in home schooling? If conservatively estimated at forty hours a week (for both instruction and lesson planning), over thirty-six weeks or nine months, it works out to 1,440 hours over the course of the year.

That seems like a lot of time. But how much is that in dollars? If the opportunity cost of those 1,440 hours are valued at just $5 per hour for time in the free labor market, this places the dollar value of the opportunity costs of home schooling at more than $7,000. This figure estimates the parents' time at just over current minimum wage, but for most parents the opportunity cost of their time will be at least twice this amount, or $14,000, and for many it will be even higher than this.

Examining the opportunity costs of home schooling, it is apparent that the offer to reclaim some lost tax revenues to use at private schools will not be an attractive offer to many. Home school parents are paying opportunity costs at least four or five times the average cost of private school tuition to home school their children. Why do they do this? Because they place a higher value on the time spent educating their children than the market places on their labor. To them, it is worth it to give up several thousand dollars in lost wages rather than spend one or two thousand dollars in a private school.

A tuition tax credit or a voucher that would earmark tax money to pay for the private school bill will probably still not be worth it for most of these parents. If they are losing thousands of dollars in lost wages now, being able to spend an extra few hundred dollars at a private school will not make the difference for most.

Perhaps the most significant effect that the school choice movement will have on home schoolers is the intangible benefit of greater support and understanding for their situation. In a society in which 90 percent of students take the same accepted path—the local public school—the social pressure to conform is immense. Those who attend private schools are sometimes seen as elitists or religious oddities, and those who choose to home school are viewed with even more skepticism. As the school choice movement grows, and more and more students move out of the public school systems, alternative educational choices will be increasingly seen as more normal, regular and healthy.

As new and innovative private schools adopt some of the favored educational methods of many home schoolers—individual instruction, comforting environments, and nontraditional performance evaluation procedures—home educators will be viewed with greater respect. Hopefully, the two movements will begin to nourish one another.

PART TWO

The Home Education Alternative

[E]ven the most attentive, perceptive, and thoughtful classroom teachers could never elicit from their students the amount and intensity of feedback that home-schooling parents typically get from their children, because parents know and understand their children so much better.

John Holt
Schools and Home Schoolers: A Fruitful Partnership (1983)

5

The Historical Perspective

To gain a proper historical perspective on the education of children in the United States, it is important to place the history of home schooling, public education, and the legal history of American education in perspective.[1] This chapter provides such an analysis and provides references for those who wish to pursue further study on the topic.

HISTORY OF PUBLIC EDUCATION

As discussed in Chapter Two, "The History and Philosophy of Public Education," public schools are an established feature of American life. All states in the United States require that children attend school in one form or another.[2] Public schools have not always existed in their present form in the United States, but their historical roots reach far back into colonial and pre-colonial America and England.

The English Precedent and the American Colonies

English "Poor Laws"
"The English 'Poor Laws' of 1563 and 1601 provided the theoretical base for all educational legislation in colonial America."[3] The Poor Laws created a mandatory apprenticeship system for people between ages twelve and sixty who were unemployed; they also provided some public funds for the support of the poor while they were engaged in the apprenticeship.[4] The Poor Laws gave the American colonists "a heritage of compulsory, publicly-enforced training which was already several generations old."[5]

Massachusetts Bay Colony
The earliest traces of public education in America are found in the New England colonies, especially Massachusetts Bay. The Puritans who settled the colony, and their version of Christianity, was the primary motivation

for the colony's interest in education, since the Puritans wanted their children to be able to read and understand the Bible.[6]

> After God had carried us safe to New England, and we had builded our houses, provided necessaries for our livelihood, rear'd convenient places for God's worship, and settled the Civil Government; One of the next things we longed for, and looked after was to advance Learning, and to perpetuate it to Posterity; dreading to leave an illiterate Ministry to the Churches, when our present Ministers shall lie in the dust.[7]

Another factor that influenced the rise of education in the Massachusetts Bay colony was that the Puritan settlers tended to live together in small communities to promote agriculture, to defend themselves from the Indians, and to join in religious worship.[8] Because they lived close together, it was logistically easier for the Puritans to organize common schools for their children to attend.

Another reason education was important in the colony was that the colony had many educated leaders: "It is safe to say that such a concentration of educated men, in a new settlement, has never been duplicated. They were the intellectual leaders who gave the community its educational ideals. They doubtless influenced the passage of the educational acts and urged their enforcement."[9]

"Apparently not satisfied with the local initiative of towns . . . and especially concerned about . . . education among the lower classes, the Massachusetts General Court stepped into the picture" with the Education Acts of 1642 and 1648.[10] These Acts required all parents to provide a specified level of education for their children, including vocational training and reading skills. Parents were additionally required to instruct their children in "the principles of religion and the capital laws."[11] Parents were thus the agents for educating their children, even though the educational requirements were set by the colony.

The colony could, however, remove children from the custody of parents if they failed to carry out their duty to educate their children. Such children were placed in apprenticeships with others who were willing to educate them.[12] The Massachusetts Acts also provided for local public money to be given to masters who were doing the vocational training, or apprenticeships, of the children.[13] It is possible that this practice laid "the foundation for the support of schools and teachers through local taxation."[14]

The Massachusetts Acts were thus consistent with the earlier English Poor Laws, but the Acts also went further than the Poor Laws. The Poor Laws mandated only vocational training in an apprenticeship, while the Massachusetts Acts required vocational training as well as basic academic instruction in reading, religion, and government. In addition, the Poor Laws required training only for the poor in England, while the Massachusetts Acts required education for all children, rich and poor.[15] The Massachusetts Acts were thus a significant step toward compulsory education in the

United States. The Acts were intended to enable children to become "good" citizens who had the ability to understand the principles of government and religion and to support themselves through employment.[16] The Acts served as the model for later compulsory education legislation in the New England colonies.[17]

The Acts of 1642 and 1648 established the minimum education that parents were required to give their children, but many parents found that they were unable to do so with their limited time and resources. Thus, many parents banded together with their local town government and "voluntarily established, managed, and supported town schools."[18] These schools were established on land provided by the towns or donated by private individuals; they were supported by local property taxes and by tuition from those who could afford it.[19]

The Old Deluder Satan Act

Leaders of the Massachusetts Bay colony approved of these local town schools and decided to make them mandatory in the colony. Thus, in 1647 "The Old Deluder Satan Act" was passed.[20] It required towns with at least fifty families to set up a common town school for all children in their community. In addition, the law required towns with at least one hundred families also to establish a grammar school. The funding for these schools was to come from tuition payments or by money raised through local taxes; each town was to vote on which method of payment it would adopt.[21] The Old Deluder Satan Act did not, however, require the children of the colony to attend these schools. They were voluntary schools for parents who were unable to educate their children at home in accordance with the Massachusetts Acts of 1642 and 1648.[22]

The Old Deluder Satan Act was significant because it was the first time the state took responsibility "for the education of all children within its boundaries. In general, we may say that previous to this date most states considered that either the church, a religious denomination or society, or private agencies were responsible for education."[23] The Massachusetts Bay colony had earlier required all parents to educate their children, but it had never before supplied alternative educational arrangements to ensure that all children would be educated.

The colony of Massachusetts Bay thus established many of the foundational principles of modern public schools with The Old Deluder Satan Act of 1647 as well as the Massachusetts Acts of 1642 and 1648. These principles included the idea that while "[t]he obligation to furnish [an] education rests primarily upon parents," "[t]he state has a right to enforce this obligation" and "to determine the type and extent of education."[24]

The early Massachusetts colonial laws also set the precedent for funding public schools with money raised by local property taxes.[25]

Other New England Colonies

Voluntary public schools were formed in New England that were mostly funded with student tuition and fees, although children of the poor were sometimes allowed to attend without paying tuition, but this was apparently rare.[26] The earliest local town schools were set up by Boston in 1635 and Charlestown in 1636.[27]

Southern Colonies

There was less progress in education laws in the Southern colonies. In the South, "The assumption was that education was a private affair and that capable parents would voluntarily attend to the education of their own children."[28] There was a large underclass in the South, however, because the population was made up of largely uneducated people: farmers and planters with slaves, independent farmers (without slaves), white servants, and black slaves.[29] Many of the children were not educated, therefore, because many of the parents were uneducated. At least some of the Southern colonies, especially Virginia, established a system similar to the English Poor Laws for training orphans and the children of the poor in an apprenticeship.[30] This system was apparently motivated by a desire to give the poor the ability to support themselves so they would not become a burden on the colony. Unlike the Northern colonies, however, there was very little academic instruction provided or required by the southern colonial governments. There was also no provision for the creation of town schools outside of the home.[31]

Compulsory education was thus much less advanced in the South than in the North.

Decline of Compulsory Education in the Eighteenth Century

Loss of Religious Motives for Education

The interest in compulsory education and schools began to decline even in the northern colonies, however, in the late Eighteenth Century. This decline occurred as the New England colonies narrowed the compulsory education requirements, focusing on vocational education (apprenticeships) for children of the poor rather than on academic and vocational education for all children.[32] The most important cause of this decline was the colonists' gradual loss of their religious motive for education.

> By the end of the 17th century there was wider toleration of various religious sects and a dilution of Puritan strength. The importance of religion diminished considerably, thus depriving education of what had been its strongest *raison d'etre*—religious learning.[33]

Economic Crisis

Part of the reason religious fervor among the colonists declined was the economic problems caused by the colonists' wars with the Indians. The economic crisis led to a "general lowering of the tone and standards of society," including looser moral standards and "a marked decline in family government."[34]

The Puritan society experienced "a weakening of the religious motive, and in particular a decline in the influence of the clergy."[35] In addition, the economic troubles created an increased emphasis on vocational education because more families were poor and thus more children needed to learn a trade to support themselves.[36]

From Centralization to the New Frontiers

Another reason for this decline of interest in education was that, over time, the colonists spread out from centralized towns to new frontiers of the colonies and beyond as they settled the New World.[37] This meant that families did not live as close together as they had before, and thus it was more difficult for public schools to be organized. It also meant that "enforcement of [the compulsory education] laws affecting all children was very difficult."[38]

All of these factors taken together demonstrate that "[a]s a whole the eighteenth century mark[ed] a decline in the efforts toward compulsory education."[39]

The Reemergence of Compulsory Education

"The winning of political independence from England gave rise to a general re-evaluation of the structures and patterns of American life."[40] Compulsory education was one of the structures which benefited from this reevaluation.

It emerged again as a popular issue, especially because of the large wave of immigration to the United States in the Nineteenth Century, after the Civil War. There was a national concern that the immigrants would permanently alter the culture of the United States unless they were "Americanized," and public schools were advocated as a powerful tool for "Americanizing" immigrant children: "[F]rom its earliest years the public school was viewed as an instrument par excellence for inducting newcomers into the 'responsibilities of citizenship.'"[41]

One historian notes that Horace Mann, a leading advocate of compulsory public schooling in Massachusetts in the early 1800s, expressly desired to use public schools as a tool to forge "a common value system" for the American people.[42]

The Industrial Revolution

Compulsory public schooling also received a boost from the Industrial Revolution of the Nineteenth Century, which concentrated large masses of people in the cities near factories. This concentration of population presented a base of families with children who lived near each other and thus who could organize to form a local public school.[43] The Industrial

Revolution also encouraged education because it created a demand for more skilled and literate workers.[44]

"The years between 1779 and 1865 mark the era when the great state school systems of contemporary America took form."[45] In addition to Horace Mann in Massachusetts, leaders in the public school movement included Calvin Wiley in North Carolina, Caleb Mills in Indiana, John Pierce in Michigan, and others.[46]

The first state law to require children to attend public school, as opposed to earlier laws which mandated home schooling or created voluntary public schools, was the Massachusetts School Attendance Act of 1852. The Act declared that all children between eight and fourteen were required to attend at least twelve weeks of school each year.[47]

Other states soon followed the lead of Massachusetts, and by 1918 nearly all states had laws which provided for compulsory public education.[48] Most states also enacted laws providing that the public schools were to be supported by public tax dollars.[49] Northern states adopted compulsory public schooling laws before southern states, but "[a]fter World War I, even the southern states had adopted compulsory attendance laws to protect their children from the perceived threat of foreign influences."[50] "In effect schools grew from an uncertain infancy in 1865 into a young maturity by 1918."[51]

Opposition to Compulsory Schooling

Opposition to Any Universal Schooling
The rise of compulsory public schooling, however, was sharply criticized and opposed by at least two groups. The first group opposed any universal schooling, contending that public schools would be a "'crime and pauper-breeding system.'"[52]

Such criticism came from men such as California attorney Zachary Montgomery, who wrote *Poison Drops in the Federal Senate: The School Question from a Parental and Non-sectarian Stand-Point,*[53] and others such as Francis Livesey of Maryland. In one of his leaflets, Livesey asserted that universal schooling was responsible for the "negro problem, the servant problem, the labor problem, the tramp problem, the unemployment problem, the divorce problem, the eyesight problem, the juvenile problem, the bribery problem, and the pure food problem."[54] Livesey also proclaimed that there were "bands of able men and women who see the public school devastation, and who have set themselves resolutely at work in demand for its abolition."[55]

Opposition to Universal Schooling Without a Religious Moral Base
A second group objected not to universal schooling itself, but to universal schooling without a religious moral base. This group included Protestant Christians but was led mainly by the Roman Catholic Church.[56] "Roman Catholic doctrine taught that no education could be complete unless it was

permeated throughout with the teachings of Roman Catholicism."[57] The Catholic Church thus could not accept the public school curriculum, which sometimes included Bible reading but which never expressly promoted Catholic doctrine.[58] This led to the development of Roman Catholic parochial schools, which the Church declared should be used by its members for the education of their children.

The Church's position was codified in part by an 1884 meeting in Baltimore of the Third Plenary Council of Bishops:

> [W]e urge and enjoin Catholic parents to provide their beloved children . . . an education which is truly Christian and Catholic. Further, that they defend them throughout infancy and childhood from the perils of a purely secular education and . . . that they therefore send them to parochial schools or other truly Catholic schools.[59]

The Church's protest is thus the historical underpinning of modern Catholic schools.

Modern Developments in Compulsory Schooling

The public school movement overcame its opposition, however, and compulsory public school laws remained essentially unchanged from 1918 to 1954.[60] Then in 1954, the Supreme Court's decision in *Brown v. Board of Education*,[61] which mandated racial integration in public schools,[62] provided a crucial test of the strength of public schooling: "[S]everal states began to repeal their compulsory attendance statutes in order to circumvent the *Brown* ruling and subsequent federal court decisions requiring forced busing to achieve racial balance."[63]

The compulsory attendance statutes were eventually reenacted, however, by all states except Mississippi in 1970, and by Mississippi in 1983.[64] Compulsory public schooling and school attendance laws are now an established part of the American political landscape, despite their volatile history.

HISTORY OF HOME SCHOOLING

Children have been taught at home by their parents for many years in the United States, dating back to the colonial period. Children of people who travel frequently, such as athletes, migrant farmers, and performing artists, have long been home schooled out of necessity. In approximately the last twenty years, however, home schooling has gathered many more followers. Parents have grown more critical of declining academic standards as well as inferior teaching in the public schools.[65] Many of the people who home school their children today are evangelical Christians who seek to build a strong moral and religious foundation into their children's education. The rise of home schooling is largely due to a parental feeling of losing control over their children.[66] Many parents object to the lack of religious instruction in the public school curriculum, forced busing, and negative peer pressure.[67]

Alternatively, a New Left group has formed which contests the public schools for entirely different reasons.[68] These "secular supporters of the home schooling movement see it as a tool of protest against the restrictive school environment. . . ."[69] While the affluent more often turn to private schools, others have opted for home education.[70] It has been estimated that one million children are currently being home schooled in the United States.[71]

Even early Americans who home schooled had a home school curriculum available.[72] For example, one text was "written for family use" and required no special skill in teaching.[73] "Anyone who could read could use the book to teach others how to read."[74] As noted earlier, the New England colonists were concerned with educating their children because many of the colonists themselves were highly educated and because the colonists wanted their children to be able to understand the basic principles of Christianity and government.[75] "Education was mainly a family responsibility in colonial America, and the extent was largely left up to the individual. There were no compulsory attendance laws enforced by governments."[76] Parents had the exclusive right to direct the education of their children.[77]

Early colonial laws required that all children be educated but placed the duty to educate on the parents. Even when the first schools outside the home were established, they were voluntary schools that were designed to aid the parents in carrying out their educational duty.[78] The state's purpose was twofold: to protect a child's right to education,[79] and to Americanize the immigrant.[80] Later, during the Industrial Revolution, the schools would prepare the poor for factory work.[81]

Many prominent Americans were home schooled at least a portion of their educational lives. Some of these are: George Washington,[82] Thomas Jefferson,[83] Woodrow Wilson,[84] Franklin Roosevelt,[85] Abraham Lincoln,[86] John Quincy Adams (who went directly from home school to Harvard),[87] John Witherspoon, pastor and once president of Princeton University,[88] Benjamin Franklin,[89] Patrick Henry,[90] Florence Nightingale,[91] Booker T. Washington,[92] Thomas Edison,[93] and Robert E. Lee.[94]

The Modern Home Schooling Movement

Home schooling apparently declined in the Nineteenth Century as the compulsory public school movement gained strength. Nevertheless, home schooling is on the rise again in the late Twentieth Century.

It is difficult to document fully the historical roots of this movement, because much home schooling has been done quietly and without publicity. Nevertheless, most home schoolers agree that Dr. Raymond Moore and his wife, Dorothy, are two of the principal leaders of the modern home school movement. They are recognized Christian researchers with an extensive background in education. The story of their life's work is essentially the history of modern home schooling.[95]

The Work of Raymond and Dorothy Moore

In 1937, Dorothy Moore was a teacher in the Southern California public schools. While teaching a remedial reading class, she noticed that many of the children in the class had been placed in formal schooling at a young age. This intrigued both her and her husband as they talked together and did more reading and study on the subject in later years.

The Moores gradually became convinced that early formal schooling was not the best way to educate children. Thus, they started home schooling their own children in 1945.

Dr. Moore went on to become a child development and learning specialist, with a doctoral degree in developmental psychology and teacher education. He also gained experience working in all levels of education, including positions as a college professor, vice president, and president. In 1964, Dr. Moore joined the United States Office of Education as a Graduate Research and Programs Officer, focusing on research and curriculum. He left this post in 1967, however, because he was disenchanted by the degree to which politics influenced education policy.

In 1968, Dr. Moore and his wife helped Carl and Ella Hewitt sell a large piece of real estate in Southern California and unexpectedly received $750,000 for their efforts. The Moores used this money to activate the research arm of the Hewitt Foundation (later renamed The Moore Foundation) and began to do research on the best age for children to enter formal education. "The Moores disapproved of a New York State regents proposal for public programs that would begin at age three and a California plan that would make preschools available to all four-year-olds."[96]

Their research entailed approximately three thousand studies of children done by professors and doctoral students around the world. The research confirmed the Moores' earlier suspicion that children were not emotionally, physically, or mentally ready for formal schooling until they were at least eight to ten years old. "Their study indicated that 'no systematic research' had been used as a basis for laws lowering entry ages to six, five, or four."[97] Moore also believed that "affective characteristics, such as emotional security, self-esteem, and independence, are more important for school achievement than academic stimuli."[98] Moore also cautioned that children may sustain physiological damage from doing "close work" in preschools.[99] The Moores published these findings in several professional journals. Furthermore, the Moores maintained that a child can learn more by having his questions answered in a few hours of one-on-one tutoring than he can in an entire day in a group setting.[100]

Sheldon White, a Harvard University professor in early childhood development, encouraged them also to publish their results in popular magazines in order to reach a larger audience. Thus, the research of the Moores was the subject of stories in *Harper's Magazine* in June 1972 and *Reader's Digest* in October 1972.

The articles gained international exposure and acceptance. The publicity generated by the articles led to the Moores' receiving $257,000 in federal grant money to expand their research. Armed with this new funding and notoriety, the Moores were able to engage in an additional eight thousand studies with university researchers.

This research was supported by several well-known childhood development authorities, including an associate of Sir John Eccles, a Nobel Laureate in neurophysiology, and Dr. John Bowlby, the head of early childhood development activities for the World Health Organization. The research confirmed the Moores' earlier conclusions, and they assembled many of their findings in a 1978 book entitled *School Can Wait*.[101]

The Moores' work continued to receive publicity and international acclaim. They continued their research and writing on home schooling even as they kept up with invitations to lecture in the United States and abroad. Their public appearances included talk shows such as those of Phil Donahue and Oprah Winfrey and also the NBC morning news program "Today." They also were mentioned favorably by radio commentator Paul Harvey and were invited to make several visits to Dr. James Dobson's "Focus on the Family" radio program. Through their seminar and research activities, they were able to encourage thousands of parents to begin home schooling their children. They also testified before several state legislatures and courts about the benefits of home schooling.

Today the home school movement is firmly established. However, it is not without its critics.[102] School principals, superintendents, and teachers do not universally echo the virtues of home schooling.[103] The proponents of public schooling often view home schooling as a threat to the future of the public schools.[104] One such threat is a monetary one, since some schools could lose the state aid normally provided to the school district on the basis of each child who attends the school.[105] Proponents of public schools often argue that the public schools are better equipped to develop a child socially and academically.[106] Although some public school proponents contest the advantages of home schooling, the academic track records of home schooled children have demonstrated success.[107] Yet, such academic success has not necessarily translated into broader freedom to home school.[108] For example, public school administrators often attempt to determine the fate of home schoolers.[109] Such administrators generally have four options: they can ignore home schoolers, prosecute them for violation of compulsory attendance laws, impose regulations (whether the legislature has given guidance or not), or cooperate with them.[110] Nonetheless, many states have enacted statutes that acknowledge home schooling as an accepted means of meeting state compulsory education requirements.[111] In addition, organizations such as The Rutherford Institute provide legal defense and educational services for home schoolers. The work of the Moores and others has laid a strong foundation upon which home school proponents will be able to build in the future.

LEGAL HISTORY OF AMERICAN EDUCATION

In addition to a perspective on the history of public and home schooling, it is important to be aware of the legal history of education in the United States. The following is a survey of relevant federal law on education and some state court decisions dealing with home schooling.

Relevant Federal Law on Education

The federal Constitution itself does not explicitly or implicitly address education; there is thus no constitutional right to receive an education.[112] The Tenth Amendment states that any power not given to the federal government in the Constitution is reserved to the states or to the people generally.[113] Education is thus generally governed by state law.

Nevertheless, federal law affects state education practices in a variety of ways. This includes federal constitutional law such as the Due Process Clause of the Fourteenth Amendment.[114] "A survey of the cases reveals that most, though not all, of the Supreme Court cases on parental autonomy [over their child's education] are based on the due process clause."[115] These cases generally deal with substantive, rather than procedural, due process.[116]

The Supreme Court has acknowledged parents' rights to direct the education of their children as part of the right to privacy. Justice White has said that "The . . . parental [autonomy] rights and the privacy rights . . . may be no more than verbal variations of a single constitutional right."[117]

Whatever its exact source, parents have a constitutionally protected liberty interest in directing the education of their children.[118] The extent of this liberty interest and its balance with the interest of the state in the education of children are revealed by an analysis of the Supreme Court's case law.[119]

There are three primary Supreme Court decisions dealing with the liberty interest of parents to direct the education of their children: *Meyer v. Nebraska, Pierce v. Society of Sisters,* and *Wisconsin v. Yoder.*[120]

In *Meyer v. Nebraska,* a state law prohibited teaching a foreign language to children before the ninth grade. A teacher was convicted under this law for teaching German to an eight-year-old. The Supreme Court overturned the conviction.[121] In the course of its opinion, the Court noted that the liberty protected by the Due Process Clause includes "the right of the individual . . . to marry, establish a home and bring up children."[122] This decision "is looked upon as the starting point in a line of Supreme Court authority supporting the power of the parents over their children."[123]

Pierce v. Society of Sisters[124] extended the reasoning of *Meyer.* In *Pierce,* a state law made it virtually impossible for any child to attend a private school until the ninth grade. A group of private schools organized to sue the state, alleging that the statute was unconstitutional. The Court ruled for the private schools.[125] The Court's opinion used strong language in support of a parent's right to direct the education of his child:

> Under the doctrine of Meyer v. Nebraska . . . we think it entirely plain
> that the [statute in question] unreasonably interferes with the liberty of
> parents and guardians to direct the upbringing and education of children
> under their control. . . . The fundamental theory of liberty upon which
> all governments in this Union repose excludes any general power of the
> state to standardize its children by forcing them to accept instruction from
> public teachers only. *The child is not the mere creature of the state*; those
> who nurture him and direct his destiny have the right, coupled with the
> high duty, to recognize and prepare him for additional obligations.[126]

The Court also emphasized that the state had an interest in "reasonable regulation" of all schools,[127] thus refusing to hold that the parent had an unlimited interest in directing his child's education. Nevertheless, *Pierce* continues to stand as a strong pillar in support of the liberty interest of parental autonomy in the education of children.[128]

Pierce is an important decision for home schooling because, as Justice White noted in his concurrence in *Yoder*, *Pierce* means that the state cannot "pre-empt the educational process by requiring children to attend public schools."[129] Thus, *Pierce* implicitly opens up the possibility of home schooling.

Wisconsin v. Yoder[130] is the third step in the line of cases dealing with parental autonomy and the education of children. In *Yoder*, an Amish man refused to send his children to anything but an Amish school, which included only grades one through eight. This was inconsistent with the state compulsory school attendance law, which required children to attend school until they were sixteen. The state convicted the Amish man of violating the school attendance law, but the Supreme Court reversed the conviction. The Court noted that "the values of parental direction of the religious upbringing and education of their children in their early and formative years have a high place in our society."[131]

The Court in *Yoder* also emphasized that the parent's interest in the education of children was greater than the state's interest, noting that it was "established beyond debate" that the parent should take the "primary role" in the direction of his child's education.[132]

Applying these principles to the facts of *Yoder*, the Court emphasized the strength of the Amish man's interest in the education of his children because it was combined with the free exercise of his religion.[133] Moreover, the Court noted that the Amish children were receiving adequate instruction in the Amish private school and thus held that the state could not force the Amish man to send his children to school until they were sixteen.[134]

The Court stated once again, however, that it was not holding that a parent had an unlimited right to control his child's education: "[T]he power of the parent, even when linked to a free exercise claim, may be subject to limitation . . . if it appears that parental decisions will jeopardize the health or safety of the child, or have a potential for significant social burdens."[135] Nevertheless, *Yoder* is a strong statement about the primary role of the parent, as opposed to the state, in directing the education of children.

The *Meyer-Pierce-Yoder* line of cases thus reveals that while both the parent and the state have an interest in the education of children, the parent's interest is deemed constitutionally superior to the state's interest under the Due Process Clause of the Fourteenth Amendment.[136] In addition, these cases demonstrate that while the Supreme Court approves of compulsory education for children, it will not allow the state to require that all children be educated in the same place and in the same manner. This principle implicitly leaves open the possibility of home schooling.

Thus, while the Supreme Court has not directly addressed home schooling,[137] the *Meyer-Pierce-Yoder* line of cases sets the stage for consideration of several state court decisions which have expressly approved of home schooling.

Some State Court Decisions Dealing with Home Schooling

Massachusetts
The earliest state court decision mentioning home schooling is from the state where public schooling has its longest history.[138] In *Commonwealth v. Roberts*,[139] the Massachusetts Supreme Court dealt primarily with parents who wanted to send their children to a private school, but it also mentioned home schooling. It noted that the state's compulsory school attendance law required children to attend public or private school or to be "otherwise instructed." The court interpreted this provision to "permit instruction . . . by the parents themselves, provided it is given in good faith, and is sufficient in extent."[140]

Indiana
A 1904 Indiana decision established the principle that the state could not force all children to be educated in the same manner.[141] In *State v. Peterman*,[142] a parent was convicted of violating the state's compulsory school attendance law when the parent employed a private tutor to educate his child and sent the child to the tutor's home instead of the local public school for daily classes. The court reversed the conviction, holding that the attendance law was intended "to secure to the child the opportunity to acquire an education," not to dictate the "means or manner" of the education.[143] Thus, the court established the principle that the state could not force all children to be educated in the same means and manner. This implicitly opened up the possibility of home schooling.

Washington

A 1912 Washington decision, however, held that home schooling was not a permissible means of satisfying a state compulsory school attendance law. In *State v. Counort*,[144] state law provided that all children must attend public or private school. Two parents who home schooled their children contended that home schooling fit the definition of "private school," but the Washington Supreme Court sustained their conviction for failing to obey the school attendance law. "Private school" was not defined by the attendance law itself, but the court declared that "private school" meant only an institution of the "same character of school as the public school, a regular, organized, and existing institution, making a business of instructing children of school age in the required studies and for the full time required by the laws of this state."[145] *Counort* was apparently a minority result, however, because, as the cases below reveal, a majority of early state court decisions on home schooling approved of the practice.

Oklahoma

Contrary to *Counort,* a 1922 Oklahoma decision held that home schooling was a form of education that satisfied the state's compulsory school attendance law. In *Wright v. State*,[146] two Oklahoma parents who were members of the Seventh-Day Adventist Church wanted to train their children to become missionaries and believed that sending their children to public school would hinder this goal. The parents both had teaching degrees, and they instructed their child at home in a variety of subjects. The child had an advanced education for her age, but the parents were convicted by the state for violating the state's compulsory school attendance law. The Oklahoma Supreme Court reversed the conviction, holding that education of children in nonpublic schooling was forbidden only if it was "manifestly inadequate" or done "for the sole purpose of evading the proper education of a child."[147] In addition, the court declared that whether nonpublic schooling was done in "good faith" and whether it was "equivalent" to public schooling were matters to be left to a jury to decide in each individual case.[148]

Wright built on the foundation of *Peterman* and *Roberts* by approving home schooling. This trend continued with *People v. Levisen*.[149] The parents in *Levisen* were also Seventh-Day Adventists who were home schooling their children and who were convicted of failing to obey the state's compulsory school attendance law. The Illinois Supreme Court reversed the conviction by citing *Roberts* and noting that "[t]he object [of the attendance law] is that all children shall be educated, not that they shall be educated in any particular manner or place."[150] The opinion was more specific than earlier state court decisions, however, on the limitations of parental rights to home school their children. The court declared that home school parents have "the burden of showing that they have in good faith provided an adequate course of instruction in the prescribed branches of learning."[151] In addition, the court noted that the home school education must be "at least commensurate with the standards prescribed for the public schools."[152] The child's academic progress may have persuaded the judge to rule in favor of the home schoolers since the child outscored her public school peers.[153]

New Jersey

A 1967 New Jersey decision continued the state court trend of accepting home schooling as a legitimate method of educating children. In *State v. Massa*,[154] the state compulsory school attendance law required children to be educated in a public school or its equivalent. The state acknowledged that such equivalent education could occur through home schooling, even by parents without teaching certificates, but it argued that the parents in this case had provided inadequate home schooling for their child. The court rejected the state's contention and held that the parents had provided their child with an education which was equivalent to the public schools.[155] In defining "equivalent" within the meaning of the school attendance law, the court declared that it meant equivalence of academic instruction rather than equivalence of social interaction.[156] Thus, home school parents were not required to give their children the level of social interaction and contact that the children would have in public school.

CONCLUSION

Home schooling stands on a firm legal foundation. An analysis of its legal history reveals United States Supreme Court decisions that open up the possibility of home schooling as a method of satisfying state compulsory school attendance laws for children.[157] The legal history of home schooling in state courts is even more positive, with many state courts expressly approving of home schooling in decisions from as early as 1922.[158] This legal history does not provide unlimited rights, however, for home school parents. Nevertheless, a firm legal foundation has been laid for the modern home school movement by these federal and state court decisions. The legal history of education combines with the history of public and home schooling to reveal that home schooling is a long-standing method of educating children which deserves the praise and support it is receiving today.

6

Dimensions of the Contemporary Home Education Movement

The dimensions of an individual home school are not Olympian:

> Parents need only be loving, responsive, and reasonably consistent, and salt these qualities with a little imagination, common sense, and willingness to follow a few simple suggestions. . . .[1]

Nonetheless, the matter of home education is often controversial. Parents, educators, psychologists, and others who may have occasion to consider the issue often have strong opinions on the subject. Such strong opinions make some parents feel that home schooling is sometimes "like building an ark in your backyard and hoping your neighbors won't notice!"[2]

One author described reactions to home schooling: "A few think it's a good thing, but worry that the children will grow up to be odd. It seems the ones who most often have a negative reaction to home teaching are those who feel some responsibility for the kids, such as grandparents, neighbors, and the people at church. . . . On the other hand, it is common for people to feel threatened by anyone who is doing something different."[3]

These and other responses may be, in part, because critics of home education often "do not have a good general picture of home-schooling. Some may be basing their views on sketchy information or on one or two worst cases involving poor programs or even child abuse."[4] The following overview of some aspects of contemporary home education will help provide a "good general picture" of home education for critics and supporters of the notion.

Although the "profile of home schoolers shows them to be very normal people, different only because they are determined to provide the kind of education that they believe their children should have,"[5] a precise delineation of all the dimensions of home education is somewhat difficult. For example, demographic information about home schools is often based upon reports from organizations that supply curriculum and other materials which are supplemented by interviews and questionnaires.[6] "Systematically collected data are rare."[7] Thus, information about income and education levels of home educators may be derived from information maintained by publishers and sellers of commercial educational materials or home education magazines. Such information may or may not accurately reflect the demographics of the home school population, since it may safely be assumed that at least some of the home school community does not purchase commercial educational materials. Although valid information may be obtained through surveys and questionnaires, this information may be greatly influenced by factors such as size of the respondent pool, skill of the surveyor in framing and analyzing the study, etc. Moreover, it may be assumed that some portion of the home school community will not provide any personal information, whether out of religious conviction, privacy concerns, or outright fear of misguided social or educational authorities.[8]

Nevertheless, the available information may be useful, for it at least presents a picture of *some* home school families, and it is therefore possible, to some extent, to imagine that part of the picture that is not documented as well. Furthermore, available information may be useful in refuting misconceptions about home schools and home educators.

INCREASING NUMBERS

During the 1980s, there was a resurgence in the number of home schools, primarily as a result of the decreasing educational quality that was becoming characteristic of America's public schools.[9] Criticism of the public schools and alienation of parents from the public schools are cited among the most fundamental reasons why home schooling has gained growing public support since the late seventies.[10] Perhaps as a result of "[t]he social activism of the sixties as well as the social tensions of the seventies and eighties,"[11] many state laws have, in the last twenty years, become more permissive with respect to home education.[12] According to *The Washington Post*: "Home schooling, once seen as an option only for conservative Christians, has become increasingly popular among Washington area parents who don't believe that public schools can effectively educate their children or who fear for their children's safety."[13] According to the article: "In Maryland and Virginia, an estimated 5,600 children are being home schooled. . . . Only 90 children were being taught at home in Maryland in 1985 . . . compared with more than 1,600 today. Virginia officials say they've seen a leap from slightly more than 1,000 home schooled children in the 1985-86 school year to about 4,000 students today. . . . The U.S. Department of Education estimates that 350,000 children nationwide are being educated by their parents today, compared with 15,000 during the early 1980s."[14]

One estimate in 1982 projected that the number of children in home schools in the United States today would be as high as one million.[15] Another estimate is that "upward of half a million children are being taught in the home, twice the number estimated in 1984 and perhaps only half the actual number, given the reluctance of some parents to register with state departments of education."[16] In 1980, the National Association for the Legal Support of Home Schools estimated that there were approximately twenty-five thousand students in home schools.[17] By 1988, that figure had quadrupled to over one hundred thousand families who taught their children at home,[18] and by the fall of 1990, only two years later, the estimated number of home schooled children in the United States had tripled to three hundred thousand.[19] One 1990 survey estimated that there are about 474,000 children in home schooling families who are of school age, a total greater than the number of public school children in the states of Delaware, Vermont, Wyoming, and the District of Columbia combined.[20]

Thus, although there may be variances in the rate of home school growth or the precise number of home schooled children, the fact that the number of home schools is increasing is not in dispute.[21] Despite this growth, however, some observers predict that "home education will never involve more than five to ten percent of the population."[22] Predictions such as this may be based upon factors such as rising divorce rates that produce one-parent families, increasing numbers of families where both parents work outside the home, and the fact that some parents view home teaching as too great a challenge.[23]

RELIGIOUS DIVERSITY

Although the "Independent Fundamental/Evangelical" denomination remains the religious preference of the greatest number of home schoolers in the United States (26 percent),[24] there is documented religious diversity among home schoolers. According to one report:

> Religious affiliation appears to vary widely depending on the subpopulation. However, most are affiliated with Protestant groups. . . . The largest of these [groups] were "mainline Protestant" (Lutheran, Baptist, Methodist, Episcopalian, Presbyterian, etc.); 22% were in other churches, including Mormons, Jehovah's Witnesses, and lesser known groups, identified, for example, as "Self-Realization Fellowships" and "Reformed Congregation of the Goddess." Finally, 4% said they were part of a "Spiritual-Unity" movement."[25]

In another survey, 16 percent of the respondents classified themselves as part of a denomination "other" than Baptist, Methodist, Assembly of God, New Age, or other widely-known denominations and religions represented throughout the United States.[26] This makes the "Other" category the third largest religious affiliation in the survey, placing it ahead of sixteen out of a possible nineteen other mainline churches in America that were shown on the survey.[27] According to one commentator, the "orthodox and the progressive, the Fundamentalist Christian and the libertarian, the urban, the rural, the social skeptic, the idealist, the self-sufficient and the paranoid"[28] are numbered among American home school families.

Therefore, while the results of various studies consistently indicate that the population of home educators is mostly Protestant, assertions that home schooling is only a "fundamentalist" phenomenon are unfounded. As has been shown, the evidence is clear that a significant percentage of home school families are part of a denomination or religion other than Protestantism or Christianity.

INCOME LEVELS

Some research shows that home schooling families now tend to have a higher income level than the average American family.[29] One survey showed that the two income groups best represented in home schools were in the $25,000-$34,999 range (26 percent) and the $35,000-$49,999 range (30 percent).[30] The same survey showed that 24 percent earned an annual income of $50,000 or above, while only 20 percent of home school families earned less than $20,000.[31] Another study reported that 45 percent of its respondents earned $35,000 to $49,000, while 26 percent earned $10,000 to $19,000. Yet another study reported that 50 percent of its respondents earned more than $30,000.[32]

Other research indicates, to the contrary, that the income level of home school families is somewhat lower than average. For example, one commentator found that "Very few home schooling families are affluent" and further stated: "[T]oday's home schooling movement may be partially explained as an attempt by families of modest means to provide the kind of education they feel their children need, which they are convinced the public schools not only deny but in significant ways openly subvert."[33] Another author found that the median annual income of home schooling families falls somewhere between $20,000 and $30,000.[34] And a 1987 study reports that "average income was solidly between the $15,000-30,000 and $30-45,000 ranges, with the majority (45%) in the $15-30,000 range."[35]

In general, however, surveys regarding the income level of home school families suggest that home education families have a slightly higher annual income than their contemporaries.[36]

LEVEL OF EDUCATION

The academic quality of home instruction is often criticized by opponents of home education, and the issue of teacher certification is a key element in this criticism.[37] By 1989, six states had passed laws requiring a home tutor to be certified.[38] Courts, however, will often support home schooling as long as the education is not proved to be "inferior" to that offered by the traditional educational system.[39] "Few people realize that the homeschooling movement is populated by a large number of educators or ex-educators—parents who teach or who have taught in the schools but keep their children out of them."[40]

One survey of education levels indicated that "59% of mothers and 72% of fathers had undergraduate or graduate degrees. Another 33% and 23% of mothers and fathers had some college, while only 7% and 4% respectively had only a high school diploma."[41] Another researcher states: "The educational level and socioeconomic status attained by home-school operators seems to be considerably higher . . . than that of the comparable general population."[42]

The foregoing is supported by another study that indicates that most home school parents have completed college (43 percent), and many have earned graduate degrees.[43] The parents of home school families are most often either professional or semi-skilled workers.[44]

Alvin Toffler, in his book *Future Shock*, predicted, more than twenty years ago, increased numbers of home schools by well-educated parents:

> As levels of education rise, more and more parents are intellectually equipped to assume some responsibilities now delegated to the schools. Near Santa Monica, California, where the RAND Corporation has its headquarters, in the research belt around Cambridge, Massachusetts, or in such science cities as Oak Ridge, Los Alamos or Huntsville, many parents are clearly more capable of teaching certain subjects to their children than are the teachers in the local schools. With the move toward knowledge-based industry and the increase of leisure, we can anticipate a small but significant tendency for highly educated parents to pull their children at least partway out of the public education system, offering them home instruction instead. . . .[45]

MOTIVATION FOR HOME SCHOOLING

Motives Are Varied

The motivation of parents to educate their children "are as varied as the families and children involved."[46] According to one summary:

> Some parents object to the political or cultural values they find in public and private schools. Others do not like the instructional methods. Many agree with the late John Holt that children learn best in an unstructured environment in which the child sets the pace and direction. Many parents wish to spend extended time with their young children before enrolling them in school. Sometimes, recognizing the needs of a precocious child, a family decides that only a highly individualized program will permit

that child to attain his or her highest potential. Still other parents want to give special attention to a child who is having trouble adapting to school for any of a variety of reasons. . . .

[S]ome parents choose home instruction because they are "committed to providing a more informal, individualized, and responsive style of learning. . . . These parents often birth their children at home, clothe them in natural fibers, feed them natural foods." Many parents undertake home-schooling as a matter of long-standing religious tradition: Mormons who operate "kitchen schools" for a few neighborhood children aged 5 to 7; Seventh-Day Adventists, many of whom believe that younger children should remain at home; the Amish, who often remove their children from school after grade 8. Today, however, the largest growth in home-schooling appears to be among devout Christian parents who are unhappy with the secular nature of the public schools and have not found a suitable religious school.[47]

Just as there are many different types of families with many different belief systems who educate their children in the home, there are many different reasons why parents choose home education.

David and Micki Colfax write:

[H]omeschooling is not all of a piece. It is characterized by considerable variety in content and style. Some parents commit themselves and their children to homeschooling almost from the moment the children are born, others drift into it, and still others consider it years after their children are having trouble in school.

Some teach their children at home for very clearly defined political, religious, philosophical, or pedagogical reasons, while others—perhaps even a majority—would be hard-pressed to say why, exactly, they teach their children at home. Some parents see homeschooling as a short-term solution to a temporary problem, while others are committed to homeschooling over the long term. Some teach their children at home because of what *is* being taught in the schools, while others choose to homeschool because of what is *not* being taught. There are those who teach their children at home because the schools are too rigid, while others do so because the schools are not structured to their liking. And some regard homeschooling as a radical action, while others see it as an essentially conservative undertaking.[48]

One author has asserted: "A fundamental motive for home schooling as it emerged in the alternative school movement was a desire for the individuality—eccentricity perhaps—of free choice."[49] This author continues:

This choice is very important for certain types of parents: "countercul-ture" adults who disagree with the restraints of conventional schools, strict religious parents who cannot accept the moral relativism of public schools or society at large, and parents whose children appear to learn well in a home setting and poorly at school.[50]

Finally, this author concludes: "For the most part, home schooling has been confined to three groups: the religious conservatives, the counterculture individualists, and the parents of talented and gifted students."[51]

Religious Conviction

Most home school experts have found that religious conviction is the primary reason for a parent's choice of this alternative education, although, as noted above, there is ample religious diversity among such parents. Some estimate that as many as 75 percent of all home school parents choose this alternative education out of religious conviction.[52]

According to one report:

Adventists, Amish, Methodists, and many fundamentalists try to apply the biblical injunction to "be not conformed to this world" (Romans 12:2) by avoiding the public schools. . . . Many Christian home educators home teach their children not only to inculcate religious values, but also to reinforce the wife's homemaking role. Concerning children, the New Testament instructs Christian parents to "bring them up in the discipline and instruction of the Lord" (Ephesians 6:4, NASB). Former feminist, now born-again Christian traditionalist Mary Pride (1985) holds that home schooling is not just an educational option. It is part of a biblical pattern of home-centered work for the wife. Religiously oriented conference speakers Bill Gothard (1984) and Gregg Harris (1985) concur in this view and promote it to thousands of American women annually.[53]

While "[r]eligious reasons are the prime motivation in the majority of the cases, [they are] seldom mentioned as the *only* reason[s]."[54] Often, there are other factors, as discussed below, that contribute to the parents' decision to educate their children at home.

Quality of Education Atmosphere

According to one study performed at Princeton University, there are three basic reasons for a parent's choice of home education: "quality of teaching, quality of moral atmosphere, and quality of social atmosphere."[55] This study suggests that parents of home school children are "as or more concerned about non-academic factors as about their children's academic progress."[56]

This conclusion is supported by a Gallup Poll showing that, according to the American populace, the biggest problem in the public schools is the lack of discipline, not the lack of quality academics.[57]

Another important reason home educating parents cite their decision to home school concerns academics.[58] As shown in Chapter Seven, "The

Straw Men: Socialization and Academics," academic achievement is an overarching concern of home educators, and the available evidence indicates that home educators have met the challenge successfully.[59]

While the performance of students in public school classrooms has seen a dramatic decline in recent years,[60] the results from the standardized tests taken by home school students have revealed that home schoolers, as a whole, perform extremely well, scoring significantly higher than the national average in every area.[61]

The average score of home educated students is at the 80th percentile, while the national average is at the 50th percentile.[62] This means that for every one hundred American students who are tested, a home school student will score higher than seventy-nine of them. In light of these statistics, one can see why many parents who are concerned about their child's scholastic achievement choose home education. According to one home school parent: "Most [parents home school] because they think their children get a better education at home."[63]

Flexibility, Informality and the Tutorial Method

Home school researchers find that another major reason for the choice of home education is the flexibility and informality that the method affords.[64] A 1991 study regarding parents of gifted children who chose home education revealed: "The most common reason is the flexibility of scheduling, materials, and methods."[65] This flexibility of scheduling not only benefits the gifted student but the average student as well, by permitting individualized learning which is more meaningful for the child.[66] Home school advocate John Holt argues that children are naturally curious learners and that formal education tends to stifle this natural learning instead of promoting it.[67] By giving children the time and freedom to expand and explore on their own, their internal motivation to learn is developed.[68]

The Tutorial Method

An important part of the educational effectiveness of home instruction is the proved tutorial method it embodies.[69] Developmental psychologist Dr. Raymond Moore asserts that the tutorial method is superior to group instruction because a child has greater opportunity to receive answers to his questions.[70] The classroom teacher simply does not have the time for such individual concern and attention. Moore avers that children thrive on routines that involve a few children who share the same family values.[71] Moore further states that tutoring makes much more efficient use of time; indeed, he insists that a child can learn more in two hours or less by being tutored than in a whole day of classroom group instruction.[72] Children are then free to engage in other activities that provide useful learning experiences apart from academia.

With home schooling, learning becomes a part of the daily life of each child and family, not a separated activity that takes place from 8:30 A.M. to 2:30 P.M. five days a week nine months a year. One home school parent noted that with the method of home education the days "pass with no sense that learning is separate from life, an activity that begins at a specific point in the morning and arbitrarily ends at another in the afternoon. Instead, learning proceeds *from* our children, spurred by their interests and questions."[73]

Another commentator writes that the requirements for conformity and restrictions on individual initiative are major forces in influencing parents to remove their children from institutional schools.[74]

More Time with Children

Home schools provide an opportunity for parents to spend more time with their children and, thus, an opportunity to be more important in their lives. In today's public schools, peers are often a more significant influence upon young people than are their parents.[75]

For instance, the average child spends a mere fourteen minutes per week in conversation with his parents,[76] while he or she is presumably influenced by peers and teachers at school for approximately thirty hours each week during the school year. According to one 1989 study, 53 percent of American parents "spend less than two hours per week looking after their children, and 42% of them do not read to their youngsters."[77]

The alternative of home education has the potential to change these statistics. For example, of the ten reasons families choose to home school, four address the advantage of additional time with and influence upon children:

Home schooling makes quality time available [for parents] to train and influence children in all areas in an integrated way. . . . Parents can control destructive influences such as various temptations, false teaching, and negative peer pressure. Children gain new respect for their parents as teachers. The family experiences unity, closeness, and enjoyment of each other.[78]

As two Washington state parents have said: "We want to be the most influential people in our children's lives . . . [we] want to provide the best for each child along the way."[79]

Socialization

Opponents of home schooling argue that even if children do receive a better education at home, they will lack the proper socialization skills needed to be functional members of society.[80] They believe that children taken out of school miss the opportunity to enjoy vital contacts with their peers.[81] Most home schooling parents, however, encourage social encounters either with other home schooling families or by enrolling their children in extracurricular classes such as music and ballet or the Boy Scouts.[82]

Home educators decry the socialization their children will receive at school. Dr. Raymond Moore, in particular, distinguishes between "positive socialization," based on a stable family life, and "negative socialization," a me-first attitude, peer dependency, and the rejection of family values.[83] John Holt suggests that peer groups in school have a negative effect on children—that children learn from peers that it is "smart" to smoke cigarettes, drink alcohol, and even turn to drugs.[84]

Home school parents view home schooling as a means of protecting their young from the "rivalry, ridicule, competition and conflicting moral values they believe are associated with much of the socialization that takes place in schools."[85] One home schooling mother remarked: "We want our children to be peer-independent."[86]

Indeed, research has shown home schooled children to be remarkably self-reliant and less susceptible to peer pressure than the average American student:[87] "[T]he self-concept of home-schooling children [is] significantly higher than that of the conventionally schooled population."[88] The research indicates further:

> Insofar as self-concept is a reflector of socialization, it would appear that few home-schooling children are socially deprived. Critics of the home school should not urge self concept and socialization rationales. These factors apparently favor home schoolers over the conventionally schooled population.[89]

Pure Pleasure

Yet, for all of these logical and technical reasons that many parents give for educating their children at home, many parents educate their children at home primarily because it is enjoyable and fulfilling for the entire family. According to one public school English teacher, who educates his children at home: "[I]t is a life our family likes, and this is our chief reason for continuing to homeschool."[90] Another home educator agrees: "We're not committed to home education forever—only for as long as [my wife] and the boys enjoy it."[91]

SIZE OF THE HOME SCHOOL

According to one survey, the most frequent number of children in home school families is three (34 percent), followed in order by two children (28 percent), four children (20 percent), five children (9 percent), six or more children (5 percent), and finally, one child (4 percent).[92] The average home school family in the 1990 nationwide study conducted by the National Education Research Institute consisted of 3.2 children and was therefore approximately 64 percent larger than the average 1988 American family.[93]

CONCLUSION

Thus, it seems clear that the home school community is not homogeneous. It is diverse and includes virtually all denominations and religions that are represented in America. There are many distinguishing characteristics of home school families, including higher than average income, Christian religious affiliation, more than the average number of children etc.; but there exist many different reasons and advantages that parents cite as motivation for their decision to home educate—some religious, some social, some academic. Of course, some families choose home schooling simply because it is a system that the whole family enjoys. But most important in our consideration of the home school movement is the noted outstanding achievement of home school students.[94]

Since academic and social success for students is more important than the means of education, "it might be wise," as one commentator has suggested, "as well as less expensive for states to allow parents whose children are progressing well at home to pursue this private alternative of home schooling."[95]

7

The Straw Men: Socialization and Academics

The resurgence and growth of home schooling has caused this educational option to be scrutinized intensely by the legal and educational communities, as well as by the general public. The recent increase in home schooling has sparked debate concerning its effectiveness and outcomes. Advocates of home schooling frequently cite greater academic achievement and healthier, more adaptive socialization of children as reasons for and benefits of home schooling, while critics of home schooling voice concerns about these same issues.

In the debate over the effectiveness and outcomes of home schooling, both advocates and critics frequently make reference to "*a priori* appeals to logic"[1] and/or anecdotal evidence to support their viewpoints. Empirical data and information are required to make sound and informed home schooling decisions; this is particularly so when decisions must be made regarding the allowance and regulation of home schooling.

This chapter will briefly review existing empirical research on learner outcomes of home schooling in the areas of academic achievement, cognitive development, social-emotional or affective development, and socialization. The studies reviewed will generally proceed from least to most recent.

Possible explanations for home school outcomes, a critique of the use of standardized tests to evaluate home schooling, brief comments on the research designs used in home schooling research, and considerations for future research will follow.

It is hoped that this discussion of empirical studies on the effectiveness and outcomes of home schooling will aid those in the legal and educational communities and parents in making sound and informed decisions, and in defending their right and decision to educate their children at home.

137

ACADEMIC ACHIEVEMENT AND COGNITIVE DEVELOPMENT

Studies of Pre-compulsory School Attendance Age Children

The first four studies reviewed below focus on children of pre-compulsory school attendance age. While these studies do not address home schooling specifically, they do speak to the home environment with a parent present and its effect on the cognitive development of young children.

Dr. Brian Ray, an Assistant Professor of Science Education at Seattle Pacific University who has extensively studied home schooling, states: "The evidence from these studies suggests that the home environment, with a parent present, is cognitively challenging and productive for very young children. The . . . studies may suggest that the home environment is even a superior environment in some ways."[2]

Cognitive Growth of Four-year-olds from Low Socioeconomic and Spanish-speaking Backgrounds (1979)

In 1979, a study was conducted of four-year-olds from low socioeconomic and Spanish-speaking backgrounds to compare the cognitive growth of home-based versus center-based intervention programs.[3] Four groups of children were administered the Leiter International Performance Scale (LIPS); two groups of children were involved in the "Home Instruction and Teaching Program," a third group of children were randomly selected from a local preschool program, and the final group of children had no previous or current preschool experience.[4]

One of the study's findings most relevant to this discussion was: "'No significant differences were found in acquired cognitive skills between home based and preschool participants.'"[5] The researcher concluded: "Home based programs can be as effective as center based programs in increasing cognitive skills. . . . Low socioeconomic parents can be effective teachers of their own children."[6]

Cognitive Demands on Four-year-old Girls in Home and Nursery School (1982)

The cognitive demands made by mothers and nursery school teachers on thirty four-year-old girls were studied in 1982.[7] Fifteen of the girls were described as middle-class and fifteen as working-class. The researchers observed the girls at nursery school with the teacher(s) in the morning and at home with their mother in the afternoon and recorded "the number of cognitive demands, per each of four categories, made on the child. . . ."[8] The study found significant differences in the following areas:

(1) Cognitive demands were used more frequently by mothers of both social class groups than by teachers.
(2) More often cognitive demands were not answered by children at school than at home.
(3) There were fewer questions asked by children at school.

(4) There was no social class difference in the hourly rate, percent, or range of cognitive demands addressed to children at home or school.[9]

Expressions of Curiosity in Home and Nursery School (1983)

In another study, the questions of four-year-old girls at home and at nursery school, and the answers of their mothers and teachers, were documented. The subjects were thirty four-year-old girls (fifteen middle-class and fifteen working-class). Specifically their purpose was:

> [T]o see whether young children's questions, especially their "why" questions, were more frequent in certain contexts, settings [home v. nursery school] and social class groups than in others. We assumed that such questions were potentially valuable both as expressions of curiosity and also because they provided occasions for adult [sic] to enlarge the child's understanding.[10]

The researchers recorded "the number of questions asked by the children, the nature of the questions, the context of the questions, and adult responses to the questions (five categories)."[11] The findings relevant to this chapter were:

(1) Many more questions were asked by children at home than at school.
(2) 10 of the 15 working-class girls asked no "why" questions at school.
(3) Most children's questions were asked when the adult was stationary for a prolonged period of time and was not too busy—a context rare at school.
(4) Persistent questioning (at least 22 turns of adult-child conversation) was rare at school compared to at home.
(5) "[T]eachers asked a far larger proportion of questions than did mothers. . . ." (p. 279)
(6) "[T]he children seem to learn very quickly that their role at school is to answer, not to ask questions." (p. 279)
(7) Most "why" questions and persistent questioning concerned non-play objects and events, especially those outside of the present context; most school conversations were just the opposite.
(8) Working-class girls were particularly affected by the school setting; asked fewer questions, asked more procedural questions, and exhibited less curiosity.[12]

Language Development at Home and School (1983)

In 1983, a group of educators examined "the language use and language development of middle- and working-class four-year-old girls at home and at school."[13] They looked at "the complexity of the speech of the children, their use of language for complex thinking, complexity of the language of the mothers used toward their children, and children's and mothers' talk together. Eleven cognitive, and one 'no code,' categories were designated."[14]

They also examined complexity of the language teachers used toward the children, and teachers' and children's talk together. Their findings indicated:

(1) Mothers used language for complex purposes more often than did teachers, when expressed as hourly rates.

(2) Teachers addressed more complex language to middle-class than to working-class children.

(3) Children used language for complex purposes more at home than at school.

(4) The school setting reduced the working-class children's usage of complex language more than it did the middle-class children's.

(5) Both adults and children had a wider range of language use at home than at school.[15]

These findings led the researchers to conclude:

[I]n their own milieu [home], working class children display all the essential verbal cognitive skills (p. 540). Furthermore, despite widespread belief in the benefits of nursery school . . . the evidence suggests that they [children] are much more likely to receive this ["measured attention to the child's language needs"] from their mothers than from teachers (p. 541), and certainly this study suggests that children's intellectual and language needs are much more likely to be satisfied at home than at school.[16]

In summary:

[The researcher] found no significant differences in acquired cognitive skills between preschool and home based groups of four-year-olds. [Other researchers] found that more cognitive demands were placed on four-year-olds at home by mothers than at nursery school by teachers. [Other researchers] found children to ask significantly more questions at home than at school, and [these researchers] found significantly more complex language used at home by children and parents than at school by teachers and children.[17]

Home Environment Can Be Cognitively Challenging

The preceding studies seem to indicate the home environment with a parent present can be a cognitively challenging environment for children of precompulsory school attendance age and in fact may be more challenging and conducive to cognitive development than conventional nursery schools.

STUDIES OF COMPULSORY SCHOOL ATTENDANCE AGE CHILDREN

The following studies involve compulsory school attendance age children, or children from six to seventeen years old.

Development of Isolated Students Compared with Conventionally Schooled Children (1979)

In 1979, the Western Australia Department of Education (WADE) published a report on the effectiveness of its Isolated Students Matriculation Scheme (ISMS), a program of correspondence courses developed by the government for rural students who are far from a conventional school.[18] The study compared the ISMS students "in which the majority of school learning was done at home"[19] with conventionally schooled students. The measure on which the students were compared was the Tertiary Admissions Examinations (TAE). "In 1977, 21 ISMS students took the TAE, and 25 took it in 1978."[20] WADE stated, "[T]hey consider 'the main indicator of the Scheme's success . . . [to be] academic achievement.'[21] The department of education concluded: 'The overall performance of these groups [1977 and 1978] has been satisfactory.'"[22] WADE did not explain the meaning of "satisfactory."

Performance on Standardized Achievement Tests (1981)

A nationwide survey of 221 home schooling families in forty-four states was conducted in 1981.[23] Of these families, 40.3 percent utilized standardized achievement tests ("Iowa, Stanford Achievement, California, Metropolitan, and 'others'").[24] The surveyor concluded that "children's achievement rated above average for those who reported using standardized achievement tests"; however, the researcher did not support his conclusion with any data, and, because parents were responsible for reporting achievement test results, the validity of this finding was lessened.[25]

Performance on California Achievement Test (1983)

Sixty-six Texas home schooling families were surveyed in 1983, and the scores of sixteen children were reported (whose scores were reported by their parents) on the reading, mathematics and language sections of the California Achievement Test (CAT).[26]

[The surveyor] . . . simply listed the actual grade of each of the 16 children . . . and the grade level that each child scored on the three CAT subjects. The youth ranged in age from grade 1.9 to 11.6, and the averages of their three scores were on the average 1.04 grades above their actual grade level.[27]

Performance on Curriculum Required by Washington State (1985)

In 1983, two experimental programs were approved using the parent as tutor under the supervision of a certified teacher by the Washington State Board of Education.[28] The programs were the Family Centered Learning Alternatives (FCLA) and the Center for Christian School Services (CCSS) and were said to include "families in a number of communities and cities across the state. They reported a combined enrollment of over 500 students in grades K-8."[29] The programs had to meet requirements set by the state board of education:

Included in these requirements, the certified teacher would . . . :
- supervise parents and monitor students (up to 20),
- provide training and/or guidance to parents,
- assess student ability, administer standardized tests, and evaluate student progress,
- assure that records required by the SPI were maintained, and
- assume that student participation in weekly socialization and PE activities were carried out.

Among other things, the parent would:

- tutor his or her own children only,
- attend training sessions,
- meet regularly with supervising teacher (at least every three weeks),
- guide student's daily work,
- keep daily records of time on task, and
- meet with student 180 days for sufficient hours to meet state requirements.[30]

A review of students' work was conducted by SPI personnel with the following findings:

The review of student work indicated that within centers as well as between centers students were progressing through curriculum which ranged from very experimental . . . to highly structured . . . the informal review indicated that regardless of the method used, all students were performing activities in the broad curriculum areas required by the state.[31]

Students were assessed in the areas of reading, language/English and mathematics through the Stanford Achievement Test (SAT). The scores from a hundred students were used in the study. These students had remained in the program from Spring of 1984 to Spring of 1985. The study found "the K to 8 children in the Parent as Tutor Program averaged the following percentile scores: reading, 62; language, 56.5; and math, 53. . . ."[32] More specifically, it found:

The median reading "scores were above average and in the majority of cases were well above [the national] average." . . . "The median reading scores for grades two (FCLA), three (CCSS, FCLA), and five (FCLA) fell at or below the national average." . . . The median scores in language/English for most grades "fell between the second and third quartiles (above average)" while the "median language scores for grades three (CCSS), and five and six (CCSS and FCLA) fell below the national median." . . . In math, "The median score for grades two, four, six and seven for both sites [CCSS and FCLA] fell at or above the national average" while the "math scores for grades one (CCSS), three (CCSS and FCLA), five (CCSS and FCLA) and eight (FCLA) fell below the national average."[33]

The study concluded that "the majority of the scores were average, or above average, in Reading, Language and Math."[34]

Case Study on Home Schooler Performance on Standardized Tests (1985)

A 1985 case study of three home schooling families reported the scores of five children who had been administered standardized tests (some of the tests had been administered by the children's parents and some had been administered by local public schools).[35] "The average (for 69 scores reported) score was at the 86th percentile level."[36]

Case Study of Home School Performance on SAT (1985)

A 1985 case study was conducted regarding three home schooling families who used the Stanford Achievement Test (SAT) to measure achievement.[37] Two children's scores were reported: "The first grade child averaged seventh grade on seven test areas, and the third grade child averaged grade 8.3 on seven test areas."[38]

Case Study of Home School Performance on Peabody Individual Achievement Test (1985)

A 1985 case study of five children using a different standardized test indicated less positive results than the previous two case studies.[39] The children were administered the Peabody Individual Achievement Test (it was implied that the researcher administered the test). "Only three of the five children could be examined for achievement gain over the period of one year; [the researcher] concluded that the results were equivocal."[40]

Hewitt-Moore Child Development Center Curriculum

In a home schooling court case, the Hewitt Research Foundation, a not-for-profit organization promoting home schooling, declared: "'North Dakota home schoolers average about 83 percentile points on their standardized tests' . . . 22 percentiles higher than the rest of North Dakota school youth," a finding which was subsequently reconfirmed.[41]

In 1986, the Hewitt Research Foundation conducted a study of academic achievement of home schoolers using Hewitt-Moore Child Development Center curriculum.[42] They found:

In a random sampling of Hewitt-Moore Child Development Center Curriculum students, including many who recently had come to home schooling from other schools, the standardized test average ranged between 78 and 80 percent, with those scoring higher who have been with Hewitt longer. This is consistent with past figures.[43]

Researchers reporting a study completed by the Hewitt Research Foundation found:[44]

The researchers mailed questionnaires to 50 families with whose court cases the foundation had been in some way involved. Of the 50 families, 30 responded but 3 responses were incomplete. The remaining 27 responses were tabulated and the result was that the average test score of this group ranked these children in the 80.1 percentile on standardized tests compared to the national norm of 50.0.[45]

None of the research studies described above mentioned the type of standardized tests used and how these tests were administered.

Alaska Centralized Correspondence Study Program

The Alaska Department of Education (ADE) operates Alaska's Centralized Correspondence Study Program (CCS). This "'is a complete K-12 education program delivered to students at home through the mails' . . . open to any Alaskan resident who has not completed high school, and is public education paid for by the people of the state. . . ."[46] The program was initially developed for those students living too far away to attend public school and has been offered since 1939.[47] However, "Since 1976 the state has also offered this program to students who have access to bussed transportation."[48] The home instructor, usually a parent, "is under the supervision of an advisory, certificated, teacher who is located in Juneau, Alaska."[49]

In the spring of 1984, the Alaska Department of Education issued a report on CCS students' Science Research Associates (SRA) reading and math test scores.[50] Fifty-three percent of the April 1984 CCS students were tested ("apparently 354 tested; unclear reporting").[51]

For the 22% of the home study students who were tested "on-site" (not at their homes), "9 of the 12 grades were above the 75th percentile in reading" . . . 8 of the 12 grades were above the 60th percentile in language, and 9 of the 12 grades were above the 60th percentile in math. When one includes the home study students who took their tests at home, their composite test scores were even higher than those just listed.[52]

In the spring of 1985, the Alaska Department of Education again assessed the CCS students' academic achievement.[53] Students' achievement was measured via the SRA reading, language, math and science test scores, and the Alaska Statewide Assessment reading and math test scores.[54] The results of the study were as follows: "From 1981 to 1985, fourth and eighth grade home study reading and math scores on the Alaska test (ASA) averaged 10.6% higher than their Alaskan peers."[55]

In terms of 1985 SRA data, the following grades and corresponding subjects were considered:

- K, 1—reading and math
- 2, 3—reading, math, and language
- 4-11—reading, math, language, and science.

The following findings were reported:

(1) For grades K-6, CCS students scored at least six percentiles higher than conventionally schooled Alaskans on all comparisons; with the majority of these above the 80th percentile of the SRA norm.

(2) For grades 7-11, CCS students were 2-27 percentiles higher than Alaskan user norm on 17 comparisons and equal on three comparisons; with the majority of these at or above the 70th percentile of the SRA norm.[56]

In 1986, the Alaska Department of Education conducted a study "purposed to examine 1981 data in order to (a) assess the achievement of CCS students compared to Alaska and national norms, (b) assess the long-term effects of CCS enrollment on achievement, and (c) compare pre- and post-CCS achievement."[57] Achievement was measured via the students' scores on the California Achievement Test (CAT), form C, levels 11-19, reading and math sections, and on the Alaska Statewide Assessment (ASA) in reading and math.[58] The results regarding the California Achievement Test were as follows:

The CAT reading scores for CCS grades 1-3 were .58 to 1.31 standard deviations (SD) higher than the norm. Grades 4-8 reading scores were .67 to 1.12 SD higher than the norm. Grades 1-8 math scores of children taught at home were .42 to 1.31 SD higher than the norm, with the exception of grade five which was .21 SD higher than the norm. . . . The CCS student scores were significantly . . . higher than the theoretical distribution. Three other findings follow:

(1) Those 4-8 grade students in CCS two years or more scored significantly higher on the CAT than those in it less than two years . . . (.61 SD higher in math and .83 SD higher in reading).

(2) The scores of 4-8 grade students after CCS involvement were significantly greater than before CCS study . . . (.29 SD greater in math, and .43 SD greater in reading).

(3) On the ASA, CCS students scored higher than the Alaska averages in reading and math (by 14.27% in fourth grade reading and by 8% in eighth grade reading; by 7.7% in fourth grade math and by 6% in eighth grade math).[59]

The Alaska Department of Education 1981 study has been summarized as follows:

> A sample of 193 CC/S enrollees in grades one through eight was chosen, of which 37 declined to take part in the study. . . . The California Achievement Test was used for math and reading . . . the Alaska Statewide Assessment Tests were administered to all first through eighth grade students in the spring of 1981. . . . All tests were administered to CC/S students by the home teachers following the instructions of the publishers. . . . The results demonstrated that correspondence students' performances were verbally superior in grades one through three; fourth graders scored slightly higher than the national average, and grades five through eight performances were all substantially higher than the national average in verbal skills. In math all but the fifth graders scored at least one third of a standard deviation above the national average. On the Alaska Statewide Assessment Tests, the CC/S fourth and fifth graders consistently outperformed their Alaska classroom counterparts on all subtests.[60]

As a result of the above three studies:

> It can be reasonably concluded that for the types of students involved in Centralized Correspondence Study, the program has not caused them to drop below their state and national peers in terms of math, reading, language, and science achievement. It appears that Alaska's home study program has allowed students to achieve at least as well as their Alaskan peers and better than national norms.[61]

Illinois Study of Home Schooled Students (1986)
A study of fifty-eight home schooling families with seventy-four children from Illinois was conducted in 1986.[62] The families came from a five-county area in northeastern Illinois. Subjects for the study were located by "networking from two known home-school support groups to over a dozen other support groups."[63] In order to participate, students had to meet certain criteria: "a) the child's having been home schooled for two or more years and b) he/she having a birthdate that would place the student in the third through sixth grade for the calendar year 1985-1986."[64] The students were administered the Iowa Tests of Basic Skills by "two independent researchers . . . enlisted to conduct the in-home testing. This entailed two half-day sessions over a two-month period in the spring of 1986."[65]

The subjects were divided into three categories for comparison:

> The first group involved all the students who participated, and their scores on the Iowa Tests of Basic Skills were compared to the national norms for all students taking the test. The second group consisted of

home-schooled children whose parents indicated that their children "would be in a private school if they were not home-schooled." This group included 58 students and was used to compare with the national norms for Catholic School students. The Catholic Schools are the only private school group that have published national norms and also use the Iowa Tests of Basic Skills. The third group involved 34 home-schooled students who were considered of "high socio-economic" status. This determination was based on parents' education and employment. This third group was used to compare with national norms of other high socio-economic status students.[66]

The findings of the study indicated that in all grade levels from third through sixth grade the home schooled students' "'Average Tested Grade Equivalent Scores' were higher than the actual 'School-Grade Level' these . . . students would have normally been in."[67] "Home-schooled students outperformed their traditionally educated counterparts in all areas (vocabulary, reading, language skills, and work study skills) except mathematics."[68] After further examining the mathematics section, it was found that the area of mathematics computation was responsible for the low total math score of home schooled students.[69] The weakness in this area has been attributed to "the result of a lack of drilling in the average home-school setting."[70] In conclusion, the researchers state:

> The growing evidence that home-educated students are not disadvantaged academically by their home-school setting is becoming more apparent. If anything, a case could be made for their "relative academic success."[71]

Survey of Home School Legal Defense Association Members

[A] random sampling survey of 300 families from the membership list of Home School Legal Defense Association (which is a national advocacy organization well-known among the home schooling community) [was conducted that included] 591 total children in these families. The parents reported the standardized test scores of "after homeschooling results" for 241 of the students (who were apparently in grades K to 12). Scogin did not explain how or by whom the children were tested. In reading, 9% were below grade level, 18% were at grade level to 11 months above, and 73% were one year or more above grade level. In math, the corresponding figures were 21% below grade level, 29% at level, and 50% above level.[72]

Academic Achievement Comparison with Social/Emotional Adjustment of Home Schooled Children and Children in Private Schools (1986)

The academic achievement and social-emotional adjustment of home schooled children and children in private schools was surveyed in 1986 (the social-emotional adjustment findings of the study will be discussed in a later section).[73] The subjects were sixty children between the ages of seven to twelve, with twenty-eight home schooled children (twelve males and sixteen females) and thirty-two children educated in a private school (eleven males and twenty-one females):[74] "All families participating in the study resided in California. . . . Demographically, the subjects and their families represented a primarily middle-class socioeconomic status, and resided within a 20 mile radius."[75]

> In order to obtain subjects from the private schools, parents of children in the third, fourth, and fifth grades of two private religiously affiliated schools received a request for participation and brief questionnaire. Parents were asked to return the questionnaire if they were interested in participating in the study. Once the requests were returned, the parents were contacted by phone to arrange for their child to be tested.
>
> The home educated subjects were recruited through a local home education newsletter, and through networking with participants in the study. A short article was placed in the newsletter, requesting participation in the study. Parents then contacted the researcher and a testing time was subsequently arranged.
>
> All subjects in this study were individually tested at their homes. The tests were administered by either the primary researcher or a research assistant, who was trained in the standardized administration procedures of the study.[76]

The children's academic achievement and intelligence was measured using the Wide Range Achievement Test—Revised (WRAT-R) arithmetic and reading subtests and a short form of the Wechsler Intelligence Scale for Children-Revised (WISC-R) which included the Vocabulary and Block Design subtests.[77] The study found (with regard only to findings relating to academic achievement and intelligence) "no significant differences in academic achievement based on type of schooling"; "intelligence estimates for each group were strikingly similar":[78]

> In general, the results indicated that the traditionally educated group and the home educated group exhibited similar levels of test performance. Achievement test scores for the home and private school groups were in the average range, while the intelligence score estimates were in the above average range, when compared to previously established norms.[79]

Achievement Tests of New York Home Schooled Children (1986)

"[H]ome school children in New York have been scoring above average on achievement tests."[80]

Arkansas Department of Education (1986 and 1987)

In Arkansas, home-schooled students must score no more than eight months behind their expected grade level on an approved standardized test to remain in the home-schooling environment. The test must be administered by a person designated by the state board of education.[81] In 1986 . . . 81% of 430 home-schooled students who were tested on standardized achievement tests were successful in meeting requirements of the state. Arkansas' 1987 report . . . stated that over 85% of the 594 home schooled students who were tested met the state's requirements.[82]

Oregon Department of Education (1986 and 1987/1988)

In the State of Oregon, home schooled children are required to take an annual standardized test which is approved by the state and administered by a qualified non-relative, then report the score to the state. The Oregon Department of Education has issued two reports on the academic achievement of home schooled children. "During late 1986, there were 2,691 children registered as home schoolers. Valid test scores were submitted for 1,121."[83]

Some reasons for the discrepancy between the number of registered home schoolers and the number of reported test scores may include children returning to traditional schools, families moving out of the state, some families not reporting their children's test score to the state, and some children not having been tested at all.[84] The results of the 1986 testing revealed that 23.8 percent of home schooled students scored in the 91st to 99th percentile range, 52.3 percent scored in the 51st to 90th percentile range, 17.5 percent scored in the 21st to 50th percentile range, and 6.4 percent scored in the 1st to 20th percentile range.[85]

In the 1987/1988 school year, there were 3,103 registered home schoolers, and 1,658 of those reported standardized test scores to the state.[86] The results showed that 21.4 percent of home schooled students scored in the 91st to 99th percentile range, 51.2 percent scored in the 51st to 90th percentile range, 19.7 percent scored in the 21st to 50th percentile range, and 7.7 percent scored in the 1st to 20th percentile range.[87] From these studies, it is apparent that a large percentage of home schooled students scored very high.

Los Angeles Study of Home Tutorial Network (1987)

One educational researcher cites a study in her article, "An Overview of Home Instruction," which showed that children in a home tutorial network in Los Angeles scored higher than their Los Angeles public school peers on standardized tests.[88]

Comparison of SAT Scores of Alabama Home Schoolers and Public School Children (1987)

The Stanford Achievement Test (SAT) scores of home schooled and public schooled Alabama children aged six to twelve years old were compared in

1987. Sixty home schooling parents were selected for the study, with eighty-four children chosen as subjects.[89] The home schooled students' scores were compared with state norms on the SAT which the researcher obtained from the Alabama State Department of Education.[90] In order to locate subjects, the researcher used several methods.[91] Coordinators of state and local chapters of Alabama Citizens for Home Education (ACHE), an Alabama home schooling support group, were contacted. Representatives of the Hewitt Research Foundation and Holt Associates, promoters of home schooling, were contacted, with both organizations providing information on the location of home schoolers in Alabama. Families were contacted via telephone and by attendance at home schooling support group meetings; an article published in the Alabama Citizens for Home Education newsletter, *The Voice*, provided further information on the study. In order to participate in the study, parents and children had to meet certain criteria.

As the criteria for selection of parents, each parent:

(1) Must have been administering a home education program in his/her home during the 1985-1986 school year.
(2) Must have been residing in the state of Alabama at the time of data collection.
(3) Must have been home schooling at least one child between the ages of 6 and 12 years.
(4) Must have been willing to participate in the study by responding to a detailed questionnaire.
(5) Must have been able to travel to the testing location on the scheduled dates.

As the criteria for selection of children, each child:

(1) Must have been attending a home school for his/her primary education at the time of testing.
(2) Must not have been enrolled in a public school during the 1985-1986 school year.
(3) Must have been between the ages of 6 and 12 years at the time of testing.
(4) Must have been able to travel to the testing location on the scheduled dates.[92]

The families who participated in the study came from urban, suburban and rural areas.[93]

Children who participated were tested at five locations by the researcher and four trained assistants who administered the SAT during a four-week period in May and June 1986; the testing took three consecutive weekday mornings to complete.[94] Parents were given detailed questionnaires which elicited demographic information, information on the existing home school, and information on reasons and attitudes concerning home education, to be completed on the first morning of testing.[95] Parents were allowed to remain at the testing location but were not allowed to interact with their children or interfere with the testing.[96] The findings of the study indicated:

> [T]here were no significant differences between the home-schooled and public-schooled subjects in the areas of reading, listening, and mathematics for grades 1, 4, and 5 and no significant difference in mathematics scores for grade 2. However, the home-schooled second-grade students scored significantly better than the public-schooled students in reading and listening.[97]

In explaining the results, the researcher states:

> In making the comparisons between home-schooled children and public-schooled children, the number of second-grade home-schooled children who participated in the study exceeded the number of home-schooled children in each of the other grades. If a greater number of home-schooled children had been possible, significant differences in the achievement of children in the other grades might have been detected.[98]

The study also compared the home schooled students' achievement on the SAT with national norms and found:

(1) First-grade children scored above the national norm levels in reading and listening. They scored below national norm levels in mathematics.
(2) Second-grade children scored above national norm levels in reading, listening, and mathematics.
(3) Third-grade children scored above national norm levels in reading, listening, language, and mathematics.
(4) Fourth-grade children scored above national norm levels in reading, listening, and language. They scored below national norm levels in mathematics.
(5) Fifth-grade children scored at the national norm levels in reading and listening. They scored above the national norm levels in language and mathematics.
(6) Sixth-grade children scored above national norm levels in reading, listening, language, and mathematics.

It is the conclusion of this study that elementary school-age children who are home-schooled in Alabama tend to score above national norm levels on the total subject domain areas of the Stanford Achievement Test.[99]

The relationships between sex of the child, the educational background of the parent-teacher, teacher certification of the parent-teacher, and home schooled students' SAT scores were also examined. When a comparison was made between boys and girls and their achievement scores on the SAT, no statistically significant differences were found between the scores of boys and girls in grades one, two, four, and combined grades five and six.[100] There was an insufficient number of third graders to make a comparison.[101] This led to the conclusion that:

> [O]verall, home-schooled boys and home-schooled girls in Alabama perform comparably to one another on standardized achievement tests. It is the conclusion of this study that there is no relationship between the sex of the home-schooled children and their performance on standardized achievement tests.[102]

The second variable examined was parent-teacher educational background. Educational background of the parent-teacher was categorized as either junior high or high school education, one to three years of college, or four years of college or college graduate.[103] The study found no significant differences in achievement scores when children were grouped according to parent-teacher background in grades one, two, and combined grades five and six; there was an insufficient number of children for comparisons to be made in grades three and four.[104] This finding led to the suggestion:

> [H]ome-schooled children in Alabama whose parent-teachers had obtained a high school education, some college education, or a college degree perform comparably to one another on standardized achievement tests. Therefore, it is concluded that there is no relationship between the educational background of the parent-teacher and the home-schooled children's performance on standardized achievement tests.[105]

The final variable examined was the effect of teacher certification on home schooled children's achievement. For the purposes of this study parent-teachers were considered to be certified if "they had obtained, at any time, certification by a state to teach," which meant those certified in areas other than elementary education or in states other than Alabama were placed in this category.[106] This variable could not be tested for first graders in the areas of reading and listening, second graders in the area of reading, fourth graders, and combined fifth and sixth graders due to an insufficient number of children to make comparisons; however, no significant differences were found between first graders in mathematics or second graders in listening and mathematics, which led to the conclusion that:

> This finding suggests that those children in Alabama whose parent-teachers are not certified to teach perform on standardized achievement tests as well as those whose parent-teachers are certified to teach. Therefore, it is concluded that there is no relationship between the certification sta-

tus of the parent-teacher and the home-schooled children's performance on standardized achievement tests.[107]

Tennessee Department of Education Testing Study (1986, 1986/1987 and 1987/1988)

In the State of Tennessee, home schooled children are required by law to be tested. Two researchers reported on the Spring 1986 comparison of home schooled and public schooled children, information which they obtained through personal communication.[108] The Tennessee Department of Education (TDE) looked at reading and math scores of 212 home schooled students in grades two, three, six and eight. "The home-schooled outscored their public-schooled peers on 7 of the 8 comparisons."[109]

The TDE (1988) also reported grade 2 home-school SAT scores for 1986/87. The reading score average was at the 85th percentile and the math average was at the 91st percentile. The 1987/88 SAT scores in reading and math for grades 2, 5, 7, and 9 ranged from the 53rd percentile to the 88th percentile.[110]

Washington Home School Research Project (1986, 1987 and 1988)

"The Washington Home School Research Project is a private, cooperative and volunteer effort on the part of 18 individuals including home school parents and several public school educators."[111] It has been ongoing since 1985, when home schooling became legal in the State of Washington. Since home schoolers are required by law to take an approved standardized test annually, several businesses have developed which provide this service.[112]

The research method used in the Project's studies simply involved tapping into the test scores of those home schoolers utilizing several of these testing services. Different combinations of eight testing services were used for the 1986 samplings. Each of the services forwarded a set of scores for each home schooler who was tested. Thus, this sampling represented a 100% reporting of scores of those utilizing selected services for each year. Parents of these home schoolers were also asked to fill out a questionnaire dealing with various aspects of the family or their home schooling. All testing services used the Stanford Achievement Test series (SAT).[113]

Unfortunately, test scores from the home schooled students cannot be compared to Washington's public school students because the state uses another standardized test to measure achievement.[114] The home schooled students' scores are compared to national norms. The findings from the studies follow:

In the 1986 sampling 424 test scores were received; the median score was at the 68th percentile on national norms. In 1987 the sampling more than doubled to 873 students. The median scores were again in the respectable

65-66 percentile range. The highest scores were in the area of science (70th percentile) and in the verbal areas of listening (74th percentile), vocabulary (79th percentile), and word reading (76th percentile). The lowest scores were in spelling (52nd percentile) and math computation (42nd percentile). An interesting contrast to the math computation score was a relatively strong showing in math applications (65th percentile). It is apparent that this sampling of home school students perform well academically. Fears that home schooled children are at an academic disadvantage compared to conventionally educated students are not confirmed.[115]

"The median scores for the 1988 sample (n=726) was at the 65th percentile. The 1987 pattern for science and mathematics was repeated in 1988."[116]

In the 1987 study, the relationship between achievement and several other variables was analyzed. The relationship between parent education level and the achievement of home schooled students was examined. The results indicated:

[A] statistically significant positive relationship was found between parent education level and test scores, but its magnitude was weak (each year of increased parent education level was associated with an increased test score of only 2.7 normal curve equivalents, N=281). Parent education level was not a good predictor of test scores.

Interestingly, in this sample children whose primary parent (the parent most involved in the child's education) had only a 12th grade education, scored, on average, at the 58th percentile (N=94). Where both parents had, at most, 12 years of education, the mean score of the students was at the 56th percentile (N=48).[117]

A second relationship which was analyzed was the relationship between contact with a certified teacher and the achievement of home school students. Due to the small number of home school students who had contact with a certified teacher, no comparison could be made between home school students who had certified teacher contact and those who did not. However, the study looked at those students whose parent-educators were certified teachers, which was referred to as "the high extreme in teacher-contact."[118] Seventeen percent of the parents in the study were certified teachers. The study found:

In general, children of teachers scored better than children of nonteachers. However, this result did not hold when one considered students who have been educated at home two years or longer. It also did not hold when children of nonteacher parents having 16 years or more of education were compared. At the opposite extreme on a teacher contact continuum, children who had no teacher contact at all scored, as a group, at the 70th percentile on national norms (N=200).[119]

The study also examined the relationship between level of structure and hours of schooling and home schooled students' achievement as a third variable. The study showed:

> Within this sample, home school parents rate the level of "structure" in their style of home schooling as slightly toward the structured side of middle on a "very unstructured" to "very structured" continuum. The number of hours per week of "structured schooling" increases somewhat with student age and averages 16 hours per week. The test data suggests that there is virtually no relationship between level of structure or hours per week of schooling and academic outcomes (N=287); the level of structure has no value in trying to predict test scores.[120]

A fourth relationship, the relationship between the length of time the student has been home schooled and achievement, were also examined. Results indicated that "virtually no relationship was found in this data between academic outcomes and the number of consecutive years the student had been educated at home (N=268)."[121]

Fifth, the study analyzed the relationship between grade level and achievement among the home schooled. The study found "no relationship between academic outcomes and the grade level of the home schooled student within the K-9 range. The analysis was restricted to K-9 because of the small sample size at grades 10-12. However, the 28 students appearing in this sample in grades 10-12 appear to be doing well; their mean score was at the 72nd percentile on national norms."[122]

A sixth relationship examined in this study was the relationship between family income level and achievement test scores. The study found "no relationship at all between family income and academic outcomes of home schooled students (N=271)."[123]

A final relationship examined was the relationship between the degree of religious content in the home school program and the achievement of home schooled students. The findings were as follows: "This sampling, using a secular measure of academic outcomes (Stanford Achievement Test) provided no evidence supporting a relationship between the degree of religious content in the home schooling and achievement test scores in general (N=278) or in social science (N=206) or science scores (N=201) in particular."[124]

Christian Liberty Academy Achievement Study (1988)

In their discussion of a study conducted by the Christian Liberty Academy (CLA) in Arlington Heights, Illinois,[125] researchers noted that CLA had:

> [R]andomly pulled 50 test scores from the file of approximately 20,000 scores. The resulting average was two to three grade levels above the national norms. This demonstrated to CLS's [sic] satisfaction that the

home-schooled children using their curricular program were performing better than their public-school counterparts.[126]

Development of Cognitive Intellect in Experimental School and Home School (1988)

The development of cognitive intellect in six- to thirteen-year-old children was studied in 1988. Specifically, the intellectual development of two groups of children was compared: a group involved in the Pathways School (experimental group) and a group of home schooled children (comparison group).[127] The researchers also compared both these groups with the intellectual development of their age-mates in conventional schools.[128]

The Pathways School is an alternative school where home and school instruction are integrated.[129] The school was founded upon Jean Piaget's theory and model of cognitive and intellectual development and has the following characteristics:

(1) Classes met for two days per week.
(2) Each class period was 2 1/2 hours in duration.
(3) Instruction was in math and science.
(4) All other instruction was provided by the parents at home.
(5) Children's ages ranged from 6 to 13 years.[130]

The school is designed to promote "maximum intellectual growth" utilizing a teaching procedure termed "the learning cycle."[131] The learning cycle operates in this way:

The student first explores the concept to be learned using materials and basic directions provided by the instructor. That learning cycle phase is called *exploration*. Next, the students, under the guidance of the instructor, combine their ideas, data and observations which the exploration produced and identify the concept which is inherent in the data. That learning-cycle phase is referred to as *conceptual* invention. During the conceptual invention phase the language of the concept is introduced. The students next use the newly invented concept in several different ways. They might engage in additional activities, work problems, answer questions, pursue individual investigations and/or read about the uses and further descriptions of the concept. This phase leads the students to expand the concept—or idea—they have just met and is called the *expansion of the idea*. It has been shown that with such student-centered experiences children move through each level of intellectual development at a faster rate than children exposed to expositional instruction.[132]

In this study, intellectual growth "was operationally defined as the development of cognition from preoperational thought through concrete and formal operational thought."[133] Preoperational thought takes place approximately between the ages of eighteen months to seven years and is evidenced when "the child becomes able to represent something with something else—in speech, play, gestures, and mental pictures. Egocentrism declines as the child becomes more able to take other people's perspectives into account."[134] Concrete operational thought occurs approximately between the ages of seven years to eleven years and is evidenced when "the child becomes capable of a certain logic—of mentally undoing a mental or physical action so long as manipulable objects are involved. She can relate dimensions, appreciate that some aspects of objects remain the same despite changes in appearance, and classify elements into hierarchies."[135] Formal operational thought normally occurs beyond eleven years and can be seen when "the adolescent can reason on purely verbal or logical statements. She can relate any element or statement to any other, manipulate variables in a scientific experiment, and deal with proportions and analogies. She can construct whole systems of belief, become actively engaged in the world of ideas, and reflect on her own activity of thinking."[136] Piaget later "suggested that the point at which the exit from concrete thought begins is 'between 15 and 20 years and not 11 and 15 years.'"[137]

The subjects in the study were nineteen students from the Pathways School (an intact group) and eleven home schooled students, all volunteers.[138] The children ranged in age from seventy-two to 131 months.[139] The home schooled students were matched to the Pathways School students on the basis of age and sex.[140] After a pre-test it was discovered the two groups were matched in intellectual development as well.[141]

The subjects were pre-tested and post-tested after nine months of instruction on nine Piagetian tasks which "provided . . . a representative, cross-section of reasoning abilities and therefore each student's development level."[142] Each child received a composite score which placed his/her intellectual development into the concrete operational, transitional, or formal operational level.[143] "Because of the small sample sizes in this study some of the findings were collapsed into two categories: concrete and post-concrete (transitional and formal)."[144] The nine tasks included: "1) Conservation of Number Solid Amount, Liquid Amount, Length, Weight, Area and Volume; 2) Equilibrium in a Balance; and 3) Combinations of Colored Beads. Students' responses to these tasks demonstrated their: 1) conservation reasoning, 2) ability to do ratios, and 3) combinational logic, respectively."[145]

All subjects were pre-tested on the Piagetian tasks, as mentioned previously. For the next nine months each group of students received instruction.

The experimental group (Pathways School students) received intensive experiences using the learning cycle procedures and materials. The comparison group (parents without formal knowledge or education of the Piagetian Model or the learning cycle) was allowed to create a learning environment free from specified controls. In other words, parents within this group independently selected curricula materials and provided learning activities for their children according to their own choices (which may or may not have included science and math).

No attempt was made to regulate or specify how the learning environment was to be structured in the comparison group.[146]

All subjects were then post-tested. The study found that "the students in the two groups were experiencing similar treatments."[147] The researchers hypothesized this occurred because home schooling parents "1) redesigned traditional curriculum, 2) provided extensive field trip type learning experiences, and/or 3) allowed their children to explore their environments during extended free time. Obviously all of these children were given ample opportunities for intellectual growth."[148] Specifically the findings revealed:

Approximately half of each group began the investigation with a Piagetian classification of concrete operation. The experimental group (mean age=104 months) was composed of 10 concrete operational and 9 post concrete operational students. The comparison group (mean age=107 months) was proportionally similar with 6 concrete operational and 5 post concrete operational students. No statistical differences were found between the two groups regarding pretest means of either age or developmental level. After the nine months of "treatment," pre/post test gains on intellectual development were measured. . . . The gain comparing the two groups was not statistically different.[149]

The researchers then compared both groups to national averages. The national averages were based on Piaget's findings.

Piaget originally said that children began to move into the concrete operational stage between 6 and 7 years of age. He went on to say that children began to move out of this stage ". . . at about 11 or 12. . . ." . . . In 1972, however, Piaget wrote an article in which he said that the students used in the original investigation were taken from ". . . the better schools in Geneva . . . a somewhat privileged population. . . ." . . . He suggested that the point at which the exit from concrete thought begins is between 15 and 20 years and not 11 and 15 years.[150]

The data indicated "that students taught at home move into formal thought between the ages of 10 to 11," while the average child moves into formal thought beginning at age fifteen, as mentioned previously.[151] The children in this study closely parallel Piaget's "privileged" group.[152] The researchers stated "both Piaget's 'privileged group' and the home schooled groups far surpass the 'average child,' or what is referred to in the literature as national averages."[153] The researchers concluded:

The data from this study suggest that the parents of the home educated students gave their children the right kinds of experiences to foster intellectual development. In other words, the parents in this sample provided learning experiences similar to those suggested by Piaget as critical to intellectual development. From this study one could infer that the comparison group children had similar experiences to that of the experimental group even though the parents in the comparison group had no formal education in the Piagetian Model or its inherent teaching strategy—the learning cycle. Furthermore, this sample of home taught children (comparison and experimental groups) was in a learning environment that caused intellectual growth that actually *exceeded* Piaget's original "privileged population."[154]

This is the final study of academic achievement of home schooled students to be reviewed, but before preceding to socialization of home schooled children, some concluding thoughts on this topic are offered.

Home Schooled Children Are Performing Well Academically

The preceding studies indicate that home schooled children seem to be doing quite well academically. The studies consistently show home schooled children to be performing equal to or better than their conventionally schooled peers, and this finding seems to hold regardless of the parent-teacher's educational background or certification status.

SOCIAL-EMOTIONAL OR AFFECTIVE DEVELOPMENT AND SOCIALIZATION

The social-emotional or affective development and socialization of children is perhaps the outcome of home schooling which promotes the most vociferous debate. Dr. Brian D. Ray and Jon Wartes, both of whom have been extensively involved in home research, state: "According to our experience, socialization is the affective dimension most frequently (and often passionately) mentioned in discussions or debates concerning home schooling."[155] Studies involving socialization will now be reviewed.

Case Study of Home Schooling Families and Socialization (1985)

One researcher conducting a case study of four home schooling families "observed that all of the children were readily able to communicate with the researcher, made the researcher feel they were glad to participate in the study, and were engaged in groups outside the home that offered opportunities for social contacts with other children."[156]

Case Study Using Seven-point Scale (1985)

In order to assess the social development of twelve home educated children, one researcher conducted a case study in which "the researcher and mother-teachers independently rated their children, using a 7-point scale, on the first eight of twelve categories listed in the Boy Scouts of America 'Scout Law' (for example, trustworthy, loyal, helpful, and friendly)."[157] The study indicated a high degree of agreement between the ratings. According to the researcher, "the ratings suggested a higher than average level of social development in the eight categories for most of the children."[158]

Self-concept Study (1986)

A study in 1986 compared the self-concept of home schooled and conventionally schooled children in grades four through twelve. The researcher saw self-concept as relevant to socialization because it "is closely linked with values, social competence, and self-evaluation."[159] After reviewing the literature, the researcher found several factors which seem to strongly influence self-concept; these were: significant others, especially parents and peers, achievement, and instructional methods such as independent study and individualized instruction.[160] The researcher hypothesized that the self-concept of home schooled and conventionally schooled students would differ from one another due to these factors.

Subjects were randomly drawn from the mailing lists of the Hewitt Research Foundation and Holt Associates, Inc., the two largest national home schooling agencies; these mailing lists had a combined total of approximately forty-five thousand addresses.[161] Two hundred and twenty-four children participated in the study. The study compared the home schooled children's scores on the *Piers-Harris Children's Self-Concept Scale* (PHSCS) to those in the normative group who were conventionally schooled and concluded as follows:

(1) The self-concept of the home-schooling children was significantly higher . . . than that of the conventionally schooled population on the global scale and all six subscales of the PHSCS. This condition may be due to higher achievement and mastery levels, independent study characteristics, or one-on-one tutoring situations in the home-school environment. It could also be due, perhaps, to higher levels of parental interest and communication, peer independence, a sense of responsibility, and lowered anxiety levels.

(2) Insofar as self-concept is a reflector of socialization, it would appear that few home-schooling children are socially deprived. Critics of the home school should not urge self-concept and socialization rationales. These factors apparently favor home schoolers over the conventionally schooled population.

(3) The self-concept of the home-schooling children decreases significantly . . . as age and grade level rise. This, however, is not likely due to increasing number of years of home schooling, as this factor had a significantly positive effect . . . when a part of the best predictive model for self-concept. It could be due to a higher age and grade level at that time when a child entered the home-schooling environment from that of the conventional school.

(4) The factors of gender, number of siblings, locale of residence, prior conventional schooling, educational level of home-school operators, and

geographical region were not significantly related to the self-concept of home-schooling children neither when considered in isolation nor as a part of the best predictive model of self-concept.

(5) While not significantly related to self-concept when in isolation, the factors of the number of years of home schooling and the beginning school age did become, when in the presence of certain other demographic variables, significant predictors . . . in the best predictive model of self-concept in home-schooling children.

(6) Higher socioeconomic status is significantly related . . . to a more positive level of self-concept in home schoolers.

(7) An increase in the total number of home-schooling children in a family, within limits examined by this study, predicts a significant increase in the self-concept level. There could be a point of diminishing return above the limits examined by this study as a significant difference in self-concept was indicated which favored home-schooled children over those conventionally schooled.

(8) The best predictive model of self-concept in home-schooling children . . . is related to lower grade-equivalence, higher years of home schooling, higher socioeconomic status, higher number of home-schooling children in the family, and higher beginning school age. The model is statistically stable and accounts for over 12 percent of the variance in the self-concept.[162]

Comparison of Home Schooled Children and Private Religious Schools (1986)

A comparison was made in 1986 of the academic achievement and social-emotional adjustment of home schooled children and children attending two private religiously affiliated schools.[163] The methodology of the study was discussed previously in the academic achievement section and will not be discussed further.

To measure the social-emotional adjustment of the children, the researcher used the Roberts Apperception Test for Children (RATC), a projective test for children between the ages of six and fifteen. "The test consists of 16 stimulus cards, each portraying a common interpersonal theme related to children's development, such as parent-child relations, sibling rivalry, and peer conflicts."[164] The RATC provides information on eight adaptive scales; six of the adaptive scales pertinent to this study are: Reliance on Others, Support-Other (from whom the child perceives support), Support-Child ("self-sufficiency and maturity as indicated by assertiveness or the experience of positive emotions"[165]), Limit Setting (the extent to which parents or other authority figures set reasonable, appropriate limits with the child), Aggression, and Interpersonal Matrix (the child's view of interaction with, and emotional reactions of, significant others"[166]).

The study indicated that both the home school group and the private school group scored in the "well-adjusted" range of emotional functioning on the RATC. "Subjects in both groups also exhibited a low frequency of scores in the 'atypical' and 'maladaptive' categories of the RATC, thus providing another indication of adaptive social/emotional functioning on the RATC."[167]

The researcher found significant differences between the two groups in the area of peer and non-family influences.

> This finding suggests that children in the private school exhibited a greater focus on peer interaction, while the home educated children's primary focus was in the family arena. A trend toward significance[168] was also indicated in the hypothesis that home educated children would perceive a greater amount of supportive behaviors from family as opposed to non-family members.[169]

This is a characteristic which would likely please many home schooling parents. It is frequently cited as a reason for choosing to home school.

The researcher also found trends toward differences between home school and private school children in the categories of Reliance on Others, Limit Setting, Problem Identification, and Unresolved Child. In the Reliance on Others category, private school children were more likely to indicate reliance on school personnel, while the home schooled children were more likely to indicate a reliance on family members. In the Limit Setting category, home schoolers mentioned limit setting in relation to their parents twice as often as private school children, while private school children mentioned school personnel in relation to limit setting almost three times as often as home schoolers. The researcher states that this seems to indicate home school children perceive their parents as primary authority figures more frequently than privately schooled children. In the Problem Identification category:

> [C]hildren in the private school group mentioned peers when identifying problems in their stories over three times as often as the home educated subjects. This supports the significant findings that the private school subjects appeared to be more influenced by or concerned with peers than the home educated group.[170]

In the Unresolved Child category, "subjects in the home school group mentioned children in unresolved situations over three times as often as the private school group."[171] Home schoolers also showed a higher rate of refusal or rejected cards on the RATC. The researcher concludes from these findings:

> This *may* suggest that children in the private schools are more adept at resolving problems than the home educated children. It is possible that the home educated children are exposed to fewer opportunities to resolve

problematic situations on their own, due to increased amounts of parental supervision.[172]

Participants in the study (there were sixty children in the study) also completed a demographic form one question of which indicated children's participation in extracurricular activities. The home educated group had a higher percentage of participation than the private school group in play groups (64.3 percent v. 9.4 percent), organized sports (39.3 percent v. 34.4 percent), church related activities (100 percent v. 84.4 percent), and in "other" activities (67.9 percent v. 40.6 percent). The private school group had a higher percentage of participation in organized clubs than the home educated group (43.8 percent v. 32.1 percent).

Social Functions (1987)

Descriptive data on the social functions in which home schoolers are involved was obtained through a parent questionnaire which showed:

The types of social functions in which the home-schooled children participated most often included religious or Sunday school activities (98.3%), interaction with other home-schooled children (90%), and interaction with neighborhood children (88.3%). Fifty percent of the respondents indicated that their children participated in music activities, and 48.3% indicated that their children participated in sports activities. Thirty-five percent of the respondents indicated that their children participated in public or private school functions. The children in 18.3% of the families participated in neighborhood or community service organizations such as scouts. Six respondents noted other social functions in which their children participated. These included dance lessons, interaction with parents' music students, Mission Action groups, sign language classes, volunteer at hospital, and relatives and children of parents' friends.[173]

Study on Social Isolation and Social Skills (1987)

Whether home school children are being socially prepared was investigated in 1987 by having 219 parents from the State of Washington respond to a questionnaire regarding the social activities and social skills of their children.[174] The survey results indicated:

52.8% of the children spent 20 to more than 30 hours per month in organized community activities; 40% spent more than 30 hours per month with age peers outside the family; 67.9% spent 20 to more than 30 hours per month with non-age peers (youth of more than one year difference in age) outside the family. (Some of the categories and times overlapped.) Wartes concluded that home school youth are not being socially deprived.[175]

Parents rated at least 94% of their children as average or above average in each of the following skills: constructively interacting with peers, constructively interacting with adults, displaying leadership ability, and showing a sense of responsibility. The data from this study suggest that home schoolers are not being socially isolated.[176]

Social Isolation as a Parental Concern (1988)

A survey was conducted in 1988 in which parents revealed social isolation as a problem in home schooling. The researcher sent questionnaires to parents located through a systematic random sampling from the directory of a national home schooling magazine. One hundred and forty-three parents responded to the questionnaire (60 percent response rate). Approximately "25% of the parents cited social isolation as a disadvantage of home schooling. Comments ranged from lack of group participation in music and drama to the idea that extra effort must be expended to provide social contact for their children."[177]

Leadership Development (1989)

Leadership development among home and conventionally schooled students has been compared. Literature on leadership information indicates that leadership in adulthood is linked to "(1) family environment and experiences during childhood, and (2) family environment coupled with school experiences during adolescence."[178] Thus, research regarding the importance of family indicates:

> [T]he future leaders (ignoring situational considerations) are likely to come from homes where they have been given opportunities to practice problem-solving, particularly interaction problem-solving; from homes where they have been stimulated and not left to their own devices; from homes where they have been treated as a function of their level of maturity rather than babied or pushed too rapidly; from organized harmonious homes emphasizing positive incentives.[179]

The leadership literature also suggests that school activities (other than academics) and school relationships are important to the development of leadership:.

> [S]chool experiences and school relationships [take] on increasing significance in the process of leadership development. [The researcher] notes that "certain social proficiencies, if learned during adolescence, often aid in an individual's success in interacting with others as an adult. Failure or lack of opportunity to develop these proficiencies, may prove a handicap to the would-be adult leader."[180]

From the literature, the study concluded, "it is not IQ scores, socio-economic status, or grade point average that are most predictive of a student's taking on leadership roles in adulthood, but rather his or her leadership experiences while in school."[181] This led the researcher to wonder how home schooled children were faring in terms of leadership development; specifically, the major question of the study was: "Is there something occurring in that environment that adequately compensates for the extracurricular program and leadership experiences of a conventional school setting?"[182]

Thus, the study identified the conditions which comprised key ingredients in the leadership development of students and then set up three interview schedules for home schooling parents, home schooling students, and conventionally schooled students. Subjects for the study were from Washington, particularly in the rural and urban areas of Puget Sound. Interviews were conducted with fifty-five parents and eighty-seven students ages ten to twenty-one between May and October 1988, with one interview occurring in January 1989 (only home schooling families with children ten or older were interviewed, since most of the research on leadership development deals with preadolescence or adolescence). The researcher also interviewed a random sample of same age and sex students in grades five through twelve at Crista Schools (King's Elementary, King's Junior High and King's High School) in Seattle, Washington, during the fall of the 1988/1989 school year as a comparison group. The study describes the students and their parents in this school district as being extremely similar to the home schooled students with the exception of type of schooling.

Home schooling parents tended to demonstrate the same traits and qualities discussed and set forth above. The study revealed the following findings with regard to the home school students themselves:

> Of the 81 students who clearly answered the question, "which kind of school do you prefer?", 71% responded with "Home school" or "Home school!"; 15% said they liked and/or disliked both systems equally; and 7% said they preferred the conventional school. In response to the question, "What things do you do [or did you do] in your home school that you did not do [or do not do] in a conventional school?," students identified 242 experiences unique to the home school, three of which were negative (no recess, mentioned once; fewer friends, mentioned twice). Taking those experiences that were identified by at least nine per cent [sic] of the sample (ten of eighty-seven students), their responses could be grouped into five major categories.[183]

The five categories and the percentage of students choosing these categories are: 1. "Control of one's schedule (often stated as learning more because of having greater flexibility, less rigidity, more freedom in determining the schedule, or having responsibility for one's own learning)" (56 percent), 2. "Control of one's time" (52 percent), 3. "Better academic progress/learning environment" (38 percent), 4. "Greater frequency and variety of activities/field trips/travel" (36 percent), and 5. "No worry about 'being cool' or wearing the 'right things'" (9 percent).[184] The researcher acknowledges that the first two categories are closely related, and their combined percentages are over 100 percent as many students shared experiences in both categories. The conclusion from these findings is:

> What stands out in these responses is a clear indication of the value these students place on time and on having control of their time and their learning. This is significant because it is a value that stands out in the literature as a characteristic of leadership.[185]

The study also looked at the students' extracurricular activities and their ability to practice leadership. After comparing eight categories of activities (Church youth group/related church activities, Jobs/paid work, Sports, Summer camp, Music lessons/recitals, Performing groups, Scouts/youth clubs/4H [sic], and Nothing [voluntarily]), the study found three significant differences between home and conventionally schooled students' activities; these differences occurred in the activities of sports, summer camp and performing groups.[186] The researcher points out that these results are not surprising since "the students at Crista Schools have no choice but to participate in a performing group at some point beyond the fifth grade, and thus their responses provide somewhat skewed percentages compared to their public school counterparts."[187] The researcher also states:

> The home schooling students in this study are being compared to a group of college-bound students who participate in extracurricular and out-of-school activities at rates typically higher that those of other college-bound students in this state. Further, it is assumed that college-bound students participate more actively in extracurricular activities than do the non-college-bound. This adds significance to the fact that in five major areas of activity there appears to be no significant difference in the participation rates of home schooling students and King's students.[188]

The study concludes: "From the results of this study it would appear that home schooling is not generally repressive of a student's potential leadership, and may in fact, nurture leadership at least as well as does the conventional system."[189] The research discusses three other patterns which "stand out as characteristics of this state's home schooling population."[190]

> First, home schooling students have as their models parents who are leaders and who demonstrate on an ongoing basis those traits that stand out in the literature as important leader traits. . . . Second, the message that home schooling children receive from their parents, both explicitly and implicitly, is that they are special people, valued and capable members of the family, cut from extraordinary cloth. . . . And the literature insists that a child's leadership potential is profoundly nurtured by such messages.

Third, home schooled adolescents are not isolated from social interaction with their peer group nor denied participation in a variety of at-home and out-of-home organized group activities. . . . The perception of home schooled students as being isolated, uninvolved, and protected from peer contact is simply not supported by this data. To the contrary, there were a number of students who reported having increased social contact and group participation because school required less of their time.[191]

Thus, it appears home schooling does not adversely affect children's leadership development and may, in fact, nurture it.

Effect on Adolescent Microsystems (1991)

The final study to be discussed regarding the social-emotional or affective development and socialization of home schooled children is a study which examined "how the schooling process, in particular home vs. public schooling, affects the relationships in the microsystems of an adolescent."[192] Specifically, the study examined the differences between home and public schooled students' social networks. The subjects were twenty-one home schooled and twenty public schooled adolescents. The students answered "questions about the people with whom they normally interact during the course of a month. The structural and interactional features of their social networks were investigated, as well as the role of selected demographic variables in relationship to the size of their social networks."[193]

The study found:

The home schoolers had differing opportunities for interaction with contacts than the public schoolers in the areas of contact ages, origins of relationships, frequency of interaction, closeness, and supportiveness. The home and public schoolers had similar opportunities for interaction with contacts in the areas of gender, race, length of acquaintance, places of interaction (except for school), activity types, conversational topics, and family relationships. Further, church youth group size and amount of subject community involvement were related to the total size of the subjects' networks.[194]

The conclusions or overall findings of the study are as follows:

This study found overall that home schoolers are not "at risk" (as compared to a similar group of public schoolers) in terms of the total numbers of people with whom to interact, although this varies from family to family. Further, home schoolers and public schoolers are similar in the types of activities, places, and conversational topics they do and/or use in their relationships. However, home schoolers are "at risk" in the sense of feeling less closeness towards and receiving less support from their relationships overall than the similar group of public schoolers who participated in this study. Although this was not true for family relationships, it showed up clearly in friend and peer friend relationships in which the home schoolers have less opportunity to interact than the public schoolers do.[195]

Conclusions Regarding Affective Development/Socialization

This concludes the studies regarding social-emotional or affective development and socialization of home schooled children. As noted above, home schooled children have been noted to be readily able to communicate and are involved in groups outside the home that offer opportunities for social interaction with other children. Overall, it appears home school students are doing as well in their social-emotional or affective development and socialization as their conventionally schooled peers. According to one authority:

> The home-schooled also appear to be at no great risk with respect to socialization. The research indicates that their self-concept is high; they are socially/emotionally well adjusted; they are involved in many activities that are predictors of adult leadership; they are consistently engaged in social activities with peers and adults. With few exceptions (for example, Gustafson's mention of social isolation), the data suggest that home-schooled children are not socially isolated. Our many years of personal experiences with home schoolers confirm the research findings with respect to socialization.[196]

POSSIBLE EXPLANATIONS FOR HOME SCHOOL OUTCOMES

One authority has postulated seven explanations for the generally positive home schooling outcomes:

(1) Home school provides an extremely low student:teacher ratio, usually 1 to 3:1. This allows for a tremendous amount of child-adult interaction, feedback, and behavior reinforcement in the learning setting.

(2) Parents are highly involved in their children's learning, and what happens at home is clearly related to learning success. . . .

(3) Parents are "significant others" to their children, and the children will value their parents' behavior enough to imitate it. Parents who home school place high value on learning and not only value teaching their young but also enthusiastically learn themselves. Extra attention from parents may raise the self-concept of children, which is associated with improved learning. Also, many home schooling parents personally experience a renewal of interest in learning. It may be likely that children will follow the model of their parents in this regard.

(4) Some children who are labeled "disadvantaged" (socioeconomically) may actually be benefitted by staying at home for several years rather than going to a conventional school. Tizard and Hughes (1984) concluded, "Far from compensating for any inadequacies of their home, the staff were in fact lowering their expectations and standards for the

working-class children." . . . The milieu of the conventional school may often discriminate against lower socioeconomic children. It has been found that higher expectations of youth by adults, perhaps more likely at home for many children, result in greater academic performance by learners. . . .

(5) At home ". . . the learning is often embedded in contexts of great meaning to the child" . . . and the home schooled are frequently involved in learning within the framework of daily living activities. This setting is similar to some aspects of the quality, educative experiences and "learning by doing" that Dewey . . . encouraged and the active involvement in learning by discovery that Piaget and Bruner have emphasized. . . .

(6) Home school lends itself to a high degree of individualization and flexibility in terms of "curriculum" for each student. The unique characteristics of each child, whether a deficit or an asset compared to the norm, can be addressed and dealt with on a daily basis without the hindrances of institutional life and operations. Even if the average home school child spends as much as three hours in "formal" or planned learning activities, he or she is still afforded four or five more hours of the conventional school day to engage in a great variety of cognitive, affective, and psychomotor learning activities. . . .

(7) Parents at home frequently exhibit behaviors that have consistently appeared in the literature on teacher effectiveness. Among these characteristics of effective teachers are (a) teacher variability, viz. the parents use many different methods to teach their children, (b) enthusiasm, (c) task orientation, viz. once the learner is on a task, they have him or her take the time to complete it; which is what many home schoolers find they are able to do with their flexible schedules, and (d) clarity and organization in instruction to the student; which is perhaps easier for home school teachers since they have so few students.[197]

There are certainly additional plausible reasons, and this area could benefit greatly from additional research effort.

THE USE OF STANDARDIZED TESTING TO EVALUATE HOME SCHOOLING

Mandatory Annual Testing

Many states require home schooled children to take a standardized test annually and report the score to the state. In some states, children must obtain a score above an arbitrary point in order to continue home schooling or continue home schooling with less monitoring. Recently individuals in the field of testing have voiced concerns about this practice. For example:

These two phenomena taken together—use of large-scale testing programs to assist in making decisions about educational quality and the trend toward greater numbers of students enrolled in home-based educational programs—have revealed improper uses of tests and incongruities in our educational policies.[198]

One commentator discusses how standardized tests are improperly used to evaluate home schooling. His first concern is:

> [T]he use of percentile ranks or other scores (e.g., stanines, grade equivalent scores, etc.) from a norm-referenced test to make judgments about content mastery for an individual student has been soundly rejected by experts in the field of educational measurement. . . . Without measures of absolute abilities or skill levels and aptitude, the data reported from a norm-referenced test are an inadequate—and improper—source of information for use in assessing the quality/acceptability of a child's home school program.[199]

Norm-referenced tests do not provide adequate information regarding what the child has specifically learned (the individual child's abilities, skills and aptitudes); rather, norm-referenced tests provide information on how the child performed on the test in relation to other children (those children in the norm group). In home schooling, the impetus behind mandatory annual testing seems to be to assess what the child has specifically learned; thus, this type of testing does not appear to be appropriate.

Another problem with mandatory annual testing to evaluate individual home school programs is the reliance on a single test score for such an important decision. For example:

> In general, judicial and legislative bodies have, with increasing frequency, rejected reliance on a single-test score for occupational or educational decisionmaking. Ironically, however, those same institutions have been increasingly willing to accept heavy reliance on a single test score in the evaluation of home-based educational programs. The sententious proscription of that practice proffered by the American Psychological Association (APA) which states,
>
>> in elementary or secondary education, a decision or characterization that will have a major impact on a test taker should not automatically be made on the basis of a single test score. . . . A student should not be placed in special classes or schools, for example, solely on the basis of an ability test score. (American Educational Research Association [AERA], APA, & NCME, 1985, p. 54)
>
> has evidently not yet received complete acceptance by courts and legislatures.[200]

A second improper use of standardized tests is interpreting norms as standards:

[O]ne could imagine that a random sample of 1,000 home-schooled students was selected and administered a new achievement test, which was then scored and normed and for which percentiles were reported. Even assuming that student abilities were not normally distributed on the variable achievement (possibly even negatively skewed), 100 students would receive percentile scores at or below the 10th percentile by definition![201]

Courts and legislatures have succumbed to the temptation to utilize the norm-referenced test score as a measure of individual standard attainment, but not without sacrificing the integrity of educational policy. The ill-conceived, but (somewhat) logical policy based upon this current misapplication of testing postulates, in effect, that high-scoring (i.e., bright, intelligent, well-taught, coached, or test-wise) children should be afforded the option of being educated under the home-based alternative, but low-scoring (i.e., slow, learning-disabled, uncoached, test-anxious, etc.) children should not. Such policy is obviously unsatisfactory.[202]

The logic and unstated assumptions of such policy has been examined by asking the reader to consider the reverse situation: A student "who fails to achieve satisfactorily after years of public or private school attendance" is required to attend another institution or be home schooled by his/her parents.[203] By applying this standard consistently, one can see its absurdity and the inconsistency of policy between home and conventional school.

Who's to Blame?—It Depends

Another implicit assumption in policies has to do with where blame is placed when a home schooled child "fails." When this occurs "it is assumed that *the parents*, for one reason or another, did not do, or were incapable of doing, an adequate job of teaching. Thus, blame is implicitly, but immediately and indisputably, fixed upon the child's *instructor*."[204]

Yet, when a child fails in public or private school, "most often specified as culpable in the blame-affixing process are *the child's* motivation, *the child's* lack of prerequisites, or—most ironically—*the parents'* socioeconomic status, *the parents'* lack of involvement, or *the home* environment"[205] and *not the teacher*:

> Rigid, consistent application of the current implicit policy with its assumptions and consequences (e.g., removing low-achieving students from the "detrimental environment" of the home school) would, at the very least, require low-achieving public school students to be spared the harmful effects of *their* placement.[206]

Addition of Aptitude Measurement

Some may suggest a solution to using a single norm-referenced achievement test score to evaluate home school programs is to pair the achievement test with a measure of aptitude as a solution in evaluating home schooling programs. But this is not a completely satisfactory policy either: "It is well established that the reliability of almost every psychological measure increases with the age of the subject."[207] Furthermore:

> The import of this inverse relationship between test reliability and age is twofold. First, because the majority of parents begin home schooling their children in the primary grades (K-6), a policy based upon differences in achievement and aptitude would involve the use of aptitude measures at their least-reliable phase. Second, the measurement problem is compounded by the fact that the validity of the achievement measure is lessened because home-educated students are usually less familiar with the types, content, format, and context of standardized testing than is the typical child educated in the more institutional setting.[208]

An additional concern regarding the validity of standardized tests in evaluating home schooled children is that home schooled children may differ substantially from the norm group. "With any standardized test, it is expected that the test shall be administered to, and used to make comparison between, students who possess characteristics highly similar to the subjects who constituted the norm group."[209] "Nationally standardized tests are normally based on the characteristics of the typical public and private school student, not on the educational experience of the typical home-schooled student, whose educational experiences are structured in a radically different way. . . ."[210]

Due to the difference between home schooled children and children in the norm group, national norms from standardized tests may not be very applicable to home schooled children.

Criterion-referenced Tests

Some may suggest that the use of criterion-referenced tests rather than norm-referenced tests may be more appropriate in evaluating home schooling programs; however, there are several issues with this solution.[211] First, a state-mandated criterion-referenced test could potentially affect the content of the curriculum; in other words, mandated criterion-referenced testing could influence parent-educators to "teach the test." Possible consequences of this occurrence have been described: "If, in fact, a state-mandated, criterion-referenced test can exert a powerful influence over the home-based curriculum, then such a test could effectively negate the uniqueness of the home-based alternative."[212]

Content Issues

A second issue with the use of criterion-referenced tests is that in order for a criterion-referenced test to be meaningful, it needs to cover or match the same content as the home school instruction. Thus comes the recommendation:

Thus, at a minimum, careful study by parents *and* state education officials of desired content and test-matching should precede test selection. For home-educated students where curricular differences are likely to be significant . . . matching of curricula and testing programs seems especially important.[213]

The Insufficiency of Examinations as a Sole Measure

Examining the role of educational testing in general highlights a final concern regarding the use of standardized testing in evaluating home school programs:

"[T]ests are omnipresent but *largely ignored* by most educators we interviewed" [emphasis added]. . . . Elsewhere, Resnick and Resnick . . . argue that "the roots of educational testing in the United States lie in efforts to gauge the success of the schools in their various functions more than in efforts to monitor the performance of individual students" and that the "overriding role of educational testing has been to serve purposes of public accountability, program evaluation, and institutional comparison." . . . Freeman, Kuhs, Knappen, and Porter . . . specifically warn that "because the standardized tests reviewed . . . have been deliberately designed to provide 'general' measures of student achievement, the number of items testing specific content areas . . . is often too limited to provide reliable measures of individual achievement in that area." . . . They conclude that "the net result of inconsistencies between what is being taught and what is tested is an underestimate of student achievement for the curriculum as offered."[214]

Therefore, standardized tests used as a sole measure in evaluating home school programs are not good measures with which to assess individual progress and achievement. In conclusion, one researcher states:

Undoubtedly, standardized testing as a means of assessing education is customary. It is not a reasonable means of assessing home-based education. Standardized testing is designed to assess what is probably a very different population and is typically used to compare groups rather than individuals. Its homogenizing influence counteracts the desire to nurture individuality that motivates many parents to choose home-based educational programs as an alternative. Misunderstanding and misapplication of measurement principles has led to misuse of testing and test results in all fora-courts, legislatures, and policymaking. These misunderstandings have caused current policy toward home-based education to be based on faulty assumptions and have revealed logical contraindications.[215]

It has been suggested that one of the best approaches to the use of standardized testing has been offered by states such as Nebraska:

[In Nebraska,] where regular achievement testing is required "for evidence that such [home] schools are offering instruction in the basic skills, but shall not be used to measure, compare or evaluate the competency of students at such schools." . . . Such a requirement temporarily avoids the evaluation issues, but will likely facilitate greater compliance by home schoolers and provide more reliable information about that population for use by researchers and policymakers.[216]

However, new tools must be developed to assess the effectiveness of home schooling programs.[217]

There are certainly other numerous issues regarding the use of standardized testing to evaluate home school programs. However, this chapter will now proceed with brief comments on the types of research designs most typically employed in home schooling research.

RESEARCH DESIGNS IN HOME SCHOOLING RESEARCH

There has been no home schooling research on effectiveness thus far which has been a true experimental study. Experiments are ideally suited for determining causal relationships (for example, whether one variable or treatment such as home schooling *causes* another variable or effect such as high academic achievement) if extraneous influences are properly controlled. It is highly unlikely experimental research involving the effectiveness of home schooling will ever be conducted. The reason for this is that the subjects of these studies are human beings, and random assignment of human subjects to groups in home schooling research is not possible. It is therefore implausible that a researcher would be allowed to randomly select children from a specified population and randomly assign half the children to a home schooling treatment and half to a conventional schooling treatment. The home schooling effectiveness studies reviewed in this chapter consist of pre-experimental designs. These designs are unable to establish causal relationships among variables.

Pre-experimental designs contain various threats to internal and external validity. Internal validity is the extent to which a cause-effect relationship exists between two variables. External validity has to do with a study's generalizability—in other words, how well the study's findings can be generalized to other situations, settings and populations. These threats are uncontrolled rival hypotheses which account for the results rather than the treatment. The more rival hypotheses can be eliminated in a study, the more confidence one can have in the study's findings.[218]

CONSIDERATIONS FOR FUTURE RESEARCH

Home schooling is an area ripe for future research. What follows is a list of topics for future research; many of these topics are also mentioned in the home schooling literature. This is by no means an exhaustive list.

(1) Research needs to be conducted on home schooling outcomes; in other words, what components make home schooling experiences successful versus unsuccessful? Much could be learned from studying those families who do not have successful experiences with home schooling.

(2) Tests and assessments need to be developed or refined specifically for the home schooling population. This is particularly so with measures to evaluate individual home school programs.

(3) Longitudinal studies need to be conducted. It will be interesting and informative to examine the effects of home schooling as home schooled children grow to adulthood. Specifically, how do home schoolers fare in college, relationships and in the work force? Another vital area for study using longitudinal research is the development of parents as educators.

(4) The focus of home schooling outcome research needs to be expanded from core curriculum (reading and math) to include other areas such as science, social sciences, creativity, motivation, cognitive processes, independence, etc.

(5) Other aspects of the home schooled child's environment could be studied in addition to the immediate family. For example, the child's relationship with extended family, peers, the community, etc. could be studied to determine what effect these have on the child.

(6) Investigate curriculum and types of materials used by home school families.

(7) Examine the use of technology in the home school (computers, software, videos, etc.).

(8) Investigate the goals home school parents have set for their children and whether their children meet these goals.

(9) Explore creative and cooperative liaisons between home school families and schools.

(10) Explore the period when home school children reenter or leave public and private schools. Does this situation produce a transitional period, and if so, what are the characteristics of this transitional period?

(11) Home school research needs to be published in professional peer-review journals for better accessibility. The majority of research in home schooling is completed by Master's or doctoral degree candidates and comes from Master's theses or doctoral dissertations which have limited accessibility.

(12) Comparative research should attempt to obtain fairly equivalent groups to aid in ruling out extraneous variables.

SUMMARY

The research on home schooling seems to be primarily positive with regard to both academics and socialization. According to Dr. Brian Ray and Jon Wartes:

[T]he facts are gathering, and they suggest that the outcomes of home schooling cannot be easily criticized when compared to those of traditional schooling. Home-schooled students' achievement scores are generally equal to or higher than those of their peers in traditional schools. It also appears that home-schooled students are faring quite well in the area of social development.[219]

[I]t should not be assumed that what *is* ought to be. That is, we should never be satisfied to say there is one best educational system . . . for all children and all families. The data suggest that home schooling can compete with conventional schooling in terms of the major agendas of education, the academic task and the socialization of children . . . It seems that home education is a solid, viable alternative that should be readily and intelligently presented to the public at large.[220]

PART THREE

Parental and Family Rights

The colonial home was a little world . . . under whose roof the children could, if need were, learn all that was necessary for their future careers.

Arthur Calhoun
A Social History of the American Family from Colonial Times to the Present (1973)

8

American Patterns

The founding of America was quite unique in that it was seen as primarily a religious experience. The Mayflower Compact of November 11, 1620 proclaims:

> Having undertaken for the Glory of God, and Advancement of the Christian Faith, and the Honour of our King and Country, a Voyage to plant the first colony . . . Do by these Presents, solemnly and mutually in the Presence of God and one another, covenant and combine ourselves together into a civil Body Politick.[1]

To many of the early American settlers, religion was an integrated reality—unlike the fragmented religion of modern America. Their religion was something upon which they structured every aspect of their existence, even the education of the children under their authority.

THE PURITANS

This totality of religious experience was especially true of the Puritans and their views on the family and parental authority.

Although some contemporary writers have been critical of the Puritans, it is evident that their impact on American society has been considerable.[2]

The Puritans, who were prominent in New England in the Sixteenth and Seventeenth Centuries, regarded the family as a sacred and vitally important institution.[3] Indeed, maintaining proper relationships between husband and wife, and between parent and child, was seen as crucial for their very survival.[4] Children were required to submit to the authority of their parents, and the family relationship was understood to be an institution of God. The husband was seen as the head of the household.[5]

These relationships were zealously guarded and maintained as "the very ligaments by which society was held together—'the root whence church and commonwealth cometh.'"[6] An adopted maxim of the day was that "families are the nurseries of church and commonwealth; ruin families and you ruin all."[7]

The history of the early colonial period, in fact, supports this belief in the vital role of the family. As historian Arthur Calhoun points out, the success of the English colonies, in contrast to those of the French and Spanish, was largely due to the fact that they came "not as individual adventurers, but as families."[8]

The Puritans, however, did not base their high regard for the family on mere practical considerations. To them, it was an aspect of obedience to God.[9] The Bible was the single most important influence in their lives,[10] and their understanding of proper family order and government was founded upon the Scriptures and was seen as ordained by God.[11]

Parental authority, then, was understood to be God-given authority. Similarly, the duties and responsibilities of parents to their children were established and commanded by God.[12]

The orthodox devotional literature of Puritan New England, which had wide circulation at the time, reflects this same reverence for the family institution. Literature, such as John Dod's *A Godly Forme of Household Government* and Reverend William Gauge's *Of Domestic Duties*, portrayed the family as the microcosm of state, church, and school, righteously ruled by the father as head of the household.[13]

Training, educating, and bringing up one's children was the sacred right and duty of parents. The corresponding duty of children was to obey cheerfully and reverently, heeding their parents' instruction and emulating their good examples.[14] All of these views were thoroughly supported with Biblical references[15] and were constantly reinforced in sermons.[16]

HOME AND EDUCATION

To the Puritan and Pilgrim of early America, the family home or household was not only cherished as a "preeminent treasure"[17]—it was central in their lives.

As the historian Lawrence Cremin notes, the early New England colonists believed in and consistently maintained "the centrality of the household as the primary agency of human association and education."[18] Cremin further describes the family as "the principal unit of social organization in the colonies and the most important agency of popular education."[19] This was not due to a lack of alternative means, nor due to isolation. Cremin explains:

> [There was] ample opportunity for social intercourse among the members of different families and for joint sponsorship of readily accessible churches and schools. . . . It was ideology rather than geography that established the primacy of the household; for the Puritans considered the

family the basic unit of church and commonwealth and, ultimately, the nursery of sainthood.[20]

In the Puritan household, children received a good deal of sustained and systematic instruction.[21] Parents were deeply concerned that their children receive an education in order that they might understand, and thus obey, the Bible and Christian doctrine.[22]

Indeed, to the Puritan mind, learning and godliness were inseparably linked. The Bible was frequently used as a reading text. Catechisms were learned to ensure that the Scriptures would be interpreted and applied properly.[23] In addition to obtaining an understanding of the Bible, the chief concern of education was in building up godly, moral character in the child for "the practice of true piety."[24]

Even though the primary emphasis of Puritan education was religious, children were still generally taught and expected to learn "the three R's."[25] Children were thus instilled with religious and moral training and were taught how to read and write at a very early age—even by contemporary standards.[26]

Furthermore, Puritan parents, in preparing and educating their children for adult life, also instructed them in a "lawful" calling or occupation.[27] This home-centered and parent-supervised education system, as Arthur Calhoun recognizes, was effective:

> The colonial home was a little world . . . under whose roof the children could, if need were, learn all that was necessary for their future careers. The Puritans, as has been seen, were strong for the training of children for their duties here and beyond.[28]

Not all the parents of Puritan New England, though, were able, for various reasons, to teach their children reading and writing. To aid parents in fulfilling their important responsibilities,[29] the Massachusetts Bay colony enacted the School Law of 1647 (commonly called "The Old Deluder Act"). In order to prevent that "old deluder Satan" from keeping men "from the knowledge of ye Scriptures," and so "learning may not be buried in ye grave of our fathers," it was ordered that a school be established in every town of over fifty households, with the teacher being paid wages by the parents of those children who used the school.[30] Towns of more than a hundred households were also required to "set up a grammar schoole," in order to "instruct youth so farr as they shall be fitted for ye university."[31] Because the duty to provide and direct the child's education was seen as completely under the authority of parents, attendance at such schools was on a strictly *voluntary* basis.[32]

There were, then, a number of educational options available for parents, even if they were unable personally to teach their own children. Moreover, even with the establishment of town schools, households were so prominently involved in the education process that it was often difficult to distinguish "home" from "school." Cremin describes this fact of Seventeenth-Century colonial life:

> For youngsters growing up in homes in which no one was equipped to teach reading, there was frequently a neighborhood household where they might acquire the skill. And, indeed, when an occasional New England goodwife decided to teach reading on a regular basis in her kitchen and charge a modest fee, she thereby became a "dame school," or when an occasional Virginia family decided to have a servant (or tutor) undertake the task of its own and perhaps some neighbor's children, the servant became a "petty school." Such enterprises were schools, to be sure, but they were also household activities, and the easy shading of one into the other is a significant educational fact of the seventeenth century.[33]

LAW AND PARENTAL AUTHORITY

In the Puritan colonies, the state was to be guided by the church and the Scriptures.[34] It was literally a state-church, with the state being a servant of the church. As such, the state was to be a "Godly commonwealth"[35] that punished evil and strengthened and encouraged the good.[36] Thus, with the Puritans' deep concern for the welfare of the family and for maintaining proper family relationships, it naturally followed that from the outset the colony leaders promoted family life.

Of special concern to the Puritan leaders, though, was maintenance of parental authority.[37] The very well-being of the community was believed to depend upon family order and discipline.[38] As such, children in every household were brought up and trained to respect and obey their parents, with strict punishment often imposed for disobedience.[39]

Recognizing the inherent dangers that could result from dilution of parental authority, Puritan lawmakers passed a variety of laws to strengthen and reinforce that authority, backing up parents with the sanctions of the state.[40]

It is at this point that modern child-rearing philosophy is in direct conflict with Puritan views. For example, in the Massachusetts Act of 1654, magistrates were permitted to have children whipped for acts of rebellion and disobedience against their parents.[41] The language of this law reflects the great concern to uphold stable family life and parental authority:

> Forasmuch as it appeareth by too much experience, that diverse children and servants do behave themselves disobediently and disorderly towards their parents, masters and governors . . . to the disturbance of families, and discouragement of such parents and governors.[42]

Perhaps the harshest law of this sort is the 1648 enactment that permitted the death penalty in the case of a persistently rebellious and disobedient son, or where a child cursed or struck a parent.[43] This law, based upon passages from the Old Testament, gave parents the right to petition the court for the imposition of this punishment. But there is no evidence that any parent ever did so, and the law was apparently never invoked.[44]

Nevertheless, the mere fact that these offenses against parental authority were among the fifteen "capitall lawes" clearly indicates the great respect and reverence the Puritans held for that authority. The actual language of the laws is instructive of this fact:

(13) If any child, or children, above sixteen years old, and of sufficient understanding, shall CURSE, or SMITE their natural FATHER, or MOTHER: he or they shall be put to death: unless it can be sufficiently testified that the Parents have been very unchristianly negligent in the education of such children; or so provoked them by extream, and cruel correction; that they have been forced thereunto to preserve themselves from death or maiming. Exod. 21.17, Lev. 20.9 Exod. 21.15.

(14) If a man have a stubborn or REBELLIOUS SON, of sufficient years and understanding (viz) fifteen years of age, which will not obey the voice of his Father, or the voice of his Mother, and that when they have chastened him will not harken unto them: then shall his Father & Mother being his natural parents, lay hold on him, and bring him to the Magistrates and assembled in court and testify unto them, that their Son is stubborn & rebellious & will not obey their voice and chastisement, but lives in sundry notorious crimes, such a Son shall be put to death. Deut. 21, 20.21.[45]

The importance attached to parental authority and discipline is further illustrated by the fact that the courts often sent youthful offenders to their families for parental correction and punishment.[46] Pursuant to this policy, Massachusetts ordered in 1645 that, regarding such child lawbreakers, "parents or masters shall give them due correction and that in the presence of some officer if any magistrate shall appoint."[47]

Other notable laws respecting parental authority include one which forbade tailors from fashioning garments for children which were "contrary to the mind and order of their parents."[48] There was also a law requiring parental approval for a child to marry. This law, however, was tempered by the fact that parents could not "unreasonably deny any childe timely or convenient marriage."[49]

Parental authority carried with it great responsibility. Puritan leaders were, therefore, very concerned that the duties of parents were not being neglected, particularly in the area of education.[50] In 1642, the Massachusetts Bay colony enacted America's first compulsory education law, providing that "because of the great neglect of many parents & masters in training up their children" men be chosen in every town who would "take account from time to time of all parents" to see to it that their children were able to "read and understand the principles of religion and the capitall lawes of this country."[51] A penalty of twelve shillings was imposed for each instance of neglect in this area.[52] These laws also had the disturbing feature that in cases of continual neglect of such requirements, and where the child remains "rude, stubborn and unruly," the child could be removed from his parents and placed with someone who would carry out the law, i.e., "apprenticed" into another household.[53] By 1648, the law specified more clearly what was required of parents:

> The Selectman of every town . . . shall have a vigilant eye over their bretheren and neighbors, to see, first that none of them shall suffer so much barbarism in any of their families as not to endeavor to teach by themselves or others, their children and apprentices so much learning as may enable them perfectly to read the english tongue, & knowledge of the capitall lawes. . . . Also that all masters of families doe once a week (at the least) catechize their children and servants in the grounds and principles of Religion.[54]

> Children were to be able to answer the questions propounded to them from the catechism by parents or select-men. Parents were also required to teach their children some lawful calling under the statute.[55]

These statutes, Cremin notes, by and large merely compelled parents to do what they had been accustomed to doing all along.[56] Parents were being directed by law to fulfill their duty to educate their children—a traditional responsibility of parents in the Christian family.[57]

The other New England colonies soon followed the lead of Massachusetts Bay. In 1650, Connecticut required that children be taught to read English, instructed in the capital laws, and catechized weekly.[58] New Haven followed suit in 1655, New York in 1665, and Plymouth in 1671.[59] In 1665, a Connecticut law admonished that the reading of Scripture and the catechizing of children was a responsibility of "every Christian family," and the neglect of it a great sin.[60] And in 1683 an ordinance of the new colony of Pennsylvania provided that all parents and guardians of children "shall cause such to be instructed in reading and writing, so that they may be able to read the Scriptures and to write by the time they attain to twelve years of age."[61]

All of these enactments were concerned simply with the basic education of children (which occurred in the home) and should not, therefore, be confused with modern compulsory education laws which require classroom attendance at state-approved schools.[62] The responsibility for the child's education in New England (and the rest of the colonies which had no such statutes) was left solely with the parents.[63] Moreover, the power of town ministers or "selectmen" to investigate such matters of family life was quickly curtailed in these colonies by the growing acceptance of the idea that every family's household was personal. That is, the common-law principle that "every man's home is his castle" was respected.[64]

By the last quarter of the Seventeenth Century, there was a rapid decline in interest in, or a growing dislike for, the idea of compulsory education.[65] The laws were substantially weakened or qualified and then repealed outright, so that by the Eighteenth Century there were no longer any laws requiring compulsory education in New England.[66]

A suggested cause for this trend is the dilution of Puritan strength and the increasing religious toleration between the various Christian denominations.[67] Also, for a number of reasons the importance of religion had diminished among the colonists, thus depriving the compulsory education laws of their basic reason for existing—religious instruction.[68] In any event, it was not until well after the American Revolution that interest in such laws returned.[69]

HEALTH, EDUCATION AND WELFARE

Evidently the Puritans viewed the family as the health, education, and welfare institution of society. These three concerns were seen as private functions to be administered in and through the family.

As we have seen in modern times, when the state assumes these functions, the health, education, and welfare of the citizenry decline. The state is simply, and will always be, a poor and ineffective substitute for parents.

9

The Early American Family

A basic characteristic of early American society—one diametrically opposed to many modern concepts of the family—was the family's centrality in the culture. It was as if the family were the hub of the wheel of society, with all the other institutions, including education, being mere spokes. Preeminent in all this was parental authority.

EIGHTEENTH-CENTURY AMERICA

The firm belief of early Americans in the sacredness and importance of the family continued unchallenged through Eighteenth- and early Nineteenth-Century America.[1] Life was, as it had been from the Puritan beginnings, home-centered, with parental authority over children reigning unopposed.[2] This was true of the southern colonies as well as of those in the North.[3] The colonists of this period were heirs to the tradition that "stress[ed] the centrality of the household as the primary agency of human association and education."[4]

To be sure, there were many changes in colonial life during the Eighteenth and early Nineteenth Centuries. The population increased substantially. More and more new towns were established, while the older ones were built up and improved. Survival was less difficult, and life expectancy increased. Commerce and enterprise were beginning to flourish. Finally, the number of churches and schools (what few there were outside the home) increased dramatically as well, making them even more accessible to colonial families.[5]

In addition to these changes, religious toleration of all the various Christian denominations was becoming the predominant view. Also, more representative forms of government were emerging out of the Puritan governments. Historian Arthur Calhoun writes that in all this change, the "family was the one substantial institution in a nation that had discarded hierarchical religion and that reduced government to a minimum."[6]

Through all of these changes, the family remained a constant, maintaining its important role and continuing to fulfill its traditional duties and responsibilities.[7] Lawrence Cremin describes this reality of Eighteenth-Century American life:

> The household remained the single most fundamental unit of social organization in the eighteenth century colonies and, for the vast majority of Americans, the decisive agency of deliberate cultural transmission. In frontier regions marked by a pattern of dispersed settlement, it continued to educate much as it had in the early years of the middle and southern plantations, taking unto itself functions ordinarily performed by church and school. And, in the older, more settled regions, even as churches became more numerous, schools more accessible, and hamlets more common, it continued to discharge its traditional obligations for the systematic nurture of piety, civility and learning.[8]

The family also retained its function as the primary health, education, and welfare institution of society. Again Cremin recounts:

> In the beginning there was the family. In the Christian West, it was traditionally monogamous, patriarchal, and, at least until the early modern era, inclusive of other than blood relatives. It provided food and clothing, succor and shelter; it conferred social standing, economic possibility, and religious affiliation; and it served from time to time as church, playground, factory, army and court. In addition, it was almost always a school, proffering to the young their earliest ideas about the nature of the world and how one ought to behave in it.[9]

In sum, as Cremin notes, "families did more and taught more, in the process nurturing a versatility in the young that was highly significant for the development of colonial society."[10]

COLONIAL EDUCATION

Parents, of course, still had sole authority and control over the education of their children in colonial America. Although schools outside the home increased in importance as a source of education, the home or family remained steadfast as a primary source of all instruction and training.[11]

The general consensus was that education was "the concern of the individual family" and "the private function of the parent, with any state interference unjustified in terms of individual rights."[12] As a result, state involvement was generally limited to providing for the education of indigent children. As Cremin notes:

The community, acting through philanthropic agencies, religious agencies, or the state, took an interest only at points where a spirit of Christian charity impelled them to provide it for the poor.[13]

Thus, from the founding of the original colonies of Puritan New England until the early years following the adoption of the Constitution, home education was one of the major forms, if not the predominant form, of education.[14]

Indeed, many of the framers of the American founding documents received all or a substantial part of their education in the home. This includes George Washington,[15] Thomas Jefferson,[16] Patrick Henry,[17] James Madison,[18] and Benjamin Franklin.[19]

In a letter on the subject of education, George Washington expresses his belief that it is the personal duty of a parent or guardian to provide a child's education. In this letter, Washington states why his ward is not yet ready for marriage, but also reveals his view of where the responsibility of education rests:

[H]is youth, inexperience, and unripened education, is, and will be insuperable obstacles in my eye, to the completion of the marriage. As his guardian, I conceive it to be my indispensable duty to carry him through a regular course of education . . . and to guard his youth to a more advanced age.[20]

Earlier in the Eighteenth Century, Cotton Mather, a Puritan scholar, clergyman, and author, had described in detail the methods of instruction he used in educating his children at home. The description he gives us may be regarded as characteristic of the time.[21] He wrote as follows:

Some Special Points, Relating to the Education of My Children

I. I pour out continual prayers and cries to the God of all Grace for them, that He will be a Father to my Children, and bestow His Christ and His Grace upon them, and guide them with his counsels, and bring them to his glory.

And in this Action, I mention them distinctly, every One by Name unto the Lord.

II. I begin betimes to entertain them with delightful Stories, especially *Scriptural* ones. And still conclude with some *Lesson* of Piety; bidding them to learn that *Lesson* from the *Story*.

And thus, every Day at the *Table*, I have used myself to tell a *Story* before I rise; and make the *Story* useful to the *Olive Plants about the Table*.

III. When the Children at any time accidently come in my Way, it is my Custom to let fall some *Sentence* or other, that may be monitory and profitable to them.

This Matter proves to me, a Matter of some study, and labor, and contrivance. But who can tell, what may be the Effect of a *continual Dropping*?

IV. I essay betimes, to engage the Children, in exercises of Piety; and especially *secret Prayer*, for which I give them very plain and brief *Directions*, and suggest unto them the *Petitions*, which I would have them to make before the Lord, and which I therefore explain to their apprehension and capacity. And I often call upon them; *Child, don't you forget every Day, to go alone, and pray as I have directed you!*

V. Betimes I try to form in the Children a Temper of benignity. I put them upon doing of Services and Kindnesses for one another, and for other Children. I applaud them, when I see them delight in it. I upbraid all aversion to it. I caution them exquisitely against all Revenges of Injuries. I instruct them, to return good Offices for evil Ones. I show them, how they will by this goodness become like to the good God, and his glorious Christ. I let them discern, that I am not satisfied, except when they have a sweetness of Temper shining in them.

VI. As soon as 'tis possible, I make the Children learn to *write*. And when they can *write*, I employ them in writing out the most agreeable and profitable things, that I can invent for them. In this way, I propose to freight their minds with *excellent Things*, and have a deep Impression made upon their Minds by such Things.

VII. I mightily endeavor it, that the Children may betimes, be acted by principles of Reason and *Honor*.

I first beget in them a high Opinion of their father's Love to them, and of his being best able to judge, what shall be good for them.

Then I make them sensible, 'tis a Folly for them to pretend unto any wit and Will of their own; they must resign all to me, and will be sure to do what is best; my Word must be their Law.

I cause them to understand, that it is a *hurtful* and a *shameful* Thing to do amiss. I aggravate this, on all Occasions; and let them see how *Amiable* they will render themselves by well-doing.

The *first Chastisement*, which I inflict for an ordinary Fault, is, to let the Child see and hear me in an astonishment, and hardly able to believe that the Child could do so *base* a Thing, but believing that they will never do it again.

I would never come, to give a Child a *Blow*; except in case of *obstinacy*: or some gross enormity.

To be chased for a while out of *my Presence*, I would make to be looked upon, as the sorest Punishment in the Family.

I would by all possible Insinuations gain this Point upon them, that for them to learn all the brave Things in the World, is the bravest Thing in the World. I am not found of proposing *Play* to them as a Reward of any diligent application to learn what is good; lest they should think *Diversion* to be a better and a nobler thing than *Diligence*.

I would have them come to propound and expect, at this Rate, *I have done well, and now I will go to my Father, he will teach me some curi-*

ous Thing for it. I must have them count it a *Privilege*, to be taught; and I sometimes manage the Matter so, that my refusing to teach them Something, is their *Punishment*.

The *slavish* way of *Education*, carried on with raving and kicking and scourging (in *Schools* as well as *Families*), 'tis abominable; and a dreadful Judgment of God upon the World.

VIII. Though I find it a marvelous Advantage to have the Children strongly biased by Principles of *reason* and *Honor*, (which I find, Children will feel sooner than is commonly thought for): yet I would neglect no Endeavors, to have *higher Principles* infused into them. I therefore betimes awe them with the eye of God upon them.

I show them, how they must love Jesus Christ, and show it, by doing what their Parents require of them.

I often tell them of the *good Angels*, who love them, and help them, and guard them; and who take notice of them: and therefore must not be disobliged.

Heaven and *hell*, I set before them, as the consequences of their behavior here.

IX. When the Children are capable of it, I take them *alone*, one by one; and after my Charges unto them, to fear God, and serve Christ, and shun Sin, *I pray with them* in my Study and make them the Witnesses of the agonies, with which I address the Throne of Grace on their behalf.

X. I find much Benefit, by a particular method, as of *catechizing* the children, so of carrying the *repetition* of the public Sermons unto them.

The Answers of the *catechism* I still explain with abundance of brief Questions, which make them to take in the Meaning of it, and I see, that they do so.

And when the Sermons are to be *repeated*, I choose to put every *Truth*, into a *Question*, to be answered still, with, *yes*, or *no*. In this way I awaken their *Attention*, as well as enlighten their *Understanding*. And in this way I have an Opportunity, to ask, *Do you desire Such, or Such a Grace of God?* and the Like. Yea, I have an Opportunity to demand, and perhaps, to obtain their Consent unto the glorious Articles of the *new Covenant*. The spirit of Grace may fall upon them in this Action; and they may be seized by Him, and held as His *Temples*, through eternal Ages.[22]

Summing up the important role of the family as a source of education during this period in our history, Cremin writes:

[A] great deal of formal and informal education, intellectual, technical, and attitudinal, continued to take place, with the young learning mostly by imitation and partly through explanation. Reading was still taught in the home by parents and siblings, from hornbooks, catechisms, primers, and Bibles, and, as a matter of fact the common expectation that books would be read aloud in the household is probably the single most important clue to the particular stylistic cast of a good deal of early popular literature—such as was certainly the case with the novels of Samuel Richardson, *The Family Instructor* (1715) of Daniel Defoe, and the essays of Addison and Steele.[23]

Not only were basic skills and trades taught, but also "the values and behaviors associated with piety and civility were systematically nurtured."[24]

An additional distinguishing feature of Eighteenth-Century colonial education was the great "diversity of alternatives" available to parents in fulfilling their responsibility to educate their children.[25] Whether in households, churches, schools, or a combination of these, the means of acquiring an education became both more accessible and more diverse.[26] Moreover, in deciding among these various alternatives, parents had absolute discretion and authority. As one commentator notes:

> Historically, the education of children in the United States was a matter of parental discretion. Decisions to educate or not to educate, and the substance of that education—method and curriculum—were made by the parents as a right.[27]

THE FRAMERS

The success of this manner of education—that is, parental control among a diversity of alternatives, including home education—was quite remarkable. It helped produce one of the most extraordinary generations of leaders and statesmen in history, well-prepared for the founding of a new nation.[28] It is instructive to note that among the signers of the Declaration of Independence were represented, in terms of education, every conceivable combination of parental, church, apprenticeship, school, tutorial, and self-education, including some who had studied abroad.[29]

Besides the quality of the leadership, another indication of the success of Eighteenth-Century education was the remarkable degree of literacy. At the time of the Revolution, literacy rates had reached unprecedented heights,[30] and by 1800 literacy was virtually universal.[31]

The general education of the populace was such a well-known fact of life that Thomas Jefferson could unabashedly extol the wisdom of the people "without ultimately sounding like a fool."[32] Commenting on this striking degree of literacy and learning throughout the colonies, John Adams stated in 1765:

> [A] native of America who cannot read or write is as rare an appearance . . . as a comet or an earthquake.[33]

He later said:

> And I have good authorities to say, that all candid foreigners who have passed through this country, and conversed freely with all sorts of peo-

ple here, will allow, that they have never seen so much knowledge and civility among the common people in any part of the world.[34]

Furthermore, what the colonists were able to achieve in the area of education also made quite an impact on Europe. Cremin writes:

> In 1689, the question in the minds of most Europeans was whether North America was yet sufficiently civilized for habitation. A century later, the question was rather what Europe could learn from America: a new education in a new land had wrought new men who seemed to hold the future in their hands.[35]

It is important to note that the education progress in early America was essentially the result of family-oriented home education. And although the framers believed education was to be encouraged and promoted, *it was not to be compelled.* Compulsion in education, it was believed, could result in depriving parents of control over their children.

Thomas Jefferson squarely rejected the notion of compulsion in the area of education in upholding the rights of parents. He said:

> It is better to tolerate the rare instance of a parent refusing to let his child be educated, than to shock the common feelings and ideas by the forcible asportation and education of the infant against the will of the father.[36]

In other words, education, no matter how important to the well-being of the nation, was not to be placed above parental rights and traditional family authority. Thus, even though Jefferson argued for the formation of some form of public education, he never questioned the fundamental role of the family in the education of children.[37]

Other leaders and writers had a strongly felt influence in the field of education in colonial America. One popular work throughout the colonies was John Locke's *Some Thoughts Concerning Education.*[38] Locke advised all parents, in teaching their children, to begin early in the child's development with the Lord's Prayer, the creeds, and the Decalogue. This was to be followed with instruction in reading the "ordinary road of the hornbook, primer, Psalter, Testament and Bible."[39] Moreover, parents were to ensure that the Bible itself was systematically studied as the foundation of all morality.[40]

Another influential leader in the field of American education was John Witherspoon, a Presbyterian minister and president of Princeton University. His students reached positions of eminence in early America. They included a President, a Vice-president, ten Cabinet members, sixty members of Congress, and three Justices of the Supreme Court.[41] Witherspoon also was one of the signers of the Declaration of Independence.[42] In his letters on education, Witherspoon stressed the great necessity for parents "to establish as soon as possible, an entire and absolute authority" over their children.[43]

THE FIRST CONGRESS

This concern for traditional morality and family values was also reflected in the laws passed by the early Congresses. For instance, according to the Northwest Territory Code of 1788, children who disobeyed their parents might, on approval of a justice of the peace in that territory, be sent for a brief stay in jail until, as the law put it, they were "humbled."[44] Although harsh by modern standards, the concern for maintaining strong family values is evident. And the Northwest Ordinance of 1789, which provided the guidelines for the establishing of governments in the territories, also set forth the priorities of the day:

> Religion, morality, and knowledge, being necessary to good government and the happiness of mankind, schools and the means of education shall forever be encouraged.[45]

This clearly expresses the intent of the first Congress to maintain religion and traditional morality within the framework of the educational process, which at that time was essentially a family function.

THE WORKMANSHIP OF THE MAKER

It was during the Eighteenth Century that certain Enlightenment writers were articulating the nature of children and their relationship to their parents and society. One such writer, John Locke, attempted to put it in a Biblical context.[46]

In his *Second Treatise of Government* (1691), Locke characterizes the relationship between parent and child as follows:

> Adam was created a perfect man, his body and mind in full possession of their strength and reason, and so was capable from the first instant of his being to provide for his own support and preservation and govern his actions according to the dictates of the law of reason which God had implanted in him. From him the world is peopled with his descendants who are all born infants, weak and helpless, without knowledge or understanding; but to supply the defects of this imperfect state till the improvement of growth and age has removed them. Adam and Eve, and after them all parents, were by the law of nature "under an obligation to preserve, nourish, and educate the children" they had begotten; not as their own workmanship, but the workmanship of their own Maker, the Almighty, to whom they were to be accountable for them.[47]

As a preface to discussing these principles, it is emphasized that Eighteenth-Century spirituality saw God's work as the creation of an orderly, well-governed universe in which independent parts were in harmony with all others. As such, children, seen as God's creatures, were destined to take their place in the moral social order as well-developed adults.

First, as Locke articulated, children are not merely the property of their parents. They were, in his opinion, the creation of God. Therefore, instead of belonging to their parents, children belong to the Creator. Parents, then, hold children in trust for God. This means that parents, as stewards, are to take care of their children for God. The child must be raised to live the sort of life which is pleasing to the Creator. Locke says this is in accordance with the "dictates of the law of reason." As such, it is a primary moral and spiritual function of the family.

Second, although children lack the fully developed capacities of adult humans, they do not lack humanity. Locke notes that children are "weak and helpless, without knowledge or understanding." In short, children do not yet have what is required to be beings pleasing to the Creator. At early ages, they do not yet have the mental and moral development to enable them to live under the "law of reason." They are in need of care.

As potential independent beings, children, Locke reasons, are born *to* a state of equality but not *in* a state of equality. Not only does this emphasize that children have a life of their own to live someday but that things can turn out well or badly. There are no guarantees that the weak infant will become the reasoning adult. Parents thus have a moral duty to take steps to see that the "improvement of growth and age" actually comes about in producing independent adults.

Third, the child's weakness is a source of parental authority, which in turn is a source of parental obligation. Thus, parents are under a God-mandated obligation to "preserve, nourish, and educate" their children. This is not a choice parents have. In Locke's view, then, *the obligation is not to the child but to God*. Therefore, the child may not refuse the services or release their parents from this obligation.

Fourth, parents can know and do what is best for children. The obvious parental guide for rearing children for Locke was the Bible. Clearly, as Locke argued, it is in the interest of the Creator in maintaining an ordered universe for a child to become a well-developed, moral adult. It is also in the interests of the child and society. Finally, it is in the best interests of the parents to bring their parental obligations to a satisfactory end and to give a good accounting of themselves to the Creator.

These were the basic thoughts that circulated through Eighteenth- and Nineteenth-Century America. Basic authority was with parents, but parents had correlative obligations to rear their children in what was commonly termed "the admonition of the Lord." And it was this parental authority and obligation that was embedded in the law and protected by the courts.

10

The Sacred Right

Recognition of the family tradition by English and American law occurs primarily in cases involving parental rights. Protection of parental rights was especially strong in the early cases.

THE COMMON LAW

The common law, which governed western societies until the advent of modern statism, was essentially based upon Christian principles. Seton Hall University law professor John C. H. Wu writes: "Whatever you may say of its defects, which are incidental to all human institutions, there can be no denying that the common law has one advantage over the legal system of any country: it was Christian from the very beginning of its history."[1]

Essentially, the common law is an age-old doctrine that developed by way of court decisions that applied the principles of Christianity to everyday situations. Out of these cases, rules were established that governed future cases. This tradition, with its origin in Europe, was imported to early life in America and became part of American law.

The common law is important in this discussion because it afforded a great deal of respect to parents in dealing with their children. In fact, writes professor Bruce Hafen, the "common law has long recognized parental rights as a key concept [and] . . . as a fundamental cultural assumption about the family as a basic social, economic, and political unit."[2] For this reason, both English and American judges view the origins of parental rights "as being even more fundamental than property rights."[3]

Much of the children's rights literature argues that children should no longer be regarded as the "property" of their parents.[4] As the argument goes, the property mentality is still strongly embedded in Western culture. Although this may be true to some extent, the children-as-property view has not been taken seriously for many years. Moreover, the cases analyzed in this chapter, as well as the traditional limitations on the exercise of parental rights, indicate it was never really the common law view.[5]

The fact remains, however, that parental rights were strictly upheld in common law. As this has been expressed in American courts, parental rights to custody and control of minor children have been described by one American court as "sacred."[6] Another court noted that parental rights were a "natural law."[7] And yet another judge said that parental rights are "inherent, natural right[s], for the protection of which, just as much as for the protection of the rights of the individual to life, liberty, and pursuit of happiness, our government is formed."[8]

COMMONWEALTH v. ARMSTRONG

To illustrate how strongly early American case law favored parental rights, consider the case of *Commonwealth v. Armstrong*.[9] This Pennsylvania case was decided in 1842. It is appropriate here because it portrays the fact that many courts in early America not only protected parental rights but incorporated Judeo-Christian principles directly into their opinions.

The defendant, a Mr. Armstrong, had refused permission and expressly prohibited the complainant, a Baptist minister, from baptizing Armstrong's seventeen-year-old minor daughter (who had already been baptized in the Presbyterian church). Against the father's direct commands, and without his knowledge, the minister proceeded to baptize the girl. Upon discovering this, the father was provoked to great anger and outrage. In his excitement, the father threatened the minister with personal injury. To prevent Mr. Armstrong from acting in vengeance, the court ordered him to provide surety in the sum of $500 to keep the peace for six months toward the complainant.

The court then considered the issue of who was responsible to pay the court costs involved. This issue hinged upon which party was most at fault in causing the incident. The court ruled in favor of the father. For interfering with a father's lawful authority over his own child, the minister was ordered to pay the costs involved in the case.

Judge Lewis, speaking for the court, said:

> The authority of the father results from his duties. He is charged with the duties of *maintenance* and *education*. These cannot be performed without the authority to command and to enforce obedience. The term *education* is not limited to the ordinary instruction of the child in the pursuits of literature. It comprehends a proper attention to the *moral* and *religious sentiments* of the child. In the discharge of this duty, it is the undoubted right of the father to designate such *teachers*, either in *morals, religion* or *literature*, as *he* shall deem best calculated to give correct instruction to the child. No teacher, either in religion or in any other branch of education, has any authority over the child, *except what he derives from its parent or guardian*; and that authority may be withdrawn whenever the

parent, in the exercise of his discretionary power may think proper. . . .
[H]e may prohibit such attendance and confine it to such religious teachers as he believes will be most likely to give correct instruction and to
secure its welfare here, and its eternal happiness in the world to come. He
cannot force it to adopt opinions contrary to the dictates of its own conscience, but he has a right to its time and its attention during its minority, for the purpose of enabling him to make the effort incumbent on him
as a father, of "training it up in the way it should go." . . . *The patriar-
chal government was established by the Most High,* and, with the necessary modifications, it exists at the present day. The authority of the
parent, over the youth and inexperience of his offspring, rests on foundations far more sacred than the institutions of man. *"Honor thy father
and mother,"* was the great law proclaimed by the King of Kings. It was
the first commandment accompanied with a promise of blessing upon
those who obeyed it: while the dread penalty of death was inflicted upon
all who were guilty of its infractions. "The eye that mocketh at his father,
and despiseth to obey his mother, the ravens of the valley shall pick it out,
and the young eagles shall eat it."—Proverbs 30,17. "The stubborn and
rebellious son who will not obey the voice of his father shall be stoned
with stones that he may die, and all Israel shall hear and fear."
Deuteronomy 21,21. Abraham commanded his children, and his household after him, to keep the way of the Lord. Joshua *resolved both for himself and his house to serve the Lord.* And the house of Eli was destroyed
because his sons made themselves vile and *he restrained them not.* "My
son, keep the *instruction* of thy father and forsake not the law of thy
mother." Proverbs 1,8, 9; and Proverbs 6,20. A fool despiseth his *father's
instruction.*—Proverbs 15,5. A wise son heareth his father's instruction.—Proverbs 13,1. Cursed be he that setteth light by his father or his
mother, and all the people shall say Amen.—Deuteronomy 27,16.

It was justly remarked by Horry, Professor of Moral Philosophy, in
his treatise upon that subject, that the words "train up a child in the way
he should go," imply both the *right* and the *duty* of the parent to train it
up in the right way. That is, the way which the parent believes to be right.
The right of the father to command, and the duty of the child to obey, is
thus shown, upon the authority of the Old Testament, to have been established *by God himself.* And the teachings of the New Testament abundantly prove that, instead of being abrogated in any respect, the duty of
filial obedience was inculcated with all the solemn sanctions which could
be derived from the New Dispensation. The Fifth Commandment,
"Honor thy father and thy mother," was repeated and enjoined by St.
Paul, in his Epistle to the Colossians. Children, obey your parents in the
Lord, for this is right. Ephesians 6,1 Children, obey your parents in all
things, for this is well pleasing unto the Lord. Colossians 3,20. If anything
can give additional weight to the authority on which rests the doctrine of
filial obedience, it is the practical commentary furnished by the Saviour
himself. In his quality of GOD, it was incumbent upon him to be about

the business of his Heavenly Father, at Jerusalem, "both hearing the doctors, and asking them questions." But in his quality of MAN, he left the Temple and its teachings of wisdom, and in obedience to the wishes of his earthly parents, "he went down with them to Nazareth, and was subject unto them." Luke iv. 51.[10]

Judge Lewis then refers to various scholars who had expounded on parental rights:

[T]he duty of children to their parents is the *next in order and importance to the duty we owe God.* . . .

[It is] the duty of a parent *to educate* his children, to form them for a life of usefulness and virtue, and . . . he has a right to such authority, and in support of that authority to exercise such discipline as may be necessary for these purposes. . . .

[C]hildren are to regard their parents as standing in the most venerable and the most endearing of all earthly relations to them, as those to whom under God, they owe every thing they are, and every thing they hope to be. They are to regard them as the persons to whose kindness, care and *government* they have been *committed by God himself.*

[T]he right of the parent is to command—the duty of the child is to obey. Authority belongs to the one, submission to the other. The relation . . . is established by our Creator. The failure of one party does not annihilate the obligations of the other. If the parent be unreasonable, this does not release the child. He is still bound to honor and obey and reverence his parent.[11]

Judge Lewis then discusses the common law principles:

The doctrines of the common law are in accordance with these principles. It is the duty of the parent to maintain and educate the child, and he possesses the resulting authority to control it in all things necessary to the accomplishment of these objects. The law has assigned no limits to the authority of the parent over the child, except that it must not be exercised in such a manner as to endanger its safety or morals. . . . 1 Blackstone, 450; 2 Kent's Commentaries, 205. . . .

The highest judicial power in the Commonwealth dare not attempt to estrange the child from the religious faith of its parents. . . . Shall any man, high or low, be allowed to invade the domestic sanctuary—to disregard the parental authority established by the Almighty . . . to seduce [the child] away from its filial obedience—or even to participate in its disregard of parental authority. . . . God forbid that the noblest and holiest feeling of the human heart should be thus violated—that the endearing relation of parent and child should be thus disturbed—that the harmony of the domestic circle should be thus broken up—and that the family altar itself should be thus ruthlessly rent in twain and trodden in the dust. . . .

The principle of parental authority and filial obedience has its home in the human heart—is in accordance with the law of nature, and will ever be near and dear to every good man of every religion under the sun. . . . There is no limit to that authority save that which is necessary for the preservation of the health and morals of the child.[12]

As to the claim of another over the children of a particular parent, Judge Lewis notes:

This proceeding cannot be justified under any claim founded upon the rights of conscience. The child whose *conscience* stimulates it to open rebellion against the lawful authority of its father, stands more in need of proper instruction and discipline under that authority than any other. If every child, under a claim founded upon the supposed rights of conscience, were allowed to carry into effect every decision of its immature judgment, where is that to end? Shall it be allowed, under this pretence, to violate the law of God? to repudiate the Christian religion? . . . to disregard the holy institution of marriage? . . .

It is dangerous to depart from established principles. Parental authority is not to be subverted so long as it is exercised within the limits which the law has prescribed. It is the duty of the parent to REGULATE THE CONSCIENCE OF THE CHILD, by proper attention to its education; and there is no security for the offspring during the tender years of its minority but in obedience to the authority of its parents, in all things not injurious to its health or morals.[13]

Unfortunately for the Baptist minister involved, he had "transcended the divine and human law, in disregarding the authority of the father over his own offspring while in its minority. This is the opinion of the constitutional authority—the result of our conscientious convictions of the law."[14]

The eminent jurist James Kent, a giant of early American law who wrote the classic *Commentaries on American Law*, wrote to Judge Lewis commending him for his decision. Kent considered it a "just explanation and application of the parental authority" and stated his intent to put it in his *Commentaries*.[15] Moreover, the *Armstrong* case is cited as a leading authority as late as 1908.[16]

PLENARY PARENTS' RIGHTS

The rights of parents over the children under their care, as the *Armstrong* case indicates, were nearly absolute. Moreover, the early case law indicates that parental rights were established as one of the earliest forms of authority.

In fact, earlier judicial philosophy and some modern judicial decisions imply that the parent-child relationship "antedates the state in much the same sense as natural individual rights are thought to antedate the state in

American political philosophy."[17] Thus, before there was a state of any kind, there were inherent human rights. Among these were those parental rights preserved within the context of the family. Professors Philip B. Heymann and Douglas E. Barzelay write:

> *Our political system* is superimposed on and *presupposes a social system of family units*, not just of isolated individuals. *No assumption more deeply underlies our society than the assumption that it is the individual [parent] who decides whether to raise a family*, with whom to raise a family *and*, in broad measure, *what values and beliefs to inculcate in the children who will later exercise the rights and responsibilities of citizens and heads of families.* . . .
>
> . . . *[T]he family unit does not simply co-exist with our constitutional system; it is an integral part of it.* In democratic theory as well as in practice, it is in the family that children are expected to learn the values and beliefs that democratic institutions later draw on to determine group directions. *The immensely important power of deciding about matters of early socialization has been allocated to the family, not to the government.*[18]

The power of parents, the early court decisions indicate, is essentially plenary. This means it should prevail over the claims of the state, other outsiders, and the children themselves "unless there is some compelling justification for interference."[19] As a 1925 decision by the Rhode Island Supreme Court notes:

> Immemorially the family has been an important element of our civil society, one of the supports upon which our civilization has developed. Save as modified by the Legislature, in domestic affairs the family has remained in law a self-governing entity under the discipline and direction of the father as its head. These fundamental principles are traceable to ancient customs and usages and are fixed by tradition and evidenced by the decisions of the courts. *Anything that brings the child into conflict with the father or diminishes the father's authority or hampers him in its exercise is repugnant to the family establishment* and is not to be countenanced save upon positive provisions of the statute law.[20]

Similarly, the Supreme Court of Mississippi, as late as 1960, held:

> The kind and extent of education, moral and intellectual, to be given to a child and the mode of furnishing it are left largely to the discretion of the parents. . . . Unless shown to the contrary, the presumption is that natural parents will make the best decisions for their offspring. . . . [T]his important parental right is protected by common law principles. It is also a right protected by the due process clauses of the Federal and State

Constitutions. . . . *The family is the basis of our society.* [The parent in the case] has an interest in [the education of his children] which lies on a different plane than that of mere property. Moreover, a child has no higher welfare than to be reared by a parent who loves him and who has not forfeited the right of custody. The agencies of our democratic government are obligated to preserve that right which is not recognized in a totalitarian society.[21]

STATE INTERFERENCE

Although parental authority has plenary overtones, it is not completely unrestricted. Thus compelling justification for state interference in parent-child relationships was recognized both at common law and in early decisions.

This is implied by the Englishman Sir William Blackstone in his *Commentaries on the Laws of England*, published between 1765 and 1770. The *Commentaries* were popular in Great Britain, but by 1775 more copies of the *Commentaries* had been sold in America than in all of England.[22] Blackstone's *Commentaries*, then, were extremely influential on the development of both early American law and culture.[23] Blackstone states:

The ancient Roman laws gave the father a power of life and death over his children; upon this principle, that he who gave had also the power of taking away. But the rigor of these laws was softened by subsequent constitutions. . . . The power of a parent, by our English laws is much more moderate; but still sufficient to keep the child in order and obedience. He may *lawfully* correct his child, being under age, *in a reasonable manner*; for this is for the benefit of his education.[24]

A Nineteenth-Century English court enunciated the justifications for judicial interference in parental authority:

A father has a legal right to control and direct the education and bringing up of his children until they attain the age of twenty-one years . . . and the Court will not interfere with him in the exercise of his paternal authority, except (1) where by his gross moral turpitude he forfeits his rights, or (2) where he has by his conduct abdicated his parental authority.[25]

It is evident that the Judeo-Christian worldview affected English jurisprudence concerning parental rights and the early development of the law on parental rights in America. This included state interference where it was *clear* that the parents had forfeited their rights. Moreover, courts in America have increasingly expressed a "lower tolerance for serious physical harms inflicted by parents on their children."[26] This is not difficult to understand in light of the rise of child abuse in modern society.

Notwithstanding the exceptions, *parental authority in normal family situations is still vital.* However, as we enter the Twenty-first Century, the older concept of the "sacred" parental rights falls into more and more question.

11

Modern Parental Rights: Issues and Limits

Donald was like many other fifteen-year-olds. His parents divorced when he was younger, and his mother remarried. He and his stepfather lived in a state of tension, with his mother caught in the middle. Sometimes Donald behaved outrageously just to test his stepfather. For example, one night he stole liquor from his parents and got drunk on the front porch. Similar behavior added to the tension, although at no point during these years was Donald harmed or abused.

Unlike most fifteen-year-olds who rebel against their parents, however, Donald had an escape route. His natural father lived nearby, and he offered considerable freedom and independence from strict rules—if only Donald would come to live with him. One summer Donald accepted the offer.

Six years later, Donald became a college football player with straight A's and received Academic All-American honors. But the intervening years would not have predicted the happy outcome. Living in his father's home, Donald wrecked a vehicle and amassed many speeding tickets. For a time, his grades fell substantially. He attended alcohol-related functions with impunity, although he was under the legal drinking age. And his mother suffered as she watched her youngest son forget the lessons she had tried so hard to teach.

Although mother and son are now reconciled, the mother will never forget the judge who took her son away.

After Donald went to live with his father, the father sued for legal custody. When the hearing came, the judge cleared everyone from the courtroom except for Donald. The judge asked the fifteen-year-old boy what he wanted to do. No one else testified. Donald said he wanted to live with his natural father, and the judge entered a decision accordingly.

In a moment, the mother watched fifteen years of parenting eliminated from the equation. On that day a judge gave parents' rights to a child.[1]

This chapter will consider three components of modern parental rights. First, historical parental rights will be compared with present rights. Second, consideration will be given to what it means to be a "parent" in modern society, since the "typical" family of two children, their natural mother, and their natural father (with both parents being married) no longer universally exists. Third, remaining parental rights will be reviewed.

HISTORICAL PARENTAL RIGHTS

The rights of parents today are rather pale in comparison to parents' rights in past years. At one time, children were sometimes seen as part of the father's economic household, and accordingly he held great control over them. Nineteenth-century legal doctrines held: "A father, and after his decease, a surviving mother, is entitled to the services of their children, and to the products or earnings of such children during their minority. . . ."[2] Children were legally accorded higher status than slaves, but they had relatively little independence in their own right.

EARLY AMERICAN LAW

Nineteenth-Century legal experts adopted a Judeo-Christian view of the family, especially in regard to the duties owed by a parent to his children. One commentator explained:

> The duty of parents to their children embraces their maintenance, protection, and education. This is said to rest upon a principle of natural law; but perhaps it may be more reasonably referred to the implied obligation which parents assume in entering into wedlock, and by bringing children into the world.[3]

Thus, it was generally agreed that parents have three duties towards their children: first, "maintenance" (or providing for physical needs); second, "protection"; and third, "education." These three duties exactly coincide with the three duties the Bible set forth as owed to children by their parents.[4]

However, the Nineteenth-Century legal system did not provide any remedy for a violation of these duties.[5] It is in this respect that Nineteenth-Century parental rights were more expansive than those today; moral and ethical obligations existed, but neither the common law, nor statutory law provided a remedy against a parent who violated these obligations.

One of the strongest rights held by parents in the 1800s was the right to discipline their children. One treatise explained:

The parent may lawfully correct or chastise his child, being under age, in a reasonable manner; but he cannot inflict a cruel and excessive punishment; and the question of excessive punishment is one for a jury.[6]

At first glance, this power to discipline might seem rather limited, since parents could only punish their children in a reasonable manner. However, the key element was that the issue of excessiveness was a jury question, and at the time neither women nor minorities served on juries,[7] and many states required that jurors be landowners. This resulted in a situation where the only jury members were white male landowners, who were then called upon to determine whether other white male landowners had used excessive discipline. Such a system probably did not produce excessive concern for the rights of children, as each jury member had an economic interest in protecting his control over his own household. Furthermore, the law presumed that the punishment was proper,[8] thus requiring a tremendous showing of proof to actually convict a parent of excessive punishment.

Thus, early American law did not scrutinize the relationship between parents and children. Certain moral and ethical duties existed, but these duties did not generally result in adverse legal consequences for violations. As abuses of parental power became more commonplace, however, states began to regulate family relationships. Our current legal system reflects these efforts to protect the welfare of children and the restriction of parental rights.

SHIFTING DEFINITION OF A PARENT

The concept of *parent* is being revolutionized in contemporary society. Today traditional concepts such as "Mommy," "Daddy," and "family" have, in some cases, given way to "egg donor" (the mother), a "sperm donor" (the father), and a "parent-child relationship."[9] As the number of nontraditional parental relationships has increased, new forms of conflict have emerged between the various classes of "parents." For example, foster parents seek increased legal status over the natural parents, and surrogate mothers seek protection from contractual parents.

The rights of a parent over his or her child often now depend on the legal relationship between the parent and the child. Foster parents and contractual parents receive the least protection, and natural parents in an intact marriage receive the most protection. In the following discussion, two types of parent-child relationships will be examined: natural parents and legal parents. The powers of the state to interfere with decisions by these parents will be compared.

Natural Parents

Currently, states almost universally prefer the "formal" family over competing claims.[10] The formal family consists of a child, its natural mother, and its natural father, with its parents married according to applicable state law.[11]

If the child is not born within a marriage, however, states may differ as to how they treat the natural parents. For example, the rights of the natural father may receive less legal protection than those of the natural mother.[12]

At one time, for example, the State of Illinois conclusively presumed that every father of a child born out of wedlock was unfit to have custody over the child;[13] yet, this presumption did not apply to the natural mother of the child.[14] The Supreme Court has held, however, that a natural father cannot be presumed to be an unfit parent absent a showing of actual unfitness.[15]

The rights of natural fathers are questioned most often when the biological mother marries a man other than the child's biological father and the mother's husband seeks to adopt the child. Where the natural father has developed a relationship with his child, he may seek to protect his stake in his child's life, and he may oppose any attempt by the mother's husband to adopt the child. In other cases, the natural father may have wholly ignored the child until he received notice of the pending adoption. Basically, the rights of a natural father currently depend on the concept of an "opportunity interest." At one end of the spectrum is the natural father who has committed himself to raising his child, even though he is not legally married to the child's mother. The other extreme is a father who has ignored his child for years and whose interest in the child begins only when someone else petitions for adoption.[16] According to the Supreme Court, the "mere existence of a biological link does not merit . . . constitutional protection."[17] Instead, courts look at the opportunity a biological father utilized to develop a relationship with his child:

> When an unwed father demonstrates a full commitment to the responsibilities of parenthood by "com[ing] forward to participate in the rearing of his child," . . . his interest in personal contact with his child acquires substantial protection under the [Constitution].[18]

A natural father's commitment does not have to be very great to receive legal protection, although his legal standing is stronger with each increasing degree of commitment.

For example, in New York an unwed father simply has to mail a letter to the "putative father registry" to ensure that he receives notice if someone else wishes to adopt the child.[19] Thus, when an unwed father in New York commits himself to his child, he gains the right to know about proceedings affecting his child's welfare.

More importantly, the biological father who grasps his "opportunity interest" cannot be deprived of his right to prevent other people from adopting his child,[20] although this right is not absolute. Generally, a child born in wedlock cannot be adopted without the consent of each living parent who has neither voluntarily surrendered parental rights nor been judged to be unfit.[21]

Many states, however, require only the consent of the mother when the child is born out of wedlock.[22] Such a requirement would be unconstitutional if applied to a father who has developed a strong relationship with his child.[23] But if the father has not legitimated his child through requisite legal proceedings,[24] then the state does not give him veto power over a potential adoption.[25]

Furthermore, if an indigent father has attempted to grasp his opportunity interest, the state must provide him with an attorney to represent his interests, at state cost.[26]

If a state has enacted a guardianship statute, there is a presumption favoring a natural parent's custody of a minor child.[27] This means that a biological father is favored for custody of his child, rather than another adult or the welfare authorities, unless he is shown to be parentally unfit.[28]

Surrogate Parents

Although natural parents are often legally preferred over strangers to the child, there are circumstances when natural parents might be superseded in their relationship with their child. Under current legal doctrines, natural parents may not be displaced by contractual parents. In the surrogate situation, couples who are unable to have children of their own, for a variety of reasons, make a contract with a woman who is capable of bearing children (the surrogate). Under the terms of the contract, the surrogate agrees to complete a pregnancy and relinquish the child to the husband and wife, usually in return for money. The childless couple might prefer this surrogate method over adoption because the husband can actually donate his sperm to the surrogate mother, thus creating a biological link that is generally not possible through adoption.

The most common problem with surrogate arrangements occurs when the surrogate mother, who carried the child through pregnancy and gave birth to it, decides she does not want to relinquish the child according to the contract. This problem is compounded when the surrogate contract is oral rather than written.[29]

One of the most publicized of these cases is the "Baby M" case.[30] A married couple, William and Elizabeth Stern, chose not to have children together because of certain risks of pregnancy for Elizabeth due to her multiple sclerosis. In return for $10,000, Mary Beth Whitehead agreed to be inseminated by William's sperm, to carry the child to term, and then to deliver the child to the Sterns. The written arrangement apparently held special significance for William, since most of his family had been destroyed in the Holocaust. As his family's only survivor, he wanted to continue his bloodline; adoption would not provide the genetic link he desired.[31]

After the child's birth, Mary Beth relinquished the baby to the Sterns, despite her strong feelings of regret. She later became "deeply disturbed, disconsolate, [and] stricken with unbearable sadness . . . [nor could she] eat, sleep, or concentrate on anything other than her need for her baby."[32] Attempting a compromise, the Sterns surrendered the child to Mary Beth for one week, apparently on the understanding that after this time she would terminate her parental rights. Instead, Mary Beth took the baby from New Jersey and fled to Florida. The Sterns felt that they had no choice but to institute legal proceedings to obtain the child.[33] On a preliminary trial, the Sterns were awarded custody of "Baby M," as the baby girl was called.

The Supreme Court of New Jersey refused to enforce the surrogacy contract, largely because it involved the use of money in connection with an adoption.[34] Under the New Jersey statutory scheme, it is a high misdemeanor for any person to pay or accept money in connection with the adoption of a child.[35] Furthermore, New Jersey provides that a parent can relinquish his or her parental rights only on a voluntary basis, unless there has been a finding of parental unfitness.[36] It was clear that Mary Beth was not willing to relinquish her parental rights over "Baby M," and no court had found her unfit to serve as the child's parent. Last, the court held that surrogacy contracts such as the one between the Sterns and Mary Beth violated public policy.[37]

Having invalidated the surrogacy contract, the court was left with two natural parents, William and Mary Beth, each of whom was married to someone else, and their child, "Baby M." Taking the "best interests of the child" into account, the Court decided that custody should remain with William and Elizabeth Stern.[38] After a new trial to determine her visitation rights, a lower court granted Mary Beth Whitehead liberal unsupervised visitation rights with "Baby M."[39]

Thus, the subject of surrogate parenting raises many concerns about the rights of the respective parties involved, and the legal system has not yet found a resolution satisfactory to all potential interests.

Grandparents

Grandparents occupy a unique family position. Since they are older, they may have wisdom from many years of living. Since they have reared children, they may have practical knowledge concerning children. Thus, the first generation often desires, or may be requested, to help the second generation raise the third generation.

Occasionally, however, the second generation does not want interference from the first generation. In these cases, a child's parent may deny the child's grandparents meaningful opportunities for forming a relationship, and as a result the grandparents might resort to the legal process to obtain visitation rights.

In *Roberts v. Ward*,[40] for example, a young woman gave birth to a child out of wedlock. She lived with her parents for several years, and they assisted in the raising of the child. When the parents objected to the young woman's unrestricted lifestyle,[41] she moved out of their home and refused to allow them any contact with their grandchild.

Recognizing that the "relationships between children and their grand-parents are often particularly special, close, and rewarding,"[42] the Supreme Court of New Hampshire decided that the grandparents had legal standing to sue for visitation rights in relation to their grandchild—even over the mother's objections.[43] The court based its decision on what would be in the best interests of the grandchild, granting the grandparents standing to sue, not on *their own behalf*, but rather on the *grandchild's behalf*.[44] Thus, at least one court has recognized the interest of grandchildren in developing a relationship with their grandparents.

In another case, with facts similar to those in *Roberts v. Ward*, the Supreme Court of Utah held that grandparents may be granted custody of their grandchildren as well as visitation rights.[45]

Nonetheless, the issue of custody is not completely resolved. The District of Columbia, for example, creates a strong presumption favoring a natural parent, over all other persons, for custody over the parents' chil-dren.[46] Under this statute, unless the natural parent is shown by clear and convincing evidence to have abandoned the child or to be unfit to serve as the child's custodian, the grandparent may not be given custody of the child.[47] Only if the clear and convincing standard is met can a grandparent displace a parent as guardian of the child.

Although not always explicit in statutory language, courts appear to favor biological grandparents over strangers to the child. In some cases, grandparents may be favored over a child's parents, but usually only if a high evidentiary burden is met. This balance may serve to protect the unique position of grandparents in the family structure without unduly interfering with the rights of the parents.

Legal Parents and Guardians

A "legal parent" is a person who has no biological relationship to a child but who has established a parent-child relationship under the law. There are two main types of legal parent relationships: adoptive relationships and fos-ter relationships.

Adoption was unknown at common law.[48] The institution of adoption is a result of modern social values, especially the concern that children who are unwanted by one family might be better cared for by another family. In some cases, parents who are unable to care for their child voluntarily agree to place the child with another family. Physicians, ministers, and counselors might assist in these private adoptions. In other circumstances, a state wel-fare agency might seek parents for a child in its care. This is known as an "agency placement."

One line of adoption cases involves women who offer their children up for adoption but then attempt to revoke the process. Courts have not been sympathetic to these mothers.

In one recent case, an unwed teenage girl gave birth to a healthy baby.[49] The girl had difficulty caring for her child, so other family members expressed an interest in adopting the baby, and the teenage mother had given her written consent. However, the adopting family members then changed the baby's name and refused the natural mother visitation rights. After these developments, the girl changed her mind about consenting to the adoption. She immediately tried to revoke her consent to the adoption before any formal decree had been entered.[50] However, the Mississippi Supreme Court held that once the mother gave her written consent, she effectively "abandoned" the child.[51] Absent fraud, duress, or undue influence, a written consent to adoption is irrevocable.[52]

As noted previously,[53] one major source of litigation involving adoptions involves unwed fathers who were unaware that they even had a child until a third party petitioned for adoption. In this context, natural fathers must be accorded constitutional due process protections before their parental rights may be terminated. However, as long as the adoptive parents comply with the state's procedures regarding adoption, the law will generally consider them to be the child's only parents.

For example, the Code of Virginia provides:

Sec. 63.1-233. Legal effects of adoption.—

The natural parents . . . shall, by such final order of adoption, be divested of all legal rights and obligations in respect to the child. . . . Any child adopted *under the provisions of this chapter* shall . . . be, to all intents and purposes, the child of the person or persons so adopting him, and . . . shall be entitled to all the rights and privileges, and subject to all the obligations, of a child of such person or persons born in lawful wedlock.[54]

Under the Virginia statutory scheme, adoptive parents stand in the exact position of persons who are the natural parents of a child, but *only if they follow the procedures outlined in Virginia law*.[55] Other states use similar statutory schemes. Adoptive parents receive the maximum protection afforded to natural parents, provided that they follow the state's procedures regarding adoption. As long as the natural parents are afforded due process protection, the adoptive parents will displace the natural parents' rights.

Another aspect of legal parenting is foster care. Such care has no basis in natural rights as it is wholly based on state statutory schemes. When a natural family is unable to care for a child for a temporary or extended period, and adoption is not desirable or possible, the child may be placed in a foster home.[56] Usually the state department of social services will retain legal custody during the period of foster care, but only because the natural parents agree to give up custody until they can provide proper care. When the natural home environment has stabilized, the child may be returned to his or her natural home.

Two criticisms have been made with respect to foster care. First, it is mostly used for children from low-income families and minorities rather than children from middle-income families.[57] Second, it is common for a child in foster care to be placed with more than one family during the period of foster care,[58] which may seriously disrupt a child's life, especially in his or her formative years.

Because foster care usually results from an agreement between the state and the natural parents, foster parents are not accorded legal rights over the foster child. Even if the child remains in a single foster home for more than a year, the natural parents may regain their child as soon as the obligations in their agreement with the state are met.[59] Should the natural parents prove unfit to regain custody of their child, the foster parents may have preference over other non-family members to adopt the child. Otherwise, the foster parents do not gain any rights which would displace the rights of the natural parents.

The Government as Parent

Usually the American government functions in three parts: First, the legislature makes the laws; second, the courts interpret the laws; and third, an executive (the President or a state's governor) executes the laws. This, however, has not always been the case. In earlier days, courts often made law according to individual cases rather than according to legislative enactments. This body of law was known as "common law," and when the first settlers came to America from England, the new country continued to rely on the common law for its legal foundations. Judges made law by deciding the cases before them.

As the decades passed, however, legislatures assumed a larger role in lawmaking. Legislatures prohibited judges from making laws on a case-by-case basis and passed statutes mandating how cases should be decided. One of the areas which was changed by statute was family law. State legislatures passed many laws regulating the family and gave state regulatory agencies the power to enforce the laws. In most states these agencies are called "Departments of Social Services." Since the common law was replaced by statutory law, however, these departments may only act pursuant to specific legislative grants of power and in accordance with federal and state constitutional requirements. They can no longer act independently on a case-by-case basis.

Constitutional protection of the family against intrusive state laws may be found in the Fourteenth Amendment to the United States Constitution, part of which states:

> No State shall make or enforce any law which shall abridge the privileges or immunities of citizens of the United States; nor shall any State deprive any person of life, liberty, or property, without due process of law; nor deny to any person within its jurisdiction the equal protection of the laws.[60]

There are two key provisions in this language: the Due Process requirement and the Equal Protection Clause.[61]

The Due Process Clause provides that no state can interfere with a family unless proper and fair procedures are used, and even then certain limits apply to the state's exercise of power. For example, the state cannot take a parent's child away without a court hearing, and it must have reason to sever the family ties. Under the Equal Protection Clause, no state can treat people in dissimilar ways if those people are basically in the same situation.

A typical state law is the Illinois Minors Requiring Authoritative Intervention Act, passed in 1987. The law states:

> 803-3. Minor Requiring Authoritative Intervention. Those requiring authoritative intervention include any minor under 18 years of age
> (1) who is
>   (a) absent from home without consent of parent, guardian or custodian, or
>   (b) beyond the control of his or her parent, guardian or custodian, in circumstances which constitute a substantial or immediate danger to the minor's physical safety; and
> (2) who, after being taken into limited custody for [twenty-one days] and offered interim crisis intervention services, where available, refuses to return home after the minor and his or her parent, guardian or custodian cannot agree to an arrangement for an alternative voluntary residential placement or to the continuation of such placement.[62]

This law is ostensibly intended to help families where the parents are unable to control their children. Many of these children are runaways. In a prior time, these children might have been called "delinquents." Today they are called "minors requiring authoritative intervention," or "MRAIs." While it may be no surprise that some parents have difficulty in providing a suitable home environment for their children, the degree of state intervention permitted by this statute appears excessive.

First, a law enforcement officer may take the child into "limited custody" for twenty-one days—without first obtaining a warrant;[63] second, a state agency provides "crisis intervention services" to the child and to the parents;[64] and third, if the child refuses to return home, he or she can be declared a ward of the state or declared to be an emancipated minor, *even if the parents want their child to return home.*[65]

Soon after enactment of this law, a group of parents sued the State of Illinois.[66] Their legal challenge illustrates how the government has come to make important family decisions. The parents alleged that the Act violated their fundamental right to bear and raise their children. Under the Fourteenth Amendment, if a state interferes with a fundamental right, it must justify its intrusion with a compelling interest, and its actions must be narrowly drawn to attain that interest.[67] Otherwise, if the right at issue is not fundamental, then a state must justify its actions only on a rational basis.[68] Thus, the parents were arguing that the Minors Requiring Authoritative Intervention Act violated a fundamental right, so that the court would be required to require the State of Illinois to justify its law with a compelling reason.

The Supreme Court of Illinois agreed that the Act interfered with family relationships in a significant way and that the Act could be justified only by a compelling state interest.[69] However, the court held that the state, indeed, has a compelling interest in protecting the welfare of children,[70] and it found that the Act is narrowly tailored to protect children without interfering unnecessarily with parental authority.[71]

For those children who are genuinely abused or neglected, and for those children who refuse to submit to the authority of their parents, these authoritative intervention statutes may protect children, as the court held. However, it is equally clear that these laws offer a way for some children to escape parental requirements rather than comply with them. The dissenter to the court's opinion wrote:

> The provisions at issue thus empower a minor to choose to remain outside the home, in the custody of the State, for three weeks, and grant to the minor a veto over any request by the parent for his return, regardless of the circumstances presented and whether or not the best interests of the minor would be served by his return home.[72]

Parents hold a fundamental right to raise their children without undue interference by the government, but the government retains a substantial ability to act as parent when natural parents have failed in their duties.[73]

Parental challenges to state interference have been largely unsuccessful. In one situation, the State of Wisconsin took children away from the custody of three families and then charged the parents for the costs of the children's care.[74] A New York case held that the Department of Social Services must show that a child is "abused or neglected" only by the standard of a preponderance of the evidence, over a parent's objection that a stricter evidentiary burden should be used.[75] As a final example, the Supreme Court of Nebraska decided that the Department of Social Services does not have to attempt to reunify a family before seeking to terminate parental rights.[76]

Throughout these proceedings, courts consider primarily the "best interests of the child." Ideally this determination would be used only in situations of equipoise. For example, when a child's parents divorce and each parent is equally able to provide a good home for the child, the "best interests of the child" could be used to determine how custody should be apportioned between the parents. Unfortunately, courts often use the doctrine to grant custody to substitute families, such as foster families, to the disadvantage of a child's natural parents.[77] This results in economic and cultural factors being taken into consideration in deciding child custody and parental rights issues.[78]

EFFECT OF THE CHILD ABUSE PROBLEM ON PARENTAL RIGHTS

In today's society, a major issue affecting parental rights is that of child abuse. This issue presents tremendous difficulty to all persons involved.[79] According to Department of Health and Human Services data, in 1984 there were 19,319 alleged perpetrators of child abuse.[80] Of these, 76 percent were parents of the victims. In 1986, there were 21,744 alleged child abusers. Of these, 78 percent were the victims' parents. To help combat child abuse, many states have imposed reporting duties on non-parents who have substantial dealings with children.[81] Professionals such as physicians, nurses, counselors, and teachers, as well as government officials such as police officers, fire-fighting personnel, and social workers, are required in many states to report suspected incidents of child abuse.[82]

In *R.S. v. State*,[83] a parent challenged Minnesota's Reporting of Maltreatment of Minors Act. Under the Act, local welfare and law enforcement officials were empowered to interview suspected victims of child abuse without notifying the parents beforehand or seeking parental consent.[84] The case involved the question of whether an unconsented interview violated familial privacy when the basis for the interview was an anonymous report and when no perpetrator had been identified. Holding against the parent, the Supreme Court of Minnesota wrote:

> The reasons for interviewing without parental consent when a parent is the alleged abuser are obvious. Children who are abused often have conflicting loyalties. They may lie to protect a parent. They may be afraid to reveal the truth. Their responses may be influenced by an abusive parent. An equally valid rationale supports permitting school interviews when the perpetrator is unknown.[85]

Many good points are made by the court. Children who are abused by their parents may be confused because of conflicting loyalties, and it might be helpful if welfare agencies could determine, in an efficient manner, whether parents are abusing their children. However, it is not clear that secretive interviews[86] are the best method for solving this problem.

The focus shift in American legal culture to the "best interests of the child" has resulted in a wide disarray of parent-child relationships. A child today might have several classes of parents:

(1) Biological parents;
(2) Natural parents;
(3) Stepparents;
(4) Psychological parents;
(5) Adoptive parents;
(6) Foster parents; and
(7) *Parens patriae*, or the state.

The rights of these classes of parents are not equal, and it appears that the state has broad power to interfere when it believes that the child's best interests require state action. As long as the various classes of parents are fighting amongst themselves, they cannot be united to oppose unwarranted state interference.

RIGHTS: A MATTER OF BALANCE

Until this century, the term *parents' rights* was rarely, if ever, used. However, the concept of *parents' duties* was quite commonly used.[87] Parents held such considerable power over their children that observers felt compelled to remind parents of the obligations they owed their children. The early Twentieth Century's Progressive Movement began to restrict parental power. The government began to regulate the number of hours children could work, even if such employment was in the family business. Compulsory education came into existence.[88] As the decades drifted onward, parental power waned. Amidst the reformers' cries of "Children's Rights!" other voices responded: "What about parents' rights?"

The Supreme Court case of *Pierce v. Society of Sisters*[89] stemmed the tide of government intrusion into parental rights. In *Pierce*, the State of Oregon enacted the Compulsory Education Act of 1922. Under the Act, all parents with children between the ages of eight and sixteen were required to send such children to public school, unless the children had completed the eighth grade. Failure to send their children to the public school would result in a criminal misdemeanor for each day of absence.[90] Children were allowed to attend private schools or home schools only if the public school superintendent granted permission, and then the Act required a test to be administered every three months to determine the children's progress.[91]

Justice McReynolds wrote the opinion for the Supreme Court. He clearly acknowledged a state's legitimate role in regulating schools within its borders:

> No question is raised concerning the power of the State reasonably to regulate all schools, to inspect, supervise, and examine them, their teachers and pupils; to require that all children of proper age attend some school, that teachers shall be of good moral character and patriotic disposition, that certain studies plainly essential to good citizenship must be taught, and that nothing be taught which is manifestly inimical to the public welfare.[92]

However, the state's power in this regard is not absolute. Parents hold a liberty to direct, *first*, the upbringing and, *second*, the education of children under their control.[93] Writing that the "child is not the mere creature of the State,"[94] Justice McReynolds held:

> The fundamental theory of liberty upon which all governments in this Union repose excludes any general power of the State to standardize its children by forcing them to accept instruction from public teachers only.[95]

The case of *Pierce v. Society of Sisters* makes clear that there are limits to the state's power to interfere with the ways in which parents raise their children. What is not as clear, however, is where those limits exist. The following discussion will examine these limits.

Introduction to the Right to Privacy

The "right to privacy" is not set forth in the United States Constitution. However, certain other rights suggest privacy concepts. The Third Amendment states:

> No soldier shall, in time of peace, be quartered in any house, without the consent of the owner, nor in time of war, but in a manner to be prescribed by law.[96]

Similarly, the Fourth Amendment protects people against unreasonable interference by governmental officials other than soldiers:

> The right of the people to be secure in their persons, houses, papers, and effects, against unreasonable searches and seizures, shall not be-violated. . . .[97]

The concept of privacy is extended in the Fifth Amendment to a person's words and to his real property:

> No person . . . shall be compelled in any criminal case to be a witness against himself, nor be deprived of life, liberty, or property, without due process of law; nor shall private property be taken for public use without just compensation.[98]

None of these explicit rights by itself provides for the right to privacy. Together, however, the rights form a structure which defines a certain zone of privacy.

This analysis was used by the Supreme Court in 1965 in *Griswold v. Connecticut.*[99] The State of Connecticut prohibited its inhabitants from using contraceptive devices, and it prohibited others from assisting people in the use of contraceptives.[100] Either activity was punishable by fine or imprisonment.[101] The Planned Parenthood League was prosecuted under the Connecticut law for providing services related to contraceptive use. Two of its officers were convicted.[102]

The United States Supreme Court reversed the convictions.[103] The Court described the fundamental right to privacy which it found among various other constitutional rights.[104] But the entire foundation of its opinion rested on the idea that *married persons* have the right to use contraceptives in order to prevent pregnancy:

Would we allow the police to search the sacred precincts of marital bedrooms for telltale signs of the use of contraceptives? The very idea is repulsive to the notions of privacy surrounding the marriage relationship.[105]

If the Court's doctrine ended with this analysis, parental rights would be extremely strong. Within the *marriage* relationship, parents would have tremendous privacy about their child-rearing decisions. However, in 1972 the Court continued developing its doctrine in *Eisenstadt v. Baird*,[106] where it held that *unmarried* persons have a right to use contraceptives.[107] Suddenly the right to privacy had little to do with marriage—it had to do with sexual intercourse.[108] In *Roe v. Wade*,[109] the Supreme Court extended sexual privacy further, to the decision whether to obtain an abortion.[110]

Since the Supreme Court retreated from its position that the right to privacy exists *because of the family relationship*, parental rights largely are dependent on *Pierce v. Society of Sisters* for their foundation. In this regard, parents have a right to direct, *first*, the upbringing and, *second*, the education of their children.[111] In any discussion of the parental right to direct their child's education,[112] the right of parents concerning their children's religious upbringing will be important.

Education

A series of three Supreme Court decisions in the 1920s firmly established the proposition that a parent retains primary control over a child's education.[113] In one case, the State of Nebraska had forbidden the teaching of all languages other than English in the schools. Apparently the law was a result of the anti-foreign sentiment which flourished following World War I. A private school teacher was convicted for teaching German to one of his pupils, but the United States Supreme Court reversed the conviction. According to the Court, parents have a right to engage someone to teach their children as they think appropriate, without interference by the state.

This doctrine was further strengthened in *Pierce v. Society of Sisters*,[114] discussed above, which held that a state cannot prohibit all education outside of the public schools.[115] Finally, the Supreme Court held in *Farrington v. Tokushige*[116] that parents have a liberty interest in choosing their children's teachers, curriculum, and textbooks without unreasonable interference by the state.

Together these cases guarantee that parents have certain rights with respect to their children's education. While state governments have an interest in the proper education of children within their borders,[117] parents are primarily responsible for this education. The state may not unreasonably interfere with this parental right.

Religious Upbringing

Contests over a child's religious upbringing arise most frequently in the context of child custody battles. When two people who were once married obtain a divorce, they must decide who should have custody over any children produced by the marriage. Usually one parent will obtain custody, while the other parent receives visitation rights.[118] However, the two parents may often dispute whether the other is obeying the custody arrangement. One such area of dispute will be the religious upbringing of the child, especially when the two parents do not share the same religious faith.

According to the courts, the determination of a child's religious upbringing is generally left to the custodial parent.[119] This means that, under normal circumstances, if the custodial parent refuses to train a child in a certain religion, the non-custodial parent cannot sue to amend the custody agreement simply on those grounds.[120] These decisions are especially important when the custodial parent desires to send the child to a religious school and the non-custodial parent disagrees with the decision.[121] However, the custodial parent can agree in the custody arrangement to give the non-custodial parent some control in the child's religious upbringing.[122]

The difficulty usually arises while the children are visiting with the non-custodial parent who disagrees with the custodial parent's decision regarding their children's religious upbringing. The non-custodial parent may use the visitation time to express his different religious views. In *Pardue v. Pardue*,[123] a Louisiana court held that the custodial parent has a right to demand that her decisions about the child's religious upbringing be maintained while the child is visiting with the non-custodial parent.[124]

In fact, according to the Louisiana court the non-custodial parent's visitation rights can be conditioned on his compliance with the custodial parent's decisions.[125]

Facing a similar situation, a New York appellate court ruled that a non-custodial parent may be ordered not to teach his children about his religion when the custodial parent has decided to raise the children in a different religion.[126]

It should be noted that not all courts agree that the non-custodial parent may be wholly prohibited from teaching the children about his religion. The Massachusetts Supreme Court, for example, has held that the custodial parent must *prove* that the different religious teachings by the non-custodial parent are harmful to the children in order to prohibit such teachings.[127] Ordinarily, however, a child's religious upbringing is wholly within the discretion of the custodial parent.

Modern Medicine

Many are familiar with the following scene: Two parents come to the emergency room at a local hospital with their child, who appears to be gravely ill. Doctors and nurses quickly perform various diagnostic tests. A blood analysis offers a life-threatening conclusion: leukemia. The doctors will need to examine the bone marrow to be certain of the diagnosis, and for this particular child a blood transfusion is required immediately. A nurse approaches the parents for written permission—but the parents refuse to give their consent. They belong to a religious sect which teaches that the act of receiving blood products will prevent an individual from resurrection and everlasting life after death.[128]

This scene is not commonplace, but its incidence is rising. Numerous groups or individuals believe that aspects of modern medical treatment preclude spiritual salvation. Increasing numbers of Christians also are refusing aspects of modern medical treatment. Today courts seem willing to allow adult believers to refuse medical treatment, even to the point of death.[129] The difficulty arises when parents who adhere to these religious beliefs wish to prevent medical treatment for their children. According to these parents, medical treatment places their child's eternal salvation in jeopardy; but without the procedure death certainly will result.[130]

When the welfare of a child is at stake, courts are not willing to allow parents to refuse medical treatment for their children, even if the parents' religious beliefs preclude such treatment. In fact, parents have been convicted of reckless homicide,[131] first-degree manslaughter,[132] and involuntary manslaughter[133] for failing to obtain necessary medical treatment for their children. Parents also may be convicted of child abuse.[134] These cases demonstrate that the courts do not agree that a parent's religious convictions can shield a child from interference by the state.[135]

The rule appears to be that the state has a compelling interest in preserving a child's life, but, without some showing of harm, the state may not interfere with parental discretion between subjective treatments.[136]

When the State Comes Marching In

The outer limits of the conflict between modern medicine and parental rights are demonstrated by the 1905 Supreme Court case *Jacobson v. Massachusetts*.[137] According to the case, by the end of February 1902, the City of Cambridge, Massachusetts, was experiencing serious outbreaks of smallpox. Under the laws of Massachusetts, Cambridge was empowered to force a vaccination upon all the inhabitants of the city. Failure to comply with the vaccination carried criminal penalties. At the time, eleven states also enforced compulsory vaccination laws.[138]

Mr. Jacobson was convicted under the Massachusetts law when he refused to be vaccinated and when he refused to allow his son to be vaccinated. He had received a smallpox vaccination earlier in his life and had become extremely ill; his son similarly became ill when he was vaccinated. Jacobson believed that both he and his son would again become ill if vaccinated under the Cambridge program.[139]

The Supreme Court characterized the issue as follows: "Was defendant exempted from the operation of the statute simply because of his dread of the same evil results experienced by him when [he was] a child and had observed in the cases of his son and other children?"[140] Because the state had decided that the public's health was in peril, the Court upheld Jacobson's conviction for refusing to be vaccinated.[141] Justice Harlan wrote the opinion for the Court:

We are not prepared to hold that a minority, residing or remaining in any city or town where smallpox is prevalent . . . may thus defy the will of its constituted authorities, acting in good faith for all, under the legislative sanction of the State. If such be the privilege of a minority then a like privilege would belong to each individual of the community, and the spectacle would be presented of the welfare and safety of an entire population being subordinated to the notions of a single individual. . . .[142]

In order to protect children from harm, states have even taken custody of the child away from the parent while medical treatment is being provided.[143] As one court noted, although "parents may be free to become martyrs themselves, they are not free, under identical circumstances, to make martyrs of their children."[144]

CONCLUSION

Although parents often do not retain the same degree of control over their children that parents held in previous generations, it is clear that they nevertheless hold important rights. Parents may make choices about the way they should train and raise children. It is only when these parental decisions approach the bound of unreasonableness that the state governments will interfere. One clear boundary exists when the child's welfare is in danger, such as when medical treatment is necessary. But within the range of decisions where a child's welfare is not in peril, parents are free to use their best judgment about their children.

PART FOUR

Constitutional Issues

[A] State's interest in universal education, however highly we rank it, is not totally free from a balancing process when it impinges on fundamental rights and interests, such as those specifically protected by the Free Exercise Clause of the First Amendment, and the traditional interest of parents with respect to the religious upbringing of their children.

Supreme Court Chief Justice
Warren Burger
Wisconsin v. Yoder (1972)

12

Free Exercise of Religion

The First Amendment provides that "Congress shall make no law respecting religion, or prohibiting the free exercise thereof."[1] Thus, "[t]he door of the Free Exercise Clause stands tightly closed against any governmental regulation of religious beliefs as such."[2] For example, the Supreme Court has held that "Government may neither compel affirmation of a repugnant belief . . . nor penalize or discriminate against individuals or groups because they hold religious views abhorrent to the authorities."[3]

The Free Exercise Clause, however, "does not prevent the government from regulating behavior associated with religious beliefs."[4] In *Sherbert v. Verner*,[5] the United States Supreme Court "rejected challenges under the Free Exercise Clause to governmental regulation of certain overt acts prompted by religious beliefs or principles, for 'even when the action is in accord with one's religious convictions, [it] is not totally free from legislative restrictions.'"[6]

This has been also true in the area of education. "Free exercise claims in the context of educational requirements have a long history."[7] The claims of religious persons in connection with education, however, often conflict with the state's recognized interest in educating America's youth.[8] The area of home education represents one such clash between the state's interest in education and the free exercise rights of parents and their children.

This constitutional struggle raises two free exercise issues. First, courts must consider whether the Free Exercise Clause protects the parental right to home educate.[9] Second, if such a right exists, courts then must consider to what extent the government can infringe upon this exercise of religious beliefs.[10] Until recently it would have been difficult for the state to constitutionally encroach upon free exercise rights, but with its 1990 decision *Employment Division v. Smith*,[11] the Court has made it easier for the state to regulate the religious lives of Americans under the guise of a "neutral, generally applicable law."[12]

This chapter examines free exercise jurisprudence, first discussing the traditional test the Supreme Court has used to determine whether the state has violated the Free Exercise Clause, and then explaining the framework the Court is currently using. Whether the right to home school is constitutionally protected and how state regulations of home education will withstand judicial scrutiny will then be examined. Finally, litigation strategies for approaching free exercise challenges will be proposed.

FREE EXERCISE JURISPRUDENCE
The Traditional Framework

As in other areas of constitutional law,[13] the U.S. Supreme Court has established a zone of "no interference" in free exercise jurisprudence. Any governmental effort to regulate or trample upon an individual's religious *beliefs or opinions* is constitutionally intolerable.[14] An attempt to restrict or encroach upon *acts or practices* motivated by these religious beliefs is not always so constitutionally intolerable; in some cases, "even when the action is in accord with one's religious convictions, [it] is not totally free from legislative restrictions."[15]

Just as the individual's right to act upon his religious beliefs is not absolute, there are limitations on the state's ability to infringe upon the right to free exercise of religion. Consequently, the key issue in free exercise cases focuses on the point at which the state may interfere with religious practices. To answer this question, the Supreme Court adapted its compelling state interest test to free exercise claims.

This analysis consists of three separate inquiries. The court first must consider whether the state action infringes upon the individual's free exercise rights.[16] Courts invariably have found the presence of a burden if the governmental act places the individual between Scylla and Charybdis,[17] meaning that the state coerces the individual "to choose between following the precepts of her religion"[18] and so forego some statutory benefit, and "abandoning one of the precepts of her religion"[19] in order to comply with the law.

If the state activity produces an encroachment on the individual's religious rights, the state must proffer a compelling state interest to justify the burden on free exercise.[20] "When clear and present danger of riot, disorder, interference with traffic upon the public streets, or other immediate threat to public safety, peace, or order, appears," the Court has found a clear compelling state interest.[21] If the conduct does not reach this level, the Court has established a high barrier for the state to surmount to prove a compelling state interest: "[N]o showing merely of a rational relationship to some colorable state interest [will] suffice; in this highly sensitive constitutional area, '[o]nly the gravest abuses, endangering paramount interests, give occasion for permissible limitation.'"[22]

Finally, if the state proves it possesses such an interest, the court must consider whether accommodating the individual "'will unduly interfere with fulfillment of the governmental interest.'"[23] In other words, "the government must accommodate a legitimate free exercise claim unless pursuing an especially important interest by narrowly tailored means."[24] If the state cannot achieve this goal without impairing its compelling interest, "the Free Exercise Clause does not require the State to accommodate . . . religiously motivated conduct."[25]

The seminal case *Sherbert v. Verner*[26] is a good example of the Court's application of the compelling state interest analysis. The plaintiff in *Sherbert*, a member of the Seventh-Day Adventist Church, refused to work on Saturday, her denomination's Sabbath.[27] Her employer discharged her because of her religious conviction.[28] Unable to find another job because of her religious beliefs, the plaintiff filed a claim for unemployment compensation benefits.[29] The South Carolina Employment Security Commission, however, denied her claim, maintaining that her "restriction upon her availability for Saturday work brought her within the provision disqualifying for benefits insured workers who fail without good cause, to accept 'suitable work when offered . . . by the employment office or the employer. . . .'"[30] The state supreme court upheld its finding, rejecting any claims that the denial of benefits violated any constitutional principles.[31]

Writing for the United States Supreme Court, Justice Brennan reversed the South Carolina Supreme Court's decision, employing the compelling state interest test. First, the Court found that disqualifying the plaintiff from receiving benefits infringed upon the free exercise of her religious beliefs. Justice Brennan stated:

> The ruling forces her to choose between following the precepts of her religion and forfeiting benefits, on the one hand, and abandoning one of the precepts of her religion in order to accept work, on the other hand. Governmental imposition of such a choice puts the same kind of burden upon the free exercise of religion as would a fine imposed against [the plaintiff] for her Saturday worship.[32]

Second, the Court addressed whether the state had proved a compelling state interest in overriding the plaintiff's religious beliefs. Initially, the Court removed the plaintiff's conduct from the "automatic" compelling state interest category because the conduct did not substantially threaten "public safety, peace or order."[33] The Court then turned to the interests that the state maintained justified the encroachment: 1. "a possibility that the filing of fraudulent claims by unscrupulous claimants feigning religious objections to Saturday work might . . . dilute the unemployment compensation fund";[34] and 2. the finding that such deceptive filing practices might "also hinder the scheduling by employers of necessary Saturday work."[35] The Court rejected both contentions, first finding that the state had failed to make such argument at the state supreme court level. In addition, despite the failure to raise such an issue, according to the Court:

[T]here is no proof whatever to warrant such fears of malingering or deceit as those which the [state] now advance[s]. Even if consideration of such evidence is not foreclosed by the prohibition against judicial inquiry into the truth or falsity of religious beliefs . . . it is highly doubtful whether such evidence would be sufficient to warrant a substantial infringement of religious liberties.[36]

Despite some criticism of the use of compelling state interest in the free exercise context,[37] the Court consistently applied it to such cases[38] until the 1990 term when it unequivocally rejected the strict scrutiny analysis in free exercise cases.[39]

In that case, *Employment Division, Department of Human Resources v. Smith*,[40] the Court addressed the issue of:

[W]hether the Free Exercise Clause of the First Amendment permits the State of Oregon to include religiously inspired peyote use within the reach of its general criminal prohibition on use of that drug, and thus permits the State to deny unemployment benefits to persons dismissed from their jobs because of such religiously inspired use.[41]

In *Smith*, the plaintiffs were discharged from their jobs because they used peyote "for sacramental purposes" at an off-duty service of the Native American Church, of which both were members.[42] Ingesting peyote constituted a violation of Oregon drug law, which at the time only provided an exemption for medical purposes.[43] The plaintiffs applied for unemployment benefits, but the unemployment benefits commission denied compensation because "they had been discharged for work-related 'misconduct.'"[44]

The Supreme Court held that the failure to exempt the use of peyote for sacramental purposes did not amount to a constitutional violation.[45] Justice Scalia, writing for the Court,[46] began his analysis by acknowledging the competing views for construing the Free Exercise Clause. One method of interpretation contends that "'prohibiting the free exercise [of religion]' includes requiring any individual to observe a generally applicable law that requires (or forbids) the performance of an act that his religious belief forbids (or requires)."[47] The second and, according to the Court, the preferred reading construes the text "to say that if prohibiting the exercise of religion . . . is not the object of the [law] but merely the incidental effect of a generally applicable and otherwise valid provision, the First Amendment has not been offended."[48]

The Court maintained that it has "never held that an individual's religious beliefs excuse him from compliance with an otherwise valid law prohibiting conduct that the State is free to regulate."[49] The Supreme Court thus concluded that "the right of free exercise does not relieve an individual of the obligation to comply with a 'valid and neutral law of general applicability on the ground that the law proscribes (or prescribes) conduct that his religion prescribes (or proscribes)."[50]

The Court, furthermore, rejected the use of the compelling state interest test in the free exercise context,[51] finding that:

> "[W]e are a cosmopolitan nation made up of people of almost every conceivable religious preference," . . . and precisely because we value and protect that religious divergence, we cannot afford the luxury of deeming *presumptively invalid*, as applied to the religious objector, every regulation of conduct that does not protect an interest of the highest order.[52]

Two situations, however, appear to fall outside the scope of *Smith*. The Court implicitly created an exception calling for the compelling state interest test:[53] namely, if a plaintiff challenges a "neutral, generally applicable law" based, not on the Free Exercise Clause alone, but on "the Free Exercise Clause in conjunction with other constitutional protections, such as freedom of speech, and of the press."[54] This is the "hybrid" approach.

In addition, the second exception provides that "where the State has in place a system of individual exemptions, it may not refuse to extend that system to cases of 'religious hardship' without compelling reason."[55]

Thus, with one decision the Supreme Court rewrote its free exercise jurisprudence. If an individual claims that he or she deserves an exemption from a "neutral, generally applicable statute," the exemption will be denied without any balancing of the interests involved unless the individual can satisfy two limited exceptions.

FREE EXERCISE CHALLENGES TO HOME SCHOOL LAWS

Two main challenges under the Free Exercise Clause exist for home educators: 1) does the Free Exercise Clause protect home schooling when pursued because of sincerely held religious beliefs?;[56] and 2) is governmental regulation of home schools impermissible?

The Right to Pursue an Education at Home— Is It Constitutionally Protected?

The Court's holding in *Smith* will no doubt be applied to the first challenge, whether home schooling because of religious beliefs is a constitutional right. A compulsory attendance statute constitutes a "neutral, generally applicable law."[57] Unless the parents can demonstrate that the statute was enacted solely to preclude home education, the fact that a statute prohibits home schooling without exemptions, following the Supreme Court's logic, merely reflects an incidental burden on the parents' exercise of their religious beliefs and does not violate the Free Exercise Clause.[58]

The hybrid claim exception, however, should provide an escape from *Smith*.

Sincerely Held Religious Beliefs

First, parents must establish that their desire to educate their children at home is based on sincerely held religious beliefs and that the state action burdens the exercise of those beliefs.[59] In evaluating religious beliefs, the court's inquiry is limited. It must decide only whether the beliefs are actually religious, and whether they are sincerely held;[60] the court cannot question or reject beliefs because they seem "incomprehensible."[61] Thus, "to have the protection of the Religion Clauses, the claims must be rooted in religious belief,"[62] and not in secular or philosophical beliefs.[63] The court also must consider the sincerity of the belief, meaning the belief must be "based upon a power or being, or upon faith to which all else . . . is ultimately dependent . . . [and] occupies in the life of its possessor a place parallel to that filled by . . . God."[64] Finally, parents must demonstrate that they possess these sincerely held religious beliefs. The Supreme Court has rejected the requirement that a tenet, church doctrine, or denomination supports the belief in question:

> Undoubtedly, membership in an organized religious denomination, especially one with a specific tenet forbidding [or prescribing the alleged action], would simplify the problem of identifying sincerely held religious beliefs, but we reject the notion that to claim the protection of the Free Exercise Clause, one must be responding to the commands of a particular religious organization.[65]

In addition, parents need not show that other members of their religious sect share their beliefs:

> [T]he guarantee of free exercise is not limited to beliefs which are shared by all of the members of a religious sect. Particularly in this sensitive area, it is not within the judicial function and judicial competence to inquire [who] more correctly perceived the commands of their common faith. Courts are not arbiters of scriptural interpretation.[66]

In summary, to prevail under *Smith* as it now stands, parents must show a sincerely held religious belief that they are required to home school their children and must demonstrate that the state has burdened the exercise of those beliefs.

Religious Claim Coupled with Another Constitutional Claim

Second, the parents must challenge the statute on at least two grounds—a free exercise claim in conjunction with another constitutional claim. In the home school situation, the best combination may be a free exercise challenge along with a parental rights claim.[67] The *Smith* Court explicitly recognized this winning combination, favorably citing *Wisconsin v. Yoder*[68] as an example of where the Court has required states to accommodate religious beliefs by exempting individuals from "neutral, generally applicable laws." One federal appellate court has subsequently indicated that such a hybrid claim would remove a challenge from the *Smith* framework.[69]

A winning combination does not necessarily amount to a victory in court; rather, it means victory in the sense that the claim remains subject to the compelling state interest test and not to the *Smith* rule. Thus, if the compulsory attendance law affects the pursuit of religious education at home and if the plaintiff alleges a hybrid claim, the court should engage in a strict scrutiny analysis. This means, as previously discussed, that the state must prove a compelling state interest and that, if such an interest is demonstrated, the state must be able to accommodate an individual's religious beliefs without unduly comprising that interest.[70]

Although it was decided nearly twenty years prior to the *Smith* decision, *Yoder* best exemplifies the Court's treatment of the hybrid claim of religious-plus-parental rights. *Yoder* involved the clash between the state's interest in educating children until they reach the age of sixteen years and the belief of the Amish religious order that Amish children should not attend organized school beyond the eighth grade.

The state charged three parents with violation of Wisconsin's compulsory state attendance laws because they had not enrolled their teenage children in any public or private school or complied with any other recognized exception to the attendance statute.[71] The parents were tried and convicted although they maintained that "their children's attendance at high school, public or private, was contrary to the Amish religion and way of life. They believed that by sending their children to high school, they would not only expose themselves to the danger of the censure of the church community, but . . . also endanger their own salvation and that of their children."[72] The Wisconsin Supreme Court invalidated their conviction, and the state appealed.[73]

While the state has an interest in educating its children, according to the Court:

> [Such concern] is not totally free from a balancing process when it impinges on fundamental rights and interests, such as those specifically protected by the Free Exercise Clause of the First Amendment, and the traditional interest of parents with respect to the religious upbringing of their children so long as they, in the words of *Pierce*, "prepare [them] for additional obligations."[74]

Thus, the Supreme Court reasoned that the state could compel attendance beyond the eighth grade if "it appear[ed] either that the State does not deny the free exercise of religious belief by its requirement, or that there is a state interest of sufficient magnitude to override the interest claiming protection under the Free Exercise Clause."[75]

First, the Court evaluated the quality of the Amish religious claims. After engaging in an in-depth analysis of the Amish tradition, the Court concluded:

[The] Amish objection to formal education beyond the eighth grade is firmly grounded in [its] central religious concepts. They object to the high school, and higher education generally, because the values they teach are in marked variance with Amish values and the Amish way of life; they view secondary school education as an impermissible exposure of their children to a "worldly" influence in conflict with their beliefs.[76]

Thus, "in the Amish belief higher learning tends to develop values they reject as influences that alienate man from God."[77] The Court, however, was "careful to determine whether the Amish religious faith and their mode of life are, as they claim, inseparable and interdependent."[78] The Court stated that "[a] way of life, however virtuous and admirable, may not be interposed as a barrier to reasonable state regulation of education if it is based on purely secular considerations; to have the protection of the Religion Clauses, the claims must be rooted in religious belief."[79] After examining the record, the Court found ample evidence to support "the claim that the traditional way of life of the Amish is not merely a matter of personal preference, but one of deep religious conviction, shared by an organized group, and intimately related to daily living."[80]

The Court determined that the compulsory attendance law clearly and unequivocally interfered with the exercise of the Amish's religious beliefs and pointed to the classic Hobson's choice the Amish faced: comply with the law and compromise their religious beliefs, or violate the statute and follow their religious tenets.[81]

The Court then considered the quality of the state's interest in universal compulsory education. The state argued that this interest "is so great that it is paramount to the undisputed claims of [the Amish parents],"[82] an argument that the Court rejected. While the Court recognized that the state has an interest in educating its youth to prepare them to be effective citizens and to function independently in society, it found that "an additional one or two years of formal high school for Amish children in place of their long-established program of informal vocational education would do little to serve those interests."[83] The Court recognized that the Amish system of education produces hard-working and self-reliant citizens; it prepares its youth for life as Amish adults which does not require advanced book learning.[84]

The Court also rejected the proposition that leaving school early would fail to prepare the Amish to be effective citizens, pointing to the fact that compulsory education is a recent development in history and that the democratic process worked before the advent of such an educational system.[85]

The successful arguments in Yoder should be equally applicable to the home school situation.[86] While the religious beliefs shared by individual parents wishing to home school their children may not require home education or may not have the historical or traditional character of the Amish, there are other aspects of the Court's reasoning that support finding a constitutional right to home school one's children.

Thus, home school litigants should consider focusing on the failure of the public schools and many private schools to teach the type of values they wish to instill in their children, pointing to the teaching of secularism, relativism, and materialism—principles contrary to most religious tenets.[87]

The state may argue that home schooling fails to prepare individuals to function in modern society and in a democracy; however, such contentions can be countered, just as the Amish litigants did in *Yoder*.[88]

STATE ATTEMPTS TO REGULATE HOME SCHOOLS: WHEN DO THESE REGULATIONS ENCROACH UPON THE RIGHT TO FREE EXERCISE?

States "which provide for home instruction generally require that parents adhere to one or more criteria in order to insure that acceptable standards are being maintained."[89] Usually such statutes specify:

(1) the qualifications of the home instructor; (2) the curriculum or course of study which is to be taught; (3) the amount of time to be spent in instruction each day; (4) the number of days the child must be taught during the year; (5) the standardized tests the child must take to determine his or her progress; and (6) the reports the parents must periodically submit to school officials to verify compliance with the law.[90]

Although "there is no doubt as to the power of a State, having a high responsibility for education of its citizens, to impose reasonable regulations for the control and duration of basic education,"[91] such a responsibility "is by no means absolute to the exclusion or subordination of all other interests."[92]

The question then becomes to what degree, if any, the state may regulate the home school. Where a "neutral, generally applicable law" is at issue, the *Smith* framework may be relevant; however, there may be two avenues to avoid this unfavorable holding.

First, in situations where the statute is applicable only to home educators, home school advocates could argue that the law is neither neutral nor generally applicable—the conditions triggering the *Smith* analysis.[93] It could be argued that the law is not designed to address a general social concern, but rather to encroach upon the ability of parents to home school their children.[94]

Second, parents should be able to establish the hybrid claim of religion-plus-parental rights, the exception to the *Smith* holding.[95]

In either case, the court should use the compelling state interest test. State courts, in general, have found that the state's interest in education, although it may burden the exercise of religious beliefs, is compelling, and that the regulations it uses are the least restrictive means available for accomplishing their goal.[96] Consequently, because binding precedent in federal courts is sparse,[97] home school litigants may wish to consider a federal forum to adjudicate their claims.[98]

In state or federal court, there appear to be two keys to winning such a case. The vast majority of courts has recognized that the state has an interest in regulating home education in furtherance of its obligation to educate its youth.[99] Litigants could argue that this interest is not compelling, but this is a more difficult argument.[100] There is ample precedent supporting the proposition that while parents have the right to educate their children outside the public school environment, "they have no constitutional right to provide their children with [such an education] unfettered by reasonable government regulation."[101] Because of the challenging nature of arguing that the state does not possess a compelling state interest, litigants should consider focusing attention on the other components of the free exercise/strict scrutiny analysis. Although in many cases the issue of the sincerity of the parents' religious beliefs and the burden the state regulations impose on them is undisputed,[102] the litigation often will turn on whether the state has burdened the exercise of religious beliefs or whether the state is using the least restrictive means available to regulate home schools.

First, home school advocates should consider challenging the existing regulations as an impermissible burden on their right to exercise their religious beliefs. The religious beliefs must be sincere and held by parents but not necessarily by other members of their denomination.[103] With respect to the burden, parents have argued that any approval requirement or any other method which constitutes the state's authority to approve or disapprove the home school program "would be an act of apostasy."[104] The burden, however, does not have to be direct or to be inherently conflicting with the religious beliefs:

> An indirect burden upon one's religious beliefs occurs when compliance with a challenged law or regulation is not inherently inconsistent with those beliefs, but the law or regulation operates so as to make more practically difficult the practice of those religious beliefs. . . . Nevertheless, "[i]f the purpose or effect of a law is to impede the observance of one or all religions or is to discriminate invidiously between religions, that law is constitutionally invalid even though the burden may be characterized as being only indirect."[105]

The parents must establish that the regulations "interfere with [the] right to pursue a religious education in the home."[106]

Second, the litigants must show that the state has neglected to meet its burden of proving that the regulation is the least restrictive means available for furthering its interest in education.[107] This is a balancing test; if the state cannot accommodate the individual's interest without impairing its own substantial interest, the state's claim will override. For example, one could argue that the teaching certification requirement imposed by many states is not the least restrictive way of ensuring that children receive a proper education.

Consider this hypothetical situation. A college professor with a doctorate in history wants to home educate his children. Under some state statutes, he would be unable to do so.[108] Although he is well-educated and entrusted with the education of college students, the state prohibits him from teaching his own children at home.[109] When litigating this issue, the professor would offer other viable alternatives to the state regulation.[110] Certainly the home school proponent also could argue that the only reasonable alternative is no regulation.[111]

LITIGATION STRATEGIES: A SUMMARY

First, it is important for litigants using the Free Exercise Clause as the basis of their claims to establish that the decision to home educate their children is firmly rooted in sincerely held religious beliefs.[112] Parents, although it may be helpful, need not demonstrate that this belief is shared by other members of one's religious sect or that the belief itself directly compels home education. Rather, the parents may argue that they believe they have a duty to inculcate in their children certain religious values and that teachings—such as materialism, secular humanism, and relativism[113]—in public schools and in many private schools conflict with these values. It is important that litigants argue that this interest is more compelling than the interest alleged by the state.

Litigants should counter claims that home educated children are not "properly educated." Some courts have implied that home schooling does not qualify as an educational opportunity.[114] Parents should direct the court's attention to the teaching of secular subjects in addition to religious matters and to children's success on standardized tests to overcome this false assumption.[115]

Second, in order to avoid the unfavorable results foreshadowed by the *Smith* holding, litigants must challenge any burdens on home schooling on at least two fronts. As previously discussed,[116] a free exercise claim in conjunction with a parental rights challenge should provide the requisite tandem to trigger the strict scrutiny analysis.[117] In addition, home school advocates also should consider challenging the state's action based on the Establishment Clause.[118] The *Smith* Court explicitly objected to a freestanding Free Exercise claim;[119] it did not state that a litigant could not proffer two challenges based on the two religion clauses.

Finally, because of the *Smith* decision and other Supreme Court decisions unfavorable to individual liberties, a litigation trend is quickly emerging: the state constitutional challenge. Because state constitutional "First Amendment/religious liberties" language frequently differs from the federal Constitution, and because states may grant more rights under their constitutions than the federal courts grant under the United States Constitution, many litigants are relying on this avenue to provide relief to their clients.[120] As Justice Brennan stated:

[S]tate courts cannot rest when they have afforded their citizens the full protections of the federal Constitution. State constitutions, too, are a font of individual liberties, their protections often extending beyond those required by the Supreme Court's interpretation of federal law. The legal revolution which has brought federal law to the fore must not be allowed to inhibit the independent protective force of state law—for without it, the full realization of our liberties cannot be guaranteed.[121]

More importantly, federal courts, including the Supreme Court, cannot reverse state court decisions construing state constitutions.[122]

CONCLUSION

Litigating a free exercise claim is a difficult and challenging task, particularly in the area of home schools. Because of the recognized state interest in education, litigants must make it difficult, if not impossible, for the state to prove that its educational interest is paramount to the right to home educate one's child without unconstitutional governmental interference.

13

Freedom of Speech and Formation of Belief

Although many parents who opt to educate their children at home do so for religious reasons, other parents who choose the home school option do so because they have secular concerns about state-sponsored or state-regulated education. These reservations often include misgivings about the stifling effect of structure and organization in the classroom, instruction in subjects such as sex education, or the transmission of certain values such as competitiveness and worldly success that may be emphasized in traditional school environments.

Parents are not alone in realizing the value of home education. Some experts within the field of education itself have increasingly extolled the virtues of home education on entirely secular grounds.[1] One noted author in the field of education has concluded:

> [E]ven the most attentive, perceptive, and thoughtful classroom teachers could never elicit from their students the amount and intensity of feedback that home-schooling parents typically get from their children, because parents know and understand their children so much better.[2]

In *The Third Wave*, Alvin Toffler also advocates an increase in the number of students educated at home:

> Families should be encouraged to take a larger—not smaller—role in the education of the young. Parents willing to teach their own children at home should be aided by the schools, not regarded as freaks or lawbreakers.[3]

The success of the majority of home educators is beyond dispute.[4] For example, the State of Alaska has been giving standardized tests to its home-educated children for years, and they have consistently scored above the national average.[5] This success is representative of students across the country. In a 1982 article in the Teachers College Record of Columbia University, Dr. Raymond Moore cited a study which found that children across the country who are educated at home usually scored well above the national average on standardized tests.[6]

In spite of this success, however, many parents who are not motivated by religious concerns have sought to exercise their rights as parents and have found their decisions hindered by compulsory education laws.[7] This chapter will discuss a constitutional defense for home schooling that is grounded in the Free Speech Clause of the First Amendment of the Constitution.[8]

COMPULSORY PUBLIC EDUCATION AS A VIOLATION OF THE FIRST AMENDMENT

The Free Speech Clause

In spite of the fact that non-religious parents would not be expected successfully to raise a constitutional defense based upon the Free Exercise Clause, such parents may still have an available constitutional defense based upon the Free Speech Clause.[9]

The Free Speech Clause is found in the First Amendment of the Constitution, which is a part of the Bill of Rights. The Bill of Rights was adopted by its framers in order to enumerate the rights of the people upon which the government may not intrude.[10]

There are two major theories which attempt to explain the motivation of the framers with respect to the constitutional protection of free speech.[11] The first theory highlights the role of freedom of expression in the promotion of self-government and as "the linchpin of constitutional democracy."[12] Interpreted as a whole, the Free Speech Clause protects the dissemination of ideas, whether those ideas are political, religious or moral. To this end, the Free Speech Clause protects the right to proselytize, to meet and discuss ideas with others, to popularize ideas through literature, and to attempt to implement ideas through legislative means.[13]

The motivation behind the protection of ideas may be found in the close relationship between the freedom of expression and self-government. Democracies are premised upon the hope that people, if exposed to a wide variety of ideas and beliefs, will analyze the strengths and weaknesses of each argument and consequently attempt to implement the wisest plan of action. The Free Speech Clause, therefore, promotes the existence of a "marketplace of ideas" which leads to a successful democracy.[14] As one theorist argues:

> When men govern themselves, it is they—and no one else—who must pass judgement upon wisdom and unfairness and danger. And that

means that unwise ideas must have a hearing as well as wise ones, unfair as well as fair, dangerous as well as safe, un-American as well as American. Just so far as the citizens who are to decide an issue are denied acquaintance with information or opinion or doubt or disbelief or criticism which is relevant to that issue, just so far the result must be considered ill-considered, ill-balanced planning for the general good. *It is that mutilation of the thinking process of the community against which the First Amendment to the Constitution is directed.*[15]

The United States Supreme Court has also recognized the crucial role of the Free Speech Clause of the First Amendment in a democratic society. As Justice William Brennan stated:

The Nation's future depends upon leaders trained through wide exposure to that robust exchange of ideas which discovers truth "out of a multitude of tongues, [rather] than through any kind of authoritative selection."[16]

Thus, according to this theory, the government has not only a responsibility to protect the freedom of speech, but an interest in promoting the expression of a variety of viewpoints in order to ensure wise decision-making by its electorate.

A second theory holds that the constitutional protection of free speech is ultimately an attempt to protect the growth of the individual.[17] According to this theory, individuals are on a never-ending quest for self-realization, and this quest begins with the development of the mind. The government protects the freedom of expression, therefore, in order to facilitate the ideological exchanges that ultimately push one's intellect toward maturity.

The development of the mind, in turn, leads to the development of personality or character. As people begin to form beliefs and hold opinions, they begin to interact with their peers in a manner that is uniquely their own. This presentation of *persona* is a necessary element of self-realization.[18] As one constitutional authority recognizes:

The freedom to have an impact on others—to make the statement implicit in a public identity—is central to any adequate conception of the self.[19]

An individual must, therefore, have the right to "the development of his own personality and the realization of his own potential free from government interference" if he or she is ever to achieve self-realization.[20] Any governmental action that inhibits the formation or expression of ideas necessarily prevents the individual from realizing his or her unique potential.

Thus, one theory stresses the contribution of free expression to the maintenance of the state, and the other theory stresses the benefits that free expression confers upon the individual.

The Freedom of Belief

Upon examination of the philosophical underpinnings of the freedom of expression, it becomes clear that one of the rights protected by the Free Speech Clause is the right to hold and express beliefs that are *not held by the state or the majority of its citizens.* Although this right is not expressly articulated in the Free Speech Clause, the United States Supreme Court has, importantly, found that any attempt by the government to regulate thoughts and beliefs is an invasion of the "sphere of intellect and spirit which it is the purpose of the First Amendment to our Constitution to reserve from all official control."[21]

The existence of a "freedom of belief" that is protected by the Free Speech Clause guarantees of the First Amendment was first expounded by the Supreme Court in a 1943 case, *West Virginia State Board of Education v. Barnette.*[22] In the height of patriotic fervor surrounding the military campaign against Germany and Japan, the West Virginia Board of Education adopted a resolution requiring that a salute to the American flag become "a regular part of the program of activities in the public schools," and that both teachers and students were required to "participate in the salute honoring the Nation represented by the Flag; provided, however, that refusal to salute the Flag be regarded as an act of insubordination, and shall be dealt with accordingly." Specifically, the resolution called for a "stiff-arm" salute, which was to be accompanied by the recitation of the Pledge of Allegiance to the Flag. Any student who refused to comply with the terms of the resolution was guilty of insubordination, which resulted in his or her expulsion from school.[23]

Members of the Jehovah's Witnesses denomination brought suit in the United States district court, asking for an injunction to prohibit enforcement of the regulations against the members of their denomination. According to the lawsuit, Jehovah's Witnesses believe that a flag is a graven image which they are not allowed to bow down to or serve.[24] The Witnesses believed that they were obliged to follow God's law, even if it came into conflict with the law of the state, and for this reason they refused to salute the flag.[25] This refusal caused the West Virginia government to expel the children from school, to threaten to send the children to juvenile reformatories, and to prosecute the parents for causing the delinquency of a minor.[26]

The United States Supreme Court held that since the student's refusal to salute did not create a clear and present danger which would justify the curtailment of First Amendment freedoms, West Virginia had no authority to coerce the Witnesses into expressing a belief their religion forbade them from espousing.[27]

It was of no consequence to the Court, however, that the student's beliefs stemmed from religious doctrine. As Justice Jackson stated:

> While religion supplies appellees' motive for enduring the discomforts of
> making the issue in this case, many citizens who do not share these reli-

gious views hold such a compulsory rite to infringe constitutional liberties of the individual.[28]

Instead, the Court found the state's regulations to be a violation of the freedom of belief, a First Amendment freedom which is "susceptible of restriction only to prevent grave and immediate danger to interests which the State may lawfully protect."[29] Although showing respect to the Flag and fostering national unity were noble goals that a state has an interest in promoting, the Court said:

If there is any fixed star in our constitutional constellation, it is that no official, high or petty, can prescribe what shall be orthodox in politics, nationalism, religion, or other matters of opinion or force citizens to confess by word or act their faith therein. If there are any circumstances which permit an exception, they do not now occur to us.[30]

In the 1961 case *Torcaso v. Watkins*,[31] the Supreme Court again found the First Amendment freedom of belief to be sufficient grounds to negate a state legislative enactment. Article 37 of the Declaration of Rights of the Maryland Constitution states:

[N]o religious test ought ever to be required as a qualification for any office of profit or trust in this State, other than a declaration of belief in the existence of God. . . .[32]

Mr. Torcaso had been appointed to the position of Notary Public, but upon receiving his appointment, refused to profess a belief in God, as required by the Maryland statute. He was, therefore, denied his commission and brought suit in a Maryland Circuit Court. Both the Maryland Circuit Court and eventually the Maryland Court of Appeals denied his request for commission.[33] They held that Torcaso was not being coerced to express a belief against his will because:

The petitioner is not compelled to believe or disbelieve, under threat of punishment or other compulsion. True, unless he makes the declaration of belief he cannot hold public office in Maryland, but he is not compelled to hold office.[34]

Writing for the Supreme Court, Justice Black disagreed with the state's rationale, and, remanding the case to Maryland, held that Maryland's religious test for public office could not be enforced against Torcaso.[35]

The Supreme Court held that neither a state nor the federal government may require a person to profess a belief in order to hold office.[36] Although the case concerned the right of the state to coerce an individual to espouse a particular religious belief, the rationale is equally applicable to any belief—political, moral, or ethical—that a citizen may hold. Thus, the state

may not impose its values upon anyone, no matter how widely held those
values may be.

The freedom of belief was expanded to include written expression in
the case of *Wooley v. Maynard*.[37] George Maynard was a resident of New
Hampshire and a member of the Jehovah's Witnesses denomination. The
legislature of New Hampshire enacted legislation that made it a crime
"knowingly [to obscure] . . . the figures or letters on any number plate,"
which included the New Hampshire state motto, "Live Free or Die."[38] Mr.
Maynard found this motto to be objectionable because it would be contrary
to his faith to:

> [B]e coerced by the State into advertising a slogan which [he finds]
> morally, ethically, religiously and politically abhorrent.[39]

In order to express his objection, Maynard covered up the motto on his
license plate. He was thereafter arrested on three separate occasions by New
Hampshire law enforcement officials and spent fifteen days in jail.[40]

The United States Supreme Court found that the state had infringed
upon Maynard's freedom of belief by forcing him to express an ideological
viewpoint with which he vehemently disagreed. In doing so, the Court elaborated on the concept of freedom of belief:

> A system which secures the right to proselytize religious, political, and
> ideological causes must also guarantee the concomitant right to decline
> to foster such concepts.[41]

In the case of *Abood v. Detroit Board of Education*,[42] handed down
about a month after the *Wooley* decision, the freedom of thought and belief
was expanded to include not only the right to decline to express a particular viewpoint, but also to include the right to decline to support or promote
an ideology.

In *Abood*, the Detroit Board of Education implemented a plan where
its teachers were to be represented by the Detroit Federation of Teachers
Union. Teachers who chose not to join the Union were nevertheless required
to pay dues in order to prevent "freeloading"—i.e., some teachers refusing
to join the union, knowing they would still receive the benefits of representation.[43]

A group of non-union teachers filed a class action suit against the
Detroit Board of Education for forcing them to comply with the plan. These
teachers were unwilling to pay dues because they claimed that some of their
money would be used by the union to endorse political candidates and to
promote other ideological causes unrelated to the union's primary function
of collective bargaining.[44] The Supreme Court found the mandatory dues
to be a violation of the freedom of belief:

For at the heart of the First Amendment is the notion that an individual should be free to believe as he will, and that *in a free society one's beliefs should be shaped by his mind and his conscience rather than coerced by the State*.[45]

Although the freedom of belief is not specifically mentioned in the Free Speech Clause, judicial enforcement of the right is consistent with the major interpretations of the Free Speech Clause.[46] The common strand running through these four cases is that the state may not compel an individual to express a certain viewpoint, either verbally, as was the case in *Barnette* and *Torcaso*, through the written word, as in *Wooley*, or through indirect means such as financial support, as in *Abood*. These prohibitions are necessary as a means of promoting the diverse points of view that lead to a more successful democracy and as a means of fostering the growth of the individual.

Compulsory State Education as a Violation of the Freedom of Belief

Requiring children to attend a public school or a private school which is subject to state requirements violates the freedom of belief. Education plays a crucial role in the formation of the individual. The process of education not only shapes the intellect, but also, more subtly, the character of its students. Thus:

Education, both public and private, is inevitably a system of manipulation of consciousness. This manipulation of consciousness takes the form of the inculcation and indoctrination of certain ideologies and values in young minds.[47]

Even instruction in apparently value-free subjects such as mathematics or chemistry impresses upon students ideas about structure, hierarchy, and relationships. For example, the following are types of value transmission:

[T]he role models teachers provide, the structure of classrooms and of teacher-student relationships, the way in which the school is governed, the ways in which the child's time is parceled out, learning subdivided and fragmented, attitudes and behaviors rewarded and punished.[48]

The Supreme Court has affirmed that public education is, by necessity, a medium for the transmission of values and ideas from the state to the minds of students by describing education as "a principal instrument in awakening the child to cultural values"[49] and as "inculcating fundamental values necessary to the maintenance of a democratic political system."[50] In *Wisconsin v. Yoder*, the Court gave specific examples of the type of indoctrination that takes place in schools:

The high school tends to emphasize intellectual and scientific accomplishments, self-distinction, competitiveness, worldly success, and social life with other students.[51]

When the state requires its children to be educated at an accredited institution of learning, be it public or private, it creates the potential for enforceable inculcation of the state's values.

This potential represents the type of governmental intrusion that the Free Speech Clause is attempting to prohibit. Thus, the Free Speech Clause was included in the Bill of Rights in order to foster the "marketplace of ideas" which leads to a successful democracy.[52] On the other hand, state-regulated education leads to a homogenous society with little cultural or intellectual diversity. As John Stuart Mill theorized in the Nineteenth Century:

> A general State education is a mere contrivance for moulding people to be exactly like one another: and as the mould in which it casts them is that which pleases the predominant power in the government, whether this be a monarch, a priesthood, an aristocracy, or the majority of the existing generation; in proportion as it is efficient and successful, it establishes a despotism over the mind. . . .[53]

Many educational experts believe that this "despotism over the mind" is occurring in America today because of the large proportion of citizens being educated in public schools:

> Critics in the field of education argue that schools have flattened cultural diversity and personal individuality in setting up strict programs of learning which are identical on each grade level throughout the nation. These critics view the present system of mass education as promoting conformity, anti-intellectualism, passivity, alienation, classism and hierarchy.[54]

The Free Speech Clause arguably prohibits the government from impeding an individual's progress towards self-realization.[55] Governmental control of education, however, limits the development of the mind and the personality when it requires students to internalize the values of the state and the majority. If formation and development of belief are controlled by the state, then there is no real freedom of expression. Simply put, it is impossible to express a dissenting or unique point of view without first being allowed to develop it.[56] As two commentators write:

> Free expression makes unfettered formulation of beliefs and opinions possible. In turn, free formulation of beliefs and opinions is a necessary precursor to the freedom of expression. If the government were to regulate the development of ideas and opinions through, for example, a single television monopoly or through religious rituals for children, freedom

of expression would become a meaningless right. The more the government regulates formulation of beliefs so as to interfere with personal consciousness, the fewer people can conceive dissenting ideas or perceive contradictions between self-interest and government sustained ideological orthodoxy. If freedom of expression protected only communication of ideas, totalitarianism and freedom of expression could be characteristics of the same society.[57]

The free speech rights of the people are only truly protected, therefore, when the state plays a passive role in the formation of beliefs by its citizens. Requiring public or private education that is regulated by the state is no less a violation of the freedom of belief than forcing a child to say the Pledge of Allegiance or requiring the payment of union dues which are then donated to political candidates. An educational system where the state is allowed to control the transmission of values denies children the right to develop ideas which may be contrary to those of the majority. This, in turn, not only limits the growth of the individual, but it also makes for a less successful democracy. In this way, denying parents the opportunity to educate their children at home is a violation of the freedom of belief.

ABRIDGING CONSTITUTIONAL RIGHTS

Rights, such as the freedom of belief, that are protected by the First Amendment are considered "fundamental" rights.[58] In order to abridge a fundamental right, the state must show that its actions promote a compelling state interest and that the means chosen to achieve that interest are the least restrictive means possible.[59]

Compelling State Interest

It is settled in law and American tradition that parents are primarily responsible for the education of their children. As the Supreme Court held in *Wisconsin v. Yoder*:[60]

> The history and culture of Western civilization reflect a strong tradition of parental concern for the nurture and upbringing of their children. This primary role of the parents in the upbringing of their children is now established beyond debate as an enduring American tradition.[61]

The state, it is argued, may only interfere with the domain of the family for two reasons.[62] First, the state may intrude upon the domain of the family to protect various state interests, including "public health, safety, morals, or general welfare."[63] This justification for interference is called the state's "police power."[64]

Second, the doctrine of *parens patriae* allows the state to interfere with the domain of the family in order to protect the individual interests of the child where the parent has failed to do so. If a parent abuses or neglects his or her child, the state has the right to step in and protect the child.[65] It is always initially assumed, however, that a parent is acting in the best interests of his or her child, and the state, therefore, bears the burden of showing parental abuse or neglect when justifying its actions on *parens patriae* grounds.[66]

The state has traditionally claimed to have two compelling interests in the education of children within its boundaries: one that is based upon its "police power" and another that is based upon the doctrine of *parens patriae*.[67] Since an educated citizenry is necessary to preserve a properly functioning democracy, the state has argued that it has the right to ensure that future citizens are receiving an education that will enable them to "participate effectively and intelligently in our open political system."[68] This interest is commonly called the "operation of the franchise" or the "collectivist interest" and is based on the state's police power to promote the general welfare.[69]

The state also claims to have an interest in ensuring that future citizens become self-reliant and self-sufficient participants in society. This interest derives from the *parens patriae* doctrine, as the state, in this instance, is acting in the best interests of the child rather than acting in its own interests.[70]

The collectivism or operation of the franchise justification for state regulation of education has been recognized as a legitimate "state" interest. Courts have consistently recognized this justification as valid and have, therefore, allowed for some state regulation of education.[71]

It is more difficult, however, for the state to justify an abridgement of First Amendment rights on *parens patriae* grounds. The interest at stake is not primarily the interest of the state but that of the child. While the state may assert an interest in the development of the child, that interest in development has traditionally been subrogated to that of the parent. As the Supreme Court held in *Prince v. Massachusetts*:[72]

> It is cardinal with us that the custody, care and nurture of the child reside first in the parents, whose primary function and freedom include preparation for obligations the state can neither supply nor hinder.[73]

Thus, the State's interest in the child is a secondary one:

> The state may have a residual, secondary interest in the well-being of the child, but it has such an interest in all of its citizenry. The primary interest in developing skills to enable successful community interaction as an adult belongs to the child. While the state often intercedes on behalf of citizens too weak or otherwise unable to protect their own interests, it does so usually *in the absence of all other safeguards*. In the present context, the parent provides the first line of safeguards for the child. The courts have continually stated that the parent is presumed to act in the best interest of the child. If the parent fails in this respect then the state

can intercede as the presumption of acting in the child's best interest is rebutted. At most, the state has an interest in insuring that the parent is acting in the child's best interest.[74]

This subrogation has been justified in three ways: 1. the parent's heightened sensitivity to the needs of their children; 2. the likelihood that parents will act in their children's best interest because of the inherently close relationship; 3. promotion of diversity by allowing parents to control the development of their children, while state oversight would lead to social homogenization.[75]

Therefore, a state can only show a compelling interest using a *parens patriae* grounds upon making three showings. First, it must be shown that the child does not have the mental competence or maturity of an adult. Second, it must be shown that the child's parents are unfit or unwilling to care for him or her adequately. Finally, the state must show that it is acting only in the best interest of the child.[76]

Least Restrictive Means

Even if a state shows a compelling interest in the operation of the franchise, it must also show that the means it has adopted to achieve that interest is the one which least infringes the First Amendment rights in question. It does not follow that prohibiting or prohibitively regulating home schooling is the least restrictive means possible of preparing children to operate the franchise.

First, home education is permissible in the overwhelming majority of states.[77] It would be difficult, therefore, for a non-complying state to argue that it has a compelling interest in the prohibition of home schooling since the majority of states see no need for prohibitive regulation.

Second, as standardized tests show,[78] students in home schools often receive better educations than students in public or accredited private schools. Voters who were educated at home, therefore, should be just as capable of exercising the franchise as voters who were educated in the public school system.

Neither does a teacher certification requirement qualify as the least restrictive means of protecting the franchise. As one commentator has stated:

> It does not appear unreasonable and would satisfy the concerns the state has in certification to allow a parent to produce proof of proficiency other than by a state certificate. . . . Given the desirability of an alternative standard, adherence to certification as the exclusive method of teacher approval would appear untenable.[79]

Furthermore:

> It may be a convenient administrative rule to require state certification but it cannot stand as the only way to qualify as an instructor when to do so

would cut off otherwise qualified individuals wishing to instruct their own or other children.[80]

In the case of *State v. Nobel*,[81] the court specifically found that requiring parents who educate their children at home to obtain state certification was not the least restrictive means of achieving the state's goals.[82]

CONCLUSION

Whether the First Amendment is seen as a vehicle for the promotion of successful self-government or as a governmental promise not to interfere with the growth of the individual, compulsory education laws contradict the intent of First Amendment guarantees.

When public schools and state-regulated private schools control the formation of ideas by their students, such schools are ultimately violating the freedom of belief.

Since the freedom of belief is a fundamental one, it may only be abridged by the government in order to achieve a compelling state interest and only by the least restrictive means possible. Usually the only compelling interest the state has in compulsory education is the protection of the franchise. Yet, the franchise can be protected through general oversight as opposed to teacher certification requirements or curriculum mandates. Any regulation of home schools that amounts to more than a general oversight is a violation of the Free Speech Clause of the First Amendment.

14

Right to Privacy
and Due Process

Privacy has been held by the Supreme Court to be a fundamental right.[1] This chapter will review the expansion of this right of privacy to include parental decisions regarding the education of their children, especially the decision to home school. Consideration will be given to the history of the fundamental right of privacy, including the dicta of Supreme Court decisions, and the strict scrutiny analysis as applied to a proposed fundamental right of privacy that includes the decision to home school.

HISTORY

Early in the Twentieth Century, the Supreme Court repeatedly held that the Due Process Clauses of the Constitution could be properly construed to protect unenumerated, substantive rights that were not otherwise listed in the Constitution.[2] While the focus of the early Twentieth Century Court was on the protection of economic liberties under the doctrine of substantive due process, the Court in more recent decades has used this same doctrinal approach to protect non-economic liberties such as the right of privacy.

The doctrine of substantive due process adopted by the Court in the late Nineteenth and early Twentieth Centuries is based on the theory (still followed by the Court today) that the concept of liberty embraces unenumerated rights that are protected by the Due Process Clauses of the Constitution.[3]

JUDICIAL ANTECEDENTS
Education Cases
The United States Supreme Court has acknowledged parental rights in four critical cases involving education that define the limits on the power of the states to regulate education.[4]

In *Meyer v. Nebraska*,[5] a private tutor was convicted of violating a state law prohibiting the teaching of foreign languages to children of elementary school age.[6] Although parental rights were not expressly at issue in *Meyer*, the Court said that "[the teacher's] right to teach and the right of parents to engage him to instruct their children . . . are within the liberty of the [Fourteenth] amendment."[7] Thus, in 1923 the Supreme Court established that the state's control over education is not absolute and that parents have a liberty interest in their child's education.[8] The Court noted that the liberty protected by the Due Process Clause of the Fourteenth Amendment includes the right "to acquire useful knowledge, to marry, establish a home and bring up children."[9]

Meyer thus represents the beginning of a line of Supreme Court authority supporting the rights of parents over their children.

Two years after *Meyer*, in *Pierce v. Society of Sisters*,[10] the Supreme Court held that an Oregon statute that compelled public school attendance and prohibited any other form of education was unconstitutional.[11] *Pierce* stands for the proposition that the state may not compel attendance at a public school without allowing the parent to choose a private education alternative.[12]

The *Pierce* Court stated:

> The child is not the mere creature of the state; those who nurture him and direct his destiny have the right, coupled with the high duty, to recognize and prepare him for additional obligations.[13]

The Court went further in describing the importance of parents' rights, noting that such rights are fundamental to the American system of government and common notions of liberty.[14]

Two years after *Pierce*, the Supreme Court considered, in *Farrington v. Tokushige*,[15] Hawaii's attempt to regulate all the aspects of a private school as part of an effort to Americanize all students (including the Japanese).[16] In effect, the regulations would have destroyed the foreign language schools.[17] The Supreme Court held in *Farrington* that Japanese parents had the right to direct their children's education free from unreasonable state restrictions.[18] From *Farrington* comes the proposition that the state may not, by extensive regulation, render the distinction between public and private alternatives meaningless.[19]

The above trilogy of cases arose at the time the Court was utilizing the notion of *substantive due process*. It was during this period that the Court recognized parents' rights to guide the education of their children.[20]

In the years following these cases, theories of economic due process fell into general disfavor with the Court. Nonetheless, the Court did not purport to *abandon* the substantive due process protection of noneconomic rights such as those involved in the education trilogy. The doctrine reemerged through the general right of privacy and other fundamental rights. Despite the trend away from the use of substantive due process, the Court continued to hold that the right of parents to guide the education of their children is important to the very fabric of our society.[21]

After *Farrington*, the Court did not address the issue of parental rights and the state's asserted interest in education until 1972, when it decided *Wisconsin v. Yoder*,[22] the landmark case upholding the right of a parent to be the primary decision-maker regarding his or her child's education.[23]

In *Wisconsin v. Yoder*, the Court exempted Amish children from state compulsory attendance laws both because the religious freedom of the parents and their common law parental rights had been infringed and because the state failed to prove an overriding interest in keeping the children in school.[24] The plaintiffs in *Yoder* were parents, unlike the earlier trilogy where the plaintiffs were teachers or private schools. The Court employed a balancing approach in deciding *Yoder*[25] and indicated that its opinion should be narrowly construed.[26] Chief Justice Burger stated:

> [T]his case involves the fundamental interest of parents, as contrasted with that of the State, to guide the religious future and education of their children. The history and culture of Western civilization reflect a strong tradition of parental concern for the nurture and upbringing of their children. This primary role of the parents in the upbringing of their children is now established beyond debate as an enduring American tradition.[27]

The Question After *Yoder*: Is There a Secular Equivalent?

After *Yoder*, an unanswered question remains: Is there a secular equivalent to *Wisconsin v. Yoder*?

To resolve this question with respect to home education, it must be determined whether home education is a fundamental constitutional right requiring the application of the strict scrutiny test to the review of state compulsory education statutes.[28]

The strict scrutiny test, as applied to state action, requires the state to show it is advancing a compelling interest through a narrowly drawn or least restrictive means.[29] This analysis recognizes the importance of the parents' fundamental rights as well any compelling interest of the state.[30]

If home education is not a fundamental right, then the regulations must only rationally and/or substantially relate to the achievement of important government objectives.[31]

Since the United States Supreme Court has yet to review a home instruction question based solely on the right of privacy, it may be helpful to review the dicta of other Supreme Court decisions (in chronological order) to see whether a constitutionally grounded fundamental right of parental or familial privacy can reasonably be construed to protect home education as a choice by parents.

Fundamental Right of Privacy

In *Griswold v. Connecticut*,[32] the United States Supreme Court expressly recognized the existence of the right of privacy and held that this right is protected by the United States Constitution against undue governmental infringement.[33] The striking aspect of the *Griswold* case was that a majority of the Court expressly described the right of privacy as an unenumerated right protected independently by the Due Process Clauses of the Fifth and Fourteenth Amendments to the United States Constitution.[34]

The concept of liberty in the Due Process Clauses of the Fifth and Fourteenth Amendments[35] was held to protect personal rights that are fundamental; such liberty is not confined to the specific terms of the Bill of Rights.[36]

Thus, the privacy penumbra[37] of *Griswold v. Connecticut* is a continuance or modification of the substantive due process approach[38] and accordingly, the Court held, based on *Pierce*[39]: "[T]he right to educate one's child as one chooses is made applicable to the states. . . ."[40]

The majority opinion in *Griswold* also postulates that this right of privacy is a fundamental right within the penumbra of protection afforded by the First, Third, Fourth, and Ninth, as well as the Fifth and Fourteenth Amendments.[41]

The progeny of *Griswold v. Connecticut*[42] arguably support a fundamental right of parental home education choice under the privacy penumbra. For example, in *Stanley v. Georgia*[43] the Court recognized the "[f]undamental . . . right to be free, except in very limited circumstances, from unwanted governmental intrusions into one's privacy,"[44] and in *Stanley v. Illinois*[45] the Court noted that "the rights to conceive and to raise one's children have been deemed essential."[46]

Despite its religious context and the effort of Chief Justice Burger to limit the case to the specific situation of the Amish, *Yoder* has possibilities for constitutional protection of parental autonomy:[47]

> The values of parental direction of the religious upbringing and education of their children in their early and formative years have a high place in our society. . . .[48] The history and culture of western civilization reflect a strong tradition of parental concern for the nurture and upbringing of their children. This primary role of the parents in the upbringing of their children is now established beyond debate as an enduring American tradition.[49]

However, in *San Antonio School District v. Rodriguez*[50] the Court declined, in the context of an attack on the state's redistricting and financing plan, to recognize a fundamental right to education.[51] Justice Brennan, in the dissent, argued for a classification of education as a fundamental right.[52] *Rodriguez* held that the right to education was not fundamental[53] and therefore not worthy of special protection.[54]

The year after *Rodriguez*, in *Roe v. Wade*,[55] the Supreme Court stated:

[D]ecisions make it clear that only personal rights that can be deemed "fundamental" . . . are included in this guarantee of personal privacy. They also make it clear that the right has some extension to activities relating to marriage . . . child rearing and education. . . .[56]

In *Doe v. Bolton,*[57] Justice Douglas recognized several fundamental rights:

[F]reedom of choice in the basic decisions of one's life . . . education and the upbringing of children.[58]

In *Cleveland Bd. of Educ. v. LaFleur,*[59] the Court cited *Pierce* and *Meyer* in noting that it:

[H]as long recognized that freedom of personal choice in matters of marriage and family life is one of the liberties protected by the Due Process Clause of the Fourteenth Amendment.[60]

In *Paul v. Davis*[61] the Court noted:

While there is no "right to privacy" found in any specific guarantee of the Constitution, the Court has recognized that "zones of privacy" may be created by more specific constitutional guarantees and thereby impose limits upon government power . . . personal rights found in this guarantee of personal privacy [include] . . . matters relating to marriage, procreation, conception, family relationships and child rearing and education.[62]

In *Runyon v. McCrary*[63] the Court found:

[T]he *Meyer-Pierce-Yoder* parental right and the privacy right . . . may be no more than verbal variations of a single constitutional right.[64]

In *Cook v. Hudson*, Chief Justice Burger reiterated his concern for these parental interests:

[F]ew familial decisions are as immune from governmental interference as parents' choice of a school for their children, so long as the school chosen otherwise meets the educational standards imposed by the State.[65]

In *Moore v. City of East Cleveland,*[66] the importance of the family as a social entity was affirmed:

This Court has long recognized that freedom of personal choice in matters of marriage and family life is one of the liberties protected by the Due Process Clause of the Fourteenth Amendment. . . . A host of cases, tracing their lineage to *Meyer v. Nebraska* ... and *Pierce v. Society of Sisters* ... have consistently acknowledged a private realm of family life which the State cannot enter.[67]

Decisions may not be distinguished according to the subject matter. Where the core set of values relates to the family, childbearing, custody and education are not to be treated differently:

> [O]ur decisions establish that the Constitution protects the sanctity of the family precisely because the institution of the family is deeply rooted in this Nation's history and tradition. It is through the family that we inculcate and pass down many of our most cherished values, moral and cultural.[68]

> If any freedom not specifically mentioned in the Bill of Rights enjoys a "preferred position" in the law it is most certainly the family.[69]

In *Carey v. Population Services International*,[70] the Court cites the *Meyer* and *Pierce* education cases as privacy right cases.[71]

In *Parham v. J.R.*,[72] the Court upheld the right of parents to commit their minor children to a state mental institution.[73] The parents' decision to place a child in a mental hospital, if erroneous, must be more harmful to the child and her future than would a comparable if less drastic choice of educational setting. Hence, the great deference paid by the Court to parental decisions concerning the child's institutionalization suggests that no less a deference should adhere to parental choices in education.[74] The Court in *Parham* stated:

> Our jurisprudence historically has reflected Western civilization concepts of the family as a unit with broad parental authority over minor children.... The law's concept of the family rests on a presumption that parents possess what a child lacks in maturity, experience, and capacity for judgment required for making life's difficult decisions. More important, historically it has recognized that natural bonds of affection lead parents to act in the best interests of their children.[75]

The Court set up a rebuttable presumption that parents do act in the best interests of their children, and therefore parental decision-making is given priority in the American constitutional framework.[76]

In *Bowers v. Hardwick*,[77] the Court stated that the right to privacy extended to child-rearing and education decisions.[78]

A state court decision worthy of mention because the court upheld the parents' right to choose home education for philosophical reasons is *Perchemlides v. Frizzle*.[79] In *Perchemlides*, the trial court stated the rationale preventing governmental intrusion into one's fundamental privacy right regarding education:

There will remain little privacy in the "right to privacy" if the state is permitted to inquire into the motives behind parents' decisions regarding the education of their children.[80]

Two other state cases dealing specifically with parental liberty and home instruction are noteworthy.

In *Commonwealth v. Roberts*,[81] the Massachusetts Supreme Court upheld the parental liberty to instruct children at home, noting the purpose of the compulsory education statute was that "all the children shall be educated, not that they shall be educated in any particular way."[82]

A South Carolina trial court held, in *Calhoun County Department of Education v. Page*,[83] that the parents' right to teach their children in a home school "is a basic constitutional 'liberty' guaranteed by the U.S. Constitution and the fourteenth amendment of the U. S. Constitution."[84]

PRIVACY AS A FUNDAMENTAL RIGHT

The United States Supreme Court has specifically recognized the right of privacy as a fundamental right. The traditional parental right is arguably also fundamental.[85]

There is support for a fundamental privacy right of parents to choose home education for their children. This support is found in the Supreme Court pronouncements in the *Meyer*[86] line of educational cases (substantive due process), in *Yoder*[87] (historical and traditional rights of parents), and in the *Griswold*[88] line of privacy cases (privacy of family-related decisions),[89] as well as in the considerable dicta in other Supreme Court cases.

To support the recognition of fundamental rights under the right of privacy, the Supreme Court relies on the holdings in *Pierce*[90] and *Meyer*[91] to create the context in which a right may be defined as fundamental. For example, in *Roe v. Wade*,[92] the Court recognized a mother's right to abort her baby as a fundamental right within the right of privacy.[93] In reaching its decision, the Court stated in dicta that the right of privacy extends to other rights such as "child rearing and education."[94]

Thus, parents may argue that their long recognized right to guide the rearing and education of their children is fundamental under either a privacy or liberty theory and that, therefore, courts should subject any state infringements of this right to strict scrutiny analysis. Such an analysis would limit, though not eliminate, the state's ability to regulate schools.[95]

Compelling State Interests

Given that parents have a fundamental right to make the educational decisions for their children, the state may intrude into this protected area to override the parental prerogative only when justified by a compelling state interest.[96] The state has the burden of proving that its compelling interest is based on either its police power to act in the interest of the community, or its *parens patriae* power to act in the interest of a neglected individual.[97]

The Supreme Court has not yet decided the question of whether to resolve the conflict by balancing the interests involved or by applying the recent Supreme Court strict scrutiny analysis.[98] The 1972 *Wisconsin v. Yoder*[99] decision is the most recent Supreme Court case to touch directly on this conflict, and there the Court chose to balance the interests involved.[100]

Since *Yoder*, the Supreme Court has revised much of its general analysis of the First and Fourteenth Amendments from a balancing of rights or interests to a strict scrutiny framework.[101] The Supreme Court now applies strict scrutiny to state infringements on fundamental rights.[102]

If a court applies strict scrutiny analysis to home education issues, it must define exactly what the state's interest in education involves and whether the state's regulatory scheme is the least restrictive means of achieving this interest.[103] The state in *Yoder* advanced three interests to support its compulsory attendance statute:

(1) [S]ome degree of education is necessary to prepare citizens to participate effectively and intelligently in our open political system if we are to preserve freedom and independence.[104]

(2) [E]ducation prepares individuals to be self-reliant and self-sufficient participants in society.[105]

(3) [Preparation] for the life style that they may later choose, or at least to provide them with an option other than the life they have led in the past.[106]

The sole interest which emanates from the nature of the state is the first interest listed. The state in the particular form in which it exists in the United States requires for its continued existence at least the nominal participation of citizens in its process by voting. Were the citizens unable to operate the franchise, the nature of the state would change. Therefore, the state has some interest in ensuring that its citizens are educated to an adequate level, enabling them to operate the machinery of state.[107]

The other two interests are, however, of a different order. Far from being interests directly vital to the state, they are individual interests of a child. While the state may assert a secondary or surveillance interest in ensuring that the parents are fulfilling their duties in regard to these other two interests,[108] such an interest is only secondary; it is not a compelling interest. It only becomes a primary and controlling interest if the parent fails to protect the child's welfare.[109] Therefore, the state may not interfere with the traditional and fundamental right of parents to pass values, beliefs, language, culture, and family identity on to their children based on an interest in socialization, Americanization, or cultural enhancement.

The state does not have a primary interest in developing self-reliance and self-sufficiency in children. This is the interest of the child, and only when the parent fails may the state step in to protect the welfare interests of the child.

Only the interest of the state in the operation of the franchise is inherent in the nature of the state and thus bears the potential of rising to a compelling level.[110] Although the Supreme Court has not found the state interest in education compelling, it has made clear that this interest is important to society.[111]

When a fundamental right clashes with a compelling state interest, due process requires that the state must show that it has chosen the least restrictive means to achieve its interest. Thus, at the most, the state may only use the least restrictive means to regulate home education.[112]

The only reasonable regulation of home education which is not prohibitive appears to be a requirement that the result of home education be sufficient to maintain the franchise.[113] Thus, for example, a system of testing should be used only to determine if home school instruction has met this requirement.[114] Teacher certification requirements, which are generally favored by teacher's unions, tests the skill of the parents, not the students, and therefore are not in line with the expressed interests of the state. Where the interests of the state in an educated populace are met and validated through ends-oriented means, means-oriented requirements are overly intrusive and unnecessary.[115]

CONCLUSION

The right of privacy has been found to be a constitutionally protected fundamental right. The Supreme Court has arguably expanded this fundamental right through a long line of cases to include the parents' right to direct the education of their children and to be the primary decision-makers in this arena. Since this right has fundamental protection, the courts must apply the strict scrutiny test to any infringement of this right, including parents' decision to educate their children at home. This makes home schooling a constitutionally viable option.

15

Ninth and Tenth Amendment Concerns

The Ninth Amendment[1] and the Tenth Amendment[2] to the United States Constitution deal with the repository of powers and rights not expressly enumerated or delegated to the United States. At first glance, the nexus between these amendments and home schoolers may appear non-existent or irrelevant.

To the contrary, these constitutional provisions may at some point prove useful in defending home school autonomy against *federal* intervention. Although federal intrusion into matters of home school education has to date been non-existent, federal programs such as America 2000,[3] which contain "national standards" for education, may well become an issue affecting home education.

This chapter thus discusses the Ninth and Tenth Amendments and their relationship to federal educational programs and home schools.

THE NINTH AMENDMENT

Education is a right, although not enumerated in the Constitution, "retained by the people" under the Ninth Amendment to the Constitution.

Education of the American citizenry is not a power delegated to the federal government by the Constitution. Nor does the Constitution prohibit such education by the states. Therefore, according to the Tenth Amendment, it is a power reserved to the states respectively, or to the people.

In his dissent in *Palmer v. Thompson* in 1971, Justice Douglas wrote:

[T]he right of the people to education . . . like the right to pure air and pure water, may well be [a right] . . . "retained by the people" under the Ninth Amendment.[4]

History and Purpose

The Ninth Amendment to the Constitution reads as follows:

> The enumeration in the Constitution of certain rights, shall not be construed to deny or disparage others retained by the people.[5]

A part of the Bill of Rights that was ratified in 1791, the Ninth Amendment was adopted, along with the Tenth Amendment, to ensure that the federal government was to be a government of express and limited powers.[6]

James Madison declared: "[T]he great object in view is to limit and qualify the powers of Government, by excepting out of the grant of power those cases in which the Government ought not to act, or to act only in a particular mode."[7] Having "analogous residual purposes,"[8] the two amendments were intended to be complementary: the Ninth dealing with rights "retained by the people," the Tenth with powers "reserved" to the states or the people.[9]

Widespread distrust of the federal government fed the drive for the adoption of the Bill of Rights.[10] The great debate over the incorporation of the Bill of Rights into the federal Constitution was exemplified by the debate over the need for a provision like that contained in the Ninth Amendment.

Those who opposed a Bill of Rights did so on grounds that specifying certain rights might result in the denial of the existence of unspecified rights. For example, George Washington wrote in a letter to Lafayette: "[T]he people evidently retained everything which they did not in express terms give up."[11] Advocates of a Bill of Rights were concerned that individual liberties would be lost under a Constitution that did not expressly declare them reserved.

The Ninth Amendment therefore served as a compromise, a "mere precaution" in the words of Madison, to prevent the misapplication of the maxim that an affirmation in particular cases implies a negation in all others.[12] The Ninth Amendment thus confirmed the framers' intent that rights not specified in the Bill of Rights were not thereby surrendered to the federal government.[13]

For more than a century and a half, the Ninth Amendment appears to have "layed dormant," receiving only perfunctory treatment from courts and commentators.[14]

After World War II, however, heightened concern for human rights inspired extolling the "forgotten" Ninth Amendment for its value in the promotion of individual liberty.[15]

Finally, in 1965 the Ninth Amendment was fully "revived" by Justice Goldberg's concurring opinion in *Griswold v. Connecticut*,[16] in which he was joined by Chief Justice Warren and Justice Brennan.[17]

The majority opinion in *Griswold* held that the right to marital privacy, although not expressly listed in the Constitution, was created by "penumbral rights" emanating from the specific guarantees in the First, Third, Fourth, Fifth, and Ninth Amendments.[18]

Justices Goldberg, Warren and Brennan, however, found that this right of privacy was specifically protected by the Ninth Amendment.[19] They explained: "The language and history of the Ninth Amendment reveal that the Framers of the Constitution believed that there are additional fundamental rights, protected from governmental infringement, which exist alongside those fundamental rights specifically mentioned in the first eight constitutional amendments."[20]

Commentators discussing the historical origins of the Ninth Amendment following the *Griswold* decision have found that the framers of the Constitution intended it not only to safeguard unenumerated natural rights of a fundamental character,[21] but also to signal the existence of *federal constitutional rights* beyond those specifically enumerated in the Constitution.[22] Another commentator finds the Ninth Amendment to be a veritable "fountain of law."[23]

Those who do not agree with such an expansive reading of the Ninth Amendment nevertheless recognize the specific function of the amendment in maintaining those rights guaranteed by the laws of the states.[24] These state rights, according to one author, represent "entitlements derived from both natural law theory and the hereditary rights of Englishmen."[25]

Although the United States Supreme Court has rejected the contention that there exists an implied fundamental right to education in the context of redistricting to allocate equal funding for schools,[26] the Court stated in the same opinion that the goals of effective speech and informed electoral choice by an educated citizenry were "indeed goals to be pursued by a people whose thoughts and beliefs are freed from governmental interference . . . [and] not values to be implemented by judicial intrusion into otherwise legitimate state activities."[27]

THE TENTH AMENDMENT

The Tenth Amendment reads as follows:

> The powers not delegated to the United States by the Constitution, nor prohibited by it to the States, are reserved to the States respectively, or to the people.[28]

History and Purpose

While the preceding eight amendments enumerated specific individual rights that neither the state nor federal government could infringe without a rational or compelling justification, the Ninth and Tenth Amendments were added to forestall both the implication of unexpressed *powers* and the disparagement of unenumerated *rights*.[29]

Implications for Education

President George Bush devised a federally controlled plan to standardize the nation's education system, called "America 2000."[30] By briefly tracing the origins of the compulsory education laws in the United States, this chapter shows how such a plan violates the Ninth and Tenth Amendments to the United States Constitution by imposing federal control of a right retained by the people and reserved to the states.[31]

In addition, by imposing homogeneity of thought in American schools,[32] federal programs like America 2000 risk destroying the fundamental fibers of a nation once committed to the ideals of freedom and diversity.[33]

The movement toward universal education came shortly after the Civil War and was especially strong at the beginning of the Twentieth Century.[34] The United States Department of Education was established in 1867, and by 1918 compulsory school attendance laws were enacted in all the states.[35]

The goal of mass education was "good citizenship," described as "a man who could read and write, whose mind had been disciplined, and who had received appropriate character education" in order to effectively and intelligently participate in the democratic process.[36]

But the goal of compulsory school attendance until age sixteen was often motivated by different concerns. Although partly motivated by humanitarian instincts to protect children from exploitation, compulsory education laws were also supported by organized labor who sought to eliminate cheap child labor that not only depressed wages generally but also displaced adult workers.[37]

Chief Justice Burger, in granting an exception for Amish children from Wisconsin's compulsory education law, noted the parallel between the growth of school attendance laws and child labor laws.[38] According to the Chief Justice, the common age limit of these two kinds of statutes was "coordinated to achieve their related objective": children under the age of sixteen were not to be employed under conditions hazardous to their health or in work that should be performed by adults.[39]

There were many problems with this new centralization of education. As one authority states: "Thousands of recalcitrant or slow-witted children who in former times would have dropped out of school . . . now became the responsibility of the school. . . . Moreover, the school was now forced to enroll many new groups of children for whom the traditional program had no particular meaning, use, nor appeal. In effect, the burden of compulsory attendance tended to force differentiation of school purposes and curricula in order that the educational needs of a heterogeneous population might be met."[40] For example, curriculum makers were torn by what one author described as "six orientations": religion, discipline, scholarship, vocation, individual needs, and society.[41]

Another problem with the new centralization of education was the administration and supervision of school systems ministering to these thousands of children.[42] By 1918, American education had become "big business," employing over 650,000 teachers, enrolling over 25 percent of the American people, and with public school property valued at close to $2 billion.[43]

The system became politicized: "In many states . . . the chief state school office was a political plum, to be handed out after election along with other lucrative posts."[44]

On the other hand, the city school superintendency was often "the center of struggles between organized pressure groups for control of the school."[45] "[T]he alarming number of untrained, and sometimes corrupt, incompetents" was appalling, for "[h]ere too, the danger was far too prevalent that the post would be either a political reward or a convenient sinecure for retired party men."[46]

A century has gone by, and the same problems remain. With all states and the District of Columbia having enacted compulsory education laws,[47] state regulation of the public schools has created a bureaucracy with which many parents are unsatisfied, and thus they are choosing to opt their children out of the system altogether.[48] Increased federal involvement may further this trend.

AMERICA 2000

America 2000 is a nine-year federal plan to upgrade the nation's educational system by imposing "National Assessment Tests" in the fourth, eighth and twelfth grades to measure the achievement of students in "core" subjects in relation to "World Class Standards."[49] It calls for the creation of "New American Schools" and encourages adults to join the new "Nation of Students."[50] President Bush outlined six "National Education Goals" which communities are "asked"[51] to adopt if they wish their schools to be considered for federal funds.[52]

Federal funds will undoubtedly provide an advantage their recipients to the detriment of those school districts not wishing to submit to federal government control and to those students who choose not to conform to the federally established agenda. This nation's tradition of educational diversity[53] and local control is thus threatened.

President Bush has attempted to distinguish his establishment of national so-called "World Class Standards" from the imposition of a national curriculum, but Thomas A. Shanker, executive director of the National School Boards Association, admitted that it "clearly moves the country toward that."[54]

Moreover, the America 2000 government publication itself states: "In time there could be 110,000 New American Schools"[55] after stating on page 5 that there are presently 110,000 American public and private schools.[56] The intent is evidently to achieve federal control of the education system nationwide. It is unclear, however, *who* will be deciding the appropriate standards by which to measure the nation's education.

President Bush handpicked a "National Education Goals Panel" charged with the task of deciding "what school children should know in five core subjects,"[57] thus leaving open the question whether this undoubtedly partisan group would change every four years to reflect the political party in power and, consequently, whether the American educational system and so-called "World Class Standards" would change with it. As of this writing, President Clinton's plans in this regard are not yet implemented.

New standardized tests are not the answer to the American educational crisis.[58] "The expectation that any new tests will revolutionize education is no wiser than the hope that a new kind of thermometer will cure a cold," said Michael H. Kean, test committee chairman of the Association of American Publishers.[59] Keith Geiger, president of the National Education Association, asserts: "This country does not need another multiple choice test."[60]

Moreover, the director of a school association believes that America 2000 depends too much on testing: "It seems to me you don't fatten cattle by weighing them. You've got to feed them."[61] The inefficiency of standardized tests has been shown time and time again.[62]

The cultural bias of testmakers often discriminates against women and minorities.[63] "For reasons that experts have not fully explained, boys consistently outscore girls on the widely used [SAT] tests, and the performance gap between the two sexes has been growing every year."[64]

The so-called "core" subjects being tested necessarily involve topics chosen by a select few, and it is a matter of luck whether the student has actually studied them. Schools adapt their curriculum to teach test-taking skills and strategies such as how to increase the probability of answering correctly on what students have familiarly dubbed "multiple guess" questions. The individual's opportunity for organization and articulation of thought, which is the most vital skill for successful communication and interaction within society, may be lost as a result.

Creativity and ingenuity, the very hallmarks of the above-average student, cannot be tested. Standardized tests tend to measure the ability to take tests rather than the knowledge of the particular test-taker.[65]

The progress of the individual, or lack thereof, may be generally ignored. Hard work, dedication and effort are not rewarded by standardized tests. Individuals are instead reduced to a common-denominator grouping, a category of achievement level based on arbitrary and capricious standards.[66] "Blind grading" may reduce the opportunity for discrimination by an individual teacher, but it often substitutes the majority's biases on a purely written test, and as Chief Justice Burger noted in *Wisconsin v. Yoder*, "There can be no assumption that today's majority is 'right.'"[67]

President Bush asserted that these tests will be voluntary[68] but, by the same token, pressured colleges and employers to take their results into account.[69]

Those who have not conformed to the new system will undoubtedly suffer discrimination, although America 2000 does not stipulate what should be done with children who do not pass the national assessment tests. In any case, it must be remembered that it is the child's teacher who observes the child on a daily basis and thus can best judge that student's progress and achievement in relation to the curriculum that has been taught, not in relation to a test and list of standards chosen by the political majority.

Neither is increased federal involvement in local and state education policy the solution to America's educational crisis. Centralization will aggravate the inefficiency of the system by complicating its administration with red tape, not to mention the high costs of maintaining such a bureaucracy.[70]

CONCLUSION

Increased federal control of education arguably violates the Ninth and Tenth Amendments to the United States Constitution.

In upholding the right of parents to choose to educate their children in a private school, the United States Supreme Court declared: "The fundamental theory of liberty upon which all governments in this Union repose excludes any general power of the State to standardize its children. . . ."[71] It is "those who nurture [the child] and direct his destiny [that] have the right, coupled with the high duty, to recognize and prepare him for additional obligations."[72]

Decisions affecting education should be made by the people as a right retained by them under the Ninth Amendment to the federal Constitution.

16

Equal Protection of the Law

The Fourteenth Amendment to the United States Constitution commands that no person shall be denied equal protection of the law by any state:

> [N]or shall any state . . . deny to any person within its jurisdiction the equal protection of the laws.[1]

The Fourteenth Amendment, including the Equal Protection Clause, applies to all state actions that attempt to classify individuals for different benefits or burdens under the law.[2] The United States Supreme Court has used concepts of equal protection to ensure that all individuals are accorded fair treatment in the exercise of their fundamental rights or the elimination of distinctions based on impermissible criteria.

Thus, the Supreme Court holds that in some circumstances the review of legislative classifications, for equal protection purposes, is a permissible part of the judicial function, particularly since it involves only the requirement that the government either forego an action or include within it all persons of a similar position.[3]

The method of analysis under the equal protection guarantees relates only to whether or not the state action classifies persons. If the means the law employs to achieve its end is the classification of persons for differing benefits or burdens, it will be tested under the equal protection guarantee. The Equal Protection Clause guarantees that similar individuals will be dealt with in a similar manner by the state. If the state classification relates to a proper state purpose, then the classification will be upheld. Equal protection analysis tests whether the state's classification is properly drawn.[4]

In reviewing any classification, it must be determined whether or not the persons classified by the law for different treatment are in fact dissimilar. Usually the purpose of the legislation will be examined in order to determine whether persons are similarly situated in terms of the state classification.[5] Thus, the Supreme Court will test the law "in its application" to determine whether the classification established is permissible.[6]

This chapter will address, in concept, the equal protection issues involved in state statutes which allow an exception to compulsory public school attendance in the form of home education. It will consider the requirements of teacher certification and student testing, with special attention to the constitutionality of such requirements in light of equal protection issues.

STATUTORY ANALYSIS

Overview

Statutes in every state and the District of Columbia require some form of school attendance.[7] Many states expressly provide for alternative educational experiences such as home schools.[8] These laws are ostensibly designed to ensure that children receive an adequate education while protecting the state's asserted interest in its future citizens.[9]

Compulsory attendance laws, however, may not compel all children to attend only public schools. In 1925, in *Pierce v. Society of Sisters*,[10] the Supreme Court held that children could attend public, private, or parochial schools. Other alternatives to public education are also available. For example, many states have enacted legislation which, under certain conditions, provide that a child may be educated at home.[11] State attendance laws providing for home instruction generally require that parents adhere to one or more criteria in order to ensure that acceptable standards are being maintained.[12] Typically, such laws specify:

(1) The qualifications of the home instructor;
(2) The curriculum or course of study which is to be taught;
(3) The amount of time to be spent in instruction each day;
(4) The number of days the child must be taught during the year;
(5) The standardized tests the child must take to determine his or her progress; and
(6) The reports the parents must periodically submit to school officials to verify compliance with the law.[13]

Of these criteria, the certification and testing requirements are the most susceptible to equal protection classification questions.

Certification Requirements

Some state statutes require some type of certification of the home instructor.[14] If these statutes do not have similar requirements for teachers in private schools, the statute arguably sets up a scheme of classification which raises a question of equal protection. This statutory scheme would discriminate in the treatment of two groups of people who are otherwise alike in the utilization of legally authorized alternatives to compulsory attendance statutes. "To determine whether a viable equal protection issue exists in this context, the right which is ostensibly violated must be identified."[15]

If the regulation adversely affects a suspect class or abridges a fundamental right protected by the Constitution (typically, a First or Fourteenth Amendment right),[16] then the court must scrutinize the statute in question and shift the burden of proof to the state.[17] The state must then demonstrate by clear and convincing evidence that either 1. the statute does not, in fact, abridge the right as alleged; or 2. even though the statute does abridge the right as alleged, the abridgement is justified by a compelling state interest.[18]

The asserted state interest in the education of unemancipated youth, which has been used to support enactment of compulsory attendance statutes, has been identified as follows:

(1) The need for a citizenry adequately educated to operate the franchise;
(2) The demand of individuals to be self-reliant and self-sufficient members of the community; and
(3) The demand of individuals to be culturally viable.[19]

Of these, only the first warrants action by the state to protect and preserve the state through its police power (which encompasses compulsory education statutes). The remaining two interests warrant action by the state to protect the child through *parens patriae* action only when the parents or lawful custodians of the child are unfit to provide for the needs of the child.[20]

An analysis of the dicta in various Supreme Court decisions[21] arguably supports the proposition that a fundamental right of privacy in child-rearing is violated by a classification scheme according different treatment to private and home schools.

Once a fundamental right is implicated, the court should apply a strict scrutiny standard that upholds a statute's constitutionality only if a compelling state interest supports the state's classification scheme.[22] In addition, if there are other reasonable ways to achieve the state's goals with less burden on the constitutionally protected activity, a state must not choose the way of greater interference, but must choose the less drastic means.[23]

While the Supreme Court has yet to decide this issue, courts in states in which the equal protection question has been raised have thus far found this challenge unfounded.[24]

For example, in California, the compelling state interest justifying the differential treatment was a state entitlement "to establish a system whereby it can be known, by reasonable means, that the required teaching is being done."[25] The court further reasoned that teachers in private schools would be under the direct supervision of their school authorities at all times and thus the state could meet its interest in ensuring that the teaching does indeed occur.[26]

In Florida, parents not certified as private tutors were not permitted to proclaim their homes to be private schools (there was no statutory regulation of the establishment of private schools) and thus exempt their children from the compulsory attendance requirement.[27] The court did not discuss a compelling state interest that would support the classification scheme, and there was no discussion of the Supreme Court cases dealing with the fundamental right of privacy.[28]

A Virginia court gave deference to the state legislature's intent in creating separate and distinct categories of exemptions for private schools and home schools.[29] The court failed to discuss a compelling state interest, prior Supreme Court cases, or fundamental privacy rights in child-rearing.[30]

The preceding cases rejected an equal protection challenge to differing state requirements for private and home teacher qualifications, although this statutory discrepancy (separate treatment for private and home schools) has all but disappeared.[31] Even so, the analysis may be applied to other criteria.

Testing Requirements

Statutory testing requirements fall into two categories. In the first, no constitutional issue exists because the mandatory testing requirements are the same for public, private, and home students, and the second occurs where states require testing for public school children and home school children but require no testing of privately schooled children.

> The policy arguments discussed [above], providing the basis for an equal protection challenge to differential certification requirements of private and home instructors, have an equivalent application to those statutes mentioned above that require the testing of students learning at home and not those attending private schools.[32]

An example may be found in Arkansas, where a court found that the state's regulation of home schooling, but not private schools, did not violate equal protection rights of parents who taught their children at home, since the state's regulation was rationally related to its asserted interest in ensuring that its citizens were being properly educated.[33]

Other Adjudication

In New Mexico, the exclusion of home instruction by parent, guardian, or custodian from satisfying the requirements of the state's compulsory attendance laws was held not a violation of equal protection requirements.[34]

A Maine court has held that the distinction between home schooling programs and private schools was merely an educational decision, not an unconstitutional classification. As such it was subject only to rational basis scrutiny, which it passed.[35]

CONCLUSION

Historically, the equal protection challenge to the state compulsory attendance statutes has not met with success. However, it may be argued that by failing to give deference to prior Supreme Court opinions recognizing privacy rights in education, as well as failing to define a compelling state interest in support of their classification schemes, states that dismissed challenges of unequal protection did not apply a strict scrutiny standard in upholding their statutes.

Thus, as one commentator has stated: "In view of the Supreme Court's opinions concerning the role of government in education, then, an equal protection argument might remain a viable challenge."[36]

17

Parental Liberty

In the late Nineteenth Century and early quarter of the Twentieth Century,[1] the Supreme Court entered into one of the most activist periods of its history.[2] Commonly known as the *Lochner* era,[3] the Supreme Court, in an almost unprecedented move, recognized a number of constitutional rights under the guise of substantive due process.[4] This judicial revolution, however, came to a halt with the ascension of a Roosevelt-packed Court in the 1930s and 1940s as the Supreme Court overturned many of these cases to protect Roosevelt's New Deal legislation.[5]

Consequently, many of the rights created in the *Lochner* era no longer exist.[6] However, one such right has withstood the test of time[7] to become one of the main weapons in the home school litigant's arsenal: the right of parents to direct the education of their children.[8] Unlike other *Lochner*-era rights, this right has expanded in scope as courts have consistently recognized the importance of family autonomy and the societal value of the family.[9] For example, Judge Roger Traynor wrote:

> The family is the basic unit of our society, the center of the personal affections that ennoble and enrich human life. It channels biological drives that might otherwise become socially destructive; it ensures the care and education of children in a stable environment; it establishes continuity from one generation to another; it nurtures and develops the individual initiative that distinguishes a free people.[10]

While the context commanding an official recognition of the right is technically different, in many other ways it is the same. In the 1920s, parents fought for the right to educate their children outside the public school system in private institutions.[11] Today the struggle continues, but for a different choice—home education. The number of parents electing to home school their children is growing at a rapid rate.[12] Although many parents

273

home educate their children for religious reasons, there are other underlying factors.[13] Many parents:

> [F]eel that home education is the best way to provide a safe environment for their children and to keep them away from the multiplying problems of assaults, drugs and vandalism. . . . Many parents cite academic failure alone. Contributing to the dissatisfaction of parents are declining scores of the Scholastic Aptitude Tests (SAT), little or no assigned homework, inflated grades, automatic promotion, below level text books and objective, rather than essay examinations.[14]

Some parents also are concerned that many college freshmen lack the fundamental skills of reading, writing, and mathematics.[15] A primary motivation, however, is that some parents believe they "are the most aware of their children's needs and are best qualified to integrate learning materials with their family's own philosophy and values."[16]

While many states allow home school as one way to satisfy compulsory school attendance, other states do not.[17] The Supreme Court, however, has yet to consider directly whether the parental right to direct the education of children includes the right to home educate. In making this argument, it is important to understand why home education should be included under this fundamental right, and to be aware of the seminal Supreme Court cases in parental rights jurisprudence.

PARENTAL RIGHTS JURISPRUDENCE— SUPREME COURT DECISIONS

The first case in which the Supreme Court acknowledged the notion of parental rights in the context of education was *Meyer v. Nebraska*.[18] The State of Nebraska enacted a law prohibiting the teaching of any modern language other than English in any school—public, private, or parochial.[19] The plaintiff, a teacher, was convicted under the state statute for teaching German in a parochial school,[20] and he challenged that conviction. The Nebraska Supreme Court found that the statute did not violate any constitutional right.[21]

The United States Supreme Court disagreed and overturned the conviction, using a substantive due process analysis. The Court first considered the scope of "liberty" as protected in the Due Process Clause of the Fourteenth Amendment:

> Without doubt, it denotes not merely freedom from bodily restraint but also the right of the individual to contract, to engage in any of the common occupations of life, to acquire useful knowledge, to marry, establish a home and bring up children, to worship God according to the dictates of his own conscience, and generally to enjoy those privileges long rec-

ognized at common law as essential to the orderly pursuit of happiness by free men.[22]

Expounding on the acquisition of knowledge aspect of liberty and the right to bring up children, the Court recognized that "it is the natural duty of the parent to give his children education suitable to their station in life."[23]

The Court then addressed the constitutionality of the Nebraska statute. While the Court understood "[t]he desire of the legislature to foster a homogeneous people with American ideals prepared readily to understand current discussions of civic matters,"[24] it nonetheless found that the statute violated the notion of liberty incorporated in the Due Process Clause. The Court found that parents have the right to have their children instructed in German, that the plaintiff had the right to teach the language, and that both rights "are within the liberty of the Amendment."[25] Unlike Plato's Ideal Commonwealth, the Supreme Court noted that American society is not one where "no parent is to know his own child, nor any child his parent."[26]

Two years later, the Supreme Court elaborated on the notion of parental rights in *Pierce v. Society of Sisters*.[27] In *Pierce*, parents and private schools challenged Oregon's authority to require children to attend public schools. Acknowledging that "[n]o question is raised concerning the power of the State reasonably to regulate all schools,"[28] the Court addressed the constitutionality of the state's action and found that the statute could not withstand judicial scrutiny.[29] The Court found that the legislation "unreasonably interfere[d] with the liberty of parents and guardians to direct the upbringing and education of children under their control."[30]

According to the Court: "The fundamental theory of liberty upon which all governments in this Union repose excludes any general power of the State to standardize its children by forcing them to accept instruction from public teachers only."[31] The Court concluded:

> The child is not the mere creature of the State; those who nurture him and direct his destiny have the right, coupled with the high duty, to recognize and prepare him for additional obligations.[32]

Therefore, the right to direct the education of one's children is protected under the Fourteenth Amendment's Due Process Clause. In *Pierce*, the Supreme Court did not address the degree, if any, to which the state could regulate private schools. Soon thereafter, however, in *Farrington v. Tokushige*[33] the Court provided a hint as to where the dividing line between permissible and impermissible interference lies. *Farrington* stemmed from a challenge to a law in the Territory of Hawaii that heavily regulated "foreign language schools." These schools, which received no public school funds, provided instruction to Korean-, Japanese-, and Chinese-speaking students.[34] All children living in the Territory were required to attend public schools or the equivalent.[35] The vast majority of children attended one of these foreign-language schools in addition to public or private school.[36]

The Territory government enacted legislation that imposed stringent restrictions upon the foreign-language schools.[37] For example, the enactment required the schools to provide a list naming the students enrolled, their sex, place of birth, residence, and parents or guardians.[38] It also required teachers in the school to acquire a permit, but in order to do so, the teachers were required to demonstrate that they "[possessed] . . . the ideals of democracy; knowledge of American history and institutions, and [knew] how to read, write, and speak the English language."[39]

Teachers and school operators, in addition, were required to sign a pledge, vowing to "direct the minds and studies of pupils in such schools as will tend to make them good and loyal American citizens."[40] Another provision of the Act granted to the Territory's Department of Education the power to "prescribe . . . the subjects and courses of study . . . and the entrance and attendance prerequisites or qualifications . . . and the textbooks used."[41] Any violation of the Act was a misdemeanor.[42]

The Court found these regulations disconcerting:

> [T]he measures adopted . . . go far beyond mere regulation of privately-supported schools where children obtain instruction deemed valuable by their parents and which is not obviously in conflict with any public interest. They give affirmative direction concerning the intimate and essential details of such schools, intrust their control to public officers, and deny both owners and patrons reasonable choice and discretion in respect of teachers, curriculum and text-books.[43]

Pointing to the recent decisions in *Meyer v. Nebraska*[44] and *Pierce v. Society of Sisters,*[45] articulating the fundamental right of parents to direct the education of their children under the Due Process Clause of the Fourteenth Amendment, the Court concluded that "The Japanese parent has the right to direct the education of his own child without *unreasonable restrictions.*"[46] Thus, the Court struck down the Hawaii enactment, stating that enforcing the legislation "would destroy most, if not all, of [the foreign language schools]; and, certainly, it would deprive parents of fair opportunity to procure for their children instruction which they think important and [not] harmful."[47]

Nearly fifty years later, the Supreme Court announced another landmark decision in the area of parental rights and affirmed the vitality of the *Meyer* and *Pierce* legacy. In *Wisconsin v. Yoder,*[48] the Court examined the parental right to direct the education of one's child in a new context—whether this right protected the parental choice to remove their children from school before they reached the age of sixteen—and in conjunction with another constitutional right—the right to exercise one's religious beliefs.

Yoder involved the clash between the state's interest in educating children until they reach the age of sixteen years and the belief of the Amish that Amish children should not attend organized school beyond the eighth grade.[49]

In *Yoder,* Wisconsin charged three parents with violation of the state's compulsory state attendance laws because they had not enrolled their teenage children in any public or private school or any other recognized exception to the attendance statute.[50] The parents were tried and convicted although they maintained that:

> [T]heir children's attendance at high school, public or private, was contrary to the Amish religion and way of life. They believed that by sending their children to high school, they would not only expose themselves to the danger of the censure of the church community, but . . . also endanger their own salvation and that of their children.[51]

The Wisconsin Supreme Court held that the conviction of the parents was invalid, and the state appealed to the United States Supreme Court.[52] The Court initially addressed the competing interests:

> There is no doubt as to the power of a State, having a high responsibility for education of its citizens, to impose reasonable regulations for the control and duration of basic education. Providing public schools ranks at the very apex of the function of a State.[53]

While the state has an interest in educating its children, according to the Court, "even this paramount responsibility was, in *Pierce,* made to yield to the right of parents to provide an equivalent education in a privately operated system."[54] Like the state's interest in education, "the values of parental direction of the religious upbringing and education of their children in their early and formative years have a high place in our society."[55] Thus, the Court said that the state interest in education:

> [I]s not totally free from a balancing process when it impinges on fundamental rights and interests, such as those specifically protected by the Free Exercise Clause of the First Amendment, and the traditional interest of parents with respect to the religious upbringing of their children so long as they, in the words of *Pierce,* "prepare [them] for additional obligations."[56]

The Court reasoned that the state could compel attendance beyond the eighth grade if "it [appeared] either that the State does not deny the free exercise of religious belief by its requirement, or that there is a state interest of sufficient magnitude to override the interest claiming protection under the Free Exercise Clause."[57]

The Court next evaluated the quality of the Amish religious claims. After engaging in an in-depth analysis of the Amish tradition, the Court concluded:

[The] Amish objection to formal education beyond the eighth grade is firmly grounded in [its] central religious concepts. They object to the high school, and higher education generally, because the values they teach are in marked variance with Amish values and the Amish way of life; they view secondary school education as an impermissible exposure of their children to a "worldly" influence in conflict with their beliefs.[58]

Thus, "in the Amish belief higher learning tends to develop values they reject as influences that alienate man from God."[59]

The Supreme Court, however, was "careful to determine whether the Amish religious faith and their mode of life are, as they claim, inseparable and interdependent."[60] The Court stated that "[a] way of life, however virtuous and admirable, may not be interposed as a barrier to reasonable state regulation of education if it is based on purely secular considerations; to have the protection of the Religion Clauses, the claims must be rooted in religious belief."[61] After examining the record, the Court found ample evidence to support "the claim that the traditional way of life of the Amish is not merely a matter of personal preference, but one of deep religious conviction, shared by an organized group, and intimately related to daily living."[62]

The Court determined that failing to exempt the Amish students clearly and unequivocally interfered with the exercise of the religious beliefs of the Amish and pointed to the classic Hobson's choice the Amish faced: comply with the law and compromise their religious beliefs, or violate the statute and follow their religious tenets.[63]

The Court then considered the quality of the state's interest in universal compulsory education. The state argued that this interest "is so great that it is paramount to the undisputed claims of [the Amish parents],"[64] an argument the Court rejected. While the Court again recognized that the state has an interest in educating its youth to prepare them to be effective citizens and to function independently in society, it found that "an additional one or two years of formal high school for Amish children in place of their long-established program of informal vocational education would do little to serve those interests."[65] The Amish system of education produces hard-working and self-reliant citizens and prepares its youth for life in Amish adulthood, which does not require advanced book learning.[66]

The Court also held that leaving school would not effect the ability of the Amish to be effective citizens in a democratic society, pointing to the fact that compulsory education is a recent development in history and that the democratic process worked sufficiently before the advent of such an educational system.[67]

Yoder is an important case in parental rights jurisprudence primarily for three reasons.

First, the Supreme Court recognized that the state's interest in education may be subordinated to the parental right to elect to educate one's children in a privately operated school system.[68]

Second, the Court's holding and reasoning intimate that the Court is more likely to deem the parental right paramount to the state's interest if the individual joins the parental right claim with another constitutional right.

Finally, while the Court tilted the scale in favor of the parental right—the religious freedom claim of the Amish in this case—it recognized that the parental right to control and direct the child's education can be subjected to reasonable state regulations.[69]

Four years later, the Supreme Court focused on the state's power to impose reasonable regulations on parental rights in the education context. In *Runyon v. McCrary*,[70] the Court addressed the issue of whether the federal Civil Rights Act "prohibits private schools from excluding qualified children solely because they are Negroes."[71]

Respondents in the case were two African-American children who had been denied admission to private schools after responding to advertisements in the "Yellow Pages" of the phone book.[72] Neither school had ever admitted an African-American student into its school or summer program.[73] The parents filed suit under the federal Civil Rights Act, alleging that their rights to contract in the same manner as whites had been violated.[74] Both the federal district court and court of appeals ruled in favor of the parents, and the schools appealed to the United States Supreme Court.[75]

First, the Court noted the limited questions the appeal raised—for example, "[W]hether §1981 prohibits private, commercially operated, nonsectarian schools from denying admission to prospective students because they are Negroes, and, if so, whether that federal law is constitutional as so applied."[76] The Court quickly rejected the schools' argument that the provisions of the federal Civil Rights Act did not reach acts of private discrimination, pointing to ample precedent in the area.[77]

The Court then focused on the issue more relevant to the discussion of the parental right to direct the education of one's child. The schools maintained that applying the statute to them violated certain constitutional rights—namely, the rights of free association and privacy, and the parental right to direct the child's education.[78]

With respect to the freedom of association claim, the Court found that applying the statute to private schools in no way interfered with the teachings of these schools and that, while the First Amendment protects the right of parents to send their children to schools that promote segregation, "it does not follow that the *practice* of excluding racial minorities from such institutions is also protected by the same principle."[79]

The Court stated that the Constitution does not protect discrimination and that although "[i]nvidious private discrimination may be characterized as a form of exercising freedom of association protected by the First Amendment . . . it has never been accorded affirmative constitutional protections."[80]

The Court then turned to the parental rights question. First, the Court examined prior Court cases affirming the parental right to direct the education of one's children, focusing on the limits of this right. According to the *Runyon* Court, this fundamental right only proscribed the state from interfering with the parental power to decide where their children would attend school and the freedom of private schools to teach certain subjects and values.[81] The Court concluded that the application of federal civil rights provisions to private schools in no way infringed this right:

> No challenge is made to the petitioner schools' right to operate or the right of parents to send their children to a particular private school rather than a public school. Nor do these cases involve a challenge to the subject matter which is taught at any private school. Thus, the [schools] remain presumptively free to inculcate whatever values and standards they deem desirable. *Meyer* and its progeny entitle them to no more.[82]

In its examination of the right to privacy, the Court reaffirmed its view that the parental right was a limited concept:

> The Court has repeatedly stressed that while parents have a constitutional right to send their children to private schools and a constitutional right to select private schools that offer specialized instruction, they have no constitutional right to provide private school education unfettered by reasonable government regulation.[83]

The fact that the parental right to direct the education of one's children is subject to reasonable governmental regulation is not a new concept. The *Runyon* decision, however, shows the Court examining the scope of the parental right in a novel way. While *Meyer* and its progeny took an expansive approach of the parental right, the *Runyon* Court had a more restrained view of the right. The *Runyon* Court's approach, in all likelihood, may be explained by the context of the case: invidious racial discrimination.

When dealing with racial inequities, the Court invariably has restrictively construed constitutional rights, particularly First Amendment freedoms.[84] The Court wanted to end the discriminatory practices of these private schools, and its reasoning reflects this result-oriented approach.

The future of the parental right to direct the education of one's child, therefore, is not endangered. In fact, in post-*Runyon* decisions the Supreme Court has affirmed the importance of family autonomy and parental rights.

For example, in a recent holding, *Employment Division, Dept. of Human Resources v. Smith*[85] the Court recognized the vitality of the parental right.[86] The Court stated that a free exercise claim alone did not warrant strict scrutiny of an offensive state statute; however, the Court pointed to the parental right-religious right claim as sort of an iron hybrid claim, intimating that any state action infringing on these rights would be subject to heightened scrutiny.[87]

In other cases outside the education context, the Supreme Court has reiterated the importance of the family in American society.[88] For example, in *Moore v. City of East Cleveland*,[89] the Supreme Court struck down a housing ordinance with a restrictive definition of the word *family*. The city charged a grandmother for violating the housing code.[90] Living with the woman were her son and two grandsons, only one of which was related to the son living in the house.[91] The city stated that the second grandson was an illegal occupant.[92] The Supreme Court held that while generally it grants deference to legislative decisions, such deference was impossible "[w]hen a city undertakes such intrusive regulation of the family."[93] The Court noted its precedents, including *Pierce v. Society of Sisters*[94] and *Meyer v. Nebraska*,[95] recognizing family autonomy:[96] "Our decisions establish that the Constitution protects the sanctity of the family precisely because the institution of the family is deeply rooted in this Nation's history and tradition. It is through the family that we inculcate and pass down many of our most cherished values, moral and cultural."[97]

Recognizing that while the family was not beyond regulation, the government must justify any interference with the family with a compelling state interest.[98] In this case, the Court found that the state could not withstand strict judicial scrutiny.[99]

PARENTAL RIGHTS AND HOME INSTRUCTION: SOME CONCLUDING THOUGHTS

None of the cases discussed in the previous section expressly addresses the right of parents to home educate their children. However, these decisions provide two general principles.

First, parents have the fundamental right to direct the education of their offspring.

Second, this right is not absolute. In some contexts, the state has the authority to impose reasonable regulations on this right,[100] but in other contexts the state power is subordinated to the parental right.

These two principles raise two questions: 1. does the parental right with respect to education include the right to home school; and 2. should the right exist, to what degree is it immune to state regulation?

These principles and unanswered questions comprise the framework lower federal courts and state courts have inherited for building home school jurisprudence.[101]

While most states have provided a home school option for compulsory education, some states have not.[102]

Nevertheless, in any state it is important for parents to argue that denying them the home school alternative infringes upon their fundamental right to direct the education of their children. This position would accord home education, finally, the status of a constitutionally protected right, meaning parents would not have to rely on legislatures to provide the home school option. The right would be automatic.

In addition, inclusion under the fundamental parental right serves another purpose. The parental right to direct the education of one's child is currently somewhat subject to reasonable government regulations.[103] In any other context, the state would merely have to demonstrate a rational basis for imposing regulations on home schools; however, establishing home education as a facet of a fundamental right entitles home schoolers to strict scrutiny of state regulations.[104]

This means that if courts recognize home education as a fundamental right, any state attempt to supervise or restrict this right must be justified by a compelling state interest, a difficult standard for the state to meet. Since parents will be subjected to such regulations, it is to their benefit for the state to be required to proffer a compelling state interest in, rather than a rational basis for, its regulations.

18

Vagueness Issues

The Fourteenth Amendment prohibits the state from depriving "any person of life, liberty, or property, without due process of law."[1] The underlying purpose of due process is to ensure fundamental fairness, and an important component of fundamental fairness is the "vagueness doctrine."[2]

The vagueness doctrine provides that any statute which "either forbids or requires the doing of an act in terms so vague that men of common intelligence must necessarily guess at its meaning and differ as to its application, violates the first essential of due process of law."[3] As a result, courts will strike down, or "void," any such statute. In essence, the doctrine prohibits "wholesale legislative delegation of lawmaking authority to the courts."[4]

The vagueness doctrine is another way for home school litigants to challenge state legislation adversely affecting home education. Relying on the vagueness doctrine may not produce the best result because it does not proscribe the legislature from enacting regulations affecting home schools; it only requires the legislature to write legislation with sufficient clarity and definiteness.[5] Nonetheless, it is an important claim to raise in home education litigation because many statutes concerning home instruction fail to define clearly what parents must do to comply with statutes regulating the home education of their children.[6]

This chapter defines the scope of the vagueness doctrine, examining important Supreme Court opinions articulating the doctrine's boundaries. It also evaluates recent decisions in the area of home education and discusses the ramifications and implications of such decisions in order to provide guidance to future litigants considering asserting a vagueness claim.

THE BOUNDARIES OF THE VAGUENESS DOCTRINE

The vagueness doctrine does not require legislators to draft statutes with "mathematical certainty"[7] or courts to void statutes that could have been written with more clarity and definiteness.[8] The Supreme Court has acknowledged that some language possesses an "inherent vagueness."[9] In fact, the Court has found that statutory language can be "marked by 'flexibility and reasonable breadth, rather than meticulous specificity' . . . [if] it is clear what the ordinance as a whole prohibits."[10]

Drawing a bright line between "reasonable breadth" and impermissible vagueness is difficult since there is no "yardstick of impermissible indeterminacy."[11] Nevertheless, the Supreme Court has devised a two-part standard to guide courts, legislatures, and citizens in defining the concept. Two distinct components comprise this test: 1. providing fair notice and warning; and 2. preventing arbitrary and discriminatory enforcement.[12] Justice Marshall elaborated on this standard in *Grayned v. City of Rockford*:[13]

> First, because we assume that man is free to steer between lawful and unlawful conduct, we insist that laws give the person of ordinary intelligence a reasonable opportunity to know what is prohibited, so that he may act accordingly. Vague laws may trap the innocent by not providing fair warning. Second, if arbitrary and discriminatory enforcement is to be prevented, laws must provide explicit standards for those who apply them. A vague law impermissibly delegates basic policy matters to policemen, judges, and juries for resolution on an *ad hoc* and subjective basis, with the attendant dangers of arbitrary and discriminatory application.[14]

This test is not evenly applied to all cases. The degree to which a statute is scrutinized under this statute depends on the type of interest at issue.[15]

At one end of the scale, "economic regulation is subject to a less strict vagueness test because its subject matter is often more narrow, and because businesses, which face economic demands to plan behavior carefully, can be expected to consult relevant legislation in advance of action."[16] In addition, "[t]he Court has also expressed greater tolerance of enactments with civil rather than criminal penalties because the consequences of imprecision are qualitatively less severe."[17]

On the far end of the scale, however, "the most important fact affecting the clarity that the Constitution demands of a law is whether it threatens to inhibit the exercise of constitutionally protected rights."[18] Courts will require greater specificity from laws encroaching upon the exercise of First Amendment rights, for example,[19] because "[u]ncertain meanings inevitably lead citizens to 'steer far wider of the unlawful zone' . . . than if the boundaries of the forbidden areas were clearly marked."[20] Consequently, the Court requires "a precise statute evincing a legislative judgment that certain specific conduct be . . . proscribed"[21] to ensure that "the legislature has focused on the First Amendment interests and determined that other governmental policies compel regulation."[22] Courts treat statutes affecting constitutionally protected rights differently in another respect as well. Ordinarily when a litigant challenges the constitutionality of a statute, courts require that the litigant have standing, or that the law is unconstitutional as applied to him or her.[23] A litigant "who engages in some conduct that is clearly proscribed cannot complain of the vagueness of the law as applied to the conduct of others."[24] The Court has created an exception to this general rule in the First Amendment area:[25] a litigant may challenge "a statute on the ground that it violates the First Amendment rights of third parties not before the court, even though the law is constitutional as applied to that [litigant]."[26]

Thus, a law affecting First Amendment freedoms "will be struck down in its entirety, even if the conduct of the particular party challenging the statute would be prohibited by an appropriately narrowed law."[27] The Court's motivation behind this principle is clear: "[T]hose whose expression is 'chilled' by the existence of [an] . . . unduly vague statute cannot be expected to adjudicate their own rights, lacking by definition the willingness to disobey the law."[28]

There are, however, limits to this exception. Courts permit a facial challenge only "if a law reaches a 'substantial amount of constitutionally protected conduct.'"[29] When considering a facial challenge, courts must examine any limiting construction that a state court or administrative agency has offered in an attempt to avoid constitutional problems.[30]

To fully understand the vagueness doctrine, it is beneficial to see how the Court has applied the analysis to two specific cases, *Grayned* and *Kolender v. Lawson*.[31]

Grayned is one of the landmark cases in vagueness doctrine jurisprudence. The appellant was among a group demonstrating a hundred feet from a high school because the principal refused to respond to complaints of African-American students.[32] Among a smaller group of protesters arrested after ignoring a warning to disband,[33] the appellant was convicted for violating an anti-picketing ordinance that prohibited picketing or demonstrating within 150 feet of a school while the school was in session.[34] The ordinance further provided:

> [N]o person, while on public or private grounds adjacent to any building in which a school or any class thereof is in session, shall willfully make or assist in the making of any noise or diversion which disturbs or tends to disturb the peace or good order of such school session or class thereof.[35]

Among other claims, the constitutionality of the ordinance under the vagueness doctrine was challenged. While the Court ultimately found the statute invalid on other grounds,[36] it rejected the appellant's vagueness claim.[37] Applying the vagueness test in a more rigid fashion because of the First Amendment interests and the penal nature of the ordinance,[38] the Court found that the ordinance provided fair notice and minimal guidelines that would avoid arbitrary enforcement. Justice Marshall, writing for the Court, stated:

> We do not have here a vague, general "breach of the peace" ordinance, but a statute written specifically for the school context, where the prohibited disturbances are easily measured by their impact on the normal activities of the school. Given this "particular context," the ordinance gives "fair notices to those to whom [it] is directed." . . . [T]he ordinance here clearly "delineates its reach in words of common understanding."[39]

Furthermore, unlike recent statutes that the Court examined, the current ordinance did "not permit punishment for the expression of an unpopular point of view, and it contains no broad invitation to subjective or discriminatory enforcement."[40] The ordinance specifically required that:

> (1) the "noise or diversion" be actually incompatible with normal school activity; (2) there be a demonstrated causality between the disruption that occurs and the "noise or diversion"; and (3) the acts be willfully done.[41]

Thus, while the language of the ordinance was flexible, the legislature drafted the law with specific requirements and sufficient notice to would-be violators and thus avoided a successful vagueness challenge.

The ordinance at issue in *Kolender v. Lawson*,[42] however, did not reach the necessary level of definiteness and specificity.[43] A convicted criminal defendant challenged a "a criminal statute that requires persons who loiter or wander on the street to provide a 'credible and reliable' identification and to account for their presence when requested by a peace officer under circumstances that would justify a stop under the standards of *Terry v. Ohio*."[44] Justice O'Connor, writing for the Court, held that the language "credible and reliable" was unconstitutionally vague.[45] In particular, the Court was troubled because the language "encourages arbitrary enforcement by failing to describe with sufficient particularity what a suspect must do in order to satisfy the statute"[46] and because such enforcement could suppress First Amendment liberties.[47] A suspect violates the ordinance "unless 'the officer [is] satisfied that the identification is reliable.'"[48] Clearly, Justice O'Connor observed, "the full discretion accorded to the police to determine whether the suspect has provided a 'credible and reliable' identification necessarily entrust[s] law-making 'to the moment-to-moment' judgment of the policeman on his beat."[49]

While the statute may have a compelling interest in fighting crime,[50] such an interest does not excuse an ordinance that "furnishes a convenient tool for 'harsh and discriminatory enforcement by local prosecuting officials, against particular groups deemed to merit their displeasure.'"[51]

VAGUENESS AND HOME EDUCATION

Essentially, the "void-for-vagueness doctrine requires that a penal statute define the criminal offense with sufficient definiteness that ordinary people can understand what conduct is prohibited and in a manner that does not encourage arbitrary and discriminatory enforcement."[52] In the context of the First Amendment, or more specifically home schools, the latter requirement may be the most significant.[53]

If the legislature fails to provide minimal guidelines, enforcement personnel may suppress First Amendment rights such as those protected by the religion clauses,[54] according to their predilections or whims.[55]

This is particularly true in the home school context. Legislators draft general compulsory attendance statutes, providing criminal sanctions if violated, with limited exemptions.[56] State legislatures generally delegate exemption decisions and approval and regulatory procedures to local school boards in the name of local autonomy.[57] In situations where the legislature has neglected to draft minimal guidelines for local school boards to follow, a vagueness issue emerges. Not only may home educators be unaware of when they are violating the compulsory attendance statutes, but such statutes may be open to construction on an *ad hoc* and arbitrary basis.[58]

Many home school litigants have asserted vagueness claims, and the courts addressing this issue have produced an incoherent vagueness jurisprudence in the home school context.

Contrasting two recent federal district court decisions provides a sampling of this disparate treatment of the vagueness claims of home educators.

In *Blackwelder v. Safnauer*,[59] a federal district court judge rejected a home school litigant's claim that New York's home instruction statute was unconstitutionally vague.[60] The New York statute provided that any child instructed outside the public schools must receive "substantially equivalent" instruction to public school students and that a "competent" teacher must provide such instruction.[61] Parents who wished to pursue such an educational path were required to prove that their home schools met the "substantially equivalent" and "competent" instructor requirements.[62] Local school boards were responsible for ensuring that such parents satisfied these standards, and their decisions were subject to review by the state education commissioner.[63] The plaintiff parents, however, argued:

> [T]hat New York's requirement that minors taught outside the public school system must receive instruction from a "competent" teacher that is at least "substantially equivalent" to that provided students in public schools fails to provide sufficiently concrete standards of conduct for those who wish to educate their children at home . . . [and contended]

that the manner in which the state evaluates homeschooling programs gives the superintendents . . . throughout the state unbridled discretion in determining whether a particular program provides the statutorily required level of instruction.[64]

The federal district court judge rejected these claims.[65] First, the judge held that the language in question did not lack reasonable definiteness and clarity. According to the court: "The terms 'competent' and 'substantially equivalent' are not in and of themselves 'so lacking in meaning as to be invalid.' . . . [T]hey . . . establish a comparative standard that makes direct reference to the minimum educational standards that must be maintained in the state's public schools."[66]

In support of its conclusion, the court pointed to the comprehensive regulations to guide local school districts in fashioning their curriculums and advisory guidelines for establishing a home education program[67] promulgated by the New York Department of Education and to the detailed curriculum descriptions provided by local school boards.[68] The court concluded: "When read in conjunction with the various regulations that complement the [statute the] statute 'communicates its reach in words of common understanding.'"[69]

Turning to the argument that the district school boards possessed too much discretion in applying the statute, the court found that districts did not have unbridled discretion in applying the compulsory law statute. Although the application of the statute may vary between districts, the court refused to equate such disparity with vagueness.[70] The statute provides a basic framework for all districts to follow, and that, according to the court, is sufficient.[71] In addition, the court emphasized that parents can obtain a preliminary construction of the statute before they act: "A party's ability to clarify the meaning of a regulation and modify his behavior accordingly, either through the party's own inquiry or through an administrative process, can ameliorate any vagueness problems that might otherwise be created by the terms of that regulation."[72]

According to this court, comprehensive regulations saved the statute despite the disparity in application.

Jeffery v. O'Donnell[73] provides a striking contrast to the *Blackwelder* decision. *Jeffery* stemmed from a home educator's federal civil rights claim challenging the constitutionality of Pennsylvania's compulsory attendance law.[74] This statute included the general compulsory attendance policy, but it also provided an exemption: "Regular daily instruction in the English language, for the time herein required, by a *properly qualified tutor*, shall be considered as complying with [the compulsory attendance law], if such instruction is satisfactory to the proper district superintendent of schools."[75] In addition, although the state department of education promulgated regulations requiring that students outside the public school must be educated by a "properly qualified tutor" and that private tutoring is subject to the approval of local school boards, the regulations failed to define the term "properly qualified tutor."[76]

The court engaged in a stringent vagueness analysis because of the First Amendment rights at issue.[77] Although the court initially found that the regulations did not encroach on the plaintiffs' First Amendment rights, it recognized that "the amendment is indeed implicated at any time the rights of parents and religious freedom conflicts [sic] with the right of the state in exercising its legitimate power to set standards for education."[78]

The court first distinguished the current statute from the statute at issue in *Blackwelder*. According to the court, New York's extensive regulations and review procedure presented a situation remarkably different from that in Pennsylvania.[79] While Pennsylvania argued that "traditionally education requires local input . . . plaintiffs [did] not dispute vagueness on this ground. Rather, they assert[ed] vagueness because neither parents nor the district superintendents have a standard by which to determine what is satisfactory."[80]

The Pennsylvania plaintiffs alleged that the structure of the statute "leaves them with as many definitions of qualifications for tutors and instructional standards as there are district superintendents."[81] For example, the plaintiffs discovered that thirty-four different definitions of "properly qualified private tutor" exist and that "disparity abounds" in the standards used to determined "satisfactory" curricula.[82] The plaintiffs also found that, upon inquiry, the state board of education provides local school districts with "a packet with various documents from seven different school districts. Each represents a unique policy, and there is no discernible pattern among them."[83] Furthermore, parents who were denied approval to home educate were provided one appeal before courts under the local school board's jurisdiction, "as opposed to an appeal provided by statute or uniform regulations."[84]

The court concurred with the argument of the plaintiffs, concluding that the statute was an affront to the values the vagueness doctrine was designed to protect:[85]

> A person of ordinary intelligence cannot reasonably steer between the lawful and unlawful to avoid criminal prosecution. There exists no standards for determining who is a qualified tutor or what is a satisfactory curriculum in any district. Superintendents of school districts, while exercising a legitimate and constitutional function of managing their districts according to the unique character of each district, nevertheless make their decisions on an *ad hoc* basis which can result in the dangers of arbitrary and discriminatory application. While some circumstances allow the luxury of awaiting judicial clarifications, the threat to sensitive First Amendment freedoms mandates judicial intrusion in the form of declaring the particular provision of the law unconstitutional for vagueness.[86]

As suggested by the contrast between *Jeffrey* and *Blackwelder*, "disparity abounds"[87] in the judicial treatment of vagueness claims in the home instruction context. Such disparity, however, may be natural given that there are fifty separate state compulsory attendance statutes[88] and at least fifty different state judiciaries construing them. It is difficult to transfer the reasoning of one state court to another;[89] however, certain language has been universally troublesome for courts because of vagueness problems.

For example, several courts have addressed claims that the term "private schools" is unconstitutionally vague.[90] One court voided a statute for failing to define this language sufficiently. In *State v. Popanz*,[91] a home educator was convicted for violating Wisconsin's compulsory attendance law. He defended on the ground that his children attended a private school—an exception to the compulsory law.[92] The state, however, asserted that the defendant did not satisfy the "private school" exemption because he failed to follow the compliance procedure articulated by the local district school administrator.[93] The parent challenged his conviction, claiming that the lack of definition and established exemption procedures was unconstitutionally vague.

The court found that the statute failed to satisfy the vagueness test articulated in *Grayned*. First, after examining the compulsory attendance statute and education rules and regulations, the court observed that the legislature and state board of education had neglected to define "private school" and to provide any criteria for assisting local school districts in determining when an instructional program is a private school.[94] The court stated that such a definition or criteria should exist, so parents and courts would not have to guess at the meaning of "private school."[95]

Second, the court found that because the statute did not define the term "private schools," "the determination of what constitutes a 'private school' apparently rests solely in the discretion of the school attendance officer of the district."[96] In the defendant's school district, anyone "seeking to comply with [the exemption to compulsory attendance] must consult the district school administrator to find out what the administrator considers a 'private school' and must comply with the procedure set forth by that particular administrator."[97]

In *Popanz*, the administrator had no written criteria or established procedure; thus, no one could ascertain the district's standards.[98] The court found in this context that determining what constitutes a "private school" was subject to arbitrary and discriminatory application.[99] It concluded:

> The persons who obey the law should not have to guess at what the phrase "private school" means. They should have some objective standards to guide them and their attempts to "steer between lawful and unlawful conduct." . . . Furthermore, standards cannot lie only in the minds of persons whose duty it is to enforce the laws. . . . [T]he statute fails to provide fair notice to those who would seek to obey it and also lacks sufficient standards for proper enforcement.[100]

At least one court, however, has found that such language is not vague.

In *Burrow v. State*,[101] the court refused to consider the vagueness issue because the parents raising the claim lacked standing.[102] An Arkansas statute required all children to attend a "public, private, or parochial school."[103] Because the statute did not define the term "school," the parents, who were convicted of violating the attendance law because they home educated their children,[104] claimed the statute was unconstitutionally vague. They argued that the language failed to provide a fair warning of whether home instruction constituted a private school.[105]

The court, however, declined to hear their claim. Pointing to the principle that those to whom the law clearly applies do not have standing to assert a vagueness claim,[106] the Arkansas Supreme Court found abundantly clear the meaning of the word *school*: "The common understanding of this phrase connotes an *institution* to which a child is sent. . . . We think someone of average intelligence would readily recognize that [home education does] not constitute a school within the common understanding of the word."[107]

Therefore, since the court did not equate *home school* with *school*, the parents were in clear violation of the attendance statute by home educating their children rather than sending them to an institution.[108]

Another phrase that is often the subject of litigation is "essentially equivalent." Many statutes provide that a school is established if the courses are taught by an instructor with "essentially equivalent" or "substantially equivalent" qualifications or credentials as public school teachers or that nonpublic school coursework must be "equivalent" to that received in public schools.[109]

Courts have divided over whether such language presents vagueness issues. For example, in *State v. Newstrom*,[110] the court found that "essentially equivalent" as used to define an adequate instructor was impermissible under the vagueness doctrine.[111] Although the state encouraged the court to place a limiting construction on the language to include only instructors with college degrees, the court refused, finding that a narrow construction would circumvent the legislative intent to provide a flexible construction.[112] In this case, however, the legislature had crossed the line from reasonable flexibility to vagueness.[113] The court found that the statutory language must be more clear in order to survive a vagueness challenge.[114]

As previously noted, it is difficult to compare and contrast these cases because of the different contexts in which they are decided. Different states have different statutes, and the language surrounding problematic phrases reflects a variety of situations.

From these cases, nonetheless, one can discern certain common threads between these cases; if such "red flags" appear in a statute or regulatory scheme, litigants should be concerned with potential vagueness problems.

First, the fact that a statute fails to define a term does not in itself present a vagueness problem if the legislature or state board of education has promulgated regulations that provide guidelines for defining the term and if these are available to local school districts and citizens.[115]

Second, litigants also should consider a vagueness claim if the local school board has not established a formal procedure for exempting parents from the compulsory attendance law or reduced its procedures and if it appears that the local school district official appears to have no pattern in making such determinations.[116]

Third, courts also have been troubled by the inability of parents to appeal local school boards' findings on exemption.[117]

CONCLUSION

Home school litigants, if faced with any of these or equivalent statutory construction problems, should consider raising a vagueness claim. Winning based on this claim does not mean that the state will no longer enact statutes that affect home schools; however, the vagueness doctrine mandates fair notice as to the procedures for establishing a home school and as to whether home education is permissible under compulsory attendance statutes, and also prevents arbitrary and discriminatory enforcement of such statutes. Parents are entitled to proceed with their plans knowing where they stand before the law.

In many cases, considering the growing hostility of courts toward promoting a vigorous Free Exercise Clause, asserting a vagueness claim may provide the best opportunity for winning the case.[118]

19

Private School Defense

The compulsory attendance laws in some states require children to attend either a public or private school.[1] For parents desiring to educate their children at home in these states, an important question is whether certain nonpublic teaching arrangements, such as home schools, can be qualified as "private schools" within the meaning of the compulsory attendance statute.

Thus, the issue of whether a home school is considered a private school arises most frequently in those states where applicable compulsory education statutes do not contain an exception for home instruction.[2] In these states, unless a child is enrolled in a public school or a certified private or parochial school, compulsory attendance laws would be in effect.[3]

The courts have issued differing opinions on this issue, disagreeing on the meaning of the word *school*.

WHAT IS A SCHOOL?

Narrow Definition

One view interprets *school* narrowly and holds that a school is an established, ongoing institution holding itself out to the public as a place where children are given instruction. These courts seem to focus on the state's interest in the educational base of its citizens, the desirability of having children associate with other children, and an assurance that the state's interest in the education of children is being served.[4]

Broad Definition

The definition of a school under the opposing view is more broad. *School* is seen as a learning *situation* that may qualify as a school if it meets certain basic requirements. Thus, a home school would qualify as a private school under this view, provided that the instruction given is equivalent to that offered in public schools.[5]

CASE LAW ADOPTING THE NARROW DEFINITION OF *SCHOOL*

One of the earliest cases considering this question was *State v. Counort*.[6] There, the court held that a "private school" was a school having the character of an institution organized by private individuals for the purpose of providing education.[7] The court stated that a private school must have "the same character of school as the public school, a regular, organized and existing institution, making a business of instructing children of school age. . . ."[8]

The court stated further: "For home instruction to be acceptable under this view, it would seem to have to become so institutional in character as to lose any intimate homelike quality."[9]

Several courts following *Counort* have provided additional criteria to assist in determining whether or not a home school is a private school.

The *quality of the instruction* given is often a determining factor. For example, in *State v. Lowry*,[10] home instruction was held not to constitute instruction in a private school.[11] The primary reason seemed to be the fact that the parent, although a qualified teacher, failed to fulfill all the statutory requirements for the classes that were taught.[12] Therefore, according to the *Lowry* court, for a home instruction program to qualify as a private school, it must at least meet the course of instruction requirements of the statute.[13]

Another often-cited reason for not classifying home schools as private schools is that home schooling does not provide the *socialization* a child would acquire in another group learning institution.[14]

Another court said that supervision of individual home schools would create *great administrative problems* for the state at great cost.[15]

Often a court will look to the *qualifications of the one doing the teaching* (usually a parent) to determine whether or not the home school should qualify as a private school. Thus, in *People v. Turner*,[16] the court said that the only substitute for a public school was an approved private school or tutoring by a qualified teacher, and since the instructor in that case was not certified as a teacher, the teaching arrangement would not qualify as a private school.[17] The fact that the instruction actually given the children may have been satisfactory did not qualify the instruction procedure as a private school.[18]

Similarly, in *State ex rel Shoreline School Dist. v. Superior Court for King County, Juvenile Court*,[19] it was conceded that the child was receiving book learning at home that was comparable to that of the public schools.[20] Nonetheless, the court held that the mother's school could not be considered a private school in view of the statutory provisions requiring that teachers of schools, both public and private, hold a teaching certificate, and requiring that private schools make reports of certain matters to public officials. Neither requirement had been met in this case.[21]

Thus, many courts adhere to a strict interpretation of *private school*. In these jurisdictions, private school status may be limited to instances where there is some type of institutionalized learning, with certified teachers, specific courses of instruction, and a variety of students.

CASES FINDING HOME SCHOOLS TO BE PRIVATE SCHOOLS

Many courts have recognized home schools as private schools. One of the first cases to so hold was *State v. Peterman*.[22] There, the court expressly rejected the notion that a private school meant an accepted school, organized and conducted as such by a person possessing necessary qualifications and having the proper equipment.[23] The court focused on the educational aspects of a school: "A school in the ordinary acceptation of its meaning, is a place where instruction is imparted to the young. . . . We do not think that the number of persons, whether one or many, make a place where instruction is imparted any less or more a school."[24]

In *People v. Levisen*,[25] the court supported the notion that home schools are legitimate private schools. The court noted: "[T]he object is that all children shall be educated, not that they shall be educated in any particular manner or place."[26] Academic training was the most essential element of a school.[27] However, the court emphasized that parents could not evade their responsibility to educate their children.[28] Parents still have to show that they in good faith have provided an adequate course of instruction.[29]

Recent decisions indicate an increased judicial willingness to accord private school status to home schools when there is such a statutory provision. For example, in *Strosnider v. Strosnider*,[30] the court found that a nonpublic learning arrangement qualified as a private school. Mrs. Strosnider had created a "school" for nine children, three of whom were not her own.[31] The school's teacher was her daughter, who had no college education and was not certified as a teacher.[32] Nevertheless, the court found that this situation qualified as a private school because the Strosnider children attended classes in a building separate from their home and were instructed by a teacher not their parent.[33]

In *Roemhild v. State*,[34] the court allowed a home schooling arrangement to qualify as a private school. In this case, the court said that the Georgia compulsory attendance statute was defective in that it did not adequately define "private school." The court said that a person of ordinary intelligence, who wanted to avoid the statute's penalties, must have fair notice as to what constituted a private school, and thus the court voided the statute as vague and allowed the home school arrangement to stand.[35]

Similarly, a Texas court, after finding that the legislature had not adequately defined "private school," concluded that as long as a home school had a written curriculum and taught five core subjects in a bona fide manner, it was a private school.[36]

CONCLUSION

Courts that refuse to find that home schools constitute private schools seem to do so either because the person doing the teaching is not a certified teacher or because the parents failed to comply with state statutory requirements, such as allowing visitation by the state.[37]

Courts also tend to scrutinize carefully the enactments of state legislatures. In states where legislatures have expressly provided for home schools, courts have refused to blur the statutorily created distinctions between private schools and home instruction.[38]

Where there is no separate home school provision, courts seem to desire that states explicitly define *private school*. Where states do not, courts will often find that the statutes are too vague and will decide that home schools are indeed private schools.[39]

The problem of defining a home school as a private school is initially one of statutory construction. However, if a home instruction program meets the minimum statutory requirements for a school, a court would have difficulty finding that it is not a private school.

20

Establishment Clause Issues

The Establishment Clause of the First Amendment reads: "Congress shall make no law respecting an establishment of religion."[1]

At first glance, this constitutional provision seems to share little common ground with home education. Yet, while home schools may not present the image of the religious institution—such as a church, "brick and mortar" religious school, or hospital—that courts traditionally have encountered in Establishment Clause cases, many home schools are *de facto* religious communities.[2]

Although few home school litigants have asserted Establishment Clause claims, court decisions addressing such challenges have not been based upon the ground that home schools fall outside the scope of this constitutional provision.[3]

Home school litigants, therefore, should consider asserting an Establishment Clause claim in addition to other constitutional challenges when facing a state statute that prohibits or regulates home schooling.

In challenging state actions affecting home education under the Establishment Clause, home school advocates should consider making two distinct claims: 1. state action affecting home education fails the traditional *Lemon* test; and 2. in certain circumstances, the state is exhibiting an impermissible preference among religions.

This chapter discusses the details of alleging such claims and the pertinent Establishment Clause jurisprudence. It also evaluates how courts have treated such claims in the home school context.

USING THE *LEMON* TEST TO CHALLENGE INTERFERENCE WITH HOME EDUCATION

Defining the Scope of the Establishment Clause

The Debate

Constitutional scholars and historians have considered the proper construction of the Establishment Clause,[4] disagreeing primarily on its historical context.[5]

One view, that of the strict separationists, supports the Jeffersonian view that separation protects the state from the church and the Madisonian view that both religion and state will meet their ultimate achievement only if they remain independent.[6] The second view is that historical records show that the framers did not intend for the First Amendment to require strict separation, but rather intended for government to show "positive toleration" and accommodation of religion.[7]

While the First Amendment was enacted in 1791, it was not until 1947 that the Supreme Court provided its definitive construction of the Establishment Clause.[8] In the seminal case *Everson v. Board of Education*,[9] the Supreme Court held that, at a minimum, the Establishment Clause means:

> Neither a state nor the Federal Government can set up a church. Neither can pass laws which aid one religion, aid all religions, or prefer one religion over another. Neither can force nor influence a person to go to or to remain away from church against his will or force him to profess a belief or disbelief in any religion. No person can be punished for entertaining or professing religious beliefs or disbeliefs, for church attendance or non-attendance. No tax in any amount, large or small, can be levied to support any religious activities or institutions, whatever they may be called, or whatever form they may adopt to teach or practice religion. Neither a state nor the Federal Government can, openly or secretly, participate in the affairs of any religious organizations or groups and *vice versa*.[10]

Concluding its discussion on the historical meaning of the provision, Justice Hugo Black, writing for the majority of the Court, elected to adopt a strict separatist view of the Establishment Clause as its official construction of this constitutional provision: "In the words of Jefferson, the clause against establishment of religion by law was intended to erect a 'wall of separation between church and State.'"[11]

The Court ruled that essentially the First Amendment had erected a high and impregnable wall between the church and state.[12] Although the Court has found that "there is room for play in the joints productive of a benevolent neutrality which will permit religious exercise to exist without sponsorship and without interference,"[13] the Court, in general, has maintained a barrier between religion and government and has "long recognized that underlying the Establishment Clause is 'the objective . . . to prevent, as far as possible, the intrusion of either [church or state] into the precincts of the other.'"[14]

The Supreme Court's *Lemon* Test

To guide lower courts, citizens, and governmental entities in determining when state or religious action impermissibly penetrates the barrier between the two institutions, the Supreme Court developed a three-part balancing test in *Lemon v. Kurtzman*:[15] "First, the statute must have a secular legislative purpose; second, its principal or primary effect must be one that neither advances nor inhibits religion . . . ; [and] finally, the statute must not foster 'an excessive government entanglement with religion.'"[16] If the government violates any one of the Establishment Clause prongs, the court must strike the action down.[17]

The most litigated prong of the *Lemon* test is "excessive entanglement," which is the prong developed to combat one of the "main evils against which the Establishment Clause was intended to afford protection . . . active involvement of the sovereign in religious activity."[18]

Factors of Excessive Entanglement

There are three factors to examine in determining whether governmental regulation of home schools represents excessive governmental entanglement in religion: "[T]he character and purposes of the institutions that are benefited, the nature of the aid that the State provides, and the resulting relationship between the government and the religious authority."[19]

Perhaps the key element is the *resulting relationship* between religious entities and the state, particularly in the case of home schools. While parents have the constitutional right to send their children to private schools, and many possess the statutorily-created right to home school their offspring, the Court has held that "they have no constitutional right to provide their children with private school education unfettered by reasonable government regulation. Indeed, the Court in *Pierce* expressly acknowledged 'the power of the State reasonably to regulate all schools, to inspect, supervise and examine them, their teachers and pupils.' . . ."[20] Therefore, "total separation is not possible in an absolute sense. Some relationship between government and religious organizations [and home schools] is inevitable."[21] The issue is then to determine at what point permissive incidental and limited entanglement[22] becomes impermissible excessive entanglement. Such an inquiry is not facile because "that . . . line . . . is a blurred, indistinct, and variable barrier depending on all the circumstances of a particular relationship."[23] Courts have been hesitant to uphold a state program or regulation if it produces a "comprehensive . . . continuing state surveillance" of a religious institution, particularly a religious school.[24] For example,[25] in *Aguilar v. Felton*[26] the Court struck down New York City's use of "federal funds to pay the salaries of public employees who teach in parochial schools,"[27] which New York City had been doing in an effort to assist local schools in meeting "the needs of educationally deprived children from low-income families."[28] Taxpayers challenged the program, arguing that it violated the Establishment Clause.[29] While the Court found that the "state aid [did] not have the primary effect of advancing religion, the provision of such aid may nonetheless violate the Establishment Clause owing to the nature of the interaction of church and state in the administration of that aid to parochial institutions."[30]

The program was problematic for two reasons. First, aid was "provided in a pervasively sectarian environment."[31] In addition:

> [B]ecause assistance is provided in the form of teachers, ongoing inspection is required to ensure the absence of a religious message. In short, the scope and duration of New York City's Title I program would require a permanent and pervasive state presence in the sectarian schools receiving aid.
>
> This pervasive monitoring by public authorities in the sectarian schools infringes precisely those Establishment Clause values at the root of the prohibition of excessive entanglement. . . . In short, the religious school, which has as a primary purpose the advancement and preservation of a particular religion must endure the ongoing presence of state personnel whose primary purpose is to monitor teachers and students in an attempt to guard against the infiltration of religious thought [in the special programs].[32]

The program, furthermore, was impermissible because it mandated substantial contact between government and sectarian school officials to discuss scheduling, assignments, and other information regarding the program. Also, in the words of the Court, "the program necessitates 'frequent contacts between the regular and the remedial teachers (or other professionals), in which each side reports on individual student needs, problems encountered, and results achieved.'"[33]

The Supreme Court concluded that the "program can only produce 'a kind of continuing day-to-day relationship which the policy of neutrality seeks to minimize.'"[34]

Courts frequently find that governmental interference does not rise to the level of excessive entanglement.

New Life Baptist Church Academy v. Town of East Longmeadow[35] and *Dole v. Shenandoah Baptist Church*[36] represent two cases in this category.

In *New Life Baptist Church Academy*,[37] the First Circuit Court of Appeals upheld "state rules and procedures for determining the adequacy of the secular education" that church schools provide.[38] The controversy arose because:

> [A] child cannot satisfy Massachusetts' compulsory school attendance laws by attending a private school unless the local school committee

"approves" the education that the private school provides. A school committee must "approve" the private school when the school meets certain minimal statutory criteria and also offers a secular education comparable to that provided in the town's public schools.[39]

The Academy argued that the "approval" requirement, which required the state to examine "teaching credentials of those who teach secular subjects"[40] and to make "occasional visits to the school,"[41] violated the Establishment Clause.[42] The court of appeals, however, rejected this contention. It concluded that the "approval" requirement did not involve the requisite pervasive state interference.

First, the School Committee's method of operation did not require "any 'pervasive state presence in the sectarian schools' or 'frequent contacts between [state and private school] teachers.'"[43] In addition, the Committee's methods did not create a "comprehensive, discriminating and continuing state surveillance."[44] Finally, finding the visits to the Academy to be merely for "checkup" purposes, the court concluded that the proposed implementation did not violate the purposes underlying the Establishment Clause.[45]

In *Shenandoah Baptist Church*,[46] the church argued that the application of the Fair Labor Standards Act to its school offended Establishment Clause values.[47] It "complain[ed] that the government inspection, monitoring, and review required to implement the Act intrude into church affairs."[48] The Fourth Circuit Court of Appeals, however, found that the intrusion did not violate the Establishment Clause,[49] holding that "'the recordkeeping requirements of the Fair Labor Standards Act, while perhaps more burdensome in terms of paperwork, are not significantly more intrusive into religious affairs' than fire inspection and building and zoning regulations."[50]

This sampling of Establishment Clause cases demonstrates that the line between constitutional and unconstitutional action is often blurred. A result in one case may differ from another because of subtle nuances in the state's program or procedure.

Applying the *Lemon* Test to Laws Affecting Home Education

State regulation of home instruction touches upon sensitive constitutional issues.[51] State requirements that subject parents to an approval procedure before granting them an exemption to compulsory attendance laws may be met with parental refusal to submit to such a process.[52] Such parents have argued that the state does not have the authority to regulate religiously-motivated home education.[53] Precedent intimates, as previously discussed, that litigants will have a difficult time winning if this is the sole argument.[54]

Alternative arguments that provide a chance at winning under an Establishment Clause claim exist. The strongest arguments of home school litigants who claim excessive entanglement of the government with their religion occur in primarily two situations: 1. where the state questions the parents' sincerely held religious beliefs in the exemption-granting and approval processes; and 2. where the state impermissibly regulates home education once the exemption is obtained.

Every state has a compulsory attendance statute requiring children, until the age of sixteen, to attend "school."[55] Generally, for parents to educate their children at home, they must prove that they qualify for one of the compulsory attendance exemptions.[56]

State Inquiry into Religious Beliefs

Those choosing the home school option because of religious beliefs often attempt to satisfy the religious exemption requirement, subjecting themselves, at times, to imposing and personal state questions about their religious beliefs. Such an intrusion also can arise during the approval process as the state evaluates curriculum and textbooks the home instructor intends to use.[57] During this process, undoubtedly "situations of conflict between secular educational goals and religious norms" emerge.[58]

Questioning religious beliefs of families seeking a religious exemption invades an intimate and personal area. Just as probing into a church's dogma or the sectarian practices of a religious school is precisely "the kind of government surveillance the Court has previously held to pose an intolerable risk of government entanglement with religion,"[59] the state's questioning of parental religious beliefs creates the same result.

The state may attempt to counter these objections, arguing perhaps that an inquiry into the religious beliefs of parents applying for an exemption can be completed with minor questioning. The *de minimis* nature of the investigation, however, is not sufficient to overcome the entanglement difficulties, as the Supreme Court stated in *NLRB v. Catholic Bishop of Chicago*.[60] There, the Court said that the state's actions "will necessarily involve inquiry into the good faith of the position asserted by the clergy-administrators. . . . It is not only the conclusions that may be reached . . . which may impinge on rights guaranteed by the Religion Clauses, but also the very *process of inquiry*."[61]

The state also may contend that its questioning procedure is no more intrusive than a court's evaluation of sincerely held religious beliefs, meaning it will ask only if the beliefs are religious and if they are sincerely held.[62] Such an inquiry, however, will not end with this line of questioning.

Consider this hypothetical situation. In order for parents to home educate their children, the hypothetical state must approve their home instruction program.[63] Such a procedure may involve examining the curriculum and textbooks:[64]

> If, for example, school officials require instruction in science, should they approve or disapprove a home education program which includes only "creation science"? It is easy to imagine how disapproval of such a program could lead to a "Scopes-in-reverse" trial.[65]

Such a situation places an unconstitutional burden on parents to defend their belief in teaching creationism and to argue that it constitutes "equivalent instruction."[66] To the school officials, this belief may seem "incomprehensible,"[67] but the state may only question whether the beliefs are religious and sincerely held and not whether the tenets are reasonable or valid.[68]

Subjecting parents to extensive interrogation about their religious beliefs is exactly what the Supreme Court has expressly prohibited. The parents are being required to prove the unprovable. Yet: "Men may believe what they cannot prove. They may not be put to the proof of their religious doctrines or beliefs."[69]

Placing parents in such a position thus fosters excessive entanglement between religion and government.[70]

Excessive or Questionable State Regulation

A second excessive entanglement claim concentrates on the extent to which the state regulates the home educators once the exemption is obtained.

Some home school litigators have declined to raise any Establishment Clause challenges, claiming that to use this defense is conceding that the state can regulate home schools.[71] Home educators, however, may have difficulty in convincing a court that the state has *no* authority to monitor their mode of instruction in light of Supreme Court precedent supporting the contrary conclusion in the private school context[72] and of recent federal and state court decisions finding that such authority exists in the home school context.[73]

In fact, some home school litigants have acquiesced on that point, focusing their attention on the degree to which the state may regulate home instruction, and it is with this argument that the case may be won or lost.[74]

Home school cases containing challenges based on the Establishment Clause are sparse.[75] Nevertheless, guidelines can be discerned from the existing cases and other cases to direct the attention of litigants to certain questionable regulations. For example, although the court ruled against the plaintiff parents, litigants can learn important lessons from *Blackwelder v. Safnauer*.[76] Plaintiffs filed an action under the federal Civil Rights Act,[77] challenging New York's statute governing home schools based on, among other constitutional claims, the Establishment Clause.[78] The school district in which the plaintiffs resided required that parents choosing to home educate their children seek approval from the district by submitting "a proposed calendar, curriculum, list of textbooks, syllabus and standardized testing schedule (if appropriate) for review by a representative of the school district."[79] Furthermore, the parents were required to inform the state's representative of the credentials and "life and occupational experiences" of the instructors.[80] The school district conditioned final approval on the results of a visit to the site of the home school by a group of representatives.[81] In addition to the initial visit, one or two other visits were scheduled during the school year.[82]

The plaintiff parents, who chose home schooling for religious reasons, refused to comply with all of the procedures.[83] The court, however, held that such requirements did not violate any constitutional rights. Relying on the *Lemon* analytical framework, the court found the excessive entanglement most problematic.[84] The court, however, rejected the plaintiff's argument that the prearranged home visits fostered excessive entanglement, finding for the proposition that the state in fact has the power to inspect all schools.[85]

The court also dismissed the plaintiff's reliance on *Aguilar v. Felton*.[86] Comparing the situation in *Aguilar* with the case before it, the *Blackwelder* court found that the entanglement did not rise to the level found in *Aguilar*, mainly because *Blackwelder* did not involve state aid to a sectarian entity,[87] frequent visitations, or any interference with religious training.[88]

Guidance

Several principles can be discerned from this decision and other home school cases which may serve as a guide to future litigants.

First, there are some types of restrictions that fall into the bright line area, meaning that the regulation is either overwhelmingly permissible or impermissible. For example, many states require parents to subject home schooled pupils to standardized testing to measure progress.[89] Courts traditionally have not considered such testing excessive entanglement.[90] Rather, the Supreme Court has held "that the State has a substantial and legitimate interest in insuring that its youth receive an adequate secular education"[91] and that giving such tests to sectarian schools serves as a "means of ensuring that minimum standards are met."[92]

Other state regulations will generally be deemed invalid. For example, courts, based on Supreme Court precedent, have found or intimated that questioning of the religious nature of instruction is intolerable.[93]

On the other hand, the status of certain types of regulations remains unclear; courts have divided on several popular methods of supervision and approval. For example, some courts have found laws requiring home school parents to be certified teachers unconstitutional,[94] while other courts have found that teacher certification represents the least restrictive means of supervising home instruction.[95]

Courts also appear divided over the issue of in-home visits. One court has held that the state can supervise home education through "infrequent, unobtrusive home visitation, at a time to be mutually agreed upon."[96] Another court, however, has intimated that in-home visits are impermissible if the state uses other means of monitoring the students' development, such as standardized testing or progress reports.[97]

If home school litigants believe the state has crossed the boundary between permissible and excessive entanglement, the key to winning such an argument, in light of the cases examined, may be to paint "[t]he picture of state inspectors prowling the halls of [the home] and auditing classroom instruction [that] surely raises" images of excessive entanglement.[98]

DISCRIMINATION AMONG RELIGIONS

In a limited number of cases, a second Establishment Clause claim is available. Apparently, in a few cases the state grants religious exemptions to one religious group—the Amish—and denies all other applicants the exemption regardless of their sincerely held religious beliefs.[99]

One court, examining the issue as Equal Protection and Establishment Clause claims, held that the preferential treatment was constitutionally permissible,[100] finding that the plaintiffs had failed to demonstrate that their situation was remotely similar to that of the Amish.[101] According to the court: "This narrowly drawn accommodation to one religious view does not require the state, under the establishment clause, to accommodate all others."[102]

The analysis of the court, however, is incomplete. The court neglected to discuss the preferential treatment doctrine articulated in *Larson v. Valente*:[103] Any statute that focuses exclusively on religious organizations and that grants denominational preferences must be treated as suspect and must apply strict scrutiny—the compelling state interest test—in determining its constitutionality.[104]

In *Larson*,[105] the Unification Church challenged a Minnesota statute that "impos[ed] certain registration and reporting requirements upon only those religious organizations that solicit more than fifty per cent of their funds from non-members," arguing that such discriminatory treatment violated the Establishment Clause.[106] Rejecting arguments that the Unification Church was not a religious organization,[107] the Court found that the statute in fact violated the Establishment Clause; however, it used a slightly different First Amendment analysis than the traditional *Lemon* test. Justice William Brennan, writing for the Court, recognized that "The clearest command of the Establishment Clause is that one religious denomination cannot be officially preferred over another."[108] Citing historical support for the principle, the Court stated: "This constitutional prohibition of denominational preferences is inextricably connected with the continuing vitality of the Free Exercise Clause."[109] Justice Brennan also pointed to precedent to bolster this doctrine:

> Since *Everson v. Board of Education* this Court has adhered to the principle, clearly manifested in history and logic of the Establishment Clause, that no State can "pass laws which aid one religion" or that "prefer one religion over another." This principle of denominational neutrality has been restated on many occasions. In *Zorach v. Clauson*, we said that "[t]he government must be neutral when it comes to compensation between sects." In *Epperson v. Arkansas*, we stated unambiguously: "The First Amendment mandates governmental neutrality between religion and religion.... The State may not adopt programs or practices ... which 'aid or oppose' any religion.... This prohibition is absolute."[110]

Thus, the Court applied a strict scrutiny analysis to the statute, but this adaptation of this test differs slightly from the free exercise compelling state interest test.

First, the Court asked whether the statute showed a preference among denominations.[111] This first question is unique and acts as a substitute for the free exercise inquiry as to whether an individual has sincerely held religious beliefs that are burdened by the state action.[112] The Court then asked the traditional questions: did the state demonstrate a compelling state interest, and if so, did it use the least restrictive means possible to further that interest?[113]

In *Larson*, the state did not withstand this heightened judicial analysis because it failed to satisfy the final requirement.[114]

Some question how this result interacts with the 1971 decision *Gillette v. United States*.[115] In *Gillette*, the Court held that when a statute asserts a "valid secular reason" as its purpose, the law withstands any Establishment Clause claim.[116] Commentators, however, have suggested that *Larson* displaces the *Gillette* principle.[117] For example, Professor Jesse Choper suggests that if a valid secular reason "were all that the Court had required in *Larson* . . . it would have had no problem upholding the Minnesota statute."[118] Professor Choper summarized the current state of the law: "Laws that explicitly deal with the subject of religion, and result in a preference of some religions over others, fall into a separate category of government action."[119]

State statutes that provide a home school religious exemption and only extend exemption status to certain religious groups are thus subject to the compelling state interest test under *Larson*. While the state may argue that the statute is a neutral law with a disparate impact among religious groups,[120] *Larson* clearly discredits such a proposition.[121] Thus, if a state consistently grants the religious exemption to the Amish to the exclusion of other groups, it must offer a compelling state reason for its preferential treatment.[122]

The state may focus on the special treatment given to the Amish in *Wisconsin v. Yoder*.[123] The *Yoder* Court did point to the history and tradition of separation and non-conformity the Amish community shared.[124] What the state suggests in making its argument, however, is disconcerting; that suggestion implies that the religious beliefs requiring parents to home school their children are less sincere for non-Amish parents than for Amish parents. As previously discussed, courts will more than likely find such assumptions intolerable.

CONCLUSION

Challenging home instruction statutes under the Establishment Clause is not the easiest challenge to make. The majority of cases addressing home education issues have addressed claims based on the Free Exercise Clause and the fundamental right of a parent to direct the education of one's child.[125]

Nevertheless, this situation may work to the litigant's advantage because most courts will be deciding without restrictive precedent. The key to successful litigation of an Establishment Clause claim may be to show that the government has gone too far (above and beyond any "reasonable" regulation). As such, the argument would be that the supervision in question fosters excessive entanglement and that other methods of supervision are available and feasible.

21

Neutral Decision-maker Requirements

In states where there are compulsory attendance laws, the local public school officials generally have the exclusive and discretionary authority to enforce them. In approval states, these school officials often set up arbitrary requirements and qualifications for those desiring home school to follow.[1] In these states, a home school is subject to the "approval" by the appropriate school official, usually the local school superintendent or school board. In these states, home schools may be disapproved at the whim of the officials. Officials cite test scores, certification requirements, evaluations, etc. as reasons for not approving a home school, often with no evidence at all to support the assertions, or contrary to the evidence.

An argument can be made that such unilateral discretion on the part of the school officials violates the due process rights of parents.

The Fourteenth Amendment provides that life, liberty, and property may not be taken away from an individual unless he receives "due process"—i.e., fairness.[2] The right to an impartial decision-maker is required by due process in every case.[3] The argument is based on the fact that the money a school district receives from the state or federal government is directly related to the number of students that are enrolled. Thus, the greater the number of students enrolled in a given district, the more money the district receives; and the more money the district receives, the more money the school official can make. Thus, it is easy to see how the decision-makers (the superintendent or the board) may become biased and incapable of making an impartial decision. They often have a direct financial incentive not to approve home schools.

Home schools not only take revenue away from the public schools, they also impact the school system's reputation. School officials may see this as a direct affront.

In addition, often public school officials genuinely believe that they know what is best for the children. They believe their school system is superior to a home school, and they do not understand why some parents would prefer other means of education for their children.

Therefore, bias is inherent in the decision of a school authority to approve or disapprove a home school, regardless of financial incentives. "Local public school boards, their employees, agents, the State education officials, and the Superintendent of Public Instruction, are all advocates of public education. The very nature of their position demands a high degree of loyalty to both the form and philosophy of public schooling."[4]

CASE LAW REGARDING NEUTRAL DECISION-MAKING

The Supreme Court's examination of the impartiality requirement has been structured by a distinction between personal and institutional conflicts of interest.[5] Personal bias is always impermissible.[6] Institutional bias occurs when the decision-maker is a member of an administrative agency that performs a dual function of investigation and adjudication.[7] The Court is more tolerant of bias in this category.[8] The Court will disqualify decision-makers who in fact have no actual bias if they might reasonably *appear* to be biased.[9]

One of the foremost cases in this area is *Tumey v. Ohio*.[10] In *Tumey*, the mayor served as judge in prohibition law cases. If defendants were convicted, the mayor received, as compensation for his services as judge, the amount of his costs in each case, in addition to his regular salary, while the city received the fine levied. If the defendant were acquitted, neither the city nor the mayor received anything.

The Supreme Court held that the scheme violated the Due Process Clause in two different ways.

First, the mayor had direct, personal, and pecuniary interests in the costs which he received from convictions.[11]

Second, the mayor was "charged with the business of looking after the finances of the village" and had a strong "official motive to convict and to graduate the fine to help the financial needs of the village."[12] Thus, the official need not have received a personal financial gain. The Due Process Clause would have been violated even if only the governmental entity received the funds.

Ward v. Village of Monroeville,[13] like *Tumey*, involved an Ohio statute authorizing mayors to sit as judges in traffic offense cases. The mayor did not have a pecuniary interest, so the first test of *Tumey* was not implicated. However, the mayor possessed "wide executive powers" and "exercised general overall supervision of village affairs."[14] The village derived a major part of its resources from the fines and fees imposed by the mayor in the cases he heard.[15] Even though the mayor had no personal financial incentive, the Court nevertheless found a due process violation. The Court stated: "[T]he test is whether the mayor's situation is one 'which would offer a possible temptation to the average man as judge to forget the burden of proof required to convict the defendant, or which might lead him not to hold the balance nice, clear and true between the State and the accused.'"[16]

Thus, the question of a school superintendent's impartiality will often depend on whether or not the superintendent is serving in an adjudicative, as opposed to a strictly administrative or prosecutorial, capacity.

The Supreme Court has held that the rigid requirements of *Tumey* and *Ward* are designed for officials performing judicial or quasi-judicial functions.[17] Thus, those serving adjudicative functions are held to strict impartiality. However, administrators who serve adjudicative functions are presumed to be unbiased.[18] This presumption can be overcome by showing that the decision-maker has a personal or institutional financial interest in the outcome of the decision made.[19]

A Kentucky district court, in a teacher-dismissal setting, considered four factors in determining whether or not a decision-making board or official had a disqualifying personal bias:

(1) Was the decisionmaker's role in initiating charges merely a procedural step, or did it imply a closed mind on the issue of guilt.

(2) Were the facts disputed so that a possible lack of impartiality might create a serious risk of an erroneous decision based on tainted findings of fact.

(3) Did the decisionmaker have a personal interest, relating to either money or prestige, in seeing that the termination be upheld.

(4) Was there personal animosity between the employee and the decisionmaker.[20]

These four factors can also apply when evaluating the administrator's decisions in the home school arena. By balancing these factors, it should be easy to overcome the presumption of fairness applied to the school official.

Wolkenstein v. Reville[21] involved the determination by the school district's superintendent and chief executive officer of an illegal strike by the district's teachers. The superintendent denied hearings to several of the striking teachers who were challenging his decision. The court found that "in evaluating the objections filed by the teachers, [the superintendent] was deciding the purely legal question whether the excuse alleged for absence was sufficient as a matter of law."[22] Thus, the strict impartiality of due process was required.

The same argument could be true for officials making determinations about home school requirements. They are deciding the purely legal questions of whether the home school is sufficient as a matter of law. Although the official is entitled to a presumption of impartiality, the party making the assertion of bias (the parents) can rebut the presumption by a showing of pecuniary or institutional interest.[23]

HOME SCHOOL CASES INVOLVING THE NEUTRAL DECISION-MAKER DEFENSE

In the few cases where this issue was brought up in the context of home schooling, the courts have not been favorable to parents. The decision of the school official has been given great deference.

In *State v. Toman*,[24] public school officials were given authority to decide whether or not to grant requests by home school families for exemption from the compulsory attendance laws.[25] The court refused to address their due process argument of bias because the family did not seek to obtain an exemption until after they were charged with the violation.[26] "Having failed to request an exemption for the time in which the statutory violation occurred, the Tomans cannot now raise objections to the exemption statute as a defense to their convictions."[27]

Therefore, the neutral decision-maker defense may only be pertinent if the home school family requests relief from the administrator *before* they are charged with a violation of the compulsory attendance law.

Parents seeking to use the neutral decision-maker defense must be fully prepared with the facts and evidence of bias. In *State v. Brewer*,[28] the court "decline[d] to hold as a matter of law, that the probability of actual bias on the part of public school officials approaches a constitutionally impermissible level and there is no factual evidence in this record which reflects an actual bias on the part of these particular public school officials."[29] Thus, it may be that if home schoolers have specific and detailed evidence of bias, a court will be more likely to hear their case and rule in their favor.

Blackwelder v. Safnauer[30] is another example demonstrating the need for thorough and specific evidence. The Court held in this case that the plaintiffs presented no evidence other than statements of conclusion in support of their contention that the school district would have a financial incentive to withhold approval for their home schooling programs. Statements of conclusion were not enough.[31]

Second, this Court held that even if a financial incentive did exist, a school superintendent in New York is not responsible for assuring that the money necessary to run his school system is provided.[32] This meant that the school superintendent was too far removed from the financial policy of the school district to raise an inference of bias.[33]

Third, there was no evidence to indicate that the incremental increase in state aid that might result if children attending home instruction were enrolled in public schools would be so great as to be considered "substantial and vitally important" to the fiscal well-being of the state's school districts.[34] The Court seemed to infer this requirement of substantiality from the fact that *Tumey* and *Ward* put great emphasis on the fact that the revenues generated by the mayor's court were substantial and important to the village's fiscal well-being.[35]

Finally, the Court stressed that any decision made by a superintendent regarding home schools was subject to review.[36] However, it has been held that the "procedural safeguard" of appeal does not serve to cure a due process violation.[37] If the initial decision-maker was biased, it is a violation of due process, regardless of whether or not the decision is subject to appeal. However, *Ward* was a criminal case, and this ruling may not apply in the civil context.[38]

Thus, in home school cases where parents have not been convicted of violating the compulsory attendance laws, the availability of an appeal may serve to negate the neutral decision-maker argument.

Some cases have turned on the classifications of the school official's activities and duties—i.e., whether or not the school official is performing judicial functions or administrative ones. For example, if an official has a good deal of discretion in his decision-making, his role will be considered more adjudicatory. For example, in *State v. Anderson*,[39] the local school board was required by statute to monitor whether school-age children were attending a school that had been approved by the county superintendent of schools and the superintendent of public instruction. The court held that the local school board's act was a ministerial function rather than a discretionary, decision-making function and was distinguishable from the function of the mayor-city judge in *Tumey v. Ohio*.[40] The local school board simply monitored the child's attendance and had no role in the discretionary act of approving or not approving the home school. Thus, although the local school board had a financial interest in having students attend public school, the board had no decision-making authority and thus there could be no due process violation.

Similarly, in *People v. DeJonge*,[41] the DeJonges contended that their due process rights were violated by the requirement that they have their home school approved by the biased superintendents of the public school system. The Court noted that there was no approval *process*: "A state approved nonpublic school is simply a school which complies with the requirements."[42] The DeJonges did not comply with the teacher certification requirements. The Court reasoned that because of this noncompliance, the hearing officer need not exercise discretion, and thus the result would be the same regardless of the partiality of the magistrate.[43]

CONCLUSION

It appears that some school officials may be unable to make impartial decisions regarding home schools since they may have financial, institutional, and reputational interests in limiting home schools.

The due process requirement of a neutral decision-maker protects parents from such impermissible overreaching by school officials. However, courts are apparently reluctant to overturn a school administrator's ruling on the grounds that the official was biased. There is a strong presumption in favor of the officials' neutrality.

The neutral decision-maker defense should not be used as an afterthought. Courts demand strong evidence; simple assertions of financial interest will not suffice. However, the more discretion a school official has, the more likely a court will be to scrutinize the evidence.

The neutral decision-maker defense is a valid defense, but the deference courts show to administrators is difficult to overcome. Nonetheless, courts may be more likely to rule in the parents' favor if the parents present specific and detailed arguments as to why school officials are not neutral decision-makers.

22

Compelling State Interest

In constitutional law jurisprudence, the Supreme Court has developed a multi-layered analysis for determining whether state action has impermissibly interfered with constitutionally protected rights.

The rational relation test—the catch-all test—comprises the bottom tier and requires the government to demonstrate that its action has a legitimate governmental end and that the regulation has a rational relation to that end.[1]

In equal protection cases, an intermediate tier exists; when a quasi-suspect class, such as illegitimacy[2] or gender,[3] is present, the court engages in a heightened scrutiny analysis. In these cases, the state must demonstrate an important governmental interest that has a substantial relationship with the state act[4] or that its intrusion has a substantial relation to a legitimate state interest.[5]

The top layer is strict scrutiny analysis—often avoided by the state, but desired by the individual because of the high standards the state must meet to justify its encroachment.

Subjecting government to strict scrutiny is the exception rather than the rule.[6] Only selective situations trigger the use of the compelling state interest test. In equal protection cases, for example, courts will use the compelling state interest test if the offended individual is a member of a suspect class,[7] such as race,[8] or if a fundamental right is at stake.[9] In the 1920s, the Supreme Court also recognized substantive due process rights that were entitled to strict scrutiny when offended;[10] however, this *Lochner*-era jurisprudence slowly eroded,[11] and few of these rights still remain, one of them being the right of parents to direct the education of their children.[12] In the First Amendment area, the Court frequently has applied the compelling state interest test. For example, in freedom of speech cases the Court requires the state to withstand strict scrutiny when it engages in content-based discrimination[13] and seeks to prohibit speech in a public forum.[14]

In addition, state action that demonstrates a preference among religions is also subject to strict scrutiny.[15]

Until recently, such an analysis was used in the free exercise context.[16] Prior to *Employment Division, Dept. of Human Resources v. Smith*,[17] when a statute adversely affected an individual's free exercise rights, the Supreme Court, unless the state could proffer a compelling state interest, would grant an individual an exemption from the statute.[18] Today, however, the Court will not grant the same individual a religious exemption from a neutral, generally applicable statute and does not use the compelling state interest test.[19]

In *Smith*, the Court implicitly reserved strict scrutiny for two limited circumstances. The first occurs if a plaintiff challenges a "neutral, generally applicable law" based not on the Free Exercise Clause alone, but on "the Free Exercise Clause in conjunction with other constitutional protections, such as freedom of speech, and of the press."[20] In addition, the second exception provides that "where the State has in place a system of individual exemptions, it may not refuse to extend that system to cases of 'religious hardship' without compelling reason."[21]

For home school litigants, understanding the compelling state interest test is important in alleging that the statute violates three distinct rights: parental right to direct the education of one's child; Establishment Clause violation of discrimination among religions; and free exercise rights in limited situations. Because the parental right and free exercise claims are the most commonly used in home school litigation, this chapter will focus on the strict scrutiny analysis in those contexts.

This chapter first examines the meaning of strict scrutiny, pointing to two Supreme Court cases to illustrate the theory in practice. It then will discuss the three aspects of the strict scrutiny analysis in the home school context.

DEFINING STRICT SCRUTINY

The compelling state interest test consists of three separate inquiries. The court first must consider whether the state action infringes upon an individual's constitutionally protected rights.[22] Two separate parts comprise this aspect of the strict scrutiny analysis. First, the litigant must prove that a constitutional right is at stake.[23] Then the litigant must demonstrate that the state has burdened this right. Courts invariably have found the presence of a burden if the individual proves that he faces the paradigm of Hobson's choice: comply with the state action and forego the exercise of a constitutionally protected right, or exercise the right and risk state sanctions.[24]

If the state activity places an individual in this precarious situation, the burden shifts to the state, and the state must then proffer a compelling state interest to justify the infringement.[25] This is a high barrier for the state to cross. In some cases the compelling state interest is obvious. For example: "When clear and present danger of riot, disorder, interference with traffic upon the public streets, or other immediate threat to public safety, peace, or order, appears," the Court consistently has found a clear compelling state interest.[26] If the conduct does not reach this level, the Court nonetheless may find a compelling state interest; however, "no showing merely of a rational relationship to some colorable state interest [will] suffice; in this highly sensitive constitutional area, '[o]nly the gravest abuses, endangering paramount interests, give occasion for permissible limitation.'"[27]

Finally, even if the state proves it possesses such an interest, it must satisfy the final requirement of the compelling state interest analysis. This final phase often is referred to as the least restrictive means aspect of strict scrutiny. At different times, however, the Supreme Court has used different language to describe this inquiry.

Sometimes the Court will ask whether accommodating the individual "'will unduly interfere with fulfillment of the governmental interest.'"[28] At other times, however, the Court will state that "the government must accommodate a legitimate free exercise claim unless pursuing an especially important interest by narrowly tailored means."[29] If the state cannot achieve this goal without impairing its compelling interest, the Constitution does not require accommodation on the part of the state.[30] Whether the slight nuances in the terminology make a difference is unclear, but the gravamen of this prong is that the state must regulate with the least restrictive means possible.

Two classic cases exemplify the Supreme Court's application of the compelling state interest: *Sherbert v. Verner*[31] and *Wisconsin v. Yoder*.[32] The seminal case *Sherbert* is a good example of the Court's application of the compelling state interest analysis in a Free Exercise Clause context. While *Smith* basically eliminated the test in the majority of cases, understanding strict scrutiny is vital when a hybrid claim exists or when a neutral, generally applicable statute is not involved.[33]

The plaintiff in *Sherbert*, a member of the Seventh-Day Adventist Church, refused to work on Saturday, her denomination's Sabbath.[34] Her employer discharged her because of her religious conviction.[35] Unable to find another job because of her religious beliefs, the plaintiff filed a claim for unemployment compensation benefits.[36] The South Carolina Employment Security Commission, however, denied her claim, maintaining that her "restriction upon her availability for Saturday work brought her within the provision disqualifying for benefits insured workers who fail without good cause, to accept 'suitable work when offered . . . by the employment office or the employer.'"[37] The state supreme court upheld its finding, rejecting any claims that the denial of benefits violated any constitutional principles.[38]

Writing for the United States Supreme Court, Justice Brennan reversed the South Carolina Supreme Court's decision, employing the compelling state interest test. First, the Court found that disqualifying the plaintiff from receiving benefits infringed upon the free exercise of her religious beliefs. Justice Brennan stated:

The ruling forces her to choose between following the precepts of her religion and forfeiting benefits, on the one hand, and abandoning one of the precepts of her religion in order to accept work, on the other hand. Governmental imposition of such a choice puts the same kind of burden upon the free exercise of religion as would a fine imposed against [the plaintiff] for her Saturday worship.[39]

Second, the Court addressed whether the state had proven a compelling state interest to override the plaintiff's religious beliefs. Initially, the Court removed the plaintiff's conduct from the "automatic" compelling state interest category because it did not substantially threaten "public safety, peace or order."[40] The Court then turned to the interests that the state maintained justified the encroachment: 1. "a possibility that the filing of fraudulent claims by unscrupulous claimants feigning religious objections to Saturday work might . . . dilute the unemployment compensation fund";[41] and 2. such deceptive filing practices might "also hinder the scheduling by employers of necessary Saturday work."[42] The Court rejected both contentions, first finding that the state had failed to make such argument at the state supreme court level. In addition, despite the failure to raise such an issue, according to the Court:

[T]here is no proof whatever to warrant such fears of malingering or deceit as those which the [state] now advance[s]. Even if consideration of such evidence is not foreclosed by the prohibition against judicial inquiry into the truth or falsity of religious beliefs . . . it is highly doubtful whether such evidence would be sufficient to warrant a substantial infringement of religious liberties.[43]

Yoder also provides a good example of how the Court applies the compelling state interest and is useful to examine because it presents a hybrid claim—religion-plus-parental rights.

Yoder involved the clash between the state's interest in educating children until they reach the age of sixteen and the Amish religious order's belief that mandated that its children not attend organized school beyond the eighth grade.[44] The state charged three parents with violation of Wisconsin's compulsory state attendance laws because they had not enrolled their teenage children in any public or private school or any other recognized exception to the attendance statute.[45] The parents were tried and convicted although they maintained that "their children's attendance at high school, public or private, was contrary to the Amish religion and way of life. They believed that by sending their children to high school, they would not only expose themselves to the danger of the censure of the church community, but . . . also endanger their own salvation and that of their children."[46] The Wisconsin Supreme Court held their conviction invalid, and the state appealed to the United States Supreme Court.[47]

While the state has an interest in educating its children, according to the Court:

> [Such concern] is not totally free from a balancing process when it impinges on fundamental rights and interests, such as those specifically protected by the Free Exercise Clause of the First Amendment, and the traditional interest of parents with respect to the religious upbringing of their children so long as they, in the words of *Pierce*, "prepare [them] for additional obligations."[48]

Thus, the Court reasoned that the state could compel attendance beyond the eighth grade if it "appear[ed] either that the State does not deny the free exercise of religious belief by its requirement, or that there is a state interest of sufficient magnitude to override the interest claiming protection under the Free Exercise Clause."[49]

First, the Court evaluated the quality of the Amish religious claims. After engaging in an in-depth analysis of the Amish tradition, the Court concluded:

> [The] Amish objection to formal education beyond the eighth grade is firmly grounded in [its] central religious concepts. They object to the high school, and higher education generally, because the values they teach are in marked variance with Amish values and the Amish way of life; they view secondary school education as an impermissible exposure of their children to a "worldly" influence in conflict with their beliefs.[50]

Thus, "in the Amish belief higher learning tends to develop values they reject as influences that alienate man from God."[51]

The Court, however, "was careful to determine whether the Amish religious faith and their mode of life are, as they claim, inseparable and interdependent."[52] The Court stated that "[a] way of life, however virtuous and admirable, may not be interposed as a barrier to reasonable state regulation of education if it is based on purely secular considerations; to have the protection of the Religion Clauses, the claims must be rooted in religious belief."[53]

After examining the record, the Court found ample evidence to support "the claim that the traditional way of life of the Amish is not merely a matter of personal preference, but one of deep religious conviction, shared by an organized group, and intimately related to daily living."[54] The Court then determined that the earlier court's decision clearly and unequivocally interfered with the exercise of the Amish's religious beliefs and pointed to the classic Hobson's choice the Amish faced: comply with the law and compromise their religious beliefs, or violate the statute and follow their religious tenets.[55]

The Court then considered the quality of the state's interest in universal compulsory education. The state argued that this interest "is so great that it is paramount to the undisputed claims of [the Amish parents],"[56] an argument the Court rejected. While the Court recognized that the state has an interest in educating its youth to prepare them to be effective citizens and to function independently in society, it found that "an additional one or two years of formal high school for Amish children in place of their long-established program of informal vocational education would do little to serve those interests."[57] The Amish system of education produces hard-working and self-reliant citizens; it prepares its youth for life as Amish adults which does not require advanced book learning.[58]

The Court also rejected the proposition that leaving school early would fail to prepare the Amish to be effective citizens, pointing to the fact that compulsory education is a recent development in history and that the democratic process worked before the advent of such an educational system.[59]

STRICT SCRUTINY AND HOME SCHOOLS

The typical home school case represents the paradigm constitutional law case: the state "interest" versus the individual. The court must conduct a balancing test to decide which interest is paramount.[60]

The state will assert that it has an interest not only in the education of its youth, but also in the quality of that education.[61] On the other hand, parents will maintain that their interest is two-fold: the right to direct the education of their children,[62] and the right to exercise religious beliefs that require home education.[63] Except in rare cases, the court will find, or the parties will concede,[64] that the state has an interest in education and that the parents have a constitutionally protected right to home educate their children, but that neither interest or right is absolute.[65]

Thus, since these two interests often cancel each other out, the result of the litigation often turns on the resolution of the final phase of the compelling state interest test: whether the regulation is the least restrictive means to further the state's interest.[66] Regardless of this reality, it is important for home school litigants to comprehend the intricacies of each phase, particularly the aspects in which the state has the burden of proof.

Phase I: Proving That the State Has Burdened a Constitutionally Protected Right

Home school advocates should maintain that the regulations place an impermissible burden on their right to exercise their religious beliefs or to direct the education of their children. Demonstrating the right to direct the education of one's children is the least difficult to prove. Even though the Supreme Court has yet to place home education within the scope of this right, most courts have acknowledged home education as a right.[67] Anything that interferes with exercising that right clearly is a burden.

Proving the existence of sincerely held religious beliefs is somewhat more challenging. First, parents must establish that their desire to educate their children at home is based on sincerely held religious beliefs and that the state action burdens the exercise of those beliefs.[68] In evaluating religious beliefs, the courts serve a rather limited role. A court's only role is to decide whether the beliefs are actually religious and whether they are sincerely held;[69] the court cannot question or reject beliefs, even though they seem "incomprehensible."[70] According to the Court: "[T]o have the protection of the Religion Clauses, the claims must be rooted in religious belief,"[71] and not in secular or philosophical beliefs.[72] The court also must consider the sincerity of the belief, meaning it must be "based upon a power or being, or upon a faith to which all else . . . is ultimately dependent . . . [and] occupies in the life of its possessor a place parallel to that filled by . . . God."[73]

Finally, parents must demonstrate that they possess these sincerely held religious beliefs. The Supreme Court has rejected the principle that a tenet, church doctrine, or denomination supports the belief:

> Undoubtedly, membership in an organized religious denomination, especially one with a specific tenet forbidding [or prescribing the alleged action], would simplify the problem of identifying sincerely held religious beliefs, but we reject the notion that to claim the protection of the Free Exercise Clause, one must be responding to the commands of a particular religious organization.[74]

In addition, parents need not show that other members of their religious sect share their beliefs:

> [T]he guarantee of free exercise is not limited to beliefs which are shared by all of the members of a religious sect. Particularly in this sensitive area, it is not within the judicial function and judicial competence to inquire [who] more correctly perceived the commands of their common faith. Courts are not arbiters of scriptural interpretation.[75]

In summary, parents must articulate a sincerely held religious belief that they are required to home school their children and must demonstrate that the state has burdened the exercise of those beliefs.

With respect to the burden, parents have argued that any approval requirement or any other method which constitutes the state's authority to approve or disapprove the home school program would violate their religious beliefs. The burden, however, does not have to be direct or to be inherently conflicting with the religious beliefs:

> An indirect burden upon one's religious beliefs occurs when compliance with a challenged law or regulation is not inherently inconsistent with those beliefs, but the law or regulation operates so as to make more practically difficult the practice of those religious beliefs. . . . Nevertheless, "[i]f the purpose or effect of a law is to impede the observance of one or

all religions or is to discriminate invidiously between religions, that law is constitutionally invalid even though the burden may be characterized as being only indirect."[76]

The parents simply must establish that the regulations "interfere . . . with [the] right to pursue a religious education in the home."[77]

Phase II: The Compelling State Interest

The state has the stringent task of proving that "the social purpose served by the challenged regulation is so essential that the loss in freedom is clearly outweighed by the benefit."[78] In addition, "[t]he essence of all that has been said and written on the subject is that only those interests of the highest order and those not otherwise served can overbalance legitimate claims to the free exercise of religion." Yet, while the Supreme Court has set the barrier high to justify encroachment, the vast majority of courts have recognized that although the state cannot prohibit home education, it has an interest in regulating such instruction in furtherance of its obligation to educate its youth.[79]

Litigants can argue that this interest is not compelling, and that is the more difficult argument. There is ample precedent supporting the proposition that while parents have the right to educate their children outside the public school environment, "they have no constitutional right to provide their children with [such an education] unfettered by reasonable government regulation."[80] The resolution of this issue will turn on the manner in which the state phrases its interest and the goals the state seeks to attain with its supervision of home schools. The following represent interests that the home school litigant can substantially undermine and show that the state has no compelling interest in these areas.

Socialization

When parents inform their friends and family that they have decided to home educate their children, the most common response is, "What about their social development?" In their continuous attempts to supervise home education, states also have expressed this concern.

For example, some state legislatures have attempted to hold home educators not only to academic but also to social standards, meaning that for a state to approve a home school, the parents must demonstrate that their method of education provides "equivalent social contact and development" to that found in public schools.[81] The general public and government thus share a common fear that any child who is home educated will be deprived of any social contact with his or her peers. A state that alleges such a concern as a basis for regulating home instruction is operating under a fallacious assumption.

When faced with such an assertion, the home school litigant should attempt to discover the real motivation behind this "socialization" interest: producing individuals who can communicate and relate with their peers or who conform with their peers. Either incentive represents a faulty assertion. Alleging that school is the only way children meet other children ignores reality. Many children today have numerous other ways of meeting peers—Scouts, church, Little League, camp, etc. Asserting such an interest, therefore, "den[ies] that opportunities for socialization vary within and beyond school settings"[82] and should not reach the level of a compelling state interest.

Typically, asserting that interest serves as a pretext for the real motivation underlying the socialization issue: *conformity*. This form of socialization, however, is the precise reason many parents proffer for wanting to home educate their children.[83] According to many parents, placing a child in an institutional setting where he or she is subject to constant peer pressure and to the inculcation of different sets of values is actually detrimental to the child's personal development. It appears that "[w]hat the opponents of parent-controlled education really want is government socialization of children."[84] Such an approach, however, precludes children from developing their own opinions and views.

Because "our society is divided into highly vocal, highly politicized separate value groups and communities of interest, who differ vastly on desired educational content and theory,"[85] a governmental interest in this aspect of socialization should be nonexistent and certainly should not qualify as a compelling state interest. If the state alleges such an interest, courts should give deference to parental control of social development because: 1. parents are more sensitive to their child's needs than the state can possibly be; 2. parents will probably act in the child's best interest because of the close familial relationship; and 3. the parental right to control the child's upbringing preserves the diversity of American society and serves as a barrier to state indoctrination.[86]

Producing an Effective Citizenry

In *Wisconsin v. Yoder*,[87] the Supreme Court flatly rejected the state's argument that its interest is that of producing self-reliant and effective citizens.[88] While an interest in an educated citizenry dates back to Jeffersonian philosophy,[89] any state argument that institutional schooling provides the only opportunity for learning about the democratic process is a fallacious assumption.

As the *Yoder* Court aptly pointed out, our society did not require compulsory attendance until recently, and the democratic process operated sufficiently before then.[90] Parents, as members of this democracy, are capable of teaching their children about the governmental process and the importance of patriotism; however, it seems that parents may properly refuse to teach such citizenship values.[91] In fact, the teaching of these values may prompt many parents to remove their children from public school. Again, the parent, rather than the school, should be the one entrusted with instilling such values into children.[92]

Phase III: The Least Restrictive Means

If the state proves that it has a compelling state interest in regulating home education, it also must demonstrate that the intrusion is the least restrictive means available for furthering its interest in education.[93] This is a balancing test; if the state cannot accommodate the individual's interest without impairing its own substantial interest, the state's claim will override. There are a myriad of ways to approach this issue, two of which will be focused upon in this discussion.

The first, and broader, approach requires the home school litigant to argue that the entire approval and exemption procedure is not the least restrictive method available. Every state has a compulsory attendance statute, requiring children, until the age of sixteen, to attend "school."[94] Generally, for parents to educate their children at home, they must prove that they qualify for one of the compulsory attendance exemptions.

Those choosing the home school option because of religious beliefs typically attempt to satisfy the religious exemption requirement, subjecting themselves, at times, to imposing and personal questions about their religious beliefs. Such an intrusion also can arise during the approval process as the state evaluates curriculum and textbooks the home instructor intends to use.[95] During this process, undoubtedly "situations of conflict between secular educational goals and religious norms" emerge.[96] Questioning religious beliefs of families seeking a religious exemption encroaches into an intimate and personal area. The least restrictive means to granting the home school exemption thus calls for an automatic exemption where the state, without questioning the parents, permits them to home school their children.[97]

In the second approach, the litigation focuses on the degree to which regulations burden the home education program. One possibility of a restriction with minimal interference is standardized testing. Many states require parents to subject home schooled pupils to standardized testing to measure progress.[98] Courts traditionally have not considered such testing overly restrictive.[99] Rather, the Supreme Court has held "that the State has a substantial and legitimate interest in insuring that its youth receive an adequate secular education"[100] and that giving such tests to sectarian schools serves as a "means of ensuring that minimum standards are met."[101]

On the other hand, legislation requiring teaching certification is arguably an overly restrictive way of ensuring that children receive a proper education. Consider again this hypothetical situation. A college professor with a doctorate degree in history wants to home educate his children. Under many state statutes, he would be unable to do so. Although he is well-educated and entrusted to teach college students, the state prohibits him from teaching his own children at home.[102] Such a measure assumes that only certified teachers are qualified to teach. Considering the quality of students—or lack thereof—the public schools are producing today with certified teachers, and the fact that programs such as Teach for America and many private schools do not require teacher certification, such a requirement seems overly burdensome.

Another regulation that is possibly overly restrictive involves in-home visits. Courts appear divided over the issue of in-home visits. One court has held that the state can supervise home education through "infrequent, unobtrusive home visitation, at a time to be mutually agreed upon."[103] Another court, however, has intimated that in-home visits are impermissible if the state uses other means of monitoring the students' development, such as standardized testing or progress reports.[104]

PART FIVE

Legislative Factors

*The fundamental theory of liberty upon which all govern-
ments in this Union repose excludes any general power of the
State to standardize its children by forcing them to accept
instruction from public teachers only. The child is not the mere
creature of the State; those who nurture him and direct his destiny have the right, coupled with the high duty, to recognize
and prepare him for additional obligations.*

Supreme Court Justice James McReynolds
Pierce v. Society of Sisters (1925)

23

Administrative Searches or "Child Welfare" Investigations

On November 5, 1987, the death of six-year-old Lisa Steinberg stunned New York City. Lisa was beaten to death by her adoptive father, a Manhattan attorney, in the climax of what had been a long, sordid story: another child tied to a playpen and covered with his own urine; a lover's face disfigured by repeated beatings; Steinberg's heavy use of narcotics; the discovery that both children were adopted illegally; and a system of child protective services ("CPS") that had apparently broken down.[1]

This and other heartbreaking stories have created an "unprecedented public awareness of and anger over the seemingly insoluble problem of child abuse and neglect."[2] In response to the public outcry, some courts have held that investigatory home visits by child protective services are "exempt from the fourth amendment's warrant requirement."[3] Thus, America continues its struggle to strike a balance in the competition between the government's interest in public safety and the individual's right to privacy as protected by the Fourth Amendment.[4]

In particular, American homes have always been given the highest protection by the Fourth Amendment.[5] The balance between these interests is usually maintained with the procedural safeguard of search warrants. The issue remains largely unresolved, however, as to whether state agents must obtain a warrant when conducting a home visit pursuant to state educa-

329

tional provisions or while investigating allegations of child abuse or neglect.[6]

THE IMPORTANT INTERESTS

The United States Supreme Court has asserted that "education is perhaps the most important function of state and local governments,"[7] seeing education as important to the maintenance of "our basic institutions, and [noting] the lasting impact of its deprivation on the life of the child."[8] "[S]ome degree of education is necessary to prepare citizens to participate effectively and intelligently in our open political system if we are to preserve freedom and independence."[9] Education also plays a vital role in giving individuals the ability to lead economically productive lives that benefit society as a whole.[10]

The right to privacy, especially in the home, is also a very important right: "Home searches have historically been considered the gravest sort of intrusion. The home is where one's expectation of privacy is greatest; it is where one's right to be let alone—the most comprehensive of rights and the right most valued by civilized men—finds its strongest expression."[11] Since people have the highest expectation of privacy in their homes, the Fourth Amendment gives the most protection to it.

The right to privacy found in the penumbra of the rights in the first ten constitutional amendments arguably protects home education.[12] The combination of the parental rights cases[13] and the *Griswold*[14] line of cases gives great protection to parental decisions on education based on a fundamental privacy right.[15] This is a fundamental right that deserves judicial deference. One commentator described the justification for that deference:

> [P]arents typically possess a sensitivity to the child's personality and needs that the state cannot match, and . . . the closeness of the familial relationship provides strong assurance that parents will use their special knowledge of the child to act in his best interests. Finally, the parental right of control serves the interests of all citizens in preserving a society in which the state cannot dictate that children be reared in a particular way. If the state could control the upbringing of children, it could impose an orthodoxy by indoctrinating individuals during the formative period of their lives.[16]

Yet, the state's interest in public safety also is important.[17] One of the key reasons for having a government is the protection of the health, welfare, and safety of the people. If a citizen's activities are a threat to the public safety, a limited intrusion on that person's rights is justified.[18] An important interest underlying investigations of ongoing or imminent criminal activity is that of protecting the safety of the public.[19]

The state's interest is thus secondary to the parent's interest. "It becomes a primary and compelling interest only if the parent fails to protect the child's welfare."

> While the state often intervenes on behalf of other citizens too weak or otherwise unable to protect their own interests, it does so usually in the absence of all other safeguards. In the present context [home education], the parent provides the first line of safeguards for the child. The courts have continually stated that the parent is presumed to act in the best interests of the child. If the parent fails in this respect then the state can intercede since the presumption of acting in the child's best interest is rebutted. At most, the state has an interest in ensuring that the parent is acting in the child's best interest.

Thus, the state's regulation of the home education choice must be narrowly tailored to determining the child's educational progress.[20] The parental right to raise and educate children is a fundamental right, and the state's interest in public safety and the welfare of the child is compelling. "When a fundamental right clashes with a compelling state interest, due process dictates that the state must show that it has chosen the least restrictive means to achieve its interest. Thus, the state may only use the least restrictive means to regulate home education."[21]

THE FOURTH AMENDMENT

The Fourth Amendment to the United States Constitution provides the framework for protecting two of these competing interests: public safety and the right to privacy in American homes. The Fourth Amendment states:

> The right of the people to be secure in their persons, houses, papers and effects, against unreasonable searches and seizures, shall not be violated, and no Warrants shall issue, but upon probable cause, supported by Oath or affirmation, and particularly describing the place to be searched, and the persons or things to be seized.[22]

However, the Fourth Amendment bars only unreasonable searches and seizures.[23] The Supreme Court has traditionally held that the term "reasonable" means pursuant to a warrant.[24] In emphasizing how essential the Fourth Amendment guarantees are to the liberty of American citizens, Justice Bradley wrote that the Fourth Amendment applies:

> [T]o all invasions on the part of the government and its employees of the sanctity of a man's home and the privacies of life. It is not the breaking of his doors and the rummaging of his drawers that constitutes the essence of the offense; but it is the invasion of his indefensible right of personal security, personal liberty and private property . . . it is the invasion of this sacred right.[25]

The general rule is that a searching officer must first get a warrant from a neutral magistrate. The warrant must be in writing and must direct an officer to search for personal property and must be signed by a magistrate.[26] A search warrant "interposes an orderly procedure involving judicial impartiality whereby a neutral and detached magistrate can make informed and deliberate determinations on the issues of probable cause."[27] "An issuing magistrate must meet two tests: 'He must be neutral and detached, and he must be capable of determining whether probable cause exists for the requested arrest or search.'"[28] This ensures that the search is necessary and justifiable.

The issue of probable cause is a complex one. It exists when an officer knows facts and circumstances, knowledge that comes from a trustworthy source, which would cause a reasonable person to believe that an offense has been or is being committed.[29] An officer has probable cause to search when there is a substantial probability that evidence of an offense will be found in a particular place.[30]

ADMINISTRATIVE SEARCHES

The Supreme Court has recognized that some searches constitutionally may be made without probable cause, as long as they are reasonable. These searches are called administrative searches. Administrative searches are usually distinguished from criminal searches on functional terms: an administrative search is not conducted as part of a criminal investigation.[31]

Nonetheless, the Court has shown concern that occupants of the place to be inspected would not know whether they were required to allow the inspection, not know the limits of the inspector's power to search, and not know whether the inspector was working with proper authorization.[32] The Court recognized that a system of search without warrant would leave the occupant subject to the same dangers the Fourth Amendment was designed to prevent; i.e., searches/investigations would be conducted without the protection of a disinterested party issuing a warrant.[33]

The reasonableness of the administrative search is determined by balancing the interests of public safety and individual privacy.[34] "It is generally assumed that the problems to which they [administrative searches] are addressed could not be adequately dealt with under the usual Fourth Amendment restraints and that consequently the practices must be judged by somewhat different standards."[35]

For example, in *Camara v. Municipal Court*,[36] a building inspector entered an apartment building to make a routine annual housing inspection for possible violations of the local housing code. Suspecting that Camara was illegally using his leasehold as a personal residence, the inspector demanded to be allowed to inspect the premises. Camara refused, then filed a petition for a writ of prohibition after he was charged with refusing to permit a lawful inspection.[37] The Court held that Camara had a constitutional right to refuse inspection of his property since the inspector did not have a warrant.[38] There is a lesser showing of probable cause necessary for these administrative searches: the officer needs only to show evidence of a violation.[39] It should be noted that an Alabama court has, in relying on *Camara*, held that the "power of the courts to permit invasions of the privacy protected by our federal and state constitutions, is not to be an exercise upon a showing of reasonable or probable cause that a crime is being or is about to be committed or a valid regulation is being or is about to be violated" and that unsworn hearsay is not sufficient to "rise to reasonable or probable cause."[40] The Court applied the standard in the setting of an Occupational Safety and Health Act inspection as follows:

> A warrant showing that a specific business has been chosen for an OSHA search on the basis of a general administrative plan for the enforcement of the Act derived from neutral sources, such as, for example, dispersion of employees in various types of industries across a given area, and the desired frequency of searches in any of the lesser divisions of the area, would protect an employer's Fourth Amendment rights.[41]

Thus, the magistrate must determine that there are reasonable legislative or administrative standards to be followed and that the proposed inspection would follow those standards, especially in determining who is to be subject to the inspection.[42]

EXCEPTIONS TO THE WARRANT RULE

There are three main exceptions to the rule that all searches must be made pursuant to a warrant issued. The first exception is the "pervasively-regulated" business exception first introduced in *Colonnade Catering Corp. v. United States*:[43]

> Certain industries have such a history of government oversight that no reasonable expectation of privacy could exist for a proprietor over the stock of such an enterprise. Liquor and firearms are industries of this type; when an entrepreneur embarks upon such a business, he has voluntarily chosen to subject himself to a full arsenal of governmental regulation. . . .[44]

The theory of this exception is that citizens are on notice that searches will be conducted in certain areas of commerce and that citizens engaged in such commerce have impliedly given consent to such searches by working in that industry.[45]

The second exception occurs when there are exigent circumstances. Exigent circumstances are usually found if there is imminent danger of the destruction of evidence or when there is a risk that a suspect will escape.[46]

The third exception occurs when an officer has a reasonable articulable suspicion of wrongdoing and obtaining a warrant would unduly hamper law enforcement. The foundation case for this exception is *Terry v. Ohio*,[47] in which the suspect, who was "casing" a store, was searched for weapons.[48] To be reasonable, the search must be based on the officer's particularized, objective belief and must be justified in scope and related to the purpose of the search.[49] This is less than the traditional probable cause required for a warrant.

There are three criteria that must be met to excuse the warrant requirement: first, a "substantial" government interest must underlie the regulatory scheme at issue; second, warrantless inspections must be necessary for the advancement of the regulatory scheme; and third, the regulatory scheme must "provid[e] a constitutionally adequate substitute for the warrant."[50]

Another way an inspector can conduct a search without a warrant is if the occupant consents to the search.[51] The consent must be voluntarily given, however, and not result from duress or coercion.[52]

EDUCATIONAL HOME VISITS

Educational home visits are often conducted pursuant to the certification of home schooling parents.[53] Home visits of this nature clearly fall under the definition of "search" contemplated by the Fourth Amendment.[54] The decision regarding a home visit is generally made by the educational agency of the state.[55] This agency is not neutral, since it has an incentive to attract as many students as possible to the public school and so obtain more funding and, in any case, generally admits to a theoretical bias in favor of public education.

By using their homes as schools, parents do not forfeit their expectations of privacy in them.[56] Even if home schools were determined to be commercial enterprises, it is unlikely that the highly regulated industry exception would be applicable. Although the government interest in protecting children is a substantial interest, home visits have not been shown to be necessary for the advancement of the regulatory scheme. There are other less restrictive means of ensuring the proper education of children, such as standardized test scores.[57] Most officials would also be able to obtain a search warrant if necessary under the lower probable cause standard for administrative searches. Moreover, the concern remains that home schooling parents would be unable to ascertain the scope of an inspector's authority without a warrant. Thus, the heavily regulated industry exception would probably not apply so as to permit a warrantless search of home school facilities.

In discussing a related subject, welfare inspections, two commentators have said:

> *Camara* reasoning would seem to be equally applicable here, for the primary concern in this context is that the search be related to a coherent policy followed by the agency and not merely an excuse for harassing a

particular unpopular welfare recipient. Thus it would suffice that a particular home visit was in accordance with an established schedule to make such visits at designated intervals or was undertaken upon a "watered-down" probable cause showing that the child's welfare was in danger. As for the warrant requirement, no reason is apparent why it would be impractical in this context, provided of course it is recognized that warrantless action may be undertaken upon a suspicion that the child is in some immediate jeopardy.[58]

The situation between welfare inspections and home schooling inspections is almost identical. There is no reason why a warrant should not be required, and the warrant requirement would help ensure that people with unpopular beliefs are not harassed.

The exigent circumstances exception would not be available in most home school situations since it is allowed only where there is immediate danger and investigatory home visits are generally conducted as part of a routine investigation, not as the result of an emergency situation.

The frustration of government regulation exception would also probably be unavailable. Again, there are other means of determining whether a child's home school education is sufficient to satisfy any interest of the state. In addition, there is no satisfactory reason why obtaining a warrant would frustrate the regulatory scheme. "One empirical study found that, on average, magisterial review of warrant applications took less than three minutes."[59]

The only other way a warrantless search could be conducted is if the parents consented to the inspection.[60] For example, consent might be given by home school parents who feel comfortable allowing an educational inspector to come into their home. Consent might be invalid, however, where parents feel compelled to allow the inspector in because of feared or anticipated reprisals such as charges of educational or other neglect. In *Blackwelder v. Safnauer*,[61] parents of home schooling children refused to allow inspections, then brought suit against the state, challenging New York's statutory scheme.[62] They claimed that the threat of educational neglect proceedings deprive parents of the opportunity to voluntarily consent to searches.[63] The court disagreed and granted summary judgment on the grounds that refusing to allow on-site inspections does not necessarily mean a finding of educational neglect is unavoidable, since such a finding is appealable to a Family Court judge.[64]

This finding is subject to criticism. It could be seriously argued that *no* wholly voluntary consent to investigatory home visits to home schools is possible. Even if the finding of educational neglect is appealable, the threat of adverse state action is a threat most parents would take very seriously, and many would not be willing to accept such a risk. Economic considerations, in addition to those of time, adverse publicity, and impact on the home school, all seem to preclude willing acceptance of educational neglect or child abuse allegations by the investigator, regardless of the administrative structures available for appeal and eventual success on the part of the parents.

Another court decided this issue differently than the New York court did. On August 7, 1986, in *Kinstedt v. East Greenwich School Committee*,[65] the practice of home visits was struck down in Rhode Island, and the Commissioner held in a written opinion:

> [I]t is our view that both the 4th Amendment and also the constitutionally derived right to privacy and autonomy which the U.S. Supreme Court has recognized, protect individuals from unwanted and warrantless visits to the home by agents of the state.[66]

Furthermore, the Commissioner wrote:

> [I]n view of the legal and constitutional considerations, we are unable to perceive any rationale whereby a home visitation requirement would be justifiable under circumstances such as these.[67]

CONCLUSION REGARDING EDUCATIONAL HOME VISITS

Educational home visits by home school inspectors are administrative searches governed by *Camara*.[68] Accordingly, the probable cause requirement is less strict than in a criminal case.[69] Probable cause necessitating home school inspections would involve balancing the two protected interests of health and welfare of children and familial privacy.[70] More than likely, none of the exceptions to the warrant requirements would be applicable since investigatory home school visits are generally not time-dependent searches and there are other less restrictive alternatives—for example, standardized testing—available to satisfy the interests of the state. In addition, there is a colorable argument that voluntary consent is not possible, so a search without a warrant is unreasonable *per se*.

Home school parents should ask to see a search warrant if an inspector requests admission to their homes. Further, home school parents should carefully read the warrant and ensure that the inspector acts only within the authorized scope set out in the warrant. But if such a warrant is issued, it is a court order, and parents should obey the court order as such.

CHILD WELFARE INVESTIGATIONS

Allegations of child abuse and child neglect are often made against parents who home school their children. When state officials are notified of suspected abuse or neglect, they often respond by sending child welfare investigators to the home to conduct a search.[71] Concerns for privacy are inherent in these investigations, just as they are inherent in educational home school visits. There is perhaps an even heightened concern in connection with child welfare investigations, since many child welfare investigations are of a broader scope than a home visit to inspect a home school. For example, "Should the investigator determine that the child's environment presents an immediate danger, he may remove the child from the home without prior judicial approval and order any physical, psychological or psychiatric examinations he deems necessary."[72]

Child welfare investigations are administrative searches rather than criminal searches since "nearly every state has expressly declared the policy underlying such investigations to be the protection and welfare of the child, not the apprehension and punishment of the alleged abuser."[73]

Warrantless searches have been permitted under the child protection arena. Child abuse investigations have fallen under the third exception listed above, where the burden of meeting the Fourth Amendment's warrant requirement would frustrate governmental regulation,[74] although "the Supreme Court has never created a general exemption from the warrant requirement for searches conducted to protect children."[75]

As noted above, the heavily regulated industry exception would not be applicable to searches of home schools since home schools occur in the context of a private home.

The exigent circumstances exception might apply in some circumstances (such as if the investigator heard or saw abuse of the child while she was ringing the doorbell), but not in most. The third exception of the heavy burden would be inapplicable in many circumstances:

> One empirical study found that, on average, magisterial review of warrant applications took less than three minutes. Any undue delay is a function not of the warrant process itself, but of poor administration: officers are either incapable of preparing the warrant application themselves or they cannot find an available magistrate to issue the warrant.[76]

In these circumstances, it does not appear that requiring a warrant would unduly burden governmental regulation, so the exception would not apply. The same consent concerns discussed above with respect to educational home visits are present, perhaps even to a greater degree, in the context of child welfare investigations. Parents who are being investigated for child abuse or neglect would be frightened that if they did not cooperate with the investigator, their children would be removed from their home temporarily or permanently.

FOURTEENTH AMENDMENT CONSIDERATIONS

The Supreme Court has recognized that "freedom of personal choice in matters of family life is a fundamental liberty interest" protected by the Due Process Clause of the Fourteenth Amendment.[77] This freedom is protected not only by procedural safeguards but also by substantive protections. A violation of these rights must further some legitimate state interest that outweighs the individual's rights. The governmental interference must also be no greater than is reasonably necessary to serve that interest.[78] The privacy interest protected by the Fourteenth Amendment as applied to home visits implicates the Fourth Amendment rights as discussed above.

Therefore, the above analysis (that privacy interests can only be protected by requiring that a warrant be obtained by investigatory agencies) would be controlling with respect to a substantive due process claim under the Fourteenth Amendment.

Procedural due process may also be at issue if there are vague or overbroad statutes. For example, home visits were held to be unconstitutional in two New York county court decisions: *In the Matter of Dixon*,[79] and *In the Matter of Standish*.[80] In *Dixon*, the court held:

> This Court firmly believes that the insistence of the Hannibal Central School District authorities to effect the desired on-site inspection was arbitrary, unreasonable, unwarranted, and violative of the Respondents' [home school parents'] due process rights guaranteed under the Fifth Amendment of the Constitution of the U.S. The school district cannot expect to put itself in the position of conducting the inspection then turning around and impartially or objectively determining whether the program subject to that inspection meets the required criteria for valid home instruction.[81]

Regarding protection from self-incrimination, the court explained: "The Respondents, further, cannot reasonably be put in a situation where they in effect are being forced to give evidence that might be used against them at a future date."[82] The court concluded that the home visit requirement is both "unconstitutional and unenforceable." This reasoning of the decision was confirmed *In the Matter of Standish*.[83]

ESTABLISHMENT CLAUSE CONCERNS

The Establishment Clause of the First Amendment forbids the enactment of any law "respecting an establishment of religion."[84] The main concern is to avoid "sponsorship, financial support, and active involvement of the sovereign in religious activity."[85] The test for determining whether a state action violates the Establishment Clause was formally enunciated in *Lemon v. Kurtzman*.[86] "First, the statute must have a secular legislative purpose; second, its principal or primary effect must be one that neither advances nor inhibits religion . . . finally, the statute must not foster an excessive governmental entanglement with religion."[87] The purpose prong of the test is clearly satisfied. The test "asks whether government's actual purpose in enacting the statute is to endorse or disapprove of religion."[88] The state has asserted its interest in the education of children.[89]

This secular purpose has been supported by the Supreme Court,[90] so the first prong is satisfied.

The second prong requires that the state action—for example, the home school visits—not have the primary effect of advancing or inhibiting religion.[91] Justice O'Connor interpreted this as meaning, "What is crucial is that a government practice not have the effect of communicating a message of government endorsement or disapproval of religion."[92] It does not seem that home visitation requirements would advance religion. However, an argument can be made that by conducting a home visit, the state is inhibiting home educators from practicing their religion.

The third prong of the *Lemon* test is also problematic. The third prong requires there not be too much entanglement with religion by the state.[93] The *Blackwelder* Court rejected the argument that home visits involve excessive entanglement, holding that such visits are simply part of the general regulatory power given to states.[94] It cited *Pierce v. Society of Sisters*[95] and *Board of Education v. Allen*[96] and said: "The state has the power 'reasonably to regulate all schools, to inspect, supervise and examine them, their teachers and pupils.'"[97]

The court distinguished *Aguilar v. Felton*,[98] where the Court struck down the practice of using federal funds to pay the salaries of public teachers in parochial schools.[99] First, it said *Aguilar* involved state financial aid to sectarian institutions.[100] Since the home schoolers in *Blackwelder* were getting neither direct nor indirect financial aid, *Aguilar* was inapplicable.[101] Second, the nature of the inspections in *Aguilar* were quite different, since they were regular and pervasive. The home school visits at issue in *Blackwelder* were only conducted once or twice a year.[102] For those reasons, the Court decided the home visits did not violate the First Amendment.[103]

Although *Aguilar* is apparently distinguishable from *Blackwelder*, the degree of entanglement could be greater in states other than New York. Some local home visit provisions give the local public school system the right to come into the religious home school, review the religious instructional materials being used, discuss the family's religious instructional program, and observe the actual instruction.[104] With this much intervention, a court may determine that the home visit excessively entangles the state with religion.

CONCLUSION

Home visits and child welfare investigations may be challenged on constitutional grounds, especially where the state's investigator does not have a warrant. Without a warrant, a parent may refuse to allow the investigator into her home. As noted above, if the investigator has a warrant, the parent should carefully read the warrant and know and enforce the limitations of the warrant, even if they "have nothing to hide." All parents, including those who are home schooling their children, should know and exercise their constitutional rights.

Home visits are a poor way to ensure the quality of home schools. As most teachers know, learning takes place over a period of time. Students and teacher both can have bad days. Unless home visits are conducted on a regular basis, there is no way for the investigator to know from a home visit what the educational process is really like at the home school. Other methods of evaluating a home school program are more accurate and less intrusive.

24

Home Educators in the Military

Home schools can be an important source of stability for children in military families. The disruption associated with frequent moves, often to new countries and new cultures, can be greatly mitigated, especially for young children, through education in the home. As one mother and home educator writes: "The Air Force may ask us to pack up and move in thirty days (yes, we've done it), but our homeschooling lifestyle goes with us."[1] She continues: "We have moved six times in twelve years. Since we homeschool, the children are saved the traumas of changing schools, moving midyear, testing to determine grade level, and having to relearn skills and subjects because they are taught differently all over the world."[2]

Moreover, home education can greatly lessen the security risks associated with living, in some cases, amidst terrorist activities, political instability, anti-American protests, and military conflict.

Finally, home education provides military families a unique opportunity to experience in-depth the local culture and geography.[3]

This chapter will review the military's treatment of home schooling, both domestically and abroad. It will also discuss general American constitutional concepts affecting military families who educate their children at home, both internationally and domestically.

OVERSEAS MILITARY HOME SCHOOLS
LOCATED ON U.S. BASES

Currently, there is "only one true place the military home schooler can move to and be sure of no confrontation—that is to live and serve in a foreign country."[4] Former Secretary of Defense Richard Cheney has stated that "in country," military families are "subject to local regulations, but overseas, home education is a recognized option."[5]

There are currently some 2,460,806 people enlisted in the United

States Armed Forces.[6] Those people reportedly have 1,647,795 children.[7] The United States has bases in twenty countries, although the American military will be leaving the Philippines soon.[8] Education is an important issue for parents who are living on these bases abroad.

The American government provides schools for military families living on these bases. There are currently 270 schools in those twenty foreign countries.[9] "The schools were established by Congress to provide an education of high quality for eligible minor dependents of Defense Department military and civilian personnel on official overseas assignments. Education may be provided to other youngsters on a space-available, tuition-paying basis."[10] These schools are run by the Department of Defense Dependents Schools (DoDDS).[11] There are approximately 131,000 children in DoDDS schools overseas.[12]

DoDDS does not have a policy favoring or disfavoring home schooling. The internal policy is to accommodate parents who wish to home school.[13] As noted above, the military must offer a free and appropriate education, but the military may not force a family to enroll in the DoDDS school. The base commander has the authority to oversee the education of children on base and can call a military member into his office and inquire into the home school curriculum.[14] If the commander does not believe the child is getting an adequate education, the military member may be transferred back to the United States, or base privileges such as shopping on base can be withdrawn.[15] The commander's discretion is great, making this the most likely trouble spot for home schooling overseas.

OVERSEAS MILITARY HOME SCHOOLS LOCATED OFF BASE

While the United States military has bases in only twenty countries, there are military and Department of Defense personnel stationed in almost every country in the world.[16] Since there are no DoDDS schools in those countries which host no U.S. base, education becomes even more of a concern. In general, parents are not subject to the education laws of the country they are stationed in, because foreign countries view the education of service personnel children as an American concern.[17] The military person's state of legal residence and the education laws there are also irrelevant once the family is placed overseas.[18]

Department of Defense Dependents Schools regulations recognize the right to home school and provide that if an adequate alternative is not available, the government will provide the home school materials to the military family.[19] The regulation describes what the government will finance but also states: "This regulation is not intended to preclude DoD sponsors (military members) from enrolling their dependents in non-DoD schools at no expense to the U.S. Government."[20]

Rights guaranteed by the United States Constitution are also protected for military people stationed overseas.[21] In one opinion, the Supreme Court has stated: "The Constitution of the United States is a law for rulers and people, equally in war and in peace, and covers with the shield of its protection all classes of [persons], at all times, and under all circumstances."[22]

Although the Supreme Court has not directly addressed the issue, most circuits "have applied the Constitution extraterritorially and required the United States government to conform to constitutional proscriptions when acting overseas."[23] Therefore, all the constitutional rights discussed below also apply to service personnel stationed overseas and to their families, regardless of the spouse's or children's citizenship.

DOMESTIC MILITARY HOME SCHOOLS

As discussed above, families who live on military bases have the same rights as other citizens of the United States, regardless of whether they are overseas; the home is a zone of privacy that the government may not intrude upon unnecessarily.[24] Citizens and others in the United States have a right to be free from government control in their own homes as long as their actions do not threaten the health, safety or welfare of society.[25]

The Free Exercise Clause of the First Amendment makes this particularly true in the case of the practice of religion. As long as their actions do not threaten others, people are free to practice their religion in their own homes. Many families who home school their children do so out of religious conviction and believe that they are practicing their religion by educating their children in this manner. The fact that the government owns the property on the base is irrelevant. Thus, the government may not limit a protected right on property it owns any more than it can limit rights on a citizen's own private property.[26]

THE PROPER ROLE OF THE MILITARY

Despite the fact that military members have the same constitutional rights as others in the United States, the Supreme Court often allows the military to limit the exercise of those rights by its members. Supreme Court Chief Justice Earl Warren summarized the problem when he said:

> Determining the proper role to be assigned to the military in a democratic society has been a troublesome problem for every nation that has aspired to a free political life. The military establishment is, of course, a necessary organ of government; but the reach of its power must be carefully limited lest the delicate balance between freedom and order be upset. The maintenance of the balance is made more difficult by the fact that while the military serves the vital function of preserving the existence of the nation, it is, at the same time, the one element of government that exercises a type of authority not easily assimilated in a free society.[27]

In totalitarian countries, it is the military that controls life, not the political organs of government.[28] The American colonists rejected abuse of military power when they wrote the Declaration of Independence and complained that "the King had subordinated the civil power to the military, that he had quartered troops among them in times of peace, and that through his mercenaries he had committed other cruelties."[29]

The threat of the military was of great concern to the drafters of the Constitution. James Madison summarized their worries in *The Federalist Papers*:

> The veteran legions of Rome were an overmatch for the undisciplined valor of all other nations, and rendered her the mistress of the world. Not the less true is it, that the liberties of Rome proved the final victim of her military triumphs; and that the liberties of Europe, as far as they ever existed, have, with few exceptions, been the price of her military establishments. A standing force, therefore, is a dangerous, at the same time that it may be a necessary, provision. On the smallest scale it has its inconveniences. On an extensive scale its consequences may be fatal. On any scale it is an object of laudable circumspection and precaution. A wise nation will combine all these considerations; and, whilst it does not rashly preclude itself from any resource which may become essential to its safety, will exert all its prudence in diminishing both the necessity and the danger of resorting to one which may be inauspicious to its liberties.[30]

Among other things, it was the fear of military powers that spurred the writing and adoption of the Bill of Rights.[31] Because the military has the potential to affect greatly the lives of United States citizens, the military establishment should not be treated as "an enclave beyond the reach of the civilian courts."[32]

HOW JUSTICE IS ADMINISTERED IN THE MILITARY

The primary sources of law for the military, like the civilian world, are statutes and case law.[33] As one commentator has noted: "[A]n individual entering the armed forces experiences a relaxation or loss of some constitutional and due process protections otherwise available to civilians."[34]

Nonetheless, in the area of the Fourth Amendment and home visits,[35] the same constitutional protections generally apply.[36] There are differences, however. The military authorizes military commanders, as well as "magistrates," to issue search warrants.[37] There is thus a potential for abuse.[38] This is especially true for administrative searches: "The military system, however, allows the government much greater latitude in the conduct of administrative inspections."[39] Military commanders have broad authority to conduct inspections[40] of their units, including areas where military members have a reasonable expectation of privacy.[41]

The Uniform Code of Military Justice (U.C.M.J.)[42] is the foundation of military law.[43] As mentioned above, however, the base commander has a great deal of discretion under the U.C.M.J. A court-martial is convened when a commander sets it up.[44] Because of this, "[critics] of the military justice system are most disturbed about command control of the court-martial machinery and the unfair influence it can have on an adjudication."[45] On the appellate level, the Court of Military Review may review both facts and law, and the highest court is the United States Court of Military Appeals, a civilian court that reviews only law.[46]

HOW THE CONSTITUTION APPLIES TO THE MILITARY

Although service members have the same constitutional rights as civilians, the Constitution applies to them somewhat differently. The United States Supreme Court reviews decisions in the military justice system when they involve constitutional matters, but the Court treats a case differently when it is initially raised in a military court rather than a civilian court.[47] The First Amendment in general will be discussed below, since the reasons for home schooling may extend beyond freedom of religion alone.

THE SEPARATE COMMUNITY

The justification for treating the military differently than the rest of society has been that the military is a "separate society."[48] This rationale has led to less protection of the constitutional rights of members of the military.[49] The Court articulated this rationale when it said, "[T]he military constitutes a specialized community governed by a separate discipline from that of the civilian."[50] As a result of this different treatment, Supreme Court Justice Jackson stated:

> [J]udges are not given the task of running the Army. The responsibility for setting up channels through which such grievances can be considered and fairly settled rests upon the Congress and upon the President of the United States and his subordinates. The military constitutes a specialized community governed by a separate discipline from that of the civilian. Orderly government requires that the judiciary be as scrupulous not to interfere with legitimate Army matters as the Army must be scrupulous not to intervene in judicial matters.[51]

The Supreme Court applied this standard to the First Amendment in *Parker v. Levy*[52] saying: "While the members of the military are not excluded from the protection granted by the First Amendment, the different character of the military community and of the military mission requires a different application of those protections."[53]

The Court based its distinction on two characteristics: "[A]s a matter of history and practice, there is a fairly clear body of social norms peculiar to the military and known to all reasonable personnel";[54] and, "a military organization is a hierarchy based on response to command, that the successful performance of its mission depends on effective response to command, and that this requires more pervasive regulation of the individual than is found in civilian society."[55]

In the separate-community cases, a member of the military claims infringement of a constitutional right while the government argues military necessity, "that the functioning of the armed forces justifies its (the claim's) denial even if it would be granted against another agency or for a person not subject to military law."[56]

REFUTATION OF THE SEPARATE COMMUNITY

Today the military is no longer a separate community. It interacts with civilian society every day.[57] Most of the jobs in the military are civilian-type work,[58] and thus "[t]he typical or common member of the armed forces is not an alien outcast but is one of us. He comes out of a civilian background, participates in civilian society when off duty, enjoys and exercises political rights, and will probably return to civil life when it is to his advantage to do so."[59] Only 17 percent of enlisted personnel are trained for combat,[60] and "[t]he duties of a military computer programmer, truck mechanic, or cook are not intrinsically different from his or her civilian counterpart, it is argued, and the full rigors of traditional military discipline are no more needed in these jobs than they would be in a civilian corporation."[61]

Obedience is necessary to the military, but unquestioning obedience can be "dangerous and illegal."[62] Allowing the military to infringe on military members' First Amendment rights discourages moral accountability, as evidenced by the Nuremberg and My Lai incidents.[63] "Requiring obedience, yet demanding that the soldier act as a moral agent when presented with unlawful orders, places an extraordinary burden on the young men and women who comprise the American military. It is morally indefensible, then, to short circuit the process through which autonomous decisions must be made."[64]

Exposure to dissent or varying viewpoints will not necessarily harm servicepersons' attitudes and performance,[65] especially since "[t]he serviceperson is exposed to the complete array of persuasions when off-base or watching television or participating in any other 'civilian' activities. They have probably already been exposed to these 'harmful viewpoints' for most of their entire lives."[66]

Allowing expression of speech and religion will benefit the military rather than harm it. Suppressing dissent leads to low morale and hostility.[67]As one authority writes: "Mindless censorship will certainly disturb discipline and loyalty."[68] Supreme Court Justice Brennan has noted: "The forced absence of peaceful expression only creates the illusion of good order; underlying dissension remains to flow into the more dangerous channels of incitement and disobedience."[69] Soldiers who have been allowed to express themselves freely seem better able to resist brainwashing and to assume the "complex responsibilities of modern warfare."[70]

THE FIRST AMENDMENT AND THE MILITARY

In reviewing the law in this area, one commentator says: "[A]s the law currently stands, the mere invocation of military necessity is sufficient to trump a serviceperson's claims that his or her first amendment rights have been violated by the military."[71] The United States Supreme Court's first foray into the area of the military and the First Amendment was *Parker v. Levy*.[72] Levy was an officer and a doctor who trained medical personnel.[73] He expressly told his students that they should refuse to go to Vietnam.[74] The Army court-martialed him for "conduct unbecoming an officer and a gentleman"[75] and for "disorder and neglects to the prejudice of good order and discipline in the armed forces."[76] Levy argued that the two articles of the U.C.M.J. were void for vagueness under the Due Process Clause and overbroad in violation of the First Amendment.[77]

The Supreme Court did not apply conventional First Amendment vagueness and overbreadth analysis to the case.[78] A very deferential standard of review was used, and the Supreme Court upheld Levy's conviction.[79] This case made clear that "military necessity emerges as a 'talismanic incantation' which spells doom for the constitutional rights of the serviceperson. Contrary to the civilian cases, the presumption is actually against the First Amendment interest in the military setting."[80]

PARKER'S PROGENY

Two years later, the Supreme Court decided that prior approval of all political speeches and political literature before distribution on a military base was constitutional in *Greer v. Spock*.[81] The Court did not enunciate any standard of review; it merely trusted the base commander's decision about what constitutes a threat to his troops.[82]

A more recent decision further signals the Supreme Court's deferential views in *Brown v. Glines*.[83] *Brown* likewise dealt with distribution of political materials, this time, petitions.[84] The Court again deferred to the commander's judgment, this time as to whether application of a prior restraint regulation was constitutional.[85]

These cases illustrate that the military may take action severely abridging freedom of speech (prior restraint) which would not be tolerated by a civilian branch of the government.

GOLDMAN V. WEINBERGER: THE ABYSS[86]

The most extreme example of Supreme Court deference to military decisions is found in *Goldman v. Weinberger*.[87]

Goldman was a military psychologist who worked in a hospital on base.[88] He was also a religious Jew who covered his head at all times.[89] An Air Force regulation stated that "[h]eadgear will not be worn . . . [w]hile indoors except by armed security police."[90] The Court upheld the Air Force regulation without actually considering Goldman's constitutional claim.[91] The Court deferred to the professional judgment of the military. The Court seemed to be saying that as long as the military claimed necessity, their decisions would be immune from judicial scrutiny.[92]

The Supreme Court presented Goldman with an unconscionable choice: violation of a significant religious practice every day or court-martial.[93] The Court did not require the government to show any connection between Goldman wearing a yarmulke and a potential risk.[94] Justice O'Connor, in dissent, noted:

> The Court rejects Captain Goldman's claim without even the slightest attempt to weigh his asserted right to free exercise of his religion against the interest of the Air Force in uniformity of dress within the military hospital. No test for Free Exercise claims in the military context is even articulated, much less applied. It is entirely sufficient for the Court if the military perceives a need for uniformity.[95]

A REAL STANDARD OF REVIEW

Justice O'Connor's dissent provides a standard for reviewing military decisions that deal with the First Amendment. One commentator concludes: "By drawing on existing precedent in free exercise adjudication, she concluded that the government must demonstrate an 'unusually important interest' to deny a free exercise claim, and in addition, 'the government must show that . . . the means adopted is the least restrictive or essential, or that the interest will not otherwise be served.'"[96] Further, this test, as Justice O'Connor recognized, "is sufficiently flexible to take into account the special importance of defending our Nation without abandoning completely the freedoms that make it worth defending."[97]

"There is no principle to explain why the courts are less able to evaluate the relationship between a military regulation and its purported aim, than the relationship between a securities regulation and its purported aim. A substantive review of the merits does not mean that the courts must become military experts any more than it means they must be scientific experts to decide patent cases."[98] But the Supreme Court is presumably an expert on constitutional law. It can and should decide whether the military is infringing on vital First Amendment freedoms.[99] As Chief Justice Warren once said: "[O]ur citizens in uniform may not be stripped of basic rights simply because they have doffed their civilian clothes."[100]

MILITARY HOME SCHOOLS AND THE ESTABLISHMENT CLAUSE

Another issue to be considered is whether allowing military parents to home school would violate the Establishment Clause of the First Amendment.[101] In determining whether military authorities' acquiescence in home schooling by military families is constitutional with respect to the Establishment Clause, consideration must be given as to whether the action has a secular purpose, whether it advances or inhibits religion, and whether it creates an excessive entanglement between religion and government.[102]

Applying the *Lemon* test to the matter of home schooling by military families, it appears that the government/military would not violate the Establishment Clause by allowing military parents to educate their children at home on United States military property or elsewhere despite their status as military personnel. The secular purpose would be to recognize the constitutional right of parents to choose the education they want their children to receive.[103] Permitting military home schools would not unconstitutionally advance religion because military parents would not be required to educate their children at home; the government would merely be recognizing the constitutional rights of parents and the options such parents wish to be available to them. The entanglement between government and religion would be minimal since the government would play only a very limited role, analogous to the role the states play when allowing non-military parents to home school their children.

The Court has found similar practices permissible:

> It obviously is not unconstitutional, for example, for a group of parishioners from a local church to go caroling through a city park on any Sunday in Advent or for a Christian club at a public university to sing carols during their Christmas meeting. *Cf. Widmar v. Vincent*, 454 U.S. 263 (1981). The reason is that activities of this nature do not demonstrate the government's allegiance to, or endorsement of, the Christian faith.[104]

Just as government is not unconstitutionally endorsing religion by allowing carolers to sing Christmas carols on public property, the military would not be endorsing religion by merely allowing military parents to teach their children at home in a religious manner.

CONCLUSION

Military families should not incur special legal difficulties as a result of home schooling their children on United States military bases, domestically or overseas. Most military regulations that have been upheld have applied to the members of the military and their conduct. Since it would generally be the non-military parent who would be primarily responsible for the home education of military families, military authorities should not be concerned with the home education aspects of the military family's life.

The courts have been very deferential to the military. This attitude has the potential to harm not only individual personnel, but the military itself, and even American society. As Earl Warren noted:

> Legislative or executive action eroding our citizens' rights in the name of security cannot be placed on a scale that weighs the public's interest against that of the individual in a sort of "count the heads" fashion. Democracy under our Constitution calls for judicial deference to the coordinate branches of the Government and their judgment of what is essential to the protection of the Nation. But it calls no less for a steadfast protection of those fundamentals imbedded in the Constitution, so incorporated for the express purpose of insulating them from possible excesses of the moment. Our history has demonstrated that we must be as much on guard against the diminution of our rights through excessive fears for our security and a reliance on military solutions for our problems by the civil government, as we are against the usurpation of civil authority by the army.[105]

The young men and women who make up the United States military deserve the same liberty they protect for the rest of society. As a former Chief Justice of the Supreme Court writes: "Today, as always, the people, no less than their courts, must remain vigilant to preserve the principles of our Bill of Rights, lest in our desire to be secure we lose our ability to be free."[106]

PART SIX

Practicalities

While the family still has the primary moral and legal responsibility for the character development of children, it often lacks the power or opportunity to do the job, primarily because parents and children no longer spend enough time together in those situations in which such training is possible. This is not because parents do not want to spend time with their children. It is simply that conditions have changed.

Professor Urie Bronfenbrenner
Two Worlds of Childhood: U.S. and U.S.S.R. (1970)

25

Making Allies of Your Family, Friends and the Public

> You will encounter many different responses to your decision to home school. Some will laud you as a brave, angelic super-mom and others will think you are nuts. I have found that the general public, with the exception of an occasional schoolteacher, are very positive toward the idea. A few think it's a good thing, but worry that the children will grow up to be odd.[1]

This experience is more than likely representative of many reactions experienced by home schoolers when they discuss their educational choices with those who are not educating their children at home. Such reactions are generally the result of a lack of information or familiarity with home education.

As discussed in Chapter Three, "Freedom and Educational Diversity," it is imperative from the perspective of national interest that the home education alternative be preserved in the United States. From a constitutional and personal liberty perspective, educational diversity is critical.

Since home education is but one form of education among several, and since home education may not be a suitable choice for all parents, it becomes important, for the preservation of educational diversity, that home educators and non-home educators understand and support the educational choices of each other. Such understanding and support may be greatly facilitated by information and communication.[2]

Thus, home schoolers should be informed about contemporary public and private education, and non-home schoolers should be informed about issues affecting contemporary home education.

It is relatively easy for home educators to be knowledgeable about public and private education. Many sources of information such as books, magazines, and newspapers are available that can provide historical and current information on and analysis of education matters. Colleges and universities have relevant information, in addition to information that may be obtained from one's elected political representatives. Many churches and other organizations also disseminate their views on education.

It many not be as easy to obtain information regarding home education. Certainly, informative and reliable information exists, but access to it might not be as familiar for those not involved in home schooling.

Thus, it is important that home schoolers make a commitment to making information available to non-home schoolers about the subject.

RED FLAGS

As with any controversial issue, there are certain words or statements that tend to generate hostility for one reason or another. Therefore, in attempting to share information with non-home schoolers, home educators should consider strategies that are non-confrontational.

According to some commentators: "People are especially offended by statements like those [below]. Even if it *is* how you really feel, refrain from saying so, and avoid the strife and misunderstanding which would follow . . .".[3]

- "As a Christian, I could never send my children to public school!"
- "God has only given parents the job of teaching their children."
- "I plan to home school clear through high school."
- "I don't want my children with all those other kids."
- "I don't want my kids to go through what I went through."
- "College isn't important. I want her to be a good wife and mother."[4]

GRANDPARENTS

Two authors on home schooling write:

> It seems the ones who most often have a negative reaction to home teaching are those who feel some responsibility for the kids, such as grandparents, neighbors, and the people at church. These people know you well enough to remember some of the dumb things you've done in the past. They may have reason to worry. . . . Therefore listen and prayerfully consider whatever they may have to say.[5]

Thus, it seems that an important place to begin making information available about home education is at home—with grandparents, neighbors, and the people at church.

Something that home educators may not always consider is that "at times our parents and in-laws have their own problems with peer pressure.

They have to consider what they will tell their friends, when asked where their grandchildren go to school. If everyone thinks you are crazy, it is a reflection on them."[6]

Thus, it has been suggested that home schooling parents express to their own parents how much they value the education, particularly the college education, they received.[7] Grandparents should be reassured that home schooling represents an attempt to reach the educational goals valued by the grandparents and transmitted by them to their children.

To the extent that the grandparents wish to listen, home schooling parents should describe the curriculum being used and the experiential learning of their grandchildren. This will give them something to discuss when they are handling the pressure of their own peers.

Home schoolers should give grandparents, neighbors, and people at church (and others, for that matter) the "freedom to hold and express their opinions" and "try not to make [home schooling] an issue."[8]

If these approaches are unsuccessful and family members remain hostile, one home school family suggests:

> Unless they are paying off your mortgage, ignore them. If they persist, suggest that they foot the bill for a second-rate but entirely respectable education at an expensive private school. Or send them a copy of this book [*Homeschooling for Excellence*, by David and Micki Colfax].[9]

Ignoring the issue if family discussions are unsuccessful will probably better preserve family relationships than arguing *ad nauseum* and further inflaming emotions. And, despite family views on educational choice, it is, of course, always important to preserve family relationships.

NEIGHBORS

Home educators should base any discussion with non-home schoolers on the notion that the other parties to the conversation *also* care about their children, the nation, and good education. Thus, home educators should consider the following advice:

- Don't try to talk anyone into home schooling.
- Don't talk too much about it. Give short answers to questions. . . . They were probably just being polite.
- Thank people for advice, comments, and observations. Thank God for those who offer it!
- Be interested in and enthusiastic about what other people are doing with their kids . . . home schooling or not.[10]

Home educators should consider and formulate their own answers to the most common questions or concerns of non-home schoolers.

In order to respond to the all-too-familiar concerns about socialization and academics, home school parents should be familiar with the published information on these issues.[11]

For non-technical issues, home school parents should assess and discuss their own experience. For example, one noted home school author writes:

> Some have suggested that by teaching our sons at home we are shelter-ing them from reality. "What's it going to be like when they have to go out into the *real world*?" was the refrain. Grant's performance at Harvard provided an easy, if somewhat misleading answer; for what the question reveals is an inability to comprehend the fact that homeschool-ing provided our boys with "real world" experiences they would never have encountered in a conventional learning situation. Because they have learned to value and make good use of their time, they have developed skills that most children simply do not have the time or opportunity to acquire.[12]

Home educators should be mindful that what others *observe* about their educational choices may be even more important than what the home schooling parents or their children *say* about it. Thus, home educators should ensure that they exemplify a "caring parent, good neighbor and a responsible citizen."[13] If this is the case, the neighbors are more likely to believe that the home schooling parents "know what [they] are doing, [and] that [they] are doing [their] children a favor."[14]

Finally, home educators should *be involved*. Home educators should be involved in their home schools, as most are, of course. But they should also be fully informed about *all* educational issues. And they should be will-ing to discuss these matters with others as neighbors and citizens and elicit their support.

THE CHURCH

Many of the suggestions regarding neighbors also apply in connection with the church. If the decision to home school was motivated by religious beliefs,[15] home schooling parents should share this with the members of their church and encourage their support.

THE AUTHORITIES

Home educators should never compromise their beliefs or their right to edu-cate their children in the manner they choose. Nonetheless, the state has asserted an interest in the education of future voters and wage-earners and in the welfare of its citizens, and these interests have been recognized by the courts.[16]

Thus, home educators *must know their rights* and must know the inter-play between their rights, the United States Constitution, and the various state laws that may apply to them.[17]

To the extent that the requirements of the state are *reasonable* and do not represent an unconstitutional infringement of their rights, home school parents should consider compliance with such requirements.

To the extent that the state's requirements are *unreasonable* or represent an unconstitutional infringement of their rights, home school parents should promptly seek the advice of a competent attorney.[18]

In this regard, home school parents should consider contacting a local attorney who could become familiar with their family and their home school. The attorney could obtain information about home school laws and issues from organizations such as The Rutherford Institute and, thus, would be in an enhanced position to help should the home school family need legal representation.

Home school families should also be informed about and active in state and local school politics,[19] for this is where policies and laws important to home education are created or revised. Home school parents should also introduce themselves to and establish relationships with local school authorities. As one authority has said: "Be open. . . . Don't act guilty or sneaky. . . . You're not selling drugs. . . ."[20] Thus:

> Often parents and educational administrators each view the other groups as adversaries. Parents are frightened when they hear about school people whose unreasonable actions are apparently motivated by a desire to protect teachers' jobs, to assure tax dollars from the state, or simply to control the situation. And educators who misunderstand school at home, or confuse parents wanting to educate their own children with those who don't care, often feel an obligation to be tough. Communication reduces misunderstanding, and a demonstration of good faith and cooperation eases restrictions.[21]

CONCLUSION

Home school parents should make every effort to make allies of grandparents, neighbors and church members. These efforts will pay off in support for the particular home school and its students and in support of educational diversity and freedom of school choice.

To the extent that it does not infringe or compromise their rights, home school parents should make allies of the politicians and other authorities who have the power to affect their home schools.

These efforts will be most successful when approached by fully informed parents who know their rights and their jobs as home educators—and who defend and perform them with excellence.

26

Legislation and Lobbyists

There are two avenues through which citizens can alter laws adversely affecting home education. Previous chapters in this book have detailed the legal route. This chapter concentrates on the second course: the legislature. In addition to challenging the validity of home school laws in court, interested citizens can band together to lobby their legislatures for amendments to or repeals of existing overly intrusive or vague statutes or enactments of more favorable laws.

This chapter is not intended to serve as an exhaustive treatise on lobbying techniques; rather, its purpose is to offer the home education advocate some basic guidelines for their own lobbying activities.[1] In addition, while many books focus on lobbying Congress, this chapter concentrates on state legislatures—the true battleground for educational reform. Because of the difficulty in examining lobbying in the context of fifty states, this chapter is a general discussion of lobbying. The citizen lobbyist, therefore, must scrutinize closely his or her state's laws regarding lobbying in order to determine applicable restrictions.

Initially, this chapter discusses lobbying in general terms, examining its benefits and operating rules. It then offers advice on how to prepare for the different phases of lobbying: organizing volunteers, drafting the legislation, finding legislative sponsors, and building legislative support. It concludes with suggestions for lobbying strategies for home education proponents.

WHAT IS LOBBYING?

Lobbying is the process through which "citizens can both instigate changes in the law and affect the outcome of the legislative process by exerting influence over their elected representatives."[2] One commentator has provided a more technical definition: "the stimulation and transmission of a communication, by someone other than a citizen acting on his own behalf, directed

at a governmental decision-maker with the hope of influencing his decision."[3] In essence, the lobbying process serves as "an extension of the right
to be heard and an exercise in democracy."[4] Lobbying provides citizens the
opportunity to act outside the voting booth and to hold those they elect to
office continuously accountable to their constituents.[5]

While there are disadvantages to lobbying,[6] the advantages are overwhelming. First, the citizen lobbyist does not need years of experience to
engage in this activity. While lobbying is challenging and must be done in
a professional manner to be successful, a citizen group does not have to hire
a "professional" to do the job. Frequently, citizen volunteers from the group
serve as more "convincing" spokespersons than the experts.[7] Citizen advocates generally present compelling and credible testimony or presentation
because of their personal stake in the legislation at issue.[8] For example, sup-
pose a group of home educators seek to repeal a statute requiring the certification of home instructors. A parent who cannot afford the time or
money to acquire certification or the parent with a doctorate in English who
can teach college freshmen but who is prohibited from teaching her own
child can bring the reality of the legislation's impact to the attention of legislators. Now the politicians have faces to place with the numbers their
work affects.[9] While a professional may have more working knowledge, the
novice can learn quickly through talking with experienced lobbyists and
reading about the legislative process beforehand.[10]

Second, as lobbyists, home educators have the opportunity to educate
not only legislators but also the general public with thorough and accurate
information about home education.[11] By faithfully and exhaustively representing one's view, legislators will come to rely on one's group for reliable
and comprehensive information,[12] a tremendous advantage in building a
legislative coalition. The public benefits from lobbying as well.[13] While
undoubtedly these groups offer biased accounts of the issues, they nonetheless "make a valuable contribution to people's understanding of political
issues" because they simply increase awareness of crucial debates.[14]

Third, a lobbyist has the opportunity not only to suggest changes in the
law, but also to outline how the legislature should make those changes.[15]
Home school proponents can write their own legislation as a proposal and
can find sponsors to support their version,[16] which means home school parents have an opportunity to mold their own future.

Finally, home schoolers should not allow financial constraints to preclude their lobbying efforts.[17] There are numerous ways in which the citizen lobbyist group can minimize their financial burdens without harming
their cause.[18] For example, look within your own advocacy group for volunteers—persons with knowledge and expertise who strongly believe in
your cause and who will work for free, and also persons who may not have
the expertise but who have a home computer or access to printing services.[19]

Another suggestion for saving money involves efficiency in training
volunteers. For example, schedule one intensive training session for the volunteers, requiring one-time compensation for contributors and instruc-

tors.[20] Mailing with second-class postage and using folding newsletters instead of envelopes are additional ways to trim the budget.[21]

Before embarking on a detailed examination of the actual lobbying process, it is important to discuss central, underlying rules which lobbyists should remember as they begin their campaigns. The most significant rule to observe is to know the issue you are representing.[22] In order to "secure reliable and comprehensive information" for legislators,[23] lobbyists must have an understanding of the primary and ancillary issues.[24] The home school advocates must learn about the existing home education legislation and must be able to convey why it does not work, how it should be changed, why your proposal is the best solution, and how it will affect other interests. Through brainstorming and intense preparation, citizen lobbyists can predict potential questions and avoid surprise when a representative asks a distant but related and pertinent question,[25] and the coalition will be prepared to counter any adversarial attempts to refute its information. Preparation is fundamental to lobbying success.

Such preparation and understanding permits lobbyists to follow the second rule: be honest and accurate.[26] First, lobbyists must be truthful in discussing their cause.[27] If your lobbying group has earned the reputation of consistently providing honest information, the legislators will respect your answers and opinions.[28] On the other hand, any mispresentations to a legislator could jeopardize a trusting relationship.[29] In politics, "honesty is not so much a matter of virtue as of necessity. Lobbyists simply cannot do the job if there are any doubts about their credibility."[30] Second, lobbyists must be reliable in providing information. Lobbyists should seek to "create a dependency": whenever legislators need information, they come to your group.[31] To build such a relationship, you must develop the reputation as "providing the right kind of information at the right time."[32]

Lobbyists also must remember to properly assess the opposition.[33] Regardless of the issue, opponents will emerge. This is true in the home education context, where advocates face the education establishment. Lobbyists should seek to neutralize the opposition by discrediting their strongest arguments. Read their literature, and understand their viewpoint in search of ways to counter their attack.[34] Home educators should learn why the education establishment opposes pro-home school laws and must prepare strong counterarguments to undermine opponents' reasoning.[35] For example, in challenging opposition based on socialization concerns, refer the legislators to the countless studies showing that home education promotes socialization and personal development.[36] If home school lobbyists cannot provide answers to these concerns, they may lose legislative support.

Perhaps more important than knowing the opposite view is recognizing allies both outside and inside the legislative hall.[37] Finding the right allies outside the legislature can help your cause build a stronger support system among the legislators.[38] "You can broaden your influence far beyond the membership of your group if you can legitimately claim the endorsement of other organizations. . . . [T]hese groups can lend you time, money, manpower and expertise which may be otherwise unavailable to you."[39] Unfortunately, few are willing to work for free; be prepared to offer other coalitions legitimate reasons why they should help you and to demonstrate how it will benefit them.[40]

Home school lobbyists also should find "friendly" staff members.[41] Having as an ally a staff member of a powerful or fence-sitting legislator is valuable because such persons have tremendous influence over their legislative bosses. Legislators "are spread thinly over many issues and many competing demands. Staff, on the other hand, are able to concentrate and follow up on individual projects, ideas and promises. They are the ones who . . . hammer out compromises with staff peers [and] prepare their [bosses] to speak forcefully and persuasively."[42] Because of the staff's role, "it comes as no surprise that politically savvy associations often spend more time on the cultivation of staff" than on legislators.[43] If a home educator can convince a staff member of the importance of his cause, the staff member, in turn, can persuade the legislator of its significance.

Finally, lobbyists must remember their ultimate goal: to move their bill through the legislature.[44] To accomplish this objective, lobbyists should be prepared to compromise.[45] The key, however, is to know how to yield without compromising the legislation's original purpose. A home school advocacy group should discuss ahead of time to what degree, if any, it is willing to be flexible.[46] "Lay . . . out all the possible options along the way [to] avoid the typical fatal mistake of novice lobbyists: agreeing to compromise before adequate consultation" with all members of the group.[47]

STEP #1: PREPARING TO LOBBY

Before approaching legislators with the proposed legislation, there are preliminary steps a lobbyist group must take to achieve success. Initially an organizational meeting is necessary.[48] For example, a state-wide association of home educators should sponsor a training meeting for interested members. The association should try to recruit members from across the state, representing as many districts as possible.[49] At this meeting, delegate general responsibilities to the majority of volunteers.[50]

Perhaps the most important goal of this meeting involves finding a selected number of individuals to serve as the core of the lobbying group— the people whom the larger group trust to guide the entire process.[51] This group will serve as the decision-making committee and will break down into smaller subcommittees to accomplish specific tasks such as drafting the legislation.[52] When looking for persons to fill these positions, search for individuals who are dedicated and committed for the long term, persons who are respected, persistent, flexible, and open-minded.[53]

Members of this committee, before proceeding further, should establish clearly what changes in the law their cause seeks to accomplish. With these objectives expressly stated, the project can move forward. Members should select, perhaps by secret balloting to avoid hurt feelings, certain individuals to prepare fact sheets, write speeches, and keep records.[54] It is also important to establish a communication network, setting up a pyramid system for letter writing and phone calls for when the time comes to make contact with legislators.[55] Finally, after determining the deadline for filing bills with the legislature, devise a realistic timeframe for the lobbying process, including the deadline for drafting the bill, a lobbying day, and days for letter campaigns; then plan how you will adhere to this plan.[56]

STEP #2: DRAFTING THE LEGISLATION

When drafting the legislation, lobbyists have several options. First, the group could find a legislator who is willing to write the proposed legislation.[57] While this option may be the least troublesome for lobbyists in that they are free of the burden,[58] it is problematic for two reasons. Lobbyists will have to keep a close watch over the process to ensure that the politician properly represents your objectives.[59] In addition, finding a legislator with the time to write the bill may be difficult, if not impossible.[60] Generally, "[l]egislators are much more likely to sponsor bills that are already written."[61] Thus, the preferable options call for other parties to perform the task.

The lobbying association could find an attorney who is willing to serve as the author.[62] Perhaps one of the group's members is an attorney who will volunteer for the task.[63] If not, finding an outside attorney is not impossible.[64] Many lawyers are interested in helping public interest groups and often offer their services free of charge.[65] Their expertise could prove invaluable.

If using an attorney is not feasible,[66] the lobbying group itself can draft the legislation. Choosing this option requires following two simple maxims: do it early, and do it right.[67] Bearing in mind the filing deadline and allowing for "bureaucratic delays," establish a firm yet realistic schedule.[68] Time is of the essence; if lobbyists cannot meet the filing deadline, the process is futile.

Proper drafting, however, is also important. Even if the group meets the deadline, a sloppy or poorly structured bill could spell disaster. The effort could lose supporters, or, even worse, it could gain passage with serious structural defects. Carefully draft the legislation so it will accomplish your objectives.[69] Consequently, before trying to write the bill, discuss and understand the group's goals, and calculate all of the possible ramifications of these objectives.[70] Once this task is accomplished, the drafting stage begins. Many tools exist to help citizen lobbyists draft their legislation.[71] Many states publish bill-drafting handbooks, and such manuals also are available through such groups as the American Bar Association or the American Law Institute.[72]

As you actually draft the legislation, be certain that the language selected is unambiguous.[73] Use an introductory paragraph to make the legislative intent undeniable.[74] Define any terms that may be open to various interpretations.[75] After completion of a first draft, circulate it among the drafting group for criticism and suggestions.[76] Upon receiving commentary, continuously refine the product until ultimately it unequivocally states your objectives.[77]

STEP #3: FINDING A SPONSOR

Approximately one month prior to the filing deadline, the search for a sponsor should begin.[78] Finding the proper sponsors for a bill can be a difficult task because there are many underlying factors to consider in making this decision.[79] Every good sponsor shares at least two traits. The legislator must be dedicated to the cause; he or she must believe strongly in the issue and must be sufficiently committed to not abandon the cause midway through the campaign.[80] For home school advocates, finding a legislator who is familiar with home education or is vocally critical of public education or the education establishment is highly beneficial. Not only will the lobbying group not have to spend precious time educating the sponsor, but the sponsor's knowledge and expertise will be apparent as he or she persuades other legislators of the bill's value. Second, the sponsor commands the respect of his or her peers.[81] Legislators are more likely to listen to a colleague who is admired and known for his or her integrity. These individuals have tremendous influence and bargaining power.[82]

One other possible factor to consider is whether the sponsor is a member of the committee to which the bill possibly could be directed.[83] It also may be beneficial to find bipartisan co-sponsors and so avoid a party division over the issue.[84]

In making these choices, research legislators carefully.[85] Public information, such as that found in newspaper and magazine articles, is plentiful and contains vital information about the candidates.[86] In addition, examine the legislative voting record to see how the sponsor has voted in the past.[87] Ask members of the press and other organizations for their opinions. Do not be afraid to talk with prospects before officially asking them to serve as sponsors.[88] In essence, lobbyists should be well informed before making this crucial decision.

STEP #4: GAINING LEGISLATIVE SUPPORT

While sponsors alone undoubtedly will attract numerous supporters for the bill, lobbying groups cannot depend on them to win passage. Lobbyists still have work to do, and in this phase of the process, networking and mobilizing volunteers is fundamental.

First, the core members of the group must devise a fact sheet containing all of the vital information about home education it wants to relate to legislators.[89] The importance of this document cannot be overstated. This three- to four-page product generally "outlines the fact of the particular issues and your position."[90] Because home instruction may be a foreign concept to many politicians, and because many lobbyists are novices, the fact sheet provides your lobbyists the key information to give legislators in letters and meetings.[91] Provide pertinent information, showing the academic success of home schooled children and their promising futures.[92] Consider including the following information:

(1) Statement of the issue;
(2) Statement of your group's position;
(3) Status of proposed legislation or administrative action;
(4) List of reasons to support (or oppose) pending legislation or administrative action;
(5) Proposed action you wish [him or her] to take.[93]

With the fact sheet serving as the foundation, home school advocates should use two lobbying procedures: personal meetings and letter-writing campaigns.[94] With respect to personal contacts, initially plan a lobbying day early in the process in which volunteers arrange meetings with their Representative or Senator, key committee members, staff, and even opponents to discuss the bill.[95] At these meetings lobbyists should present legislators an information packet containing a copy of the bill and any other necessary information.[96] If possible, many of these lobbyists should be parents who home school or individuals who have been home educated because they can best educate legislators about the advantages and successes of home education.[97] At these pre-scheduled meetings, make it clear who you are and what group you represent.[98] Get to the point, be concise, and be friendly and courteous, bearing in mind their time constraints.[99] Disclose all vital information at the meeting because it may be the only chance to speak with this legislator in such an environment.[100] Before the meeting concludes, summarize the main points, thank the legislator for taking time to meet, and discuss the next step.[101]

Intensive letter-writing campaigns also are important because letters "[remind legislators] how strongly constituents feel."[102] Letters also "legitimize [lobbying] activities."[103] Because staff screen letters, ensure that your letters are good enough to make it to the legislators' desks.[104] Avoiding form letters is the first step in surviving the screening process.[105] Rather, make the letters personal and informative. Suggest to the letter writers that they include information from the fact sheet, but that they elaborate on only one or two issues to avoid overkill.[106] Enclose pertinent literature such as newspaper and magazine articles to bolster your statements.[107] One lobbying expert has suggested that a good letter should contain the following elements:

(1) Brief description of your organization and its objectives;
(2) Description of the issue;

(3) Status of current law and/or pending legislation;
(4) Effect of passage or defeat of legislation on the [legislator's] constituency;
(5) Your group's position with regard to the issue;
(6) Request for specific action on the[ir] part;
(7) Reaffirmation of your group's interest in his position on this issue.[108]

These two steps are fundamental in building a strong legislation foundation.

Soon the pace will quicken: the sponsor will introduce the bill, it will be referred to a committee, and the committee will schedule a hearing.[109] The hearing represents the next pivotal step in the lobbying journey. Individuals testifying before the committee must convince the members that the problem home educators are facing is serious, but that the "solution is both reasonable and workable."[110] "The more they understand about each issue, the more they [will] understand the big picture as your group sees it."[111] The hearing, therefore, represents a golden opportunity for home education advocates to educate legislators about home schools.[112] Your group should select a small number to testify, but make certain that their testimony will have a resounding impact.[113] Consider a speaker whom the home school regulations overly burden[114] or perhaps an impartial[115] expert in child psychology to refute any socialization concerns.[116] Preparation is essential in developing the concise but informative testimony necessary to hold the members' attention.[117] Be persuasive and show conviction, remembering that your job is to convince the committee of the merits of your cause.[118] Behind the scenes, talk to the chairpersons, committee members, and the staff of committee members, and assign volunteers to contact their legislators on the committee.[119] Pay careful attention to uncommitted members, giving them additional time to discuss the issue.[120] Make certain everyone understands the bill.[121]

If the bill survives the committee vote, it will go to the Rules Committee, which will calendar it for the floor debate.[122] It then will go before the entire legislative body for debate and a vote.[123] Your goal is now within visible reach.[124] Understand how the debate process works, and be prepared to supply legislators with last-minute information.[125] Basically it is time to stay out of the way and let the legislature function.[126]

LOBBYING STRATEGIES FOR HOME EDUCATION ADVOCATES

One of the most intimidating aspects of lobbying for home education is the opposition—the education establishment.[127] Like any other opposing force, however, it can be neutralized. Home education lobbyists can undermine many of its arguments. For example, consider the classic concern educators and legislators invariably raise: socialization.[128] Lobbyists should find citizen volunteers who home educate their children to talk with legislators or to testify at committee hearings to refute this concern. Parents should tell legislators that one factor motivating home education is "negative socialization" in institutional schools and that home education actually protects children from unhealthy peer influence.[129] Parents also should discuss how home education prepares children for life better than does institutional schooling because in home schools these children learn to communicate with both adults and their peers.[130] In reality individuals rarely communicate primarily or only with people their own age; they must deal with older people as well. Home education prepares children for that reality.[131]

Opponents also express concern that home schools deny their students the opportunity to participate in sports.[132] Such a concern, however, is no longer valid. Lobbyists should point to the emergence of Little League, city recreation leagues, and, more recently, home school teams.[133] While sports are valuable because they teach sportsmanship and provide exercise, home education lobbyists should ask legislators and opponents what the real purpose of school is—education.[134]

Through personal contact with legislators and testimony at committee hearings, home education advocates have the opportunity to *educate* legislators about home instruction.[135] During personal meetings and committee testimony, lobbyists should discuss the academic success of these students, pointing to the number who attend college.[136] Provide legislators with studies and literature containing statistics, and be available to answer their questions.[137] The key lies in overcoming the classic, negative stereotype of home schools. To minimize apprehension, lobbyists may wish to bring their children themselves to talk with legislators so the politicians can see firsthand how bright, articulate, and normal they are.

Lobbying is not an easy task. It requires hard work, long hours, and dedication, but for home education advocates, it may provide the best opportunity to spread the word about the benefits of home instruction. Even if your efforts fail the first time, persevere, learn from your mistakes, and try again. In time a majority of the legislators will begin to understand the importance of your cause, and your efforts will be rewarded.

27

Litigation: Maps and Land Mines

Although home schooling is an increasingly widespread practice,[1] there are still states and school districts that impede home schools in a variety of ways. Thus, the rights of home schoolers must sometimes be defended in court.

Even though various organizations[2] may provide them with information and legal support, it is important for home school families to have their own basic understanding of the issues involved in home school litigation.[3] This basic understanding will enable home school families either to foresee and avoid legal problems or to take action that will make it easier for an attorney fully to defend their rights.

Thus, this chapter will highlight various issues that are often the subject of litigation. While there is very little the home school family may be able to control with respect to constitutional issues, home school families have more control over the facts that may play a role in litigation concerning their particular home school. As noted in Chapter Twenty-six, "Legislation and Lobbyists," they may also exert significant influence in connection with legislation that affects them.

SIGNIFICANT CONTEMPORARY HOME SCHOOL LITIGATION ISSUES

Permissibility of Home School Under State Statutes

Home school litigation may be triggered by fundamental issues concerning whether home schooling is, in fact, even permitted by state education laws.[4] For example, one state education agency has interpreted its state education laws in a very narrow way, thus making it essentially impossible for home schoolers to operate in the state. In this case, a class action lawsuit was filed on behalf of home school families in Texas.[5]

A Texas law enacted in 1915 required all school-aged children to attend public school, except for those children who were "in attendance upon a private or parochial school," although the Texas legislature did not define the term "private school."[6] Until 1981, the Texas Education Agency (TEA)[7] had agreed that home schooling fell within the definition of "private school." There was no change in the law in 1981, but the TEA nevertheless changed its policy and declared that home schooling would no longer be considered a form of private school:

> [E]ducating a child at home is not the same as private school instruction and, therefore, not an acceptable substitute. . . . Correspondence courses are not a legal substitute for attendance at a public or private school.[8]

After this change in the TEA's interpretation of the law, Texas parents who were home schooling their children were in violation of the law, since their children were not in a public or private school. The TEA therefore began criminal prosecutions of these parents, as required by Texas law. There were 150 such prosecutions, with eighty going to a full trial. "In each prosecution the position of [the TEA] was that it did not make any difference what was taking place in the home because the home could not qualify as a private school."[9]

A lawsuit was then filed alleging that the actions of the TEA violated the civil rights of the home school families.[10]

Both the Texas trial court and the Texas Court of Appeals ruled in favor of the home school families and against the TEA. The Texas Court of Appeals noted that "[t]he conduct of the [TEA] towards [home school parents] amounts to bad faith, arbitrary, capricious and unreasonable conduct and is harassment."[11] As of this writing, the TEA has appealed the case to the Texas Supreme Court[12] and the case is scheduled for argument in January 1993.

Regardless of the ultimate outcome of this case, it demonstrates that interpretation of a state's education law by the state administrative agency responsible for education can dramatically affect such basic questions as whether home schooling is permitted by state law.

Home school families, therefore, should be informed and involved with political developments regarding home schooling, especially policy decisions by a state agency for education.[13]

Certification of Home School Teachers
Another issue in home school litigation concerns state requirements for certification of home school teachers to ensure that such teachers have the "basic skills" needed for teaching their children at home.[14]

For example, in 1990 the South Carolina legislature enacted a law that required all home school parents to have a high school diploma and to pass an Educational Entrance Examination (EEE) to demonstrate that they had sufficient skills to teach their children.[15] Before enforcing the EEE requirement, however, the legislature ordered that a study be performed to deter-

mine the validity of the EEE requirement.[16] This validity study was conducted by a thirty-three member panel which issued a fourteen-page report
after a one-day meeting; the report found that the EEE requirement was
valid.[17]

A lawsuit was filed alleging that the EEE requirement was unconstitutional and that the validity study was inadequate.[18] The South Carolina
Supreme Court held that the EEE requirement was constitutional but
agreed that the validity study was inadequate.[19] Although the South
Carolina Supreme Court's ruling is not binding on any other state, it may
be that other state courts confronted with these issues will follow the lead
of South Carolina and require extensive validity testing of proposed "basic
skills" requirements for home school parents.

Regulatory Issues

Periodic Visits

Home school litigation can also be sparked by challenges to state regulation of various aspects of the home school. For example, some states and
local school districts attempt to require home school parents to open the
home school to periodic visits or other review by school officials or social
workers.[20]

Curriculum Review

Other states may seek to impose curriculum review requirements on the
home school.[21] At least one state court has upheld a state law which
required home school curriculum to be approved by the state education
commissioner, despite free exercise of religion objections from home school
parents.[22] Some states have formulated regulations which effectively require
the education of home school children to be supervised by licensed teachers if the home school parents are not licensed teachers.[23]

Legislative Review

In one case dealing with regulation of home schools, a state court ruled that
a state education agency which seeks to impose extensive regulations on
home schools must submit the proposed regulations to periods of public
notice and opportunity to comment before enforcing the regulations.[24]

Another state's court, however, rejected a home schooler's objections
to a state statute regulating home schooling, ruling that the home schooler's
membership in a state association of independent schools did not exempt
the home schooler from meeting the separate requirements of the state home
school statute.[25]

Written Progress Reports

School districts also sometimes attempt to require home schoolers to submit written reports on the progress of their home schooling.[26]

In Missouri, for example, a school district ordered a home school family to submit a report which included "subjects taught, activities engaged in, portfolios of student work, evaluations and evidence of progress, and other written documentation demonstrating 1000 hours of instruction."[27]

In Indiana, a school district required home schoolers to "provide information on their student performance objectives, the method of evaluation to be utilized, the number of minutes of instructional time, and a schedule for achieving each objective."[28] In many cases home schoolers have been able to avoid some or all of these reporting requirements without resorting to litigation.[29]

Some states maintain an official record of all home schooling families by requiring them to submit a general written record of basic information such as the location of the home school and the names and ages of the children in the home school.[30] These states may or may not seek to impose other regulations on the home school.[31] Some home school parents object to the registration requirement, but in at least one case registration requirements have been upheld despite a home school parent's objections that the registration requirement infringed on her free exercise of religion.[32]

Subsequent Public School Enrollment

Home schoolers also may face some difficulty when they seek to enroll their children in public school.[33] In *Vandiver v. Hardin City Board of Education*,[34] a student who was taken out of public school and home schooled for the tenth grade reentered public school in the eleventh grade.

The public school refused to grant the student credit for the home school academic work, however, because the student refused to take equivalency tests to demonstrate that his home school academic work was equivalent to the tenth grade public school academic courses.[35]

The student refused to take the tests because he had used different books than those which were used in the public schools and thus felt that the tests would be an undue burden on him. He asserted that this violated his free exercise of religion because it infringed on his belief that "God would not allow me a bigger burden than I could carry."

A federal appeals court rejected this free exercise argument, however, holding that the student's religious beliefs did not exempt him from the generally applicable requirement of taking the equivalency tests.[36]

Other Issues Sometimes Litigated

Other cases illustrate further the various types of issues that may result in litigation.

In *Murphy v. Arkansas*[37] a federal appeals court upheld a state law that required home school parents to allow state education officials to administer a standardized achievement test to home schooled children.[38] The parents were allowed to select one test from a list of nationally recognized tests, but if the child did not score within eight months of his grade level on the test, then the child was no longer allowed to be home schooled.[39] The home school parents argued that this law violated their free exercise of religion in the supervision of their child's education, but the court disagreed.[40] The court held that the achievement test requirement was the least restrictive means of achieving the state's compelling interest in "ensur[ing] that its citizens are being properly educated."[41]

In *Maine v. Friel*[42] the Maine Supreme Court upheld the truancy conviction of a home schooling father despite his contention that his religious beliefs supported home schooling.[43] The court said that the father had failed to demonstrate any sincerely held religious belief that would require him to home school his daughter.[44]

In another case, a mother who received federal welfare benefits objected to participating in a work incentive program required of all welfare recipients because she asserted that her religious beliefs required her to home school her children.[45]

THE TENSION

Many of these home school litigation cases are, quite simply, the result of tension between the interests asserted by the state and those of the home school family in the education of children. This struggle will more than likely continue into the indefinite future since both the state and the home school family have recognized interests in this area. While the courts and the law have recognized a state interest in the education of its citizens and in preventing the abuse of children, parents have the right to guide the education and values of its children without unreasonable interference from the state.[46]

The litigation that often results from this tension may thus involve the protection of a variety of legal rights. Such rights include those guaranteed by the federal Constitution,[47] such as equal protection of the law,[48] free exercise of religion,[49] and freedom of speech.[50]

Home schoolers may also be able to obtain protection through rights granted by their state's constitution and statutes.[51]

Regardless of the specific rights involved in a particular case, however, it is always prudent for the home school family to be prepared for the possibility of home school litigation.

BEING PREPARED FOR LITIGATION

Home schoolers who are familiar with the material described above and in earlier chapters of this book will often possess the information needed to resolve any difficulties with their local school districts and school boards over various home school issues. Unfortunately, in some cases there may be no way to resolve a dispute except through legal action. All home schoolers should bear this in mind with respect to any dispute about their home school so they can take steps that will assist their attorney in defending their rights.

For example, one current case involves a challenge to Iowa's requirement that parents furnish information about their home schooling to the public school authorities.[52] Two parents have brought this challenge after being convicted for failing to provide the required information.[53] Although the parents attempted to compromise with the state by providing the information after they were charged, the state still continued the prosecution.[54] In circumstances such as this, despite good faith efforts by home schooling parents, the state has forced the family into litigation.

Some of these steps are based on common sense, while others are necessitated by the rules of the legal system. It should be emphasized that these steps are described only as general guidelines and do *not* constitute the giving of legal advice.[55] Home schoolers involved in a dispute should always consult a competent attorney for legal advice regarding their specific situation.

Use Care in Discussions and in Writing

One of the most important things home schoolers can do in a dispute is to be very careful what they say and what they write to the opposing party. Words spoken or written in haste or anger may prove to be damaging when repeated later in a courtroom. Specifically, home schoolers should not admit any liability or guilt in connection with any charge or alleged violation. An opposing party may attempt to intimidate a home schooler with threats of prosecution, civil lawsuits, or fines, but home schoolers should simply refuse to make any admissions of liability or guilt without first consulting their attorney.

Consult an Attorney Before Permitting Home Visits

The general rule of consulting an attorney applies if school officials attempt to subject home schoolers to involuntary home visits. Unless the officials have a search warrant, they generally do not have the right to enter one's home, even if there is a police officer with them.[56] Such officials also have no right to inspect or remove any home school records without a search warrant.[57]

Always Make Written Notes of Conversations and Meetings

Home schoolers involved in a dispute should be especially careful when receiving telephone calls from the opposing party. It may be wise to purchase an answering machine that allows the home schooler to screen calls so parents can be prepared in advance of any conversations with or requests from the opposing party.[58]

It is helpful for home schoolers to make notes of any meetings or conversations they may have with the opposing party. Such notes may be useful as evidence in a trial; they also enable home schoolers to remember accurately their side of the story and thus give accurate testimony at trial, if necessary.

It is important to make these notes during, or as soon as possible after, a meeting or conversation occurs so the incident is still fresh in one's mind when making the notes.

Maintain Good General Records

In addition to keeping notes on specific incidents, home schoolers should maintain good records in general. These records should include materials that document the activity of the home school, such as grade reports or portfolios of student work. Home schoolers should also keep a copy of all correspondence they send to or receive from the opposing party.

A good rule is, when in doubt, *don't* throw it out; that is, keep a record of everything that might be significant at a later time. An attorney representing a home schooler's case will have a much easier time assembling the needed evidence and information if the home schooler has maintained accurate and complete records.

Be Careful and Be Diligent

This is the general principle behind all of these steps. In most cases it is not necessary to live in fear of school officials or non-home schoolers in general. If a dispute arises, however, then it is crucial to be very careful in revealing information or answering questions about home schooling. Maintain thorough records, but also maintain the confidentiality of these records as much as possible. If you are unsure of what to do in a specific situation, contact an attorney before answering questions or otherwise giving out any information.

CONCLUSION

Home schooling is a thriving, leading-edge development in contemporary American education.[59] It has been shown to be an effective means of educating children,[60] but disputes nevertheless sometimes arise with state and local education officials, and some of these may result in litigation.

Home school families with a basic understanding of the issues involved in litigation will be better able to avoid such litigation or at least to be prepared for it, should it be necessary. Moreover, a prepared home school family will be able to assist their attorney in defending their rights.

Part Seven

Freedom

The Sacred Rights of Mankind are not to be rummaged for among old parchments or rusty records. They are written, as with a sunbeam, in the whole volume of human nature, by the Hand of Divinity itself, and can never be erased or obscured by mortal power.

Alexander Hamilton
(1757-1804)

Fiction

28

Freedom in Education

There is much wisdom in the Supreme Court's pronouncement that children are not the mere creatures of the state. This thought echoes the sentiments of an earlier time when freedom was at a pinnacle in America.

Before the Nineteenth Century, education was considered primarily a family concern. Within the family, the child, as student, learned both religion and the necessary vocational and academic skills to become a self-sufficient individual and informed citizen.

Today, however, the family function of education and value orientation has been radically altered and largely replaced by the state-financed system of public education. The child, as student, is no longer socially oriented solely by his family. To the contrary, most children are now nurtured to an overwhelming degree by the state. Moreover, the compulsory nature of the public educational process has the effect of turning students into captive audiences for government-controlled curricula:

> [E]ducation poses a constitutional problem because it has become (and was intended to become) a uniquely state activity: the state not only formally educates through the public school system but it also defines the end of education through its control over the curriculum and the certification of both public and private schools.[1]

Regardless of the legitimacy of the state's alleged interest in education, the state's authority over education must stop short of any measures or actions that conflict with fundamental rights guaranteed by the United States Constitution. The state should seek to avoid constitutional problems by allowing for freedom in education.

In other words, within the context of the compulsory education laws, the state must permit those parents who so choose to develop intellectual and religious areas in the lives of their children beyond those developed in the public schools.

The state, then, should encourage and protect the minority viewpoint that supports the alternative of home education. It should seek to promote rather than to punish diversity and pluralism. This is the essence of the American Constitution and particularly of the Bill of Rights. As James Madison told the First Congress, the limitations of the Bill of Rights point "sometimes against the abuse of executive power, sometimes against the legislative, and in some cases, against the community itself; or, in other words, against the majority in favor of the minority."[2] This is what true freedom and choice are all about.

APPENDIX

Legislative Status

This chapter summarizes and references the various state statutes affecting home education as of June 1992.

ALABAMA

In Alabama, the compulsory attendance statute will be satisfied if instruction is given by a private tutor, or if the statutory requirements of a church school program or private school program are met.[1]

If a parent chooses to home school through a church program, the following elements must be present: the program must be operated as a ministry of a local church, a group of churches, a denomination and/or associations of churches; it shall maintain non-profit status and receive no state or federal funding; and the program must offer grades kindergarten through twelve or any combination thereof.[2] In addition, the parent shall file enrollment and attendance records with the local public school, which are signed by the administrator of the church school.[3] No teacher certificate is required here.[4]

If a parent chooses to home school with a private tutor, or by qualifying as a private school, enrollment and attendance records must be kept and filed.[5] In addition, the teacher must be state certified, instruction must be offered in the same branches of study required in public schools, and instruction must be given for at least three hours a day between 8:00 A.M. and 4:00 P.M., for 140 days per calendar year.[6]

ALASKA

A student provided with comparable education to that of public school education by private tutoring, correspondence study, an alternative educational experience, or the utilization of a religious or private school program will be excused from compulsory public school attendance.[7]

A private tutor giving instruction to a child at home must be certified, in compliance with Alaska Statute § 14.20.020.[8] To be eligible for certification, the applicant must have a baccalaureate degree from a properly qualified institution.[9] Teaching by private tutor is the only home school option in Alaska which requires a teaching certificate.

Correspondence study must be approved by the Department of Education, if used as a form of home schooling.[10]

A child may be taught at home through the use of an alternative educational experience when the program serves the child's educational interests, but this must be put in writing and must be approved by the school board. In addition, the child must be excused from school by the school administrator.[11]

A religious or private school is exempt from the compulsory attendance law[12] when: notice, enrollment reports and school calendar forms are filed annually;[13] monthly records are maintained;[14] the school operates on a regular schedule, with holidays and vacations, for 180 days per year;[15] it receives no direct state or federal funding.[16] In addition, a religious school is statutorily defined as one operated by a church or other religious organization.[17]

Further, the religious or private school must choose and administer a nationally standardized test to each student participating in the fourth, sixth and eight grade.[18] The school shall maintain records of the test for the student's parents and shall make composite test results available for review by the department.[19]

A home school complying with these requirements may qualify as a religious or private school and is exempt from the state compulsory attendance law.[20]

ARIZONA

A student may be instructed at home if the county school superintendent is satisfied the student is receiving instruction in at least reading, grammar, mathematics, social studies and science.[21]

A home school cannot qualify as a private school to avoid statutory requirements of home schooling. Under the private school exemption to compulsory school attendance, the legislature states, "For the purposes of this paragraph, 'private school' means a non-public institution other than the child's home where instruction is imparted."[22]

The parent or legal guardian must provide proof of the child's identity to the county school superintendent within thirty days of commencement of home instruction.[23] If this requirement is not complied with, the local law enforcement agency of the student's school district will investigate.[24]

The instructor of a home school program must pass a proficiency examination in reading, grammar and mathematics no later than six months after home instruction has begun.[25]

Finally, the student must annually take all sub-tests of a nationally standardized, non-referenced achievement test chosen by the parent (except for the essential skills examination prescribed in Arizona's education statute).[26] The child may take a nationally standardized norm-referenced achievement test which is part of a home school academic program if it is provided with the curriculum.[27]

The parent must file with the county school superintendent, on an annual basis, a copy of the results of the achievement test and an affidavit stating the child is being taught at home.[28]

ARKANSAS

Arkansas defines a home school as one primarily conducted by legal guardians or parents for their own children.[29] In order to begin instruction, parents must first: agree to annual testing, inform the school district of a student who is in need of special education services, and provide notice[30] of intent to home school to the local school superintendent by August 15 or December 15, depending on the semester in which instruction will begin.[31]

Annual testing is required for all students seven years and older, at the expense of the parent or guardian.[32]

When test results are unsatisfactory,[33] a remediation program should be implemented by the teacher/parent.[34] However, unsatisfactory performance by a child eight years or older will result in forced attendance at public, private or parochial school other than the home school.[35]

However, the student may continue with home schooling at any time if a satisfactory score is achieved on the same test as taken previously, sometime before the next school year.[36]

The Department of Education retains authority to make exceptions to force public school attendance when "improvement on test scores indicates that continued home instruction would not be adverse to the child's interest."[37]

CALIFORNIA

Instruction by a certified tutor is exempt from compulsory public school attendance.[38] Instruction must be for no less than three hours per day 175 days per year, and the tutor must hold a valid state credential for the grade that is taught.[39]

Pupils attending private schools are exempt from compulsory public school attendance as well. Here there are no teacher certification requirements,[40] although a home school cannot function as a private school under California's compulsory education law.

In *People v. Turner*, a 1954 case where parents home schooled their children without valid state credentials, the *Turner* court held that a home school cannot qualify as a private school to circumvent the teacher qualification requirement.[41]

The court stated that a mere reading of the education statutes "clearly indicates that the legislature intended to distinguish between private schools, upon the one hand, and home instruction by a private tutor or other person, on the other."[42] They further stated that if the term "private school" encompassed home instruction by a parent of private tutor, "there was no necessity to make specific provision exempting the latter."[43]

COLORADO

Nonpublic home-based education is recognized as a legitimate alternative to compulsory classroom attendance.[44] It is "the sequential program of instruction for the education of a child which takes place in a home, which is provided by the child's parent or guardian or by an adult relative of the child designated by the parent, and which is not under the supervision and control of a school district. . . . This educational program is not intended to be and does not qualify as a private and nonprofit school."[45]

When the legislature drafted this statute, they intended to make any regulation of home study very flexible, with minimum state controls.[46] This intent is demonstrated in the lenient guidelines for teacher qualification.

The teacher of a Colorado home school is not subject to the "Teacher Certification Act of 1975," which provides for the certification of Colorado school teachers.[47]

To begin instruction, the parent must notify the local school district in writing fourteen days before beginning the program.[48] Notice must be filed each year the parent continues home schooling.[49]

The home school education program must be conducted for an average of four hours per day 172 days per year and must teach statutorily mandated subject matter.[50] Finally, parents must comply with statutory testing requirements.[51]

Parents are required to keep records of attendance data, test and evaluation results, and immunization records[52] which the local school district superintendent may review, given probable cause to believe the home school program is not in compliance with Colorado's statutory guidelines.[53]

A parent may also home school by qualifying as a parochial or independent school. In a recent Colorado case, *People in Interest of D.B.*, four children were enrolled in a Christian school while perusing course work at home.[54] The school district filed suit against the father, arguing that because studies were conducted in the home, instruction must be given by a certified teacher or under a state-approved home study program.[55] The court held the father was in compliance with the compulsory attendance law, stating, "[S]ince the district has not challenged the adequacy of the education provided by the academy, the matter of sufficiency of the children's attendance is between them and the independent school in which they are enrolled."[56]

CONNECTICUT

Connecticut's compulsory school attendance law allows the parent to provide instruction in the home which is equivalent (as determined by the board of education of the district in which the client resides) to public school instruction.[57] The parent or person in control of the child must be able to show the education is comparable.[58]

DELAWARE

Instruction proven to be equivalent to public school instruction is acceptable.[59] Proof of equivalency must be provided by examination and officially endorsed by a witness of the Superintendent of School Districts and the state board of education.[60]

DISTRICT OF COLUMBIA

Private instruction considered by the board of education to be equivalent to public school education is acceptable.[61]

Parents must submit forms demonstrating equivalence, which contain the following information: hours of instruction, subject matter taught, textbooks used, qualifications of the teacher, and a copy of academic transcripts.[62]

The teacher's qualifications must be substantially equivalent to public school teachers, although certification is not necessary.[63]

In addition, proper records of attendance must be kept and made available to school attendance officers, for enforcement purposes.[64]

Education must consist of three hours of instruction per day, five days per week.[65]

FLORIDA

Florida statutes define home education as "sequentially progressive home instruction of a student in his or her home by his or her parent or guardian. . . ."[66] When home education follows the statutory requirements, it will satisfy the compulsory attendance laws of the state.[67]

Florida includes a child protection clause in the home education statute which mandates that the parent/teacher must not be guilty of perpetrating child abuse or actual neglect or abuse of a child.[68]

In order to teach in a home school, the parent must hold a Florida teaching certificate[69] or (in lieu of the certificate) file notification of intent to home school with the superintendent within thirty days of establishment of the program,[70] maintain records of instruction for two years,[71] and provide for annual evaluation of the student.[72]

Florida parents without teaching certification are prohibited from "teaching a child at home under the guise that a private school has been established," to avoid complying with the state requirements of a home school.[73]

The Florida Administrative Code allows a private tutor to home school a child if the tutor holds a valid Florida certificate for the subjects and grade levels taught, adheres to the state attendance requirements,[74] and keeps records and reports required by the state and school board.[75]

Evaluation must show the child's progress is equal to his or her ability level and must be reported to the school superintendent.[76] Home schooling will be discontinued if the school superintendent believes the pupil's performance is not satisfactory.[77]

GEORGIA

The legislature recognizes home study programs as acceptable alternatives to public school attendance, if they meet statutory requirements.[78]

Initial notification of intent to home school must be given to the superintendent by September 1 and within thirty days of commencement of the program.[79] For each additional year the parent continues to home school, notice must be given by September 1.[80] Notice must include the child's name and age, location of the home study program, and the dates the program will cover.[81]

The parent/teacher must have a high school diploma or equivalent, or employ a tutor with a baccalaureate college degree.[82] Parents may teach only their own children in the home study program.[83]

Home school programs are required to teach reading, language arts, mathematics, social studies and science for 180 school days, four and a half hours per day, over a twelve-month period.[84] Parents must annually give their assessment of the student's progress in these subjects and must keep these records for three years.[85]

The parent must submit monthly attendance records to the superintendent.[86]

Students will be required to take nationally standardized tests at least every three years, beginning at grade three.[87]

The Attorney General of Georgia has stated that it is theoretically possible to classify a home school program as a private school.[88] He added, whether the instruction satisfies the requirements of compulsory school attendance depends on the facts of each case.[89] Although a private school must comply with the same curriculum, scheduling, attendance and notice requirements as a home school, there are no testing or teacher certification requirements listed in the statutes for private schools.[90]

A private school must be privately controlled and continuously run, and any building used for the private school must meet all the state and local health and safety standards.[91]

HAWAII

Public school attendance is not compulsory "where the child is enrolled in an appropriate alternative educational program as approved by the superintendent" or the representative of the superintendent "in accordance with the plans and policies of the department of education,"[92] or when proper notice is submitted to the school district, as specified by department rules.[93]

Children must take standardized tests in grades three, six, eight and ten.[94] In addition, an annual progress report of the child's test performance, written evaluation, or a narrative assessment must be given annually to a local principal.[95]

IDAHO

The local school district board of trustees has discretion to determine whether a child is receiving instruction comparable to public school instruction, in order to excuse the child from compulsory public school attendance.[96]

Because the word "comparably" is not defined by statute, school boards vary from district to district as to what guidelines home schoolers must follow to achieve comparability. (Some school districts, as a result, require parents to be certified.) Home schoolers may contact their local board of trustees announcing their intention to home school and submitting their curriculum for "approval," so the trustees can determine if it is in fact "comparable."[97]

ILLINOIS

Students who attend private or parochial schools which meet the state statutory requirements are exempt from compulsory public school attendance.[98] It is a statutory requirement that private schools (and home schools which qualify as private schools) teach the branches of education taught to children in public schools, in the English language.[99]

In *People v. Levisen*, parents who were prosecuted for home schooling claimed they fell under the private school exemption from compulsory public school attendance.[100] The Illinois Supreme Court held:

> "[P]rivate school," when read in the light of the manifest object to be attained, includes the place and nature of the instruction given to this child. The law is not made to punish those who provide their children with instruction equal or superior to that obtainable in the public schools. It is made for the parent who fails or refuses to properly educate his child.[101]

Yet, the parents must show "they have in good faith provided an adequate course of instruction in the prescribed branches of learning."[102]

Parents must show "a type of instruction and discipline having the required quality and character."[103]

This decision made properly executed home educating legal in Illinois.

INDIANA

Compulsory public school attendance is excused if a child is being taught at another school in the English language,[104] with instruction equivalent to that given in the public school.[105]

The court decides what equivalent instruction is.[106] In one case, home schooling was held to be equivalent, based on the following facts: parents fully complied with statutory enrollment and attendance requirements, and parents made frequent use of the public library, and the curriculum was found to be acceptable.[107] In another case a parent who employed a teacher (formerly of the public school) to teach his child was found to be in compliance with the compulsory education statute.[108]

The Prosecuting Attorney of Indiana uses the following factors to measure equivalency:

(1) Student performance objectives including development of reading, writing and computation skills;
(2) The method to achieve the performance objectives;
(3) The time period (1 calendar year or less) in which the performance objectives are to be accomplished and a schedule for achieving each objective;
(4) The method of evaluation to be utilized to determine progress toward the objectives and to summarize and periodically report the results of the evaluation;
(5) The adult responsible for discipline and supervision of the children and achievement of each instructional objective; and
(6) The instruction is provided in a school day of reasonable length and results in significant progress toward the performance objectives stated.[109]

IOWA

Each home school class a student takes must be: equivalent to the same class taught in public school, approved by the local school board, and taught by a certified teacher.[110]

Iowa courts determined that a certified teacher is one licensed by the state, and equivalent instruction is that which is equal in kind and amount to instruction provided in public schools.[111] Equivalent instruction must be approved by the local school board.[112]

Iowa has provided guidance regarding what constitutes equivalent instruction in regulations entitled "Equivalent Instruction Standards."[113]

All public and nonpublic schools (including home schools) are responsible for meeting Iowa's educational standards. The state provides required curriculum for pre-kindergarten, kindergarten, grades one through six, seven and eight, and nine through twelve.[114] When a nonpublic school is unable to meet these requirements, exemption may be requested from the state board of education.[115] A party may receive an exemption for two years, and annual renewal may be granted.[116] In order to renew, proof of achievement must be given in all the basic skill areas of the curriculum.[117] This can be accomplished through testing or evaluation.[118]

If a representative or member of an established local congregation of a church or denomination holds to tenets which conflict with those embodied in Iowa's educational standards, an exemption from compulsory public school attendance may be granted for two years.[119] Annual renewal may be granted, after proof of achievement is shown.[120]

Reports of children under private instruction, not in an accredited or approved school, must be furnished to the school district.[121] These reports must include: the child's name, period of private instruction, the name and address of the instructor, and an outline of the curriculum.[122]

KANSAS

Each child must either attend a public, private, denominational or parochial school under the state compulsory education statute.[123]

The Supreme Court of Kansas held that to be classified as a private school, the courses of instruction must include those required by statute,[124] and the children must be taught by a competent instructor for the prescribed time as required in the statute.[125]

KENTUCKY

Kentucky has not provided for home schooling in its statutes. However, a home school may be exempt from compulsory public school attendance by qualifying as a private, church or parochial school.[126] The board of education of the district in which the child resides has the discretionary authority to exempt a student from compulsory public school attendance.[127]

All nonpublic schools must give notice of students attending the school to the local board of education.[128] Home schools should send a letter with this information during the first two months of the school year.[129]

Attendance records of all nonpublic school students must be kept in a register provided by the state in the same manner kept in the public schools.[130]

It is unconstitutional to require teachers to be certified.[131] The Kentucky Supreme Court held that "a bachelor's degree . . . is an indicator of the level of achievement, but is not a sine qua non the absence of which establishes that private and parochial school teachers are unable to teach their students to intelligently exercise the elective franchise."[132]

In addition the court held it is unconstitutional to prescribe textbooks for private, church or parochial schools.[133] In fact, the only state involvement allowed with nonpublic schools is monitoring students through standardized achievement testing.[134] Only if the results of these tests show failure of the state to reasonably accomplish their constitutional purpose of compulsory attendance may approval of the nonpublic school be withdrawn.[135]

LOUISIANA

Louisiana's compulsory school attendance statute allows home study when it offers the same quality of education as public school education and is approved by the board of education.[136]

To start a home study program, the parent must apply[137] to the Board of Elementary and Secondary Education and receive approval of the program.[138] The application must include a birth certificate of the child and verification that the child has scored comparable to public school students in the same grade level on a standardized examination.[139]

The parent must apply for renewal on an annual basis to home school, by October or within twelve months of the initial application.[140] Satisfactory evidence must be submitted to prove the quality of home education, including: subjects taught, lists of books and materials, copies of the student's work and standardized tests, statements by witnesses of the child's progress.[141] Based upon this evidence, the renewal will be approved or denied.

MAINE

Students receiving equivalent in a program approved by the commissioner are exempt from the state compulsory attendance law.[142] Parents must submit an application to the commissioner, as well as the local board, who may submit comments to the commissioner.[143] If the application for equivalent home instruction is denied, the parents may resubmit it to the commissioner, who will reconsider it.[144] The local board is not required to play any role in the approval or oversight of home instruction.[145]

Home schooling programs are qualified equivalent instruction programs that are distinguished from "private schools," where there is "enroll[ment of] two or more unrelated students."[146] All home schools must be in compliance with The Rules for Equivalent Instruction Programs, which require "teacher competence, compliance with state curriculum and calendar standards and assessment of students' academic progress."[147] The state has made these rules flexible, allowing for testing options.[148] Under these rules, teachers must be eligible for state certification or be "assisted by a satisfactory support system."[149]

Those receiving equivalent instruction must file a certificate with the local school office, which includes their name, residence, attendance information, and the signature of the person in charge of the school.[150]

MARYLAND

The compulsory attendance statute of the state does not apply to students receiving regular, thorough instruction in the same studies taught in public schools.[151]

MASSACHUSETTS

Parents who wish to home school their children must submit a proposal, which will be considered by school committees or the school superintendent of the child's local county.[152] The proposal is evaluated based on the curriculum, hours of instruction, length of school year, competency of instructors, textbooks, and instructional aids. Other requirements may be mandated, such as testing, evaluations, or other subjects to be taught.[153]

A home school program must be approved prior to the removal of children from public schools, and parents must be able to prove the home school will comply with state requirements.[154]

MICHIGAN

Home instruction comparable in time and subject matter[155] to instruction given in public schools, and a "nonpublic school which teaches subjects comparable to those taught in public schools to children of corresponding age and grade as determined by the course of study for the public schools of the district within which the nonpublic school is located,"[156] will satisfy the compulsory public school attendance statute.[157]

All instruction other than in public schools must be given by state certified teachers.[158] Candidates for a teacher certificate must receive forty hours "in a program of general or liberal education" and 180 hours of indirect teaching to receive a Bachelor's degree in education.[159]

In a recent decision a Michigan appellate court determined that the "Nonpublic School and Home School Compliance Procedures" which required certain filing procedures could not be enforced because they were improperly promulgated.[160]

Failure to comply with statutory requirements will result in a misdemeanor, with imprisonment up to ninety days.[161]

MINNESOTA

Minnesota allows home instruction which is in compliance with the state Compulsory Instruction and Reporting statutes.[162] Education is mandatory for children between seven and sixteen years of age, for 170 days per year.[163] Instruction must be provided in reading, writing, literature, fine arts, mathematics, science, social studies, history, geography, government, health and physical education from English textbooks.[164]

Instructors must either hold a Minnesota teaching license for the field and grade level being taught, be directly supervised by someone with the above qualifications, or pass a teacher competency examination, have a baccalaureate degree, or have the child's performance properly assessed by a nationally norm-referenced standardized achievement examination.[165]

All home schooled children must take a nationally norm-referenced standardized achievement examination and score above the 30th percentile and at the proper grade level of children of the same age in order to avoid further evaluation of abilities and performance.[166]

Parents must report the child's name, age and address; the instructor's name and evidence of compliance with teaching requirements; a plan for the year's curriculum; and a quarterly report card for each subject area taught.[167]

If a "school" was accredited by one of the six recognized accrediting agencies, its only responsibility to the state was to report to the appropriate school district superintendent the names, addresses and ages of the students.[168]

MISSISSIPPI

A child enrolled in a legitimate home instruction program is exempt from compulsory public school attendance.[169]

The parent or guardian must complete a "certificate of enrollment" which must include: the child's name, address, and birthday; the parent's or guardian's name and address; a description of the type of education given; and the parent's or guardian's signature.[170]

MISSOURI

In Missouri, home school attendance which complies with statutory requirements satisfies the state compulsory attendance law.[171] A "home school" is defined as one with: a primary purpose of private or religious-based instruction; student age between seven and sixteen, with no more than four unrelated students participating; no tuition fees charged for instruction; and a thousand hours of instruction per calendar year given in subjects "consonant with the pupil's age and abilities."[172]

The parent is required to keep records of activities, subjects taught, samples of the child's school work, and evaluations of the child's progress which are evidence of regular instruction.[173] The parent has the option of reporting home school attendance.[174]

MONTANA

Students may be exempt from compulsory public school attendance when enrolled in a qualified home school and instructed by a parent.[175] A qualified home school is one which notifies school authorities upon commencement of the program, properly maintains attendance and disease immunization records, gives instruction for 180 days, meets the local health and safety regulations, and provides comparable instruction to that of public schools.[176]

NEBRASKA

A school is exempt from state compulsory education laws when it has "elected not to meet approval or accreditation requirements" and has complied with the state law and regulations relating to such exemptions.[177]

To operate a home school as a private school, parents must send a signed statement that the requirements for approval and accreditation and the rules and regulations of the state board of education are violative of the parent's sincerely held religious beliefs.[178] Parents must submit proof of: meeting health, fire and safety standards; meeting attendance requirements;[179] and offering a program of instruction leading to the acquisition of basic skills in language arts, math, science, social studies, and health.[180]

A parent/teacher or designated instructor of the home school program must either take portions of a nationally recognized teacher competency exam (designated by the state board of education) or give evidence which shows competency to provide instruction in basic skills, by offering transcripts, a diploma, or other evidence of formal education.[181]

The state board of education has the power to establish rules and regulations relating to student testing and monitoring of the private education program.[182]

If these statutory requirements are not complied with, parents will be subject to prosecution pursuant to the state compulsory attendance statute or any statutes relating to habitual truancy.[183]

NEVADA

Students instructed in homes are exempt from provisions of the state Private Elementary and Secondary Education Act.[184]

Parents must provide evidence that the student is "receiving at home . . . equivalent instruction of the kind and amount approved by the state board of education."[185] The parent must give proper notice, including: an annual calendar of instruction; a sample weekly schedule; a list of instructional materials, teaching methods and annual goals.[186] In addition, the parent must be certified, consult with a certified teacher, or enroll the student in an approved correspondence course; keep attendance records; provide 180 days of instruction; and have the student tested in grades one, two, four, five, seven and eight with tests used in the public schools.[187]

NEW HAMPSHIRE

New Hampshire allows the alternative of home education to public or private school attendance[188] Home education is planned, supervised teaching and activities provided by a parent for his own child.[189]

Notice must include the student's name, address, birth date, subjects to be taught, and information on the curriculum which will be used.[190] Notice must again be given upon termination of the home schooling program.[191]

The curriculum includes the following subjects: the history of the constitutions of New Hampshire and the United States, science, mathematics, language, government, health, reading, writing, spelling and exposure to and appreciation of art and music.[192]

Proper records must be maintained for two years, including a listing of materials used and samples of the student's work.[193]

The student's progress must be evaluated on an annual basis by completing one of the following: evaluation in a manner approved by a qualified school official, written evaluation by a certified or public school teacher, testing with a national student achievement test (and scoring above the fortieth percentile), or testing with a state student assessment test.[194] If the child does not exhibit progress acceptable for children the same age and ability level, the parent will be responsible to provide remedial instruction for one year to prepare the child for reevaluation.[195] Failure to show the requisite progress after one year of remedial instruction will result in termination of the home school program.[196]

NEW JERSEY

Students receiving equivalent instruction elsewhere (which is "thorough and efficient") than in the public school will be excused from public school attendance.[197] Instruction which is equivalent [198] must be demonstrated on the academic level only.[199]

Parents may be found guilty of being disorderly persons for providing home education which is not equivalent to public school education[200] or by giving haphazard instruction in the home.[201]

NEW MEXICO

Attendance at a home school satisfies state attendance requirements.[202]

The state defines "home school" as "the operation by a parent, guardian or other person having custody of a school age person of a home study program which provides a basic academic education program including but not limited to reading, language arts, mathematics, social studies and science."[203]

NEW YORK

School instruction may be given at a public school or "elsewhere" if it is substantially equivalent to public school instruction.[204]

The teacher must be competent and must instruct in English, with English textbooks (unless an exception is made by the proper school official).[205]

The "[l]ocal public school board of education, through superintendent of schools, is responsible for ascertaining whether home taught child receives instruction substantially equivalent in time and quality to that provided by public school."[206] Parents must allow the home school program to be evaluated by the proper school official,[207] while the state has the duty to make sure the home school requirements are being complied with.[208]

Yet, proof of instructional equivalency to "instructions given to minors of like age and attainments at public school falls on parents."[209]

When a good faith effort is not made to give adequate education, the court will rule against the parents.[210]

NORTH CAROLINA

"The legality of home schools was established by the North Carolina Supreme Court in *Delconte v. North Carolina*, 313 N.C. 384, 329 S.E.2d 636 (1985)."[211]

Delconte stated that one of the four ways by which students may be educated is that of a home school qualifying as a nonpublic school.[212] To qualify as a nonpublic school, the home school must maintain attendance, testing and disease immunization records, must operate on a regular schedule, must be subject to health and safety inspections, and must administer standardized tests.[213]

Also, to qualify as a nonpublic school, the home school must be accredited by the state board of education or the Southern Association of Colleges and Schools and must be an active member of the North Carolina Association of Independent Schools or receive no funding from the state.[214]

"Parents who establish a school in their home to educate their school-age children must have their home school recognized by the Office of Nonpublic Schools and meet the requirements of Article 39, Chapter 115C in order to meet the requirements of the Compulsory Attendance Law."[215]

NORTH DAKOTA

Home education in North Dakota is defined as "an educational program for students based in the child's home and supervised by the child's parent or parents."[216]

Parents must on an annual basis, thirty days before the beginning of the semester, file a statement of intent to home school.[217] This notice must include the courses[218] to be taught and activities to be performed; the par-

ent's name, address, qualifications, and oath to comply with the state regulations; and the student's name, address, birth date and grade.[219]

Parents may be qualified to teach home instruction if they are certified
or certifiable to teach or, as an alternative, have a high school diploma or
its equivalent and are supervised by a certified teacher.[220] The supervisory
teacher must spend one hour per week with a single student and an additional half hour for each additional student in a home school and must
report to the supervisor on the student's progress two times per year.[221]

Parents must keep records of academic progress of the student, along
with standard achievement test results.[222] These records must be furnished
to school officials upon request.[223]

A Quality Assurance section has been added to chapter 15 which will be
in effect until June 30, 1993.[224] This section mandates annual standard
achievement testing, with tests used in public schools in the student's local
school district or state-approved private or parochial schools.[225] If the student
scores below the 13th percentile on these tests, a professional evaluation for
learning deficiencies will be performed.[226] If the results of the evaluation show
the student is handicapped or is developmentally disabled, special instruction
may be necessary; however, the parent may continue to instruct the child.[227]

OHIO

Ohio defines "home education" as that which is "primarily directed and
provided by the parent or guardian of a child ... of compulsory school age
and ... not enrolled in a nonpublic school."[228]

In order to begin home instruction, proper notice must be given and
must include the following information: the school year for which instruction will be given, the parent's and teacher's names and addresses, the
child's name and birth date,[229] a commitment to give instruction in the
statutorily required courses,[230] an outline of the curriculum, as well as a list
of textbooks and other teaching materials to be used.[231]

Parents must give additional assurance in the notice that the home
schooled child will receive a minimum of nine hundred hours of instruction
per year and that the teacher is qualified.[232]

The superintendent has the power to determine whether a program is
in compliance with the state home school requirements.[233] Compliance will
result in the child's excuse from school attendance, while noncompliance
will result in the denial of excuse from attendance.[234]

At the end of the year, students must demonstrate adequate progress
by showing one of the following: comparable proficiency to other students
in their grade level, through results of an approved nationally normed,
standardized achievement test; or a written review of the child's work
demonstrating progress commensurate with the child's abilities; or an
approved alternative.[235] The assessment must be conducted by an
approved individual, and a report must then be sent to the superintendent
by the child's parents.[236]

If the child's progress isn't satisfactory, in order to continue home schooling, remediation must be commenced until satisfactory progress is demonstrated.[237] The superintendent will determine whether the child's progress is satisfactory during remediation and may revoke the excuse from school attendance following a due process hearing if performance is unsatisfactory.[238]

In *Gardini v. Moyer*, a recent Ohio case, a divorced father sued for change of custody of his children from the children's mother to himself.[239] He claimed there was a change in circumstances which would warrant this change, that of the mother's efforts to home school her children.[240] The court held that the children were endangered by the home school environment and the effects it would likely have on their future, and therefore a change of custody from the mother to the father was in order.[241]

OKLAHOMA

"Other means of education may be provided" for children than education in the public school system.[242]

The board of education recognizes home schools as "other means of education," and the governor declared in 1989 that ". . . the State of Oklahoma is committed to excellence in education," and "[m]aximum, individualized preparation for citizenship and life work is provided by home education . . . ," after he declared the week of May 1-7 to be National Home Education Week.[243]

"Education can be furnished without attendance at any school,"[244] but the education must be supplied "in good faith and equivalent in fact to that afforded by the State."[245]

Subject matter equivalency would involve the teaching of basic skills of learning prescribed for the state public school system,[246] and time equivalency would involve holding classes for 180 days per year.[247]

OREGON

Children proving to the school board that they have received instruction comparable to public school instruction may be exempt from compulsory public school attendance.[248] Before home instruction may begin, notice must be given to the superintendent in writing, acknowledged by the superintendent in writing, and passed on to the school district superintendent.[249]

Children must show progress in order to stay in the home school program by performing satisfactorily on an annual exam (the parent may choose the exam from a state-provided list of approved exams).[250]

PENNSYLVANIA

Properly executed home education programs will satisfy the compulsory attendance statute of Pennsylvania.[251] The state defines a home education program as one conducted by a parent, guardian, or a person who has legal custody of the child.[252]

To commence home instruction, proper notice of intent to home school must be filed.[253]

If a home school is relocated, the state requires proper notice as well.[254]

The state has mandated that students be taught for 180 days or nine hundred hours at the elementary level[255] and 990 hours at the secondary level.[256]

Parents must keep a portfolio of the following records: materials used; samples of the student's work; nationally normed standardized test results[257] taken in third, fifth and eighth grade; and an annual evaluation by a qualified individual.[258]

If the public school district superintendent believes the home school program may be lacking, the portfolio of the student may be examined.[259] After an examination, one of the following results will occur: the program will be determined to be satisfactory; the parent will have to supply additional information to prove compliance with home school requirements; the child will go through remedial education; or the child will automatically be enrolled in the public school district, due to deficiencies of the program.[260]

If a parent or supervisor of a home school program is out of compliance with state regulations, they will not be eligible to supervise a program again for twelve months.[261]

RHODE ISLAND

Students perusing home instruction which is approved by the student's local school committee will be excused from public school attendance.[262]

SOUTH CAROLINA

Parents may teach children in the home if a district board of trustees approves of the home schooling program.[263]

For approval, a program must be taught: for four and a half hours per day for 180 days per year,[264] by a parent with a high school diploma (or equivalent)[265] or a college degree,[266] in the basic areas of reading, writing, mathematics, science and social studies (and in grades seven through twelve, composition and literature).[267]

For approval, parents also must keep a portfolio of records of the curriculum and activities used, samples of student work, and evaluations of the student's academic progress.[268]

In addition, students must have access to a library and be tested annually,[269] and the student's parent must waive district board liability for any possible future educational deficiencies resulting from home schooling.[270]

The legal counsel for Greenville County School District indicated in his January 22, 1991, opinion that a home school classifying itself as a private school or associating with other home schools in an organization could not avoid necessary compliance with South Carolina's home school regulations, discussed above.[271]

SOUTH DAKOTA

A child is excused from compulsory school attendance when provided with competent instruction given to no more than twenty-two students per instructor in the basic skills of language arts and mathematics for periods equal to those in public school instruction.[272]

An application must be filed in order to commence home instruction, which must include the location of instruction and the names of the instructors.[273] Teacher certification is not necessary, although an authorized official may investigate the competency of the teacher.[274] The child must take annual nationally standardized achievement tests, and the home school program may be viewed by a representative of the department of education throughout the year.[275]

TENNESSEE

Tennessee defines a home school as one headed by a parent or guardian for their children which meets for the same number of days per year as public schools meet.[276] A local superintendent may allow home schoolers to use public school facilities for special needs courses when laboratories or other special facilities may be needed.[277]

Notice must be given before the beginning of each year and must include the child's name, age, and grade level, the location of the school, the curriculum, the planned hours of instruction, and teacher qualifications.[278]

A home school teacher must have a high school diploma or its equivalent for teaching kindergarten through eighth grade and a college degree for teaching ninth grade through twelfth grade.[279]

Instruction must be given for four hours per day minimum; students must be vaccinated and receive health examinations; records of attendance must be maintained; and students must be given standardized tests[280] in second, fifth, seventh and ninth grades along with public school students in the child's school district.[281]

TEXAS

A private or parochial school may be attended in lieu of public school attendance.[282] In a recent statutory amendment to the state compulsory attendance statute, the legislature used the following language: "Nothing in this act applies to students in attendance upon a private or parochial school which includes home schools in accordance with § 21.033, Education Code."[283]

In *Leeper v. Arlington Indep. School Dist.*, the court ruled that "home schools can legally operate as private schools in Texas"; "home schools must be conducted in a bona fide manner, using a written curriculum consisting of reading, spelling, grammar, math and a course in good citizenship"; "further prosecution of bona fide home schoolers in Texas" is enjoined; and "the State Board of Education" may suggest methods of inquiry "concerning curricula and standardized test scores, in order to ascertain if there is compliance with the declaration contained in this judgment."[284]

UTAH

A home schooled student is exempt from Utah's compulsory education requirements if the program operates in accordance with the law.[285]

VERMONT

A home study program fulfills Vermont's school attendance requirements.[286]

VIRGIN ISLANDS

Children may be home instructed upon proper notice if the program follows the board of education's rules.[287] The board reserves the right to test the student.[288]

VIRGINIA

Home instruction by a parent is an acceptable alternative to public school attendance if the statutory requirements are met.[289]

The parent/teacher must either hold a baccalaureate degree, be a qualified teacher, teach from an approved correspondence course, or demonstrate the ability to adequately educate the child through the home study program.[290]

The parent is responsible for giving proper notice, providing a description of the curriculum and evidence of teacher qualification, and showing either satisfactory test results of the student or an evaluation of the student's achievements that demonstrates an adequate level of growth and progress.[291]

WASHINGTON

A student may be exempt from state-required public school attendance when receiving proper home-based instruction.[292]

Home instruction must be planned, supervised for one hour per week by a certified teacher, and meet statutory criteria such as subject matter[293] and time requirements.[294] Unless the parent is qualified by receiving forty-five college hours or completing a course in home-based instruction or is deemed to be qualified by the superintendent, the program must be supervised by a certified person.[295]

The legislature has stated that the teacher and subject matter requirements of the home-based instruction statute will be "liberally construed."[296]

WEST VIRGINIA

A student will be qualified for an exemption from compulsory school attendance when instructed in the home if the program is approved by the county board of education.[297]

"Instruction must be given for a time equal to the school term of the county."[298] Also, notice of intent to home school must be submitted along with the name and address of the child to be instructed and evidence of adequate teaching qualifications[299] and the annual administration of standardized tests.[300]

To continue with home education each year, the student must score above the fortieth percentile on the standardized test.[301]

WISCONSIN

The compulsory attendance statute is waived for students receiving home-based private education which meets the statutory requirements.[302]

A home-based program must be religiously motivated or for a private purpose, must be conducted for 875 hours per year, and must include specific subjects in its curriculum[303]

WYOMING

Home-based education is included in Wyoming's definition of a private school.[304] It is defined by the state as "a program of educational instruction provided to a child by the child's parent or legal guardian or by a person designated by the parent or legal guardian. An instructional program provided to more than one family unit does not constitute a home-based educational program."[305]

The program must meet the requirements of a "basic academic educational program," which is one that "provides a sequentially progressive curriculum of fundamental instruction in reading, writing, mathematics, civics, history, literature and science."[306] Parents are not required to teach anything which is in conflict with its religious doctrines and do not have to exclude any "concept, topic or practice consistent with its religious doctrines."[307]

NOTES

CHAPTER ONE: *The Crisis in Contemporary Public Education*

1. John Gatto, "Why Schools Don't Educate," reprinted in *The Blumenfeld Education Letter*, Vol. 6., No. 5 (Letter #57) (May 1991), p. 1.
2. Sam Blumenfeld, "The Great American Math Disaster: Where Is God in All This?," *Home School Digest* (Fall 1991), p. 35.
3. James Kilpatrick, *The Idaho Statesman* (December 21, 1989), p. 8A.
4. Avis Carlson, *Small World Long Gone—A Family Record of an Era* (Evanston, IL: Schori Press, 1975), pp. 83-4.
5. *Id.*
6. R. Freeman Butts and Lawrence A. Cremin, *A History of Education in American Culture* (New York: Holt, Rinehart and Winston, 1953), p. 330.
7. *Id.* at 518-23. Interestingly, there is a major shift among African-American academics regarding desegregated schools. As Wisconsin state assemblywoman and choice advocate Polly Williams said, "I'm for education, not integration." "Afrocentric Schools—Fighting a Racist Legacy," *U.S. News & World Report* (December 9, 1991), pp. 74, 76. The new concept is "Afrocentric" education; i.e., there is a broad commitment to recognition of African-American history and culture and the hurdles that African-American students face by "being black in a society with a legacy of racism. Such 'sympathy' translates into caring and high expectations." *Id.* According to *U.S. News & World Report*: "The Afrocentric strategy seems to be paying off academically. A recent study of 82 black private schools nationwide found that over 60 percent of the schools' students were scoring above national averages in reading and math." *Id.* Critics, including former U.S. Secretary of Education William Bennett, comment that such schooling substitutes "racial pride for academic achievement and promote[s] tribalism and racial resentment at the expense of a shared national heritage." *Id.* at 74.
8. Marvin Cetron and Margaret Gayle, *Educational Renaissance* (New York: St. Martin's Press, 1991), p. xii.
9. Butts and Cremin, *supra* note 6, at 523-25.
10. NCEE, *A Nation at Risk: The Imperative for Educational Reform* (Washington, D.C.: Government Printing Office, 1983), p. 1.
11. *See* Jeanne A. Allen, "An Agenda for George Bush's Education Summit," No. 106, *Policy Insights* (September 1989).

12. *See America 2000—An Education Strategy* (Washington, D.C.: U.S. Dept. of Education, 1991). In his program, President Bush proposed to institute a system of voluntary national examinations that would establish world-class standards in five core subjects; achieve global superiority in math and science by the year 2000; promote parental "choice" in education; recognize outstanding achievement by teachers, administrators, and students; and entirely revamp existing school design through the expenditure of $535 million in start-up funds for 535 "New American Schools." *Id.* at 53-4.

13. It must be noted that there is not only disagreement about what "excellence" really means, but also a good deal of apprehension among many groups involved with public education about the concept as it is described in America 2000. For example, the term "World-class Standards" connotes to some, "standards promoting a one-world view." Moreover, some commentators fear that public education has intertwined information and skills with attitudes and beliefs to the extent that the academic achievement tests referred to in America 2000 could well amount to national psychological profile assessments. *See generally* Beverly K. Eakman, *Educating for the New World Order* (Portland, OR: Halcyon House, 1991).

14. *See generally* Ina V.S. Mullis, *Accelerating Academic Achievement: A Summary of Findings from 20 Years of NAEP*, prepared by Educational Testing Service under a grant from the National Center for Education Statistics, Office of Educational Research and Improvement, U.S. Dept. of Education (September 1990). "The low levels of academic achievement in our country today have failed to improve appreciably since the publication of *A Nation at Risk*, despite the education reform movement." *Id.* at 77.

15. Barbara Kantrowitz and Pat Wingert, "A Dismal Report Card," *Newsweek* (June 17, 1991), p. 64. A study produced for the U.S. Department of Education indicated that, in 1990, "The mathematical skills of our nation's children are generally insufficient to cope with either on-the-job demands for problem solving or college expectations for mathematical literacy." Ina V.S. Mullis, *The State of Mathematics Achievement*, Report No. 21-ST-03 by National Assessment of Educational Progress, 1990 Assessment of the Nation and the Trial Assessment of the States, prepared by Educational Testing Service under contract with the National Center for Education Statistics Office of Educational Research and Improvement, U.S. Dept. of Education (June 1991), p.1, *citing Everybody Counts: A Report to the Nation on the Future of Mathematics Education*, Lynn Steen, ed. (Washington, D.C.: National Research Council, National Academy Press, 1989).

16. Arthur Powell, Eleanor Farrar, and David Cohen, *The Shopping Mall High School: Winners and Losers in the Educational Marketplace* (Boston: Houghton Mifflin Company, 1985), p. 325.

17. Jeannie Oakes and Martin Lipton, *Making the Best of Schools: A Handbook for Parents, Teachers, and Policymakers* (New Haven, CT: Yale University Press, 1990), p. 129.

18. *Id.* at 131.

19. *Id.*

20. *Id.*

21. *Id.* at 132.

22. *Id.* at 134.

23. *Id.* at 148-49.

24. *Id.* at 149.

25. Edward Fiske, "Changes Planned in Entrance Test Used by Colleges," *The New York Times* (January 3, 1989), p. I:1 col. 3. The ACT is taken by one million

high school juniors and seniors each year; about 1.2 million students take the SAT in addition to, or instead of, the ACT. Most of the nation's colleges and universities prefer the SAT for admitting students. *See* Deirdre Carmody, "Minority Students Gain on College Entrance Tests," *The New York Times* (September 12, 1989), p. I:16 col. 4.

Since 1969 the National Assessment of Educational Progress (NAEP) has periodically conducted assessments of what America's students know and can do in various subject areas such as reading, mathematics, science, writing, history/geography, and other fields. NAEP is a congressionally mandated project of the National Center for Education Statistics, the U.S. Department of Education. The Commissioner of Education Statistics is responsible, by law, for carrying out the NAEP project through competitive awards to qualified organizations. NAEP reports directly to the commissioner, who is also responsible for providing continuing review, including validation studies and solicitation of public comment, on NAEP's conduct and usefulness. The NAEP produces the annual *Nation's Report Card*, which documents and publishes these assessments. The annual *Nation's Report Card* may be ordered from The National Assessment of Educational Progress, P.O. Box 6710, Princeton, NJ 08541-6710.

26. Oakes, *supra* note 17, at 143.
27. *Id.* at 144.
28. *Id.*
29. *Id.* at 146.
30. *Id.* at 138.
31. *Id.* at 141.
32. *Id.* at 142-3.
33. NCEE, *A Nation at Risk*, *supra* note 10, at 1.
34. Peter S. Hlebowitsh, "Playing Power Politics: How *A Nation at Risk* Achieved Its National Stature," 23 *J. Res. Dev. Educ.* 82 (Winter 1990) remarked: "The members of the NCEE were an impressive lot, made up of four college presidents, three school administrators, two university professors, two administrative officials from private foundations, two school board members, one former state governor, one former state education official, one retired business executive, one educational consultant, and one foreign language teacher." *Id.* at 86.
35. *A Nation at Risk*, *supra* note 10, at 1.
36. *Id.* at 2-3.
37. Hlebowitsh, *supra* note 34, at 82.
38. August Franza, 71 *Eng. J.* 4:36 (April 1982).
39. Some critics of *A Nation at Risk* argue that the report does not identify the true underlying problems of the system. *See* William E. Gardner, "*A Nation at Risk*: Some Critical Comments," 35 *J. Teach. Ed.* 1:13-15 (January-February 1984).
40. Milton Goldberg and James Harvey, "*A Nation at Risk*: The Report of the National Commission on Excellence in Education," 65 *Phi Delta Kappan* 1:14, 15 (September 1983).
41. *A Nation at Risk*, *supra* note 10, at 6.
42. *Id.* at 7.
43. *Id.*
44. In the 1982 Gallup Poll of the public's attitudes toward the public schools, 80 percent of those polled felt that education is extremely important to one's future success. *See* 64 *Phi Delta Kappan* 1: 37, 46 (September 1982). In addition to the 80 percent, 18 percent thought education was fairly important. *Id.*
45. *A Nation at Risk*, *supra* note 10, at 17.

46. *Id.* at 8-9. *See also* Goldberg, *supra* note 40, at 15.
47. *A Nation at Risk, supra* note 10, at 18.
48. *Id.*
49. *Id.*
50. *Id.* at 20.
51. *Id.* at 20-1.
52. *Id.* at 9.
53. *Id.* at 24 (emphasis in original).
54. *Id.*
55. *Id.* at 27.
56. *See, e.g., A Nation at Risk, supra* note 10, at 28.
57. *Id.* at 29.
58. *Id.* at 30. *See also* Bill Marshner, "Bringing New Teachers to the Classroom," No. 104, *Policy Insights* (July 1989).

> Unless a new source of classroom talent is found soon, every state will face a grave shortage of qualified teachers. . . . Over the next five years, in order to fill new openings or to replace teachers who retire or leave the profession, America will need to find more than 1 million new teachers. In the same five years, at current rates of enrollment, all teachers colleges and education departments combined will graduate only about 625,000 men and women. . . . If we want America's laboratories and universities to be the world's leaders tomorrow, we have no choice but to employ *real* science teachers *today* in our elementary and secondary classrooms, where future vocations to science are being won or lost. . . . So, if a state forces its school districts to hire only those math/science teachers whom the establishment considers "certified," then this year, and each year for the foreseeable future, nine out of every 10 districts will get no one at all. America will compete for her future with nine-tenths of her school systems sitting on the sidelines.

> *Id.*

59. *Id.* at 32.
60. *Id.*
61. *Id.* at 36.
62. Gardner, *supra* note 39, at 15.
63. "Public's Attitudes Toward the Public Schools," 65 *Phi Delta Kappan* 1:33, 45 (1983).
64. "The Exodus," *U.S. News & World Report* (December 9, 1991), p. 66.
65. NCEE, *Meeting the Challenge: Recent Efforts to Improve Education Across the Nation* (Washington, D.C.: United States Dept. of Education, November 1983).
66. *Id.* at 6.
67. *Id.* at 1.
68. "The Exodus," *supra* note 64, at 67.
69. Shirley Chisholm, "Literacy: Democracy's Basic Ingredient," 12 *Adult Literacy Bas. Ed.*, 2:57, 58 (1988).
70. Audrey Pendleton, *Young Adult Literacy and Schooling: A Summary Report* (Washington, D.C.: National Center for Educational Statistics, 1988), p. 3.
71. *Id.* at 12.
72. *Id.* at 3.
73. Jonathan Kozol, *Illiterate America* (New York: New American Library, 1985), p. 10.
74. *Id.*
75. *Id.* at 12.

76. *Id.* at 5.
77. "Together, all federal, state, municipal, and private literacy programs in the nation reach a maximum of 4 percent of the illiterate population." *Id.* at 5.
78. *Id.* at 57.
79. *Id.* at 62.
80. *Id.* at 60 (*quoting* Maya Pines, *Revolution in Learning* [New York: Harper & Row, 1967]).
81. *Id.* at 63.
82. *Id.*
83. *Id.* at 4.
84. *Id.* at 64.
85. *Id.* at 65.
86. "Once out of school, nearly 60% of all adult Americans have never read a single book, and most of the rest read only one book a year. Alvin Kernan, author of *The Death of Literature*, says that reading books 'is ceasing to be the primary way of knowing something in our society.' He also points out that bachelor's degrees in English literature have declined by 33% in the last 20 years and that in many universities the English courses are largely reduced to remedial reading." *Imprimis* (February 1992). Moreover, "Recent surveys by dozens of organizations also suggest that up to 40% of the American public is functionally illiterate; that is, our citizens' reading and writing abilities, if they have any, are so seriously impaired as to render them, in that handy jargon of our times, 'dysfunctional.'" *Id.*
87. E. D. Hirsch, Jr., *Cultural Literacy: What Every American Needs to Know* (New York: Vintage Books, 1988).
88. *Id.* at 2 (emphasis added).
89. *Id.* at 33-4.
90. *Id.* at 218, endnote 10.
91. *Id.* at 110.
92. *Id.* at 112.
93. *Id.* at 113.
94. *Id.* at 150.
95. *Id.* at 149.
96. *Id.* at 22.
97. Gatto, *supra* note 1, at 2.
98. John Yang, "Bush Unveils Education Plan," *The Washington Post* (April 19, 1991), p. A:1 col. 2. *See also* "The Exodus," *supra* note 64, at 67. "Disenchantment with the traditional public schools is also at the root of the Bush administration's recent proposal to build 535 'New American Schools.'" *Id.*
99. *Id.* Columnist Dave Barry remarked, "Here is the ironic thing: America produces 'smart' bombs, while Europe and Japan do not; yet our young people don't know the answers to test questions that are child's play for European and Japanese students." *See* "Math R Not Us," *The Washington Post Magazine* (April 28, 1991), p. 52 col. 2.
100. Yang, *supra* note 98, at A1 col. 2 (graphic).
101. Rene Sanchez, "Battling Student Boredom," *The Washington Post* (April 15, 1991), p. D7 col. 5. The national dropout rate for Hispanic students, in addition, rose to 35.7 percent in 1989. *See* Julie Johnson, "Hispanic Dropout Rate Is Put at 35 Percent," *The New York Times* (September 15, 1989), p. I:12 col. 1.
102. Yang, *supra* note 98, at A:8 col. 1 (graphic).
103. Various legislative mandates are currently under consideration in connection with implementation of America 2000. Regardless of the final form of such

legislation, legitimate concerns about "national achievement tests" remain. Whether such tests are voluntary or not is irrelevant. To the extent that the results of such tests become the basis of assessments of teacher ability, school efficacy, and curriculum design, there will be a proportionately strong incentive to teach what the tests measure in order to avoid jeopardizing one's career, government funding, and commercial advantage. Such tests inevitably have an effect even on sectarian and home schools, for the students of these schools will be required, one way or the other, to perform well against these measurements in order to avoid jeopardizing their rights to attend such schools, enter state universities, etc. *See* Mary Jordan, "Nationwide Tests Urged for Schools," *The Washington Post* (January 25, 1992), p. A1:

> Since the nation's birth, the U.S. education system has been decentralized, with testing and curriculum decisions made at the local level. Although the curriculum standards and national tests are to be voluntary, education leaders said there would be strong pressure—such as possible federal funding and business support—for the states to adopt the higher standards.

Id.

104. *See generally* Powell, *The Shopping Mall High School: Winners and Losers in the Educational Marketplace, supra* note 16.
105. *Id.* at 1.
106. *Id.* at 2.
107. Cetron and Gayle, *supra* note 8, at 69.
108. Powell, *supra* note 104, at 3.
109. Sanchez, *supra* note 101, at D1 col. 4.
110. *Id.* at D7 col. 6.
111. *Id.* at D1 col. 6.
112. In some areas, non-school consequences may attend dropping out of school. West Virginia, for example, bars high school dropouts from obtaining a driver's license until age eighteen. *See* "Youth Bitter over Ban on Driving by Dropouts," *The New York Times* (October 5, 1989), p. III:13 col. 1.
113. Paul Hill, "Can Public Schools Survive?," *U.S. News & World Report* (December 9, 1991), p. 78.
114. Powell, *supra* note 104, at 67. At preparatory schools, for example, teachers are "handpicked" and "not assigned from union seniority rolls, and the emphasis is on liberal-arts degrees rather than education-school training. They usually give their instructors much more control than public schools allow over what's taught in each course, and they limit bureaucracy by having teachers perform administrative duties and by having administrators teach." "Preparatory Schools—Shaking off an Elitist Past," *U.S. News & World Report* (December 9, 1991), pp. 72-3.
115. *Id.* at 68-70. Accusations have been made that these treaties go so far that students are assigned to nonexistent courses and are actually running errands and performing other chores. *See, e.g.,* "'Phantom Class' Report Investigated in Bronx," *The New York Times* (August 9, 1989), p. II:4 col. 6.
116. Powell, *supra* note 16, at 70.
117. *Id.* at 76.
118. *Id.* at 77.
119. *Id.* at 82.
120. *Id.* at 78.
121. *Id.* at 80.
122. *Id.* at 86.

123. *Id.* at 92.

124. Barry, *supra* note 99, at 52 col. 3.

125. Powell, *supra*, note 16, at 106.

126. Samuel Blumenfeld, "The SAT Disaster of 1991—National Verbal Score Hits New Low and the Dumbing Down Goes On," *The Blumenfeld Education Letter*, Vol. 7, No. 12 (Letter #64) (December 1991), p. 6.

127. *See, e.g.*, "Education: America 2000," *Fac-Sheet* #67, Plymouth Rock Foundation. "All told . . . spending for education has more than doubled since 1980 . . . but American students still rank at or near bottom in international scholastic comparison." *Id.* at 1, *quoting* Secretary Lamar Alexander.

128. John Chubb, "Can Public Schools Survive?," *U.S. News & World Report*, p. 78.

129. Edward Fiske, "Historic Shift Seen in School Finance," *The New York Times* (October 4, 1989), p. II:9 col. 1.

130. Parochial school systems have successfully reduced bureaucracy and related costs. For example, the "archdiocese of Washington, D.C. . . . runs its 50,000-student school system with a central administration of just 17 people; by contrast, the District of Columbia public schools support their 81,000-student enrollment with a headquarters bureaucracy of 1,500. Not surprisingly, Catholic schools educate students less expensively than do public schools. They spend only about half as much per student, though their budgets are spared . . . at times [the] heavy expense of enrolling large numbers of students with special needs, as public schools must." "Parochial Schools, An Evolving Mission," *U.S. News and World Report* (December 9, 1991), p. 71.

131. Hill, *supra* note 113, at 78.

132. Philip Quigg, "S.A.T.'s: Don't Shoot the Test-makers," *The New York Times* (April 16, 1989), p. XXI:22 col. 1.

133. Various commentators have asserted that at least some of the decline may be attributed to factual errors in secular textbooks. For example, "A recent *Human Events* magazine published the drama going on in the State of Texas over 200 factual errors uncovered in brand-new high school American history textbooks under consideration by the Texas State Board of Education." Dr. Paul A. Kienel, "Gablers Discover Amazing Factual Errors," in *Secular Human Events* (December 28, 1991), p. 28.

134. Edward Fiske, "College Testing Is a Hard Habit to Break," *The New York Times* (January 15, 1989), p. IV:28 col. 4. The Educational Testing Service has annual revenues of $226 million from administering the SAT. Its competitor, the American College Testing Program (which administers the ACT) has annual revenues of $50 million. *Id.*

135. David Barton, *To Pray or Not to Pray: A Statistical Look at What Has Happened Since 39 Million Students Were Ordered to Stop Praying in Public Schools* (Aledo, TX: Wallbuilder Press, 1988), p. 58.

136. *Id.* at 59.

137. *Id.* at 60.

138. "Modest Gains Seen in Improving Schools," *The New York Times* (November 8, 1989), p. II:13 col. 4.

139. Carmody, *supra* note 25, at I:16 col. 4.

140. *Id.* Figures such as these continually give rise to criticism of the SAT as being biased against minority students.

141. Blumenfeld, *supra* note 126, at 1. *See also* Samuel Blumenfeld, "The SAT Disaster of 1990—National Verbal Score Hits Bottom As the Dumbing Down of America Continues Apace," *The Blumenfeld Education Letter*, Vol. 5, No. 11 (Letter #51) (November 1990), p. 1.

142. *Id.*

143. Fiske (January 15, 1989), *supra* note 134, at IV:28 col. 4.
144. William Glaberson, "U.S. Court Says Awards Based on SAT's Are Unfair to Girls," *The New York Times* (February 4, 1989), p. I:1 col. 2.
145. Tessa Melvin, "Allegations of Cheating Prompt Investigation," *The New York Times* (July 2, 1989), p. XXII:1 col 1.
146. Sam Howe Verhovek, "New York Cancels Regents Exam After Newspaper Carries Answers," *The New York Times* (June 21, 1989), p. I:1 col. 5.
147. *Id.*, at II:4 col. 5.
148. A 1991 *Time*/CNN poll indicated that "78% of those polled said voluntary Bible classes should be allowed on public school grounds; 78% favored voluntary Christian fellowship groups on public school grounds; 73% favored prayer before athletic games; 56% favored church choir practices on school grounds; 78% favored prayer in public schools; 89% favored silent meditation; 55% said there was too little religious influence on our students." David Aikman and Richard Ostling, "America's Holy War," *Time Magazine* (December 9, 1991), p. 64:

> For God to be kept out of the classrooms or out of America's public debate by nervous school administrators or overly cautious politicians serves no one's interests. That restriction prevents people from drawing on this country's rich and diverse religious heritage for guidance, and it degrades the nation's moral discourse by placing a whole realm of theological reasoning out of bounds. The price of that sort of quarantine, at a time of moral dislocation, is—and has been—far too high.

Id. at 68.
149. "Crosscurrents on Dress in High Schools," *The New York Times* (September 13, 1989), p. II:10 col. 4.
150. Neil Lewis, "Metal Detectors Deemed Success and Will Expand in Schools," *The New York Times* (September 6, 1989), p. II:2 col. 4.
151. *Id.* at col. 1.
152. Felicia Lee, "Teachers' Leader Argues for More Metal Detectors," *The New York Times* (December 7, 1989), p. II:12 col. 4.
153. Joseph Berger, "Ferocity of Youth Violence Is Up, a School Official Says," *The New York Times* (November 11, 1989), p. I:31 col. 5.
154. *USA TODAY*, August 28, 1991.
155. Felicia Lee, "When Violence and Terror Strike Outside the Schools," *The New York Times* (November 14, 1989), p. II:1 col. 3.
156. *Id.*
157. Joseph Berger, "Judgment Replaces Fear in Drug Lessons," *The New York Times* (October 30, 1989), p. I:1 col. 2.
158. *Id.*
159. Barton, *supra* note 135, at 140.
160. *Id.* at 141.
161. *Id.* at 140.
162. *Education Newsline*, August/September 1991.
163. Felicia Lee, "In Age of AIDS, Sex and Drugs Are Classroom Topics," *The New York Times* (December 26, 1989), p. II:1 col. 1.
164. *MMWR*, Vol. 41, No. 14 (April 10, 1992), p. 237 (citations omitted).
165. "Condom Roulette," *Washington Watch*, Vol. 3, No. 4 (January 1992).
166. La. Att. Gen. Op. No. 87-399 (1987).
167. La. Rev. Stat. Sec. 17:281 (D) (1982).
168. La. Att. Gen. Op. No. 87-399.
169. Mich. Att. Gen. Op. No. 6521 (1988).

170. Mich. Comp. Laws Ann Sec. 380.1507(4) (West 1992).

171. *Id.* Sec. 380.1169 (1990).

172. Mich. Att. Gen. Op. No. 6521 *Citing* Mich. Comp. Laws. Ann. Sec. 380.1170(3) (West 1992).

173. Tenn. Stat. Sec. 49-6-1303 (1990).

174. Wash. Stat. 28A Sec. 230.070(4) (1990).

175. Lee, *supra* note 163.

176. Seth Mydans, "School Offers Day Care for Teenage Mothers," *New York Times* (December 27, 1989), p. I:20 col. 1. Furthermore, "In the last decade, sexual activity among 15-year-old girls has increased 50%. This has given the U.S. the highest adolescent pregnancy rate among industrial nations." *World News Digest* (August 30, 1991).

177. *Alfonso v. Fernandez*, 584 N.Y.S. 2d 406 (1992), 1992.

178. 8 N.Y.C.R.R. 135.3(c)(2).

179. *Alfonso*, 584 N.Y.S. 2d at 410.

180. *Id.*

181. *Id.*

182. Cal. Civil Code Sec. 34.5 (1990).

183. Gatto, *supra* note 1, at 5.

184. Whittle Communications, a Knoxville, Tennessee, corporation of which Christopher Whittle is chairman, plans to spend some $60 million during the next three years in researching the "new American school." Samuel L. Blumenfeld, "Can Chris Whittle Succeed? His Is the Most Revolutionary Plan for American Education in 150 Years," *The Blumenfeld Education Letter*, Vol. 6, No. 7 (Letter #59) (July 1991).

   According to Blumenfeld:

   The proposed "Whittle schools" would serve all children, including the handicapped and others with special needs, from pre-school to 18. . . . As part of its three-year research effort, Whittle will devise ways to offer this education less expensively than the average per-pupil cost in the nation's public schools, currently estimated by the Education Department at $5,638 per year. The tuition charged for each school would be just below the per-pupil cost of public education in its community.

   Id. at 2.
   Blumenfeld continues that:

   The Whittle plan is the handwriting on the wall writ large. Sooner or later some entrepreneur, deeply involved with the new technology, would see the challenge of American education and seize the opportunity to provide Americans with an educational scheme more in line with the 21st century than the 19th. Of course, the movement toward privatization and decentralization has been underway for the last ten years. The home-school movement has been the most dramatic indicator of these trends.

   Id. at 3. "If he [Whittle] educates 2 million children on a tuition basis, he will be saving the taxpayers over $10 billion a year." *Id.* at 4. Of course, according to Blumenfeld:

   [What Whittle] will need more than his hi-tech delivery system is a sound philosophy of education, sound teaching of the basic academic skills, and a wide range of subject-matter software. . . . In short, the Whittle plan may indeed do for education what Edison did for lighting and recording—open the way for unlimited possibilities. Parents will finally have educational choice in the full sense of the word. No longer will they have to put their children in the hands of strangers with peculiar ideologies. They will be able to choose what they want their children to learn.

Id.

   Another foray into education by big business is that of Educational Alternatives Inc. (EAI) of Minneapolis and Johnson Controls World Services of Cape Canaveral. In 1991, these organizations signed a five-year contract with the Dade County, Florida, school system and thus became the nation's first for-profit enterprise to help operate a public school. The group is also negotiating to operate several elementary schools in Baltimore, Maryland. "For-Profit Schools—Investment in Learning," *U.S. News & World Report* (December 9, 1991), p. 76.

185. For example, "in response to shifting demographics, many of the nation's 8,600 Catholic elementary and secondary schools are adapting to a new mission. Like parochial schools sponsored by the Lutheran, Episcopal and Methodist churches, Catholic schools today are educating large numbers of inner-city minority students, many of whom are non-Catholic. Nationally, minority enrollment has risen from 11 percent to 23 percent of the Catholic-school population since 1970." "Parochial Schools—An Evolving Mission," *supra* note 130, at 68.

186. According to one observer:

   Many of the nation's 1,500 prep schools—nonreligious private schools that attract top students with rigorous academic standards—are no longer the lily-white enclaves they once were. In 1990, members of minority groups represented 13 percent of the total prep-school enrollment of 400,000, up from 5 percent in 1970. At prestigious New England boarding schools, minority representation is even higher: 18 percent at Deerfield, 25 percent at Andover and Choate Rosemary Hall and 31 percent at Phillips Exeter. . . . Choate Rosemary Hall in Wallingford, Conn., for instance, where John F. Kennedy attended classes, is working with 13 urban Connecticut school systems to include 70 public-school students in its extensive summer-school program.

"Preparatory Schools—Shaking Off an Elitist Past," *supra* note 114, at 72.

187. "Home Schooling—Schooling in Family Values," *U.S. News & World Report* (December 9, 1991), p. 73.

188. Thomas Toch, "Choice About School Choice: How Far Should We Go?," *The Education Digest*, Nos. 44-8 (November 1991), p. 77.

CHAPTER TWO: *The History and Philosophy of Public Education*

1. For a discussion of *A Nation At Risk* and other issues in American Schools, *see* Chapter One, "The Crisis in Contemporary Public Education."
2. N. Ray Hiner, "Look into Families: The New History of Children and the Family and Its Implications for Educational Research," *Education and the American Family*, William J. Weston, ed. (New York: New York University Press, 1989), p. 5.
3. For a discussion of this subject, *see* Chapter Five, "The Historical Perspective," Chapter Eight, "American Patterns," Chapter Nine, "The Early American Family," and Chapter Ten, "The Sacred Right."
4. Gerald L. Gutek, *Education in the United States* (Englewood Cliffs, NJ: Prentice-Hall, Inc., 1986), p. 1.

5. John D. Pulliam, *History of Education in America* (New York: Macmillan, 1991), p. 17.
6. John I. Goodlad, *A Place Called School* (New York: McGraw-Hill, 1984), p.40.
7. Gutek, *supra* note 4, at 2.
8. Pulliam, *supra* note 5, at 18.
9. *Id.* at 19.
10. *Id.*
11. Gutek, *supra* note 4, at 1-2.
12. *Id.* at 4.
13. S. Alexander Rippa, *Education in a Free Society* (New York: David McKay Co. Inc., 1967), p. 19.
14. *Id.*
15. *Id.*
16. Gutek, *supra* note 4, at 5.
17. *Id.*
18. Rippa, *supra* note 13, at 21.
19. Pulliam, *supra* note 5, at 29.
20. *Id.* at 30.
21. *Id.*
22. Lawrence A. Cremin, *American Education: The Colonial Experience, 1607-1783* (New York: Harper & Row, 1970), pp. 124-5. The law empowered the selectmen of each town "to take account from time to time of all parents and masters, and of their children, concerning their calling and employment of their children, especially of their ability to read and understand the principles of religion and the capital laws of this country," and authorizing them, with the consent of any court or magistrate, to "put forth apprentices the children of such as they shall [find] not to be able and fit to employ and bring them up."
23. Pulliam, *supra* note 5, at 30.
24. Gutek, *supra* note 4, at 8. The prelude to the act reads, "It being one chief point of the olde deluder, Satan, to keep men from knowledge of the Scriptures . . . it is therefore ordered that every township in this jurisdiction, after the Lord has increased them to the number of fifty householders, shall then forthwith appoint one within their town to teach all such children as shall resort to him to write and read." Jon Barton and John Whitehead, *Schools on Fire* (Wheaton, IL: Tyndale House Publishers, Inc., 1980), p. 63.
25. Pulliam, *supra* note 5, at 30.
26. Gutek, *supra* note 4, at 8.
27. *Id.* at 9.
28. Pulliam, *supra* note 5, at 31.
29. Gutek, *supra* note 4, at 9.
30. *Id.*
31. Pulliam, *supra* note 5, at 31.
32. *Id.*
33. Gutek, *supra* note 4, at 9.
34. R. Freeman Butts and Lawrence A. Cremin, *A History of Education in American Culture* (New York: Holt, Rinehart and Winston, 1953), pp. 118-19.
35. Gutek, *supra* note 4, at 10.
36. Cremin, *supra* note 22, at 394.
37. Gutek, *supra* note 4, at 10.
38. *Id.* at 2.
39. *Id.* at 11.
40. *Id.* at 12.
41. Butts and Cremin, *supra* note 34, at 107.

42. Pulliam, *supra* note 5, at 25; Butts and Cremin, *supra* note 34, at 107.
43. Gutek, *supra* note 4, at 13-14.
44. *Id.* at 14.
45. *Id.*
46. Rippa, *supra* note 13, at 11.
47. Gutek, *supra* note 4, at 15.
48. Pulliam, *supra* note 5, at 26.
49. Gutek, *supra* note 4, at 16.
50. Pulliam, *supra* note 5, at 27.
51. *Id.* at 28.
52. Gutek, *supra* note 4, at 2.
53. *Id.* at 18.
54. Butts and Cremin, *supra* note 34, at 16-17.
55. *See* note 44, *supra.* In 1671, Governor Sir William Berkeley of Virginia expressed this idea when he said, "I thank God, that there are no free schools nor printing, and I hope we shall not have them these hundred years, for learning has brought disobedience, and heresy, and sects into the world, and printing has divulged them, and libels against the best government." Pulliam, *supra* note 5, at 20.
56. Gutek, *supra* note 4, at 18.
57. Pulliam, *supra* note 5, at 20.
58. *Id.* at 21.
59. *Id.*
60. *Id.*
61. *Id.* at 23.
62. *Id.* at 24.
63. *Id.* at 39-40.
64. Gutek, *supra* note 4, at 27.
65. *Id.*
66. Rippa, *supra* note 13, at 54.
67. Butts and Cremin, *supra* note 34, at 43-44 (emphasis in original).
68. Pulliam, *supra* note 5, at 46.
69. *Id.*
70. *Id.*
71. *Id.*
72. Gutek, *supra* note 4, at 30.
73. *Id. See also* John W. Whitehead, *The Rights of Religious Persons in Public Education* (Wheaton, IL: Crossway Books, 1991), p. 41.
74. Pulliam, *supra* note 5, at 48.
75. Gutek, *supra* note 4, at 31.
76. Pulliam, *supra* note 5, at 48.
77. Gutek, *supra* note 4, at 31.
78. *Id.* at 33-34.
79. *Id.* at 35.
80. *Id.* at 37.
81. *Id.* at 39.
82. Pulliam, *supra* note 5, at 49.
83. Saul K. Padover, *Thomas Jefferson and the Foundations of Freedom* (Coronado, CA: D. Van Nostrand, 1965), p. 75.
84. Gutek, *supra* note 4, at 42.
85. Padover, *supra* note 83, at 184.
86. "This bill proposes to lay off every county into small districts of five or six miles square, called hundreds, and in each of them to establish a school for teaching reading, writing, and arithmetic. The tutor to be supported by the hundred, and

every person in it entitled to send their children three years gratis, and as much longer as they please, paying for it. These schools to be under a visitor, who is annually to chuse the boy, of best genius in the school, of those whose parents are too poor to give them further education, and to send him forward to one of the grammar schools, of which twenty are proposed to be erected in different parts of the country, for teaching Greek, Latin, geography, and the higher branches of numerical arithmetic. Of the boys thus sent in any one year, trial is to be made at the grammar schools one or two years and the best genius of the whole selected, and continued six years, and the residue dismissed. By this means twenty of the best geniuses will be raked from the rubbish annually, and be instructed, at the public expense, so far as the grammar schools go. At the end of six years' instruction, one half are to be discontinued (from among whom the grammar schools will probably be supplied with future masters); and the other half, who are to be chosen for the superiority of their parts and disposition, are to be sent and continued three years in the study of such sciences as they shall chuse, at William and Mary college, the plan of which is proposed to be enlarged . . . and extended to all the useful sciences. The ultimate result of the whole scheme of education would be the teaching of all the children of the state reading, writing, and common arithmetic: turning out ten annually of superior genius, well taught in Greek, Latin, geography, and the higher branches of arithmetic: turning out ten other annually, of still superior parts, who, to those branches of learning, shall have added such of the sciences as their genius shall have led them to: the furnishing to the wealthier part of the people convenient schools, at which their children may be educated, at their own expense. . . . Of all the view of this law none is safe, as they are the ultimate guardians of their own liberty. For this purpose the reading in the first stage, where they will receive their whole education, is proposed, as has been said, to be chiefly historical. History by apprising them of the past will enable them to judge of the future."
Ryland W. Crary and Louis A. Petrone, *Foundations of Modern Education* (New York: Alfred A. Knopf, 1971), pp. 113-14.

87. Gutek, *supra* note 4, at 43.
88. Pulliam, *supra* note 4, at 49.
89. Gutek, *supra* note 4, at 51.
90. Henry Steele Commager, "Schoolmaster to America," *Noah Webster's American Spelling Book* (New York: Columbia University, 1958), p. 6.
91. Gutek, *supra* note 4, at 52. It is estimated that fifteen million copies of the speller were sold by 1837.
92. *Id.* at 53.
93. Butts and Cremin, *supra* note 34, at 145.
94. Gutek, *supra* note 4, at 82.
95. *Id.*
96. *Id.* at 83.
97. Pulliam, *supra* note 5, at 60.
98. Gutek, *supra* note 4, at 87.
99. *Id.*
100. Rippa, *supra* note 13, at 91.
101. *Id.* at 92.
102. Gutek, *supra* note 4, at 87.
103. *Id.*
104. *Id.*
105. Pulliam, *supra* note 5, at 62.
106. *Id.* at 63.
107. Gutek, *supra* note 3, at 94.

108. *Id.* at 95.
109. Lawrence A. Cremin, *American Education: The National Experience, 1783-1876* (New York: Harper & Row, 1980), p. 137.
110. Gutek, *supra* note 4, at 95.
111. *Id.* at 97.
112. *Id.*
113. Lawrence A. Cremin, *The American Common School: An Historical Conception* (New York: Columbia University, 1951), pp. 62-63.
114. Gutek, *supra* note 4, at 97.
115. *Id.*
116. *Id.* at 101.
117. *Id.* at 102.
118. *Id.*
119. *Id.*
120. Crary and Petrone, *supra* note 86, at 238.
121. Pulliam, *supra* note 5, at 66.
122. Gutek, *supra* note 4, at 59.
123. *Id.*
124. Rippa, *supra* note 13, at 101.
125. *Id.* at 102.
126. Gutek, *supra* note 4, at 69.
127. Cremin, *supra* note 109, at 77.
128. Rippa, *supra* note 13, at 55.
129. Gutek, *supra* note 4, at 72.
130. *Id.* at 77.
131. Pulliam, *supra* note 5, at 67.
132. Gutek, *supra* note 4, at 111.
133. Cremin, *supra* note 109, at 389.
134. *Id.*
135. Gutek, *supra* note 4, at 112.
136. *Id.* at 113.
137. *Id.*
138. Pulliam, *supra* note 5, at 84.
139. *Id.* at 85.
140. *Id.* at 89.
141. Gutek, *supra* note 4, at 115.
142. *Id.*
143. Gutek, *supra* note 4, at 117.
144. 30 Mich. 69 (1874)
145. *Id.* at 70.
146. *Id.* at 84.
147. Pulliam, *supra* note 5, at 91.
148. *Id.* at 92.
149. Rippa, *supra* note 13, at 284.
150. *Id.*
151. Gutek, *supra* note 4, at 118.
152. *Id.* at 199.
153. *Id.*
154. *Id.*
155. *Id.* at 200.
156. *Id.* at 206-207.
157. *Id.* at 207.
158. *Id.*

159. *Id.*
160. *Id.*
161. James A. Johnson, Harold W. Collins, Victor L. Dupuis, and John H. Johansen, *Introduction to the Foundations of American Education*, 8th edition (Boston: Allyn and Bacon, 1991), p. 438.
162. Gutek, *supra* note 4, at 210.
163. *Id.*
164. *Id.* at 211.
165. *Id.* at 211-12.
166. *Id.* at 214.
167. *Id.*
168. *Id.* at 215.
169. *Id.* at 218-19.
170. *Id.*
171. *Id.* at 219.
172. *Id.*
173. *Id.* at 220.
174. Pulliam, *supra* note 5, at 173.
175. *Id.*
176. *Id.*
177. *Id.*
178. *Id.*
179. *Id.* at 220-21.
180. *Id.* at 145-46.
181. Gutek, *supra* note 4, at 225.
182. *Id.*
183. *Id.*
184. *Id.* at 222.
185. *Id.* at 223.
186. *Id.* at 226.
187. *Id.* at 227.
188. *Id.*
189. *Id.*
190. *Id.* at 226-27.
191. Pulliam, *supra* note 5, at 175.
192. Gutek, *supra* note 4, at 227.
193. Gerald L. Gutek, *Education and Schooling in America* (Englewood Cliffs, NJ: Prentice-Hall, Inc., 1983), pp. 64-5.
194. Gutek, *supra* note 4, at 227.
195. *Id.*
196. *Id.*
197. *Id.* at 228.
198. *Id.* at 233.
199. *Id.*
200. *Id.* at 233-34.
201. *Id.* at 234.
202. *Id.*
203. *Id.*
204. *Id.* at 237.
205. *Id.* at 239.
206. *Id.*
207. *Id.*
208. *Id.*

209. *Id.* at 240.
210. *Id.* at 240-41.
211. *Id.* at 241.
212. *Id.* at 244.
213. *Id.*
214. *Id.* at 245.
215. *Id.*
216. *Id.*
217. *Id.*
218. *Id.* at 246.
219. *Id.* at 251.
220. *Id.*
221. *Id.*
222. Pulliam, *supra* note 5, at 177.
223. *Id.*
224. Gutek, *supra* note 4, at 257-58.
225. *Id.* at 258.
226. *Id.*
227. *Id.*
228. *Id.*
229. *Id.* at 259.
230. *Id.* at 263.
231. *Id.*
232. *Id.* at 265.
233. *Id.* at 264-65.
234. *Id.* at 265.
235. *Id.* at 268-69.
236. *Id.* at 268.
237. Pulliam, *supra* note 5, at 151.
238. Gutek, *supra* note 4, at 261.
239. *Id.* at 272.
240. *Id.*
241. *Id.* at 271-72.
242. *Id.* at 273.
243. *Id.*
244. *Id.*
245. *Id.*
246. *Id.*
247. *Id.*
248. Pulliam, *supra* note 5, at 149.
249. *Id.*
250. Gutek, *supra* note 4, at 275.
251. *Id.*
252. *Id.*
253. Pulliam, *supra* note 5, at 150.
254. Gutek, *supra* note 4, at 279.
255. *Id.*
256. *Id.*
257. *Id.* at 280.
258. *Id.* at 281.
259. *Id.* at 294.
260. *Id.*
261. Pulliam, *supra* note 5, at 129.

262. Gutek, *supra* note 4, at 295.
263. *Id.* at 296.
264. *Id.* at 297-301.
265. *Id.*; Pulliam, *supra* note 5, at 151.
266. Gutek, *supra* note 4, at 299.
267. *Id.* at 300.
268. *Id.* at 309.
269. *Id.*
270. *Id.*
271. *Id.*
272. *Id.* at 311.
273. *Id.*
274. *Id.* at 312.
275. *Id.* at 319.
276. *Id.*
277. *Id.* at 320.
278. *Id.*
279. *Id.* at 322.
280. *Id.* at 323.
281. *Id.* at 326.
282. *Id.*
283. *Id.* at 327.
284. *Id.*
285. *Id.* at 328.
286. *Id.* at 330.
287. *Id.*
288. *Id.* at 340.
289. *Id.*
290. *Id.* at 336, 340-41.
291. Ronald Reagan, "Excellence and Opportunity: A Program of Support for American Education," 66 *Phi Delta Kappan* No. 1 (September 1984), pp. 13-5. *Cited in* Gutek, *supra* note 4, at 339.
292. *Id.* at 338-39.
293. *See* Chapter One, "The Crisis in Contemporary Public Education" for a discussion of President George Bush's education program, America 2000.

CHAPTER THREE: *Freedom and Educational Diversity*

1. Aldous Huxley, *Brave New World* (Garden City, NY: Doubleday, Doran & Co., Inc., 1932), pp. 20-3, 31-2.
2. Jane A. Van Galen, "Ideology, Curriculum, and Pedagogy in Home Education," 21 *Education and Urban Society* No. 1 (November 1988), pp. 54-5.
3. *See also* Chapter Two, "The History and Philosophy of Public Education," and Chapter Five, "The Historical Perspective."
4. J. Gary Knowles, "Introduction: The Context of Home Schooling in the United States," 21 *Education and Urban Society* No. 1 (November 1988), p. 6.
5. Stephen Arons, *Value Conflict Between American Families and American Schools. Final Report to National Institute of Education* (Amherst, MA: University of Massachusetts, 1981) (ERIC ED 210 786), p. 5.
6. John W. Whitehead, *Parents' Rights* (Wheaton, IL: Crossway Books, 1985), p. 73.
7. Arons, *supra* note 5, at 5.
8. *Id.* at 5-6.

9. *Id.* at 6.
10. *Id.*
11. Knowles, *supra* note 4, at 6.
12. *Id.*
13. *Id.*
14. Israel Zangwill, *The Melting Pot*, Vol. I (New York: Macmillan, 1926).
15. Knowles, *supra* note 4, at 6.
16. Arons, *supra* note 5, at 6.
17. *Id.*
18. Harold Hodgkinson, "Reform Versus Reality," *Phi Delta Kappan* (September 1991), p. 10.
19. *Id.* at 11.
20. *Id.*
21. *Id.* at 10-1.
22. *Id.* at 11, 14.
23. *Id.* at 10.
24. Donna Jackson, "Making a Choice," *New Woman* (April 1992), p. 68.
25. Whitehead, *supra* note 6, at 143.
26. *Id.* at 142-43.
27. *Id.* at 141.
28. *Id.* at 142.
29. *Id.*
30. *Id.*
31. *Id.* at 141.
32. *Id.*
33. *Id.* at 144.
34. *Id.*
35. *Id.* at 146.
36. *Id.*
37. *Id.*
38. Urie Bronfenbrenner, *Two Worlds of Childhood: U.S. and U.S.S.R.* (New York: Russell Sage Foundation, 1970), p. 101. Study summarized in Whitehead, *supra* note 6, at 147.
39. Bronfenbrenner, *supra* note 38, at 101.
40. *Id.*
41. *Id.*
42. *Id.*
43. *Id.* at 102.
44. *Id.* (emphasis supplied).
45. Albert Bandura, D. Ross, and S. A. Ross, "Imitation of Film-mediated Aggressive Models," 66 *Journal of Abnormal and Social Psychology* (1963), pp. 3-11. Study summarized in Arnold S. Kahn, ed., *Social Psychology* (Dubuque, IA: Wm. C. Brown Publishers, 1984), pp. 174-5.
46. Bandura, *supra* note 45, at 3-11.
47. Bronfenbrenner, *supra* note 38, at 101-02.
48. Whitehead, *supra* note 6, at 37-8.
49. *Id.* at 38.
50. *Id.* at 37.
51. *Id.* at 38.
52. *Id.*
53. Stephen Arons, *Compelling Belief: The Culture of American Schooling* (New York: New Press, 1983), p. 211.

54. For a list of values home schooling parents believe are taught in the schools and commonly object to, *see* Arons, *supra* note 5, at 24-6.
55. Van Galen, *supra* note 2, at 54-5.
56. Arons, *supra* note 53, at 205.
57. *Id.*
58. 268 U.S. 510 (1925).
59. Arons, *supra* note 53, at 208.
60. *Id.*
61. *Id.*
62. *Id.*
63. *Id.* at 205.
64. *Id.* at 198.
65. *Id.* at 199.
66. *Id.* at 211.
67. *Id.* at 198.
68. *Id.*
69. *Id.* at 205.
70. *Id.* at 205-06.
71. *Id.* at 207.
72. *Id.* at 206.
73. *Id.*
74. *Id.* at 206-07.
75. *Id.* at 212.
76. *Id.* at 195.
77. *Id.*
78. *Id.* at 197.
79. *Id.* at 131.
80. Arons, *supra* note 5, at 142.
81. John W. Whitehead, *The Rights of Religious Persons in Public Education* (Wheaton, IL: Crossway Books, 1991), p. 22, and Jackson J. Spielvogel, *Hitler and Nazi Germany: A History* (Englewood Cliffs, NJ: Prentice Hall, 1988), p. 172.
82. William L. Shirer, *The Rise and Fall of The Third Reich* (New York: Simon and Schuster, 1960), p. 249.
83. *Id.*
84. *Id.*
85. Spielvogel, *supra* note 81, at 172.
86. Hannsjoachim W. Koch, *The Hitler Youth* (New York: Stein and Day, 1975), p. 166.
87. Shirer, *supra* note 82, at 252.
88. Koch, *supra* note 86, at 166.
89. *Id.* at 170.
90. Shirer, *supra* note 82, at 253, 255.
91. Arons, *supra* note 53, at 88.
92. Whitehead, *supra* note 81, at 29.
93. Whitehead, *supra* note 6, at 38.
94. Arons, *supra* note 5, at 143.
95. *Id.* at 196.
96. *Id.*
97. *Id.* at 195.
98. *See generally* John W. Whitehead and Wendell Bird, *Home Education and Constitutional Liberties* (Wheaton, IL: Crossway Books, 1984).

99. David Colfax and Micki Colfax, *Homeschooling for Excellence* (New York: Warner Books, 1988), p. xv.
100. Van Galen, *supra* note 2, at 52.
101. Kahn, *supra* note 45, at 34-5.
102. *Id.* at 35.
103. *Id.*
104. *Id.* at 38.
105. *Id.*
106. *Id.* at 39.
107. *Id.*
108. *Id.* at 40.
109. *Id.* at 154.
110. John M. Darley and Paget H. Gross, "A Hypothesis Confirming Bias in Labeling Effects," 44 *Journal of Personality and Social Psychology* (1983), pp. 20-33. Study summarized in Kahn, *supra* note 45, at 39-40.
111. Darley, *supra* note 110, at 20-33.
112. Kahn, *supra* note 45, at 154.
113. K. K. Dion, E. Berscheid, and E. Walster, "What Is Beautiful Is Good," 24 *Journal of Personality and Social Psychology* (1972), pp. 285-90. Study summarized in Kahn, *supra* note 45, at 154.
114. K. K. Dion, "Young Children's Stereotyping of Facial Attractiveness," 9 *Developmental Psychology* (1973), pp. 183-88. Study summarized in Kahn, *supra* note 45, at 154.
115. M. Clifford and E. Walster, "The Effect of Physical Attractiveness on Teacher Expectation," 46 *Sociology of Education* (1973), p. 248. Study summarized in Kahn, *supra* note 45, at 155.
116. D. A. Landy and H. Sigall, "Beauty Is Talent: Task Evaluation as a Function of the Performer's Physical Attractiveness," 29 *Journal of Personality and Social Psychology* (1974), pp. 299-304. Study summarized in Kahn, *supra* note 45, at 155.
117. T. F. Cash, B. Gillen, and D. S. Burns, "Sexism and 'Beautyism' in Personnel Consultant Decision Making," 62 *Journal of Applied Psychology* (1977), pp. 301-10. Study summarized in Kahn, *supra* note 45, at 155.
118. K. K. Dion, "Physical Attractiveness and Evaluation of Children's Transgressions," 24 *Journal of Personality and Social Psychology* (1972), pp. 207-13. Study summarized in Kahn, *supra* note 45, at 155.
119. N. Cavior and L. R. Howard, "Facial Attractiveness and Juvenile Delinquency Among Black and White Offenders," 1 *Journal of Abnormal Child Psychology* (1973), pp. 202-13. Study summarized in Kahn, *supra* note 45, at 155.
120. M. G. Efran, "The Effect of Physical Appearance on the Judgement of Guilt, Interpersonal Attraction, and Severity of Recommended Punishment in a Simulated Jury Task," 8 *Journal of Experimental Research in Personality* (1974), pp. 45-54. Study summarized in Kahn, *supra* note 45, at 155.
121. Kahn, *supra* note 45, at 496.
122. Camille B. Wortman, Elizabeth F. Loftus, and Mary Marshall, *Psychology* (New York: Alfred A. Knopf, 1981), p. 57.
123. R. Rosenthal and K. L. Fode, "Three Experiments in Experimenter Bias," 12 *Psychological Reports* (1963), pp. 491-511. Study summarized in Kahn, *supra* note 45, at 19.
124. R. Rosenthal and K. L. Fode, "The Effect of Experimenter Bias on the Performance of the Albino Rat," 8 *Behavioral Science* (1963), pp. 183-89. Study summarized in Donald H. McBurney, *Experimental Psychology* (Belmont, CA: Wadsworth Publishing Company, 1983), pp. 132-3.

125. Robert Rosenthal, *Experimenter Effects in Behavioral Research* (New York: Appleton-Century-Crofts, 1966). Study summarized in Wortman, *supra* note 122, at 57-8.
126. Van Galen, *supra* note 2, at 52.
127. Whitehead, *supra* note 81, at 22.
128. Van Galen, *supra* note 2, at 57.
129. *Id.* at 56.
130. *Id.* at 57.
131. Malcolm Knowles, *Self-Directed Learning* (Chicago: Association Press, 1975), p. 18.
132. *Id.*
133. *Id.* at 18-21, 60.
134. *Id.* at 19.
135. *Id.*
136. *Id.*
137. *Id.*
138. *Id.* at 19-21, 60.
139. *Id.* at 20, 60.
140. *Id.* at 19-20, 60.
141. *Id.* at 20, 60.
142. *Id.*
143. *Id.*
144. *Id.*
145. *Id.* at 20-1, 60.
146. *Id.* at 21, 60.
147. *Id.*
148. *Id.* at 21. The paragraph here is paraphrased from a discussion by Malcolm Knowles on the need for both types of learning.
149. *Id.*
150. Alvin Toffler, *Future Shock* (New York: Bantam Books, 1970), p. 414.
151. *Id.*
152. Richard Nelson Bolles, *What Color Is Your Parachute?* (Berkeley, CA: Ten Speed Press, 1990), p. 37.
153. Gretchen Morgensen, "How to Get a Better Paying Job," *New Woman* (March 1992), p. 112.
154. John W. Gardner, *Self-Renewal* (New York: Harper & Row, 1963), p. 12.
155. Colfax, *supra* note 99, at 38-48.
156. *Id.* at 40-1.
157. *Id.* at 39.
158. *Id.* at 40.
159. *Id.* at 41-2.
160. *Id.* at 42-3.
161. *Id.* at 44.
162. *Id.*
163. *Id.*
164. *Id.*
165. *Id.* at 45.
166. *Id.* at 46-7.
167. *Id.* at 47-8.
168. *Id.*
169. *Id.* at 48.
170. Thomas Toch, "Choice About School Choice: How Far Should We Go?," 57 *The Education Digest* (November 1991), pp. 44-8.

171. *Id.* at 46.
172. *Id.*
173. *Id.*
174. *Id.*
175. *Id.* at 47.
176. *Id.* at 47-8.
177. *Id.* at 47.
178. *Id.* at 48.
179. *Id.* at 49.
180. Hodgkinson, *supra* note 18, at 15.
181. *Id.* at 11.
182. *Id.* at 15.
183. *Id.*
184. *Id.* at 15-16.
185. *Id.* at 16.
186. *Id.*
187. *Id.*
188. *Id.* at 12.
189. Whitehead, *supra* note 6, at 37-8.
190. Arons, *supra* note 53, at 195.
191. *Id.* at 196, 197.
192. Whitehead, *supra* note 6, at 38.
193. Colfax, *supra* note 99, at 38-48.
194. Toch, *supra* note 170, at 46-7.
195. *Id.* at 47-8.
196. *Id.* at 48.
197. Hodgkinson, *supra* note 18, at 15.

CHAPTER FOUR: *Free Market Choice in Education*

1. James R. Rinehart and Jackson F. Lee, Jr., *American Education and the Dynamics of Choice* (Santa Monica, CA: Praeger, 1991), p. 8.
2. Myron Lieberman, *Public School Choice: Current Issues/Future Prospects* (Lancaster, PA: Technomic, 1990), p. 3-4.
3. In the 1991 poll, 62 percent of the respondents were in favor of a moderate school program that would allow students to attend any public school of their choice in their community. Stanley M. Elam, Lowell C. Rose, and Alec M. Gallup, "The 23rd Annual Gallup Poll of the Public's Attitudes Toward the Public Schools," in *Phi Delta Kappan* 41, 47-48 (September 1991). Furthermore, 50 percent approved of a more drastic restructuring known as a voucher system that would allow families to get back tax dollars and spend them at any school of their choosing. *Id.* at 47. This figure was up from an average of about 45 percent approval since the poll began in 1970. *Id.*
4. Fifty-seven percent of minorities favored the first plan (freedom of choice among public schools) as opposed to 50 percent of the population at large. *Id.* at 47-48. And 69 percent of minorities said that the voucher system of choice between public and private schools should be instituted as opposed to 62 percent of all respondents. *Id.* at 48.
5. Secretary of Education Lamar Alexander has indicated that eighteen states had passed such legislation between 1989 and early 1992. Carol Innerst, "Administration Tries New Paths to School Choice," *The Washington Times* (January 31, 1992), p. A3.
6. These are Minnesota, Iowa, and Milwaukee.

7. While a presidential candidate, Bill Clinton proposed that states adopt public school choice plans; President George Bush went further and advocated nationwide limited voucher plans. *See* Fred Barnes, "Logjam; White House Watch," *The New Republic* (May 11, 1992), p. 10.

8. Myron Lieberman, *Privatization and Educational Choice* (New York: St. Martin's Press, 1989), pp. 5-13, Rinehart & Lee, supra note 2, at 12-13.

9. See *infra* notes 105-108 and accompanying text.

10. For a discussion of this executive order generally, see James Ott, "Bush Order Opens Door for Airport Privatization," *Aviation Week and Space Technology* (May 11, 1992), p. 24. This order generated immediate talk about the privatization of Baltimore-Washington International Airport; *see* "State of Maryland Resistant to Sale of BWI Airports" (May 12, 1992), p. 186, and Los Angeles International Airport, *see* Bill Boyarsky, "Quayle Here with a Legitimate Issue: The Sale of LAX," *Los Angeles Times* (May 22, 1992), at B2.

11. *See* Jack Kemp, "A New Agenda for Ending Poverty; Give People a Stake in Their Own Communities," in *The Washington Post* (May 3, 1992), p. C7. *See* Carl F. Horowitz, "Jack Kemp's 'Perestroika': A Choice Plan for Public Housing Tenants," *Heritage Foundation Reports* (March 26, 1992), available on NEXIS.

12. *See* James Cook, "A Mailman's Lot Is Not a Happy One," *Forbes* (April 27, 1992), p. 82.

13. *See* William D. Eggers, "Economic Reform in Eastern Europe: A Report Card," *Heritage Foundation Reports* (April 23, 1992), available on NEXIS.

14. One example is Zaire. *See* "Zaire to Privatize National Airline, Post and Telecommunications," *Agence France Press* (July 28, 1991).

15. For information about Mexico, see Jacqueline Gold, "Removing the Dead Hand of State," *Financial World* (March 3, 1992), p. 39. For information about Canada, see Doug Kelly, "Shutdown of Agencies a 'Streamlining' Step," *The Financial Post* (February 26, 1992), sec. 1, p. 27.

16. In May 1992, extensive news coverage was given to the National Assessment of Educational Progress's study showing that television viewing time is growing, while students have virtually stopped reading either for homework or for pleasure, have stopped visiting their libraries, and have extremely low levels of comprehension and retention of the materials they do read. "News Conference with: Lamar Alexander, Secretary of Education, and Emerson Elliott, Action Commissioner of Education, on: Reading In and Out of School: Factors Influencing the Literacy and Achievement of American Students in Grades 4, 8 and 12, in 1988 and 1990," May 28, 1992. *Federal News Service*, available on NEXIS. Additionally, recent studies continue to show American children and teenagers scoring at or near the bottom of international math and science tests. For a discussion of one recent example, see Barbara Kantrowitz and Pat Wingert, "An 'F' in World Competition," *Newsweek*, February 17, 1992, p. 57.

17. Rinehart and Lee, *supra* note 1, at 3.

18. *Id.*

19. *Id.*; Lieberman, *supra* note 2, at 3.

20. *Id.* at 3; *Rinehart, supra* note 1, at 55.

21. Lieberman, *Public School Choice, supra* note 2, at 3-4.

22. "Choosing Better Schools: The Five Regional Meetings on Choice in Education" (Washington, D.C.: U.S. Dept. of Education, 1990), p. 6; *Survey of Magnet Schools: Analyzing a Model for Quality Integrated Education* (Washington, D.C.: U. S. Dept. of Education Office of Planning, Budget, & Evaluation, 1983), p. 10.

23. Lieberman, *Public School Choice, supra* note 2, at 3.

24. *Survey of Magnet Schools, supra* note 22, at 11, 13.

25. Lieberman, *Public School Choice, supra* note 2, at 4.
26. *Educating Our Children: Parents and Schools Together—A Report to the President* (Washington, D.C.: Secretary of Education, 1989).
27. Ruth Randall and Keith George, *School Choice: Issues and Answers* (Washington, D.C.: Nat'l Educ. Serv. 1991), 166-9.
28. *Choosing Better Schools, supra* note 22, at 8; *see also* Randall *supra* note 27, at 167-8 (discussing eligible students).
29. Lieberman, *Public School Choice, supra* note 2, at 62; *Choosing Better Schools, supra* note 22, at 7.
30. *See, e.g., Choosing Better Schools, supra* note 22, at 8 (*citing* Minnesota as an example); Lieberman, *Public School Choice, supra* note 2, at 62.
31. *Choosing Better Schools, supra* note 22, at 7.
32. *See id.*
33. John E. Chubb and Terry M. Moe, "Politics, Markets And America's Schools" (Washington, D.C.: The Brookings Institute, 1990), p. 210.
34. Lieberman, *Public School Choice, supra* note 2, at 2.
35. *Id.* This term is also sometimes applied to interdistrict choice.
36. *Choosing Better Schools, supra* note 22, at 7.
37. *Id.;* Lieberman, *Public School Choice, supra* note 2, at 2.
38. Chubb and Moe, "Politics, Markets and America's Schools," *supra* note 33, at 206.
39. *Id.*
40. *Id.* at 210.
41. *Id.* at 210-11.
42. *Id.*
43. *Id.* at 211.
44. *Id.*
45. *Id.*
46. *Id.*
47. *Id.* The school precludes the potential for all students to rank the same school as number one by offering a variety of programs. Also, this potential problem was minimized because of the proximity factor. *Id.*
48. *Id.* Those students not receiving their first choice could apply for a transfer the next year. *Id.*
49. *Id.*
50. *Id.* at 210.
51. *Id.*
52. *Id.*
53. *Id.*
54. *Id.* at 210-12.
55. According to Dr. Lieberman, these include: contracting out public education to non-government workers, either for-profit or non-profit; franchising of certain services within the public school systems; having volunteers provide more services in the schools; selling off certain public school assets; constructing or purchasing of facilities by private parties who then lease them to the public schools; and load shedding—complete withdrawal of the government from the business of education. Lieberman, *Privatization, supra* note 8, at 6-8.
56. Milton Friedman, *Capitalism and Freedom* (Chicago: University of Chicago Press, 1962), pp. 91-105.
57. Chubb and Moe, "Politics, Markets, and America's Schools," *supra* note 33, at 191.
58. Lieberman, *Privatization, supra* note 8, at 118.

59. Minn. Stat. Ann. § 290.01, subd. 19b (1992); Iowa Code Ann. §§ 422.9(2)(f)(1992); 422.12(2)(1992).
60. Lieberman, *Privatization, supra* note 8, at 118.
61. Friedman, *supra* note 56, at 89.
62. John E. Coons and Stephen D. Sugarman, "Credits v. Subsidies: Comment on the California Tuition Tax Credit Proposal," in *Private Schools and the Public Good: Policy Alternatives for the Eighties*, Edward McGlynn Gaffney, Jr., ed. (Notre Dame, IN: University of Notre Dame Press, 1981), pp. 106, 108.
63. *Id.*
64. 413 U. S. 756 (1973).
65. For commentary, see Roger A. Freeman, "Educational Tax Credits," in *The Public School Monopoly: A Critical Analysis of Education and the State in American Society*, Robert B. Everhart, ed. (San Diego, CA: Pacific Institute, 1982), p. 471.
66. *Nyquist*, 413 U.S. at 764 *citing* N.Y. Laws 1972, c. 414, § 2, amending N.Y. Educ. Law, Art. 12-A, §§ 559-563 (Supp. 1972-73).
67. *Id.* at 765 *citing* N.Y. Laws 1972, c. 414, §§ 3, 4, & 5, amending N.Y. Tax Law §§ 612 (c),(j) (Supp. 1972-1973).
68. *Id.* at 783.
69. *Id.* at 791.
70. 463 U.S. 388 (1983).
71. *Id.* at 401.
72. *Id.*
73. *Id.* at 398-99.
74. *Id.* at 396-97.
75. *Id.* at 396-97 n.6.
76. *Id.* at 396-97, n.6 (*Committee for Public Educ. v. Nyquist*, 413 U.S. 756, 790 n.49).
77. *Id.* at 391.
78. Minn. Stat. § 290.01, subd. 196(3)(1992) (footnote omitted).
79. *Id.*
80. *Id.*
81. It is interesting to note that New York's plan has not yet been repealed, although it has been invalidated by the Court. Also, in 1972 Louisiana adopted a tuition tax credit plan similar to the one passed by New York. La. Rev. Stat. 47:85-87 (1991). Following *Nyquist*, the United States District Court of the Middle District of Louisiana held the Louisiana statutes unconstitutional in *Seegers v. Traigle*, La. Tax Ct. Rep. (CCH) ¶ 200-471 (M. D. La. Dec. 27, 1973); La. Tax Ct. Rep. (CCH) ¶ 200-472 (M. D. La. Jan. 7, 1974) (addendum to original opinion). However, as one commentator indicates, some confusion may ensue in researching tax credits because the statutes have not been repealed, while the *Seegers* decision was not published in West's National Reporter System. John H. Runnels Note, "The Constitutionality of Louisiana Aid to Private Education," 44 La. L. Rev. 865, 871-72 (1984). This may lead the unfamiliar to believe that the plan is still valid.
82. Iowa Code § 422.9 (2)(f)(1992).
83. Iowa Code § 422.12(2)(1992).
84. Minn. Stat. Ann. § 290.01, subd. 196(3)(1992).
85. Iowa Code § 422.9(2)(f); Iowa Code § 422.12(2)(1992).
86. Iowa Code Ann. §§ 422.9(2)(f); 422.12(2)(1992).
87. Iowa Code Ann. §§ 422.9(2)(f); 422.12(2)(1992).
88. *Mueller & Allen*, 463 U.S. 388, 396 n. 6.

89. Jesse H. Choper, "The Establishment Clause and Aid to Parochial Schools—An Update," 75 Cal. L. Rev. 5, (1987), at 9 *citing Mueller* 463 U.S. at 411 (Marshall, J. dissenting).

90. 474 U.S. 481 (1986).

91. *Id.* at 483.

92. *Id.*

93. Choper, *supra* note 89, at 13.

94. *Witlers*, 474 U.S. 490 (Powell, J. concurring).

95. *Id.* at 490-92 (Powell, J. concurring).

96. *Id.* at 490 (White, J., concurring); *Id.* at 493 (O'Connor, J., concurring).

97. Choper, *supra* note 89, at 13.

98. *Id.*

99. As this book went to press, California voters were seeking to get a voucher referendum on the ballot that would allow vouchers of $2,500 to each school-aged child. *See* Vlae Kershner, "Educators Want to Keep School Choice Off Ballot: They Urge Californians Not to Sign Petitions," *San Francisco Chronicle* (January 22, 1992), p. A11. If passed, this referendum would be the first real statewide experiment with school choice. The California school voucher initiative is presently scheduled to appear on the ballot in June 1994.

    Vermont has a school choice program on the books that allows school districts to make tuition payments to private high schools and public high schools outside of that district on behalf of students. 16 Vt. Stat. Ann. § 822 (1991). The specific purpose of this plan, originally, was to provide secondary education to students residing in districts without high schools. Lieberman, *Privatization, supra* note 8, at 244. Payments to religious denominational high schools under this plan, which is similar to a voucher in plan except that the tuition payments are authorized to go directly to the school instead of to the parents, were ruled unconstitutional by the Vermont Supreme Court in 1961. *Swart v. South Burlington Town Sch. Dist.*, A.2d 514 (1961). However, Lieberman reports that "several religiously oriented private schools have continued to receive tuition payments." Lieberman, *Privatization, supra* note 8, at 245.

100. For one story describing the experiment, see Terry Eastland, "School Choice Clears a Hurdle," *The Washington Times* (March 3, 1992), p. F:1.

101. Wisc. Stat. § 119.23 (1989-90).

102. *Id.* The bill was heavily influenced by the Brookings Institute study by Chubb and Moe in "Politics, Markets and America's Schools," according to the Wisconsin Supreme Court. *Davis v. Grover*, 480 N. W. 2d 460 at 471, n.21.

103. See *id.* at 465-77.

104. "Abandoning the Motherland; Learning by Choice; Pearl Harbor Remembered," transcript from the "MacNeill-Lehrer News Hour," Monday, December 2, 1991, #4216, available on NEXIS.

105. *Remarks by Pres. George Bush at Milwaukee, Wis.—Bush-Quayle Fundraiser Milwaukee, Wis., Federal News Service*, March 16, 1992, available on NEXIS.

106. Linda Chion-Kenney, "Education; The Choice Debate, A Patch to Better Schooling or an Elitist Plum?," *The Washington Post* (February 10, 1992), p. B:5.

107. See Carol Innerst, "Administration Tried New Paths to School Choice," *The Washington Times* (January 31, 1992), p. A:3.

108. Associated Press, "Senate Rejects School Choice Tax Credits," *Chicago Tribune* (January 24, 1992), p. 6.

109. Joel Spring, "The Evolving Structure of American Schooling," in *The Public School Monopoly*, p. 77.

110. *Id.* at 82.
111. *Id.* at 84-5.
112. *Id.* at 84.
113. *Id.* at 85-6.
114. Chubb and Moe, *Politics, Markets & America's Schools, supra* note 33, at 3.
115. Spring, in *Public School Monopoly, supra* note 109, at 89.
116. *See id.* at 90-1 (discussing the reasons underlying this evolution).
117. *Id.* at 90-2.
118. Examples of federal intrusion into local curriculum decisions that Springer cites include the National Defense Education Act of 1958 and the establishment of the National Institute of Education in the 1970s. *Id.* at 95-100.
119. Friedman, *supra* note 56, at 85-107.
120. *Id.* at 85.
121. *Id.* at 85-6.
122. *Id.* at 87-9.
123. *Id.* at 89.
124. *Id.*
125. Governments could require a minimum level of schooling financed by giving parents vouchers redeemable for a specified maximum sum per child per year if spent on "approved" educational services. Parents would then be free to spend this sum and any additional sum they themselves provided on purchasing educational services from an "approved" institution of their own choice. The educational services could be rendered by private enterprises operated for profit or by non-profit institutions. The role of government would be limited to insuring that the schools met certain minimum standards, such as the inclusion of a minimum common content in their programs, much as it now inspects restaurants to insure that they maintain minimum sanitary standards. *Id.* at 89.
126. *Id.* at 90.
127. *Id.* at 91.
128. *Id.*
129. *Id.*
130. *Id.* at 93-4.
131. *Id.* at 94.
132. Muriel Cohen, "School Plan Draws Fire: Educators Say Additional Funds Vital to Fuel Massachusetts 2000," *The Boston Globe* (October 24, 1991), Metro/Region, p. 25. Rinehart and Lee have estimated the amount of increase in money spent on education during the time that dissatisfaction with the system has been increasing:

> To gain a better perspective on the real burden education places on the average taxpayer, we can look at the proportion of personal income spent for this purpose. In 1950 approximately 2.5 percent of the nation's personal income went toward education. In 1987 this figure was 4.6 percent in spite of a declining student population. These figures represent an 84 percent increase in the share of personal income going for education.

Rinehart, *supra* note 1, at 7.
133. *Id.* at 25.
134. *Id.*
135. Lieberman, *Privatization, supra* note 8, at 294-96.
136. *Id.*
137. Minn. Stat. § 290.01(1991); Iowa Code § 422.9(1991).
138. Minn. Stat. § 290.01(1991); Iowa Code § 422.9(1991).

139. However, note that both states exclude certain classes from deductions. Minnesota law appears to allow a deduction for tuition but not for textbooks and transportation for "extracurricular activities including sporting events, musical or dramatic events, speech activities, driver's education," or similar programs. Minn. Stat. Ann. § 290.01, subd. 196(3)(1992). The Iowa code, which does not allow deductions for transportation at all, appears to differ only in that respect. Iowa Code Ann. §§ 422.9(2)(f)(1992); 422.12(2)(1992). In any case, home educators seeking to take advantage of these provisions should seek the advice of a competent tax advisor.

140. *See* Chapter Six, "Dimensions of the Contemporary Home Education Movement."

141. Lieberman, *Privatization, supra* note 8, at 281, *citing* Brian D. Ray, "A Comparison of Home Schooling and Conventional Schooling: With a Focus on Learner Outcomes," *Science* (Corvallis, OR: Oregon State University, Department of Science, Mathematics, and Computer Education, 1986), pp. 5-6.

142. Presumably, most plans will come to include religious education. Although the Milwaukee school experiment does not allow vouchers to be used in parochial schools, Wis. Stat. § 119.23 (1989-90), the Minnesota and Iowa plans allow deductions for parochial schools, though not for religious textbooks. Also the voucher system proposed by President George Bush in his 1993 budget plans included granting vouchers for use in private religious schools. *See* Chion-Kenney, *supra* note 106.

143. Jon Wartes, *Report From the 1986 Home School Testing* (Washington Home School Research Project, 1987), p. 16, *quoted* in Lieberman, *Privatization, supra* note 8, at 369, n. 15.

144. *Id.*

145. *Id.* at 281 *quoting* Ray, *supra* note 141.

CHAPTER FIVE: *The Historical Perspective*

1. For a discussion of "The Crisis in Contemporary Public Education," *see* Chapter One, and of "The History and Philosophy of Public Education," *see* Chapter Two.

2. Lawrence Kotin and William Aikman, *Legal Foundations of Compulsory School Attendance* (Port Washington, NY: Kennikat Press, 1980). *See also* Note, "Home Education v. Compulsory Attendance Laws: Whose Kids Are They Anyway?," 24 Washburn L.J. 274, 278, n. 51 (1985).

3. Kotin and Aikman, *supra* note 2, at 9.

4. *Id.*

5. *Id.* at 10.

6. Marcus W. Jernegan, "The Beginnings of Public Education in New England, Part I," 23 School Review 319, 325, 330 (May 1915). *See also* George Cressman and George Bereday, *Public Education in America*, 2nd ed. (New York: Harper, 1961). "In general, it is true that the first motives in education were primarily religious," p. 28. In fact, it has been asserted that the "chief purpose [of colonial education] was to support revealed religion." Clinton Rossiter, *Seedtime of the Republic: The Origin of the American Tradition of Political Liberty* (New York: Harcourt, Brace, 1953), p. 120.

7. Jernegan, "Beginnings I," *supra* note 6, at 330, *quoting New England's First Fruits* (London: R.O. and G.D. for Henry Overton, 1643).

8. *Id.* at 325-29.

9. *Id.* at 326.

10. R. Freeman Butts and Lawrence Cremin, *A History of Education in American Culture* (New York: Holt, 1953), p. 101. The full text of the 1642 act is set out in Marcus W. Jernegan, "Compulsory Education in the American Colonies Part I," 26 School Review 731, 735, n. 1 (December 1918).

11. Kotin and Aikman, *supra* note 2, at 11, *quoting Records of the Governor and Company of Massachusetts Bay in New England,* 1642.

12. *Id.*

13. *Id.* at 13.

14. *Id.*

15. *Id.* at 11.

16. *Id.* at 12.

17. *Id.* at 14.

18. *Id.* at 17.

19. *Id.*

20. *Id.* at 17. This 1647 law was so named because of the belief that Satan "used ignorance to keep people from knowledge of the Scriptures."

21. *Id.* at 18.

22. *Id.* at 19.

23. Jernegan, "Compulsory American I," *supra* note 10, at 739.

24. Kotin and Aikman, *supra* note 2, at 19.

25. *Id.* For a table of the dates of compulsory education laws in the New England colonies, *see* Marcus W. Jernegan, "Compulsory Education in the American Colonies Part II," 27 School Review 24, 42 (January 1919).

26. Butts and Cremin, *supra* note 10, at 101. But *see* Jernegan "Compulsory American II," *supra* note 25, at 42, n. 1, *quoting* a 1644 town law which stated: "Also that if any poore body hath children or a childe, to be put to school and not able to pay for their schooling, that the Towne will pay it by rate."

27. Marcus W. Jernegan, "The Beginnings of Public Education in New England Part II," 23 School Review 361, 378 (June 1915). Additional local education acts are discussed at 378-80.

28. Marcus W. Jernegan, "Compulsory Education in the Southern Colonies," 27 School Review 405, 422 (June 1919).

29. *Id.* at 412. There was thus apparently a much lower concentration of educated leaders in the southern colonies than in the northern colonies.

30. Butts and Cremin, *supra* note 10, at 105.

31. Kotin and Aikman, *supra* note 2, at 20.

32. Marcus W. Jernegan, *Laboring and Dependent Classes in Colonial America 1607-1783* (Chicago: University of Chicago Press, 1931), p. 114.

33. Kotin and Aikman, *supra* note 2, at 23, *citing* Newton Edwards and Herman Richey, *The School in the American Social Order* (Boston: Houghton Mifflin Co., 1947), p. 108-09.

34. Jernegan, "Compulsory American II," *supra* note 25, at 26.

35. *Id.* at 41.

36. *Id.* at 27.

37. Jernegan, *Laboring, supra* note 32, at 114.

38. *Id.*

39. *Id., supra* note 32, at 41. One exception to this general rule was the development of religious schools in the so-called "middle colonies" (Pennsylvania, New York, New Jersey). They included "schools established by an individual congregation or minister, by neighboring churches as a cooperative undertaking, or by religious societies organized on a wider basis." Butts and Cremin, *supra* note 10, at 111.

40. Kotin and Aikman, *supra* note 2, at 24.

41. Lawrence Cremin, *The Transformation of the School* (New York: Alfred A. Knopf, 1961), p. 66.
42. *Id.* at 9-10.
43. *See* Note, "Home Education in America: Parental Rights Reasserted," 49 UMKC Law Review 191, 193 (1981).

  It should be noted, however, that child labor law reform was needed to get children out of the factories so they would be able to attend the local public schools. *See* Kotin and Aikman, *supra* note 2, at 36-68.
44. Kotin and Aikman, *supra* note 2, at 27.
45. Butts and Cremin, *supra* note 10, at 241.
46. *Id.* at 242.
47. Kotin and Aikman, *supra* note 2, at 25.
48. *Id.* at 25-6.
49. *Id.* at 25, n. 48; *see also* Butts and Cremin, *supra* note 10, at 246 and following.
50. 24 Washburn L.J., *supra* note 2, at 277.
51. Butts and Cremin, *supra* note 10, at 404.
52. *Id.* at 362.
53. 1886.
54. Butts and Cremin, *supra* note 10, at 362-63.
55. *Id.*
56. St. Thomas: 1983.
57. *Id.*
58. *Id.* at 386-87.
59. *Id.* at 364, *quoting* Ellis, "Parochial and Public Schools: A Point of View," 14 Educational Forum 21-37 (1949).
60. 24 Washburn L. J., *supra* note 2, at 277.
61. 347 U.S. 483 (1954).
62. 24 Washburn L.J., *supra* note 2, at 277.
63. *Id.* at 277-78.
64. *Id.*
65. Michael S. Shepherd, *The Home Schooling Movement: An Emerging Conflict in American Education* (Ph.D. dissertation, East Texas State University, 1986), p. 1.
66. *Id.* at 12.
67. *Id.*
68. *Id.* at 59.
69. *Id.*
70. *Id.* at 1.
71. Phone interview with Dr. Raymond Moore, January 23, 1992. Dr. Moore emphasized that this figure includes approximately 400,000 children of migrant farmers. *See also* Chapter Six, "Dimensions of the Contemporary Home Education Movement."
72. Shepherd, *supra* note 65, at 15-6, *quoting* Edward Power, *The Transit of Learning: A Sound and Cultural Interpretation of American Educational History* (Sherman Oaks, CA: Alfred Publishing Co., 1979), p. 66.
73. *Id.*
74. *Id.*
75. *See supra*, notes 6-19 and accompanying text.
76. Clarence Carson, *The Colonial Experience* (Wadley, AL: American Textbook Committee, 1987), pp. 124-25. *See also* Chapter Eight, "American Patterns," Chapter Ten, "The Sacred Right," and Chapter Seventeen, "Parental Liberty."
77. Shepherd, *supra* note 65, at 15.
78. *See supra*, notes 21-8 and accompanying text.

79. Shepherd, *supra* note 65, at 17.
80. *Id.* at 18-9, *paraphrasing* Robert Baker, "Compulsory Education in the United States: Big Brother Goes to School," 3 Seton Hall L. Rev. 102 (1972).
81. *Id.*
82. John C. Fitzpatrick, *George Washington Himself* (Indianapolis: Bobbs-Merrill Co., 1885).
83. Saul K. Padover, *Jefferson: A Great American's Life and Ideals* (New York: Mentor Books, 1942).
84. Shepherd, *supra* note 65, at 115.
85. *Id.*
86. *Id.*
87. *Id.*
88. Varnum Lansing Collins, *President Witherspoon* (Princeton, NJ: Princeton University Press, 1925), p. 11.
89. Carl Van Doren, *Benjamin Franklin* (The Haddon Craftsman, 1938), pp. 11-2.
90. Lawrence Cremin, *American Education: The Colonial Experience, 1607-1783* (New York: Harper and Row, 1970), pp. 479-85.
91. Sarah H. Tooley, *The Life of Florence Nightingale* (London: Cassell and Company, Ltd., 1911), p. 35.
92. Booker T. Washington, *Up From Slavery* (New York: Doubleday, Page & Co., 1925), p. 31.
93. Matthew Josephson, *Edison* (New York: McGraw-Hill, 1959), p. 20.
94. William Johnstone, *Robert E. Lee: The Christian* (Arlington Heights, IL: Christian Liberty Press, 1989), p. 27.
95. The following summary of their life's work is based on a January 23, 1992, phone interview with Dr. Moore and on a document entitled "February 1991 White Paper—History on Homeschooling" by Dr. Moore.
96. Shepherd, *supra* note 65, at 61, *paraphrasing* Raymond and Dorothy Moore, *Better Late Than Early* (New York: E. P. Dutton, 1975), p. 58.
97. *Id.* at 64, *paraphrasing* Dr. Moore, *supra* note 96, at 10.
98. *Id.* at 65, *quoting* Christopher Johnson, "Early Schooling Doesn't Necessarily Mean Better Schooling," 61 *Phi Delta Kappan* 220-21 (November 1979).
99. *Id.* at 63.
100. *Id.* at 116.
101. Raymond Moore and Dorothy Moore, *School Can Wait* (Provo, UT: BYU Press, 1979).
102. Shepherd, *supra* note 65, at 3.
103. *Id.*
104. *Id.*
105. *Id.* at 14, *paraphrasing* *Sheridan Road Baptist Church v. Michigan*, as cited in Defendant's First Supplemental Brief, *Texas v. Hardie*, Precinct [sic] Dallas County, No. 2566-83. *See also* Chapter Four, "Free Market Choice in Education."
106. *Id.* at 3. For a discussion of this issue, *see* Chapter Seven, "The Straw Men: Socialization and Academics."
107. *Id.* at 6.
108. *Id.* at 9.
109. *Id.*
110. *See* Appendix, "Legislative Status."
111. Comment, "Texas Homeschooling: An Unresolved Conflict Between Parents and Educators," 39 Baylor L.R. 469, 471, n. 24 and following (1987).
112. The Supreme Court held in *San Antonio School Dist. v. Rodriguez*, 411 U.S. 1 (1973), that education was not a fundamental right because it was not expressly

or impliedly mentioned in the text of the Constitution. *Id.* at 35. The Supreme Court has emphasized, however, that education is an issue of vital national concern. *See Brown v. Bd. of Ed.*, 347 U.S. 483, 493 (1954) ("education is perhaps the most important function of state and local governments").

113. U.S. Constitution, Tenth Amendment. *See also* Brendan Stocklin-Enright, "The Constitutionality of Home Education: The Role of the Parent, the State and the Child," 18 Willamette L. Rev. 563, 565 (1982).

114. ". . . No State shall make or enforce any law which shall abridge the privileges or immunities of citizens of the United States; nor shall any State deprive any person of life, liberty, or property, without due process of law. . . ." U.S. Constitution, Fourteenth Amendment.

115. Stocklin-Enright, *supra* note 113, at 567.

116. *Id.*

117. *Runyon v. McCrary*, 427 U.S. 160, 178 n. 15 (1976). *See also* Chapter Fourteen, "Right to Privacy and Due Process."

118. The general term "liberty interest" is used in the same sense as in the Stocklin-Enright article. *See* Stocklin-Enright, *supra* note 113, at 568.

119. *See also* Chapter Eight, "American Patterns"; Chapter Nine, "The Early American Family"; Chapter Ten, "The Sacred Right"; Chapter Eleven, "Modern Parental Rights: Issues and Limits"; Chapter Fourteen, "Right to Privacy and Due Process"; and Chapter Seventeen, "Parental Liberty."

120. *Meyer v. Nebraska*, 262 U.S. 390 (1923); *Pierce v. Society of Sisters*, 268 U.S. 510 (1925); *Wisconsin v. Yoder*, 406 U.S. 206 (1972).

121. *Meyer*, 262 U.S. at 403.

122. *Id.* at 399.

123. Stocklin-Enright, *supra* note 113, at 569.

124. 268 U.S. 510 (1925).

125. *Id.* at 536.

126. *Id.* at 534-35 (emphasis supplied).

127. *Id.* at 534.

128. *See, e.g., Smith v. Employment Div.*, 494 U.S.872, 110 S.Ct. 1595, 1601 (1990) (*Pierce* acknowledged "the right of parents . . . to direct the education of their children").

129. *Yoder*, 406 U.S. at 239. Later state court decisions reemphasize this principle. *See, infra*, notes and accompanying text.

130. 406 U.S. 206 (1972).

131. *Id.* at 213-14.

132. *Id.* at 232.

133. *Id.* at 214.

134. *Id.* at 235.

135. *Id.* at 233-34, *citing Prince v. Mass.*, 321 U.S. 158 (1943). In *Prince*, the Court upheld the conviction of a legal custodian of a child for using the child to distribute literature in violation of state child labor laws, even though the literature was religious material:

> And neither rights of religion nor rights of parenthood are beyond limitation. Acting to guard the general interest in youth's well being, the state as *parens patriae* may restrict the parent's control by requiring school attendance, regulating or prohibiting the child's labor, and in many other ways. . . . [T]he state has a wide range of power for limiting parental freedom and authority in things affecting the child's welfare; and . . . this includes, to some extent, matters of conscience and religious conviction.

Prince, 321 U.S. at 166-67 (footnotes omitted).

136. The Supreme Court has generally not addressed the interest of the *child* in his education, except for Justice Douglas's dissent in *Wisconsin v. Yoder*, 406 U.S. 206. For more on this topic, *see* 24 Washburn L.J., *supra* note 2, at 283.

137. Although it should be noted that Chief Justice Burger once wrote in a concurring opinion that "[f]ew familial decisions are as immune from governmental interference as parents' choice of a school for their children" (*citing Meyer*, *Pierce*, and *Yoder*). *Cook v. Hudson*, 429 U.S. 165, 166 (1976).

138. Kotin and Aikman, *supra* note 2, at 133.

139. 159 Mass. 372, 34 N.E. 402 (1893).

140. *Roberts*, 34 N.E. at 403.

141. This agrees with Justice White's later concurrence in *Yoder*.

142. 32 Ind. A. 665, 70 N.E. 550 (1904).

143. *Id.*, 70 N.E. 552 (no citation for quote given by court).

144. 69 Wash. 361, 124 P. 910 (1912).

145. *Id.*, 124 P. at 911-12.

146. 21 Okla. Crim. 430, 209 P. 179 (1922).

147. *Id.*, 209 P. at 180.

148. *Id.* at 180-81.

149. 404 IL 574, 90 N.E.2d 213 (1950).

150. *Id.*, 90 N.E. 2d at 215.

151. *Id.*

152. *Id.*

153. Shepherd, *supra* note 65, at 10, *paraphrasing People v. Levisen*, 90 N.E.2d 213 (Il. 1950).

154. 95 N.J. Super. 382, 231 A.2d 252 (1967).

155. *Id.*, 231 A.2d at 257.

156. *Id.*

157. *See supra*, notes 113-137 and accompanying text.

158. *See supra*, notes 138-156 and accompanying text.

CHAPTER SIX: *Dimensions of the Contemporary Home Education Movement*

1. Raymond and Dorothy Moore, *Home-spun Schools* (Waco, TX: Word Books, 1982), p. 12. Among other things, *Home-spun Schools* contains vignettes of the home schools of many types of families such as "The Nurse and the PR Man," "New York Banker," "The Army Wife and the Intelligence Officer," "The Oil Man and the Housewife," and "We Single Girls." *See also* Raymond and Dorothy Moore, *Home-grown Kids* (Waco, TX: Word Books, 1981).

2. Rae Holtzendorff, quoted in Luanne Shackelford and Susan White, *A Survivor's Guide to Home Schooling* (Wheaton, IL: Crossway Books, 1988), p. 3.

3. Shackelford, *supra* note 2, at 3-4.

4. Patricia M. Lines, "An Overview of Home Instruction," 69 *Phi Delta Kappan* (March 1987), p. 510.

5. Cheryl Gorder, *Home Schools: An Alternative*, 3rd ed. (Tempe, AZ: Blue Bird Publishing Co., 1990), p. 11.

6. Lines, "An Overview of Home Instruction," *supra* note 4, at 510. For example, "[i]n the early Seventies, only a handful of educational institutions enrolled children in a home curriculum or provided curriculum packages designed for parents teaching their children at home. These included the Calvert School, Home Study International, the International Institute, and the state of Alaska. Between 5,000 and 6,000 children in grades K through 8 were estimated to be enrolled in or receiving curricular materials from these organizations. Based on interviews with those familiar with the movement and on two questionnaires . . .

it appears that 50% to 75% of all parents engaged in home-schooling today design their own curricula rather than use the services or materials from these institutions. Assuming that this was also true in the early Seventies, between 10,000 and 15,000 children were probably being schooled at home during that period." *Id.* at 510-11.

7. *Id.* at 511.

8. According to two commentators: "There is no definite figure on home schools because many families do not want to be studied or counted. Fearing prosecution and harassment from state authorities, a large but uncertain number of parents simply hide their children." John Whitehead and Wendell Bird, *Home Education and Constitutional Liberties* (Wheaton, IL: Crossway Books, 1984), p. 18.

9. For a discussion of this issue, *see* Chapter One, "The Crisis in Contemporary Public Education."

10. Michael S. Shepherd, "Home Schooling: Dimensions of Controversy, 1970-1984," 31 *Journal of Church and State* 1 (Winter 1989), p. 101.

11. Michael S. Shepherd, "The Home Schooling Movement: An Emerging Conflict in American Education," doctoral thesis presented to the Graduate School of East Texas State University (May 1986), p. 25.

12. *See generally* Appendix, "Legislative Status." *See also* Shepherd, "The Home Schooling Movement," *supra* note 11, p. 137, *et. seq.*

    By the end of 1986, every state permitted home instruction in some form and only a few strictly regulated it. Lines, "An Overview of Home Instruction," *supra* note 4, at 514.

13. Stephen Buckley, "Home Schooling on Rise," *The Washington Post* (May 26, 1992), p. 1.

14. *Id.*

15. John Naisbitt, *Megatrends: Ten New Directions Transforming Our Lives* (New York: Warner, 1982), p. 144.

16. Greg Monfils, "On Home Schooling," Vol. XIII *US Air Magazine*, No. 3 (March 1991), p. 13.

17. David Guterson, "When Schools Fail Children," *Harper's Magazine*, November 1990.

18. Gorder, *supra* note 5, at 8.

19. Guterson, *supra* note 17, at 58. *See also* Anthony Cook, "When Your Home Is the Classroom," *Money* (September 1991), p. 107.

20. The National Home Education Research Institute, "A Nationwide Study of Home Education: Family Characteristics, Legal Matters, and Student Achievement" (Seattle, WA, November 16, 1990). Study commissioned by the National Center for Home Education in Paeonian Springs, Virginia, and conducted by Dr. Brian Ray, reported in the *Home School Court Report*, Home School Legal Defense Association (December 1990).

21. *See* Patricia M. Lines, "Home Instruction: Characteristics, Size and Growth" (Washington, D.C.: Office of Research, U.S. Department of Education, 1987).

22. Shepherd, "The Home Schooling Movement," *supra* note 11, at 136.

23. *Id.* and sources cited therein.

24. "Nationwide Study," *supra* note 20, at 3.

25. Lines, "Home Instruction," *supra* note 21, at 10.

26. "Nationwide Study," *supra* note 20, at 4.

27. *Id.* The survey included nineteen denominations and an "Other" category from which the respondents to the survey could choose.

    The list included the following (with the percentages rounded): Adventist (1.2 percent), Amish (.5 percent), Assembly of God (7.6 percent), Baptist (18 percent), Catholic (3.3 percent), Episcopal (.3 percent), Independent Charismatic

(14.2 percent), Independent Fundamental/Evangelical (26.2 percent), Jewish (.1 percent), Latter Day Saints (Mormon) (.6 percent), Lutheran (1.2 percent), Mennonite (1 percent), Methodist (.9 percent), Muslim (0 percent), Nazarene (.9 percent), New Age (.3 percent), Pentecostal (2.8 percent), Presbyterian (2.8 percent), Reformed (2.6 percent), and "Other" (16.3 percent). As can be seen above, the five largest representations (excluding the "Other" category) came from the Independent Fundamental/Evangelical, Baptist, Independent Charismatic, Assembly of God, and Catholic denominations.

28. Guterson, *supra* note 17, at 59.
29. Dr. John Wesley Taylor V, "Self-Concept in Home-schooling Children," a study using randomized sample of 224 participants drawn from the mailing lists of two home schooling agencies, Holt Associates, Inc. and Hewitt Resource Foundation.

    Although this study focused upon socialization and self-concept in home school children, it also provided certain other demographic information on home school families. Dr. Taylor found that "[t]he educational level and socioeconomic status attained by home-school operators seems to be considerably higher . . . than that of the comparable general population." *Id.* Complete copies of this study (in book form) by Dr. Taylor may be obtained by writing to University Microfilms International, 300 N. Zeeb Rd., Ann Arbor, MI 48106.

    Dr. Lines has published her statistics regarding income in her study, "Home Instruction: Characteristics, Size and Growth," *supra* note 21, at 8-9.
30. "Nationwide Study," *supra* note 20, at 3.
31. *Id.*
32. Lines, "Home Instruction," *supra* note 21, p. 8.
33. Sheperd, "Dimensions" *supra* note 10, at 101-02.
34. Guterson, *supra* note 17, at 59.
35. Sonia K. Gustafson, "A Study of Home Schooling: Parental Motivations and Goals" (Woodrow Wilson School of Public and International Affairs, Princeton University, 1987).
36. Lines, *supra*, note 21, at 8.
37. Sheperd, *Dimensions*, *supra* note 10, at 104.
38. *Id. See also* Appendix, "Legislative Status."
39. *Id.* at 105. *See also* Sheperd, "The Home Schooling Movement," *supra* note 11, at 13.
40. Guterson, *supra* note 17, at 59. *See also* Gorder, *supra* note 5, at 11.
41. Gustafson, "A Study of Home Schooling: Parental Motivations and Goals," *supra* note 34, p. 1.
42. Taylor, "Self-concept in Home-schooling Children," *supra* note 30, at 2.
43. "Nationwide Study," *supra* note 20, at 3. This survey found that nearly 43 percent of parents involved in home school families have completed four or more years of college. The study also revealed that the average level of educational attainment for home schooling mothers was more than fourteen years of formal training, while the fathers had completed fifteen years of formal education. *Id.*
44. Gorder, *supra* note 5, at 11.
45. Alvin Toffler, *Future Shock* (New York: Random House, 1970), pp. 359-60.
46. Lines, "An Overview of Home Instruction," *supra* note 4, at 510.
47. *Id.*
48. David and Micki Colfax, *Homeschooling for Excellence* (New York: Warner Books, 1988), pp. 37-8.
49. Shepherd, "The Home Schooling Movement," supra note 11, at 160.
50. *Id.* at 160-61.

51. *Id.* at 158.
52. *Id.* at 48. Cook gives a slightly lower estimate, citing that "perhaps two-thirds of the parents who keep their kids home do so for religious reasons." Cook, *supra* note 19, at 107.
53. Shepherd, "The Home Schooling Movement," *supra* note 11, at 162-63.
54. *Id.* at 12. *See also* Lines, "Home Instruction: Characteristics, Size and Growth," *supra* note 21, at 8.
55. Gustafson, *supra* note 34, at 1.
56. *Id.*
57. 1980 Gallup Poll of the Public's Attitude Toward the Public Schools, cited in Gorder, .*supra* note 5, at 13. For a more detailed discussion of these issues, *see* Chapter One, "The Crisis in Contemporary Public Education."
58. *See* Chapter One, "The Crisis in Contemporary Public Education."
59. *See* Chapter Seven, "The Straw Men: Socialization and Academics."
60. *See* Chapter One, "The Crisis in Contemporary Public Education."
61. "Nationwide Study," *supra* note 20, at 5; *see also* Guterson, *supra* note 17, at 59; Eric Miller, "Home Schooling—Does It Pass the Test?," *Rural Living* (September 1991), p. 14.

    Virtually every study of the home schooling movement, even those conducted by state boards of education, reveals that home schoolers score significantly higher than the national average on standardized tests. For a detailed discussion of the academic performance of home school students, *see* Chapter Seven, "The Straw Men: Socialization and Academics."
62. *Id.*
63. Gorder, *supra* note 5, at 13. In its study of December 1990, the Home School Legal Defense Association cites some possible reasons for this significant gap in student achievement:

    > [T]he home education environment naturally causes higher achievement because of factors such as low student-to-teacher ratio, flexibility that is possible in a small, private setting, close contact between parent and child, and the enhanced opportunity to individualize curriculum and methodology to meet the gifts and limitations of a particular child. "Nationwide Study," *supra* note 20, at 5.

64. Gustafson, *supra* note 34, at 1.
65. "Research. Gifted Children in Home School," *The Moore Report* (July/August 1991), p. 1.
66. Shepherd, *Dimensions*, *supra* note 10, at 103, *citing* Hal Bennett, *No More Public School* (New York: Random House, 1972), Chapter 1.
67. John Holt, *Teach Your Own* (New York: Delacorte Press, 1981), Chapter 1.
68. *Id.*
69. Whitehead and Bird, *supra* note 8, at 98.
70. Raymond Moore, "Home Schooling: An Idea Whose Time Has Returned," *Human Events* (September 15, 1984), p. 12-3.
71. Raymond Moore, "Research and Common Sense: Therapies for Homes and Schools," 84 *Teachers College Record* (Winter 1982), p. 372.
72. Moore, "Home Schooling," *supra* note 70.
73. Guterson, *supra* note 17, at 60.
74. Miller, *supra* note 31, at 13. The research of Gustafson supports these reasons of flexibility and informality as well. Gustafson, *supra* note 34.
75. *See generally* Whitehead and Bird, *supra* note 8.
76. Gorder, *supra* note 5.
77. *Id. citing* a 1989 Priority Management Systems Report.

78. Welch and Short, "Home School Questions and Answers," *The Teaching Home* (April/May 1991), p. 7.
79. Gorder, *supra* note 5, at 14.
80. For a detailed discussion of the socialization issue, *see* Chapter Seven, "The Straw Men: Socialization and Academics."
81. Shepherd, *Dimensions, supra* note 10, at 107.
82. *Id.* at 108. *See also* Gustafson, *supra* note 34, at 2.
83. *Id.*
84. Holt, *supra* note 66, at 49-50.
85. Shepherd, *Dimensions, supra* note 10, at 108.
86. *Id.*
87. Guterson, *supra* note 17, at 62.
88. Taylor, *supra* note 30, at 1.
89. *Id.*
90. Guterson, *supra* note 17, at 60.
91. Cook, *supra* note 19, at 109.
92. "Nationwide Study," *supra* note 20, at 2.
93. *Id.* at 3.
94. On standardized achievement tests, the home schooled students performed at or above the 80th percentile on national norms in terms of their reading, listening, language, math, science, social studies, basic battery, and complete battery scores. "Nationwide Study," *supra* note 20, at 1.
95. Shepherd, *Dimensions, supra* note 10, at 113.

CHAPTER SEVEN: *The Straw Men: Socialization and Academics*

1. Brian D. Ray, "A Comparison of Home Schooling and Conventional Schooling: With a Focus On Learner Outcomes" (hereinafter, "A Comparison"), p. 16. (Paper presented in partial fulfillment of the comprehensive written examinations for the doctoral degree in the Science, Math, and Computer Science Education Department at Oregon State University, 1986) (ERIC Document Reproduction Service No. ED 278 489).
2. Brian D. Ray, "Home Schools: A Synthesis of Research on Characteristics and Learner Outcomes" (hereinafter, "A Synthesis"), p. 21 *Education and Urban Society* (November 1988), p. 21.
3. F. E. Perkel, "The Effects of a Home Instruction Program on the Cognitive Growth of a Selected Group of 4-year-olds" (doctoral dissertation, University of Southern California, 1979), *Dissertation Abstracts International*, Vol. 40, p. 1859A, *cited in* Ray, "A Comparison," *supra* note 1, at 20-2.
4. A discussion and critique of the research design and methodology involved in Perkel's study and the Leiter International Performance Scale can be found in Ray, "A Comparison," *supra* note 1, at 20-2. In this paper Brian Ray provides critical evaluation of the research design and methodology of most of the studies to be presented in this chapter. A general discussion of the use of standardized tests in evaluating home schooling effectiveness and some comments on the research designs utilized in the home schooling research will follow later in the chapter.

    For more about specific standardized tests, *see Mental Measurements Yearbooks*, O. K. Buros, ed. (Highland Park, NJ: The Gryphon Press, 1938-1978):

    The *Mental Measurements Yearbooks* . . . are a series of eight yearbooks which critically evaluate most of the currently available published tests. Each yearbook supplements rather than replaces the earlier editions, so that it is occasionally necessary to consult earlier volumes to obtain complete coverage of a test. One or more experts review tests especially for the MMYs, and the yearbook gives excerpted journal reviews as well. . . . In addition, each review entry contains test title, age or grade levels, publication date(s), special comments, number and type part scores, author(s), publishers, references, and bibliographic information. There are 1,184 tests listed. The MMYs also list recent books on testing and include excerpted book reviews. Names and addresses of 309 test publishers are listed in the 8th MMY.

Anthony J. Nitko, *Educational Tests and Measurement: An Introduction* (New York: Harcourt Brace Jovanovich, Inc., 1983), pp. 482-3.

5. Perkel, "Effects," *supra* note 3, *cited in* Ray, "A Comparison," *supra* note 1, at 21.

It is important to understand the definition of the term "significant difference" as it is used in educational and psychological research studies. *Significant difference* is a statistical concept. When a study reports that a significant difference between two groups was found, it means the null hypothesis has been rejected. The null hypothesis states there is no difference between the two groups. Thus, when statistics demonstrate there is a significant difference, the null hypothesis is rejected, signifying there is a difference between the two groups. In Perkel's study, no significant differences were found between the home-based and preschool groups, and the null hypothesis was accepted.

A significant difference indicates that the difference occurring between the groups is a true difference rather than a random occurrence. It is important not to assign more meaning or weight to a significant difference than it merits. A significant difference does not provide any information about cause and effect. For example, when a significant difference is found between two groups it does not prove the researcher's hypothesis is correct. It may be that another variable or an interaction between several variables is the reason or cause for the difference and not the variable or cause the researcher postulated.

6. Ray, "A Comparison," *supra* note 1, at 22.

7. B. Tizard, M. Hughes, G. Pinkerton, and H. Carmichael, "Adults' Cognitive Demands at Home and at Nursery School," 23 *Journal of Child Psychology and Psychiatry* (1982), pp. 105-16, *cited in* Ray, "A Comparison," *supra* note 1, at 22-4.

8. Ray, "A Comparison," *supra* note 1, at 22.

9. *Id.*, at 23.

10. B. Tizard, M. Hughes, H. Carmichael, and G. Pinkerton, "Children's Questions and Adults' Answers," 24 *Journal of Child Psychology and Psychiatry* (1983), p. 276, *cited in* Ray, "A Comparison," *supra* note 1, at 24-6.

11. Ray, "A Comparison," *supra* note 1, at 24.

12. *Id.* at 25.

13. B. Tizard, M. Hughes, H. Carmichael, and G. Pinkerton, "Language and Social Class: Is Verbal Deprivation a Myth?," 24 *Journal of Child Psychology and Psychiatry* (1983), pp. 533-42, *cited in* Ray, "A Comparison," *supra* note 1, at 26-7.

14. Ray, "A Comparison," *supra* note 1, at 26.

15. *Id.* at 26-7.

16. *Id.* at 27.

17. *Id.* at 27-8.

18. Western Australia Department of Education, *Innovations in Rural Education: The Isolated Students Matriculation Scheme in Western Australia and the*

Chidley Educational Centre (Western Australia: author, 1979), cited in Ray, "A Comparison," *supra* note 1, at 29, in Ray, "A Synthesis," *supra* note 2, at 22, and in Brian D. Ray and Jon Wartes, "The Academic Achievement and Affective Development of Home-schooled Children," in *Home Schooling: Political, Historical, and Pedagogical Perspectives*, Jane Van Galen and Mary Anne Pittman, eds. (Norwood, NJ: Ablex Publishing Corporation, 1991), p. 52.

19. Ray and Wartes, *supra* note 18, at 52.
20. Ray, "A Comparison," *supra* note 1, at 29.
21. Western Australia Department of Education, *supra* note 18, at 16, *cited in* Ray, "A Synthesis," *supra* note 2, at 22.
22. Ray, "A Synthesis," *supra* note 2, at 22.
23. G. A. Gustavsen, "Selected Characteristics of Home Schools and Parents Who Operate Them" (doctoral dissertation, Andrews University, 1981), *Dissertation Abstracts International*, Vol. 42, pp. 4381A, 4382A, *cited in* Ray, "A Comparison," *supra* note 1, at 5-7, 28, and Ray, "A Synthesis," *supra* note 2, at 22.
24. Gustavsen, *supra* note 23, at 4381A, 4382A, *cited in* Ray, "A Comparison," *supra* note 1, at 28.
25. Ray, "A Comparison," *supra* note 1, at 28.
26. N. J. F. Linden, "An Investigation of Alternative Education: Home Schooling" (doctoral dissertation, East Texas State University, 1983), *Dissertation Abstracts International*, Vol. 44, p. 3547A, *cited in* Ray, "A Comparison," *supra* note 1, at 7-8, 29-30.
27. Ray, "A Comparison," *supra* note 1, at 30.
28. Washington State Superintendent of Public Instruction, *Washington State's Experimental Programs Using the Parent as Tutor Under the Supervision of Washington State Certified Teacher, 1984-1985* (Olympia, WA: author, 1985). Study described in Brian D. Ray, "Parent as Tutor Experimental Program in Washington State," 1 *Home School Researcher* No. 4 (December 1985), pp. 29-31 (ERIC Document Reproduction Service No. ED 307 016) (hereinafter "Parent as Tutor").
29. Ray, "Parent as Tutor," *supra* note 28, at 29-30.
30. *Id.*
31. *Id* at 30.
32. Washington State Superintendent of Public Instruction, *supra* note 28, *cited in* Patricia M. Lines, "An Overview of Home Instruction," 68 *Phi Delta Kappan* (March 1987), p. 513, and Ray, "A Synthesis," *supra* note 2, at 22.

    The following definition and interpretation of percentiles (percentile ranks) may be beneficial: "The *percentile rank* is a *number that tells what percentage of the persons in a defined group have scored lower than the raw score in question.*" Anthony J. Nitko, *Educational Tests and Measurement: An Introduction, supra* note 4, at 72.

    For example, if a student received a raw score of 46 and was told he or she scored in the 84th percentile, it means 84 percent of the class or group taking the test scored lower than the student. Scoring in the 50th percentile is interpreted as an average score as 50 percent of the scores in the group fall below this score. Scoring above the 50th percentile is interpreted as scoring above average.
33. Ray, "Parent as Tutor," *supra* note 28, at 30.

    Definitions and interpretations of the median and quartiles may prove helpful in understanding the findings. "The *median* is *the point on the score-scale which is so located that the same number of scores are above it as are below it.*" Nitko, *supra* note 4, at 59. The median is ". . . not affected by the numerical values of extremely high or low scores" and can be viewed as being representative of the "typical score" of a group. *Id.* at 63.

Quartiles are special percentiles; the second quartile is "the score point below which fifty percent of the scores fall," or the 50th percentile. *Id.* at 73. The third quartile is "the score point below which seventy-five percent of the scores fall," or the 75th percentile. *Id.* Thus, scoring between the second and third quartiles is interpreted to be above average.

34. Ray, "Parent as Tutor," *supra* note 28, at 30.
35. P. L. Reynolds, "How Home School Families Operate on a Day-to-day Basis: Three Case Studies" (unpublished doctoral dissertation, Brigham Young University, 1985), *cited in* Ray and Wartes, *supra* note 18, at 48.

A case study is a type of research design in which a single subject, group or phenomenon is studied in detail commonly through observational methods.

Most case studies are based on the premise that a case can be located that is typical of many other cases; that is, the case is viewed as an example of a class of events or a group of individuals. Once such a case has been located, it follows that in-depth observations of the single case can provide insights into the class of events from which the case has been drawn. Of course, there is no way of knowing how typical the selected case really is, and it is therefore rather hazardous to draw any general conclusions from a single case study. The main justification for case studies is that they have the potential to generate rich subjective data that can aid in the development of theory and empirically testable hypotheses.

Walter R. Borg and Meredith Damien Gall, *Educational Research: An Introduction* (New York: Longman, Inc., 1983), pp. 488-89.
36. Ray and Wartes, *supra* note 18, at 48.
37. P. L. Reynolds and D. D. Williams, *The Daily Operations of a Home School Family: A Case Study*. Paper presented at the Annual Meeting of American Educational Research Association, 1985. (ERIC Document Reproduction Service No. ED 256 080), *cited in* Ray, "A Comparison," *supra* note 1, at 32.
38. Ray, "A Comparison," *supra* note 1, at 32.
39. B. A. S. Schemmer, "Case Studies of Four Families Engaged in Home Education" (unpublished doctoral dissertation, Ball State University, 1985), *cited in* Ray and Wartes, *supra* note 18, at 48.
40. Ray and Wartes, *supra* note 18, at 48.
41. Ray, "A Comparison," *supra* note 1, at 30-1, *citing* Hewitt Research Foundation, "North Dakota Trial Results Pending," 3 *The Parent Educator and Family Report* No. 2 (1985), p. 5, and Hewitt Research Foundation, "Study of Home Schoolers Taken to Court," 4 *The Parent Educator and Family Report* No. 1 (1986), p. 2.
42. Hewitt Research Foundation, "On Home-schooling Figures and Scores," 4 *The Parent Educator and Family Report* No. 2 (1986), pp. 1-2, *cited in* Ray, "A Comparison," *supra* note 1, at 31.
43. Ray, "A Comparison," *supra* note 1, at 31.
44. Eugene A. Frost and Robert C. Morris, "Does Home-schooling Work? Some Insights for Academic Success," 59 *Contemporary Education* No. 4 (Summer 1988), p. 224. It is unclear whether Frost and Morris are referring to the 1986 study discussed above, as they do not cite a reference for or date of the study. In the 1986 study discussed above, Brian D. Ray reports no sample size was given in *The Parent Educator and Family Report* article in which the study was described. Since Frost and Morris's article gives a sample size for the study they describe, it would seem this is a separate study.
45. Frost and Morris, *supra* note 44, at 224.

46. M. M. Madden, ed., "Home Study by Correspondence," 7 *Method: Alaskan Perspectives* No. 1 (1986), *cited in* Ray, "A Comparison," *supra* note 1, at 33.
47. Frost and Morris, *supra* note 44, at 224.
48. *Id.*
49. Ray, "A Comparison," *supra* note 1, at 33.
50. Alaska Department of Education, *Summary of SRA Testing for Centralized Correspondence Study April/May 1984* (Juneau, AK: author, 1984), *cited in* Ray, "A Comparison," *supra* note 1, at 35.
51. *Id.*
52. Alaska Department of Education, *supra* note 50, *cited in* Ray, "A Synthesis," *supra* note 2, at 23.
53. *Id.*
54. Ray, "A Comparison," *supra* note 1, at 36, *citing* Alaska Department of Education, *supra* note 50.
55. B. Falle, "Standardized Tests for Home Study Students: Administration and Results," 7 *Method: Alaskan Perspectives* (1986), 22-24, *cited in* Ray, "A Synthesis," *supra* note 2, at 23.
56. Ray, "A Comparison," *supra* note 1, at 36-7, *citing* Alaska Department of Education, *supra* note 50.
57. Ray, "A Comparison," *supra* note 1, at 33.
58. *Id.*
59. *Id.* at 34. Some information on the statistical concepts of the standard deviation and the theoretical distribution (also referred to as normal distribution, normal curve and bell-shaped curve) may aid the reader in understanding the study's findings.

The standard deviation is a statistical measure which describes the variability of scores about a central measure, the mean (or average). The standard deviation "is a measure of the extent to which scores in a distribution, on average, deviate from their mean." Borg and Gall, *Educational Research: An Introduction, supra* note 35, at 365.

A relationship exists between the standard deviation and the theoretical or normal distribution. Typically when frequency distributions of achievement test scores are graphed, with the horizontal axis (or baseline) designating scores and the vertical axis designating the number of students receiving particular scores, a normal distribution or curve results.

A normal curve, often referred to as a bell-shaped curve because of its shape, is symmetrical, with the majority of scores clustered close to the mean and increasingly fewer scores occurring further from the mean. The horizontal axis or baseline can be divided into equal units. "Each unit is one standard deviation in length. It can be shown mathematically that, if a distribution of scores forms a normal curve, each standard deviation above or below the mean will include a fixed percentage of the scores." *Id.* at 366. These percentages can also be converted into percentiles.
60. Sue Green, "Research on Alaska Home Schoolers," in J. Holt and D. Richoux, eds., *Growing Without Schooling* No. 40, p. 11 (available from Growing Without Schooling, 729 Boylston Street, Boston, Massachusetts 02116), *cited* in Frost and Morris, *supra* note 44, at 224.

While it appears this is a description of the same 1986 published report from the Alaska Department of Education utilizing 1981 data, Frost and Morris do not supply an Alaska Department of Education reference for this study and this assumption cannot be confirmed.
61. Ray, "A Synthesis," *supra* note 2, at 24.

62. The Illinois study was cited in Frost and Morris, _supra_ note 44, at 225-26. However, Frost and Morris do not supply a reference for this study.

63. Frost and Morris, _supra_ note 44, at 225.

64. _Id._

65. _Id._

66. _Id._

67. _Id._

68. _Id._ at 226.

69. _Id._

70. _Id._

71. _Id._

72. Ray and Wartes, _supra_ note 18, at 47, _citing_ L. A. Scogin, _Home School Survey_ (1986).

73. Mona Maarse Delahooke, "Home Educated Children's Social/Emotional Adjustment and Academic Achievement: A Comparative Study" (doctoral dissertation, California School of Professional Psychology, 1986), _Dissertation Abstracts International_, Vol. 47, p. 475A.

74. _Id._ at 44.

75. _Id._ at 44-5.

76. _Id._ at 45.

77. _Id._ at 46-7.

78. _Id._ at 59, 62.

79. _Id._ at 82.

80. Ray, "A Synthesis," _supra_ note 2, at 20, _citing_ S. Feinstein, "Domestic Lessons: Shunning the Schools, More Parents Teach their Kids at Home," _The Wall Street Journal_ (October 6, 1986), pp. 1, 17.

81. Ray and Wartes, _supra_ note 18, at 49.

82. _Id._, _citing_ Arkansas Department of Education, _Arkansas Department of Education News Release, July 21, 1986_ (Little Rock, AR: author, 1986), and Arkansas Department of Education, _Arkansas Department of Education, News Release, July 27, 1987_ (Little Rock, AR: author, 1987).

83. Oregon Department of Education, _December 1, 1986 Homeschool Data Report_ (Salem, OR: author, 1986), _cited in_ Ray and Wartes, _supra_ note 18, at 49.

84. Ray and Wartes, _supra_ note 18, at 49.

85. _Id._ at 50. Information taken from Table 2.1.

86. Oregon Department of Education, _March 1, 1988 Homeschool Data Report_ (Salem, OR: author, 1988), _cited in_ Ray and Wartes, _supra_ note 18, at 49.

87. Ray and Wartes, _supra_ note 18, at 50.

88. Patricia M. Lines, "An Overview of Home Instruction," 68 _Phi Delta Kappan_ No. 7 (March 1987), p. 513. No reference for the study was given in the article.

89. Jennie Finlayson Rakestraw, "An Analysis of Home Schooling for Elementary School-age Children in Alabama" (doctoral dissertation, University of Alabama, 1987), p. 64, _Dissertation Abstracts International_, Vol. 49, p. 725.

90. Rakestraw, _supra_ note 88, at 67.

91. _Id._ at 62.

92. _Id._ at 63.

93. _Id._ at 65.

94. _Id._ at 64-5.

95. _Id._ at 65-6, 68.

96. _Id._ at 66-7.

97. Ray and Wartes, _supra_ note 18, at 47.

98. Rakestraw, _supra_ note 88, at 127-28.

99. _Id._ at 138.

100. *Id.* at 129.
101. *Id.*
102. *Id.*
103. *Id.* at 80, 82.
104. *Id.* at 130.
105. *Id.*
106. *Id.* at 84.
107. *Id.* at 131-32.
108. Ray and Wartes, *supra* note 18, at 49.
109. *Id.*
110. *Id.*, at 49-50, *citing* Tennessee Department of Education, *Tennessee Statewide Averages, Home School Student Test Results, Stanford Achievement Test, Grades 2, 5, 7, and 9* (Nashville: author, 1988).
111. Jon Wartes, "The Washington Home School Project: Quantitative Measures for Informing Policy Decisions," 21 *Education and Urban Society* No. 1 (November 1988), p. 42.
112. Ray and Wartes, *supra* note 18, at 44.
113. *Id.* at 44-5.
114. *Id.* at 45.
115. Wartes, *supra* note 110, at 46.
116. Ray and Wartes, *supra* note 18, at 45.
117. Wartes, *supra* note 110, at 47.
118. *Id.* at 47-8.
119. *Id.* at 48.
120. *Id.*
121. *Id.*
122. *Id.* at 49.
123. *Id.*
124. *Id.*
125. Frost and Morris, *supra* note 44, at 224. The authors of this article do not provide a reference for the study, and the date of the study is unknown; therefore, this writer has taken the liberty of listing the date of the study as the date of the article.
126. *Id.*
127. David Neal Quine and Edmund A. Marek, "Reasoning Abilities of Home-educated Children," in 4 *Home School Researcher* No. 3 (Brian D. Ray, ed.) (September 1988), p. 3 (ERIC Document Reproduction Service No. ED 329).
128. *Id.*
129. *Id.* at 2.
130. *Id.* at 2-3.
131. *Id.* at 3.
132. *Id.* For more information on the learning cycle teaching procedure, *see* J. W. Renner and E. A. Marek, *The Learning Cycle and Elementary School Science Teaching* (Portsmouth, NH: Heinemann Educational Books, Inc., 1988).
133. Quine and Marek, *supra* note 126, at 3. For more information on Piaget's model, *see* B. Inhelder and J. Piaget, *The Growth of Logical Thinking from Childhood to Adolescence* (New York: Basic Books, Inc., 1958).
134. Howard Gardner, *Developmental Psychology: An Introduction* (Boston: Little, Brown and Company, 1982), p. 67.
135. *Id.*
136. *Id.*
137. Quine and Marek, *supra* note 126, at 6.
138. *Id.* at 3-4.

139. *Id.* at 4.
140. *Id.*
141. *Id.*
142. *Id.*
143. *Id.*
144. *Id.*
145. *Id.*
146. *Id.*
147. *Id.* at 4-5.
148. *Id.* at 5.
149. *Id.*
150. *Id.* at 5-6. For more information regarding the age children enter into and leave the concrete operational stage, *see* Jean Piaget, *Psychology of Intelligence* (Patterson, NJ: Littlefield and Adams, 1963), p. 148, and Jean Piaget, "Intellectual Evolution from Adolescence to Adulthood," 15 *Human Development* No. 1 (1972), pp. 10-24.
151. Quine and Marek, *supra* note 126, at 6.
152. *Id.*
153. *Id.*
154. *Id.* at 6-7.
155. Ray and Wartes, *supra* note 18, at 52.
156. Schemmer, *supra* note 39, *cited in* Ray and Wartes, *supra* note 18, at 56.
157. Reynolds, *supra* note 35, *cited in* Ray and Wartes, *supra* note 18, at 56.
158. Ray and Wartes, *supra* note 18, at 56.
159. John Wesley Taylor V., "Self-Concept in Home schooling Children" (doctoral dissertation, Andrews University, 1986), p. 53, *Dissertation Abstracts International*, Vol. 47, p. 2809.
160. Taylor, *supra* note 158, at 180-81.
161. *Id.* at 181-82.
162. *Id.* at 186-89.
163. Delahooke, *supra* note 72, at 475.
164. *Id.* at 48.
165. *Id.* at 50.
166. *Id.* at 51.
167. *Id.* at 82.
168. The phrase "trend toward significance" means the data indicated a pattern or relationship between two variables, but the relationship *was not* shown to be statistically significant.
169. Delahooke, *supra* note 72, at 83.
170. *Id.* at 85.
171. *Id.*
172. *Id.* (emphasis supplied by the author).
173. Rakestraw, *supra* note 88, at 725.
174. Jon Wartes, *Washington Homeschool Research Project Report from the 1986 Homeschool Testing and Other Descriptive Information about Washington's Homeschoolers* (Woodinville, WA: author, 1987), *cited in* Ray and Wartes, *supra* note 18, at 54 and in Ray, "A Synthesis," *supra* note 2, at 25.
175. Ray, "A Synthesis," *supra* note 2, at 25, *citing* Wartes, *supra* note 173.
176. Ray and Wartes, *supra* note 18, at 55, *citing* Wartes, *supra* note 173.
177. S. K. Gustafson, "A Study of Home Schooling: Parental Motivation and Goals," 4 *Home School Researcher* No. 2, pp. 4-12 (ERIC Document Reproduction Service No. ED 307 016), *cited in* Ray and Wartes, *supra* note 18, at 56-7.

178. Linda Montgomery, "The Effect of Home Schooling on the Leadership Skills of Home Schooled Students," 5 *Home School Researcher* No. 1 (March 1989), p. 36 (ERIC Document Reproduction Service No. ED 329).

179. Bernard M. Bass, *Leadership, Psychology, and Organizational Behavior* (Westport, CT: Greenwood Press Publishers, 1960), *cited in* Montgomery, *supra* note 177, at 37.

180. Montgomery, *supra* note 177, at 37.

181. *Id.* at 38.

182. *Id.*

183. *Id.*, pp. 40-1.

184. *Id.* at 41.

185. *Id.*

186. *Id.* at 42.

187. *Id.*

188. *Id.* at 43.

189. *Id.*

190. *Id.*

191. *Id.* at 43-4.

192. April Dawn Chatham, "Home vs. Public Schooling: What About Relationships in Adolescence?" (doctoral dissertation, University of Oklahoma, 1991), *Dissertation Abstracts International*, Vol. 52, p. 2100.

193. *Id.*

194. *Id.*

195. *Id.*

196. Ray and Wartes, *supra* note 18, at 57.

197. Ray, "A Comparison," *supra* note 1, at 45-7.

198. Gregory J. Cizek, "Applying Standardized Testing to Home-based Education Programs: Reasonable or Customary?," 7 *Educational Measurement Issues and Practice* No. 3 (Fall 1988), p. 12.

199. *Id.* at 15. Norm-referenced tests compare an individual's performance on a particular test with the performance of others on the test (the norm group). A norm-referenced test "reflects the position of an examinee in a group which took the test." Nitko, *supra* note 4, at 24. This provides a reference for the individual's performance on a test and make the individual's score more meaningful. "When absolute interpretations of test performance are required—for example, when instructional decisions about learners need to be made," norm-referenced tests are insufficient. *Id.* at 357.

200. Cizek, *supra* note 197, at 15. Mr. Cizek is quoting from: American Educational Research Association, American Psychological Association, and National Council on Measurement in Education, *Standards for Educational and Psychological Testing* (Washington, D.C.: American Psychological Association, 1985).

201. Cizek, *supra* note 197, at 15. The term "negatively skewed" means the majority of the group received high scores.

202. *Id.* at 16.

203. *Id.*

204. *Id.*

205. *Id.*

206. *Id.*

207. *Id.* Reliability refers to consistency of test scores; that is, a test taker should receive approximately the same test score if he/she took the test several times in order for the test to be reliable.

208. *Id.* Validity of a test means the test is measuring the construct it is designed to measure; for example, an intelligence test would measure intelligence. If a test is valid it is a true measure of the construct.

209. *Id.*

210. *Id.* at 17.

211. Criterion-referenced tests describe "the performance repertoire of an examinee—the kinds of tasks an examinee with that score is able to do." Nitko, *supra* note 4, p. 24.

212. Cizek, *supra* note 197, at 16.

213. *Id.* at 17-8.

214. *Id.* at 18, *citing* L. B. Resnick, "Introduction: Research to Inform a Debate," 62 *Phi Delta Kappan* (1981), p. 624; D. P. Resnick and L. B. Resnick, "Standards, Curriculum, and Performance: A Historical and Comparative Perspective," 14 *Educational Researcher* (1985), p. 11; D. Freeman, T. Kuhs, L. Knappen, and A. Porter, *A Closer Look at Standardized Tests*, Research Series No. 53 (East Lansing, MI: Michigan State University, Institute for Research on Teaching, 1979), pp. 2, 11.

215. *Id.*

216. *Id.*

217. *Id.*

218. For specific information on the weaknesses of pre-experimental designs, *see* Donald T. Campbell and Julian C. Stanley, *Experimental and Quasi-experimental Designs for Research* (Chicago, IL: Rand McNally College Publishing Company, 1963).

A critique of home school research appears in Cheryl Wright, "Home School Research: Critique and Suggestions for the Future," 21 *Education and Urban Society* No. 1 (November 1988), pp. 96-113.

219. Ray and Wartes, *supra* note 18, at 59.

220. *Id.* at 59-60.

CHAPTER EIGHT: *American Patterns*

1. Isidore Stan, Lewis Paul Todd, and Merle Curtis, *Living American Documents* (New York: Harcourt, Brace, and World, 1961), p. 5.

2. *See generally* Perry Miller, *The New England Mind—The Seventeenth Century* (Cambridge, MA: Harvard University Press, 1954); *The Puritans* (New York: Harper and Row, 1963); *Orthodoxy in Massachusetts, 1630-1650* (Cambridge: Harvard University Press, 1933).

3. Willystine Goodsell, *A History of the Family as a Social and Educational Institution* (New York: Macmillan, 1915), p. 353.

4. George Haskins, *Law and Authority in Early Massachusetts* (New York: Macmillan, 1960), p. 80.

5. Edmund Morgan, *The Puritan Family: Religion and Domestic Relations in Seventeenth Century New England* (New York: Harper and Row, 1966), pp. 42-6, 106. *Also see* Arthur Calhoun, *A Social History of the American Family from Colonial Times to the Present*, Vol. 1 (New York: Arno Press, 1973), pp. 41, 47, 83; Goodsell, *supra* note 3, at 353.

6. Haskins, *supra* note 4, at 80.

7. Calhoun, *supra* note 5, at 75.

8. *Id.* at 51.

9. Morgan, *supra* note 5, at 25-8, 106; Goodsell, *supra* note 3, at 353; Calhoun, *supra* note 5, at 41, 47, 83. *Also see* Susan Tiffin, *In Whose Best Interest* (Westport, CT: Greenwood Press, 1982), p. 16.

10. Lawrence Cremin, *American Education: The Colonial Experience, 1607-1783* (New York: Harper and Row, 1970), p. 40. Cremin notes that the Bible, throughout the Seventeenth Century, remained the single most important influence in the lives of Anglo-Americans.

11. Calhoun, *supra* note 5, at 41, 47, 83. On p. 72, Calhoun quotes the Colonial Records of Connecticut (1643) on this point: "The prosperity and well being of the Commonwealth doth much depend upon the well government and ordering of particular families, which in an ordinary way cannot be expected when rules of God are neglected in laying the foundation of a family state." *Also see* Morgan, *supra* note 5, at 25-8, 106. Tiffin, *supra* note 9, at 16. Goodsell, *supra* note 3, at 353.

12. Calhoun, *supra* note 5.

13. Cremin, *supra* note 10, at 50.

14. *Id.* at 51, 52.

15. *Id.* at 51.

16. *Id.* at 124.

17. Calhoun, *supra* note 5, at 67.

18. Cremin, *supra* note 10, at 124.

19. *Id.* at 135.

20. *Id.* at 135, 136.

21. *Id.* at 128.

22. Morgan, *supra* note 5, at 87-108. *See also* Ellwood Cubberly, *The History of Education* (New York: Houghton Mifflin, Co., 1920), pp. 374, 360. Calhoun, *supra* note 5, at 75.

23. Cremin, *supra* note 10, at 130. The texts used included *The New England Primer* (1690), *The Westminster Catechism* (1647), and John Cotton's *Milk for Babes, Drawn Out of the Breasts of Both Testaments* (1646).

24. Cremin, *supra* note 10, at 49.

25. Harvey Wish, *Society and Thought in Early America* (New York: Longmans Green, 1950), p. 55.

26. Calhoun, *supra* note 5, at 110.

27. Cremin, *supra* note 10, at 133.

28. Calhoun, *supra* note 5, at 124.

29. *See* E. Alice Beshoner, "Home Education in America: Parental Rights Reasserted," 49 UMKC Law Review 191, 191-92 (1981).

30. Massachusetts School Law of 1647, *Records of the Governor and Company of Massachusetts Bay in New England*, 1647, Vol. 11, p. 203. *See also* Henry Steele Commager, ed., *Documents of American History* (New York: Appleton-Century-Crofts, Inc., 1949), p. 29. *See also* Chapter Two, "The History and Philosophy of Public Education," and Chapter Five, "The Historical Perspective."

31. *Records, supra* note 30, at 203.

32. Cubberly, *supra* note 22, at 365, 366. Beshoner, *supra* note 29, at 191, 192.

33. Cremin, *supra* note 10, at 129. *Also see* William T. Davis, *History of the Town of Plymouth* (Philadelphia: J. W. Lewis & Co., 1885), p. 52.

34. Haskins, *supra* note 4, at 78-81. Cubberly, *supra* note 22, at 365, 374. It was literally a state-church, with the state being a servant of the church.

35. *See* Thomas Barnes, *The Book of the General Lawes and Libertyes Concerning the Inhabitants of the Massachusetts* (San Marino, CA: The Huntington Library, facsimile of the 1648 edition, 1975), p. 6.

36. Haskins, *supra* note 4, at 79. *See for example* the preamble or introduction of the General Court to the Inhabitants of Massachusetts, in *The Book of the*

General Lawes and Libertyes Concerning the Inhabitants of the Massachusetts (Cambridge, 1648), p. A-2.

37. Haskins, *supra* note 4, at 81.
38. Calhoun, *supra* note 5, at 71.
39. Goodsell, *supra* note 3, at 397.
40. Haskins, *supra* note 4, at 81. Calhoun, *supra* note 5, at 119.
41. Calhoun, *supra* note 5, at 119. Goodsell, *supra* note 3, at 400.
42. As quoted in Calhoun, *supra* note 5, at 119.
43. *The Book of the General Lawes and Libertyes*, *supra* note 36, at 6.
44. Haskins, *supra* note 4, at 81. Calhoun, *supra* note 5, at 121.
45. *The Book of the General Lawes and Libertyes*, *supra* note 36, at 6.
46. Calhoun, *supra* note 5, at 77. Haskins, *supra* note 4, at 81.
47. Calhoun, *supra* note 5, at 77.
48. *Id.* at 120.
49. *The Book of the General Lawes and Libertyes*, *supra* note 36, at 12.
50. Calhoun, *supra* note 5, at 74.
51. Massachusetts School Law of 1642, *Records of the Governor and Company of Massachusetts Bay in New England*, (June 14, 1642), pp. 6, 7.
52. *The Book of the General Lawes and Libertyes*, *supra* note 36, at 11.
53. *Id.*
54. *Id.*
55. *Id.*
56. Cremin, *supra* note 10, at 124.
57. *Id.* at 119. Similarly, in England, King Henry VIII ordered parsons and vicars to admonish parents to "teach children regarding the Christian faith." *Id.*
58. *Id.* at 125.
59. *Id.*
60. Calhoun, *supra* note 5, at 74.
61. Cremin, *supra* note 10, at 125.
62. Beshoner, *supra* note 29, at 191.
63. John Miller, *The First Frontier: Life in Colonial America* (New York: Delacorte Press, 1966), pp. 224, 225. The same was also true in the southern colonies. Cremin, *supra* note 10, at 135, 136. *Also see* Calhoun, *supra* note 5, at 229-44.
64. Calhoun, *supra* note 5, at 75.
65. Lawrence Kotin and William Aikman, *Legal Foundations of Compulsory School Attendance* (Port Washington, NY: Kennikat Press, 1980), p. 20.
66. *Id.* at 20, 21.
67. Newton Edwards and Herman Richey, *The School in the American Social Order* (Boston: Houghton Mifflin Co., 1947), pp. 108, 109. Other reasons suggested are the impracticalities of enforcement in frontier America and the social breakdown due to the Indian wars. Kotin and Aikman, *supra* note 65, at 22, 23.
68. Edwards and Richey, *supra* note 67, at 108, 109; Kotin and Aikman, *supra* note 65, at 23.
69. *Id.* at 20, 21.

CHAPTER NINE: *The Early American Family*

1. Willystine Goodsell, *A History of the Family as a Social and Educational Institution* (New York: Macmillan, 1915), p. 353; Lawrence Cremin, *American Education: The Colonial Experience, 1607-1783* (New York: Harper and Row, 1970), pp. 479-85.

2. Arthur Calhoun, *A Social History of the American Family from Colonial Times to the Present*, Vol. 11 (New York: Arno Press, 1973), pp. 54, 138; Cremin, *supra* note 1, at 479-85.

3. Calhoun, *supra* note 2, at 229-44.

4. Cremin, *American Education*, *supra* note 1, at 124.

5. *Id.* at 479-485.

6. Calhoun, *supra* note 2, at 11.

7. *Id.*

8. Cremin, *American Education*, *supra* note 1, at 480, 481.

9. *Id.* at 113.

10. *Id.* at 135.

11. *Id.* at 479-85, 113, 124-29, 135; Lawrence Cremin, *The American Common School, An Historic Conception* (New York: Bureau of Publications, Teachers College, Columbia University, 1951), pp. 87, 88.

12. Cremin, *The American Common School*, *supra* note 11, at 87, 88.

13. *Id.* at 88.

14. Cremin, *American Education*, *supra* note 1, at 478-85, 113, 124-29, 135.

15. John C. Fitzpatrick, *George Washington Himself* (Indianapolis: Bobbs-Merrill Co., 1933), p. 19.

16. Cremin, *American Education*, *supra* note 1, at 483.

17. *Id.*

18. *Id.*

19. Carl Van Doren, *Benjamin Franklin* (The Hadden Craftsman, 1938) p. 11-2.

20. John C. Fitzpatrick, ed., *The Writings of George Washington*, Vol. 3 (Washington, D.C.: United States Government Printing Office, 1932), p. 130.

21. Cremin, *American Education*, *supra* note 1, at 486.

22. *Diary of Cotton Mather*, Vol. 1 (New York: Frederick Ungar Pub. Co., 1957), pp. 534-37.

23. Cremin, *American Education*, *supra* note 1, at 482-83.

24. *Id.* at 483.

25. *Id.* at 479, 549, 550.

26. *Id.*

27. James Tobak and Perry Zirkel, *Home Instruction: An Analysis of the Statutes and Case Law*, 8 University of Dayton Law Review 13-4 (1982).

28. Cremin, *American Education*, *supra* note 1, at 550.

29. *Id.* at 550.

30. *Id.* at 543.

31. Pierre Samuel Dupont de Nemours, *National Education in the United States of America* (Newark, DE: University of Delaware Press, 1923), pp. 3, 4. *Also see* Cremin, *supra*, note 1, at 543.

32. *As quoted* in Cremin, *American Education*, *supra* note 1, at 550.

33. *As quoted* in Charles Adams, ed., *The Works of John Adams*, Vol. III (Boston: n.p., 1851), p. 456.

34. *Id.*

35. Cremin, *American Education*, *supra* note 1, at 267.

36. Saul K. Padover, *Jefferson* (New York: Harcourt-Brace, 1942), p. 396.

37. Cremin, *American Education*, *supra* note 1, at 442, 440.

38. *Id.* at 277, 278.

39. *As quoted* in James Axtell, ed., *The Educational Writings of John Locke* (Cambridge, MA: Cambridge University Press, 1968), pp. 153-59, 241, 260, 313, 314.

40. *Id.*

41. Cremin, *American Education*, *supra* note 1, at 301.

42. *Id.* at 466.
43. *The Works of the Rev. John Witherspoon,* 2d ed., Vol. IV (Philadelphia: William Woodward, 1802), p. 133.
44. Calhoun, *supra* note 2, at 57, 58.
45. Ord. of 1787, July 13, 1787, Art. 3, reprinted in *Documents Illustrative of the Formation of the Union of American States* (Washington, D.C.: United States Government Printing Office, 1927), p. 52.
46. *See* Howard Cohen, *Equal Rights for Children* (Totowa, NJ: Rowman and Littlefield, 1980), pp. 5-7, for a discussion of John Locke's views on children and parents.
47. John Locke, *Second Treatise of Government* (Indianapolis: Bobbs-Merrill, 1952), p. 33.

CHAPTER TEN: *The Sacred Right*

1. John C. H. Wu, *Fountain of Justice* (Beaverton, OR: International Scholarly Book Services, 1980), p. 65.
2. Bruce C. Hafen, "Children's Liberation and the New Egalitarianism: Some Reservations About Abandoning Youth to Their 'Rights,'" 1976 Brigham Young Law Review 605, 615.
3. *Id.* at 615-16.
4. *See, e.g.,* Harriet Philpel, "Minor's Rights to Medical Care," 36 Albany Law Review 462 (1972).
5. *But see Poe v. Gerstein,* 517 F.2d 787, 789 (5th Cir. 1975).
6. *In re Hudson,* 13 Wash. 2d 673, 685, 126 P.2d 765, 771 (1942).
7. *People ex rel. Portnoy v. Strasser,* 303 N.Y. 539, 542, 104 N.E.2d 895, 896 (1952).
8. *Lacher v. Venus,* 177 Wis. 558, 569-70, 188 N.W. 613, 617 (1922).
9. *Commonwealth v. Armstrong,* 1 Pa. L. J. 393 (1842).
10. *Id.* at 393-95 (emphasis in original).
11. *Id.* at 395-96 (emphasis in original).
12. *Id.* at 396-97.
13. *Id.* 397-98 (emphasis and capitalization in original).
14. *Id.* at 398.
15. *Id.*
16. William Mack, ed., 29 *Cyclopedia of Law and Procedure* (New York: American Law Book Co., 1908), p. 1548. Other older cases upholding parental rights include: *Denton v. James,* 107 Kan. 729, 193 P. 307 (1920); *Hardwick v. Board of School Trustees,* 54 Cal. App. 696, 205 P. 49 (1921); *Norval v. Zinsmaster,* 57 Neb. 158, 77 N.W. 373 (1898); *State ex rel. Kelley v. Ferguson,* 144 N.W. 1039 (Neb. 1914); *People v. Turner,* 55 IL 208 (1870); *Stapleton v. Poynter,* 111 Kentucky 264 (1901); *Jamison v. Gilbert,* 38 Okl. 751, 135 P. 342 (Okl. 1913); *Rulison v. Post,* 79 IL 567 (1875); *Lacher v. Venus,* 177 Wis. 558, 569-70, 188 N.W. 613 (Wis. 1922); *Commonwealth v. Roberts,* 159 Mass. 372 (1893); *State v. Peterman,* 32 Ind. App. 665, 70 N.E. 550 (1904); *Board of Education v. Purse,* 101 Ga. 422 (1897); *Roller v. Roller,* 37 Wash. 242 (1905); *Tremain's Case,* 1 Strange 167 (1719).
17. Hafen, *supra* note 2, at 616.
18. Philip B. Heymann and Douglas E. Barzelay, "The Forest and the Trees: *Roe v. Wade* and Its Critics," 53 Boston University Law Review 765, 772-73 (1973) (emphasis supplied).
19. Hafen, *supra* note 2, at 617.

20. *Matarese v. Matarese*, 17 R. I. 131, 132-133, 131 A. 198, 199 (1925) (emphasis supplied).
21. *In re Guardianship of Faust*, 239 Miss. 299, 305-07, 123 So. 2d 218, 220-21 (1960) (emphasis supplied).
22. Perry Miller, *The Life of the Mind in America* (London: Victor Gallanez, 1966), p. 115.
23. Daniel Boorstin, *The Mysterious Science of the Law* (Magnolia, MA: Peter Smith, 1958), p. 3.
24. William Blackstone, *Commentaries on the Laws of England*, Vol. 2, George Tucker, ed. (Philadelphia: William Birch Young and Abraham Small, 1803), p. 452 (emphasis supplied).
25. *In re Agar-Ellis*, 24 Ch. D. 317 (C.A.) (1883).
26. Hafen, *supra* note 2, at 618.

CHAPTER ELEVEN: *Modern Parental Rights: Issues and Limits*

1. *See Rose v. Rose*, 340 S.E.2d 176 (1985).
2. G. Field, *The Legal Relations of Infants, Parent and Child, and Guardian and Ward* 68 (1888) (*citing Jenness v. Emerson*, 15 N.H. 486 [1844] and *Moore v. Welton*, 6 Conn. 547 [1827]).
3. Field, *supra* note 2, at 57. *See also* John Whitehead, *Parents' Rights* (Wheaton, IL: Crossway Books, 1986), p. 56.
4. *E.g.*, "maintenance," 2 Corinthians 12:14; "protection," Matthew 19:13 and Matthew 19:14; "education," Proverbs 22:6, Proverbs 1:8, Ephesians 6:1-3, and Colossians 3:20-1.
5. *See, e.g., Kelley v. Davis*, 49 N.H. 187, 188-89 (1870).
6. Field, *supra* note 2, at 66.
7. *Cf. Batson v. Kentucky*, 476 U.S. 79 (1986).
8. Field, *supra* note 2, at 67.
9. *See, e.g.,* W. Wadlington, *Cases and Other Materials on Domestic Relations* (Westbury, NY: Foundation Press, 1990), p. 299. Professor Wadlington euphemistically calls these nontraditional family relationships "private-ordering arrangements." *Id.* at 82.
10. *Lehr v. Robertson*, 463 U.S. 248, 257 (1983); *see also Smith v. Organization of Foster Families for Equality and Reform*, 431 U.S. 816, 823 (1977) ("'. . . parents are entitled to bring up their own children unless the best interests of the child would be thereby endangered. . . .'"—*quoting* New York Soc. Serv. Law sec. 384-b(1)(a)(ii) (McKinney Supp. 1976-77).
11. Marriage is especially important in relation to inheritance laws.
12. Courts used to rely, for example, on the "tender years" doctrine in awarding custody of young children. Using this doctrine, courts held that during its "tender years," a child needed to be with its mother rather than its father. Over time this presumption has been largely invalidated.

    However, in recent years some courts again have come to favor the mother's custody of young children. In *Rose v. Rose*, 340 S.E.2d 176 (W.Va. 1985), the Supreme Court of West Virginia held that the "primary caretaker" of a young child should be preferred for custody. Since in many families the mother stays at home to care for the child while the father works, usually the "primary caretaker" will be the mother. It appears that the "primary caretaker" presumption may replace the "tender years" doctrine in favoring mothers rather than fathers for the custody of young children.
13. *In re Stanley*, 45 IL 2d 132, 256 N.E.2d 814 (1970).
14. *Stanley v. Illinois*, 450 U.S. 645, 649 (1972).

15. *Id.* at 649.
16. *See, e.g., In the Matter of Karen A.B.*, 513 A.2d 770 (Del. 1986).
17. *Lehr*, 463 U.S. at 261.
18. *Id.* (*quoting Caban v. Mohammed*, 441 U.S. 380, 392, 99 S. Ct. 1760, 1768 (1978).
19. *Id.* at 264.
20. *Caban*, 441 U.S. 394. *But see Adoption of C.J.H., W.L.H., and T.A.H.*, 803 P.2d 214 (Mont. 1991) (consent of natural father who has not met his support obligations is not required).
21. *Quilloin v. Walcott*, 434 U.S. 246, 248 (1978). In *Adoption of Eder*, 312 Or. 244, 821 P.2d 400 (Or. 1991) (*en banc*), the Supreme Court of Oregon held that a parent's consent to adoption cannot be presumed by her failure to provide a "minimal expression of concern"; voluntary consent must be given.
22. *See, e.g., id. citing to* Ga. Code sec. 74-403(3) (1975). Note, however, that there is also some movement towards allowing fathers to adopt children who are born out of wedlock without the mother's consent. *Bridges v. Nicely*, 304 Md. 1, 497 A.2d 142 (Md. App. 1985).
23. *See Caban*, 441 U.S. at 394.
24. *Quilloin* at 249. Under due process guarantees, a state may not give a natural mother a mechanism to preclude the child's natural father from attempting to be declared as the child's father. *Adoption of Kelsey S.*, 4 Cal.Rptr.2d 615 (Cal. 1992).
25. *Id.* at 256.
26. *Matter of K.L.J.*, 813 P.2d 276 (Alaska 1991); *Zockert v. Fanning*, 310 Or. 514, 800 P.2d 773 (Or. 1990).
27. *Appeal of H.R.*, 581 A.2d 1141, 1152 (D.C. App. 1990).
28. *Id.* According to the Supreme Court, a biological father cannot be presumed to be unfit. *Stanley v. Illinois*, 405 U.S. 645 (1972).
29. *See, e.g., Bryant v. Cameron*, 473 So.2d 174 (Miss. 1985). In Mississippi, an enforceable consent to adoption may not be given prior to three days after the child's birth, and such consent must be in writing. *Id.* at 177, 178, *citing* Miss. Code Ann. Sec. 93-17-5 (1972).
30. *In the Matter of Baby M*, 109 N.J. 396, 537 A.2d 1227 (N.J. 1988).
31. Facts taken from *id.* at 1235.
32. *Id.* at 1236.
33. *Id.*
34. *Id.* at 1240.
35. *Id.*
36. *Id.* at 1242.
37. *Id.* at 1246.
38. *Id.* at 1261.
39. *In the Matter of Baby M*, 225 N.J.Super. 267, 542 A.2d 52 (N.J.Super.Ch. 1988).
40. 493 A.2d 478 (N.H. 1985).
41. The Supreme Court of New Hampshire noted that during the grandchild's ten years of life, she had no less than ten different homes and five different schools, apparently due to the mother's unrestricted lifestyle. *Id.* at 480.
42. *Id.* at 482.
43. *Id.*
44. *Id. See also In the Matter of the Guardianship of Nemer*, 419 N.W.2d 582 (Iowa 1988) (consent to adoption by a child's parents did not terminate the relationship between the child and his natural grandparents; it was in the best interests of the child for the grandparents to receive visitation rights).

45. *Coppedge v. Harding*, 714 P.2d 1121 (Utah 1985).
46. *See* D.C. Code sec. 21-101 (1989).
47. *Shelton v. Bradley*, 526 A.2d 579, 580 (D.C.App. 1987).
48. *See supra* notes 3-8 and accompanying text for an explanation and discussion of the common law.
49. *Id.*
50. *Id.*
51. *Id.* at 694.
52. *Id. See also Porter v. Hoffman*, 592 A.2d 482 (Maine 1991); *Pierce v. Pierce*, 279 Ark. 62, 648 S.W.2d 487 (1983); *McCluskey v. Kerken*, 278 Ark. 338, 645 S.W.2d 948 (1983); *In re Doe's Adoption*, 87 N.M. 253, 531 P.2d 1226 (1975); *In re Adoption of Graves*, 481 P.2d 136 (Okla. 1971); and *In re Adoption of Dailey*, 20 Ark. App. 180, 726 S.W.2d 292 (1987). However, Section 8(b) of the Uniform Adoption Act states:

> A consent to adoption may be withdrawn prior to the entry of a decree of adoption if the Court finds . . . that the withdrawal is in the best interest of the individual to be adopted.

Grafe v. Olds, 556 So.2d at 694.
53. *See supra* notes 10-28 and accompanying text.
54. Va. Code sec. 63.1-233 (1986) (emphasis supplied).
55. *Id.*
56. *Smith v. Organization of Foster Families for Equality and Reform*, 431 U.S. 816, 823 (1977).
57. *Id.* at 833-34.
58. *Id.* at 837.
59. *Id.* at 855-56.
60. U.S. Const., Amend. XIV.
61. *See* Chapter Fourteen, "Right to Privacy and Due Process," and Chapter Sixteen, "Equal Protection of the Law," for a detailed discussion of these issues with respect to home education.
62. Ill. Stat. Ann. ch. 37, par. 803-3 (Smith-Hurd 1988).
63. Ill. Stat. Ann., ch. 37, par. 803-4 (Smith-Hurd 1988).
64. Ill. Stat. Ann., ch 37, par. 803-5 (Smith-Hurd 1988).
65. Ill. Stat. Ann., ch. 37, par. 803-24 (Smith-Hurd 1988). *See People v. R.G.*, 131 Ill. 2d 328, 137 Ill. Dec. 588, 546 N.E.2d 533 (Ill.), *cert. denied*, 110 S.Ct. 1491 (1989).
66. *People v. R.G.*, 546 N.E.2d at 536.
67. *Id.* at 540, *citing Roe v. Wade*, 410 U.S. 113 (1973).
68. *Id.* at 540 *citing Kelley v. Johnson*, 425 U.S. 238, 244 (1976).
69. *Id.* at 541.
70. *Id.*
71. *Id.* at 546.
72. *Id.* at 552 (Miller, J., dissenting).
73. The primary Supreme Court decision on this subject is *Prince v. Massachusetts*, 321 U.S. 158 (1944), where a state law prohibited minors under the age of twelve from selling merchandise in public places. *Id.* at 160-61. This law was one portion of a broader statutory scheme regulating against child labor. The Court upheld the law, *id.* at 171, noting that a parent's control over his or her child is not absolute, especially in matters affecting the child's health or welfare. *Id.* at 166. For similar state decisions, *see City of Panora v. Simmons*, 445 N.W.2d 363 (Iowa 1989) (upholding city curfew for minors over assertion that it violated parental rights) and also *Hunter v. State*, 257 Ga. 571, 361 S.E.2d

787 (Ga. 1987) (upholding conviction of man for showing obscene video to child, against assertion that the child's parents approved of the activity).

74. *In the Matter of K.C., S.C., R.J.S., B.J.S., and C.W.*, 142 Wis.2d 906, 420 N.W.2d 37 (Wis. 1988) (state may require parents to reimburse the state for costs of placing children in juvenile training facilities, despite absence of finding that the parents are responsible for the conduct of the children which prompted the placement).

75. *In the Matter of Tammie Z.*, 66 N.Y.2d 1, 484 N.E.2d 1038 (N.Y. 1985).

76. *In the Interest of L.C., J.C., and E.C.*, 235 Neb. 703, 457 N.W.2d 274 (Neb. 1990).

77. *Matter of C.O.W.*, 519 A.2d 711 (D.C.App. 1987).

78. *Id.* at 713-14.

79. There are essentially three parties involved in all disputes involving the welfare of children: *first*, the parents; *second*, the children; and *third*, the state. *See* Note, "State Intrusion into Family Affairs: Justifications and Limitations," 26 Stan. L. Rev. 1383 (1974). One modern article stated its purpose by saying, "This Note suggests a proper mode for analyzing parental challenges to the state's authority to intervene in childrearing practices." *Id.* Notice the two assumptions in this statement. First, it is assumed that the state has authority to intervene in family matters. Second, it is assumed that not all parental challenges to the exercise of the state's authority will be upheld.

80. These figures are cited in *R.S. v. State*, 459 N.W.2d 680, 685 (Minn. 1990).

81. John E. B. Myers, "A Survey of Child Abuse and Neglect Reporting Statutes," 10 *J. Juv. L.* 1, 2 (1986).

82. *See* Myers, *supra* note 81, at 11-72.

83. *See supra* note 80.

84. 459 N.W.2d at 682.

85. *Id.* at 687.

86. It is hard to imagine that these interviews will be kept secret for long. When a child is called out of a classroom by the local social worker, it is likely that other children will glean the reason for the interview. When this information reaches the abusive parent through secondhand sources, it is likely that the parent's anger will be greater than if the parent had known about the interview beforehand.

87. *See* Field, *supra* note 2, at 57.

88. *See* Chapter Two, "The History and Philosophy of Public Education."

89. 268 U.S. 510 (1925).

90. *Id.* at 530.

91. *Id.* at 531.

92. *Id.* at 534.

93. *Id.* at 534-35 *citing Meyer v. Nebraska*, 262 U.S. 390 (1923).

94. *Id.* at 535.

95. *Id.*

96. U.S. Const., Amend III.

97. U.S. Const., Amend IV.

98. U.S. Const., Amend V.

99. 381 U.S. 479 (1965).

100. *Id.* at 480.

101. *Id.*

102. *Id.*

103. *Id.* at 486.

104. *Id.* at 485.

105. *Id.* at 485-86.

106. 405 U.S. 438 (1972).

107. *Id.* at 454-55.

108. An extreme extension of this theory may be seen in a recent challenge by two minor females in Florida who wished to "consent" to statutory rape. *See* "Teen Rape, or Private Sex?," *The Miami Herald*, p. 10.

109. 410 U.S. 113 (1973).

110. The right to privacy has not been extended to homosexual activity. *Bowers v. Hardwick*, 478 U.S. 186 (1988).

111. *Pierce*, 268 U.S. at 534-35.

112. This is discussed more fully in Chapter Seventeen, "Parental Liberty."

113. *Meyer v. Nebraska*, 262 U.S. 390 (1923); *Pierce v. Society of Sisters*, 268 U.S. 510 (1925); and *Farrington v. Tokushige*, 273 U.S. 284 (1927), all of which are discussed at length in Chapter Seventeen, "Parental Liberty."

114. 268 U.S. 510 (1925).

115. *Id.*

116. 273 U.S. 284 (1927).

117. *Pierce*, 268 U.S. at 534.

118. *See, e.g., In Re Marriage of Heriford*, 586 S.W.2d 769, 770 (Mo. App. 1979).

119. *Applebaum v. Hames*, 159 Ga.App. 552, 284 S.E.2d 58 (Ga. 1981).

120. *Applebaum*, 159 Ga.App. at 553, 284 S.E.2d at 60.

121. *See, e.g., Flynn v. Flynn*, 7 Conn.App. 745, 510 A.2d 1005 (Conn.App. 1986); *Asch v. Asch*, 164 N.J.Super. 499, 397 A.2d 352 (N.J. Super. Ct. 1978); *Majnaric v. Majnaric*, 46 Ohio App.2d 157, 347 N.E.2d 552 (Oh.App. 1975); and *Kilgrow v. Kilgrow*, 268 Ala. 475, 107 So.2d 885 (Ala. 1959).

122. *Marriage of Heriford*, 586 S.W.2d at 771. According to one New York court, however, these agreements can be modified so as to serve the best interests of the child. *Schwarzman v. Schwarzman*, 388 N.Y.S.2d 993, 998 (N.Y. 1976).

123. 285 S.2d 552 (La. 1973).

124. *Id.* at 555.

125. *Id.*

126. *Bentley v. Bentley*, 86 A.D.2d 926, 448 N.Y.S.2d 559 (N.Y.App. 1982); *see also Margaret B. v. Jeffrey B.*, 106 Misc.2d 608, 435 N.Y.S.2d 499 (1980).

127. *Felton v. Felton*, 418 N.E.2d 606, 610 (Mass. 1981).

128. *In the Matter of McCauley*, 409 Mass. 134, 134-35, 565 N.E.2d 411, 412 (1991).

129. *Norwood Hospital v. Munoz*, 409 Mass. 116, 120, 564 N.E.2d 1017, 1020 (Mass. 1991); *In Re Milton*, 29 Ohio St.3d 20, 505 N.E.2d 255 (Oh. 1987); *see also In the Interest of E.G.*, 161 Ill. App.3d 765, 515 N.E.2d 286 (Ill. App. 1987) (where a seventeen-year-old was permitted to refuse medical treatment on behalf of herself; the court deemed that she was "mature" and capable of making an informed decision).

130. *Custody of a Minor*, 375 Mass. 733, 379 N.E.2d 1053 (1978).

131. *Bergmann v. State*, 486 N.E.2d 653 (Ind.App. 1985).

132. *State v. Norman*, 61 Wash. App. 16, 808 P.2d 1159 (Wash. 1991).

133. *Commonwealth v. Barnhart*, 497 A.2d 616 (Pa.Super. 1985).

134. *Lybarger v. People*, 807 P.2d 570 (Colo. 1991).

135. *Id.* at 622-23, *citing Prince v. Massachusetts*, 321 U.S. 158 (1944) ("The right to practice religion freely does not include liberty to expose the community or the child to communicable disease or the latter to ill health or death").

136. *Mercy Hospital v. Jackson*, 489 A.2d 1130 (Md.App. 1985).

137. 197 U.S. 11 (1905).

138. *Id.* at 13-15.

139. *Id.* at 17.

140. *Id.* at 37.
141. *Id.* at 39.
142. *Id.* at 37-38.
143. *In Re Willmann,* 493 N.E.2d 1380, 1382 (Oh.App. 1986); *but see Matter of Appeal in Cochise County,* 650 P.2d 459 (Ariz. 1982) (where one child died as a result of withholding of medical treatment, the state cannot take custody of remaining children without showing their health to be in immediate danger).
144. *Id., citing Prince v. Massachusetts,* 321 U.S. at 170.

CHAPTER TWELVE: *Free Exercise of Religion*

1. U.S. Const., Amend. I.
2. *Sherbert v. Verner,* 374 U.S. 398, 402 (1963) (emphasis in original).
3. *Id.* quoting *Torcaso v. Watkins,* 367 U.S. 488 (1961) and *Fowler v. Rhode Island,* 345 U.S. 67 (1953).
4. *Vandiver v. Board of Educ.,* 925 F.2d 927, 932 (6th Cir. 1991).
5. 374 U.S. 398.
6. *Id.* at 403 quoting *Braunfeld v. Brown,* 366 U.S. 599, 603 (1961).
7. *Fellowship Baptist Church v. Benton,* 815 F.2d 485, 490 (8th Cir. 1987).
8. *See, e.g., Wisconsin v. Yoder,* 406 U.S. 205, 213 (1972); *Board of Educ. v. Allen,* 392 U.S. 236, 245-47 & n.7 (1968); *Brown v. Board of Educ.,* 347 U.S. 483, 493 (1954); *Pierce v. Society of Sisters,* 268 U.S. 510, 534 (1929).
9. The Supreme Court has yet to consider whether the right to home school is constitutionally protected; however, several federal and state courts have addressed this issue. *See infra* notes 57-88.
10. The First Amendment was made applicable to the states through the Fourteenth Amendment in *Cantwell v. Connecticut,* 310 U.S. 296, 303 (1940) ("The fundamental concept of liberty embodied in the [Fourteenth] Amendment embraces the liberties guaranteed by the First Amendment").
11. 494 U.S. 872 (1990).
12. For a discussion of this new test and the Court's rejection of the strict scrutiny test, *see infra* notes 39-55.
13. *See* Jennifer E. Bennett Overton, Note, "Unanswered Implications—The Clouded Rights of the Incompetent Patient Under *Cruzan v. Director, Missouri Department of Health,*" 69 N. C. L. Rev. 1293, 1324-25 & n. 238 (1991).
14. *Reynolds v. United States,* 98 U.S. 145, 166 (1878).
15. *Braunfeld v. Brown,* 366 U.S. 599, 603 (1961), *cited in Sherbert,* 374 U.S. 398, 403 (1963).
16. *See Sherbert,* 374 U.S. at 403. During this phase of the analysis, "courts may emphasize the Constitution's preferred treatment of the [F]irst [A]mendment right to free exercise of religion and the framers' intent that the Free Exercise Clause protect minority religions from persecution." Karin M. Rebescher, Note, "The Illusory Enforcement of First Amendment Freedom: *Employment Division, Department of Human Resources v. Smith* and the Abandonment of the Compelling Interest Governmental Interest Test," 69 N. C. L. Rev. 1332, 1337 (1991) *citing Smith,* 494 U.S. at 901-02 (O'Connor, J., concurring in judgment); *Reynolds,* 98 U.S. 145, 162-64 (1878).
17. Scylla is a mythical monster with six heads and twelve arms that lived opposite the whirlpool Charybdis and snatched sailors from ships. To be "Between Scylla and Charybdis" means to be between two dangers. Clarence L. Barnhard, ed., *The World Book Dictionary* (Chicago: Doubleday & Company, Inc., 1971), p. 1857.
18. *Sherbert,* 374 U.S. at 404.

19. *Id.*
20. *Id.* at 403. If no intrusion exists, the governmental action withstands judicial scrutiny. *Id.*
21. *Cantwell*, 310 U.S. at 308; see *Sherbert*, 374 U.S. at 403 ("The conduct or actions so regulated have invariably posed some substantial threat to public safety, peace or order").
22. *Sherbert*, 374 U.S. at 406 *citing Thomas v. Collins*, 323 U.S. 516, 530 (1945).
23. *Smith*, 494 U.S. at 905 (O'Connor, J., concurring in judgment) *quoting United States v. Lee*, 455 U.S. 252, 259 (1982).
24. *Bowen v. Roy*, 476 U.S. 693, 727 (1986).
25. *Smith*, 494 U.S. at 906 (O'Connor, J., concurring in judgment).
26. 374 U.S. 398 (1963).
27. *Id.* at 399.
28. *Id.*
29. *Id.* at 399-400.
30. *Id.* at 401.
31. *Id.*
32. *Id.* at 404.
33. *Id.* at 403.
34. *Id.* at 407.
35. *Id.*
36. *Id.*
37. See Michael W. McConnell, "The Origins and Historical Understanding of Free Exercise of Religion," 103 Harv. L. Rev. 1409, 1417-18 (1990). Even before the *Smith* decision, Professor McConnell foreshadowed the inevitable demise of the *Sherbert* analytical framework, pointing to the increasing numbers of Justices hostile to the doctrine. *Id.* According to Professor McConnell, members of the judiciary are engaged in a debate over exempting individuals from general statutes because of religious beliefs. *Id.* at 1417-18.

    Chief Justice Rehnquist and Justice Stevens espouse the non-exemption view which contends that "the free exercise clause exists solely to prevent the government from singling out religious practice for peculiar disability. The evil to be prevented is . . . 'laws that directly and intentionally penalize religious observance.' The remedy is to strike down the offending legislation and to treat religious institutions and practices the same way that comparable nonreligious institutions and practices are treated." *Id.* at 1418 *quoting* Robert Bork, *The Supreme Court and the Religion Clauses*," in *Turning the Religion Clauses on Their Heads: Proceedings of the National Religious Freedom Conference of the Catholic League for Religious and Civil Rights*, 83, 85-6 (1988).

    Individuals holding the exemption view, however, claim that "the free exercise clause protects religious practices against even the incidental or unintended effects of government action. The evil includes not only active hostility, but also majoritarian presuppositions, ignorance, and indifference. The remedy generally is to leave the government policy in place, but to carve out an exemption. . . ." McConnell, *id.* at 1418. Smith represents victory for the non-exemption view—the result Professor McConnell predicted.
38. Although it applied the compelling state interest test, the Court rejected every free exercise exemption claim between 1972 and 1990. *See* McConnell, *supra* note 37, at 1417 and n. 29 *citing O'Lone v. Estate of Shabazz*, 482 U.S. 342 (1987); *Goldman v. Weinberger*, 475 U.S. 503 (1986); *Tony & Susan Alamo Found. v. Secretary of Labor*, 471 U.S. 290 (1985); *Bob Jones Univ. v. United States*, 461 U.S. 574 (1983); *United States v. Lee*, 455 U.S. 252 (1982).
39. *Smith*, 494 U.S. at 886-90.

40. 494 U.S. 872.
41. *Id.* at 874.
42. *Id.* The plaintiffs were employed by a private drug rehabilitation organization. *Id.*
43. *Id.* In 1991, the Oregon Legislative Assembly amended Section 475.992 to include:

> (5) In any prosecution under this section for manufacture, possession or delivery of that plant of the genus *lopophora* commonly known as peyote, it is an affirmative defense that the peyote is being used for or is intended for use:
>
> (A) In connection with the good faith practice of a religious belief;
> (B) As directly associated with a religious practice; and
> (C) In a manner that is not dangerous to the health of the user or others who are in the proximity of the user.
>
> (6) The affirmative defense created in Subsection (5) of this section is not available to any person who has possessed or delivered the peyote while incarcerated in a correctional facility in this state.

These sections were approved by the governor on June 24, 1991.
44. *Smith*, 494 U.S. at 874.
45. The Oregon Supreme Court, affirming the state court of appeals' decision, rejected the state's argument that the denial of unemployment compensation based on the criminal nature of the misconduct was irrelevant because "the purpose of the 'misconduct' provision . . . was not to enforce the State's criminal laws but to preserve the financial integrity of the compensation fund, and since that purpose was inadequate to justify the burden that disqualification imposed on [the plaintiff's] religious practice." *Id.* at 875.

In its first hearing of the case, the Supreme Court agreed with the state, finding that the state could deny unemployment benefits to persons who engage in illegal conduct. *Employment Div., Dept. of Human Resources v. Smith*, 485 U.S. 660-70 (1988) (*Smith* I). Nevertheless, the Court remanded to the state supreme court for a determination of whether the statute in fact prohibited ingestion of peyote for sacramental purposes. *Smith*, 494 U.S. at 875-76 (*citing Smith* I, 485 U.S. at 670).

On remand the Oregon Supreme Court found that the plaintiffs' "religiously inspired use of peyote fell within the prohibition of the Oregon statute, which 'makes no exception for the sacramental use' of the drug," *id. quoting Employment Div., Dept. of Human Resources v. Smith*, 763 P.2d 146, 148 (1988), but that such a prohibition was invalid under the Free Exercise Clause. *Id.*
46. Six Justices concurred with the Court's ultimate judgment: Justice Scalia, writing for the majority, Chief Justice Rehnquist, and Justices Stevens, White, Kennedy, and O'Connor. Only five Justices, however, concurred with the Court's reasoning. Justice O'Connor authored a vehement concurring opinion, chastising Justice Scalia and the rest of the majority for its novel approach to the Free Exercise Clause. Justices Blackmun, Brennan, and Marshall agreed with Justice's O'Connor's mode of analysis, but not with her conclusion, and thus dissented.
47. *Id.* at 878.
48. *Id.*
49. *Id.* at 878-79. As Professor Laycock points out, this statement stands in striking contrast to a dissenting opinion authored by Scalia fourteen months earlier.

Douglas Laycock, "The Remnants of Free Exercise," 1990 Supreme Court Review 1, 2-3. In *Texas Monthly, Inc. v. Bullock*, Justice Scalia wrote:

> In such cases as *Sherbert v. Verner, Wisconsin v. Yoder, Thomas v. Review Bd. of Indiana Employment Security Div.*, and *Hobbie v. Unemployment Appeals Comm'n of Fla.*, we held that the free exercise clause of the First Amendment *required* religious beliefs to be accommodated by granting religion-specific exemptions from otherwise applicable laws.

Id. at 3 *quoting Texas Monthly, Inc.*, 489 U.S. 1, 38 (1989) (Scalia, J., dissenting) (emphasis in opinion) (citations omitted in article).

Numerous scholars and commentators, including Professor Laycock, have criticized the *Smith* decision. *See, e.g., id.* at 2-3; Michael W. McConnell, *Free Exercise Revisionism and the Smith Decision*, 57 U. Chi. L. Rev. 1109 (1990). Many of the complaints are justified; nonetheless, *Smith*, with all of its faults and misconstructions of the law, currently provides the analytical framework for free exercise complaints.

50. *Smith*, 494 U.S. at 879.
51. *Id.* at 887-88.
52. *Id.* at 888 *quoting Braunfeld v. Brown*, 366 U.S. 599, 606 (1961).
53. The Court never explicitly stated that this exception mandated the use of strict scrutiny; however, lower courts have construed the opinion to imply that such a result should occur. *See, e.g., Vandiver v. Hardin County Bd. of Educ.*, 925 F.2d 927, 933 (6th Cir. 1991).
54. *Smith*, 494 U.S. at 881.
55. *Id.* at 884 *quoting Bowen v. Roy*, 476 U.S. 693, 708 (1986).
56. A separate issue involves whether the right to home educate is a fundamental liberty under the Fourteenth Amendment. For a discussion of this issue, see *infra* Chapter Ten ("The Sacred Right").
57. Lower courts have extended *Smith* to include civil statutes as well as criminal statutes. *See Vandiver*, 925 F.2d at 932 *citing Salvation Army v. Department of Community Affairs*, 919 F.2d 183 (3rd Cir. 1990); *Rector, Wardens, and Members of the Vestry of St. Bartholomew's Church v. City of New York*, 914 F.2d 348 (2nd Cir. 1990); *Intercommunity Center for Justice and Peace v. INS*, 910 F.2d 42 (2nd Cir. 1990).
58. *See Smith*, 494 U.S. at 878.
59. *See Sherbert*, 374 U.S. 398, 403-06 (1963); *Yoder*, 406 U.S. 205, 215. *See also State v. Patzer*, 382 N.W.2d 631, 654 (N.D.), *cert. denied*, 479 U.S. 825 (1986) (examining parents' religious motivation to home school their children).
60. *United States v. Seeger*, 380 U.S. 163, 184-85 (1965).
61. *Id. quoting United States v. Ballard*, 322 U.S. 78, 86 (1944).
62. *Yoder*, 406 U.S. 205, 215.
63. *Id.* at 215-16; *see Seeger*, 380 U.S. at 165.
64. *Seeger*, 380 U.S. at 176.
65. *Frazee v. Illinois Dept. of Employment Security*, 489 U.S. 829, 834 (1989).
66. *Thomas v. Review Bd.*, 450 U.S. 707, 715-16 (1981).
67. For a discussion of parental rights, *see* Chapters Eleven, "Modern Parental Rights: Issues and Limits," and Chapter Seventeen, "Parental Liberty."
68. 406 U.S. 205 (1972).
69. *See Vandiver v. Board of Educ.* 925 F.2d 927, 933 (6th Cir. 1991). In *Vandiver*, the court of appeals suggested that had the plaintiff parents' claims not been barred by justiciability problems and by the statute of limitations, "the right of

parents to direct the education and upbringing of their children" could be joined with a free exercise claim to require a strict scrutiny analysis. *Id.* at 933.

Because of the recent nature of the *Smith* decision, few courts have addressed what constitutes a hybrid claim, but those that have addressed it may foreshadow how other courts may approach this analysis. For example, in *Society of Separationists v. Herman,* 939 F.2d 1207 (5th Cir. 1991), the Fifth Circuit Court of Appeals used the hybrid claim exception. *Id.* at 1216. The plaintiff was called to serve jury duty, and upon arrival, the judge asked her to take a pre-*voir dire* oath. *Id.* at 1209. The plaintiff, an American Atheist, refused, claiming that it violated her religious beliefs because it referred to God. *Id.* The plaintiff also refused to take any affirmation, with or without reference to God, because of the religious nature of the act. *Id.* The judge jailed her in contempt. *Id.* The plaintiff sued, challenging the judge's actions, and the court of appeals found that the judge had violated her right to exercise her beliefs. The court of appeals removed the case from the *Smith* analysis because it viewed her case as a "religion-plus-speech" claim. *Id.* at 1216. *See also Salvation Army v. Department of Community Affairs,* 919 F.2d 183, 185-86 (3rd Cir. 1990) (demonstrating a willingness to accept a hybrid claim of free exercise plus freedom of speech or of association and remanding to district court for further inquiry).

A winning combination does not necessarily mean a victory in court; rather, it means victory in the sense that the claim remains subject to the compelling state interest test and not to the bright line *Smith* rule. Thus, if the compulsory attendance law affects the pursuit of religious education at home and if the plaintiff alleges a hybrid claim, the court should engage in a strict scrutiny analysis, meaning, as previously discussed, that the state must prove a compelling state interest and that, if such an interest is demonstrated, the state must be able to accommodate an individual's religious beliefs without unduly comprising that interest.

70. *Smith,* 494 U.S. at 905 (O'Connor, J., concurring in judgment) *quoting United States v. Lee,* 455 U.S. 252, 259 (1982).

71. *Yoder,* 406 U.S. at 207.

72. *Id.* at 208-09.

73. *Id.* at 207.

74. *Id.* at 214 (*quoting Pierce,* 268 U.S. at 535).

75. *Id.* The Court added that it could accept "as settled, therefore, that, however strong the State's interest in universal compulsory education, it is by no means absolute to the exclusion or subordination of all other interests." *Id.* at 215 *citing Sherbert,* 374 U.S. 398; *McGowan v. Maryland,* 366 U.S. 420, 459 (1961) (separate opinion of Frankfurter, J.); *Prince v. Massachusetts,* 321 U.S. 158, 165 (1944).

76. *Id.* at 210-11. The high school experience conflicted with the Amish teaching of non-conformity and separation from the "contemporary, worldly society." *Id.* at 211.

77. *Id.* at 212. The Amish were not opposed to sending their children to elementary schools because "they view such a basic education as acceptable because it does not significantly expose their children to worldly values or interfere with their development in the Amish community during the crucial adolescent period." *Id.* During the adolescent period, the Amish teenagers engage in "learning-by-doing," meaning they must learn the skills necessary to be an Amish farmer or housewife. *Id.* at 211.

78. *Id.* at 215.

79. *Id.*

80. *Id.* at 216. The Court found particularly convincing the Amish's literal interpretation of the Biblical command to "be not conformed to this world," a command deemed fundamental to their faith. *Id.* The Court also pointed to the degree in which the Amish attitudes and beliefs toward family and home have remained static in a world that has become increasingly more conscious of the value of education. *Id.* Some courts have suggested that the history, tradition, and uniqueness of the Amish order compelled the Court to rule in the Amish's favor and that other beliefs do not merit such a result. *See, e.g., State v. Patzer,* 382 N.W.2d 631, 636-37 (N.D.), *cert. denied,* 479 U.S. 825 (1986).
81. *Yoder,* 406 U.S. at 218.
82. *Id.* at 219. The state did not challenge the sincerity of the Amish's beliefs; rather, its argument focused on its superior interest. *Id.*
83. *Id.* at 222. The Court also stated that "[i]t is one thing to say that compulsory education for a year or two beyond the eighth grade may be necessary when its goal is the preparation of the child for life in modern society as the majority live, but it is quite another if the goal of education be viewed as the preparation of the child for life in the separated agrarian community that is the keystone of the Amish faith." *Id. citing Meyer v. Nebraska,* 262 U.S. 390, 400 (1923).
84. *Id.* at 222-23. The Court rejected the state's argument that the Amish children ought to be prepared to function in modern society should they choose to leave their community, calling it mere speculation in light of the lack of evidence of attrition and the minimal burden they would be on society because of their education should they elect to leave.
85. *Id.* at 226.
86. Lower courts appear to be divided over whether home schooling is a constitutionally protected right. *See Duro v. District Attorney of Second Judicial Dist. of N.C.,* 712 F.2d 96 (4th Cir. 1983) (finding the compelling state interest paramount to the free exercise claim).
87. Home school litigants in some states may have trouble with the Court's language focusing on the "one or two years" of education that the Amish children will be missing. Some courts have refused to apply *Yoder* to home schooling parents who have not completed primary schooling in an institutional setting. *See, e.g., State v. Patzer,* 382 N.W.2d 631, 637.
88. In fact, the best interests of a democracy require educational diversity. *See* Chapter Three, "Freedom and Educational Diversity."
89. Donald H. Henderson, *et al.,* "Legal Conflicts Involving Home Instruction of School-aged Children," 64 Ed. L. Rep. 999, 1000 (1991).
90. *Id.*
91. *Yoder,* 406 U.S. at 213.
92. *Id.* at 215.
93. *See Smith,* 494 U.S. at 879-80.
94. *Id.*
95. *See supra* notes 67-88 and accompanying text.
96. *See, e.g., Blount v. Department of Educ. & Cultural Serv.,* 551 A.2d 1377 (Me. 1988).
97. *See, e.g., Vandiver v. Hardin County Bd. of Educ.,* 925 F.2d 927 (6th Cir. 1991) (discussing only the reasonableness of testing requirements for home schooled students to return to public school); *Jeffrey v. O'Donnell,* 702 F. Supp. 516 (M.D. Pa. 1988) (finding that regulations imposed on home schools did not violate the First Amendment, but that language of regulations was unconstitutionally vague); *Blackwelder v. Safnauer,* 689 F. Supp. 106 (N.D.N.Y. 1988) (finding regulations constitutionally sound).

98. One potential problem with suing in federal court is the federal judiciary's reluctance to interfere with the state court and its construction of state statutes. Such hesitance may trigger the use of the abstention doctrine. Known as *Pullman* abstention, this doctrine requires federal courts to refrain from judicial review in cases where a narrow construction of a state statute by a state court would allow a federal court to avoid a federal constitutional question. *Railroad Comm'n of Texas v. Pullman* Co., 312 U.S. 496, 499-500 (1941). "[W]here state law is uncertain and a clarification of state law might make a federal court's determination of a constitutional question unnecessary, the federal court should abstain until the state court has had an opportunity to resolve the uncertainty as to state law." Erwin Chemerinsky, *Federal Jurisdiction*, §12.2.1, at 595 (1989).

This doctrine may emerge in home school cases. For example, if a state statute does not provide explicitly for a home school alternative, rather than addressing the existence of the right to home school, the federal court may abstain, giving the state courts the opportunity to construe language to include home schooling within the definition of "school." *See*, e.g., *Delconte v. State*, 329 S.E.2d 636 (N.C. 1985). (Although the case did not involve abstention, the state supreme court broadly construed statutory language to include home schools.). If the state court does not construe the statute in a favorable way to the home school litigants, the federal court then will hear the case.

99. *See, e.g., Blount*, 551 A.2d at 1381-82 (finding that the state's interests—education and quality education—were paramount to parents' religious beliefs and the right to direct the education of their children).

100. Some parents even concede this point. *State v. Anderson*, 427 N.W.2d 316, 322 (N.D. 1988), *cert. denied*, 488 U.S. 965 (1988).

101. *Runyon v. McCrary*, 427 U.S. 160, 178 (1976).

102. *Anderson*, 427 N.W.2d at 322.

103. *Blount*, 551 A 2d. at 1380 *citing Thomas v. Review Board*, 450 U.S. 707, 715 (1981); *Dotter v. Main Emp. Sec. Comm'n*, 435 A.2d 1368, 1371 (Me. 1981). For a more detailed discussion, see *supra* notes 59-66 and accompanying text.

104. *Blount* 551 A 2d. at 1380.

105. *State v. Patzer*, 382 N.W.2d 631, 635-36 *quoting Braunfeld v. Brown*, 366 U.S. 599, 607 (1961) and *citing Sherbert*, 374 U.S. 398, 404 (1963).

106. *Vandiver*, 925 F.2d at 933. Some courts use *Yoder* as the measuring stick and expect parents to demonstrate that the burdens the regulations impose is as great as the burden the compelling state interest imposed on the Amish. *See Fellowship Baptist Church v. Benton*, 815 F.2d 485, 493 (8th Cir. 1987) (involving a religious school).

107. *State v. Anderson*, 427 N.W.2d at 322 (focusing on "least restrictive alternative" arguments since the state conceded that the plaintiff had sincerely held religious beliefs and that the plaintiff conceded the state had a compelling state interest).

108. *See* Appendix, "Legislative Status."

109. Nonetheless, courts have held that this requirement is not unconstitutional because the state's compelling interest outweighs any parental religious beliefs; *see State v. Patzer*, 382 N.W.2d 631, 637-39; *Sheridan Road Baptist Church*, 396 N.W.2d 373, 382 (Mich. 1986), *cert. denied*, 481 U.S. 1050 (1987); *People v. DeJonge*, 449 N.W.2d 899, 902-05 (Mich. App. 1989), particularly since many courts have found similar requirements to be constitutionally vague. *See infra* Chapter Eighteen, "Vagueness Issues."

110. Litigants should use care in proposing standardized tests as a "least restrictive means." Some courts view this method as problematic. *See, e.g., Blount*, 551 A.2d at 1384 (finding that testing "creates incentives to turn instruction into

exam coaching"); *Sheridan Road Baptist Church*, 396 N.W.2d at 382 (finding that testing is "an inadequate substitute because deficiencies in teaching would be discovered only after the damage has occurred"). But *see Kentucky State Bd. for Elem. & Secondary Educ. v. Rudasill*, 589 S.W.2d 877 (Ky. 1979) (finding testing suitable as a method of monitoring the work and progress of students in private and religious schools), *cert. denied*, 446 U.S. 938 (1980). For a discussion of other issues regarding testing, *see generally* Chapter Seven, "The Straw Men: Socialization and Academics."

111. Undoubtedly, while this is a potential argument, it is a difficult one. *See, e.g., Runyon v. McCrary*, 427 U.S. 160, 178 (1976) (finding that parents "have no constitutional right to provide their children with private school education unfettered by reasonable government regulation"); *Pierce v. Society of Sisters*, 268 U.S. 510, 534 (1925) (finding that "[n]o question is raised concerning the power of the State reasonably to regulate all schools"); *Blackwelder v. Safnauer*, 689 F. Supp. 106, 135 (N.D.N.Y. 1988) (finding that the state's compelling state interest justified certain regulations of home schools); *Blount*, 551 A.2d at 1381-84; *DeJonge*, 449 N.W.2d at 902-05.

112. The home school proponent, in the alternative, should argue that the mere questioning of religious beliefs constitutes a violation of the Establishment Clause (see *infra* Chapter Twenty, "Establishment Clause Issues") and the Free Exercise Clause.

113. Parents also might argue that public schools teach contrary to traditional family values, promoting divorce, single-parenting, and, in many cases, homosexual unions.

114. *Blount*, 551 A.2d at 1381.

115. For an in-depth discussion of statistics and academic findings that point to the overall success of home schooled children in academics and socialization, see *supra* Chapter Seven, "The Straw Men: Socialization and Academics."

116. See *supra* notes 67-88 and accompanying text.

117. *See Smith*, 494 U.S. at 881-82.

118. See *supra* notes 40-53 and accompanying text.

119. *See Smith* 110 494 U.S. at 879-880 (discussing free exercise claims).

120. *See, e.g., Donahue v. Fair Employment & Housing Comm'n*, 2 Cal Rptr. 2d 32 (1991).

121. William Brennan, "State Constitutions and the Protection of Individual Rights," 90 Harv. L. Rev. 489, 491 (1977).

122. *See id.* at 501 n.80.

CHAPTER THIRTEEN: *Freedom of Speech and Formation of Belief*

1. *See* Chapter Seven, "The Straw Men: Socialization and Academics."

2. Dr. John Holt, "Schools and Home Schooling: A Fruitful Partnership," 64 Phi Delta Kappan 391, 393 (February 1983).

3. Alvin Toffler, *The Third Wave* (New York: Morrow, 1980), p. 386.

4. For a detailed discussion of this issue, *see* Chapter Seven, "The Straw Men: Socialization and Academics."

5. Patricia Lines, "An Overview of Home Instruction," 68-7 Phi Delta Kappan, 510, 513 (March 1987).

6. Dr. Raymond Moore, "Research and Common Sense: Therapies for Our Homes and Schools," 84 Teachers College Record 355, 372 (Columbia University) (1982).

7. For a detailed discussion of these laws, *see* Appendix, "Legislative Status."

8. "Congress shall make no law . . . abridging the freedom of speech, or of the press; or the right of the people peaceably to assemble. . . ." U.S. Const., Amend. I.

9. *Id.*

10. *See* John W. Whitehead, *The Rights of Religious Persons in Public Education* (Wheaton, IL: Crossway Books, 1991), pp. 25-32.

11. *See generally*, Thomas Emerson, *Toward a General Theory of the First Amendment* (New York: Random House, 1966); Alexander Meiklejohn, *Political Freedom* (New York: Harper, 1960).

12. Stephen Arons and Charles Lawrence III, "The Manipulation of Consciousness: A First Amendment Critique of Schooling," 15 Harvard Civil Rights and Civil Liberties Law Review, 309, 313 (1980).

13. Meiklejohn, *supra* note 11, at 24-28.

14. *Id.*

15. *Id.* at 27.

16. *Keyishian v. Board of Regents*, 385 U.S. 589, 603 (1967).

17. Emerson, *supra* note 11, at 8-11.

18. *Id.*

19. Laurence Tribe, *American Constitutional Law*, §12-1 (Mineola, NY: Foundation Press, 1978), p. 576.

20. David B. Gaebler, "First Amendment Protection Against Government Compelled Expression and Association," 23 Boston College Law Review 995, 1004 (1982).

21. *West Virginia State Board of Education v. Barnette*, 319 U.S. 624, 642 (1943).

22. *Id.* at 624.

23. *Id.* at 626-628.

24. According to Exodus, chapter 20, verses 4 and 5:

> Do not make for yourselves images of anything in heaven or on earth or in the water under the earth. Do not bow down to any idol or worship it, because I am the LORD your God and I tolerate no rivals. I bring punishment on those who hate me and on their descendants down to the third and fourth generation.

Good News Study Bible (Nashville: Thomas Nelson Publishers, 1986).

25. *Barnette*, 319 U.S. at 629.

26. *Id.* at 630.

27. *Id.* at 642.

28. *Id.* at 634-35.

29. *Id.* at 639.

30. *Id.* at 642.

31. *Torcaso v. Watkins*, 367 U.S. 488 (1961).

32. *Id.* at 489.

33. *Id.*

34. *Id.* at 495.

35. *Id.* at 496.

36. *Id.* at 495.

37. *Wooley v. Maynard*, 430 U.S. 705 (1977).

38. *Id.* at 707.

39. *Id.* at 713.

40. *Id.* at 708.

41. *Id.* at 714.

42. *Abood v. Detroit Board of Education*, 431 U.S. 209 (1977).

43. *Id.* at 212.

44. *Id.* at 212-13.

45. *Id.* at 234-35 (emphasis supplied).
46. *See supra* notes 9-20 and accompanying text.
47. Whitehead, *supra* note 10, at 15.
48. Arons and Lawrence, *supra* note 12, at 317.
49. *Brown v. Board of Education*, 347 U.S. 483, 493 (1954).
50. *Ambach v. Norwick*, 441 U.S. 68, 77 (1979).
51. *Wisconsin v. Yoder*, 406 U.S. 205, 211 (1972).
52. Meiklejohn, *supra* note 11, at 24-28.
53. John Stuart Mill, "On Liberty," in *On Liberty and Considerations on Representative Government*, R. B. McCallum, ed. (New York: Macmillan, 1947), p. 95.
54. E. Alice Law Beshoner, "Home Education in America: Parental Rights Reasserted," 49 UMKC L. Rev. 191, 194 (1981).
55. *See generally* Emerson, *supra* note 11.
56. *Id.* at 8-11.
57. Arons and Lawrence, *supra* note 12, at 312.
58. Francis Barry McCarthy, *The Confused Constitutional Status and Meaning of Parental Rights*, 22 Georgia Law Review 975, 981 (1988).
59. Dwight Tompkins, "An Argument for Privacy in Support of the Choice of Home Education by Parents," 20 Journal of Law and Education 301, 315 (Summer 1991). For a discussion of the compelling state interest concept, *see* Chapter Twenty-two, "Compelling State Interest."
60. 406 U.S. 205.
61. *Id.* at 232.
62. *See generally*, "Developments in the Law—The Constitution and the Family," 93 Harvard L. Rev. 1157 (1980) (hereinafter, "Developments").
63. *Id.* at 1199.
64. *Id.*
65. For a discussion of the rights of parents, *see* Chapter Eleven, "Modern Parental Rights: Issues and Limits."
66. "Developments," *supra* note 62, at 1200-02.
67. David Allen Peterson, "Home Education v. Compulsory Attendance Laws: Whose Kids Are They Anyway?," 24 Washburn Law Journal 274, 282 (1985).
68. *Yoder*, 406 U.S. at 221.
69. Brendan Stocklin-Enright, "The Constitutionality of Home Education: The Role of the Parent, the State and the Child," 18 Willamette Law Review 563 (1982).
70. *Id.* at 578.
71. *Id. See also* Peterson, *supra* note 67, at 282.
72. *Prince v. Massachusetts*, 321 U.S. 158 (1944).
73. *Id.* at 166.
74. Stocklin-Enright *supra* note 69, at 578.
75. Neal M. Devins "A Constitutional Right to Home Instruction?," 62 Washington University Law Quarterly 435, 453 (1984).
76. "Developments," *supra* note 62, at 1201-02.
77. *See* Appendix, "Legislative Status."
78. *See* Chapter Seven, "The Straw Men: Socialization and Academics."
79. Stocklin-Enright, *supra* note 69, at 607.
80. *Id.*
81. *State v. Nobel*, No. S791-0114-A, Jan. 9, 1980 (Mich. Dist. Ct., Allegan County).
82. *Id.*

CHAPTER FOURTEEN: *Right to Privacy and Due Process*

1. *Griswold v. Connecticut*, 381 U.S. 479 (1965).
2. *See Lochner v. New York*, 198 U.S. 45 (1905).
3. *Griswold*, 381 U.S. at 481-82.
4. Michael Knight, "The Case for Allowing Parental Liberties Versus the State's Interest in Education: Home Education," 18 Texas Tech Law Review 1261, 1270 (1987).
5. 262 U.S. 390 (1923).
6. *Id.* at 396-97.
7. *Id.* at 400.
8. *Id.*
9. *Id.* at 402.
10. 268 U.S. 510 (1925).
11. *Id.* at 536.
12. Knight, *supra* note 4, at 1271.
13. *Pierce*, 268 U.S. at 535.
14. *Id.* The Court stated that "the fundamental theory of liberty upon which all governments in this Union repose excludes any general power of the State to standardize its children."
15. 273 U.S. 284 (1927).
16. *Id.* at 290.
17. *Id.* at 298.
18. *Id.* at 298.
19. Knight, *supra* note 4, at 1272.
20. Paul Brest and Sanford Levison, *Processes of Constitutional Decisionmaking* (Boston: Little, Brown and Co., 1985), pp. 658-60.
21. *Id.*
22. 406 U.S. 205 (1972).
23. *Id.*
24. *Id.* at 234.
25. *Id.* at 214. The First Amendment rights of the parents were balanced against the state's interest in education.
26. *Id.* at 235-36.
27. *Id.* at 232.
28. *See Sherbert v. Verner*, 374 U.S. 398 (1963) (strict scrutiny test); *Wisconsin v. Yoder*, 406 U.S. 205 (1972) (strict scrutiny test applied to home education.)
29. G. Gunther, *Constitutional Law*, 11th ed. (Mineola, NY: Foundation Press, Inc., 1985), pp. 586-93.
30. Daniel J. Rose, "Compulsory Education and Parents Rights: A Judicial Framework of Analysis," 30 Bos. Col. L. Rev. 861, 865 (1989).
31. *E.g., McGowan v. Maryland*, 366 U.S. 420 (1961) (rational basis test).
32. *Griswold*, 381 U.S. at 479.
33. *Id.*
34. The Fifth Amendment to the United States Constitution says:

> No person shall be held to answer for a capital, or otherwise infamous crime, unless on a presentment or indictment of a Grand Jury, except in cases arising in the land or naval forces, or in the Militia, when in actual service in time of War or public danger; nor shall any person be subject for the same offence to be twice put in jeopardy of life or limb, nor shall be compelled in any criminal case to be a witness against himself, *nor be deprived of life, liberty, or property, without due process of law*; nor shall private property be taken for public use without just compensation.

U.S. Const., Amend. V (emphasis supplied).

The Fourteenth Amendment to the United States Constitution says:

> ... No State shall make or enforce any law which shall abridge the privileges or immunities of citizens of the United States; *nor shall any State deprive any person of life, liberty, or property, without due process of law*. ...

U.S. Const., Amend. XIV (emphasis supplied).

35. *Id.*
36. G. Sidney Buchanan, "The Right of Privacy: Past, Present, and Future," 16 Ohio N. Univ. L. Rev. 403, 404 (1989).
37. I.e., the partly lighted area surrounding the complete shadow of a body. *Webster's New World Dictionary of the American Language*, College Edition (Cleveland: The World Publishing Company, 1962), p. 1083.
38. R. Collin Mangrum, "Family Rights and Compulsory School Laws," 21 Creighton L. Rev. 1019, 1026 (1988).
39. *Pierce*, 268 U.S. at 510.
40. *Griswold*, 381 U.S. at 482.
41. *Id.* at 484. *See generally* U.S. Const., Amends. I, III, IV, V, IX, and XIV.
42. *Id.*
43. 394 U.S. 557 (1969).
44. *Id.* at 564.
45. 405 U.S. 645 (1972).
46. *Id.* at 651.
47. B. Stocklin-Enright, "The Constitutionality of Home Education," 18 Willamette L. Rev. 563, 571 (1982).
48. *Yoder*, 406 U.S. at 213-14.
49. *Id.* at 232.
50. 411 U.S. 1 (1972).
51. *Id.* at 34.
52. *Id.* at 62.
53. Although the Court did not consider education a fundamental right, the choice of manner of education when predicated upon a fundamental right is protected. *Wisconsin v. Yoder*, 406 U.S. 232-33.
54. Four United States district courts have concluded that home education is not a fundamental right. *Scoma v. Chicago Board of Education*, 391 F.Supp. 452 (1974); *Hanson v. Cushman*, 490 F.Supp. 109 (1980); *Clonlara v. Runkel*, 722 F.Supp. 1442 (1989).

    The Eighth Circuit held that the constitutional right of privacy did not extend to protect parental decisions concerning direction of a child's education from state interference. *Murphy v. Arkansas*, 852 F.2d 1039 (1988).
55. 410 U.S. 113 (1973).
56. *Id.* at 152-3.
57. 410 U.S. 179 (1973).
58. *Id.* at 211.
59. 414 U.S. 632 (1974).
60. *Id.* at 639-40.
61. 424 U.S. 693 (1976).
62. *Id.* at 713.
63. 427 U.S. 160 (1976).
64. *Id.* at 178 n.15.
65. *Cook v. Hudson*, 429 U.S. 165, 166 (1976).
66. 431 U.S. 494 (1977).

67. *Id.* at 499.
68. *Id.* at 503-04.
69. *Id.* at 511.
70. 431 U.S. 678 (1977).
71. *Id.* at 685.
72. 442 U.S. 584 (1979).
73. *Id.*
74. Stocklin-Enright, *supra* note 47, at 573.
75. *Parham*, 442 U.S. at 602.
76. *Id.*
77. 478 U.S. 186 (1986).
78. *Id.* at 190.
79. Civil Action No. 16641 (Mass. Super. Ct., Hampshire County, Nov. 13, 1978).
80. *Id.* slip op. at 9.
81. 159 Mass. 372 (1893).
82. *Id.* at 374.
83. No. 83DR966 (S.C. Fam. Ct., Calhoun County, June 28, 1983), appeal dismissed, No. 83 CP-40-0830 (S.C. Sup. Ct. Feb. 3, 1984).
84. *Id.* slip op. at 7.
85. M. Davis, "The Constitutional Right to Home School," 55 Inter Alia 14, 15 (October 1990).
86. *Meyer*, 262 U.S. at 390.
87. *Yoder*, 406 U.S. at 205.
88. *Griswold*, 381 U.S. at 479.
89. D. E. Tompkins, "An Argument for Privacy in Support of the Choice of Home Education by Parents," Vol. 20, No. 3, Journal of Law and Education 301, 314 (1991).
90. *Pierce*, 268 U.S. at 510.
91. *Meyer*, 262 U.S. at 390.
92. *Roe*, 410 U.S. at 113.
93. *Id.* at 153.
94. *Id.*
95. Rose, *supra* note 30, at 883.
96. *See also* Chapter Twenty-two, "Compelling State Interest."
97. For a further discussion of this issue, *see* Chapter Thirteen, "Freedom of Speech and Formation of Belief."
98. Rose, *supra* note 30, at 862.
99. 406 U.S. 205 (1972).
100. *Id.* at 214.
101. J. Nowak, R. Rotunda and J. Young, *Constitutional Law*, 2d ed. (St. Paul, MN: West Publishing Co., 1983), pp. 448, 457, 1061-63. Under strict scrutiny analysis, the Supreme Court gives added protection to certain rights contained in the Fourteenth and First Amendments, rights that are essential to accepted views of individual liberty that justify strict scrutiny.
102. *Roe*, 410 U.S. 113.
103. Rose, *supra* note 30, at 864.
104. *Yoder*, 406 U.S. at 221.
105. *Id.*
106. *Id.* at 240
107. Rose, *supra* note 30, at 902.
108. Stocklin-Enright, *supra* note 47, at 578.
109. *Id.*
110. Tompkins, *supra* note 89, at 315.

111. *See* Chapter Twenty-Two, "Compelling State Interest."
112. Tompkins, *supra* note 89, at 315.
113. *See* Chapter Thirteen, "Freedom of Speech and Formation of Belief."
114. Note, "Home Education and Fundamental Rights: Can Johnny's Parents Teach Johnny?," 18:73 W.St.U. L. Rev. 731, 758 (1991).
115. Tompkins, *supra* note 89, at 320.

CHAPTER FIFTEEN: *Ninth and Tenth Amendment Concerns*

1. *See* text and discussion, *infra.*
2. *See* text and discussion, *infra.*
3. *See* discussion *infra* and Chapter One, "The Crisis in Contemporary Public Education."
4. 403 U.S. 217, 233-34 (1971).
5. U.S. Const., Amend. IX.
6. John Hart Ely, *Democracy and Distrust* (Cambridge, MA: Harvard University Press, 1980), p. 34.
7. Gales and Seton, eds., 1 *Annals of Congress*, (1834), p. 454, *reprinted in* Bennett B. Patterson, *The Forgotten Ninth Amendment: A Call for Legislation and Judicial Recognition of Rights Under Social Conditions of Today* (Indianapolis: Bobbs-Merrill, 1955).
8. Caplan, "The History and Meaning of the Ninth Amendment," 69 Va. 1. Rev. 223, 263 (1983).
9. Berger, "The Ninth Amendment," 66 Cornell L. Rev. 1, 2-3 (1980).
10. *Id.* at 4.
11. Letter from George Washington to the Marquis de Lafayette (April 28, 1788), reprinted in Vol. 29, *The Writings of George Washington*, Fitzpatrick, ed., (1939), p. 478.
12. Joseph Story, Vol. 2, *Commentaries on the Constitution of the United States*, 5th edition, Melville M. Bigelow, ed. (Boston: Little, Brown and Company, 1891), p. 653.
13. Joseph Story, Vol. 3, *Commentaries on the Constitution of the United States*, 1st ed. (Cambridge, MA: Boston, Hilliard, Gray and Company, 1833), p. 751-2.
14. *See* Caplan, *supra* note 8, at 223.
15. *Id.* at 224.
16. 381 U.S. 479 (1965).
17. *Id.* at 486.
18. *Id.* at 484.
19. *Id.* at 487.
20. *Id.* at 488.
21. E. Corwin, *The Constitution and What It Means Today*, 14th ed. (Princeton, NJ: Princeton University Press, 1978), p. 440.
22. Ely, *supra* note 6, at 34-8: *see also* B. Patterson, *The Forgotten Ninth Amendment* (Indianapolis: Bobbs-Merrill Company, Inc., 1955) (arguing for the resuscitation of the Ninth Amendment as a source of additional federal and even state rights).
23. Charles Lund Black, *Decision According to Law* (New York: Norton, 1981), p. 44.
24. *See, e.g.*, Caplan, *supra* note 8, at 227.
25. *Id.* at 227.
26. *San Antonio Independent School District v. Rodriguez*, 411 U.S. 1, 35 (1973).
27. *Id.* at 36.
28. U.S. Const., Amend. X.

29. Ely, *supra* note 6, at 36.

30. *See* Chapter One, "The Crisis in Contemporary Public Education."

31. The Ninth Amendment to the United States Constitution states:

> The enumeration in the Constitution of certain rights shall not be construed to deny or disparage others retained by the people.

The Tenth Amendment to the United States Constitution states:

> The powers not delegated to the United States by the Constitution, nor prohibited by it to the States, are reserved to the States respectively, or to the people.

32. *See, e.g.,* "World Class Standards," *America 2000: An Education Strategy* (Washington, D.C.: U.S. Dept. of Education, 1991), p. 13.

33. *See* Chapter Two, "The History and Philosophy of Public Education."

34. *See id. See also* R. Freeman Butts and Lawrence A. Cremin, *A History of Education in American Culture* (New York: Holt, Rinehart and Winston, 1953), p. 404; Newton Edwards and Herman Richey, *The School in the American Social Order* (Boston: Houghton Mifflin Co., 1947).

35. Butts and Cremin, *supra* note 34, at 415, 426.

36. *Id.* at 433.

37. *Id.*

38. *See Wisconsin v. Yoder,* 406 U.S. 205, 227 (1972).

39. *Id.* at 227.

40. Butts and Cremin, *supra* note 34, at 415.

41. *Id.* at 539-40.

42. *Id.* at 431.

43. *Id.* at 405, 429.

44. *Id.* at 452.

45. *Id.*

46. *Id.*

47. *See* Appendix, "Legislative Status."

48. *See* Chapter Six, "Dimensions of the Contemporary Home Education Movement."

49. *America 2000, supra* note 32, at 13.

50. *Id.* at 19.

51. *Id.* at 6.

52. *Id.* at 3.

53. *See* Chapter Three, "Freedom and Educational Diversity."

54. Mary Jordan, "Nationwide Test Urged For Schools," *The Washington Post* (January 25, 1992), p. A:4, col. 3.

55. *America 2000, supra* note 32, at 30.

56. *Id.*

57. Kenneth J. Cooper, "National Standards at Core of Strategy," *The Washington Post* (April 19, 1991), p. A:1, col. 1.

58. *See* Chapter One, "The Crisis in Contemporary Public Education" and Chapter Seven, "The Straw Men: Socialization and Academics."

59. Jordan, *supra* note 54, at A:4, col. 2.

60. Cooper, *supra* note 57, at p. A:8, col. 5.

61. *Id.*

62. *See* Chapter Seven, "The Straw Men: Socialization and Academics."

63. Edward B. Fiske, "Changes Planned in Entrance Test Used by Colleges," *The New York Times* (January 3, 1989), p. I:1, col. 3.

64. William Glaberson, "U.S. Court Says Awards Based on SAT's Are Unfair to Girls," *The New York Times* (February 4, 1989), p.I:1, col. 3.
65. *See* Chapter Seven, "The Straw Men: Socialization and Academics."
66. *See* Chapter One, "The Crisis in Contemporary Public Education."
67. 406 U.S. at 223.
68. *America 2000, supra* note 32, at 53.
69. *Id.* at 27.
70. *See* Chapter Four, "Free Market Choice in Education."
71. *Pierce v. Society of Sisters*, 268 U.S. 510, 535 (1925).
72. *Id.* at 535.

CHAPTER SIXTEEN: *Equal Protection of the Law*

1. U.S. Const., Amend. XIV.
2. John E. Nowak, Ronald D. Rotunda and J. Nelson Young, *Constitutional Law*, 3rd ed. (St. Paul, MN: West Publishing Company, 1986), p. 523-4.
3. *Id.*
4. *Id.* at 525-6.
5. Joseph Tussman and Jacobus tenBroek, "The Equal Protection of the Laws," 37 Calif. L. Rev. 341, 367 (1949).
6. *See* Nowak, *supra* note 2, at 526.
7. *See* Appendix, "Legislative Status."
8. *Id.*
9. *See, e.g., State v. Garber*, 419 P.2d 896 (1966). The Kansas Supreme Court held that the state had a legitimate right to enforce compulsory attendance laws as a valid exercise of police power.
10. 268 U.S. 510 (1925). "The fundamental theory of liberty upon which all governments in this Union repose excludes any general power of the state to standardize its children by forcing them to accept instruction from public teachers only." *Id.* at 535.
11. *See* Appendix, "Legislative Status."
12. Henderson, Golanda, and Lee, *Legal Conflicts Involving Home Instruction of School-aged Children* (St. Paul, MN: West Publishing Company Commentary, 1991). *See also* Appendix, "Legislative Status."
13. *Id.*
14. Only two states, Iowa and Michigan, now require that a certified teacher be involved in instruction at home. Five other states, California, Kansas, New York, Ohio, and South Dakota, require home school teachers to be "competent," "qualified," or "capable of teaching." *See* Appendix, "Legislative Status."
15. Kara T. Burgess, Note, "The Constitutionality of Home Education Statutes," 55 UMKC Law Rev. 69, 77 (1986).
16. For a discussion of the right of privacy and its application to a parent's decision to home school, *see* Chapter Fourteen, "Right to Privacy and Due Process."
17. *See* Chapter Twenty-two, "Compelling State Interest."
18. *See generally*, Comment, "Developments in the Law—The Constitution and the Family," 93 Harv. L. Rev. 1156 (1980).
19. Stocklin-Enright, "The Constitutionality of Home Education: The Role of the Parent, the State, and the Child," 18 Willamette L. Rev. 562, 578 (1982).
20. *Id.*
21. *See supra* note 14 and accompanying text.
22. *Shapiro v. Thompson*, 394 U.S. 618, 638 (1969).
23. *See* Sec. 16A, *Am. Jur. 2nd Const. Law Section* 750 (1979).
24. *See* Burgess, *supra* note 15, at 77.

25. *People v. Turner*, 263 P.2d 685, 689 (1953), appeal dismissed, 347 U.S. 972 (1954).
26. *Id.* at 688.
27. *State v. M.M.*, 407 So. 2d 987, 990 (Fla. Dist. Ct. App. 1981).
28. *See generally, id.* at 989-90.
29. *Grigg v. Commonwealth*, 297 S.E. 2d 799, 803 (Va. 1982).
30. *See generally, id.* at 800-05.
31. *See* Chapter Nineteen, "Private School Defense" and Appendix, "Legislative Status."
32. *See* Burgess, *supra* note 15, at 80.
33. *Murphy v. Arkansas*, 852 F.2d 1039, 1043-44 (1988).
34. *State of New Mexico v. Edgington*, 663 P.2d 374, 377-79 (N.M.App. 1983), *cert. denied*, 464 U.S. 940 (1983).
35. *Blount v. Department of Educational and Cultural Services*, 551 A.2d 1377, 1385-86 (1988).
36. *See* Burgess, *supra* note 15, at 78.

CHAPTER SEVENTEEN: *Parental Liberty*

1. *See* Stephen A. Siegel, "Lochner Era Jurisprudence and the American Constitutional Tradition," 70 N.C. L. Rev. 1, 3 (1991).
2. "[T]he Court in a heavy-handed way threw its 'liberty' weight around to permit courts to substitute their social and economic beliefs for the judgment of legislative bodies." R. Collin Mangrum, "Family Rights and Compulsory School Laws," 21 Creighton L. Rev. 1019, 1025 (1988).
3. For a historical and jurisprudential analysis of this period, *see generally* Siegel, *supra* note 1.
4. The standard narrative of the period offered by its critics refers to the *Lochner* era as a "deviant period" in which "the Court underconstrued the scope of congressional power and overprotected private property." *Id.* at 3.
5. *See* Siegel, *supra* note 1, at 3 *citing* David P. Currie, *The Constitution*, in *The Supreme Court: The Second Century, 1888-1896* (Chicago: University of Chicago Press, 1985), pp. 235-36.
6. Many of the substantive economic rights are longer recognized. *See* Mangrum, *supra* note 2, at 1025.
7. *Id.* at 1027.
8. *See Meyer v. Nebraska*, 262 U.S. 390 (1923); *Pierce v. Society of Sisters*, 268 U.S. 510 (1925).
9. *See* Mangrum, *supra* note 2, at 1025-32.
10. Mangrum, *supra* note 2, at 1023 *quoting DeBurgh v. DeBurgh*, 250 P.2d 598, 601 (1952).
11. *See Pierce v. Society of Sisters*, 268 U.S. 510 (1925).
12. *See* Chapter Six, "Dimensions of the Contemporary Home Education Movement."
13. Ira C. Lupu, "Home Education, Religious Liberty, and the Separation of Powers," 67 Boston U.L. Rev. 971, 971 (1987); E. Alice Law Beshoner, Note, "Home Education in America: Parental Rights Reasserted," 49 UMKC 191, 193 (1981).
14. Beshoner, *supra* note 13, at 193-94 *citing* "Should Parents Be Allowed to Educate Their Kids at Home?," 89 Instructor 30 (1979); Vernon Hope Smith, *Alternative Schools: The Development of Options in Public Education* (Lincoln, NE: Professional Educators Publications, 1974); "Why Our Schools Aren't Making the Grade," *McCalls* (September 1975), p. 48.

15. Henry C. T. Richmond, III, Note, "Home Instruction: An Alternative to Institutional Education," 18 J. Family L. 353, (1979-80).
16. Beshoner, *supra* note 13, at 193.
17. For the current status of state legislation affecting home schools, *see* Appendix, "Legislative Status."
18. 262 U.S. 300 (1923).
19. *Id.* at 397.
20. *Id.* at 396.
21. *Id.* at 397.
22. *Id.* at 399.
23. *Id.* at 400.
24. *Id.* at 402.
25. *Id.* at 400.
26. *Id.* at 401-02.
27. 268 U.S. 510 (1925).
28. *Id.* at 534.
29. *Id.*
30. *Id.* at 534-35.
31. *Id.* at 535.
32. *Id.*
33. 273 U.S. 284 (1927).
34. *Id.* at 291.
35. *Id.*
36. *Id.*
37. *Id.* at 291-96.
38. *Id.* at 293.
39. *Id.*
40. *Id.* at 293-94.
41. *Id.* at 294.
42. *Id.* at 296.
43. *Id.* at 298.
44. 262 U.S. 390 (1923).
45. 268 U.S. 510 (1925).
46. *Farrington*, 273 U.S. at 298 (emphasis supplied).
47. *Id.*
48. 406 U.S. 205 (1972).
49. *Id.*
50. *Id.* at 208.
51. *Id.* at 209.
52. *Id.* at 207.
53. *Id.* at 213 *citing Pierce v. Society of Sisters*, 268 U.S. 510, 534 (1925).
54. *Id.*
55. *Id.* at 213-14.
56. *Id.* at 214 (*quoting Pierce*, 268 U.S. at 535).
57. *Id.* The Court added that it could "accept as settled, therefore, that, however strong the State's interest in universal compulsory education, it is by no means absolute to the exclusion or subordination of all other interests." *Id.* at 215 *citing Sherbert v. Verner*, 374 U.S. 398 (1963); *McGowan v. Maryland*, 366 U.S. 420, 459 (1961) (separate opinion of Frankfurter, J.); *Prince v. Massachusetts*, 321 U.S. 158, 165 (1944).
58. *Id.* at 210-11. The high school experience conflicted with the Amish teaching of non-conformity and separation from "contemporary, worldly society." *Id.*

59. *Id.* at 212. The Amish were not opposed to sending their children to elementary schools because "[t]hey view such a basic education as acceptable because it does not significantly expose their children to worldly values or interfere with their development in the Amish community during the crucial adolescent period." *Id.* During the adolescent period, the Amish teenagers engage in "learning-by-doing," meaning they must learn the skills necessary to be an Amish farmer or housewife. *Id.* at 211.

60. *Id.* at 215.

61. *Id.*

62. *Id.* at 216. The Court found particularly convincing the Amish's literal interpretation of the Biblical command to "be not conformed to this world," a command deemed fundamental to their faith. *Id.* The Court also pointed to the degree in which the Amish attitudes and beliefs toward family and home have remained static in a world that has become increasingly more conscious of the value of education. *Id.* Some courts have suggested that the history, tradition, and uniqueness of the Amish order compelled the Court to rule in the Amish's favor and that other beliefs do not merit such a result. *See, e.g., State v. Patzer*, 382 N.W.2d 631, 636-37 (N.D. 1986), *cert. denied*, 479 U.S. 825 (1986).

63. *Yoder*, 406 U.S. at 218.

64. *Id.* at 219. The state did not challenge the sincerity of the Amish's beliefs; rather, its argument focused on its superior interest. *Id.*

65. *Id.* at 222. The Court also stated that "[i]t is one thing to say that compulsory education for a year or two beyond the eighth grade may be necessary when its goal is the preparation of the child for life in modern society as the majority live, but it is quite another if the goal of education be viewed as the preparation of the child for life in the separated agrarian community that is the keystone of the Amish faith." *Id.* (*citing Meyer v. Nebraska*, 262 U.S. at 400).

66. *Id.* at 222-23. The Court rejected the state's argument that the Amish children ought to be prepared to function in modern society should they choose to leave their community, calling it mere speculation in light of the lack of evidence of attrition and the minimal burden they would be on society because of their education should they elect to leave.

67. *Id.* at 226.

68. *Id.* at 213; *see also id.* at 215 ("We can accept it as settled, therefore, that, however strong the State's interest in universal compulsory education, it is by no means absolute to the exclusion or subordination of all other interests"), *citing Sherbert v. Verner*, 374 U.S. 398; *McGowan v. Maryland*, 366 U.S. at 459 (separate opinion of Frankfurter, J.); *Prince v. Massachusetts*, 321 U.S. at 165.

69. *Id.* at 213 (*citing Pierce v. Society of Sisters*, 268 U.S. 510).

70. 427 U.S. 160 (1976).

71. *Id.* at 163.

72. *Id.* at 163-65.

73. *Id.* at 165.

74. *Id.* at 163-64.

75. *Id.* at 165-67. An ancillary issue involved the type of the relief to which the parents were entitled. *See id.* at 166-67, 182-86.

76. *Id.* at 168.

77. *Id.* at 173-75.

78. *Id.* at 175.

79. *Id.* at 175-76 (emphasis in original).

80. *Id.* at 176 *quoting Norwood v. Harrison*, 413 U.S. 455, 470 (1973).

81. *Id.* at 176-77.

82. *Id.* at 177. The Court seemingly engaged in a selective examination of precedent to support its reasoning. For example, when *citing Wisconsin v. Yoder*, 406 U.S. 205, the *Runyon* Court stated that the *Yoder* Court "stressed the limited scope of *Pierce.*" *Runyon*, 427 U.S. at 177; *see Pierce v. Society of Sisters*, 268 U.S. 510. The *Runyon* Court stated that the *Yoder* Court observed that *Pierce*:

> [L]ent "no support to the contention that parents may replace state educational requirements with their own idiosyncratic views of what knowledge a child needs to be a productive and happy member of society" but rather "held simply that while a State may posit [educational] standards, it may not pre-empt the educational process by requiring children to attend public schools."

Id. quoting Yoder, 406 U.S. at 239 (White, J., concurring). Note, however, whom the *Runyon* Court cites for this proposition: Justice White in a *concurring* opinion. The *Yoder* majority did not focus on the limiting nature of *Pierce*. Although the *Yoder* Court recognized the state's power to impose *reasonable* regulations on the parental right to direct a child's education, it explicitly stated that *Pierce* demonstrated that the state's interest in education was not absolute. *Yoder*, 406 U.S. at 213.

83. *Runyon*, 427 U.S. at 178 (*citing Yoder*, 406 U.S. at 213; *Pierce*, 268 U.S. at 534; *Meyer v. Nebraska*, 262 U.S. at 402).

84. "'[T]he Constitution . . . places no value on discrimination.'" *Id.* at 176 *quoting Norwood v. Harrison*, 413 U.S. 455, 469 (1973). This paternal attitude of protecting racial minorities and ending discrimination has emerged in other contexts as well. *See, e.g., Bob Jones Univ. v. United States*, 461 U.S. 574 (1983) (denying a sectarian school tax exempt status because of overt discriminatory practices); *NAACP v. Claiborne Hardware*, 458 U.S. 886 (1982) (prohibiting a state from proscribing an NAACP boycott, a protest against discrimination, of white merchants despite potential of economic ruin for merchants); *In re Primus*, 436 U.S. 412 (1978) (finding that ACLU contact with a possible complainant in a civil rights claim did not constitute an ethics violation); *New York Times Co. v. Sullivan*, 376 U.S. 254 (1964) (finding that an advertisement accusing a public official of racist practices did not constitute defamatory falsehood).

85. 494 U.S. 872 (1990).

86. *See id.* at 881. Note that *Runyon* did not address sectarian schools or any religious rights claims. *Runyon*, 427 U.S. at 167.

87. *Id.* While the Court did not explicitly hold that hybrid claims—a religious claim in conjunction with any other constitutional claim—were subject to the compelling state interest test, many lower courts have construed such a requirement. *See, e.g., Vandiver v. Hardin County Bd. of Educ.*, 925 F.2d 927, 933 (6th Cir. 1991); *Society of Separationists, Inc. v. Herman*, 939 F.2d 1207, 1216 (5th Cir. 1991).

88. *See supra* note 84 and cases cited therein. Many of these cases involve the family right to privacy, which is addressed in a separate chapter; nevertheless, these cases demonstrate the paramount importance the Supreme Court has given the family. For a discussion of these cases, *see* Chapter Fourteen, "Right to Privacy and Due Process" and Mangrum, *supra* note 2, at 1027-33.

89. 431 U.S. 494 (1977).

90. *Id.* at 496-97.

91. *Id.*

92. *Id.* at 497.

93. *Id.* at 499.

94. 268 U.S. 510, 534-35 (1925).

95. 262 U.S. 390, 399-401 (1923).
96. *Moore,* 431 U.S. at 499 *citing Prince v. Massachusetts,* 321 U.S. at 166; *Roe v. Wade,* 410 U.S. 113, 152-53 (1973); *Wisconsin v. Yoder,* 406 U.S. 205, 231-33 (1972); *Stanley v. Illinois,* 405 U.S. 645, 651 (1972); *Ginsberg v. New York* , 390 U.S. 629, 639 (1968); *Griswold v. Connecticut,* 381 U.S. 479 (1965); *id.* at 495-96 (Goldberg, J., concurring); *id.* at 502-03 (White, J., concurring); *Poe v. Ullman,* 367 U.S. 497, 542-44, 549-53 (1961) (Harlan, J., dissenting); *Loving v. Virginia,* 388, U.S. 1, 12 (1967); *May v. Anderson,* 345 U.S. 528, 533 (1953); *Skinner v. Oklahoma,* 316 U.S. 535, 541 (1942).
97. *Id.* at 503-04.
98. *Id.* at 499.
99. *Id.* at 499-506.
100. *See, e.g., Runyon, supra* notes 70-84, and accompanying text.
101. With respect to the first question, most courts seemingly have provided an easy answer: the right to direct the education of one's child includes the right to educate the child at home. *See, e.g., In re Charles,* 504 N.E.2d 592, 598-600 (Mass. 1987) (both the state and court agreed that a parental right to home school exists); *State v. McDonough,* 468 A.2d 977, 979 (Me. 1983) (same); *see also Vandiver v. Hardin County Bd. of Educ.,* 925 F.2d 927, 933 (6th Cir. 1991) (stating there is a right to home education); *Hanson v. Cushman,* 490 F. Supp. 109, 112-14 (1980) (implying that the right to educate one's child at home is limited to parents who are religiously motivated to home school). For an in-depth analysis of legislation affecting home schools, *see* Appendix, "Legislative Status."
102. *See* Appendix, "Legislative Status."
103. *See Runyon v. McCrary,* 427 U.S. at 178 (1976) (*citing Yoder,* 406 U.S. at 213; *Pierce,* 268 U.S. at 534; *Meyer v. Nebraska,* 262 U.S. at 402).
104. *See* Chapter Twenty-two, "Compelling State Interest."

CHAPTER EIGHTEEN: *Vagueness Issues*

1. U.S. Const., Amend. XIV.
2. *Grayned v. City of Rockford,* 408 U.S. 104, 108 (1972).
3. *Donnally v. General Constr. Co.,* 269 U.S. 385, 391 (1926) *citing International Harvester Co. v. Kentucky,* 234 U.S. 216, 221 (1914); *Collins v. Kentucky,* 234 U.S. 634, 638 (1914).
4. John Calvin Jeffries, Jr., "Legality, Vagueness, and the Construction of Penal Statutes," 71 Va. L. Rev. 189, 189 (1985).
5. *See* Richard A. Rosen, "The (Especially Heinous) Aggravating Circumstance in Capital Cases—The Standardless Standard," 64 N.C. L. Rev. 941, 955 (discussing the vagueness doctrine in the context of capital punishment).
6. For example, many statutes provide that students are exempt from compulsory attendance if they receive "equivalent instruction," language several courts have held to be unconstitutionally vague. *See* Appendix, "Legislative Status."
7. *Grayned,* 408 U.S. at 110.
8. *Rose v. Locke,* 423 U.S. 48, 49 (1975) (*per curiam*).
9. *Id.* at 49-50 *quoting Robinson v. United States,* 327 U.S. 282, 286 (1975).
10. *Grayned,* 408 U.S. at 10 *quoting Esteban v. Central Missouri State College,* 415 F.2d 1077, 1088 (8th Cir. 1969) (Blackmun, J.), *cert. denied,* 398 U.S. 965 (1970).
11. Jeffries, *supra* note 4, at 196. "Unconstitutional indefiniteness 'is itself an indefinite concept.'" *Id. quoting Winters v. New York,* 333 U.S. 507, 524 (1948) (Frankfurter, J., dissenting).

12. *See Kolender v. Lawson*, 461 U.S. 352, 357-58 (1983); *Smith v. Goguen*, 415 U.S. 566, 572 (1974); *Grayned*, 408 U.S. at 108; *Papachristou v. City of Jacksonville*, 405 U.S. 156, 162 (1972); *Coates v. City of Cincinnati*, 402 U.S. 611, 614 (1971); *Lanzetta v. New Jersey*, 306 U.S. 451, 453 (1939); *Donnally* 269 U.S. at 391.
13. 408 U.S. 104 (1972).
14. *Id.* at 108-09 (footnotes omitted).
15. *Hoffman Estates v. Flipside, Hoffman Estates*, 455 U.S. 489, 498 (1982); *Smith*, 415 U.S. at 573 and n.10 (citations omitted); *Grayned*, 408 U.S. at 109 and n.5.
16. *Hoffman Estates*, 455 U.S. at 498; *Smith* 415 U.S. at 573 n.10; *see, e.g., United States v. National Dairy Products Corp.*, 372 U.S. 29, 36 (1963); *McGowan v. Maryland*, 366 U.S. 420, 428 (1961).
17. *Hoffman Estates*, 455 U.S. at 498-99.
18. *Id.* at 499.
19. *Id.*; *Smith*, 415 U.S. at 573 (footnote omitted); *Grayned*, 408 U.S. at 109 and n.5; *Papachristou*, 405 U.S. at 165-66; *see* Jeffries, *supra* note 4, at 196; Rosen, *supra* note 5, at 955 n. 69.
20. *Grayned*, 408 U.S. at 109 *quoting Baggett v. Bullitt*, 377 U.S. 360, 372 (1964) *quoting Speiser v. Randall*, 357 U.S. 513, 526 (1958). *See* Note, "The Void-for-Vagueness Doctrine in the Supreme Court," 109 U. Pa. L. Rev. 67, 75 (describing the Court's use of the vagueness doctrine as "the creation of an insulating buffer zone of added protection at the peripheries of several of the Bill of Rights freedoms").
21. *Grayned*, 408 U.S. at 109 n.5 *quoting Edwards v. South Carolina*, 372 U.S. 229, 236 (1963).
22. *Id.*
23. *See* Erwin Chemerinsky, *Federal Jurisdiction*, Sec. 2.3.4 (Boston: Little, Brown & Co., 1989), p. 75.
24. *Hoffman Estates*, 455 U.S. at 495. In essence, a litigant's facial challenge will succeed only if it is "impermissibly vague in all of its applications," including when applied to the litigant. *Id.* at 494-95.
25. The exception is commonly referred to as the "overbreadth doctrine." *See* Chemerinsky, *supra* note 23, at Sec. 2.3.4., p. 75. The court, however, has acknowledged that this exception applies to cases where vagueness, rather than overbreadth, is the issue. *See Kolender*, 461 U.S. at 358-59 n. 8.

   The *Blackwelder* Court held the view that this special rule may not be applicable to the Religion Clauses of the First Amendment. *Blackwelder v. Safnauer*, 689 F. Supp. 106, 126 n. 19 (N.D. N.Y. 1988), *aff'd and appeal dismissed*, 866 F. 2d 548 (2d Cir. 1989); however, *Kolender* in no way used such limiting language. It referred to the First Amendment in general, and not to specific clauses. *See Kolender*, 461 U.S. at 358-59 and n. 8.
26. Chemerinsky, *supra* note 23, at Sec. 2.3.4, p. 75. *see Kolender*, 461 U.S. at 358-59 and n.8. As the court stated in *Schaumberg v. Citizens for a Better Environment*, 444 U.S. 620 (1980): "Given a case or controversy, a litigant whose own activities are unprotected may nevertheless challenge a statute by showing that it substantially abridges the First Amendment rights of other parties not before the court." *Id.* at 643, *cited in* Chemerinsky, *supra* note 23, at Sec. 2.3.4., p. 75.
27. *Blackwelder*, 689 F. Supp. at 126 n.19.
28. Chemerinsky, *supra* note 23, at Sec. 2.3.4, p. 76. Laurence H. Tribe, *American Constitutional Law*, 1st ed., Sec. 12-32 (Mineola, NY: Foundation Press, 1978), p. 1035 *citing Gooding v. Wilson*, 405 U.S. 518, 521 (1972) (dictum). Essentially this overbreadth doctrine creates an exception to the general notions

of justiciability that prohibit third-party standing. Chemerinsky, *supra* note 23, at Sec. 2.3.4., p. 75-6 *citing Virginia v. American Booksellers Ass'n*, 108 S. Ct. 636 (1988); *Secretary of State v. J. H. Munson, Co.*, 467 U.S. 947, 956 (1984).

29. *Hoffman Estates*, 455 U.S. at 494; *Kolender*, 461 U.S. at 358-59 n. 8 (*citing Hoffman Estates*, 455 U.S. at 494).

30. *See Kolender*, 461 U.S. at 355 (*citing Hoffman Estates*, 455 U.S. at 494 n.5); Chemerinsky, *supra* note 23, at Sec. 2.3.4, p. 77 *citing New York v. Ferber*, 458 U.S. 747, 769 n.24 (1982).

31. 461 U.S. 352 (1982).

32. *Id.* at 105. There was a difference among witnesses' testimony over the actual tone of the protest and its impact on school operations.

33. *Id.* at 106.

34. *Id.* at 107. The ordinance prohibited picketing and demonstrating:

> [O]n a public way within 150 feet of any primary or secondary school building while the school is in session and one-half hour before the school is in session and one-half hour after the school session has been concluded, provided that this subsection does not prohibit of any school involved in a labor dispute.

Id. quoting Code of Ordinances, c. 28 § 18.1(i).

35. *Id.* at 107-08 *quoting* Code of Ordinances, c. 28, § 19.2(a).

36. *Id.* at 107.

37. *Id.* at 107-14.

38. *Id.*

39. *Id.* at 112 *quoting American Communications Ass'n v. Douds*, 339 U.S. 382, 412 (1950); *Cameron v. Johnson*, 390 U.S. 611, 616 (1968).

40. *Id.* at 113.

41. *Id.* at 113-14.

42. 461 U.S. 352 (1982).

43. *Id.* at 353-54.

44. *Id.* at 353 (citation omitted).

45. *Id.* at 353.

46. *Id.* at 361.

47. *Id.* at 358.

48. *Id.* at 360 (*quoting* from transcript of oral argument at 6).

49. *Id* at 360.

50. *Id.* at 361.

51. *Id.* at 360 (*quoting Papachristou*, 405 U.S. at 170 *quoting Thornhill v. Alabama*, 310 U.S. 88, 97-98 (1940). This reasoning is easily transferrable to the home school context: any interest in education should not excuse an ordinance lacking "clarity and definiteness." *Id.* at 361. Courts should be particularly cautious about arbitrary enforcement among school districts, for some officials undoubtedly harbor a grudge against parents who wish to home school their children.

52. *Kolender*, 461 U.S. at 357.

53. *See id.* at 358.

54. *E.g.*, "Congress shall make no law respecting an establishment of religion, or prohibiting the free exercise thereof. . . ." U.S. Const., Amend. I.

55. *See id.*

56. *See* Appendix, "Legislative Status."

57. *See, e.g., Blackwelder*, 699 F. Supp. at 122; *Jeffrey v. O'Donnell*, 702 F. Supp. 516, 518-19 (M.D. Pa. 1988); *Roemhild v. State*, 308 S.E.2d 154 (Ga. 1983); *State v. Popanz*, 332 N.W.2d 750, 753 n.5 (Wis. 1983).

58. *Grayned*, 408 U.S. at 108-09 (1972).
59. 689 F. Supp. 106 (N.D. N.Y. 1988).
60. *Id.* at 121-28.
61. *Id.* at 122.
62. *Id.*
63. *Id.*
64. *Id.* at 121.
65. This rejection came in spite of the use of a more rigid vagueness test because of the criminal charges. *Id.* at 125-26. The court neglected to discuss the First Amendment interests at stake.
66. *Id.* at 126-27 *quoting Textile Workers Pension Fund v. Standard Dye & Finishing Co.*, 725 F.2d 843, 856 (2nd Cir.), *cert. denied*, 467 U.S. 1259 (1984).
67. While not binding on the local districts, the home school guidelines detail information that the local school officials should receive from the parents before approving or disapproving a home education program: "a plan of instruction and a calendar for the year, syllabi, and a list of materials or textbooks to be used, a description of the background, experience and credentials of the teacher, and a plan for evaluating the academic progress of the child being taught at home." *Id.* at 125. In addition, the guidelines inform parents of their right to challenge a superintendent's findings at a hearing before the local school board and to an appeal before the state board of education. *Id.*
68. *Id.* at 127.
69. *Id. quoting Boos v. Barry*, 485 U.S. 312, 332 (1988).
70. *Id.*
71. *Id.*
72. *Id.* at 127-28 (*citing Hoffman Estates*, 455 U.S. at 498).
73. 702 F. Supp. 516 (M.D. Pa. 1988).
74. *Id.* at 517-18.
75. *Id.* at 518 (*quoting* 24 P.S. Section 13-1327) (emphasis provided by court).
76. *Id.* at 519.
77. *Id.* The plaintiffs sought to home educate their children because of their religious beliefs. *Id.*
78. *Id. quoting Wisconsin v. Yoder*, 406 U.S. 205 (1972).
79. *Id.* at 519-20. The Court recognized that *Blackwelder* held no precedential weight. *Id.* at 521.
80. *Id.* at 520-21.
81. *Id.* at 520.
82. *Id.*
83. *Id.*
84. *Id.*
85. *Id.* at 521. But *see State v. Riddle*, 285 S.E.2d 359, 366 (W. Va. 1981) (finding that similar language—"qualified to give instruction in subjects to be taught in free elementary schools"—was not vague).
86. *Jeffrey v. O'Donnell*, 702 F. Supp. at 521.
87. *Id.* at 520.
88. *See* Appendix, "Legislative Status."
89. Another reason for this disparity is the different standards courts have employed in addressing vagueness issues. While courts supposedly should require a greater degree of specificity when First Amendment issues are involved, they have demanded inconsistent levels of definiteness, some not rising to the level required. *Compare Blackwelder*, 689 F. Supp. 106 (using a loose standard) with *Jeffrey*, 702 F. Supp. 516 (requiring a higher degree of specificity).
90. *Roemhild*, 308 S.E.2d 154; *Popanz*, 332 N.W.2d 750.

91. 332 N.W.2d 750. *See also Roemhild*, 308 S.E.2d 154 (finding that the language "private school" was impermissibly vague).

92. *See Popanz*, 332 N.W.2d at 751-52.

93. *Id.* at 751-53.

94. *Id.* at 754. *See Roemhild*, 308 S. E.2d at 157-58. The *Roemhild* court found that the Georgia compulsory attendance statute "suffer[ed] from the same infirmities." *Id.* at 157. In addition, the court held that while the "word 'school' clearly puts one on notice that an organized education must be provided to the child, there are many questions concerning the scope, nature, and place of education which are left unanswered by the statute or applicable authorities." *Id.* at 158.

95. *Popanz*, 332 N.W. 2d at 755.

96. *Id.*

97. *Id.*

98. *Id.*

99. *Id.* at 755-56.

100. *Id.* at 756 *quoting Grayned*, 408 U.S. at 108. The court also was troubled because parents did not have an appeal procedure available within the education system; rather the only method of appeal was through the courts. This was insufficient, according to the *Popanz* court, because the legislature did not provide the court any guidelines to define "private school" and "[d]efining the contours of laws subjecting a violator to criminal penalty is a legislative and not a judicial function." *Id.*

101. 669 S.W.2d 441 (Ark. 1984).

102. *Id.* at 443.

103. *Id.*

104. *Id.* at 442.

105. *Id.* at 443.

106. The interpretation of this principle is erroneous.

107. *Burrow*, 669 S.W.2d at 443. *But see Popanz*, 332 N.W.2d at 755 (finding that the traditional definition of the word *school*—describing it as an institution—is not the only interpretation a citizen, school official, or court could deduce); *Roemhild*, 308 S.E.2d at 158 (same).

108. *Burrow*, 669 S.W.2d at 443.

109. *See Bangor Baptist Church v. Maine*, 549 F. Supp. 1208 (Me. 1982) ("equivalent instruction"); *Newstrom*, 371 N.W.2d at 526 ("essentially equivalent" qualifications); *State v. Moorhead*, 308 N.W.2d 60, 63-64 (Iowa 1981) ("equivalent instruction").

110. 371 N.W.2d 525 (Minn. 1985).

111. *But see Bangor Baptist Church*, 549 F. Supp. 1208, (finding "equivalent instruction" not vague); *Moorhead*, 308 N.W.2d at 63-64 (finding neither "equivalent instruction" nor "certified teacher" vague).

112. *Newstrom*, 371 N.W.2d at 529.

113. *Id.* at 532-33.

114. *Id.*

115. *Compare Blackwelder*, 689 F. Supp. at 124-27 (finding no vagueness problem because of comprehensive regulations) with *Jeffrey v. O'Donnell*, 702 F. Supp. at 520-21 (finding a vagueness problem enhanced by the absence of a statutory definition and of regulations and guidelines for local school districts to follow). *See also Moorhead*, 308 N.W.2d at 64 (finding that the state provided reasonable guidelines to assist in determining what qualifies as "equivalent instruction"); *State v. DeLaBruere*, 577 A.2d 254, 272-73 (Vt. 1990) (finding that although the compulsory attendance statute failed to provide exceptions,

the legislature clearly defined the exceptions in a later statute, and that provision was sufficient to provide fair warning).

116. *See Popanz*, 332 N.W.2d 750; *Roemhild*, 308 S.E.2d at 158.

117. *Compare Blackwelder*, 689 F. Supp. at 127 (appeals process existed) with *Jeffrey*, 702 F. Supp. at 520 (meaningful appellate avenue nonexistent). *See also Riddle*, 285 S.E.2d at 365, 366 (finding that any arbitrary and capricious action can be corrected through court action). The *Riddle* court seemingly has applied erroneously the vagueness standard. The Supreme Court has held that if a statute fosters arbitrary and discriminatory enforcement, the statute is void for vagueness. *See Grayned*, 408 U.S. at 108-09. A statute that is upheld because the courts can correct the discretionary problem undermines one of the underlying principles of the vagueness doctrine—to prevent "wholesale legislative delegation of law making to the courts." Jeffries, *supra* note 4, at 189.

118. *See, e.g., Jeffrey*, 702 F. Supp. 516 (finding that home school regulations did not interfere with the free exercise rights of parents, but that the statute did fail under the vagueness doctrine).

CHAPTER NINETEEN: *Private School Defense*

1. See Appendix, "Legislative Status."

2. *See* Appendix, "Legislative Status."

3. For example, Tex. Educ. Code §21.033 (1991) declares that:

> (a) The following classes of children are exempt from the requirements of compulsory attendance.

> (1) Any child in attendance upon a private or parochial school which shall include in its course a study of good citizenship.

The other exceptions are for mentally and physically handicapped students, expelled students, and teenage students taking high school equivalency tests. There is nothing that expressly exempts a program of home instruction.

4. *See* Chapter Twenty-two, "Compelling State Interest." *See also* 65 A.L.R.3d 1222, 1228 (1975).

5. *Id.* at 1232.

6. 124 P. 910 (Wash. 1912).

7. *Id.* at 911-12.

8. *Id.*

9. Tobak and Zirkel, "Home Instruction: An Analysis of the Statutes and Case Law," 8 U. of Dayton L. Rev. 1, 30 (1982).

10. 383 P.2d 962 (Kan. 1963).

11. *Id.*

12. *Id.* at 965.

13. *Id.*

14. *See, e.g., State v. Hoyt*, 146 A. 170-71 (N.H. 1929). *See also* Chapter Seven, "The Straw Men: Socialization and Academics."

15. *See, e.g., id.* at 171.

16. 263 P.2d 685 (Cal. App. 1953).

17. *Id.* at 689.

18. *Id.*

19. 346 P.2d 999 (Wash. 1959).

20. 346 P.2d at 1001.

21. *Id.* at 1002-03.

22. 70 N.E. 550 (Ind. App. 1904).

23. *Id.* at 551.
24. *Id.*
25. 90 N.E. 2d 213 (IL 1950).
26. *Id.* at 215.
27. *Id.* "The law is not made to punish those who provide their children with instruction equal or superior to that obtainable in the public schools."
28. *Id.*
29. *Id.*
30. 686 P.2d 981 (N.M. App. 1984).
31. *Id.* at 984.
32. *Id.*
33. *Id.* at 985.
34. 308 S.E.2d 154 (Ga. 1983).
35. *Id.* at 158-59.
36. *Leeper v. Arlington Independent School District,* No. 17-88761-85, Tarrant County, 17th Judicial Ct. (April 13, 1987), p. 3-6. (This case is currently on appeal to the Texas Supreme Court.) *See also People v. Darrah,* No. 853104 and *People v. Black,* No. 853105, Santa Maria Mun. Ct., March 10, 1986.
37. *See, e.g., State v. M.M.,* 407 So. 2d 987 (Fla. Dist. Ct. App. 1981), *Grigg v. Commonwealth,* 297 S.E. 2d 799 (1982), *In re Kilroy,* 467 N.Y.S. 2d 318 (Fam. Ct. 1983).
38. Tobak and Zirkel, *supra* note 9, at 53-5. Parents in this situation often wish to qualify as a private school to avoid the restrictions otherwise imposed upon their home school by applicable state statutes.
39. *See Roemhild v. State, supra* n.34, *Strosnider, supra* n. 30. *See also* Chapter Eighteen, "Vagueness Issues."

CHAPTER TWENTY: *Establishment Clause Issues*

1. U.S. Const, Amend. I. The Establishment Clause was made applicable to the states through the Due Process Clause of the Fourteenth Amendment. *See Everson v. Board of Educ.* 330 U.S. 1 (1947).
2. *See* Ira C. Lupu, "Home Education, Religious Liberty, and the Separation of Powers," 67 Boston U.L. Rev. 971, 982-83 (1987) (suggesting that home schools constitute a religious community). There is strong support for the proposition that the home is a school; *see Delconte v. State,* 329 S.E.2d 636, 642 (N.C. 1985) (finding that the legislature did not intend "simply by use of the word 'school,' because of some intrinsic meaning invariably attached to the word, to preclude home instruction"), and consequently that when home education is pursued because of religious beliefs it is a religious school, placing it under the definition of "church" for Establishment Clause purposes.
3. *See, e.g., Blackwelder v. Safnauer,* 689 F. Supp. 106, 142-45 (N.D.N.Y. 1988) (rejecting parents' Establishment Clause argument not because such an avenue was closed to home schoolers but because parents failed to show that the state had failed the *Lemon* test).
4. *See generally* Daniel L. Dreisbach, *Real Threat and Mere Shadow: Religious Liberty and the First Amendment* (Wheaton, IL: Crossway Books, 1987); *see* Thomas J. Curry, *The First Freedoms,* Preface (New York: Oxford University Press, 1986) (discussing the two sides of the debate).
5. Curry, *supra* note 5, at Preface; Laurence H. Tribe, *American Constitutional Law,* 2nd ed., § 14-3 (Mineola, NY: The Foundation Press, 1988), p. 1158.
6. Curry, *supra* note 4, at Preface; Tribe, *supra* note 5, at 1158-59.

7. Dreisbach, *supra* note 4, at 49; Curry, *supra* note 4, at Preface; Tribe, *supra* note 5, at 1159.

8. Dreisbach, *supra* note 4, at 47.

9. 330 U.S. 1 (1947).

10. *Id.* at 15-16 (emphasis in original).

11. *Id.* at 16 *quoting Reynolds v. United States*, 98 U.S. 145, 164 (1878). Many scholars have argued that this Jeffersonian language has been misconstrued and that the actual context of this writing does not support the Court's conclusion. *See, e.g.,* Dreisbach, *supra* note 4, at 115.

12. Dreisbach, *supra* note 4, at 47.

13. *Walz v. Tax Comm'n*, 397 U.S. 664, 669 (1970).

14. *Aguilar v. Felton*, 473 U.S. 402, 413 (1985) *citing Lemon v. Kurtzman*, 403 U.S. 602, 614 (1971).

15. 403 U.S. 602 (1971).

16. *Lemon v. Kurtzman*, 403 U.S. 602, 612-13 (1971) *quoting Walz v. Tax Comm.*, 397 U.S. 664, 674 (1970). It appears, however, that the death knell for the traditional *Lemon* test has been sounded. On the present Court there are two competing standards emerging to replace the *Lemon* test. First articulated in *Lynch v. Donnelly*, 465 U.S. 668, 687-88 (1984) (O'Connor, J., concurring in judgment), Justice O'Connor has advocated the endorsement test that has attracted support from some of her colleagues. *See, e.g., County of Allegheny v. American Civil Liberties Union*, 492 U.S. 573, 589-94 (1989) (favorably *citing* the endorsement test but failing to overturn *Lemon*). Justice O'Connor would alter the three-prong *Lemon* test to a two-step standard "[f]ocusing on institutional entanglement and on endorsement or disapproval of religion" in order to clarify the Establishment Clause analysis. *Lynch*, 465 U.S. at 689. She considers the latter the "more direct infringement . . . [because it] sends a message to nonadherents that they are outsiders, not full members of the political community, and an accompanying message to adherents that they are insiders, favored members of the political community." *Id.* at 688.

   The competing standard, articulated by Justice Kennedy in *Allegheny* (*see* 492 U.S. at 655-63) is known as the coercion test. Justice Kennedy, in his examination of Supreme Court precedent, finds that "the Establishment Clause permits government some latitude in recognizing and accommodating the central role religion plays in our society." *Id.* at 657. Prohibiting any form of endorsement, such as aid or assistance, would offend the nation's political and cultural heritage. *Id.* According to Justice Kennedy, the Establishment Clause only operates under "two limiting principles: government may not coerce anyone to support or participate in any religion or its exercise and it may not, in the guise of avoiding hostility or callous indifference, give direct benefits to religion in such a degree that it in fact 'establishes a [state] religion or religious faith, or tends to do so.'" *Id.* at 659 (*quoting Lynch v. Donnelly*, 465 U.S. at 678). Chief Justice Rehnquist and Justices White and Scalia concurred with Justice Kennedy's opinion announcing the coercion test. *Id.* at 655.

17. *Lemon*, 403 U.S. at 613-14.

18. *Id.* at 612 (*quoting Walz*, 397 U.S. at 668).

19. *Id.* at 615.

20. *Runyon v. McCrary*, 427 U.S. 160, 178-79 (1976) (citations omitted); *see Murphy v. State of Arkansas*, 852 F.2d 1039, 1041-43 (8th Cir. 1988).

21. *Lemon*, 403 U.S. at 614.

22. "Some limited and incidental entanglement between church and state authority is inevitable in a complex modern society." *Larkin v. Grendel's Den, Inc.*, 459 U.S. 116, 123 (1982).

23. *Lemon*, 403 U.S. at 614.
24. *Id.* at 619.
25. *See also Lemon*, 403 U.S. 602 (1971) (striking down two separate programs where the states provided educational resources to sectarian schools).
26. 473 U.S. 402 (1985).
27. *Id.* at 404.
28. *Id.*
29. *Id.* at 407.
30. *Id.* at 409.
31. *Id.* at 412.
32. *Id.* at 412-13 (citations omitted).
33. *Id. quoting Felton v. Secretary of Educ.* 739 F.2d 48, 65 (1984), *aff'd sub nom. Aguilar v. Felton*, 473 U.S. 402 (1985).
34. *Id.* at 414 *quoting Walz v. Tax Comm'n*, 397 U.S. 664, 674 (1970).
35. 885 F.2d 940 (1st Cir. 1989), *cert. denied*, 494 U.S. 1066 (1990).
36. 899 F.2d 1389 (4th Cir.), *cert. denied*, 111 S. Ct. 131 (1990).
37. 885 F.2d 940.
38. *New Life Baptist Church Academy*, 885 F.2d at 941.
39. *Id.* (*citing* Mass. Gen. L. ch. 76, § 1).
40. *Id.* at 952.
41. *Id.* The visits consisted "of at least one initial visit where the visitors . . . will read texts, examine teaching plans for secular courses, consider curricula, observe some classes, and discuss these matters with the school administration. The School Committee [predicted] additional visits only if the teaching credentials [were] inadequate." *Id.*
42. *Id.* It also argued that the statute infringed upon its free exercise rights. *Id.*
43. *Id.* at 953 *quoting Aguilar v. Felton*, 473 U.S. 402, 413 (1985).
44. *Id.* (*quoting Lemon*, 403 U.S. at 619).
45. *Id.* at 953-54.
46. 899 F.2d 1389.
47. *Id.* at 1399.
48. *Id.*
49. *Id.*
50. *Id. quoting Tony & Susan Alamo Found. v. Secretary of Labor*, 471 U.S. 290, 305-06 (1985).
51. For a discussion of such state regulations, *see* Appendix, "Legislative Status."
52. Lupu, *supra* note 2, at 983.
53. *Id.; see, e.g., Murphy v. State*, 852 F.2d 1039, 1041 (8th Cir. 1988) (parents argued that according to their religious beliefs, they were solely responsible for their child's education and that state testing requirements interfered with this obligation); *Blount v. Dept. of Educ. & Cultural Serv.*, 551 A.2d 1377, 1379 (Me. 1988) (parents maintained that application for state approval violated their religious rights under the Constitution); *People v. DeJonge*, 470 N.W.2d 433, 434 (Mich. 1991).
54. *See, e.g., Runyon v. McCrary*, 427 U.S. 160, 178-79 (1976) (finding that the right to direct the education of one's child is free from government regulation); *Murphy*, 852 F.2d at 1041-43; *Blount*, 551 A.2d at 1381-82. *See also* a discussion of the "hybrid" claim in Chapter Twelve, "Free Exercise of Religion."
55. David Allen Peterson, Note, "Home Education v. Compulsory Attendance Laws: Whose Kids Are They Anyway?," 24 Washburn L.J. 274, 278 (1985). *See also* Appendix, "Legislative Status."
56. *See id.*
57. Lupu, *supra* note 2, at 984.

58. *Id.*
59. *Tony & Susan Alamo Found. v. Secretary of Labor*, 471 U.S. 290, 305 (1985).
60. 440 U.S. 490 (1979).
61. *Id.* at 502 (emphasis supplied).
62. *Thomas v. Review Bd.*, 450 U.S. 707, 715-16 (1981).
63. *See* Appendix, "Legislative Status."
64. Lupu, *supra* note 2, at 984.
65. *Id.* at 984 and n.55 *citing Edwards v. Aguillard*, 107 S. Ct. 2573 (1987) for the proposition that while a state legislature cannot mandate equal time between evolution and creationism, the decision does not resolve the question of whether the state can regulate the teaching of science in private schools (footnote omitted).
66. *Id.; see Thomas*, 450 U.S. at 715-16.
67. *United States v. Ballard*, 322 U.S. 78, 86 (1944).
68. *Thomas*, 450 U.S. at 715-16. One also might argue that in this situation the state is an interested party and incapable of making an objective ruling. The state has an interest in keeping students in public schools for two key reasons: money and image. If students leave the public school system, the need for teachers and administrators will decline; positions will be cut. The school system will lose money for those positions.

    Second, removing students from public schools does not create a positive image for the public system. While many parents remove their children primarily for religious reasons, academics and safety also are contributing factors. Many parents:

    > [F]eel that home education is the best way to provide a safe environment for their children and to keep them away from the multiplying problems of assaults, drugs, and vandalism. . . . Many parents cite academic failure alone. Contributing to the dissatisfaction of parents are declining scores on the Scholastic Aptitude Test (SAT), little or no assigned homework, inflated grades, automatic promotion, below-level text books and objective, rather than essay, examinations.

    E. Alice Law Beshoner, Note, "Home Education in America: Parental Rights Reasserted," 49 UMKC L. Rev. 191, 193-94 (1981) (citations omitted). Removing students for these reasons does not promote a positive public school image. Consequently, it seems logical for public school officials to seek to keep as many students as possible from leaving.
69. *U.S. v. Ballard*, 322 U.S. 78, 86 (1944).
70. *See, e.g., Scharon v. St. Luke's Episcopal Presbytery Hosp.*, 929 F.2d 360 (8th Cir. 1991) (finding that the application of Title VII and the Age Discrimination in Employment Act to religious institutions created excessive entanglement because it required the state and the courts to question the meaning of church dogma to make certain tenets support employment decisions). Some courts have held that subjecting religious institutions to the Fair Labor Standards Act is permissible; however, in these cases the intrusion in no way conflicted with the religious beliefs of the institutions—unlike the home education scenario where intrusion frequently conflicts with home educators' religious beliefs. *See, e.g., EEOC v. Tree of Life Christian Schools*, 751 F. Supp. 700, 711 (S.D. Ohio 1990).
71. *See* Neal Devins, "A Constitutional Right to Home Instruction?," 62 Wash. U.L.Q. 435, 462 n. 167 (1984).
72. *See, e.g., Runyon v. McCrary*, 427 U.S. 160, 178 (1976) (finding that parents "have no constitutional right to provide their children with private school

education unfettered by reasonable government regulation"); *Pierce v. Society of Sisters*, 268 U.S. 510, 534 (1925) (finding that "[n]o question is raised concerning the power of the State reasonably to regulate all schools").

73. *See, e.g., Blackwelder v. Safnauer*, 689 F. Supp. 106, 135 (N.D.N.Y. 1988) (finding that the state can interfere on a limited scale with home education without violating constitutional rights), *aff'd & appeal dismissed* 866 F.2d 548 (2nd Cir. 1989); *Blount v. Department of Educ. & Cultural Serv.*, 551 A.2d 1377, 1381-84 (Me. 1988) (same); *People v. DeJonge*, 470 N.W.2d 433, 434-35 (Mich. App. 1991) (same). It should be noted that many of the cases did not involve Establishment Clause claims.

74. *State v. Patzer*, 382 N.W.2d 631, 635 (N.D. 1986) (arguing that teaching certification requirement and not state supervision in general violated their right to free exercise), *cert. denied*, 479 U.S. 825 (1986); *see DeJonge*, 470 N.W.2d at 434 (foreclosing any discussion of the least restrictive means aspect of the strict scrutiny analysis because parents asserted they would not submit to any state authority; parents lost on compelling state interest grounds).

75. Perhaps this marks a reflection of the hesitancy of litigants to raise such claims. *See supra* note 3 and accompanying text.

76. 689 F. Supp. 106 (N.D.N.Y. 1988).

77. 42 U.S.C. Section 1983 (1989).

78. *Blackwelder*, 689 F. Supp. at 112.

79. *Id.* at 113.

80. *Id.* -

81. *Id.*

82. *Id.*

83. *Id.*

84. *Id.* at 143.

85. *Id. citing Pierce v. Society of Sisters*, 268 U.S. 510, 534 (1925); *Board of Educ. v. Allen*, 392 U.S. 236, 247 (1968).

86. 473 U.S. 402 (1985); *see supra* notes 26-34 and accompanying text.

87. One may argue, however, that the fact that the state conducts these approval procedures and uses state money to do so violates the Establishment Clause. If such an argument was carried through, a court could find itself in a precarious predicament. The state has a recognized interest in the education of children. Parents have the right to home educate their children. If the state cannot spend tax dollars to supervise or regulate home instruction, which interest will the court find paramount? The court could find that if the state cannot regulate the home school program, home schools cannot exist. Such a result emphasizes the state's fundamental interest in educating their young. Or it could find that the parents, alleging a free exercise claim, have the superior interest. Prior to *Employment Division, Human Resources v. Smith*, 494 U.S. 872 (1990), the latter result would have seemed highly probable, but after *Smith*, the free exercise claim no longer, in the Court's eyes, merits special treatment. In order to survive, parents, in light of the hybrid claim exception to *Smith*, must make certain to allege other constitutional claims—Establishment Clause, freedom of association, right to privacy, and parental rights. Considering the current judicial attitude toward religion, asserting these additional claims is, in all likelihood, the only way to defeat the state's educational interest should such a situation arise.

88. *Blackwelder*, 689 F. Supp. at 144.

89. *See* Appendix, "Legislative Status."

90. In numerous cases, the Supreme Court has found that the administration of standardized tests to private religious school students does not constitute excessive entanglement. *See Wolman v. Walter*, 433 U.S. 229, 238-41 (1977)

(attacking the issue from the point of view that using tax dollars to provide testing is excessive entanglement and holding that such action does not constitute excessive entanglement).

91. *Wolman*, 433 U.S. at 240 *citing Levitt v. Committee for Public Education*, 413 U.S. 472, 479-80 (1973).

92. *Id.* at 238-41. *See also In re Charles*, 504 N.E.2d 592, 602 (Mass. 1987) (approving use of standardized tests). Some courts, however, have rejected standardized testing as a valid means of supervising home schooled students because it does not expose problems until the end of the school term. *See, e.g., Johnson v. Charles City Comm. Schools Bd.*, 368 N.W.2d 74, 81 (Iowa 1985), *cert. denied*, 474 U.S. 1033 (1985); *Sheridan Road Baptist Church v. Department of Educ.*, 396 N.W.2d 373, 382 (Mich.), *cert. denied*, 481 U.S. 1050 (1986); *State v. Rivinius*, 328 N.W.2d 220, 229 (N.D.), *cert. denied*, 460 U.S. 1070 (1982); *State v. Patzer*, 382 N.W.2d 631, 638 (N.D.), *cert. denied*, 479 U.S. 825 (1986).

93. *See, e.g., NLRB v. Catholic Bishop of Chicago*, 440 U.S. 490, 502 (1979); *Serbian Orthodox Diocese v. Milivojevich*, 426 U.S. 696, 713 (1976); *Scharon v. St. Luke's Episcopal Presbyterian Hosp.*, 929 F.2d 360, 362-63 (8th Cir. 1991).

94. *See, e.g., Mazanec v. North Judson-San Pierre School Corp.*, 614 F. Supp. 1152 (N.D. Ind. 1985) (dicta), *aff'd* 798 F.2d 230 (7th Cir. 1986); *Charles*, 504 N.E.2d at 601 (finding that home school instructors need not be certified college educated, but that school districts may inquire about instructors academic credentials).

95. *See, e.g., Patzer*, 382 N.W.2d at 639; *Sheridan Road Baptist Church*, 396 N.W.2d at 382.

96. *In re Kilroy*, 467 N.Y.S.2d 318, 321 (1983) (finding that on-site visits are the only true way of measuring the competency of instructors). *See also* Chapter Twenty-four, "Administrative Searches or 'Child Welfare' Investigations."

97. *Charles*, 504 N.W.2d at 602.

98. *Aguilar*, 473 U.S. at 414 (*quoting Lemon v. Kurtzman*, 403 U.S. at 650).

99. *Fellowship Baptist Church v. Benton*, 815 F.2d 485, 496 (8th Cir. 1987).

100. *See id.* at 496-98.

101. *Id.* at 498.

102. *Id. citing United States v. Lee*, 455 U.S. 252, 261 (1982); *Gillette v. United States*, 401 U.S. 437, 451-52 (1971).

103. 456 U.S. 228 (1982).

104. *Id.* at 246. *See also* Chapter Twenty-two, "Compelling State Interest."

105. 456 U.S. 228.

106. *Id.* at 230.

107. *Id.* at 238-43.

108. *Id.* at 244.

109. *Id.* at 245 *citing* The Federalist No. 51, p. 326 (H. Lodge, ed., 1908).

110. *Id.* at 246 *quoting Everson v. Board of Educ.*, 330 U.S. 1, 15 (1947); *Zorach v. Clauson*, 343 U.S. 306, 314 (1952); *Epperson v. Arkansas*, 393 U.S. 97, 104, 106 (1968) (citations omitted).

111. *Id.* at 246; *Hernandez v. Commissioner*, 490 U.S. 680, 695 (1989).

112. *See* Tribe, *supra* note 5, at § 14-7, at 1191 n.19.

113. *Larson*, 456 U.S. at 246-47.

114. *Id.* at 246-51. The Court also applied the *Lemon* test; however, it acknowledged that such an analysis was not necessary to the disposition of the case. *Id.* at 252.

115. 401 U.S. 437 (1971).

116. *Id.* at 454. Petitioners challenged the constitutionality of the federal conscientious objector exemption from the draft. *Id.* at 439. Particularly, the Court addressed "the question whether conscientious objection to a particular war, rather than objection to war as such, relieves the objector from responsibilities of military training and service." *Id.* Both petitioners did not object to war in general but opposed American presence in Vietnam as an "unjust" military action. *Id.* at 439-41. Petitioners claimed that the exemption provision currently protects only those who oppose all wars and that the Court, because Congress has granted a benefit to only one type of religious belief, should create another exception based on the Establishment Clause. *Id.* at 451.

     Addressing petitioners' Establishment Clause claim that the statute creates a *de facto* discrimination among religions, the Court acknowledged that government was proscribed from such preferential treatment but that petitioners did not make the required showing of such a discriminatory practice. *Id.* at 451-52. The Court held that the motivation behind such a demarcation between religious beliefs had both neutral and secular purposes—fair administration of conscription and the desire to avoid exempting individuals whose beliefs are more likely to stem from political views than from religious beliefs. *Id.* at 454. The Court concluded that any burdens felt by those denied exempt status are merely incidental to a secular and neutral statute. *Id.* at 462.

117. *See, e.g.,* Jesse H. Choper, "The Free Exercise Clause: A Structural Overview and an Appraisal of Recent Developments," 27 Wm. & M. L. Rev. 943, 958-61 (1986); Tribe, *supra* note 5, at § 14.7, at 1192. Indeed, *Larson* does not appear to be an aberration. The Court has relied on it in recent cases as its first analytical step in the Establishment Clause context. *See, e.g., Hernandez v. Commissioner,* 490 U.S. 680, 695 (1989) (asking first whether a law "facially differentiates among religions before moving to the traditional *Lemon* analysis").

118. *Id.* at 960-61. Professor Choper hints that the reason the Court upheld the statute in *Gillette* was because it involved building a national defense. *Id.* at 961; *see Gillette,* 401 U.S. at 454-60.

119. Choper, *supra* note 117, at 961. Choper commended the Court for its result in *Larson.* He explains that laws that explicitly address religion and ultimately demonstrate a preference of one religious belief over another should be treated as free exercise cases. *Id.* at 961. Although the *Larson* Court did not label its case "free exercise," "it explicitly employed a rationale that does"—strict scrutiny. *Id.*

120. *Id.* at 960.

121. *Id.* at 960-61.

122. The state does not necessarily have to state explicitly that all Amish are exempt but that no other religious group is. *See* Choper, *supra* note 117, at 960 *citing Gillette,* 401 U.S. 437 (1971). Rather the state may discriminate on the types of religious beliefs one possesses. *Id.* For example, in *Gillette,* the statute exempted individuals who opposed all wars and not those who simply opposed unjust wars. *Id.* (*citing Gillette,* 401 U.S. at 440). According to Choper, this is preferential treatment of religious beliefs. This logic can be transferred to compulsory attendance statutes. Laws discriminate among religions if they grant exemption status to the Amish because of their lifestyle and religious beliefs but deny such status to, for example, a Fundamentalist Baptist who believes that Christians should not conform to the world but do not live as the Amish do.

123. 406 U.S. 205 (1972).

124. *Id.* at 209-11.

125. For a discussion of these issues, see Chapter Twelve, "Free Exercise of Religion."

CHAPTER TWENTY-ONE: *Neutral Decision-maker Requirements*

1. *See* Appendix, "Legislative Status."
2. U.S. Const., Amend. XIV, sec. 1, which reads in pertinent part:

   ... No State shall make or enforce any law which shall abridge the privileges or immunities of citizens of the United States; nor shall any State deprive any person of life, liberty, or property, without due process of law; nor deny to any person within its jurisdiction the equal protection of the laws.

3. *Arnett v. Kennedy*, 416 U.S. 134, 197 (1974) (White, J., concurring in part and dissenting in part).
4. *State v. Brewer*, 444 N.W.2d 923, 924 (N.D. 1989) (*quoting* Defendant's argument).
5. Laurence H. Tribe, *American Constitutional Law*, 1st ed., Sec. 10-16 (Mineola, NY: Foundation Press, 1978), p. 555.
6. Robert F. Maslan, Jr., "Bias and the Londermill Hearing: Due Process or Lip Service to Federal Law?," 57 Fordham L. Rev. 1093, 1099 (1989).
7. *Id.*
8. *Id.*
9. Tribe, *supra* note 5, at 555.
10. 273 U.S. 510 (1927).
11. *Id.* at 531-32.
12. *Id.* at 533, 535.
13. 409 U.S. 57, (1972).
14. *Blackwelder v. Safnauer*, 689 F. Supp. 106, 146 (N.D.N.Y. 1988) (*quoting Ward*, 409 U.S. at 58).
15. *Id.* at 146-47.
16. *Ward*, 409 U.S. at 60 (*quoting Tumey*, 273 U.S. at 532).
17. *Marshall v. Jerrico*, 446 U.S. 238, 248 (1980).
18. *Blackwelder v. Safnauer*, 689 F. Supp. at 146.
19. *Id.*
20. *Salisbury v. Housing Authority*, 615 F.Supp. 1433, 1441 (D.C. Ky. 1985).
21. 694 F.2d 35 (2nd Cir. 1982).
22. *Id.* at 41.
23. *See generally Schweiker v. McClure*, 456 U.S. 188, 195-96 (1982).
24. 436 N.W. 2d 10 (N.D. 1989).
25. *Id.* at 11.
26. *Id.*
27. *Id.*
28. 444 N.W.2d 923 (N.D. 1989).
29. *Id.* at 925.
30. 689 F. Supp. 106 (N.D.N.Y. 1988).
31. *Id.* at 147.
32. *Id.*
33. *Id.*
34. *Id.* at 147 (*quoting Wolkenstein*, 694 F.2d at 43).
35. *Id.*
36. *Id.*
37. *Ward*, 409 U.S. at 61.
38. *See Wolkenstein*, 694 F.2d at 44.
39. 427 N.W.2d 316 (N.D. 1988).
40. *Id.* at 320; *see Tumey v. Ohio*, 273 U.S. 532, discussed at *supra* notes 10-12.

41. 449 N.W.2d 899 (Mich. App. 1989).
42. *Id.* at 907.
43. *Id.*

CHAPTER TWENTY-TWO: *Compelling State Interest*

1. *See, e.g., Bowers v. Hardwick*, 478 U.S. 186, 196 (1986); *Cleburne v. Cleburne Living Center*, 473 U.S. 432, 442 (1985).
2. *See, e.g., Matthews v. Lucas*, 427 U.S. 495, 505 (1976).
3. *See, e.g., Frontiero v. Richardson*, 411 U.S. 677, 686 (1973) (plurality opinion). Age, however, is not considered a quasi-suspect class. *See Massachusetts Bd. of Retirement v. Murgia*, 427 U.S. 307, 313 (1976). The Court has held that mental retardation also does not fall into this category. *Cleburne*, 473 U.S. at 442-43. Both are subject to the rational relation standard.
4. *Frontiero*, 411 U.S. at 686 (gender); *Cleburne*, 473 U.S. at 440-41 (same).
5. *Mills v. Habluetzel*, 456 U.S. 91, 99 (1982) (illegitimacy).
6. *Cleburne*, 473 U.S. at 440 (citations omitted).
7. *Id.*
8. *Palmore v. Sidoti*, 466 U.S. 429, 432-33 (1984); *Loving v. Virginia*, 388 U.S. 1, 11 (1967); *McLaughlin v. Florida*, 379 U.S. 184 (1964); *Strauder v. West Virginia*, 100 U.S. 303 (1880).
9. *See Kramer v. Union Free Sch. Dist., No. 15*, 395 U.S. 621 (1969) (right to vote); *Shapiro v. Thompson*, 394 U.S. 618 (1969) (right to travel); *Skinner v. Oklahoma*, 316 U.S. 535 (1942) (right to procreation). But *see San Antonio Independent Sch. Dist. v. Rodriguez*, 411 U.S. 1 (1973) (no right to education).
10. *See United States v. Carolene Products*, 304 U.S. 144, 152-53, n. 4 (1938).
11. Stephen A. Siegel, "Lochner-Era Jurisprudence and the American Constitutional Tradition," 70 N.C. L. Rev. 1, 3 *citing* David P. Currie, *The Constitution in the Supreme Court: The Second Century, 1888-1986* (Chicago: University of Chicago, 1990), pp. 235-36.
12. *Pierce v. Society of Sisters*, 268 U.S. 510 (1925); *Meyer v. Nebraska*, 262 U.S. 390 (1923); *see* R. Collin Mangrum, "Family Rights and Compulsory School Laws," 21 Creighton L. Rev. 1019, 1025. For a more in-depth discussion of parental rights, *see* Chapter Eleven, "Modern Parental Rights: Issues and Limits" and Chapter Seventeen, "Parental Liberty."
13. *See, e.g., Burson v. Freeman*, 1992 WL 107344 (U.S.), *4 (1992); *Simon & Schuster, Inc. v. Members of the New York State Crime Victims Bd.*, 112 S. Ct. 501, 509 (1991); *Arkansas Writers' Project, Inc. v. Ragland*, 481 U.S. 221, 231 (1987).
14. *United States v. Kokinda*, 110 S.Ct. 3115, 3119 (1990); *Perry Educ. Ass'n v. Perry Local Educators' Ass'n*, 460 U.S. 37, 45 (1983).
15. *Larson v. Valente*, 456 U.S. 228 (1982).
16. *See Wisconsin v. Yoder*, 406 U.S. 205 (1972); *Sherbert v. Verner*, 374 U.S. 398 (1963); *West Virginia Bd. of Educ. v. Barnette*, 319 U.S. 624 (1943).
17. 110 S. Ct. 1595 (1990).
18. *See Sherbert*, 374 U.S. at 406.
19. *Smith*, 110 S. Ct. at 1595.
20. *Smith*, 110 S. Ct. at 1601; *see Vandiver v. Hardin County Bd. of Educ.*, 925 F.2d 927, 933 (6th Cir. 1991) (stating that *Smith* created such an exception for strict scrutiny).
21. *Id.* at 1603 *quoting Bowen v. Roy*, 476 U.S. 693, 708 (1986).
22. *See Sherbert*, 374 U.S. 398, 403 (1963). During this phase of the analysis in the free exercise context, "courts may emphasize the Constitution's preferred

treatment of the [F]irst [A]mendment right to free exercise of religion and the framers' intent that the Free Exercise Clause protect minority religions from prosecution." Karin M. Rebescher, Note, "The Illusory Enforcement of First Amendment Freedom: *Employment Division, Department of Human Resources v. Smith* and the Abandonment of the Compelling Interest Governmental Interest Test," 69 N. C. L. Rev. 1332, 1335 (1991) *quoting Smith*, 110 S. Ct. at 1614 (O'Connor, J., concurring in judgment); *Reynolds*, 98 U.S. 145, 162-64 (1878).

23. *See Wisconsin v. Yoder*, 406 U.S. 205, 215-16 (1972).
24. *Sherbert*, 374 U.S. at 404.
25. *Id.* at 403. If no intrusion exists, the governmental action withstands judicial scrutiny. *Id.*
26. *Cantwell*, 310 U.S. at 308; *see Sherbert*, 374 U.S. at 403 ("The conduct or actions so regulated have invariably posed some substantial threat to public safety, peace or order").
27. *Sherbert*, 374 U.S. at 406.
28. *Smith*, 110 S.Ct. at 1614 (O'Connor, J., concurring in judgment) *quoting United States v. Lee*, 455 U.S. 252, 259 (1982).
29. *Bowen v. Roy*, 476 U.S. 693, 727 (1986).
30. *Smith*, 110 S.Ct. at 1611 (O'Connor, J., concurring in judgment).
31. 374 U.S. 398 (1963).
32. 406 U.S. 205 (1972).
33. *See Vandiver v. Hardin County Bd. of Educ.*, 925 F.2d 927, 933 (6th Cir. 1991).
34. *Sherbert*, 374 U.S. at 399.
35. *Id.*
36. *Id.* at 399-400.
37. *Id.* at 401.
38. *Id.*
39. *Id.* at 404.
40. *Id.* at 403.
41. *Id.* at 407.
42. *Id.*
43. *Id.*
44. *Wisconsin v. Yoder*, 406 U.S. 205 (1972).
45. *Id.* at 207.
46. *Id.* at 209.
47. *Id.* at 207.
48. *Id.* at 214 *quoting Pierce v. Society of Sisters*, 268 U.S. 510, 535 (1925).
49. *Id.* The Court added that it could "accept as settled, therefore, that, however strong the State's interest in universal compulsory education, it is by no means absolute to the exclusion or subordination of all other interests." *Id.* at 215 *citing Sherbert*, 374 U.S. 398; *McGowan v. Maryland*, 366 U.S. 420, 459 (1961) (separate opinion of Frankfurter, J.); *Prince v. Massachusetts*, 321 U.S. 158, 165 (1944).
50. *Id.* at 211. The high school experience conflicted with the Amish teaching of non-conformity and separation from "contemporary, worldly society." *Id.*
51. *Id.* at 212. The Amish were not opposed to sending their children to elementary schools because "they view such a basic education as acceptable because it does not significantly expose their children to worldly values or interfere with their development in the Amish community during the crucial adolescent period." *Id.* During the adolescent period, the Amish teenagers engage in "learning-through-doing," meaning that they must learn the skills necessary to be an Amish farmer or housewife. *Id.* at 211.

52. *Id.* at 215.

53. *Id.*

54. *Id.* at 216. The Court found particularly convincing the Amish's literal interpretation of the Biblical command to "be not conformed to this world," a command deemed fundamental to their faith. *Id.* The Court also pointed to the degree in which the Amish attitudes and beliefs toward family and home have remained static in a world that has become increasingly more conscious of the value of education. *Id.* Some courts have suggested that the history, tradition, and uniqueness of the Amish order compelled the Court to rule in the Amish's favor and that other beliefs do not merit such a result. *See, e.g., State v. Patzer,* 382 N.W.2d 631, 636-37 (N.D.), *cert. denied,* 479 U.S. 825 (1986).

55. *Yoder,* 406 U.S. at 218.

56. *Id.* at 219. The state did not challenge the sincerity of the Amish's beliefs; rather, its argument focused on its superior interest. *Id.*

57. *Id.* at 222. The Court also stated that "[i]t is one thing to say that compulsory education for a year or two beyond the eighth grade may be necessary when its goal is the preparation of the child for life in modern society as the majority live, but it is quite another if the goal of education be viewed as the preparation of the child for life in the separated agrarian community that is the keystone of the Amish faith." *Id. citing Meyer v. Nebraska,* 262 U.S. 390, 400 (1923).

58. *Id.* The Court rejected the state's argument that the Amish children ought to be prepared to function in modern society should they choose to leave their community, calling it mere speculation in light of the lack of evidence of attrition and the minimal burden they would be on society because of their education should they elect to leave.

59. *Id.* at 226.

60. *See* Douglas A. Laycock, "The Remnants of the Free Exercise Clause," 1990 Supreme Ct. Rev. 1, 32-33 (1990) (discussing the value of balancing interests rather than adhering to a bright line rule).

61. *See Duro v. District Attorney, 2nd Jud. Dist. of N.C.,* 712 F.2d 96, 98 (4th Cir. 1983); *Blount v. Dept. of Educ. & Cultural Serv.,* 551 A.2d 1377, 1381 (Me. 1988).

62. *See Blount,* 551 A.2d at 1380.

63. *See, e.g., In re Charles,* 504 N.E. 592 (Mass. 1987).

64. *Anderson,* 427 N.W.2d at 322.

65. *Yoder,* 406 U.S. at 213.

66. *See Anderson,* 427 N.W.2d at 322; *State v. Patzer,* 382 N.W.2d 631, 636-39 (N.D.), *cert. denied,* 479 U.S. 825 (1986).

67. *See, e.g., Charles,* 504 N.E.2d at 598-99; *State v. McDonough,* 468 A.2d 977, 979 (Me. 1983); *State v. LaBarge,* 357 A.2d 121, 124 (Vt. 1976); *see also Vandiver v. Hardin County Bd. of Educ.,* 925 F.2d 927, 933 (6th Cir. 1991) (suggesting there is a right to home education).

68. *See Sherbert,* 374 U.S. 398, 403-06 (1963); *Yoder,* 406 U.S. 205, 215. *See also State v. Patzer,* 382 N.W.2d 631, 654 (N.D.), *cert. denied,* 479 U.S. 825 (1986) (examining parents' religious motivation to home school their children).

69. *United States v. Seeger,* 380 U.S. 163, 184-85 (1965).

70. *Id. quoting United States v. Ballard,* 322 U.S. 78, 86 (1944).

71. *Yoder,* 406 U.S. at 215.

72. *Id.* at 215-16; *see Seeger,* 380 U.S. at 165.

73. *Seeger,* 380 U.S. at 176.

74. *Frazee v. Illinois Dept. of Employment Security,* 489 U.S. 829, 834 (1989).

75. *Thomas v. Review Bd.,* 450 U.S. 707, 715-16 (1981).

76. *State v. Patzer*, 382 N.W.2d 631 (N.D. 1986) *quoting Braunfeld v. Brown*, 366 U.S. 599, 607 (1961) and *citing Sherbert*, 374 U.S. 398, 404 (1963).

77. *Vandiver*, 925 F.2d at 933. Some courts use *Yoder* as the measuring stick and expect parents to demonstrate that the burdens the regulations impose is as great as the burden the compelling state interest imposed on the Amish. *See Fellowship Baptist Church v. Benton*, 815 F.2d 485 (8th Cir. 1987) (involving a religious school).

78. *Blount*, 551 A.2d 1377.

79. *See, e.g., Blount*, 551 A.2d at 1382 (finding that the state's interests—education and quality education—were paramount to parents' religious beliefs and right to direct the education of their children).

80. *Runyon v. McCrary*, 427 U.S. 160, 178 (1976).

81. *See, e.g., State v. Massa*, 231 A.2d 252, 257 (N.J. 1967) (rejecting such an argument because it, in effect, would eliminate the home school option).

82. James W. Tobak and Perry A. Zirkel, "Home Instruction: An Analysis of the Statutes and Case Law," 8 U. Dayton L. Rev. 1, 59 (1982).

83. *State v. Patzer*, 382 N.W.2d 631, 633 (N.D.), *cert. denied*, 479 U.S. 825 (1986); *see* Donald D. Dorman, Note, "Michigan's Teacher Certification Requirement as Applied to Religiously Motivated Home Schools," 23 U. Mich. J. L. Reform 733, 736 (1990). For a more detailed discussion of socialization, *see* Chapter Seven, "The Straw Men: Socialization and Academics."

84. Allan E. Parker, Jr., "Public Free Schools: A Constitutional Right to Educational Choice in Texas," 45 S.W.L.J. 825, 911 (1991).

85. *Id.*

86. Neal Devins, "A Constitutional Right to Home Instruction?," 62 Wash. U.L.Q. 435, 453 (1984) *citing* "Developments in the Law—The Constitution and the Family," 93 Harv. L. Rev. 1156, 1354 (1980).

87. 406 U.S. 205 (1972).

88. *Id.* at 222-26.

89. *Id.* at 226, n.14.

90. *Id.* at 226.

91. *See West Virginia Bd. of Educ. v. Barnette*, 319 U.S. 624 (1943); Ira C. Lupu, "Home Education, Religious Liberty, and the Separation of Powers," 67 Boston U.L. Rev. 971, 984-85 (1987).

92. *See supra* note 86 and accompanying text.

93. *State v. Anderson*, 427 N.W.2d 316, 322 (N.D. 1988) (focusing on "least restrictive alternative" arguments since the state conceded that the plaintiff had sincerely held religious beliefs and the plaintiff conceded that the state had a compelling state interest).

94. David Allen Peterson, Note, "Home Education v. Compulsory Attendance Laws: Whose Kids Are They Anyway?," 24 Washburn L.J. 274, 278 (1985).

95. Lupu, *supra* note 91, at 984.

96. *Id.*

97. This would be beneficial to parents who want to home educate their children but are not religiously motivated to pursue that route. *See Hanson v. Cushman*, 490 F. Supp. 109, 112-14 (limiting the right to home educate to parents whose religious beliefs command it). Regardless of the motive, parents should be allowed to home instruct their children.

98. *See* Tobak and Zirkel, *supra* note 82 and cases cited therein. *See also* Appendix, "Legislative Status."

99. In numerous cases the Supreme Court has found that the administration of standardized tests to private religious school students does not constitute excessive entanglement. *See Wolman v. Walter*, 433 U.S. 229, 238-41 (1977)

(attacking the issue from the point of view of using tax dollars to provide testing and holding that such action does not constitute excessive entanglement).

100. *Id.* at 240.

101. *Id. See also In re Charles*, 504 N.E.2d 592, 602 (Mass. 1987) (approving the use of standardized tests). Some courts, however, have rejected standardized testing as a valid means of supervising home schooled students because it does not expose problems until the end of the school term. *See e.g, Johnson v. Charles City Community Schs. Bd.*, 368 N.W.2d 74, 81 (Iowa (1985), *cert. denied*, 474 U.S. 1033 (1985); *Sheridan Road Baptist Church v. Department of Educ.*, 396 N.W.2d 373, 382 (Mich.), *cert. denied*, 481 U.S. 1050 (1986); *State v. Rivinius*, 328 N.W.2d 220, 229 (N.D. 1982), *cert. denied*, 460 U.S. 1070 (1982); *State v. Patzer*, 382 N.W.2d 631, 638 (N.D.), *cert. denied*, 479 U.S. 825 (1986).

102. Nonetheless, courts have held that this requirement is not unconstitutional because the state's compelling interest outweighs any parental religious beliefs; *see State v. Patzer*, 382 N.W.2d 631, 637-39 (N.D.), *cert. denied*, 479 U.S. 825 (1986); *Sheridan Road Baptist Church*, 396 N.W.2d 373, 382 (Mich.), *cert. denied*, 481 U.S. 1050 (1986); *DeJonge*, 449 N.W.2d 899, 902-05 (Mich. App. 1989). *See also* Chapter Eighteen, "Vagueness Issues."

103. *In re Kilroy*, 467 N.Y.S.2d 318, 321 (1983) (finding that on-site visits are the only true way of measuring the competency of instructors).

104. *Charles*, 504 N.E.2d at 602.

CHAPTER TWENTY-THREE: *Administrative Searches or "Child Welfare" Investigations*

1. Note, "Investigating Child Abuse: The Fourth Amendment and Investigatory Home Visits," 89 Columbia L. Rev. 1034 (1989) (hereinafter, "Investigating Child Abuse").

2. *Id.*

3. *Id.* at 1035.

4. U.S. Const., Amend. IV: "The right of the people to be secure in their persons, houses, papers, and effects, against unreasonable searches and seizures, shall not be violated, and no warrants shall be issued, but upon probable cause, supported by oath or affirmation, and particularly describing the place to be searched, and the persons or things to be seized."

5. Comment, "Protecting Children in Licensed Family Day-care Homes: Can the State Enter a Home Without a Warrant?," 25 Santa Clara L. Rev. 411, 412 (1985).

6. *See, e.g.*, "Investigating Child Abuse," *supra* note 1. *But see H. R. v. State Dept. of Human Resources*, 1992 Ala. Civ. App. LEXIS 413 (Ala. App. 1992).

7. *Brown v. Board of Education*, 347 U.S. 483, 493 (1954).

8. *Plyler v. Doe*, 457 U.S. 202, 221 (1982).

9. *Wisconsin v. Yoder*, 406 U.S. 205, 221 (1972). *See also* John W. Whitehead, *The Rights of Religious Persons in Public Education* (Wheaton, IL: Crossway Books, 1991), Chapter 1.

10. *Plyler*, 475 U.S. at 221.

11. "Investigating Child Abuse," *supra* note 1, at 1037-38.

12. For a discussion of privacy and home schooling, *see* Chapter 14, "Right to Privacy and Due Process."

13. *Meyer v. Nebraska*, 262 U.S. 390 (1923); *Pierce v. Society of Sisters*, 268 U.S. 510 (1925); *Farrington v. Tokushige*, 273 U.S. 284 (1927); *Wisconsin v. Yoder*, 406 U.S. 205 (1972). These cases set out the basic principle that parents have a fundamental right to raise and educate their children.

14. *Griswold v. Connecticut*, 381 U.S. 479 (1965). Griswold and its progeny stand for the proposition that the Bill of Rights contains a right to privacy in familial matters (i.e., contraception, marriage, abortion) within its penumbra.
15. Dwight Edward Tompkins, "An Argument for Privacy in Support of the Choice of Home Education by Parents," 20 J. of Law & Educ. 301, 308-09 (1991).
16. Note, "Developments in the Law—The Constitution and the Family," 93 Harv. L. Rev. 1156, 1353-04 (1980).
17. *United States v. Salerno*, 481 U.S. 739 (1987).
18. *United States v. Hensley*, 469 U.S. 221, 229 (1985).
19. *Terry v. Ohio*, 392 U.S. 1, 22 (1968).
20. Tompkins, *supra* note 15, at 312 *quoting* Stocklin-Enright, "The Constitutionality of Home Education: The Role of the Parent, the State and the Child," 18 Willamette L. Rev. 563, 586 (1982).
21. *Id.* at 315.
22. U.S. Const., Amend IV. The Supreme Court has held that the Fourth Amendment also applies to the states through the Fourteenth Amendment. *Ker v. California*, 374 U.S. 23, 30, (1963).
23. *Id.*
24. Note, *supra* note 11, at 1036. *See also Johnson v. United States*, 333 U.S. 10 (1948); *United States v. Jeffers*, 342 U.S. 48 (1951); *Aguilar v. Texas*, 378 U.S. 108 (1964).
25. *Boyd v. United States*, 116 U.S. 616, 630 (1885).
26. *Allen v. Holbrook*, 103 Utah 319, 331 (1943).
27. Wayne R. La Fave, Vol. 2, *Search and Seizure* (St. Paul: West Publishing Co., 1978), p. 29 (footnotes omitted).
28. Comment, *supra* note 5, at 419 (citation omitted).
29. *Brinegar v. United States*, 338 U.S. 160, 175-76 (1949).
30. *Carroll v. United States*, 267 U.S. 132, 162 (1925).
31. Collins and Hurd, "Warrantless Administrative Searches: It's Time to be Frank Again," 22 Am. Bus. L.J. 189, 190 (1984).
32. *Camara v. Municipal Court*, 387 U.S. 523, 532 (1967).
33. *Id.* at 532-33.
34. *Id.* at 536-37.
35. Wayne L. LaFave and Jerold H. Israel, *Criminal Procedure* (St. Paul: West Publishing Co., 1992), p. 217.
36. 387 U.S. 523, 526-27.
37. *Id.* at 528.
38. *Id. citing Marshall v. Barlow's Inc.*, 436 U.S. 307, 320 (1978) (warrant required for inspection of property suspected of violation of sec. 8(a) of the Occupational Safety and Health Act of 1970).
39. *Id.*
40. *H. R. v. State Dept. of Human Resources*, LEXIS 413 at 6 (*citing Camara* and *Nicaud v. State ex rel. Hendrix*, 401 So. 2d 43 (Ala. 1981).
41. LaFave and Israel, *supra* note 33, at 222.
42. 397 U.S. 72 (1970).
43. *Marshall*, 436 U.S. at 313 (citations omitted).
44. *Donovan v. Dewey*, 452 U.S. 594, 600-04 (1981).
45. *Coolidge v. New Hampshire*, 403 U.S. 443, 460 (1971).
46. 392 U.S. 1 (1968).
47. *Id.*
48. *Id.* at 19-22.
49. *Donovan*, 452 U.S. at 603.
50. *Schneckloth v. Bustamonte*, 412 U.S. 218 (1973).

51. *Id.* at 233-34.
52. *See Blackwelder v. Safnauer*, 689 F. Supp. 106 (N.D. N.Y. 1988).
53. *See id.*
54. *Cf. Daryl H. v. Coler*, 801 F.2d 893, 899-900 (7th Cir. 1986).
55. *See* Appendix , "Legislative Status."
56. *Blackwelder v. Safnauer*, 689 F. Supp. 106, 138 (N.D. N.Y. 1988), *rev'd* on other grounds, 866 F.2d 548 (1989).
57. Thompkins, *supra* note 11, at 318.
58. LaFave and Israel, *supra* note 35, at 222.
59. "Investigating Child Abuse," *supra* note 1, at 1054.
60. The consent of only one person who has joint control over the home is necessary. Thus, if one parent consents to the home visit, the search is valid as against the other parent. *U. S. v. Matlock*, 415 U.S. 164 (1974); *Illinois v. Rodriguez*, 110 S. Ct. 2793 (1990).
61. 689 F. Supp. 106 (N.D. N.Y. 1988).
62. *Id.* at 112-13.
63. *Id.* at 141.
64. *Id. See also In re Kilroy*, 467 N.Y.S.2d 318, 321 (Fam. Ct. 1983). Slip. Op. (Rhode Island Commissioner of Education, August 7, 1986).
65. Slip Op. (Rhode Island Commissioner of Education, August 7, 1986).
66. *Id.* at 5 n.12.
67. *Id.* at 7.
68. 387 U.S. 523 (1967).
69. *Marshall v. Barlow's, Inc.*, 436 U.S. 307 (1978).
70. *Camara*, 387 U.S. at 536-7.
71. According to one commentator, "[C]hild protective services are generally required to commence an investigation within 24 hours of receiving any report of abuse or neglect." "Investigating Child Abuse," *supra* note 1, at 1042. The commentator notes further that "If it appears that the child is in imminent danger or that the family may flee, however, investigations must commence immediately upon receipt of the report." *Id.*
72. "Investigating Child Abuse," *supra* note 1, at 1043.
73. *Id.* at 1050.
74. *Id.* at 1044-45.
75. *Id.* at 1051.
76. *Id.* at 1054.
77. *Smith v. Organization of Foster Families*, 431 U.S. 816, 842 (1977).
78. *Blackwelder*, 689 F. Supp. at 136.
79. No. N-37-86, Family Court of Oswego County, New York (November 21, 1988).
80. Slip op. No. N-125-86, Family Court of Oswego County, New York (December 23, 1988).
81. *Dixon*, *supra* note 78, at 5.
82. *Id.*
83. *Standish*, Slip Op., No. N-125-86.
84. *See* U.S. Const. Amend I.
85. *Walz v. Tax Comm'n*, 397 U.S. 664, 668 (1970). *See also* Whitehead, *supra* note 9, at 97-8.
86. 403 U.S. 602 (1971).
87. *Id.* at 612-13 (citations omitted). The three parts are referred to as the "three prongs of the *Lemon* test."
88. *Edwards v. Aguillard*, 482 U.S. 578, 585 (1987). The Court held that the Louisiana Balanced Treatment for Creation-Science and Evolution-Science in

Public School Instruction Act serves no identified secular purpose and that its primary purpose was the promotion of a particular religious belief and was thus unconstitutional.

89. *Yoder*, 406 U.S. at 221.
90. *Id.*
91. *Lemon*, 403 U.S. 612-13.
92. *Lynch v. Donnelly*, 465 U.S. 668, 692 (1984) (O'Connor, J., concurring).
93. *Lemon*, 403 U.S. 613.
94. *Blackwelder*, 689 F. Supp. at 143.
95. 268 U.S. 510 (1925).
96. 392 U.S. 236 (1968).
97. *Blackwelder*, 689 F. Supp. at 143.
98. 473 U.S. 402 (1985).
99. *Id.*
100. *Blackwelder*, 689 F. Supp. at 144.
101. *Id.*
102. *Id.* at 145.
103. *Id.*
104. Since not all home schooling is based upon religious beliefs, the First Amendment argument would not apply to all home schools.

CHAPTER TWENTY-FOUR: *Home Educators in the Military*

1. Ruth Cooper, "An Air Force Family Homeschools," *Home Education Magazine* (March-April 1991), p. 16.
2. *Id.*
3. Bobbie Lee Howard, "Home Schooling—A Military Adventure!," *Home Education Magazine* (March-April 1991), p. 19.
4. Michael Howard, "Home Schooling Military Style," *Home Education Magazine* (March-April 1991), p. 18.
5. *Id.* at 20.
6. *Defense Almanac* (Washington, D.C.: Department of Defense, 1991).
7. *Id.*
8. *Id.* The countries are: Belgium, Bermuda, British West Indies, Canada, Cuba, United Kingdom (England and Scotland), Iceland, Netherlands, Norway, Panama, Germany, Azores, Bahrain, Greece, Italy, Spain, Turkey, Japan, Korea, and The Philippines. *You Had a Question ?* (Washington, D.C.: Department of Defense, 1986), p. 1.
9. *Id.*
10. *Id.*
11. Public Law 95-561, 20 U.S. §921 *et. seq.* (1982), "Defense Dependents' Education Act of 1978," as amended by Public Law 99-145, "Defense Authorization Act of 1986." *You Had a Question?*, *supra* note 8, p. 13.
12. *Defense Almanac*, *supra* note 6.
13. Phone interview with Harvey Gerry, DoDDS Education Division, June 3, 1992.
14. *Id.*
15. *Id.* This measure has never been taken by any commander, but it does remain as an option. In 1990, a commander in Germany who did not like home schooling ordered no home schooling allowed. This order only lasted one day, however, after an attorney in the Judge Advocate General office informed the Commander of the Constitution. *Id.*
16. *Id.*

17. *Id.* The Status of Forces Agreement dictates how a host country will deal with military personnel. None of the countries hosting the United States deals with education of military children.

18. *Id.*

19. DS Regulation 2035.1(D)(8), March 25, 1988. This regulation provides, "Eligible DoD dependent students may be provided education in certified non-DoD schools at U.S. Government expense only at locations where DoDDS schools are not available, are operating at maximum capacity, or where, in the case of handicapped students, an appropriate educational program is not available within the DoDDS-operated school." Enrollment in local English-speaking schools is preferred to home schooling in the regulation, but the option is recognized.

20. DS Regulation 2035.1(D)(19).

21. *Reid v. Covert*, 354 U.S. 1 (1957). This case involved two women stationed with their husbands at overseas military bases. The women killed their husbands and were convicted without a jury. The Court overturned their convictions, holding that "The United States is entirely a creature of the Constitution. Its powers and authority have no other source. It can only act in accordance with all the limitations imposed by the Constitution." *Id.* at 5-6.

22. *Ex parte Milligan*, 71 U.S. 120-21 (1886).

23. *United States v. Yunis*, 681 F.Supp. 909,917 (D.D.C. 1988) *citing United States v. Pinto-Mejia*, 720 F.2d 248,259,261 (2d Cir.1983); *United States v. Marino-Garcia*, 679 F.2d 1373, 1384 (11th Cir.1982), *cert. denied*, 459 U.S. 1114 (1983); *United States v. Howard-Arias*, 679 F.2d 363, 371 (4th cir.1982), *cert. denied*, 459 U.S. 874 (1982); *United States v. Green*, 671 F.2d 46, 53 (1st Cir.1982); *United States v. Williams*, 617 F.2d 1063, 1078 (5th Cir.1980).

24. *Moore v. East Cleveland*, 431 U.S. 494, 504 n.12 (1976) *citing* Justice Harlan's dissent in *Poe v. Ullman*, 367 U.S. 497, 551-52 (1961).

25. *Stanley v. Georgia*, 394 U.S. 557, 565 (1969).

26. *Tucker v. Texas*, 326 U.S. 517, 520 (1946). *Cf. Marsh v. Alabama*, 326 U.S. 496, 508-9 (1946) (company-owned town).

27. Earl Warren, "The Bill of Rights and the Military," 37 N.Y.U. L. Rev. 181, 182 (1962).

28. *Id.*

29. *Id.* at 183-4.

30. The Federalist No. 41, at 251 (Lodge, ed., 1888).

31. Warren, *supra* note 27, at 185 *citing* Pinkney's recommendations to the Federal Convention, 2 Records of the Federal Convention 341 (Farrand, ed., 1911), and the discussion by Mason and Madison, *id.* at 617; Resolutions on Ratification of the Constitution by the States of Massachusetts, New Hampshire, New York and Virginia, reprinted in Documents Illustrative of Formation of the Union of American States, H.R. Doc. No. 398, 69th Cong., 1st Sess. 1018-20, 1024-44 (1927).

32. *Id.* at 188.

33. Ronald S. Thompson, "Constitutional Applications to the Military Criminal Defendant," 66 U. Det. L. Rev. 221 (1989).

34. *Id.*

35. See Chapter Twenty-three, "Administrative Searches or 'Child Welfare Investigations.'"

36. Thompson, *supra* note 33, at 222.

37. Mil. R. Evid. 315(d).

38. Thompson, *supra* note 33, at 224.

39. *Id.* at 225.

40. Mil. R. Evid. 313(b) defines inspection as: "an examination of the whole or part of a unit, organization . . . conducted as an incident of command the primary purpose of which is to determine and to ensure the security, military fitness, or good order and discipline of the unit, organization."

41. Thompson, *supra* note 33, at 225.

42. 10 U.S.C.A. Sec. 801-934 (West 1983 & Supp. 1987).

43. Linda Sugin, "First Amendment Rights of Military Personnel: Denying Rights to Those Who Defend Them," 62 N.Y.U. L. Rev. 855, 861 (1987).

44. *Id.* at 862.

45. *Id.* at 863.

46. U.C.M.J. art. 67, 10 U.S.C. 867 (1982).

47. Donald N. Zillman and Edward J. Imwinkelried, "Constitutional Rights and Military Necessity: Reflections on the Society Apart," 51 Notre Dame Lawyer 396, 397 (1976).

48. Jeffrey F. LaFave, "The Talismanic Incantation of Military Necessity: Is there a First Amendment in the Not-So Separate Society?," 2 J. Contemp. Legal Issues 173, 175 (1989).

49. *Id.*

50. *Orloff v. Willoughby*, 345 U.S. 83, 94 (1953).

51. *Id.* at 93-94.

52. 417 U.S. 733 (1974).

53. *Id.* at 758.

54. James M. Hirschhorn, "The Separate Community: Military Uniqueness and Servicemen's Constitutional Rights," 62 N.C.L. Rev. 177, 189 (1984). Professor Hirschhorn generally supports the separate community doctrine.

55. *Id.*

56. *Id.* at 180.

57. LaFave, *supra* note 48, at 178.

58. *Id.* at 179.

59. Hirschhorn, *supra* note 54, at 205.

60. *Defense Almanac*, supra note 6.

61. Hirschhorn, *supra* note 54, at 205.

62. LaFave, *supra* note 48, at 180.

63. *Id.*

64. Note, "Military Dissent and the Law of War: Uneasy Bedfellows," Cal. L. Rev. 871, 891 (1985).

65. William A. Johnson, "Military Discipline and Political Expression: A New Look at an Old Bugbear," 6 Harv. C.R.-C.L. L. Rev. 525, 537 (1971).

66. LaFave, *supra* note 48, at 182.

67. *Id.* at 183.

68. *Id.*

69. *Brown v. Glines*, 444 U.S. 348, 371 (1980) (Brennan, J., dissenting).

70. Johnson, *supra* 65, at 544.

71. Sugin, *supra* note 43, at 865.

72. 417 U.S. 733 (1974).

73. *Id.* at 735-6.

74. *Id.* at 736-7. He said, "The United States is wrong in being involved in the Viet Nam War. I would refuse to go to Viet Nam if ordered to do so. I don't see why any colored soldier would go to Viet Nam; they should refuse to go to Viet Nam and if sent should refuse to fight because they are discriminated against in Viet Nam by being given all the hazardous duty and they are suffering the majority of casualties. . . . Special Forces personnel are liars and thieves and killers of peasants and murderers of women and children." *Id.* at 769-70.

75. U.C.M.J. art. 133, 10 U.S.C. 933 (1982).
76. U.C.M.J. art. 134, 10 U.S.C. 934 (1982).
77. *Parker*, 417 U.S. at 752.
78. For a discussion of being void for vagueness and overbreadth, see Chapter Eighteen, "Vagueness Issues."
79. *Parker*, 417 U.S. at 756.
80. LaFave, *supra* note 48, at 189.
81. 424 U.S. 828 (1976).
82. *Id.* at 840.
83. 444 U.S. 348 (1980).
84. *Id.* at 351.
85. *Id.* at 355.
86. Sugin, *supra* note 43, at 871.
87. 475 U.S. 503 (1986).
88. *Id.* at 505.
89. *Id.* at 504.
90. Air Force Reg. 35-10, para. 1-6.h(2)(f)(1980).
91. *Id.* at 515-16 (Brennan, J. dissenting).
92. *Id.* at 509.
93. LaFave, *supra* note 48, at 197.
94. *Id.* at 197-98.
95. *Goldman*, 475 U.S. at 528 (O'Connor, J., dissenting).
96. Sugin, *supra* note 43, at 873.
97. *Goldman*, 475 U.S. at 530-31 (O'Connor, J. dissenting).
98. Sugin, *supra* note 43, at 875.
99. Hirschhorn, *supra* note 54, at 206.
100. Warren, *supra* note 27, at 188.
101. The Establishment Clause says, "Congress shall make no law respecting an establishment of religion. . . ." U.S. Const., Amend. I.
102. *Lemon v. Kurtzman*, 403 U.S. 602, 612-13 (1971). The three tests enunciated in this case are often referred to as the "three prongs of the *Lemon* test."
103. *Yoder* involved Amish parents who wanted to withdraw their children from school after the eighth grade; *Pierce* involved a private school's challenge to a compulsory education statute requiring public education.
104. *Allegheny County v. Greater Pittsburgh ACLU*, 492 U.S. 573, 612 (1989).
105. Warren, *supra* note 27, at 202.
106. *Id.* at 203.

CHAPTER TWENTY-FIVE: *Making Allies of Your Family, Friends and the Public*

1. Luanne Shackelford and Susan White, *A Survivor's Guide to Home Schooling* (Wheaton, IL: Crossway Books, 1988), p. 3.
2. *See* Chapter Three, "Freedom and Educational Diversity."
3. Shackelford, *supra* note 1, at 3 (emphasis in original).
4. *Id.* at 4.
5. *Id.*
6. *Id.* at 5.
7. *Id.*
8. *Id.* at 4.
9. David and Micki Colfax, *Homeschooling for Excellence* (New York: Mountain House Press, 1988), p. 104.
10. Shackelford, *supra* note 1, at 6.
11. *See* Chapter Seven, "The Straw Men: Socialization and Academics."

12. Colfax, *supra* note 9, at 11-2 (emphasis in original).
13. Shackelford, *supra* note 1, at 8.
14. *Id.*
15. *See* Chapter Twelve, "Free Exercise of Religion."
16. *See* Chapters Twelve through Twenty-four for a discussion of these interests and their effect on the right to educate one's children at home. *See especially* Chapter Twenty-two, "Compelling State Interest."
17. *See* Appendix , "Legislative Status."
18. Information about such an attorney may be obtained from The Rutherford Institute through its home school program. Write: The Rutherford Institute, P.O. Box 7482, Charlottesville, VA 22906; or call (804) 978-3888.
19. *See* Chapter Twenty-six, "Legislation and Lobbyists."
20. Shackelford, *supra* note 1, at 6.
21. Theodore E. Wade, Jr., *Home School Manual* (Auburn, CA: Gazelle Publications, 1991), p. 52.

CHAPTER TWENTY-SIX: *Legislation and Lobbyists*

1. There are many excellent handbooks on lobbying available. *See, e.g.* Donald deKieffer, *How to Lobby Congress: A Guide For the Citizen Lobbyist* (New York: Dodd, Mead & Co., 1981); Samuel Halperin, *A Guide for the Powerless and Those Who Don't Know their Own Power* (Washington, D.C.: The Institute for Educational Leadership, 1981); Judith C. Meredith, *Lobbying on a Shoestring* (Westport, CT: Greenwood, 1989); Dorothy Smith, *In Our Own Interest* (Seattle: Madrona Publishers, 1989).
2. Meredith, *supra* note 1, at 1.
3. Jeffrey M. Berry, *Lobbying for the People: The Political Behavior of Public Interest Groups* (Princeton, NJ: Princeton University Press, 1977), p. 11 *quoting* Lester W. Milbrath, *The Washington Lobbyists* (Chicago: Rand McNally, 1963), p. 8.
4. Smith, *supra* note 1, at 7.
5. John W. Gardner, *In Common Cause* (New York: W. W. Norton & Co., Inc., 1972), pp. 19-21.
6. Many commentators fear that special interest groups, with the power of money, threaten to undermine our democratic system because legislators may become responsive to their financial assistance rather than to their constituents. *See, e.g.,* Jeffrey M. Berry, *The Interest Group Society* (Glenview, IL: Scott, Foresman & Co., 1989), pp. 1-2. Furthermore, the mere mention of the term lobbyist "conjures up a negative stereotype: a smooth-talking arm-twister. *Id.* at 77.
7. Meredith *supra* note 1, at 13.
8. *Id.*; Halperin, *supra* note 1, at 33.
9. *See* Meredith, *supra* note 1, at 13.
10. *See* deKieffer, *supra* note 1, at 22; Meredith, *supra* note 1, at 51-2. In addition, the first-time lobbyist should read his or her state's rules and regulations pertaining to lobbying.
11. *See* Smith, *supra* note 1, at 3-4.
12. *Id.*
13. Berry, *supra* note 6, at 7.
14. *Id.*
15. DeKieffer, *supra* note 1, at 22; Smith, *supra* note 1, at 14.
16. DeKieffer, *supra* note 1, at 22.
17. *See* Meredith, *supra* note 1, at 14-20.
18. *Id.* at 15.

19. *Id.*
20. *Id.*
21. *Id.*
22. *See* deKieffer, *supra* note 1, at 13; Marc Caplan, *Ralph Nader Presents: A Citizen's Guide to Lobbying* (New York: Dembner Books, 1983), pp. 26-8; Smith, *supra* note 1, at 5.
23. Smith, *supra* note 1, at 5.
24. DeKieffer, *supra* note 1, at 13.
25. *Id.*
26. Meredith, *supra* note 1, at 7.
27. DeKieffer, *supra* note 1, at 20; Smith, *supra* note 1, at 4.
28. Smith, *supra* note 1, at 4.
29. Berry, *supra* note 6, at 81.
30. *Id.* Smith, *supra* note 1, at 10.
31. Berry, *supra* note 6, at 84; Smith, *supra* note 1, at 4.
32. Berry, *supra* note 6, at 84.
33. DeKieffer, *supra* note 1, at 17; Meredith, *supra* note 1, at 10; Smith, *supra* note 1, at 11, 65.
34. DeKieffer, *supra* note 1, at 17.
35. *See infra* notes 127-37 and accompanying text.
36. Interview with James Moon, lobbyist for the Virginia Home Educators' Association, conducted June 16, 1992. For a discussion of socialization and home education, *see* Chapter Seven, "The Straw Men: Socialization and Academics."
37. DeKieffer, *supra* note 1, at 19; *see generally* Donald R. Hall, *Cooperative Lobbying—The Power of Pressure* (Tucson: University of Arizona Press, 1969).
38. deKieffer, *supra* note 1, at 20.
39. *Id.* Consider joining forces with school choice proponents. Any legislation favoring one group generally helps the other organization. For a discussion of this relationship, *see* Chapter Four, "Free Market Choice in Education."
40. *Id.*
41. H. R. Mahood, *Interest Group Politics in America: A New Intensity* (Englewood Cliffs, NJ: Prentice Hall, 1990), p. 112; Smith, *supra* note 1, at 60-2.
42. Halperin, *supra* note 1, at 25.
43. *Id.*
44. Smith, *supra* note 1, at 11.
45. *Id.* Berry, *supra* note 6, at 83 ("politics is the art of compromise").
46. Meredith, *supra* note 1, at 16.
47. *Id.*
48. *Id.* at 15.
49. *Id.*
50. *Id.*
51. Smith, *supra* note 1, at 16. Keeping this group at a small, workable number is vital. *See id.* at 17-8.
52. *Id.* at 16.
53. Smith, *supra* note 1, at 16.
54. *Id.* at 50.
55. *Id.* at 50-1. One handbook suggests setting up a filing system to include all legislators and their staff members and the lobbying volunteers. Meredith, *supra* note 1, at 16. Such a system makes it easier to keep track of who has been assigned to do what tasks. *Id.*
56. Meredith, *supra* note 1, at 51-5; Smith, *supra* note 1, at 19.
57. Caplan, *supra* note 22, at 31.

58. *Id.*
59. *Id.* In many cases, the legislator may take control and leave the lobbying group without a voice. Smith, *supra* note 1, at 14.
60. Caplan, *supra* note 22, at 31.
61. *Id.*
62. *Id.* at 31-2; Meredith, *supra* note 1, at 14.
63. Meredith, *supra* note 1, at 14.
64. Caplan, *supra* note 22, at 32.
65. *Id.* Meredith, *supra* note 1, at 14.
66. Your group may want to consider showing an attorney a rough draft of the legislation for criticism and comment.
67. Smith, *supra* note 1, at 16.
68. *Id.* at 19-20. Assign someone to keep up with the timeframe. *Id.*
69. *Id.* at 14.
70. *Id.*
71. Remember that each state may have unique rules governing this process; thus, your group should become acquainted with the laws in your state. Caplan, *supra* note 22, at 32.
72. *Id.*
73. Smith, *supra* note 1, at 20-1.
74. *Id.* at 21.
75. *Id.* at 20-1.
76. *Id.*
77. *Id.* Consider distributing a second draft to potential legislative sponsors for their input. *Id.*
78. *Id.*
79. Caplan, *supra* note 22, at 41-2.
80. Meredith, *supra* note 1, at 60; Smith, *supra* note 1, at 34. In evaluating this characteristic, exude caution if the legislator seems overly burdened with other causes; your project may suffer. Smith, *supra* note 1, at 34-5. In addition, be certain that supporting this legislation will not create friction with the constituency—a situation that inevitably may force the sponsor to withdraw his or her support. *Id.* at 35.
81. Meredith, *supra* note 1, at 59.
82. Smith, *supra* note 1, at 35.
83. *Id.* at 34-5.
84. Lawrence Gilson, *Money and Secrecy: A Citizens' Guide to Reforming State and Federal Practices* (New York: Praeger Publishers, 1972), p. 200.
85. Caplan, *supra* note 22, at 43.
86. Smith, *supra* note 1, at 35-6.
87. *Id.* at 37; Berry, *supra* note 6, at 108-9.
88. Smith, *supra* note 1, at 37.
89. *Id.* at 69-70.
90. DeKieffer, *supra* note 1, at 61.
91. *Id.*
92. Interview with James Moon, *supra* note 36.
93. DeKieffer, *supra* note 1, at 61-2.
94. *See* Berry, *supra* note 6, at 112.
95. Meredith, *supra* note 1, at 74-6.
96. Smith, *supra* note 1, at 69-70. Remember that legislators are busy people and do not have time to read countless volumes discussing the value of home education. The more concise the presentation, the more likely they are to read it.

97. Interview with James Moon, *supra* note 36.
98. *Id.* at 73.
99. *Id.* at 71; Halperin, *supra* note 1, at 22.
100. Halperin, *supra* note 1, at 22.
101. *Id.*
102. Berry, *supra* note 6, at 112-13.
103. *Id.* at 112.
104. deKieffer, *supra* note 1, at 56-7.
105. *Id.* at 60; Halperin, *supra* note 1, at 27.
106. deKieffer, *supra* note 1, at 61. Seemingly it is a good idea to assign certain issues to certain writers; however, such action may destroy the personal touch. Rather, let the writers discuss whichever issues matter most to them. *Id.*
107. Halperin, *supra* note 1, at 28. Do not enclose the fact sheet because, according to one commentator, it makes the letter seem more formal and less palatable. deKieffer, *supra* note 1, at 60-1.
108. *Id.* at 56; *see also* Halperin, *supra* note 1, at 27-8 (discussing similar elements).
109. *Id.* at 76-9.
110. Meredith, *supra* note 1, at 66.
111. *Id.* at 67.
112. Smith, *supra* note 1, at 79. Deliver copies of the testimony in advance so legislators will be prepared to ask questions. Halperin, *supra* note 1, at 34.
113. Meredith, *supra* note 1, at 73.
114. Halperin, *supra* note 1, at 33 (discussing how legislators prefer personal stories and experience).
115. *Id.* at 32.
116. *See* Meredith, *supra* note 1, at 71-2.
117. *Id.* at 67; Halperin, *supra* note 1, at 34.
118. Halperin, *supra* note 1, at 34-5.
119. Meredith, *supra* note 1, at 69-70.
120. Smith, *supra* note 1, at 81.
121. *Id.* at 70.
122. *Id.* at 101.
123. Smith, *supra* note 1, at 103-04.
124. *Id.* at 105.
125. *Id.* at 105, 108.
126. *Id.* at 109.
127. Interview with James Moon, *supra* note 36.
128. *Id.*
129. *Id. See* Chapter Seven, "The Straw Men: Socialization and Academics."
130. Interview with James Moon, *supra* note 36.
131. *Id.*
132. *Id.*
133. *Id.* Many home schools have joined forces to form teams that compete against Christian schools. *Id.*
134. *Id.*
135. *Id.*
136. *Id.*
137. *Id.*

CHAPTER TWENTY-SEVEN: *Litigation: Maps and Landmines*

1. *See* Chapter Six, "Dimensions of the Contemporary Home Education Movement."

2. *E.g.*, The Rutherford Institute. The Rutherford Institute provides information and legal assistance to home school families through its home school program. The Institute provides litigation expertise for selected cases and assists local counsel in litigating appropriate cases. In addition, staff attorneys are available to answer questions. The Institute also produces a Home Education Reporter that contains information about relevant state statutes and containsn available information from the various state departments of education. Finally, the Institute maintains a "hotline" for home schoolers to call when they need information or assistance. The Institute also publishes a monthly magazine for home educators on a subscription basis.

3. That is one purpose of this book.

4. *See* Appendix, "Legislative Status."

5. *Leeper v. Arlington Indep. School Dist.*, No. 17-88761-85 Tarrant County 17th Judicial Ct. (April 13, 1987).

6. "Brief of Respondents," *Texas Education Agency v. Leeper* (No. D-2022, Supreme Court of Texas, 1992), p. 6.

7. The TEA is the state administrative agency that is in charge of implementing education law in Texas.

8. Brief, *supra* note 6, at 9.

9. *Id.* at 10.

10. *Leeper v. Arlington Indep. School Dist.*, No. 17-88761-85 Tarrant County 17th Judicial Ct.

11. Brief, *supra* note 6, at 17.

12. *Texas Education Agency v. Leeper*, No. D-2022 (Tex. Sup. Ct. 1992).

13. *See*, Chapter Twenty-six, "Legislation and Lobbyists."

14. *See* Appendix, "Legislative Status." *See also* "Home Schoolers Win EEE Case," *Home School Court Report*, Vol. 8, No. 1 (January-February 1992), p. 1.

15. S. C. Code Ann. Sec. 59-65-40 (A)(1)(a) (1990).

16. *Lawrence v. South Carolina State Board of Education*, 412 S.E.2d 394, 395 (S. C. 1991).

17. "Home Schoolers Win EEE Case," *Home School Court Report*, Vol. 8, No. 1 (January-February 1992), p. 1.

18. *Lawrence*, 412 S.E. 2d at 394.

19. *Id.* at 396.

20. *See* Appendix, "Legislative Status" and Chapter Twenty-three, "Administrative Searches or 'Child Welfare' Investigations." *See also* "Massachusetts Court Case Could Set Precedent on Home Visits," *Home School Court Report*, Vol. 8, No. 1 (January-February 1992), p. 5.

21. *See* Appendix, "Legislative Status."

22. *Blount v. Dept. of Educational Services*, 551 A.2d 1377 (Me. 1988).

23. *See* Appendix, "Legislative Status."

24. *Clonlara v. State Bd. of Ed.*, 469 N.W.2d 66 (Mich. App. 1991).

25. "Cases on Appeal," *Teaching Home*, Vol. X, No. 1 (February-March 1992), p. 29.

26. *See* Appendix, "Legislative Status."

27. *See* Missouri section of Appendix, "Legislative Status." *See also* "Missouri," in *Home School Court Report*, Vol. 8, No. 1, at 9.

28. *See* Indiana Section of Appendix, "Legislative Status." *See also* "Indiana," *Home School Court Report*, Vol. 9, No. 2 (March-April 1992), p. 11.

29. *See supra* notes 13 and 14 and materials cited therein.

30. *See* Appendix, "Legislative Status."

31. *Id.*

32. *State v. Kielpinsky*, 1990 Ohio App. LEXIS 2406. *See also* Chapter Twelve, "Free Exercise of Religion."
33. *Vandiver v. Hardin County Bd. of Ed.*, 925 F.2d 927 (6th Cir. 1991).
34. *Id.*
35. *Id.* at 929.
36. *Id.* at 930, 935.
37. 852 F.2d 1039 (8th Cir. 1988).
38. *Id.* at 1040.
39. *Id.* at 1040-6.
40. *Id.* at 1041.
41. *Id.* at 1043. For a state court decision reaching a similar result, *see also Bayes v. State*, 785 P.2d 660 (Idaho App. 1989). For a discussion on the validity of this position, *see* Chapter Seven, "The Straw Men: Socialization and Academics."
42. 582 A.2d 252 (Me. 1990).
43. *Id.* at 253.
44. *Id.* For more on this issue, *see also People v. DeJonge*, 470 N.W.2d 433 (Mich App. 1991) and Chapter Twelve, "Free Exercise of Religion."
45. *Hinrichs v. Goodrich*, 753 F.Supp. 261 (W.D.Wis. 1990).
46. *See* Chapter Seventeen, "Parental Liberty."
47. *See, e.g.,* Chapter Twelve, "Free Exercise of Religion" and Chapter Thirteen, "Freedom of Speech and Formation of Belief."
48. *See* Chapter Sixteen, "Equal Protection of the Law."
49. *See* Chapter Twelve, "Free Exercise of Religion."
50. *See* Chapter Thirteen, "Freedom of Speech and Formation of Belief."
51. Indeed, after the Supreme Court's ruling in *Employment Division v. Smith*, 494 U.S. 872 (1990), recourse to state constitutions and state statutes is well advised. For a discussion of this issue, *see* Chapter Twelve, "Free Exercise of Religion."
52. Iowa Rev. Code §299.4 (1972).
53. *Rivera v. Iowa*, (No. 92-326 Disc. Rev. granted March 30, 1992 Iowa Sup. Ct.).
54. *Iowa v. Rivera*, Iowa Dist. Ct. No. SP 89506A&B, Ct. (Linn County, June 18, 1991).
55. *See* statement to this effect at the beginning of the book.
56. *See* Chapter Twenty-three, "Administrative Searches or 'Child Welfare' Investigations."
57. *See id.*
58. This suggestion is based on the article "Telephones and Kids: Consider these Dangers," in *Home School Court Report*, Vol. 8, No. 1 (January-February 1992), p. 27.
59. *See* Chapter Six, "Dimensions of the Contemporary Home Education Movement."
60. *See* Chapter Seven, "The Straw Men: Socialization and Academics."

CHAPTER TWENTY-EIGHT: *Freedom in Education*

1. Note, "Freedom and Public Education: The Need for New Standards," 50 Notre Dame Lawyer 530, 531 (1975).
2. 1 Annals of Congress 454 (Gales and Seaton, eds., 1834).

APPENDIX: *Legislative Status*

1. Code § 16-28-3 (1990).
2. *Id.* § 16-28-1.
3. *Id.* §§ 16-28-7.
4. *Id.*

5. *Id.* § 16-28-5.
6. *Id.*
7. Alaska Stat. § 14.30.010 (1991).
8. *Id.*
9. *Id.* § 14.20.020.
10. *Id.* § 14.30.010(b)(10).
11. *Id.* § 14.30(010)(b)(11).
12. *Id.* § 14.45.100. This type of school is exempt from education regulations, but not regulations which relate to fire safety, physical health, sanitation, immunization and physical examinations. *Id.*
13. *Id.* § 14.45.110(a).
14. *Id.* § 14.45.110(b). Records must reflect attendance, immunizations, physical exams, standardized tests, academic achievement and courses taken. *Id.*
15. *Id.* § 14.45.110(b).
16. *Id.* §§ 14.45.200(1),(2).
17. *Id.* § 14.45.200(2).
18. *Id.* § 14.45.120(a).
19. *Id.* § 14.45.120. The student must be tested in English, grammar, reading, spelling and mathematics. *Id.*
20. No statutory confirmation; only confirmed by letter.
21. Rev. Stat. Ann. § 15-802 (1991).
22. *Id.* § 15-802(B)(2).
23. *Id.* § 15-828 B. Proof may be satisfied by a certified copy of a birth certificate, a baptismal certificate, an application for a Social Security number, original school registration records along with an affidavit stating why a birth certificate cannot be supplied, or a letter certifying the child is in legal custody of an agency representative pursuant to title 8, chapter 2. *Id.*
24. *Id.* §15-828 D.
25. *Id.* § 15-533,802(B)(1).
26. *Id.* § 15-741. A parent may choose between the following four tests: 1. Metropolitan achievement test; 2. California Achievement Test; 3. Stanford Achievement Test; 4. Iowa test of basic skills at the elementary level and test of academic proficiency (TAP) at the secondary level. *Id.* § 15-802(B)(1).
27. *Id.*
28. *Id.* § 15-802(B)(1).
29. Stat. Ann. § 6-15-501 (1991).
30. Notice must be provided on an annual basis and must include information on the student, curriculum, schedule of instruction, parent/teacher qualifications, and the school's location. According to the Arkansas statute, this information is required for statistical purposes only. *Id.* §§ 6-15-503(1)(A),(B).
31. *Id.* § 6-15-503.
32. *Id.* § 6-15-504. The test shall be the same test given to public school students. *Id.*
33. *Id.* § 6-15-505(a)(3). "Unsatisfactory test results on the standardized achievement battery shall mean, for all grades, achieving a composite score on reading, mathematics and language arts that is more than eight (8) months below the expected grade level plus, for grade 6 and above, scores on science and social studies tests which are more than eight (8) months below expected grade level." *Id.* § 6-15-505(b)(1). "Unsatisfactory test results on the minimum performance test shall mean not achieving the standard of mastery established for such test by the State Board of Education." *Id.* § 6-15-505(b)(2).
34. *Id.* When a student performs unsatisfactorily on the minimum performance test, remediation may be provided by the parent, *Id.* § 6-15-505(c). The minimum

performance test must be passed before beginning the ninth grade. *Id.* Forced attendance at a public, private or parochial school is required for unsatisfactory performance on the standardized achievement battery. *Id.* §§ 6-15-505(c),(d).

35. *Id.* § 6-15-505(a)(4).
36. *Id.*
37. *Id.* § 6-15-505(f).
38. Education Code § 48224 (West 1991), but independent study is addressed in § 51745.
39. *Id.*
40. *Id.* § 48222.
41. *People v. Turner,* 263 P.2d 685; Cal. App. Dep't. Super. Ct., *appeal dismissed,* 347 U.S. 972; (1953).
42. *Id.*
43. *Id.*
44. Rev. Stat. § 22-33-104.5(3)(c) (1990).
45. *Id.* § 22-33-104.5(2)(a),(b).
46. *Id.*
47. *Id.* § 22-33-104.5(3)(a).
48. *Id.* § 22-33-104.5(3)(e).
49. *Id.*
50. *Id.* § 22-33.104.5(3)(c), (d). The curriculum shall include "communication skills of reading, writing, and speaking, mathematics, history, civics, literature, science, and regular courses instructing in the Constitution of the United States." *Id.*
51. *Id.* § 22-33-104.5(3)(f). The child must be tested at the equivalent age for grades three, five, seven, nine, and eleven with the same national standardized achievement test used in the child's local public school district.

    Parents must submit results to an independent or parochial school or the local school district, and if scores are submitted to a parochial or independent school, the school is required to notify the local school district of any child scoring below the thirteenth percentile. *Id.* §§ 22-33-104.5(5)(a),(b).

    To continue in the home school program, the child must achieve a composite score above the thirteenth percentile. *Id.* § 22-33-104.5(5)(a). Students scoring below the thirteenth percentile will be given the opportunity to take a different version of the same test, or a different nationally standardized achievement test chosen by the parent from a list of board-approved tests. *Id.* If the child scores below the thirteenth percentile the second time, public, independent or parochial school attendance is mandatory until the next testing period. *Id.*
52. *Id.* § 25-4-901,902,903.
53. *Id.* § 22-33-104.5(3)(g).
54. *People in Interest of D.B.,* 767 P.2d 801 (Colo. Ct. App. 1988).
55. *Id.*
56. *Id.* at 802.
57. Gen. Stat. § 10-184 (1991). *See also Snyder v. Town of Newtown,* 161 A.2d 770 (Conn., 1960), *appeal dismissed,* 365 U.S. 299 (1961).
58. Conn. Gen. Stat. § 10-184 (1991).
59. Code Ann. tit. 14, § 2703 (1991).
60. *Id.* § 2703.
61. D.C. Code Ann. § 31-402 (1991).
62. Christopher J. Klicka, *Home Schooling in the United States: A Statutory Analysis,* Home School Legal Defense Association, 1989, at 10, *citing* 24 D.C. Reg. 1021.
63. *Id.*

64. *Id.*

65. *Id.*

66. Stat. § 228.041 (1991).

67. *Id.* § 232.01.

68. *Id.*

69. *Id.* § 232.02(4)(a).

70. *Id.* § 232.02(4)(b)1. Notification must be in writing, must be signed by the parent and must include the participating child's name, address and birth date. *Id.*

71. *Id.* § 232.02(4)(b)2. Records which must be maintained are reading materials, writing samples, worksheets, workbooks and creative materials, which may be inspected by the superintendent or agent with fifteen days notice. *Id.*

72. *Id.* § 232.02(4)(b)3.

73. *State v. Buckner*, 472 So.2d 1228, 1230 (Fla. 1985). *See also State v. M.M.*, 407 So.2d 987,990 (Fla. Dist. Ct. App. 1981).

74. Fla. Admin. Code Ann. r. 6A-1.044, 1.0951 (1990). *See also* Fla. Stat. chs. 232.17, 228.041(17).

75. *Id.* r. 6A-1.0951(1)-(4). Failure to comply with the code requirements will result in prosecution under the Compulsory Attendance Law. *Id.*

76. *Id.* The parent may choose the form of evaluation from the following choices: review by a certified teacher, appraisal by the district's nationally normed student achievement test administered by a certified teacher, appraisal by a state student assessment test, evaluation by a licensed psychologist or school psychologist, or measurement by a valid tool which is approved by the district school superintendent. Fla. Stat. §§ 232.02(4)(b)3, 490.003(3),(5) (1991).

77. Fla. Stat. § 232.02(4)(b)3.e (1991). The parent will be notified in writing of a pupil's unsatisfactory progress, and a one-year probationary period of remediation will begin. At the end of the period, the child will be reevaluated and must demonstrate progress commensurate with his or her ability to continue with home instruction. *Id.*

78. Code. Ann. § 20-2-690(a) (1991). One who fails to comply with all the home school requirements will be guilty of a misdemeanor and will receive a $100 fine. *Id.* § 20-2-690(d).

79. *Id.* § 20-2-690(c)(1).

80. *Id.*

81. *Id.* 20-2-690(c)(2).

82. *Id.* 20-2-690(c)(3).

83. *Id.*

84. *Id.* §§ 20-2-690(c)(4),(5).

85. *Id.* § 20-2-690(c)(8). There is no requirement that these records be submitted to education authorities. *Id.*

86. *Id.* § 20-2-690(c)(6). Printed forms necessary to carry out statutory requirements will be provided to parents by the state board of education through local school superintendents. *Id.* § 20-2-690(e).

87. *Id.* 202-690(c)(7). Records of test scores must be kept for three years, but there is no requirement that they be turned in to education authorities. *Id.*

88. 1982 Op. Atty Gen. No. U82-43.

89. *Id.*

90. *Id.*

91. Ga. Code. Ann. § 20-2-690(b)(2),(6) (1991).

92. Rev. Stat. §§ 298-9(a)(5),(6) (1990).

93. *Id.*

94. Hawaii Compulsory Attendance Exception, Regulations, 4140.4(D)(6) (1990).

95. *Id.*
96. Code § 33-202 (1991).
97. Klicka, *supra* note 62, at p.15.
98. Rev. Stat. ch. 122, para. 26-1. (1991).
99. IL Rev. Stat. ch. 122, para. 26-1.1. Branches of education must include health, metric education, physical education, safety, history, social studies, language arts, science, math, consumer education, conservation, foreign language, music, art, career education, and driver education. IL Ann. Stat. Ch. 122, paras. 27-21 to 22 (1988); IL Admin. Code tit. 23, §§ 1.420-.440 (1986).
100. *People v. Levisen*, 90 N.E.2d 213, 215 (IL 1950).
101. *Id.*
102. *Id. See also Scoma v. Chicago Board of Education*, 391 F.Supp. 452, 461 (N.D. IL 1974).
103. *Id.* In *Levisen*, the evidence of the child's education showed: the child was taught subjects comparable to those being taught in public schools; she showed a proficiency comparable to the average child of her age; she had regular hours for schooling; and there was nothing to show her education was being neglected. *Id.*
104. Code § 20-8.1-3-17.(a) (1991).
105. *Id.* § 20-8.1-3-34. Attendance, notice and enrollment in home schools must be equivalent to what is required in public schools. *Id.* § 20-8.1-3-17(c)-(h). Failure to comply with the statutory equivalency requirement is a Class B Misdemeanor. *Id.*
106. *Mazanec v. North Judson-San Pierre School Corp.*, 614 F. Supp. 1152 (N.D. Ind., 1985), *aff'd*, 798 F.2d 230 (1985).
107. *Id.*
108. *State v. Peterman*, 70 N.E. 550, 551 (Ind. Ct. App., 1904).
109. Sybil Yastrow, *Home Instruction: A National Study of State Law*, May 1989 at 101, *quoting* Steven Goldsmith, Memorandum from the Office of the Prosecuting Attorney of Marion County Indiana, February 17, 1984.
110. Admin. Code r. 670-63.3 (1991).
111. *State v. Moorhead*, 308 N.W.2d 60, 64 (Iowa 1981). The court upheld a misdemeanor conviction of a parent for violation of the compulsory attendance education requirement. *Id.*
112. Iowa Admin. Code r. 670-63.4 (1991).
113. Equivalent Instruction Standards, Chapter 63, at 1.
114. Ia. st § 256.11 (1991).
115. *Id.* § 280.3.
116. *Id.*
117. *Id.*
118. *Id.*
119. *Id.* § 299.24.
120. *Id.*
121. *Id.* § 299.4.
122. *Id.*
123. Stat. Ann. §§ 72-1111(1),(2) (1990).
124. "Courses must include civil government, and United States history, and in patriotism and the duties of a citizen, suitable to the elementary grades; in addition thereto, all accredited high schools, public, private or parochial shall give a course of instruction concerning the government and institutions of the United States and particularly of the Constitution of the United States. . . ." *Id.* § 72-1103.

125. Yastrow, *supra* note 109, at 127, *citing State v. Lowrey*, 383 P.2d 962 (Kan. 1963).
126. § 159.030.(1)(b) (1991).
127. *Id.*
128. *Id.*
129. Klicka, *supra* note 62, at 20, *quoting* Gary Bale, *Memorandum, RE: State Regulation of Private Schools*, Kentucky Dept. of Ed., January 21, 1985.
130. Ky. st. § 159.040 (1991).
131. *Kentucky State Bd. for Elementary and Secondary Educ. v. Rudasill*, 589 S.W.2d 877 (Ky., 1979).
132. *Id.* at 884.
133. *Id.*
134. *Id.*
135. *Id.*
136. Rev. Stat. Ann. § 17.236 (West 1991).
137. *Id.* Application to home school must be made within fifteen days after beginning the program. *Id.* § 17:236.1.
138. *Id.* § 17.236.1.
139. *Id.* § 17.236.1.
140. *Id.* § 17.236.1.A.
141. *Id.* § 17.236.1.C.(1). In lieu of the required materials, a parent may submit verification of the child passing a competency test approved by the state, or positive evaluation by a teacher certified to teach the student's grade level. *Id.* § 17.236.1.D.
142. Rev. Stat. Ann. tit. 20-A § 5001-A(3)(A)(West Supp. 199).
143. *Id.* § 5001-A(3)(A)(1)(c).
144. *Id.*
145. *Id.*
146. *Blount v. Dept. of Educ. & Cultural Serv.*, 551 A.2d 1377 (Me. 1988), *quoting* Rules for Equivalent Instruction Programs, 05-071 Code Me. R. ch. 130 § 1(A)(3).
147. *Blount v. Dept. of Educ. & Cultural Serv.*, 551 A.2d at 1383.
148. 05-071 Code Me. R. ch. 130, § 1(c)(2)(c)(ii).
149. *Id.* § 1(C)(2)(a)(ii)(dd).
150. § 5001-A(3)(A)(2).
151. Education Code Ann. § 7-301(a)(1) (1990).
152. Gen. L. c. 76, § 1 (1991).
153. *Care and Protection of Charles*, 504 N.E.2d 592, (Mass., 1987).
154. *Id.* at 337. The state has the right to regulate school attendance because of broad state autonomy in situations involving children. *Prince v. Com. of Mass.*, 321 U.S. 158 (1944).
155. *People v. De Jonge*, 179 Mich. App. 225 (1989), *remanded by*, 461 N.W.2d 365 (Mich., 1990), *affirmed*, 470 N.W.2d 433 (Mich. App., 1991).
156. *Id.* § 380.1516(3)(a).
157. Comp. Laws § 380.1561(3)(a) (1990). Instruction must be given to the home school student at the same grade level as public school students of the same age. *Id.*
158. *Id.* § 388.553; Mich. Stat. Ann. § 15.1923 (1991).
159. *Id.* §§ 1122(1), 1124(2),(3), 1125.
160. *Clonlara, Inc. v. State Board of Education*, 188 Mich. App. 332, 469 N.W.2d 66 (1991).
161. Comp. Laws § 380.1599 (1990).

162. Stat. §§ 120.101, 102 (1991). Parents are responsible for making sure the child receives knowledge and skills necessary for effective citizenship. *Id.*

163. *Id.* § 120.101. Subd. 5. Once students under the age of seven are enrolled in public schools, the school board may require they be subject to compulsory instruction. *Id.* Subd. 5a. The mandatory days of instruction will increase incrementally, as provided in the state Compulsory Instruction statute, with the first increase beginning in 1995. *Id.* Subd. 5b.

164. *Id.* Subd. 6.

165. *Id.* Subds. 7,8.

166. *Id.* Subd. 8. The Minnesota Court of Appeals held in *Matter of Welfare of T.K.,* 475 N.W.2d 88 (Minn. App., 1991) that removal of home schooled children from the home because the parent didn't submit to state testing requirements was premature, because these results were more severe than the penalty which would result from actual failure on the required tests.

167. *Id.* § 120.102.

168. Yastrow, *supra* note 109, at 74, *citing id.* §§ 120.101 subd. 7(6),8(d), 120.102 subd. 1(4).

169. Code Ann. § 37-13-91(3)(c) (1991).

170. *Id.*

171. Rev. Stat. § 167.031.1 (1991).

172. *Id.* § 167.031.2.(1). Six hundred hours must be taught in reading, language arts, math, social studies and science, with four hundred of the six hundred hours taught at the home school location. *Id.* § 167.031.2(2)(b).

173. *Id.* § 167.031 2(2).

174. *Id.* § 167.042.

175. Code Ann. § 20-5-102(2)(e) (1991).

176. *Id.* § 20-5-109(1)-(5).

177. Rev. Stat. §§ 79-1701(2)-(4) (1991).

178. *Id.*

179. *Id.* § 79-201. Required time of attendance is 1,032 hours for elementary students, and 1,080 hours for high school students. *Id.*

180. *Id.* §§ 79-1701(2)-(4), 79-328(5).

181. *Id.* §§ 79-1701(2)-(4).

182. *Id.* §79-328(5)(c).

183. *Id.* §§ 79-201, 79-1701(2)-(4).

184. Rev. Stat. Ann. § 394.211.1(f) (1991).

185. Klicka, *supra* note 62, at 31, *quoting Nev. Admin. Code* ch. 392.015.

186. *Id.* § 392.025.

187. *Id.* § 392.015, 392.065(3)-(8), 392.075.

188. Rev. Stat. Ann. § 193-A (1990).

189. *Id.* § 193-A:4I. A school official will help parents meet the teacher requirement and may allow someone other than the parent to teach the child. *Id.* §193-A:4II.

190. *Id.* § 193-A:5II.(a)-(d). Proper notice must be given by August 1 of each year, unless commencing instruction after August 1 where thirty days notice must be given. *Id.*

191. *Id.* § 193-A:5III.

192. *Id.* § 193-A:4I.

193. *Id.* § 193-A:6I.

194. *Id.* § 193-A:6II(a)-(d).

195. *Id.* § 193-A:6III.

196. *Id.*

197. Rev. Stat. § 18A:38-25. (1991).

198. "[E]qual in worth or value, force, power, effect, import and the like." N.J. Rev. Stat. § 18A:38-25 Note 7 (1991). *See Knox v. O'Brien*, 7 N.J.Super. 608, 72 A.2d 389 (Co. 1950).

199. *State v. Massa*, 231 A.2d 252 (N.J. Co., 1967).

200. *Massa*, 95 N.J. Super. 382.

201. *Stephens v. Bongart*, 189 A. 131 (N.J. Juv. & Dom. Rel. Ct., 1937).

202. Stat. Ann. § 22-12-2 (Michie 1991).

203. *Id.* § 22-1-2V.

204. Compulsory Education Law §§ 3204.1, 2 (McKinney 1991).

205. *Id.* § 3204.2.

206. *Id.* § 3204 Note. *See Matter of Adam D.*, 132 Misc.2d 797, 505 N.Y.S.2d 809 (N.Y. Fam. Ct., 1983).

207. *Id.* § 3204 Note 2. *See Matter of Blackwelder*, 528 N.Y.S.2d 759 (N.Y. Sup., 1988).

208. *Id.* § 3204 Note 2. *See Matter of Kilroy*, 121 Misc.2d 98, 467 N.Y.S.2d 318 (N.Y. Fam. Ct., 1983).

209. *Id.* § 3204 Note 2. *See Matter of Falk*, 441 N.Y.S.2d 785 (N.Y. Fam. Ct. 1981).

210. *Matter of Franz*, 378 N.Y.S.2d 317 (N.Y. City Fam.Ct. 1976), *aff'd*, 390 N.Y.S.2d 940 (N.Y.A.D. 2 Dept., 1977).

211. 55 Ops. Atty. Gen. 86.

212. *Delconte v. State*, 329 S.E.2d 636,640 (N.C. 1985).

213. *Id.* at 641.

214. *Id.*

215. 55 Ops.N.C. Atty. Gen. 86.

216. Cent. Code § 15-34.1-03.5 (1991).

217. *Id.*

218. For elementary grades, course work must include: spelling, reading, writing, arithmetic, language, English grammar, geography, U.S. History, civil government, nature study, elements of agriculture, physiology and hygiene. *Id.* § 15-38-07. High school students must study four units of work per year, made up of forty minutes per unit per day, in 180 days per year. *Id.* § 15-41-24. Coursework may be chosen from the following subjects: English, mathematics, science, social studies, world history, health, physical education, music, business education, economics, foreign language, industries and vocational education. *Id.* § 15-41-24.

219. *Id.* § 15-34.1-03.5.

220. *Id.*

221. *Id.*

222. *Id.*

223. *Id.*

224. *Id.*

225. *Id.*

226. *Id.*

227. *Id.*

228. Rev. Code Ann. § 3301-34-01 (1989).

229. *Id.* §§ 3301-34-03(A)(1)-(4).

230. *Id.* § 3301-34-03(A)(5). Required courses are: language, reading, spelling, writing, geography, U.S. and Ohio history, national, state and local government, mathematics, science, health, physical education, fine arts, music, first aid, safety and fire prevention. *Id.*

231. *Id.* §§ 3301-34-03(A)(6),(7).

232. *Id.* §§ 3301-34-03(A)(8),(9). A teacher may be qualified by: holding a high school diploma, its equivalent or some other appropriate credential approved by

the superintendent; or by testing at the level of a high school graduate; or by receiving supervision by a person with a college degree. *Id.*

233. *Id.* §§ 3301-34-03(C)(1),(2). The superintendent will work with the parent in order to satisfy the state requirements; yet if there is evidence that minimal educational requirements are not complied with, the superintendent may express his intent to deny excuse. A due process hearing will result, and, based on the evidence presented at the hearing, an excuse from attendance may be granted or denied. *Id.* §§ 3301-34-03(C)(2),(D).

234. *Id.*

235. *Id.* §§ 3301-34-04(B)(1)-(3).

236. *Id.* §§ 3301-34-04(A),(B)(1)(a),(B)(2)(a).

237. *Id.* §§ 3301-34-05(A)(C). During remediation parents must submit quarterly reports including curriculum used and an evaluation of the child's progress. *Id.* § 3301-34-05(B).

238. *Id.* §§ 3301-34-05(C)(D).

239. *Gardini v. Moyer*, 575 N.E.2d 423 (Ohio, 1991), *rehearing denied*, 577 N.E.2d 663 (Ohio, 1991).

240. *Id.*

241. *Id.* at 486.

242. Stat. Ann. tit. 70 § 10-105(A) (1992).

243. Klicka, *supra* note 62, at 40.

244. *Id., quoting Sheppard v. Oklahoma*, 306 P.2d 346-353 (Okl. Cr., 1957).

245. *Id., quoting* 70-129 Op. Att'y Gen. (1974).

246. The basic skills in learning include: reading, writing, English, math, science and use of numbers; citizenship, ideals of history and government of the United States and of Oklahoma and of other countries; and the United States Constitution, health, safety, physical education, and conservation. Okla. Stat. Ann. tit. 70 § 11-103 (1992).

247. *Id.* § 11-103.

248. Rev. Stat. § 339.030(3) (1991). Children may in the alternative prove they have acquired knowledge equal to that acquired in public schools, through the twelfth grade. *Id.* § 339.030(2). The parent or private teacher exemption does *not* fall within the private school exemption (which would allow the parent to avoid statutory notice and testing requirements). *State v. Bowman*, 653 P.2d 254 (Or. Ct. App. 1982).

249. *Id.* § 339.035(2)

250. *Id.* §§ 339.035(3)(a)-(e). The superintendent determines whether performance is satisfactory. *Id.* The testing requirement must be complied with. *State v. Bowman*, 653 P.2d 254 (Or. Ct. App. 1982).

251. Stat. Ann. tit. 24, § 13-1327(d) (1991). Programs for students in need of special education services (other than gifted and/or talented) must address needs and be approved of in writing by a certified special education teacher or school psychologist. *Id.*

252. *Id.* 1327.1.(a).

253. *Id.* 1327.1.(b)(1). Notice must include the student's name and age, the supervisor's name, the program site's address and telephone number, assurance that required courses will be taught, a curriculum outline, and evidence of immunization and health and medical services. *Id.*

254. *Id.* §§ 1327.1(b)(2),(3).

255. Elementary students must be taught: English, spelling, reading, writing, arithmetic, science, geography, history of the United States and Pennsylvania, civics, safety education (including fire prevention), health, physiology, physical education, music and art. *Id.* § 1327.1.(c)(1).

256. Secondary students must be instructed in: English; language; literature; speech; composition; science; geography; civics; world, United States and Pennsylvania history; general mathematics; algebra; geometry; art; music; physical education; health; safety education (dangers and preventions of fires). *Id.* § 1327.1.(c)(2). Students may be taught economics, biology, chemistry, foreign languages; trigonometry, etc. *Id.* In order to graduate, the following must be taught in grades nine through twelve: English, four years; mathematics, three years; science, three years; social studies, three years; arts and humanities, two years. *Id.* § 1327.1.(d).

257. Parents may choose a test from a list of five tests. *Id.*

258. *Id.* §§ 1327.1.(e)(1),(2).

259. Upon examination of the portfolio, if the program is not in compliance with state requirements for home education programs, the parent may be requested to provide additional information demonstrating compliance. If this request is ignored, the child will automatically be enrolled in a public school district. If the parent does respond but does not demonstrate compliance, a hearing will be held to determine whether remediation is required or the student should be enrolled automatically in the public school district. *Id.* §§ 1327.1.(h)-(l).

260. *Id.*

261. *Id.* § 1327.1(m).

262. Gen. Laws § 16-19-1 (1991).

263. Code Ann. § 59-65-40(A) (Law. Co-op. 1991).

264. *Id.* § 59-65-40(A)(2).

265. The statutory requirement that a home school instructor with a high school degree must "attain a passing score on the basic skills examination" in § 59-65-40(A)(1)(a) was determined to be unenforceable by South Carolina's supreme court, because the requirement failed to meet a standard of reasonableness. *Lawrence v. South Carolina State Bd. of Educ.*, 412 S.E.2d 394 (S.C. 1991).

266. S.C. Code Ann. § 59-65-40(A)(1) (1991).

267. *Id.* § 59-65-40(A)(3).

268. *Id.* §59-65-40(A)(4).

269. *Id.* § 59-65-40(D). Any student scoring below the appropriate promotion standard for that student's grade may be required to attend public school, receive special services as a handicapped student, or go through remedial home education. *Id.* § 59-65-40(D).

270. S.C. Code Ann. § 59-65-40(A).

271. S.C. Op. Att'y Gen. (Jan. 22, 1991).

272. Codified Laws Ann. § 13-27-3 (1991).

273. *Id.*

274. *Id.* If the instructor is incompetent, the school board may withdraw excuse from attendance. *Id.*

275. *Id.*

276. Code Ann. §§ 49-6-3050(a)(1),(b)(3) (1991).

277. *Id.* The local school board's rules will govern such use.

278. *Id.* § 49-6-3050(b)(1).

279. *Id.* §§ 49-6-3050(b)(4),(7). A parent may obtain an exemption from the requirement of a college degree from year to year. *Id. Crites v. Smith* 826 S.W.2d 459 (Tenn. App., 1991). In *Crites v. Smith*, No. 01-A-01-9101-CH00002 *4 1991 WL 169690, Sept. 4, 1991, permission to appeal was denied by the Supreme Court, February 24, 1992, because it was not unreasonable to consistently deny parents without college degrees this exemption, since a college degree was set up as the standard by the legislature. *Id.*

280. A student testing three to six months behind the student's grade level in reading, language arts, mathematics or science will be given remedial instruction designed by a licensed teacher in the student's grade level. A student testing more than one year behind on back to back tests may be required to enroll in a public, church or private school. *Id.* §§ 49-6-3050(b)(6)(A),(B),(C).

281. *Id.* §§ 49-6-3050(b)(2),(3),(5),(9).

282. Educ. Code Ann. § 21.033(a) (1991).

283. *Id.*

284. Klicka, *supra* note 62, at 47, *quoting Leeper v. Arlington Indep. School Dist.,* No. 17-88761-85 Tarrant County 17th Judicial Ct. (April 13, 1987).

285. Code Ann. § 53A-11-102. (1991).

286. Stat. Ann. tit. 16, § 1121 (1991).

287. Code Ann. tit. 17, s. 84 (1991).

288. *Id.*

289. Code Ann. s. 22.1-254.1. (1991).

290. *Id.*

291. *Id.*

292. Rev. Code § 28A.225.010(1)(b) (1991).

293. Subjects taught must include "instruction in the basic skills of occupational education, science, mathematics, language, social studies, history, health, reading, writing, spelling and the development of an appreciation of art and music." *Id.* § 28A.225.010(4).

294. Education must be "provided for a number of hours equivalent to the total annual program hours per grade level established for approved private schools under §§ 28A.195.010, 040." *Id.*

295. *Id.* §§ 28A.225.010.(4)(a)-(c).

296. *Id.* §28A.225.010(5).

297. Code § 18-8-1 (1991).

298. *Id.*

299. The home instructor must have a high school diploma or equivalent, and formal education of at least four years higher than the child being instructed. *Id.* § 18-8-1(b).

300. *Id.*

301. *Id.* If a student scores below the fortieth percentile, a remedial program must be implemented to improve the score above the fortieth percentile. If this program is not effective, home schooling must be discontinued. *Id.*

302. Stat. s. 118.15(4) (1991).

303. *Id.* § 118.165. The curriculum must include instruction in language arts, mathematics, social studies, science and health. *Id.* If the subject is not consistent with "the program's religious doctrines," it will not need to be included. *Id.*

304. Stat. § 21-4-101(a)(iii) (1991).

305. *Id.* § 21-4-101(a)(v).

306. *Id.* §§ 21-4-101(a)(vi), 21-4-102(b).

307. *Id.*

BIBLIOGRAPHY

"Abandoning the Motherland; Learning by Choice; Pearl Harbor Remembered." Transcript from "The MacNeill-Lehrer News Hour." #4216 (December 2, 1991), available on NEXIS.

Adams, Charles, ed. *The Works of John Adams*. Volume. III. Boston, 1851.

Aikman, David and Richard Ostling. "America's Holy War." *Time* Magazine (December 9, 1991).

Alaska Department of Education. *Summary of SRA Testing for Centralized Correspondence Study April/May 1984*. Juneau, AK: author, 1984.

Allen, Jeanne A. "An Agenda for George Bush's Education Summit." 106 *Policy Insights* (September 1989).

American Educational Research Association, American Psychological Association, and National Council on Measurement in Education. *Standards for Educational and Psychological Testing*. Washington, D.C.: American Psychological Association, 1985.

America 2000—An Education Strategy. Washington, D.C.: U.S. Dept. of Education, 1991.

American Jurisprudence. 2nd Const. Law Section 750 Sec. 16A (1979).

American Law Reports, 65 A.L.R.3d 1222 (1975).

Arkansas Department of Education. *Arkansas Department of Education News Release, July 21, 1986*. Little Rock, AR: author, 1986.

—— *Arkansas Department of Education, News Release, 1987*. Little Rock, AR: author, 1987.

Arons, Stephen and Charles Lawrence III. "The Manipulation of Consciousness: A First Amendment Critique of Schooling." 15 *Harvard Civil Rights and Civil Liberties Law Review* 309 (1980).

Arons, Stephen. *Value Conflict Between American Families and American Schools. Final Report to National Institute of Education*. Amherst, MA: University of Massachusetts, 1981.

—— *Compelling Belief: The Culture of American Schooling*. New York: New Press, 1983.

Associated Press. "Senate Rejects School Choice Tax Credits." *Chicago Tribune* (January 24, 1992).

Axtell, James, ed. *The Educational Writings of John Locke*. Cambridge, MA: Cambridge University Press, 1968.

Baker, Robert. "Compulsory Education in the United States: Big Brother Goes to School." 3 *Seton Hall Law Review* 102 (1972).

Bale, Gary. Memorandum, RE: State Regulation of Private Schools. Kentucky Department of Education. January 21, 1985.

Bandura, Albert, *et al.* "Imitation of Film-Mediated Aggressive Models." 66 *Journal of Abnormal and Social Psychology* (1963).

Barnes, Fred. "Logjam; White House Watch." *The New Republic* (May 11, 1992).

Barnes, Thomas. *The Book of the General Lawes and Libertyes Concerning the Inhabitants of the Massachusetts.* San Marino, CA: The Huntington Library, facsimile of the 1648 edition, 1975.

Barnhard, Clarence L., ed. *The World Book Dictionary.* Chicago: Doubleday & Company, Inc., 1971.

Barry, Dave. "Math R Not Us." *The Washington Post Magazine* (April 28, 1991).

Barton, David. *To Pray or Not to Pray: A Statistical Look at What Has Happened Since 39 Million Students Were Ordered to Stop Praying in Public Schools.* Aledo, TX: Wallbuilder Press, 1988.

Barton, Jon and John Whitehead. *Schools on Fire.* Wheaton, IL: Tyndale House Publishers, Inc., 1980.

Bass, Bernard M. *Leadership, Psychology, and Organizational Behavior.* Westport, CT: Greenwood Press Publishers, 1960.

Bennett, Hal. *No More Public School.* New York: Random House, 1972.

Berger, Joseph. "Ferocity of Youth Violence Is Up, A School Official Says." *The New York Times* (November 11, 1989).

——— , "The Ninth Amendment." 66 *Cornell Law Review* 1 (1980).

——— "Judgment Replaces Fear in Drug Lessons." *The New York Times* (October 30, 1989).

Berry, Jeffrey M. *Lobbying for the People: The Political Behavior of Public Interest Groups.* Princeton, NJ: Princeton University Press, 1977.

——— *The Interest Group Society.* Glenview, IL: Scott, Foresman & Co., 1989.

Beshoner, E. Alice. "Home Education in America: Parental Rights Reasserted." 49 *UMKC Law Review* 191 (1981).

Black, Charles Lund. *Decision According to Law.* New York: Norton, 1981.

Blackstone, William. *Commentaries on the Laws of England.* Volume 2. George Tucker, ed. Philadelphia: William Birch Young and Abraham Small, 1803.

Blumenfeld, Samuel L. "Can Chris Whittle Succeed? His Is the Most Revolutionary Plan for American Education in 150 Years." *The Blumenfeld Education Letter.* Vol. 6, No. 7 (Letter #59) (July 1991).

——— "The Great American Math Disaster: Where Is God in All This?" *Home School Digest* (Fall 1991).

——— "The SAT Disaster of 1990—National Verbal Score Hits Bottom as the Dumbing Down of America Continues Apace." *The Blumenfeld Education Letter.* Vol. 5, No. 11 (Letter #51) (November 1990).

——— "The SAT Disaster of 1991—National Verbal Score Hits New Low and the Dumbing Down Goes On." *The Blumenfeld Education Letter.* Vol. 7, No. 12 (Letter #64) (December 1991).

Bolles, Richard Nelson. *What Color Is Your Parachute?* Berkeley, CA: Ten Speed Press, 1990.

Boorstin, Daniel. *The Mysterious Science of the Law.* Magnolia, MA: Peter Smith, 1958.

Borg, Walter R. and Meredith Damien Gall. *Educational Research: An Introduction.* New York: Longman, Inc., 1983.

Bork, Robert. *The Supreme Court and the Religion Clauses. Turning the Religion Clauses on Their Heads: Proceedings of the National Religious Freedom Conference of the Catholic League for Religious and Civil Rights.* 1988.

Boyarsky, Bill. "Bill Boyarsky: Quayle Here with a Legitimate Issue: The Sales of LAX." *Los Angeles Times* (May 22, 1992).

Brennan, William. "State Constitutions and the Protection of Individual Rights." 90 *Harvard Law Review* 489 (1977).

Brest, Paul, and Sanford Levison. *Processes of Constitutional Decisionmaking.* Boston: Little, Brown and Co., 1985.

Bronfenbrenner, Urie. *Two Worlds of Childhood: U.S. and U.S.S.R.* New York: Russell Sage Foundation, 1970.

Buchanan, G. Sidney. "The Right of Privacy: Past, Present, and Future." 16 *Ohio Northern University Law Review* 403 (1989).

Buckley, Stephen. "Home Schooling on Rise." *The Washington Post* (May 26, 1992).

Buros, O. K., ed. *Mental Measurements Yearbooks.* Highland Park, NJ: The Gryphon Press, 1938-1978.

Butts, R. Freeman and Lawrence A. Cremin. *A History of Education in American Culture.* New York: Holt, Rinehart and Winston, 1953.

Calhoun, Arthur. *A Social History of the American Family from Colonial Times to the Present.* New York: Arno Press, 1973.

Campbell, Donald T. and Julian C. Stanley. *Experimental and Quasi-Experimental Designs for Research.* Chicago: Rand McNally College Publishing Company, 1963.

Caplan, Marc. *Ralph Nader Presents: A Citizen's Guide to Lobbying.* New York: Dembner Books, 1983.

_____ "The History and Meaning of the Ninth Amendment." 69 *Virginia Law Review* 223 (1983).

Carlson, Avis. *Small World Long Gone—A Family Record of an Era.* Evanston, IL: Schori Press, 1975.

Carmody, Deirdre. "Minority Students Gain on College Entrance Tests." *The New York Times* (September 12, 1989).

Carson, Clarence. *The Colonial Experience.* Wadley, AL: American Textbook Committee, 1987.

"Cases on Appeal." *Teaching Home* Vol. X, No.1 (February-March 1992).

Cash, T. F. *et al.* "Sexism and 'Beautyism' in Personnel Consultant Decision Making." 62 *Journal of Applied Psychology* (1977).

Cavior, N. and L. R. Howard. "Facial Attractiveness and Juvenile Delinquency Among Black and White Offenders." 1 *Journal of Abnormal Child Psychology* (1973).

Cetron, Marvin and Margaret Gayle. *Educational Renaissance.* New York: St. Martin's Press, 1991.

Chatham, April Dawn. "Home vs. Public Schooling: What About Relationships in Adolescence?" Doctoral dissertation, University of Oklahoma, 1991. *Dissertation Abstracts International*, Vol. 52.

Chemerinsky, Erwin. *Federal Jurisdiction. Secs. 2.3.4 and 12.2.1.* Boston: Little, Brown & Co., 1989.

Chion-Kenney, Linda. "Education; The Choice Debate, A Patch to Better Schooling or an Elitist Plum?" *The Washington Post* (February 10, 1992).

Chisholm, Shirley. "Literacy: Democracy's Basic Ingredient." 12 *Adult Literacy Bas. Ed.* 2 (1988).

"Choosing Better Schools: The Five Regional Meetings in Choice in Education." Washington, D.C.: U.S. Dept. of Education, 1990.

Choper, Jesse H. "The Free Exercise Clause: A Structural Overview and an Appraisal of Recent Developments." 27 *William & Mary Law Review* 943 (1986).

—— "The Establishment Clause and Aid to Parochial Schools—An Update." 75 *California Law Review* 5 (1987).

Chubb, John E. and Terry M. Moe. "Politics, Markets and America's Schools." Washington, D.C.: The Brookings Institute, 1990.

Chubb, John. "Can Public Schools Survive?" *U.S. News & World Report* (December 9, 1991).

Cizek, Gregory J. "Applying Standardized Testing to Home-based Education Programs: Reasonable or Customary?" 7 *Educational Measurement Issues and Practice*. No. 3 (Fall 1988).

Clifford, M. and E. Walster. "The Effect of Physical Attractiveness on Teacher Expectation." 46 *Sociology of Education*. (1973).

Cohen, Howard. *Equal Rights for Children*. Totowa, NJ: Rowman and Littlefield, 1980.

Cohen, Muriel. "School Plan Draws Fire: Educators Say Additional Funds Vital to Fuel Massachusetts 2000." *The Boston Globe* (October 24, 1991).

Colfax, David and Micki Colfax. *Homeschooling for Excellence*. New York: Warner Books, 1988.

Collins, Varnum Lansing. *President Witherspoon*. Princeton, NJ: Princeton University Press, 1925.

Collins and Hurd. "Warrantless Administrative Searches: It's Time to be Frank Again." 22 *American Business Law Journal* 189 (1984).

Commager, Henry Steele. "Schoolmaster to America." *Noah Webster's American Spelling Book*. New York: Columbia University, 1958.

——, ed. *Documents of American History*. New York: Appleton-Century-Crofts, Inc., 1949.

Comment. "Developments in the Law—The Constitution and the Family." 93 *Harvard Law Review* 1156 (1980).

—— "Protecting Children in Licensed Family Day-care Homes: Can the State Enter a Home Without a Warrant?" 25 *Santa Clara Law Review* 411 (1985).

—— "Texas Homeschooling: An Unresolved Conflict Between Parents and Educators." 39 *Baylor Law Review* 469 (1987).

"Condom Roulette." *Washington Watch*. Vol. 3, No. 4 (January 1992).

Cook, Anthony. "When Your Home Is the Classroom." *Money* (September 1991).

Cook, James. "A Mailman's Lot Is Not a Happy One." *Forbes* (April 27, 1992).

Coons, John E. and Stephen D. Sugarman. "Credits v. Subsidies: Comment on the California Tuition Tax Credit Proposal." In Edward McGlynn Gaffney, Jr., *Private Schools and the Public Good: Policy Alternatives for the Eighties.* Notre Dame, IN: Univ. of Notre Dame Press, 1981.

Cooper, Kenneth J. "National Standards at Core of Strategy." *The Washington Post* (April 19, 1991).

Cooper, Ruth. "An Air Force Family Homeschools." *Home Education Magazine* (March-April 1991).

Corwin, E. *The Constitution and What It Means Today.* 14th ed. Princeton, NJ: Princeton University Press, 1978.

Cotton, John. *Milk for Babes, Drawn Out of the Breasts of Both Testaments.* 1646.

Crary, Ryland W. and Louis A. Petrone. *Foundations of Modern Education.* New York: Alfred A. Knopf, 1971.

Cremin, Lawrence A. *American Education: The Colonial Experience, 1607-1783.* New York: Harper & Row, 1970.

―― *American Education: The National Experience, 1783-1876.* New York: Harper & Row, 1980.

―― *The American Common School: An Historical Conception.* New York: Columbia University, 1951.

―― *The Transformation of the School.* New York: Alfred A. Knopf, 1961.

Cressman, George and George Bereday. *Public Education in America.* 2nd ed. New York: Harper, 1961.

"Crosscurrents on Dress in High Schools." *The New York Times* (September 13, 1989).

Cubberly, Ellwood. *The History of Education.* New York: Houghton Mifflin, Co., 1920.

Currie, David P. *The Constitution in the Supreme Court: The Second Century, 1888-1896.* Chicago: University of Chicago Press, 1985.

Curry, Thomas J. *The First Freedoms.* New York: Oxford University Press, 1986.

Darley, John M. and Paget H. Gross. "A Hypothesis Confirming Bias in Labeling Effects." 44 *Journal of Personality and Social Psychology* (1983).

Davis, M. "The Constitutional Right to Home School." 55 *Inter Alia* 14 (October 1990).

Davis, William T. *History of the Town of Plymouth.* Philadelphia: J. W. Lewis & Co., 1885.

Defense Almanac. Washington, D.C.: Department of Defense, 1991.

deKieffer, Donald. *How to Lobby Congress: A Guide for the Citizen Lobbyist.* New York: Dodd, Mead & Co., 1981.

Delahooke, Mona Maarse. "Home Educated Children's Social/Emotional Adjustment and Academic Achievement: A Comparative Study." Doctoral dissertation, California School of Professional Psychology, 1986. *Dissertation Abstracts International.* Vol. 47.

"Developments in the Law—The Constitution and the Family." 93 *Harvard Law Review* 1157 (1980).

Devins, Neal M. "A Constitutional Right to Home Instruction?" 62 *Washington University Law Quarterly* 435 (1984).

Diary of Cotton Mather. Vol. 1. New York: Frederick Ungar Pub. Co., 1957.

Dion, K. K. *et al.* "What Is Beautiful Is Good." 24 *Journal of Personality and Social Psychology* (1972).

Dion, K. K. "Physical Attractiveness and Evaluation of Children's Transgressions." 24 *Journal of Personality and Social Psychology* (1972).

—— "Young Children's Stereotyping of Facial Attractiveness." 9 *Developmental Psychology* (1973).

Discussion by Mason and Madison. 2 Records of the Federal Convention 341. Farrand, ed. 1911.

Dreisbach, Daniel L. *Real Threat and Mere Shadow: Religious Liberty and the First Amendment.* Wheaton, IL: Crossway Books, 1987.

Dupont de Nemours, Pierre Samuel. *National Education in the United States of America.* Newark, DE: Univ. of Delaware Press, 1923.

Eakman, Beverly K. *Educating for the New World Order.* Portland, OR: Halcyon House, 1991.

Eastland, Terry. "School Choice Clears a Hurdle." *The Washington Times* (March 3, 1992).

Educating Our Children: Parents and Schools Together—A Report to the President. Secretary of Education, 1989.

Education Newsline. August/September, 1991.

"Education: America 2000." *Fac-Sheet* #67. Plymouth Rock Foundation.

Edwards, Newton and Herman Richey. *The School in the American Social Order.* Boston: Houghton Mifflin Co., 1947.

Efran, M. G. "The Effect of Physical Appearance on the Judgement of Guilt, Interpersonal Attraction, and Severity of Recommended Punishment in a Simulated Jury Task." 8 *Journal of Experimental Research in Personality* (1974).

Eggers, William D. "Economic Reform in Eastern Europe: A Report Card." *Heritage Foundation Reports* (April 23, 1992), available on NEXIS.

Elam, Stanley M. *et al.* "The 23rd Annual Gallup Poll of the Public's Attitudes Toward the Public Schools." *Phi Delta Kappan* (September 1991).

Ellis. "Parochial and Public Schools: A Point of View." 14 *Educational Forum* 21 (1949).

Ely, John Hart. *Democracy and Distrust.* Cambridge, MA: Harvard University Press, 1980.

Emerson, Thomas. *Toward a General Theory of the First Amendment.* New York: Random House, 1966.

Falle, B. "Standardized Tests for Home Study Students: Administration and Results." 7 *Method: Alaskan Perspectives* (1986).

Feinstein, S. "Domestic Lessons: Shunning the Schools, More Parents Teach Their Kids at Home." *The Wall Street Journal* (October 6, 1986).

Field, G. *The Legal Relations of Infants, Parent and Child, and Guardian and Ward* 68 (1888).

Fiske, Edward. "Changes Planned in Entrance Test Used by Colleges." *The New York Times* (January 3, 1989).

—— "College Testing Is a Hard Habit to Break." *The New York Times* (January 15, 1989).

—— "Historic Shift Seen in School Finance." *The New York Times* (October 4, 1989).

Fitzpatrick, John C. *George Washington Himself*. Indianapolis: Bobbs-Merrill Co., 1885.

Fitzpatrick, John C., ed. *The Writings of George Washington*. Vol. 3. Washington, D.C.: United States Government Printing Office, 1932.

"For-Profit Schools—Investment in Learning." *U.S. News & World Report* (December 9, 1991).

Franza, August. 71 *Eng. J.* 4 (April 1982).

Freeman, D. *et al. A Closer Look at Standardized Tests*. Research Series No. 53. East Lansing, MI: Michigan State University, Institute for Research on Teaching, 1979.

Freeman, Roger A. "Educational Tax Credits." *The Public School Monopoly: A Critical Analysis of Education and the State in American Society*. Robert B. Everhart, ed. San Diego: Pacific Institute, 1982.

Friedman, Milton. *Capitalism and Freedom*. Chicago: University of Chicago Press, 1962.

Frost, Eugene, A. and Robert C. Morris. "Does Home-Schooling Work? Some Insights for Academic Success." 59 *Contemporary Education* No. 4 (Summer 1988).

Gaebler, David B. "First Amendment Protection Against Government Compelled Expression and Association." 23 *Boston College Law Review* 995 (1982).

Gales and Seaton, eds. 1 *Annals of Congress* 454 (1834).

——— 1 *Annals of Congress*. (1834), reprinted in Bennett B. Patterson, *The Forgotten Ninth Amendment: A Call for Legislation and Judicial Recognition of Rights Under Social Conditions of Today*. Indianapolis: Bobbs-Merrill, 1955.

Gardner, Howard. *Developmental Psychology: An Introduction*. Boston: Little, Brown and Company, 1982.

Gardner, John W. *Self-Renewal*. New York: Harper & Row, 1963.

——— *In Common Cause*. New York: W.W. Norton & Co., Inc., 1972.

Gardner, William E. "*A Nation at Risk*: Some Critical Comments." 35 *J. Teach. Ed.* 1 (January-February 1984).

Gatto, John. "Why Schools Don't Educate." Reprinted in *The Blumenfeld Education Letter*. Vol. 6, No. 5. Letter #57 (May 1991).

Gilson, Lawrence. *Money and Secrecy: A Citizens' Guide to Reforming State and Federal Practices*. New York: Praeger Publishers, 1972.

Glaberson, William. "U.S. Court Says Awards Based on SAT's Are Unfair to Girls." *The New York Times* (February 4, 1989).

Gold, Jacqueline. "Removing the Dead Hand of State." *Financial World* (March 3, 1992).

Goldberg, Milton and James Harvey. "*A Nation at Risk*: The Report of the National Commission of Excellence in Education." 65 *Phi Delta Kappan* 1 (September 1983).

Goldberg. 64 *Phi Delta Kappan* 1 (September 1982).

Good News Study Bible. Nashville: Thomas Nelson Publishers, 1986.

Goodlad, John I. *A Place Called School*. New York: McGraw-Hill Book Co., 1984.

Goodsell, Willystine. *A History of the Family as a Social and Educational Institution*. New York: Macmillan, 1915.

Gorder, Cheryl. *Home Schools: An Alternative.* Tempe, AZ: Blue Bird Publishing Co., 3rd ed., 1990.

Green, Sue. "Research on Alaska Home Schoolers." *Growing Without Schooling,* J. Holt and D. Richoux, eds. No. 40, Boston, 1981.

Gunther, G. *Constituional Law,* 11th ed. Mineola, NY: Foundation Press, Inc., 1985.

Gustafson, S. K. "A Study of Home Schooling: Parental Motivation and Goals." 4 *Home School Researcher,* No. 2.

Gustafson, Sonia K. "A Study of Home Schooling: Parental Motivations and Goals." Woodrow Wilson School of Public and International Affairs, Princeton University, 1987.

Gustavsen, G. A. "Selected Characteristics of Home Schools and Parents Who Operate Them." Doctoral dissertation. Andrews University, 1981. *Dissertation Abstracts International.* Vol. 42.

Gutek, Gerald L. *Education and Schooling in America.* Englewood Cliffs, NJ: Prentice-Hall, Inc., 1983.

—— *Education in the United States.* Englewood Cliffs, NJ: Prentice-Hall, Inc., 1986.

Guterson, David. "When Schools Fail Children." *Harper's Magazine* (November 1990).

Hafen, Bruce C. "Children's Liberation and the New Egalitarianism: Some Reservations About Abandoning Youth to Their 'Rights.'" 1976 *Brigham Young Law Review* 605.

Hall, Donald R. *Cooperative Lobbying—The Power of Pressure.* Tucson: University of Arizona Press, 1969.

Halperin, Samuel. *A Guide for the Powerless and Those Who Don't Know Their Own Power.* Washington, D.C.: The Institute for Educational Leadership, 1981.

Haskins, George. *Law and Authority in Early Massachusetts.* New York: Macmillan, 1960.

Henderson, Donald H. *et al.* "Legal Conflicts Involving Home Instruction of School-aged Children." 64 *Educational Law Reporter* 999 (1991).

Henderson *et al. Legal Conflicts Involving Home Instruction of School-aged Children.* St. Paul: West Publishing Comp. Commentary, 1991.

Hewitt Research Foundation. "North Dakota Trial Results Pending." 3 *The Parent Educator and Family Report.* No. 2 (1985).

—— "On Home-Schooling Figures and Scores." 4 *The Parent Educator and Family Report.* No. 2 (1986).

—— "Study of Home Schoolers Taken to Court." 4 *The Parent Educator and Family Report.* No. 1 (1986).

Heymann, Philip B. and Douglas E. Barzelay. "The Forest and the Trees: *Roe v. Wade* and Its Critics." 53 *Boston University Law Review* 765 (1973).

Hill, Paul. "Can Public Schools Survive?" *U.S. News & World Report* (December 9, 1991).

Hiner, N. Ray. "Look into Families: The New History of Children and the Family and Its Implications for Educational Research." *Education and the American Family,* William J. Weston, ed. New York: New York University Press, 1989.

Hirsch, E. D.,Jr. *Cultural Literacy: What Every American Needs to Know.* New York: Vintage Books, 1988.

Hirschhorn, James M. "The Separate Community: Military Uniqueness and Servicemen's Constitutional Rights." 62 *North Carolina Law Review* 177 (1984).

Hlebowitsh, Peter S. "Playing Power Politics: How a Nation at Risk Achieved Its National Stature." 23 *J. Res. Dev. Educ.* 82 (Winter 1990).

Hodgkinson, Harold. "Reform Versus Reality." *Phi Delta Kappan* (September 1991).

Holt, John. *Teach Your Own.* New York: Delacorte Press, 1981.

——— "Schools and Home Schooling: A Fruitful Partnership." 64 *Phi Delta Kappan.* 391 (February 1983).

"Home Schoolers Win EEE Case." Vol. 8, No.1, *Home School Court Report* (January-February 1992).

"Home Schooling—Schooling in Family Values." *U.S. News & World Report* (December 9, 1991).

Horowitz, Carl F. "Jack Kemp's 'Perestroika': A Choice Plan for Public Housing Tenants." *Heritage Foundation Reports* (March 26, 1992), available on NEXIS.

Howard, Bobbie Lee. "Home Schooling—A Military Adventure!" *Home Education Magazine* (March-April 1991).

Howard, Michael. "Home Schooling Military Style." *Home Education Magazine* (March-April 1991).

Huxley, Aldous. *Brave New World.* Garden City, NY: Doubleday, Doran & Co., Inc., 1932.

"Indiana." Vol. 9, No. 2 *Home School Court Report* (March-April 1992).

Inhelder, B. and J. Piaget. *The Growth of Logical Thinking from Childhood to Adolescence.* New York: Basic Books, Inc., 1958.

Innerst, Carol. "Administration Tried New Paths to School Choice." *The Washington Times* (January 31, 1992).

Interview with Dr. Raymond Moore (January 23, 1992).

Interview with James Moon, lobbyist for Virginia Home Educators' Association, conducted June 16, 1992.

Interview with Harvey Gerry. DoDDS Education Division, June 3, 1992.

Jackson, Donna. "Making a Choice." *New Woman* (April 1992).

Jeffries, John Calvin, Jr. "Legality, Vagueness, and the Construction of Penal Statutes." 71 *Virginia Law Review* 189 (1985).

Jernegan, Marcus W. "Compulsory Education in the American Colonies Part I." 26 *School Review* 731 (December 1918).

——— "Compulsory Education in the American Colonies Part II." 27 *School Review* 24 (January 1919).

——— "Compulsory Education in the Southern Colonies." 27 *School Review* 405 (June 1919).

——— *Laboring and Dependent Classes in Colonial America 1607-1783.* Chicago: Univ. of Chicago Press, 1931.

——— "The Beginnings of Public Education in New England, Part I." 23 *School Review* 319 (May 1915).

——— "The Beginnings of Public Education in New England Part II." 23 *School Review* 361 (June 1915).

Johnson, Christopher. "Early Schooling Doesn't Necessarily Mean Better Schooling." 61 *Phi Delta Kappan* 220 (November 1979).

Johnson, James A. *et al. Introduction to the Foundations of American Education.* 8th edition. Boston: Allyn and Bacon, 1991.

Johnson, Julie. "Hispanic Dropout Rate is Put at 35 Percent." *The New York Times* (September 15, 1989).

Johnson, William A. "Military Discipline and Political Expression: A New Look at an Old Bugbear." 6 *Harvard Civil Rights-Civil Liberties Law Review* 525 (1971).

Johnstone, William. *Robert E. Lee: The Christian.* Arlington Heights, IL: Christian Liberty Press, 1989.

Jordan, Mary. "Nationwide Tests Urged For Schools." *The Washington Post* (January 25, 1992).

Josephson, Matthew. *Edison.* New York: McGraw-Hill, 1959.

Kahn, Arnold S., ed. *Social Psychology.* Dubuque, IA: Wm. C. Brown Publishers, 1984.

Kantrowitz, Barbara and Pat Wingert. "A Dismal Report Card." *Newsweek* (June 17, 1991).

—— "An 'F' in World Competition." *Newsweek* (February 17, 1992).

Kelly, Doug. "Shutdown of Agencies a 'Streamlining' Step." *The Financial Post* (February 26, 1992).

Kemp, Jack. "A New Agenda for Ending Poverty; Give People a Stake in Their Own Communities." *The Washington Post* (May 3, 1992).

Kernan, Alvin. *Imprimis* (February 1992).

Kershner, Vlae. "Educators Want to Keep School Choice Off Ballot: They Urge Californians Not to Sign Petitions." *The San Francisco Chronicle* (January 22, 1992).

Kienel, Paul A. "Gablers Discover Amazing Factual Errors." *Secular Human Events* (December 28, 1991).

Kilpatrick, James. *The Idaho Statesman* (December 21, 1989).

Klicka, Christopher, J. *Home Schooling in the United States: A Statutory Analysis.* Home School Legal Defense Association, 1989.

Knight, Michael. "The Case for Allowing Parental Liberties Versus the State's Interest in Education: Home Education." 18 *Texas Tech Law Review* 1261 (1987).

Knowles, Gary J. "Introduction: The Context of Home Schooling in the United States." 21 *Education and Urban Society.* No. 1 (November 1988).

Knowles, Malcolm. *Self-directed Learning.* Chicago: Association Press, 1975.

Koch, Hannsjoachim W. *The Hitler Youth.* New York: Stein and Day, 1975.

Kotin, Lawrence and William Aikman. *Legal Foundations of Compulsory School Attendance.* Port Washington, NY: Kennikat Press, 1980.

Kozol, Jonathan. *Illiterate America.* New York: New American Library, 1985.

LaFave, Jeffrey F. "The Talismanic Incantation of Military Necessity: Is There a First Amendment in the Not-So Separate Society?" 2 *Journal of Contemporary Legal Issues* 173 (1989).

LaFave, Wayne L. and Jerold H. Israel. *Criminal Prodecure.* St. Paul, MN.: West Publishing Co., 1992.

LaFave, Wayne R. *Search and Seizure.* Vol. 2. St. Paul: West Publishing Co., 1978.

Landy, D. A. and H. Sigal. "Beauty Is Talent: Task Evaluation as a Function of the Performer's Physical Attractiveness." 29 *Journal of Personality and Social Psychology* (1974).

Laycock, Douglas. "The Remnants of Free Exercise." 1990 *Supreme Court Review* 1.

Lee, Felicia. "In Age of AIDS, Sex and Drugs Are Classroom Topics." *The New York Times* (December 26, 1989).

—— "Teachers' Leader Argues for More Metal Detectors." *The New York Times* (December 7, 1989).

—— "When Violence and Terror Strike Outside the Schools." *The New York Times* (November 14, 1989).

Lewis, Neil. "Metal Detectors Deemed Success and Will Expand in Schools." *The New York Times* (September 6, 1989).

Lieberman, Myron. *Privatization and Educational Choice*. New York: St Martin's Press, 1989.

—— *Public School Choice: Current Issues/Future Prospects*. Lancaster, PA: Technomic, 1990.

Linden, N. J. F. "An Investigation of Alternative Education: Home Schooling." Doctoral dissertation. East Texas State University, 1983. *Dissertation Abstracts International*. Vol. 44.

Lines, Patricia M. "Home Instruction: Characteristics, Size and Growth." Washington, D.C.: Office of Research, U.S. Department of Education, 1987.

—— "An Overview of Home Instruction." 69 *Phi Delta Kappan* (March 1987).

Locke, John. *Second Treatise of Government*. Indianapolis: Bobbs-Merrill, 1952.

Lupu, Ira C. "Home Educaton, Religious Liberty, and the Separation of Powers." 67 *Boston University Law Review* 971 (1987).

Mack, William, ed. 29 *Cyclopedia of Law and Procedure*. New York: American Law Book Co., 1908.

Madden, M.M., ed. "Home Study by Correspondence." 7 *Method: Alaskan Perspectives* No. 1 (1986).

Mahood, H. R. *Interest Group Politics in America: A New Intensity*. Englewood Cliffs, NJ: Prentice Hall, 1990.

Mangrum, R. Collin. "Family Rights and Compulsory School Laws." 21 *Creighton Law Review* 1019 (1988).

Marshner, Bill. "Bringing New Teachers to the Classroom." No. 104 *Policy Insights* (July 1989).

Maslan, Robert F., Jr. "Bias and the Londermill Hearing: Due Process or Lip Service to Federal Law?" 57 *Fordham Law Review* 1093 (1989).

"Massachusetts Court Case Could Set Precedent on Home Visits." Vol. 8, No. 1 *Home School Court Report* (January-February 1992).

Massachusetts School of Law of 1647. *Records of the Governor and Company of Massachusetts Bay in New England*. Vol. 11, 1647; also, June 14, 1642.

McBurney, Donald H. *Experimental Psychology*. Belmont, CA: Wadsworth Publishing Company, 1983.

McCarthy, Francis Barry. "The Confused Constitutional Status and Meaning of Parental Rights." 22 *Georgia Law Review* 975 (1988).

McConnell, Michael W. "Free Exercise Revisionism and the Smith Decision." 57 *University of Chicago Law Review* 1109 (1990).

—— "The Origins and Historical Understanding of Free Exercise of Religion." 103 *Harvard Law Review* 1409 (1990).

Meiklejohn, Alexander. *Political Freedom.* New York: Harper, 1960.

Melvin, Tessa. "Allegations of Cheating Prompt Investigation." *The New York Times* (July 2, 1989).

Meredith, Judith C. *Lobbying on a Shoestring.* Westport, CT: Greenwood, 1989.

Milbrath, Lester W. *The Washington Lobbyists.* Chicago: Rand McNally, 1963.

Mill, John Stuart. "On Liberty," in *On Liberty and Considerations on Representative Government.* New York: Macmillan, 1947.

Miller, Eric. "Home Schooling—Does It Pass the Test?" *Rural Living* (September 1991).

Miller, John. *The First Frontier: Life in Colonial America.* New York: Delacorte Press, 1966.

Miller, Perry. *The Life of the Mind in America.* London: Victor Gallanez, 1966.

—— *The New England Mind—The Seventeenth Century.* Cambridge, MA: Harvard University Press, 1954.

"Missouri." Vol. 8, No. 1 *Home School Court Report* (January-February 1992).

MMWR. Vol. 41, No. 14 (April 10, 1992).

"Modest Gains Seen in Improving Schools." *The New York Times* (November 8, 1989).

Monfils, Greg. "On Home Schooling." Vol. XIII, No. 3. *US Air Magazine* (March 1991).

Montgomery, Linda. "The Effect of Home Schooling on the Leadership Skills of Home Schooled Students." 5 *Home School Researcher.* No. 1 (March 1989).

Montgomery, Zachary. *Poison Drops in the Federal Senate: The School Question from a Parental and Non-sectarian Stand-point.* 1886.

Moore, Raymond. "Home Schooling: An Idea Whose Time Has Returned." *Human Events* (September 15, 1984).

—— "Research and Common Sense: Therapies for Our Homes and Schools." 84 *Teachers College Record* 355 (Winter 1982).

Moore, Raymond and Dorothy. *Better Late Than Early.* New York: E.P. Dutton, 1975.

—— *Home-Grown Kids.* Waco, TX: Word Books, 1981.

—— *Home-Spun Schools.* Waco, TX: Word Books, 1982.

—— *School Can Wait.* Provo, Utah: BYU Press, 1979.

Morgan, Edmund. *The Puritan Family: Religion and Domestic Relations in Seventeenth Century New England.* New York: Harper and Row, 1966.

Morgensen, Gretchen. "How to Get a Better Paying Job." *New Woman* (March 1992).

Mullis, Ina V. S. *Accelerating Academic Achievement: A Summary of Findings from 20 Years of NAEP.* Prepared by Educational Testing Service under a grant from National Center for Education Statistics, Office of Educational Research and Improvement, U.S. Dept. of Education. September 1990.

—— *The State of Mathematics Achievement.* Report No: 21-ST-03 by National Assessment of Educational Progress 1990. Assessment of the Nation and the Trial Assessment of the States, prepared by Educational Testing Service under Contract with the National Center for Education Statistics Office of Educational Research and Improvement, U.S. Dept. of Education. June 1991.

Mydans, Seth. "School Offers Day Care for Teenage Mothers." *The New York Times* (December 27, 1989).

Myers, John E. B. "A Survey of Child Abuse and Neglect Reporting Statutes." 10 *Journal of Juvenile Law* 1 (1986).

Naisbitt, John. *Megatrends: Ten New Directions Transforming Our Lives.* New York: Warner, 1982.

NCEE. *Meeting the Challenge: Recent Efforts to Improve Education Across the Nation.* Washington, D.C.: United States Dept. of Education, November 1983.

—— *A Nation at Risk: The Imperative for Educational Reform.* Washington, D.C.: Government Printing Office, 1983.

New England's First Fruits. London: R.O. and G.D. for Henry Overton, 1643.

"News Conference with: Lamar Alexander, Secretary of Education, and Emerson Elliott, Action Commissioner of Education, on: Reading In and Out of School: Factors Influencing the Literacy and Achievement of American Students in Grades 4, 8 and 12, in 1988 and 1990." *Federal News Service* (May 28, 1992), available on NEXIS.

Nitko, Anthony J. *Educational Tests and Measurement: An Introduction.* New York: Harcourt Brace Jovanovich, Inc., 1983.

Note. "Freedom and Public Education: The Need for New Standards." 50 *Notre Dame Lawyer* 530 (1975).

Note. "Home Education and Fundamental Rights: Can Johnny's Parents Teach Johnny?" 73 *Washburn State University Law Review* 731 (1991).

Note. "Home Education in America: Parental Rights Reasserted." 49 *UMKC Law Review* 191 (1981).

Note. "Home Instruction: An Alternative to Institutional Education." 18 *Journal of Family Law* 353 (1979-80).

Note. "Home Education v. Compulsory Attendance Laws: Whose Kids Are They Anyway?" 24 *Washburn Law Journal* 274 (1985).

Note. "Investigating Child Abuse: The Fourth Amendment and Investigatory Home Visits." 89 *Columbia Law Review* 1034 (1989).

Note. "Michigan's Teacher Certification Requirement as Applied to Religiously Motivated Home Schools." 23 *University of Michigan Journal of Law Reform* 733 (1990).

Note. "Military Dissent and the Law of War:—Uneasy Bedfellows." *California Law Review* 871 (1985).

Note. "State Intrusion into Family Affairs: Justifications and Limitations." 26 *Stanford Law Review* 1383 (1974).

Note. "The Constitutionality of Home Education Statutes." 55 *UMKC Law Review* 69 (1986).

Note. "The Constitutionality of Louisiana Aid to Private Education." 44 *Louisiana Law Review* 865 (1984).

Note. "The Illusory Enforcement of First Amendment Freedom: *Employment Division, Department of Human Resources v. Smith* and the Abandonment of the Compelling Governmental Interest Test." 69 *North Carolina Law Review* 1332 (1991).

Note. "The Void-for-Vagueness Doctrine in the Supreme Court." 109 *University of Pennsylvania Law Review* 67, 75.

Note. "Unanswered Implications—The Clouded Rights of the Incompetent Patient Under *Cruzan v. Director, Missouri Department of Health*." 69 *North Carolina Law Review* 1293 (1991).

Nowak, J., *et al. Constitutional Law*. 2nd ed. St. Paul: West Publishing Co., 1983.

—— *Constitutional Law*. 3d ed. St. Paul: West Publishing Co., 1986.

Oakes, Jeannie and Martin Lipton. *Making the Best of Schools: A Handbook for Parents, Teachers, and Policymakers*. New Haven, CT: Yale University Press, 1990.

Ordinance of 1787, July 13, 1787, Art. 3 reprinted in *Documents Illustrative of the Formation of the Union of American States*. Washington, D.C.: United States Government Printing Office, 1927.

Oregon Department of Education. *December 1, 1986 Homeschool Data Report*. Salem, OR: author, 1986.

Orthodoxy in Massachusetts, 1630-1650. Cambridge, MA: Harvard University Press, 1933.

Ott, James. "Bush Order Opens Door for Airport Privatization." *Aviation Week and Space Technology* (May 11, 1992).

Padover, Saul K. *Jefferson: A Great American's Life and Ideals*. New York: Mentor Books, 1942.

—— *Jefferson*. New York: Harcourt-Brace, 1942.

—— *Thomas Jefferson and the Foundations of Freedom*. Coronado, CA: D. Van Nostrand, 1965.

Parker, Allan E., Jr. "Public Free Schools: A Constitutional Right to Educational Choice in Texas." 45 *Southwestern Law Journal* 825 (1991).

"Parochial Schools, An Evolving Mission." *U.S. News and World Report* (December 9, 1991).

Patterson, B. *The Forgotten Ninth Amendment*. Indianapolis: Bobbs-Merrill Company, Inc., 1955.

Pendleton, Audrey. "Young Adult Literacy and Schooling: A Summary Report." Washington, D.C.: National Center for Educational Statistics, 1988.

Perkel, F. E. "The Effects of a Home Instruction Program on the Cognitive Growth of a Selected Group of 4-year-olds." Doctoral dissertation, University of Southern California, 1979, *Dissertation Abstracts International*. Vol. 40.

Peterson, David Allen. "Home Education v. Compulsory Attendance Laws: Whose Kids Are They Anyway?" 24 *Washburn Law Journal* 274 (1985).

"'Phantom Class' Report Investigated in Bronx." *The New York Times* (August 9, 1989).

Philpel, Harriet. "Minor's Rights to Medical Care." 36 *Albany Law Review* 462 (1972).

Piaget, Jean. "Intellectual Evolution from Adolescence to Adulthood." 15 *Human Development* No.1 (1972).

—— *Psychology of Intelligence.* Patterson, NJ: Littlefield and Adams, 1963.

Pines, Maya. *Revolution in Learning.* New York: Harper & Row, 1967.

Pinkney's recommendations to the Federal Convention. 2 Records of the Federal Convention 341. Farrand, ed. 1911.

Powell, Arthur, Eleanor Farrar, and David Cohen. *The Shopping Mall High School: Winners and Losers in the Educational Marketplace.* Boston: Houghton Mifflin Company, 1985.

Power, Edward. *The Transit of Learning: A Sound and Cultural Interpretation of American Educational History.* Sherman Oaks, CA: Alfred Publishing Co., 1979.

"Preparatory Schools—Shaking Off an Elitist Past." *U.S. News & World Report* (December 9, 1991).

Priority Management Systems Report, 1989.

"Public's Attitudes Toward the Public Schools." 65 *Phi Delta Kappan* 1 (1983).

Pulliam, John D. *History of Education in America.* New York: Macmillan Publishing Company, 1991.

Quigg, Philip. "S.A.T.'s: Don't Shoot the Test-makers." *The New York Times* (April 16, 1989).

Quine, David Neal and Edmund A. Marek. "Reasoning Abilities of Home-educated Children." 4 *Home School Researcher.* No. 3. Brian D. Ray, ed. (September 1988).

Rakestraw, Jennie Finlayson. "An Analysis of Home Schooling for Elementary School-age Children in Alabama." Doctoral dissertation, University of Alabama, 1987. *Dissertation Abstracts International.* Vol. 49.

Randall, Ruth and Keith George. *School Choice: Issues and Answers.* National Education Service, 1991.

Ray, Brian D. *A Comparison of Home Schooling and Conventional Schooling: With a Focus on Learner Outcomes, Science.* Department of Science, Mathematics, and Computer Education, Oregon State University, 1986.

—— "A Nationwide Study of Home Education: Family Characteristics, Legal Matters, and Student Achievement." Study conducted by The National Home Education Research Institute. Reported in the *Home School Court Report.* Home School Legal Defense Association (December 1990).

—— "Home Schools: A Synthesis of Research on Characteristics and Learner Outcomes." 21 *Education and Urban Society* (November 1988).

—— "Parent as Tutor Experimental Program in Washington State." 1 *Home School Researcher* No. 4 (December 1985).

Ray, Brian D. and Jon Wartes. "The Academic Achievement and Affective Development of Home-schooled Children." *Home Schooling: Political, Historical, and Pedagogical Perspectives.* Jane Van Galen & May Anne Pittman, eds. Norwood, NJ: Ablex Publishing Corporation, 1991.

Reagan, Ronald. "Excellence and Opportunity: A Program of Support for American Education." 66 *Phi Delta Kappan* 1 (September 1984).

Records of the Governor and Company of Massachusetts Bay in New England 1642.

Remarks by President George Bush at Milwaukee, Wisconsin—Bush-Quayle Fundraiser Milwaukee, Wis. Federal News Service (March 16, 1992), available on NEXIS.

Renner, J. W. and E. A. Marek. *The Learning Cycle and Elementary School Science Teaching*. Portsmouth, NH: Heinemann Educational Books, Inc., 1988.

"Research. Gifted Children in Home School." *The Moore Report* (July/August 1991).

Resnick, D. P. and L. B. "Standards, Curriculum, and Performance: A Historical and Comparative Perspective." 14 *Educational Researcher* (1985).

Resnick, L. B. "Introduction: Research to Inform a Debate." 62 *Phi Delta Kappan* (1981).

Resolutions on Ratification of the Constitution by the States of Massachusetts, New Hampshire, New York and Virginia, reprinted in *Documents Illustrative of Formation of the Union of American States*, H.R. Doc. No. 398, 69th Cong., 1st Sess. 1018 (1927).

Reynolds, P. L. and D. D. Williams. *The Daily Operations of a Home School Family: A Case Study*. Paper presented at the Annual Meeting of American Educational Research Association, 1985.

Reynolds, P. L. "How Home School Families Operate on a Day-to-Day Basis: Three Case Studies." Unpublished doctoral dissertation, Brigham Young University, 1985.

Rinehart, James R. and Jackson F. Lee, Jr. *American Education and The Dynamics of Choice*. Santa Monica, CA: Praeger, 1991.

Rippa, S. Alexander. *Education in a Free Society*. New York: David McKay Co. Inc., 1967.

Rose, Daniel J. "Compulsory Education and Parents Rights: A Judicial Framework of Analysis." 30 *Boston College Law Review* 861 (1989).

Rosen, Richard A. "The (Especially Heinous) Aggravating Circumstance in Capital Cases—The Standardless Standard." 64 *North Carolina Law Review* 941.

Rosenthal, R. and K. L. Fode. "The Effect of Experimenter Bias on the Performance of the Albino Rat." 8 *Behavioral Science* (1963).

—— "Three Experiments in Experimenter Bias." 12 *Psychological Reports* (1963).

Rosenthal, Robert. *Experimenter Effects in Behavioral Research*. New York: Appleton-Century-Crofts, 1966.

Rossiter, Clinton. *Seedtime of the Republic: The Origin of the American Tradition of Political Liberty*. New York: Harcourt, Brace, 1953.

Runnels, John H. "The Constitutionality of Louisiana Aid to Private Education." 44 *Louisiana Law Review* 865 (1984).

Sanchez, Rene. "Battling Student Boredom." *The Washington Post* (April 15, 1991).

Schemmer, B. A. S. "Case Studies of Four Families Engaged in Home Education." Unpublished doctoral dissertation, Ball State University, 1985.

Scogin, L. A. *Home School Survey* (1986).

Shackelford, Luanne and Susan White. *A Survivor's Guide to Home Schooling*. Wheaton, IL: Crossway Books, 1988.

Shepherd, Michael S. "Home Schooling: Dimensions of Controversy, 1970-1984." 31 *Journal of Church and State* 1 (Winter 1989).

——— *The Home Schooling Movement: An Emerging Conflict in American Education.* Ph.D. dissertation, East Texas State University, 1986.

Shirer, William L. *The Rise and Fall of the Third Reich.* New York: Simon and Schuster, 1960.

Siegel, Stephen A. "Lochner Era Jurisprudence and the American Constitutional Tradition." 70 *North Carolina Law Review* 1 (1991).

Smith, Dorothy. *In Our Own Interest.* Seattle: Madrona Publishers, 1989.

Smith, Vernon Hope. *Alternative Schools: The Development of Options in Public Education.* Lincoln, NE: Professional Educators Publications, 1974.

Spielvogel, Jackson J. *Hitler and Nazi Germany: A History.* Englewood Cliffs, NJ: Prentice Hall, 1988.

Spring, Joel. "The Evolving Structure of American Schoooling." *The Public School Monopoly.*

St. Thomas. 1983.

Stan, Isidore, *et al. Living American Documents.* New York: Harcourt, Brace, and World, 1961.

"State of Mayland Resistant to Sale of BWI Airports." *Los Angeles Times* (May 12, 1992).

Steen, Lynn, ed. *Everybody Counts: A Report to the Nation on the Future of Mathematics Education.* Washington, D.C.: National Research Council, National Academy Press, 1989.

Stocklin-Enright, Brendan. "The Constitutionality of Home Education: The Role of the Parent, the State and the Child." 18 *Willamette Law Review* 563 (1982).

Story, Joseph. *Commentaries on the Constitution of the United States.* 1st ed. Vol. 2. Cambridge: Boston, Hilliard, Gray and Company, 1833.

——— Volume 3. *Commentaries on the Constitution of the United States.* 5th edition, Melville M. Bigelow, ed. Boston: Little, Brown and Company, 1891.

Sugin, Linda. "First Amendment Rights of Military Personnel: Denying Rights to Those Who Defend Them." 62 *New York University Law Review* 855 (1987).

Survey of Magnet Schools: Analyzing A Model for Quality Integrated Education. Washington, D.C.: U.S. Dept. of Education Office of Planning, Budget, & Evaluation, 1983.

Taylor, John Wesley, V. "Self-concept in Home-schooling Children." Doctoral dissertation, Andrews University, 1986. *Dissertation Abstracts International.* Vol. 47.

"Telephones and Kids: Consider these Dangers." Vol. 8, No. 1. *Home School Court Report* (January-February 1992).

Tennessee Department of Education. *Tennessee Statewide Averages, Home School Student Test Results, Stanford Achievement Test, Grades 2, 5, 7, and 9.* Nashville: author, 1988.

The Book of the General Lawes and Libertyes Concerning the Inhabitants of the Massachusetts. Cambridge, 1648.

"The Exodus." *U.S. News & World Report* (December 9, 1991).

The Federalist No. 41. Lodge, ed. 1888.

The New England Primer. 1960.

The Puritans. New York: Harper and Row, 1963.

The Westminster Catechism. 1647.

The Works of the Rev. John Witherspoon. 2nd ed. Vol. IV. Philadelphia: William Woodward, 1802.

Thompson, Ronald S. "Constitutional Applications to the Military Criminal Defendant." 66 *University of Detroit Law Review* 221 (1989).

Tiffin, Susan. *In Whose Best Interest*. Westport, CT.: Greenwood Press, 1982.

Tizard, B. *et al.* "Language and Social Class: Is Verbal Deprivation a Myth?" 24 *Journal of Child Psychology and Psychiatry* (1983).

—— "Adults' Cognitive Demands at Home and at Nursery School." 23 *Journal of Child Psychology and Psychiatry* (1982).

—— "Children's Questions and Adults' Answers." 24 *Journal of Child Psychology and Psychiatry* (1983).

Tobak, James, and Perry Zirkel. "Home Instruction: An Analysis of the Statutes and Case Law." 8 *University of Dayton Law Review* 13 (1982).

Toch, Thomas. "Choice about School Choice: How Far Should We Go?" 57 *The Education Digest* Nos. 44-8 (November 1991).

Toffler, Alvin. *Future Shock*. New York: Random House, 1970.

—— *The Third Wave*. New York: Morrow 1980.

Tompkins, Dwight. "An Argument for Privacy in Support of the Choice of Home Education By Parents." 20 *Journal of Law and Education* 301 (Summer 1991).

Tooley, Sara H. *The Life of Florence Nightingale*. London: Cassell and Company, Ltd., 1911.

Tribe, Laurence. *American Constitutional Law*. Sec 14-3. 2nd ed. Mineola, NY: Foundation Press, 1988.

—— *American Constitutional Law*. Sec. 12-1. 1st ed. Mineola, NY: Foundation Press, 1978.

Tussman, Joseph and Jacobus ten Broek, "The Equal Protection of the Laws." 37 *California Law Review* 341 (1949).

U.S. News & World Report. "Afrocentric Schools—Fighting a Racist Legacy" (December 9, 1991).

USA Today. August 28, 1991.

Van Doren, Carl. *Benjamin Franklin*. The Haddon Craftsman, 1938.

Van Galen, Jane A. and Mary Anne Pittman, eds. *Home Schooling: Political Historical, and Pedagogical Perspectives*. Norwood, NJ: Ablex Publishing Corporation, 1991.

Van Galen, Jane A. "Ideology, Curriculum, and Pedagogy in Home Education." 21 *Education and Urban Society*. No. 1 (November 1988).

Verhovek, Sam Howe. "New York Cancels Regents Exam after Newspaper Carries Answers." *The New York Times* (June 21, 1989).

Wade, Theodore, E., Jr. *Home School Manual*. Auburn, CA: Gazelle Publications, 1991.

Wadlington, W. *Cases and Other Materials on Domestic Relations*. Westbury, NY: Foundation Press, 1990.

Warren, Earl. "The Bill of Rights and the Military." 37 *New York University Law Review* 181 (1962).

Wartes, Jon. *Report From the 1986 Home School Testing.* Washington Home School Research Project. Woodinville, WA: author, 1987.

—— "The Washington Home School Project: Quantitative Measures for Informing Policy Decisions." 21 *Education and Urban Society.* No. 1 (November 1988).

Washington, Booker T. *Up From Slavery.* New York: Doubleday, Page & Co., 1925.

Letter to the Marquis de Lafayette (April 28, 1788), reprinted in Vol. 29, *The Writings of George Washington,* Fitzpatrick, ed. (1939).

Washington State Superintendent of Public Instruction. *Washington State's Experimental Programs Using the Parent as Tutor Under the Supervision of Washington State Certified Teacher, 1984-1985.* Olympia, WA: author, 1985.

Webster's New World Dictionary of the American Language. College Edition. Cleveland: The World Publishing Company, 1962.

Welch and Short. "Home School Questions and Answers." *The Teaching Home* (April/May 1991).

Western Australia Department of Education. *Innovations in Rural Education: The Isolated Students Matriculation Scheme in Western Australia and the Chidley Educational Centre.* Western Australia: author, 1979.

Whitehead, John W. *Parents' Rights.* Wheaton, IL: Crossway Books, 1985.

—— *The Rights of Religious Persons in Public Education.* Wheaton, IL: Crossway Books, 1991.

Whitehead, John W. and Wendell Bird. *Home Education and Constitutional Liberties.* Wheaton, IL: Crossway Books, 1984.

"Why Our Schools Aren't Making the Grade." *McCalls* (September 1975).

Wish, Harvey. *Society and Thought in Early America.* New York: Longmans Green, 1950.

"World Class Standards." *America 2000: An Education Strategy.* Washington, D.C.: U.S. Dept. of Education, 1991.

World News Digest. August 30, 1991.

Wortman, Camille B. *et al. Psychology.* New York: Alfred A. Knopf, 1981.

Wright, Cheryl. "Home School Research: Critique and Suggestions for the Future." 21 *Education and Urban Society* No. 1 (November 1988).

Wu, John C. H. *Fountain of Justice.* Beaverton, OR: International Scholarly Book Services, 1980.

Yang, John. "Bush Unveils Education Plan." *The Washington Post* (April 19, 1991).

Yastrow, Sybil. *Home Instruction: A National Study of State Law.* May 1989, *quoting* Steven Goldsmith, Memorandum from the Office of the Prosecuting Attorney of Marion County Indiana, February 17, 1984.

You Had a Question? Washington, D.C.: Department of Defense, 1986.

"Youth Bitter over Ban on Driving by Dropouts." *The New York Times* (October 5, 1989).

"Zaire to Privatize National Airline, Post and Telecommunications." *Agence France Press* (July 28, 1991).

Zangwill, Israel. *The Melting Pot* I. New York: Macmillan, 1926.

Zillman, Donald N. and Edward J. Imwinkelried. "Constitutional Rights and Military Necessity: Reflections on the Society Apart." 51 *Notre Dame Lawyer* 396 (1976).

INDEX OF CASES

GENERAL INDEX

ABOUT THE RUTHERFORD INSTITUTE

The Rutherford Institute is a nonprofit civil liberties legal and education organization, specializing in the defense of religious liberty, which includes the protection of the rights of home educators.

The Rutherford Institute has been actively involved with home schooling for over a decade. Back in 1979, John W. Whitehead, Founder and President of The Rutherford Institute, litigated the Nobel case. His victory memorialized the academic excellence and positive socialization produced by home education.

As a nonprofit civil liberties organization, The Rutherford Institute is committed to assisting all home educators, regardless of their religious affiliation or their reason for choosing home education. Our position is that parents have the primary control over the education and upbringing of their children.

From its inception, The Rutherford Institute has helped to pioneer the defense of home education. But since the home education movement is growing by more than 30 percent a year, the resulting need for legal and education assistance demands an expanded program.

In an effort to meet the growing needs of home educators, The Rutherford Institute has developed the Home School Brief and the Home Rights Hotline. These resources are geared towards helping the home education community develop into a strong and cohesive foce.

In addition to defending home schoolers, Institute attorneys also participate in legal action to protect other vital constitutional rights. The Institute has established a network of state, regional and international chapters to defend vital liberties.

To educate the public on priority issues, the Institute publishes numerous books and papers and provides educational training programs. Legal research resources are also made availabe to assist attorneys involved in First Amendment litigation.

Address: The Rutherford Institute, P.O. Box 7482, Charlottesville, VA 22906-7482, (804) 978-3888.